Yahrzeit

Liat Taiber Ben-David

JERUSALEM ♦ NEW YORK

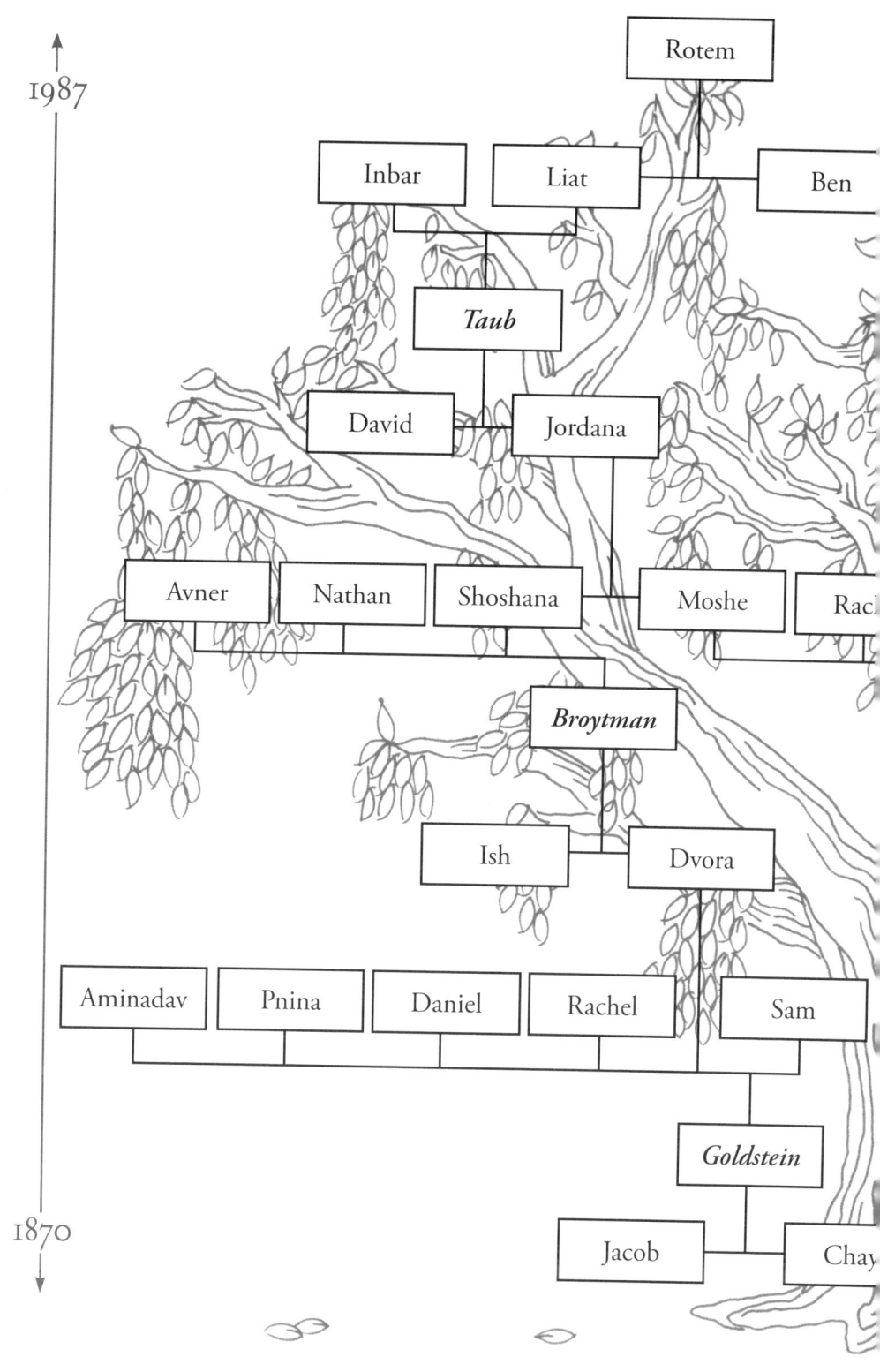

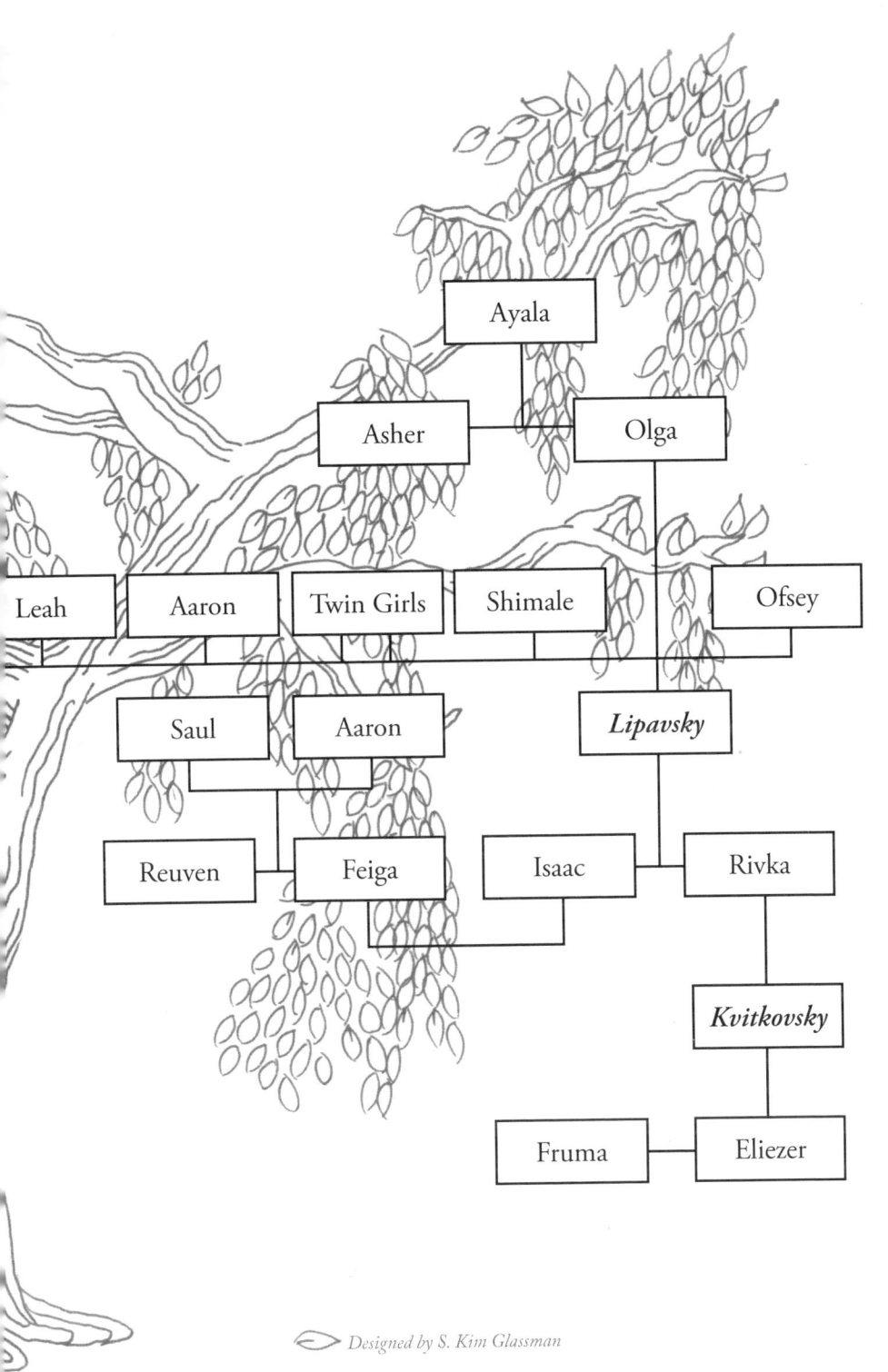
Designed by S. Kim Glassman

Copyright © Gefen Publishing House
Jerusalem 2004 / 5764

All rights reserved. No part of this publication may be translated, reproduced, stored in a retrieval system or transmitted, in any form or by any means, electronic, mechanical, photocopying, recording or otherwise, without express written permission from the publishers.

Typesetting: Raphaël Freeman, Jerusalem Typesetting
Cover Design: Studio Paz, Jerusalem

Excerpts of the song "Jerusalem of Gold" by Naomi Shemer ז״ל (pp. 254 and 256) were translated by the author.

Front cover: Painting by Nahum Gutman "Ahuzat Bayit", 1950s. Ink drawing, watercolor and glued clippings on paper. With courtesy of the Gutman family & the Gutman Museum, Tel Aviv ©.

Back cover photograph: Bobeh and Zeida in front of the Mulberry tree, Zichron Yaacov, 1940s

ISBN 965-229-333-4

1 3 5 7 9 8 6 4 2

Gefen Publishing House
6 Hatzvi Street, Jerusalem 91360, Israel
972-2-538-0247
orders@gefenpublishing.com

Gefen Books
600 Broadway, Lynbrook, NY 11563, USA
1-800-477-5257
orders@gefenpublishing.com

www.israelbooks.com

Printed in Israel

Send for our free catalogue

Our lives are not made of the people we love,
But of our love for them.
That, even death can't take away.

To my Mother,
Who taught me how to stand on the shoulders of my forefathers
And reach to the sky,

To my husband David,
Who has always created stars for me to pick,

And to our amazing children, Rotem, Roy and Bar,
Whom I teach that their children should
be the sixth generation of Sabras.

Contents

Acknowledgements ix
Introduction xi
Prologue: March, 1960 1

PART I

Chapter 1:   Rivka, 1870–1902 5
Chapter 2:   Dvora, 1882–1907 31
Chapter 3:   Rivka, 1902–1913 55
Chapter 4:   Dvora and Shoshana, 1908–1917 79
Chapter 5:   Rivka, Dvora and Shoshana, 1914–1919 .. 103
Chapter 6:   Shoshana, 1919–1930 127
Chapter 7:   Shoshana, 1930–1940 153
Chapter 8:   Jordana, 1940–1941 181

PART II

Morning: 1942–1947 203
Noon: 1947–1962 225
Evening: 1962–1987 245

Epilogue: January, 1987 261

About the Author 263

Acknowledgements

This book would never have been completed without the loving care and support of more people than I can possibly mention here. However, special thanks should be given to the following people:

Tzvia Nahor, for your everlasting friendship and love;

Susan Levin and Esti Levinson, for your encouragement, love and commitment that gave me the confidence to write this story;

Jeffrey I. Klein, for reminding me of my values and deep connection to my history and roots, and for making me believe that my story was worth telling;

Lori Abrams, for your endless energy and helpful remarks that elevated my writing to a higher level;

Ilan Greenfield, who believed in this book enough to actually publish it.

Although based on actual family stories and events, the characters and story are completely fictitious.

Introduction

An old story tells of two Jewish women who meet at a conference and start talking. After a couple of hours, when the conference is over, and it is time to leave, one says to the other: "I feel like I know you so well, I can't believe we have just started talking!" The other looks at her and says: "We haven't just started – we have been talking for 3,500 years."

In a nutshell, that is how I have always felt – in a state of constant, intimate dialogue with the spirits and the narrative of the people to which I was born.

I was born in Israel in 1960. My parents saw to it that I was highly aware of the fact that as a fourth-generation Israeli, I had a very unique pedigree – I was a daughter of the first *Aliyah* – the first wave of Jews to return to Israel as an organized group in the 1880s, after almost 2,000 years of exile. In U.S. terms, it made me an equivalent of the direct offspring of the Mayflower. Indeed, my generation was raised on the stories of the first modern Jewish pioneers – tales of strong and defiant people who had left behind the old world with its old ways, and set forth to accomplish a dream: the vision of renewed Jewish independence in the ancient homeland of the Jews. They were the giants – and I knew I was standing on their shoulders.

My grandmother used to fill my head with the songs of the land, walking me through her own experiences. She had a natural gift for storytelling, and I liked nothing better than to listen to her vivid descriptions and words of compassion that would transform her stories into my own. As I listened to her, the visions of the past became very real. I could hear the voices, see the scenes, and feel the emotions. I was fascinated by the stories of my own grandparents and great-grandparents, who were connected to an endless line of history that hailed back to biblical days.

It was as if I was always accompanied by a group of people, people who had created a very definite pathway for me to take – and who stood right behind me to make sure I took it. Traveling through my life and my country, two pillars always marched with me – the Bible and the story of the creation of the modern State of Israel, two storylines that merged into one, fantastic, logical narrative. My narrative.

My connection to this narrative is complete and undoubting, and yet, one of my greatest surprises was the lack of knowledge and understanding that was evident amongst my own people. Most of the Jewish people live in the Diaspora, and although many of them declare and indeed display a commitment to the Jewish state, they have no idea what it is like to actually live and be part of the Zionist story, an understanding that cannot be derived from history books, learned speakers, short visits or documentaries – but the kind of understanding that stems from the very small, personal, unique stories of the people who live them, day by day. I came to the realization that this phenomenon is damaging to our entire people, and that I would like to do something concrete to change it, even if in my own humble way, under difficult, disturbing circumstances.

It was October 2000. I was enjoying a beautiful family vacation in a charming little bed-and-breakfast outside of Utrecht in

The Netherlands when CNN brought the news that back home, in Israel, violence and riots between Israel and the Palestinians had erupted once again. After more than seven years of negotiations, peace talks, agreements and more than anything – very high hopes and dreams for a better future – the vision of a foreseeable peace came crashing down like a tower of cards. What was to be known in Israel and, in fact, around the world, as "The Second Intifada" was about to change my life in a direction I hadn't suspected.

When you live in a place like Israel, you grow up listening to the news every hour, and you are accustomed to the fact that every hour something new actually happens. It becomes an addiction, a second nature, so much so that taking a vacation outside of Israel means you try to listen to the news no more than once a day, preferably once every few days, hoping that nothing really bad will happen back home, knowing that if something really bad does happen it will reach you anyway. The greatest joy is the ability to say to people around you (usually other Israelis as yourself): "See? We can actually live with much less news, and the world doesn't fall apart! It's even nice and quiet for a change. This is definitely a more normal way to live, we should try it back home as well." Which, of course, we never do.

But when something really bad happens back home, and we are not there, we suddenly feel stranded. The only source of information is the TV networks and information you receive over the phone from your friends and relatives back home (and you are always certain they aren't telling you everything). The sense of solidarity with our fellow Israelis, against the background of yet another calamity that has been thrust upon us, is widespread and, although to a bystander it may look completely insane, all you want to do is get back home – directly into the heart of the catastrophe – as soon as possible.

October 2000 was no exception. The horrific scenes that came through the television screen, via CNN, were devastating, but this time there was an additional feeling stirring inside me: it was a difficult mixture of pure anger and heartbreaking frustration.

There, at the peaceful, sweet B&B in The Netherlands, CNN was showing horrific pictures of the lynch in Rammalah, when two Israeli officers accidentally wandered into the Arab town and were attacked by a mob, murdered, their bodies mutilated – all inside and around the Palestinian police headquarters. The image of one of the murderers standing at the window, waving his red, bloodied hands towards the mob in a sign of victory, a satisfied smile on his lips, and his eyes gleaming in a frenzied craze, still haunts me at night together with many, many other such horrible images.

The viciousness, brutality and cruelty of the attacks were so devastatingly fierce that all the hopes and dreams we had nurtured were not only unrealistic, but completely foolish. Sentences that I hadn't heard in many years, such as – "We will never be able to trust them again," "They don't want us here, they prefer we were all drowned in the sea," and many others, started being heard once again on the streets and sent me back a few decades in time. The feeling of betrayal was complete. We were devastated.

And yet, somehow, we were the ones being blamed. To the objective eye, watching the footage on international television, we were the perpetrators, killing innocent people, while the terror inflicted upon us was studiously avoided. Although we made – and are still making – some terrible mistakes in judgement and in action, they are no comparison to the horrific, hateful and hellish actions of terrorism, inflicted by the Palestinians. I found myself screaming and arguing, with a growing anger and frustration, at...a TV set.

I had to do something.

Less than a year later, I packed up my family and landed in the U.S. to become the Israeli representative of the Jewish Agency for Israel at the Jewish Federation of Palm Beach County. Leaving a comfortable and fulfilling position in the area of science education at Tel Aviv University, I became an emissary of Israel, and for 24 hours a day, seven days a week, I did everything in my power to tell our story, the story of a people trying desperately to fulfill their right to have a place of their own, against all odds.

It was during those 30 months when I was in the u.s. that I wrote *Yahrzeit*. Based on family stories, historic events and a great deal of imagination, *Yahrzeit* is another way for me to relate a personal side of my people's story. Although many of the names I used for my family members are real, as are many of the events and their historical backgrounds, most of the story is fictional and should be regarded as such, weaving crumbs of reality and large portions of imagination into one large web. Although Dvora and Rivka really did exist, I never met them, and know very little about them. All I know is that Dvora was a remarkably beautiful woman, and that Rivka had big blue eyes and was very kind. I never met Moshe, my grandfather, whom I understand was always full of mischief, but I know he was madly in love with my grandmother. We never had a "Yahrzeit Hanukah" candle lighting ceremony – it is complete fiction – but I know that my grandmother, Shoshana, always felt that the spirits of her family surrounded her, a feeling I willingly received from her.

They were all highly-committed Zionists, who believed so deeply in the right of the Jewish people to have a place of their own in their ancient homeland, that it was never even a question, just a simple, everyday fact. That is the spirit of their story, the spirit they have passed on to me, and the spirit I hope to pass on to my children. *Yahrzeit* is the story of four generations of dedicated, strong women, whose actions and love of their home and family is intertwined with the rebirth of the Jewish people in the Jewish homeland, the most remarkable story of the Jews in modern times. Their passion, combined with common sense, readiness for hard work, and above all – family strength, are the pillars upon which the entire story of the creation of Israel is carved.

My daughter is currently a soldier in the Israel Defense Force. It isn't easy watching her, a young girl of 19, wearing uniform. But it also fills me with pride, the pride of a people who, after 2,000 years of exile, have finally returned home – and are willing to defend it. It's the only home we have. Soon, my son will be joining the army as well, and after him – my youngest. It is part of our life, and probably will be for a very long time. But always, every single time a child is born in Israel, our very first prayer for her or him is that by the time they are 18, we won't need an army anymore. It is a prayer that is yet to be fulfilled.

Yahrzeit – the Yiddish word for "memorial day" – is a story of the memories that build a reality. Since we all have different memories, we also carve a variety of realities from them. This story is based on my reality, the reality of one daughter of the first *Aliyah* – the first Zionist immigrants who came to the Land of Israel in 1882 – who still believes that Israel is the home for the Jews.

And I will always be there to welcome those who decide to come, with the word SHALOM – Peace.

Prologue

March, 1960

The day I was born, my rather large grandmother, Beylla, took my father by the hand, squeezed it firmly and ordered him to give me his late grandmother's name. "The child," she said, "comes from a proud line of intelligent Jews, and she should carry this spirit on, both by deeds and by name." My father's grandmother's name was Leah, which, in Hebrew, means tired, easy-going, but it was as far as could be from my great-grandmother Leah's real character. My father loved to disobey his mother, so to spite her, he refused to give me his grandmother's name. But, since my own grandmother was a very strong-willed woman who usually got her way, he couldn't bring himself to defy her completely. So he discussed it with my mom, who discussed it with her mom, my rather small grandmother Shoshana.

At first my grandmother Shoshana grumbled, saying they might as well give me the name Rivka, after my late-grandfather's mother, who was "a living angel," as Shoshana always called her. All her life, Rivka had been accompanied by good spirits, Shoshana maintained, and if I had her name the same good spirits would undoubtedly *accompany me as well. But then Shoshana looked into my father's eyes and, as she adored him, reluctantly turned to my mother and told her that husbands are to be obeyed. After a long night of debate, they finally decided to call me Liat – Hebrew for "you are mine" – a gentler, more optimistic meaning than Leah, but with the remnants of Leah hidden within. Throughout my life, I have been trying to prove that I am not LEAH, and throughout my life, I have been highly aware of the long line of spirits from which I sprouted, and who have been accompanying me since the day I was born.*

PART I

Chapter 1

RIVKA

1870–1902

One day, just for the fun of it, I went with my mother, Jordana, to what we jokingly called "a witch" – a fortune teller who was famous for reading your future from the patterns left by the coffee you drank. I must admit I felt both ridiculous and curious at the same time. My cynicism led me to imagine a fortune-teller resembling a gypsy, sitting in a dark room, dressed in colorful skirts and adorned with a beaded scarf. She would be barefoot, and would have a low, husky, mysterious voice, telling me things I already knew. Little did she know that I would call her bluff instantly.

When we arrived, we entered through a regular, sun-eaten door into what looked like a completely ordinary room. There was a small coffee table near the window, with three wooden chairs assembled around it; I was struck by the bareness and simplicity of the room. Instinctively, my mother and I sat on two of them, as we waited for the fortune-teller to emerge. A minute later, the witch made her appearance – a stout woman who looked like she was in her sixties, dressed in an ordinary T-shirt and a faded skirt. Truth be told, she resembled a housekeeper more than a person of mysteries.

She handed me a white coffee cup, that had obviously seen better times, filled with dark, black coffee that looked like mud, but smelled like a fresh promise. I obeyed her instruction to drink the coffee, and turn the cup upside down and back again. She picked up the cup and looked closely at the lines, marks and endless patterns that decorated the cup. I couldn't help but think about my math lessons, in which I learn about fractals. She paused, staring deep into the black, muddy lumps that were the residue of the coffee. Then she looked up at me and with an astonished, joyous voice, she pointed at some of the newly formed fractals and said: "Look here! Can you see them?! It's amazing! There is a whole bunch of spirits guarding you!"

*

One after the other, the Yahrtzeit candles burst into life, their light cheerfully embracing Shoshana's heart with their dance. She was only twelve years old and, having been invited for the first time to her new neighbor's house to watch their strange ceremony of candles, was completely captured by the dancing lights. Shoshana's eyes burned as she watched her spirit dance around the room with the memorial flames. Dreamily, she watched Rivka, the mother of the house, kneel quietly near the Yahrzeit candles, that stood proud by the Chanukiah – the special eight-branched candelabra that is traditionally lit each day of the Hanukah holiday. The two Hanukah candles watched, embarrassed, as Rivka's hand gently caressed the Yahrzeit light.

"*Yitgadal VeYitkadash Shmei Rabbah….*" Rivka's voice was clear and soft as she whispered the traditional Jewish words of the mourner's prayer. The motion of her hand embracing the light joined the dancing Yahrzeit lights and spirits, and soon the small room was entirely filled by the vibrant, lively dance. Shoshana continued to observe, fascinated by what she saw, until Rivka's son,

Moshe, penetrated her consciousness with his voice. Loud and clear, Moshe laughingly dared the death dance: "If you haven't seen the light of *my* Yahrzeit, you haven't seen a thing!" Rivka shuddered, her slim figure projecting a strong determination that matched her gentle but steady voice as she said to her son: "Enough, my little orphan, it isn't wise to dare the spirits who control your fate."

The spirits had been with Rivka since the day she was born. Even as an infant, she could hear them from the pit of her stomach. They were the patriarchs and matriarchs of her people, and they possessed the wisdom and experience of kings and queens, who bestowed their gems on the chosen. Rivka knew she was one of their favorites. They would embed clear prophecies in her mind, either bringing the comfort of relief or the unease of disturbance. They would whisper light and shadow in her ears, providing her with a unique, bittersweet understanding. She knew what they expected of her. She respected the advice of the good spirits, for she knew that they were protective and loving, and she was filled with awe of the evil spirits, for she knew that they sought the dark sides hidden within her soul.

All of the spirits, both good and evil, were there when she was born, stood beside her as she got married, accompanied her when she gave birth to her children and were present when she had to bury some of them. They embraced her during moments of joy, love, grief and anguish. They often gave her a very clear and accurate vision of the future, a gift that made her husband, Isaac, very nervous whenever he saw evidence of it. And they all came with her on the year-long journey from Russia to the land of Israel at the turn of the twentieth century. She had arrived in Jaffa in 1903, twelve years earlier, with Isaac and their four children, openly knowing she was following Isaac's dreams and supporting his feverish, even if seemingly practical, messianic rush. Her scholar husband was about to become the assistant manager of the new Anglo-Palestine Company bank in Jaffa, his first real job since they were married.

As the ship approached the port of Jaffa, Rivka stood watching the waves of the Mediterranean Sea. It was her first time at sea, far away from home, journeying to a distant, unfamiliar place, knowing only that this had once been the land of milk and honey, but was currently a land of sun and malaria. The white foam and gentle whooshing of the water, as it hit the sides of the ship, were at once soothing and peaceful, conjuring in her mind a rhythmic melody, like the cooing sound of her mother's Yiddish lullaby.

Sleep my child, there is a bird on the tree
Oh mother, a bird I would like to be!

She was still humming the tune, her head filled with birds, when her husband, Isaac, came up behind her and cuddled her in his firm arms, whispering joyfully in her ears: "See, my dove, we are coming to the promised land!" Rivka saw the fire in Isaac's eyes while the evil spirits were snickering in the back of her mind, and the good spirits surrounded her and watched the approaching Holy Land with an astonished silence. And she was silent, too.

As the boat approached the port of Jaffa, Rivka's thoughts became clear and she began to relax, for she knew Isaac would be successful. She also knew, even then, that this journey was going to be the first of many wanderings, that would take them through the promised land, beyond and back. And she knew that Jerusalem would be the place where she would give birth to her last child, Moshe, the first and only child she would bear in the land of Israel.

Twelve years later, as she stood watching the Yahrzeit flames, all the voices, sights, smells and memories that belonged to her journeys started to float gently around her, hand in hand with her spirits, embracing her soul. Transfixed, she watched them, disturbed only by the penetration of reality that was Moshe's mocking voice.

Moshe was born with a mark of doom, and he provoked and

taunted the angel of death by pulling and pushing his heel into the angel's dark face. From the moment he was born, the angel of death pursued him, attempting to grab Moshe by his foot, but Moshe outsmarted him by pushing his heel deep into the angel's nose, directly into his twin sister's breath. Moshe was born strong and laughing, with his eyes wide open in curiosity. The sight of his beautiful face caused the Christian midwife to catch her breath; when she saw that his heel was pulling out a baby girl after him, beautiful as heaven, but completely dead, she quickly crossed herself, handed Moshe to Rivka, took her money and the dead baby girl, and fled from the house. "He who is born under the mark of death, death shall seek him, never giving in until he has him in his grasp," she mumbled, her eyes filled with fright and her feet carrying her far through the twists and turns of Jerusalem's narrow labyrinth of alleys.

Rivka didn't even hear her. Filled with maternal pride, she lay her beautiful son on her breast, carefully drinking in each one of his beautiful features. She kissed his face softly, blessing him and capturing the warm tears that fell from her eyes onto his face with her tongue.

From the very moment she had conceived, nine months earlier, she knew she was once again pregnant with twins. And with the same confidence she knew the heartless, cheating fate awaiting them. At first, she tried to defy the murmurs whispering inside her head and ignore the familiar twist of sounds in her stomach. Then she tried to persuade the voices of her feverish heart, crying and begging for the life of her unborn daughter. But the spirits that had accompanied Rivka since the day she was born would not surrender. Again and again, they would lay the image of her sacrificed daughter in front of her eyes. Grief-stricken and filled with fear, Rivka wandered through the narrow alleys of Jerusalem, her small, slim body enveloped by an aura of wonder. Her blond hair neatly tied in a bun and her deep blue eyes as blazing as the sun, Rivka was an unusual sight. She sought advice from those who speak with ghosts, saints and spirits, begging for the healing and salvation of her baby whose fate was decided before birth.

During the first months of her pregnancy, the house was decorated with colorful ribbons, red, yellow and blue, each ribbon carrying a promise of shelter and forgiveness. Garlic chains hung from the window sills, the mezuzot – the prayer boxes that every Jew affixes to his doors – were carefully checked and replaced. Every precaution possible was taken. Each Friday, the Yemenite holy man, Diwan The Wise, came from the Yemenite quarter in Jerusalem to give a special blessing against the evil eye, spraying holy water in the house until it glistened, while lighting scented leaves that choked the breath with sweetness, all part of a well-known ritual that was a famous, excellent remedy for expelling evil spirits and bringing back the saints. Rivka followed little Olga and Racheli around the house, tying ribbons around their curls and tying silk strings around Ofsey's and Aaron's wrists. Even Isaac, who at first had vigorously objected to the idolatry that had suddenly invaded his household, surrendered in the face of his wife's anxiety, and placed a chamsa – the palm against all evil – into his pocket, meticulously transferring it from the pocket of one suit to the other as he dressed handsomely each morning, hoping it would help calm down his beloved wife. But with every blessing whispered, with each ribbon added to the cheerful rainbow festival illuminating the house, Rivka could hear the voices inside her troubled stomach becoming clearer and clearer, and increasingly felt the heavy weight of fate until she finally caved in.

Isaac couldn't understand the change that had overcome Rivka in her last pregnancy. In her former pregnancies, all nine of them, she was as happy and light as a butterfly. Filled with anxiety and fear, he watched the gray and tempered ocean gushing in Rivka's eyes, and his heart filled with the prophecies of doom. Even when she reassured him, time and again, that she was happy with her pregnancy, his mind would not rest, for he had long ago learned that his wife spoke with spirits and held the knowledge of the future in her soul. He tried to ease her with gifts, showering affection and love upon her, helping her with the daily chores and returning early from his job at the bank, but nothing seemed to help: Rivka continued to walk around the house like a ghost, tears welling in the bottom of her eyes and her soul ravaged.

For nine whole months she spoke to the twins who were running inside her. She was determined to pass her narrative to her unborn daughter before her death-birth, to equip her with the love and pride of her heritage before she met the angels. Throughout her entire pregnancy, she invested her energy in the daughter within her. But now, after her daughter had been taken away, and all that was left was her son, she felt it was time to immerse herself completely in his being. Gently, she collected the tears that fell from her eyes onto his face with her mouth, drinking him in until his face shone like a baby that had been pulled out of water. "Moshe," she whispered. "I will call you Moshe, for I have pulled you out from the depths of my tragedy." To these words, the shadows cast by the candlelight started moving around the room in a slow, embracing ballet, and Rivka raised her eyes to them. Confident, the shadows reassured her that the spirits who had guarded her all her life would now guard her newborn son. And with the same confidence she knew she would have to guard him with every single drop of the ocean in her eyes. For those who are born with the mark of death, death continues to pursue them, following their every move. And no one was more familiar with the mocking deceitfulness of the angel of darkness than Rivka.

Death, the terrible angel of darkness, continued to follow her as she roamed with her family throughout the Ottoman Empire, and was still following her years later during the final journey that took her back home from Beirut to Tel Aviv. She was standing restless on the deck, watching the waves break violently and listening to the voices of her thousand spirits, that made their way from her stomach to her head. She stood there for what seemed like a lifetime, the blue in her eyes growing darker and darker, blending with the angry waves of the sea. Moshe was running around, calling her name, trying to capture her attention – "Mom, see this hat, I look like a captain!" – but she did not hear him and remained motionless until the rooftops of Jaffa appeared on the distant horizon. It was her second arrival at Jaffa port, this time without her beloved husband, and she guarded the city fiercely with her gaze when the boats came to take them to shore.

Dreamily, she floated in the tiny fisherman's boat, her black dress swaying around her like the waves, her hand firmly supported by the grasp of Moshe's, her eyes gazing into the distance, her restless mind in turmoil. Even when her firstborn son, Ofsey, who was already twenty-six and married, met them at the port and led them to the white houses of young Tel Aviv, her mind still stormed, as if creating a wedge between her and reality.

Only when she took her first steps into the entrance to the new house Ofsey had built for them was her mind suddenly put to rest. The ghosts of her thoughts suddenly burst out of her head and stabilized themselves as a wall on her right and on her left, and she passed between them. Suddenly tall, head high and proud, she passed, with slow, measured steps, and her walled thoughts were silenced in awe. Eyes wide open, she looked straight at them, at the creations of her fiery mind which stood and escorted her into the house. There they were, her brothers and her sister, their eyes lowered to the ground. Rivka looked at them, her gaze penetrating their imaginary hollow, ghostly bodies and a taste of bitter victory filled her mouth.

Standing in front of her was her mother, the wrinkles of worry all ironed from her face and her eyes lit with an approving smile. There was her Isaac, tall and slender, dressed and pressed, handsome and smiling, like he was on the day he first penetrated her soul with his smile. Standing next to him were five of their children, young and beautiful, innocent as the flowers they were, betraying no sign of the calamities that had landed on their bodies and snatched their souls.

And there was her father, Eliezer, the rich lumber merchant, nodding his head lovingly, stretching out his hand to her, his ghost leading her into the house. Slowly, she walked into the last house she would live in, her firstborn to her right and her father's ghost to her left, opening with his hands the future that she still had left. Her father's hand moved gallantly, and the door opened, as if on its own, to greet her. She could hear her father saying softly: "This is your kingdom, my plum, this is your house of rest."

The second half of the nineteenth century had been very kind to Eliezer, Rivka's father, for lumber wasn't the only thing he sold: his main business was building railroads that cut through the length and breadth of the Tzar's country. He was not only rich – he was also a scholar, a man of The Book, with his own place of honor at the synagogue of his town. But, above all, he was a kind and generous man who loved having guests at his table every Shabbat and who gave substantially to charity. He had seven children, five boys and two girls. Though he loved them all dearly, Rivka, his firstborn, had a special place in his heart. "My plum" he would call her, his loud, bass voice suddenly becoming soft. And he never tired of looking into her big, beautiful, sky-blue eyes, watching all the angels of innocence dancing in them.

When Rivka was born, the whole town whispered that Eliezer and Fruma had given birth to a daughter with eyes as blue as the sky – large, beautiful and innocent as angels from above. Her eyes were like water buckets so large and enticing that you had no choice but to drown in them. The good souls of the town came to Fruma's bedside, hanging garlands of white garlic and pomegranates above the child's head, an assurance of a long and fruitful life. The town's evil tongues whispered: "Those who have eyes as blue as water are born to roam, like waves she will sail to faraway places and her roots will always be thirsty." As Rivka grew, the blue in her eyes became deeper and richer, inviting the brave to venture nearer, while scaring the cowards away.

When Rivka was fifteen, Hershl the matchmaker started appearing at Eliezer's doorstep with a handful of propositions, all of them categorically rejected by Eliezer. One wasn't a scholar, another was not honorable, a third had madness in his family. "I am looking for a good match!" roared Eliezer at a trembling Hershl. "My Rivka is a good catch with a respectable dowry – she will make a fine wife. Don't forget that she is a Kvitkovsky! And you are offering second-hand grooms!"

Hershl fumbled for the appropriate words. "No one is good enough for your Rivka, I assure you," he tried soothingly. "But…" he hesitated, "all I have left are two young men. Both of them come from fine families, but each one…how shall I put it…each one has a thorn…a small, insignificant thorn, I assure you." Hershl quickly added before Eliezer could start screaming again, "One is an amazing scholar, elevated above all his peers at the Yeshiva, the Rabbi predicts he will be a great man. But he is poor, an orphan who has no money or profession, though his family was respected and honest…he will always depend on your generosity. The other is the son of a rich and respectable family, but he has no knowledge of The Book…he has never learned, but he does know his prayers and he is a good boy. These two are the best I have!"

Eliezer thought long and hard about Rivka's shidduch, her match made in heaven. How could he decide who is a better prospect? Who will be the true, worthy groom for his beloved daughter? On the one hand, there was the scholar, a boy of wisdom, great in studying the Torah – oh, how he will enjoy Shabbat dinners with him, discussing the finer details of commentary and interpretation of each week's portion! In his heart, Eliezer always regretted that he himself never had enough time to devote to study. Not that being a merchant was bad, God forbid, and it even gave him a good living to provide his family – but all these trimmings were nothing when compared to the sweetness of studying the Torah. And now God was giving him the opportunity to find a husband who was a scholar for his Rivka! Eliezer had no shortage of money, so he would support Rivka and her husband and, God willing, he will support Rivka's children, his first grandchildren…

But – what will happen when he, Eliezer, is gone? What will the rest of his children have to say when they have to carry the burden of supporting not only their own families but also Rivka, her husband and, God willing, their many children?…

On the other hand – the son of a rich family will never need his support. Rivka and her children will never know the embarrassment of hunger and charity, they will be his source of comfort when he is old, and the Torah is always something one can start learning if only one has the time…

Perplexed, Eliezer's mind kept swaying back and forth, until one night at dinner he looked into his daughter's big blue eyes and read the words written in their depth: he shall let Rivka choose – she alone carries the answer. " I shall call the girl and ask her," he chuckled to himself. And so he did. Eliezer called Rivka and told her of the two options.

"My plum, you are about to spend your entire life with your groom. I want to make sure you are happy. Therefore, I will allow you to choose."

Rivka's eyes grew stormy blue with anticipation as her father continued. "This Shabbat, Ezra Bernstein, the son of the linen merchant, will be honored at the Temple with an aliyah – going up to the Bimah – the prayer platform – and reading from the Torah. You will be in the women's section, hidden behind the curtain, and you will be able to see his face through the curtain. The following Shabbat, Isaac Lipavsky, the orphan, will do the aliyah and you will be able to see *his* face as well. Then you can make your choice. I will honor whatever you decide."

The following Shabbat, Rivka found herself standing in the synagogue behind the curtain in the women's section, peeking at the praying men. Dressed in her best Shabbat clothes, her heart pounding, she watched her intended groom walk up to the Bimah. With a soft, uncertain voice he stood and said the blessing. His back was broad and he kept shifting his legs from side to side. Rivka silently prayed that he would lift his eyes for a moment, just a moment, and look in her direction. When her prayer was answered, and he glanced at the women's section, his eyes met hers and she looked directly at him. Ezra looked as if he had been suddenly burned, his face turned completely red, and he quickly averted his gaze from Rivka's invasive eyes.

That entire week, Rivka walked very quietly around the house, avoiding her father's questioning gaze. She knew he was trying to capture her thoughts, seize a sign from the words floating in her soul. The truth was that she didn't know what to think, whether she liked Ezra or not, and the spirits that had always helped her before were annoyingly silent. "I still have one more groom to see," she thought. "I'll see him first, then decide."

The following Shabbat she stood once again behind the curtain when Isaac, the orphan, went up to the Bimah to bless. He was tall, slender and gentle, as though needing protection. Contrastingly, his voice was loud and clear, and the entire congregation followed his lead. Enchanted, she listened to him pray, and before she could fully understand what was happening, he raised his eyes directly at hers, and a broad smile lit his eyes, his lips, his whole body. The smile penetrated her soul like a knife, nailing her down, and an unfamiliar, sweet sense of pleasure spread throughout her entire body, from her head to the depths of her stomach and to the tips of her toes. At that moment, Rivka knew that this was the smile she wanted to see every day for the rest of her life, this was the smile she wanted to see reflected in the eyes of her children. And at that moment, she heard with full certainty the voices of the spirits that declared on the day she was born: "Isaac the orphan is to be your heavenly match."

That very same day, she announced her decision: "I want the orphan."

Isaac the orphan, Rivka's groom, was a Talmid Hacham – an excellent scholar of the Bible whom everyone predicted was likely to become a great rabbi. Orphaned at ten, he and his eight-year-old sister Feiga were left to the care of their old grandparents. Isaac, whose sharp mind was recognized from the age of three, was sent to study at the local Yeshiva – the rabbi's school. After making sure he was happy there, his grandparents took Feiga and set off with her to the Holy Land so she could be married and they could die and be buried peacefully in Jerusalem.

"You must stay here," they told Isaac when he begged to join them. "Stay and become a great rabbi. It was your parents' wish before they were slaughtered by the Cossacks…study hard and be a scholar of the Torah. It is the only way to carry on our sacred traditions. Become a rabbi and make us proud!" And with those words, they left. From that moment on, Isaac was on his own.

The whole town was joyous on the day Isaac and Rivka were married. "Even their names suggest that they were meant for each other," Rivka's father happily announced. The bride and groom had shared but a few stolen glances at each other, but these were enough to unite all the deep blue water drops from Rivka's eyes with the dancing flames in Isaac's soul into one sweeping dance, as though water and fire had been one entity since Genesis. And, as fire and water, they floated in the town streets, followed by the blessings of the good and the kind and by the whispers of the jealous and narrow-minded.

Rivka and Isaac were happy in their marriage. Rivka was very proud of her husband, who walked tall from their home every morning to his studies, and the rumors of his wisdom were the talk of the town. She was also grateful for her father's pride, who announced that he would grant the newlyweds the traditional *keset* – seven years of full financial support, on the condition that Isaac studies the Torah and becomes a great rabbi.

But nothing compared to the joy of the physical pleasure of love she had discovered, amazed, in Isaac's arms. Every morning, Isaac kissed her lips and whispered in her ears that her kisses were sweeter than the Torah itself. And every evening he slowly unbuttoned her dress, swallowing her into his soul and was swallowed into her bodily storm. He held her close, very close, his gaze drifting in the sea of her dark blue eyes, his lips whispering pleasing words into her ears, and his body making hers sway like a giant wave. Rivka, who was surprised at first by her own shamelessness, quickly replaced her surprise with pure addiction to the pleasure of being owned and owning all-at-once. She waited for him every evening, and once he returned they would shut the door of their little room and she would fall into his arms, kissing every inch of his face. He would laugh, caressing her back and holding her tight, and she would take his head and lead his lips to her breasts, her stomach, and every inch of her body. Laughing like children, excited by the discovery of themselves and each other, they made love wherever they fell – on the bed, on the floor, on the tiny dining table. They experimented, discovering a variety of ways to please each other, and enjoyed the pure relish of their lovemaking.

Rivka was so engulfed with her love that for the first time in her life she forgot to listen to the voices surrounding her – she did not heed the warning signs and forgot to appease the evil spirits. She didn't hear the whispering sounds of the demons, snickering at the saints, laughing at Rivka's addiction to the human pleasures of the flesh, rejoicing over the sacrifice they were about to demand. She also didn't know that on her wedding night, from within the materialization of his love, the first, tiny seed of doubt and action started to flicker in Isaac's soul, a seed that would grow and lead him to enlightenment, taking her and their yet unborn children to an unknown future. Isaac himself didn't realize it at that moment. If he had, he might have run away, frightened, from his newly sprouting identity – but he didn't know, and by the time he was aware of the new, independent spirit that was growing inside him, he was already in a different time and place. Seven years this sprout would grow, slowly and stubbornly, making way through concrete foundations, creating fine and irreparable cracks. Seven years would pass before Isaac would start nurturing this sprout, and yet another seven until he would begin to enjoy its fruits.

But all of this was unknown to Isaac and Rivka during those first wondrous months of 1887, and they were completely immersed in their happiness in a way that only new excited lovers can be.

Soon they were both filled with an astonished, naïve excitement when they discovered that Rivka was with child. From the moment she had conceived Rivka knew she was carrying a son, and she innocently told her husband of her knowledge. Isaac was frightened by his wife's ability to look directly into her soul and body as if they were transparent, and begged her not to say a word to anyone, so the evil spirits would not arise from their sleep and inflict danger on their yet unborn son. Rivka obeyed her husband, and nine months later their firstborn son, strong, healthy Ofsey-Joshua, was born. With kisses of happiness and laughter Rivka soothed Isaac's worries – "Don't fear, my love, I know that this son will grow to be a comfort and source of pride." And with the same confidence she whispered in Isaac's ears, only four months later, that the girl she is carrying in her womb would grow to be wise and bright-eyed as he.

Looking at his new son-in-law, Eliezer the merchant was overwhelmed by the sense of a man who had fulfilled his dreams. His beloved daughter, Rivka, was married and the mother of fine children – the fourth on the way, thank God – and her husband's name was renowned all over town for his wisdom and knowledge of the Torah. Eliezer's business was never as successful as it was during those years – his sons, now married and family men themselves, worked with their father in the lumber business. Eliezer was a generous man, and all his children lived with their families in the family mansion. Each family had its own small apartment, and each apartment overlooked a large courtyard. Most of the family activities were conducted in that court. Laundry, cooking and cleaning were entangled together amongst children who were running around, playing, studying the Torah and lending a helping hand to their mothers as the men were away working for the town paritz – governor, who officially owned the land and the business that Eliezer and his sons managed for him. Railways and castles were built throughout Russia under their strict supervision, horses and carriages continuously came and left toward the railways filled with lumber, food and people. There were always workers and helping hands that required lodging and food, and the family was always open and welcoming.

The hustle and bustle would reach its peak every Friday afternoon, as the family prepared for Shabbat. Chicken soup with large chunks of carrots, parsley and chicken, all bubbling happily together within the rich broth, was cooked all morning on the coal stoves, while from within the stoves, the sweet smell of challah bread, braided and decorated with raisins, and the aroma of apple cakes and kugels – a sweet noodle pie – spread and filled the court like a promise that made the children's smiles widen and sparkle with anticipation. Shabbat clothes were laid out, white shirts were cleaned, satin skirts and dark suits were pressed, and the best silverware was set. Children were caught and dunked into huge buckets of warm water and were scrubbed with lavender scented soap bars that drove the week's dust from their skin until they glistened. The high-spirited level of energy that was bubbling during the day, filling every little crack in the stone floors, and invading every splinter of the beams that lined the ceilings, would suddenly evaporate like a charm when the women lit the Shabbat candles at dusk. At that moment, the entire world changed and was transformed from being a busy, nervous and active circus into a quiet, enchanted and peaceful castle. A beautiful glow spread from each apartment to the court, accompanying the holy day into their homes, their lives, and their souls. Even the children miraculously calmed down, babies smiling contentedly and happy faces illuminated the court as the entire family and their guests gathered around Eliezer and Fruma's table for dinner: Shabbat had begun.

Shabbat was the best day of the week. With no conversations about work permitted, the main topics of conversation were the weekly Torah portion and scriptures, at which Rivka's Isaac excelled.

"Jerusalem is not merely a physical place," her husband eagerly stated, as he discussed the idea of redemption with his father-in-law. "It is a spiritual center, an intellectual and emotional being in the soul of every Jew…we learn that only the combination of all these aspects will bring true redemption for our people."

"We have been praying to return to our beloved Land for almost two thousand years, and, God willing, we will one day make the journey," Eliezer answered. "This country has been good enough to us, our traditions have developed here, and we know how to recognize the signs of trouble and stay away from them. Do your teachers believe that these times are different?"

"We have suffered persecution for so many years that we have grown accustomed to thinking this is the way it should be…we are always longing, always praying, never stopping our prayers, so we can find ways to turn our dreams into reality…."

"When all our young men are as fine scholars as you are, our redemption will come," Eliezer responded confidently.

"That is indeed what the Rabbis say…but the question is this," Isaac's voice was booming: "We learn that we must combine action with thoughts…when we received the Torah, our people said *na'aseh venishmah* – we shall do and we shall listen, which really means obey. We are immersed in listening, in obeying God's commandments, and now I am asking our Rabbis – what are we supposed to be doing about the DO part that should actually come before the LISTEN part...."

The children already drowsy, the younger ones fast asleep beneath the Shabbat table, Isaac and her father would continue debating for hours. How proud Rivka was! Not only was Isaac a great scholar, but he also had a strong, clear voice that made the Shabbat songs they sang at every meal sparkle and dance around the table with joy. Her pride reached new heights when she noticed Eliezer glancing around the table, his gaze falling on the curls of his grandchildren and the heads of his children. At those moments, Eliezer was filled with a sense that was stronger than pride and more important than accomplishment: he was filled with the happiness of love.

The family seemed so happy and united that Eliezer did not notice the undercurrents of tension that were stirring among his offspring until it was too late. He was surprised and angered when he suddenly noticed that the eyes of his five sons were becoming narrower and narrower, like almonds. At first, he dismissed his own reaction, telling himself that he must be wrong. But as time passed, and work increased, he was suddenly faced with the bare, ugly truth: his sons couldn't stand the idea that they were working so hard while their older sister, her husband and her children were dependent upon their support. "We are tearing our bodies with work, and they are tearing the sheets," the brothers would say to each other maliciously whenever they thought Rivka or their father were out of earshot. "What are they thinking? That we will keep working harder and harder while they continue to have baby after baby?"

The happier Rivka was, the narrower their eyes became. The more Isaac accomplished in his studies, the sharper were their whispers, cutting the air around them like dangerous knives, to the point that they ripped Eliezer's ears and squeezed an angry roar from his lips. Rivka's brothers did not dare defy their father, but Rivka could clearly feel their anger grow and feed the evil spirits whom she sensed were growing bolder. Every Friday evening, when she and her children would cross the family yard to their parents' house for the communal Shabbat dinner, she heard her sisters-in-law whisper: "Here comes the beggar!" She saw the wicked gazes in her brother's eyes. A seed of defiance she never thought existed started to grow inside her. Her lips pursed, her head high, she held little Olga's hand, Ofsey running in front, and baby Shima'le on her arm. Stubborn and proud, she joined the Shabbat table, her eyes openly defying the tension in the air. Only when Isaac sang the Shabbat blessings with her father, their voices clear and sweet, did she allow herself to calm down and happily anticipate the pleasures that awaited her at home, when the children would be asleep. Then, she knew, the whole house would be peaceful. They would listen to the quiet, confident hum of the children's breaths, and it would feel as if the whole world was standing still as her husband would lovingly caress and soothe her.

Each note that Isaac sung was accompanied by reassurance. Rivka drank the songs in, knowing that later at night she would sing them to her children, the music leading them to a dreamy slumber. Sitting at the table, she let her husband's melodies engulf her and the music lull the storm in her heart. She then directed her piercing gaze, blazing and dark blue as the night, at her brothers and their wives – and they averted their eyes, not understanding what power had made them suddenly feel stung. Even so, the brothers didn't know that their anger was food for evil spirits who quietly, eagerly, waited to strike. They were so preoccupied with their pettiness that they didn't notice the bad signs starting to close in on them until it was too late.

When Rivka gave birth to twin girls, who died of a raging scarlet fever several months later, the brothers were silenced for a while. Less than a month after the death of the twins, little Shima'le stumbled into the laundry basin and drowned at the age of two.

"Shima'le...my sweet, innocent baby...Shima'le..." The sight of Rivka's grief was overwhelming. Her sobs filled the air, creeping into the hearts of her brothers, covering the pavement with a lamentation so thick it couldn't be penetrated.

"Hush, my love, he is at peace now." Isaac's voice was gentle, concealing his own anguish.

"I want my Shima'le...." Rivka couldn't stop crying, rocking back and forth, holding the tiny dead child close to her stomach in a desperate effort to silence her deep inner voices of sorrow.

"We must bury him, Rivka," Isaac calmly stated.

"NO!"

When the twins died, she was silent, knowing that their little bodies were finally at peace. She understood that their suffering had finally come to an end, and she accepted their fate. But now she refused to let anyone touch Shima'le, continuing to hold him close, singing his favorite lullaby through her tears.

Heartbroken, Isaac embraced her, stroking her gently, his tears rolling silently down his cheeks, and whispered words of comfort tinged with despair that finally managed to seep into her soul. Her howls slowly diminished to quiet sobs. Somehow, with an inner strength that he didn't even know he possessed, Isaac convinced Rivka that they must bury the child before darkness, so he could rest with the angels. Rivka made her spirits pledge to guard her little baby and to make sure that he joined his baby sisters. Kissing Shima'le's innocent toddler face, she promised she would talk to him every day. Then, exhausted, she let Isaac take Shima'le away.

At first, Isaac was worried for Rivka's well-being, but she was a strong woman and the support of her husband and father helped her through her terrible losses. When she became pregnant again, giving birth to Aaron, the brother's poisoned minds awoke once more. When their younger sister, Blooma, married Shlomo

Pomerantz, the owner of a small soap factory, the brothers became even more vicious and the venom of their cruelty spread all over town. "Blooma," they said, "is a responsible person. She doesn't expect us all to wine and dine her. After all, let's face it," they snickered, "Rivka is too fine and her husband too delicate to work. Labor isn't for them, they are too intellectual. That's what she has us for." Blooma loved her older sister and was so afraid that the brothers would bring yet more calamity upon the family that one day she forced Shlomo to try and intervene with her brothers.

"Family is more important than anything," she argued. "They respect you, they will listen to you. You must go and set them straight!"

Shlomo was a kind man, very much in love with his new wife and on very good terms with her brothers. At first, he was reluctant to interfere, but after Blooma did not relent, crying and begging, he finally agreed. Blooma stayed behind at the soap factory while Shlomo went to talk to the brothers. They were in the middle of a conversation when suddenly they heard screams: "The factory is burning! Quick, bring water!"

The small, wooden factory burned to the ground within minutes. The whole town, including Shlomo, the brothers, Eliezer, Isaac and Rivka, searched for Blooma for hours until they realized with horror that she was gone in the fire. Ashes in his hair and craziness in his eyes, grief-stricken Shlomo ran into the house that had been his and Blooma's and a shot roared into the town air: he had killed himself to join his beloved Blooma.

The entire town was in a state of shock. During the shiva – the seven days of mourning – the people of the town came creeping, tiptoeing into the house, whispering their condolences, their eyes lowered and their spirits timid. Hardly a word was spoken. The family just sat there, numb, avoiding one another's eyes. Eliezer was out of his mind with grief and anger, the pain in his heart intensifying until it became a literal, physical pang, weakening his once strong body and proud spirit. He was about to have words with his sons when Rivka gently asked him to leave them be.

"What do you mean?" Eliezer demanded, the marks of worries and tragedy evident in his wrinkles. "I am still the head of this household, and I will not tolerate such behavior."

"Father, there is no point…." Rivka began.

"My plum, please," His voice was weak and begging. She had never heard him so miserable before. "We are family…family is more important than money…more important than the house we live in, the soil we slave…without our family and tradition, we are nothing."

"I know," Rivka spoke gently. She felt the net that her spirits had spread under her wings, supporting what she was about to say. "That's exactly why there is no point in you quarrelling with them." Watching the surprised expression sweeping over her father's face, Rivka did not blanch when she told her father her news: she and her little family were leaving.

The signs had been there for some time, and during the past few years, they had become clearer and clearer. It began with small conversations. Isaac would come home at night after a long day of study, a troubled look in his eyes. He started questioning the ways of his faith. He would engage in long conversations with Rivka, sharing with her new ideas he had heard of and worse – new ideas he had read about in hidden, forbidden newspapers and books. Ideas speaking of action instead of prayer, ideas speaking of a nation awakening, standing up for itself. Ideas that called for rejecting the past and embracing a new future instead, a future that demanded change, welcomed liberalism and advancement, a future that involved denouncing the old world and creating a new, improved one. A future that would ensure safety and prosperity for the Jewish people in their homeland. Ideas that were labeled "Enlightenment," and that men of pure, traditional Jewish faith were not supposed to embrace.

Isaac became increasingly restless. Secretly, with only Rivka knowing, Isaac started learning different languages, general history and literature. He would leave the Yeshiva early, go to the library and lose himself in an endless chain of books. He read everything he could find, eager to know more, his brilliant mind like a dry sponge placed in water, absorbing it all. Within less than a year, he had mastered French, German and English. He studied the works of the great philosophers. With each personal tragedy, his restlessness and questioning intensified. With each book he read, his confidence in the necessity of change grew stronger. He wasn't certain what kind of change he was after, but he knew he had to search for a new beginning.

With the support of her spirits, Rivka turned into his silent, accepting partner in this journey of the soul, so when Isaac announced that he was leaving for America at the end of the shiva for Blooma, she was the only one not surprised. "I am going to find a job there," he told Eliezer and the brothers, "and when I settle I will send for Rivka and the children." Knowing his daughter too well to argue, and after all that had happened, Eliezer silently accepted their decision. A few months later, Isaac was on his way, leaving Rivka behind with three children and another daughter on the way.

The following year was one of the most difficult times Rivka had known. With Eliezer too weak to protect her, she was forced to sell her silverware and give the money to her brothers for their permission to remain in the family mansion. She was treated like an outcast by her sisters-in-law, and her children were mocked as beggars by their cousins.

But most of all, Rivka missed Isaac terribly. His letters were very few but very loving, and she knew he was suffering equally. She sent him letters of reassurance, never revealing her hardship. She gave birth to Leah, who quietly died one night a few months after her birth. It was then that Rivka noticed that all the Yahrzeits – the memorial days – fell around the holiday of Hanukah. The twins, Shima'le, Leah and even Blooma – all died within the eight days of Hanukah. Understanding that this was a message from her spirits, Rivka began a habit that soon became an obsession: she began lighting all five Yahrzeit candles together with the Hanukah candles. From that year on, wherever she lived, every day of Hanukah, there would be two tables set up in the living room: one table with the five Yahrtzeit candles, dancing happily and creating gay shadows on the walls, and a table for the Chanukiah, with its candles added from day to day. Starting with the lighting of one candle on the Chanukiah each day of the holiday, one more candle would be added until the entire Chanukiah – all eight candles and the ninth server candle, the *shamash* – was ablaze.

And yet somehow, for reasons unknown, the light of the menorah was always second-best, giving way gracefully, and with awe, to the light of the memorial candles. Although happy Hanukah songs were sung, the simple words of the mourner's prayer – the Kaddish – that Rivka stubbornly insisted on singing when lighting the Yahrtzeit candles, those words were always the ones that brought peace and comfort to her soul. "*Yitgadal VeYitkadash Shmei Rabbah….*" Rivka's voice was clear as the flow of water in her eyes, as holy as the souls she had parted from, as soothing as her lullabies. It made the children dream and the adults relax. It was what the spirits of the saints wanted for Rivka. She had paid for it with blood. And she knew that, as the years went by, there would be more Yahrzeit candles to add.

Exactly one year after he had left, Isaac returned. He found a craving, hungry wife and children waiting for him, and his own longing and loneliness were drowned in his tears. He measured the children to see how much they had grown, he cried for little Leah who was born and died without him ever seeing her, he learned from Rivka all about the events that had taken place while he was gone, and then he started talking.

"I have met wonderful people," he told Rivka. "People of our own nation, Jews like us who dream of freedom and independence. Jews who believe that after two thousand years of exile, poverty and helplessness, two thousand years of praying and dreaming about the day we will return to our beloved Land of Israel, the time has come to make that dream come true. Time for combining dream with action, prayer with work – *Halacha* and *Ma'aseh*, as our scriptures teach us...."

"Where...How...?" Rivka was puzzled.

"On the train from Odessa to France, I met an amazing man with a dark beard and fire in his eyes. He talked about our future in a way no one has ever talked before...." Isaac was growing increasingly excited. "I believe he is a prophet. He will become our second Moses. His name is Theodore Herzl and he believes in establishing a Jewish state in our ancient homeland. Can you imagine?!" Rivka could taste the passion in his words. "A real state for the Jews! A home of our own! A place where we can finally decide our own fate, live our lives in peace, work for ourselves without having to hide behind a paritz and worry that he or any other bunch of hooligans will drive us away or even worse – torture and slaughter us whenever their hearts desire without anyone stopping them.... Just the idea of this Jewish renewal makes my heart sing with joy! But it won't be easy," Isaac continued in a stern voice. "There is much to be done. And we are going to start immediately."

Rivka looked at him, confused, "Will you be working for this man in America? When are we leaving?"

"America?" Isaac looked at her, puzzled, and then said in a joyful, confident voice: "We are not going to America. We are going to Eretz Yisrael! We are leaving for Palestine!"

Chapter 2

DVORA

1882–1907

Three generations of Israeli-born people led to the day I was born, a fourth generation sabra. That's what they call us Israeli-born children, sabarim, the fruit of the Sabar Cactus, for we are thorny and tough on the outside but when stripped to our hearts, we are the sweetest, most scrumptious, fruit you have ever tasted. Hardly a surprise to anyone who has plunged into the lives of the generations responsible for her being, as I have. Especially when I think of my great-grandmother, Dvora, a first Sabra herself, and her family, or when I revisit the life of Moshe, my great-grandmother Rivka's first Sabra. My forefathers came from Europe, some at the end of the nineteenth century, some at the beginning of the twentieth century, all of them determined to revive Jewish freedom and independence in the ancient Land that was promised to the Jewish people through a covenant with the Lord, at least according to the Bible. They worked very hard, had many disappointments as well as successes, losses as well as gains, and never once did they think they should have gone somewhere else. The land became part of their skin, its treasures part of their sweat, the weather part of their demeanor and the culture part of their soul. And it was all very romantically wrapped as a gift and handed to me to continue on the day that I was born.

The whole thing took no longer than two hours. From the very first contraction to the first time the baby cried, it was one of the fastest and easiest births that the midwife had ever seen. Dvora wasn't even tired when her new baby, a daughter this time, was placed in her arms. She explored each one of the baby's features with a growing sense of disappointment. This is what her daughter looks like?! The daughter of one of the most beautiful women in the entire northern part of Palestine? The daughter of the Belle of Zichron Yaacov? Her mind drifted to her son, Nathan, her firstborn, only two years old and already making girls turn their heads to look at him when he skipped by in his joyful, toddler manner. How proud she was when he was born! What a beautiful baby he was, with the large blue eyes of his father and the rosy red cheeks of his mother! Sturdy and alert, she named him Nathan – a gift given to her by God. Well, or at least given to her by her husband Ish – the best-looking man ever to ride into her small village of Zichron Yaacov since her parents founded it, twenty-four years earlier.

The village of Zichron Yaacov is perched on the Carmel mountains, south of Haifa, the large port city of the north. It was founded by a group of idealistic Jews who decided to make history by establishing a new homeland for the Jewish People on the very soil from which they were exiled almost two thousand years before. They were young and bright, very stubborn and naïve, and didn't have the slightest idea about what they were doing. They tried to grow crops, work the harsh land, stand up to a nasty climate, fight diseases and hostile enemies and raise families all at once, and it nearly cost them their lives.

Dvora's parents, Jacob and Chaya Goldstein, were part of that group. Young idealists from Romania, they arrived at the shores of the Ottoman Empire region of Palestine in 1882 with songs on their lips and prayers in their hearts, only to find that they had been thrown into a life very different than what they were used to or had imagined. Every detail of their lives, from the food they ate and the clothes they wore to the furniture they brought from their native land, seemed to sprout from the gray, drizzling skies of Romania, its dark green mountains and wide potato fields. All of that was struck by the yellow, blazing sun of Palestine, its white shores and salty air and the narrow, crowded alleys of the city swarming with men who carried amber beads in their hands, who were dressed in long robes and who wore hats that looked like upside-down red buckets on their heads. The heat made the newcomers from Europe dizzy, the salt made their breath sour, and their surroundings were like a bad dream.

But Jacob and his young wife Chaya were determined to succeed, as were the rest of the group of dreamers, and they were so stubborn about it, and were so busy trying to make it happen, that they were the first ones to stand astonished when one day they woke up and understood that their dream had actually come true: Zichron Yaacov became an established fact, a place that everyone in Palestine, including the Turks, admired. It had become the Belle of the Ball, one of the most respected of new Jewish settlements, the envy and pride of the Halutzim – the Jewish pioneers of the late nineteenth and early twentieth century.

Since she could remember, Dvora always knew she would leave Zichron Yaacov; it seemed too provincial to her, too small for her dreams and interests. Born only two years after it was established, she was brought up like most of Zichron Yaacov's children, a newly-founded aristocracy of Jewish farmers, people who worked the land for intellectual and idealistic reasons rather than practical and agricultural ones. Like the rest of the children in the village,

Dvora learned etiquette, French and embroidery and took piano lessons alongside Bible and Hebrew lessons. At home, she helped her parents with the daily chores of farming and housekeeping.

Publicly, the settlers of Zichron Yaacov called themselves the New Hebrew People, the modern aristocracy of Jewish farmers and pioneers. But when left alone with their hearts, even they had to admit that it was mostly a parade of charades, a fake act covered with French manners and dialect that, when rubbed a bit, easily betrayed their true colors: old-fashioned Jewish tradition, hallucinations that miraculously came true and a lot of back-breaking, hand-scraping hard work.

Although immersed in village life, there was always a part of Dvora that felt like an outsider in Zichron Yaacov. She was tall and beautiful, with long brown hair and dark brown eyes that pierced straight through you. Stubborn, independent and never biting her tongue before saying exactly what she thought, Dvora had a free, practical spirit that did not succumb to the romantic dreams and visions that were the food of her pioneer parents. Zichron Yaacov seemed too small for her aspirations, its inhabitants too plain. As Dvora grew older, she longed for the city – any city, a place where the excitement of a normal day would be far more profound than the village herd going up the hill and back down the main street to the stalls. A place where the food would be finer than grapes, goat cheese and olives, and your hands would not be rough from the harshness of working in the fields. A place where people did not have to worry endlessly about the Arab herdsmen allowing their goats to trample on, and feed from, the village crops, the delicate plants that they worked so hard to grow, the leaves that would bring the food of tomorrow. It was a common sight: someone would run from the fields that surrounded the foot of the hill all the way up into the village, yelling, "The herds are in the fields again!" At that signal, everyone would stop what they were doing and grab anything they could find – a plow, a broomstick, a hoe – and rush down to the fields to drive the animals away. The Arab shepherds always stood by, laughing, mocking and teasing the settlers, until suddenly the Turkish soldiers would appear, always accusing the settlers of provocation, threatening to arrest them and refusing to leave until a handsome bakshish – bribe – was paid, a few gold coins that added humiliation and fear to the farmers' growing anguish and frustration.

"Can I come, too?" Dvora's voice was eager. "Please?"

"Jaffa is no place for young girls. You should stay home with the others and help your father while we are gone." Her mother was busy packing the wagon and her strict, direct voice brought tears to Dvora's eyes. There was no room for debate. Chaya and Dvora's older brothers were going all the way south to Jaffa to buy supplies for their farm, and Chaya was terrified by the prospect of having her growing daughter subject to the dangers of the road. The children knew that when Chaya used this direct tone, they had better remain silent. All except Dvora.

"I'm not a young girl anymore! I'm fourteen years old and I can take care of myself!" Dvora's foot stamped the ground angrily. "Papa, please let me go! Just this once!"

Jacob looked into his beautiful daughter's eyes. He wasn't certain what the longing in them indicated, but he did not have the heart to ignore it. Sighing, he turned to his wife. "It can't hurt," he said, avoiding direct contact with Chaya's astonished gaze. "The boys will take care of you both. Ruth will stay and help out with the farm and the young ones."

Chaya started to protest, but Jacob cut her short. "Let her have some fun. She needs it."

An hour later, Dvora was on her way to Jaffa with her mother and older brothers for three whole, glorious days. She was speechless with delight. Chaya was speechless with anger.

For the rest of her life, Dvora would never forget her first visit to the city of Jaffa. She ignored her mother's demand to sit quietly in the wagon. Thirsty for excitement, her body already showing the promise it would keep when she would become a fully-developed woman, Dvora's head was raised high and her eyes looked openly and shamelessly at the astonishing sights all around her as the wagon entered the city of Jaffa. She didn't notice the lustful, staring eyes of the Turks following her, whose gaze bathed in the sun that gleamed on her shining, loose hair and revelled in the dreams that her ripening body reflected.

Jaffa was a crowded, busy place, with small and ancient alleyways, colorful shops filled with anything you could imagine. Devora focused all of her senses on drinking in her new surroundings, oblivious to all else. The major port of entry into the land, Jaffa was an exciting crossroads. There were people of different hues, shapes and attire: Turks, Armenians, Arabs, Germans, Bedouins, Christians, Jews and many, many others were running around, creating a frenzied, vivid and energetic place with an international flair; some of them were wearing long, strange dresses she had never seen before, some walking calmly, beads in their hands. Others were sitting peacefully at the entrance to their shops, smoking long pipes, copper trays with very black coffee in very small cups and plates with sweets on them at their feet, while people shouted or rushed by. The alleyways carried a crowded sensation of scents, a combination that made her dizzy and curious – scents of leather, wood, spices, fish and brass. It bore no resemblance to the insignificant, airy and flower-filled fields where she and her siblings had grown up only a few mule-driven hours away.

"What a composition of man-made mess," her oldest brother, Sam, murmured under his breath as they walked through the steamy alleyways.

"It's amazing that people actually live like this," Daniel, brother number two, remarked. "Look how crowded everything is."

"And smelly," Sam added.

"How can you say that?!" Dvora demanded, "It's fascinating…" Her voice trailed as her eyes caught a glimpse of a rich, colorful pile of leather bags. She inhaled the intoxicating scent of leather and her eyes sparkled at the scenes rushing all around her. She felt very much alive, a feeling that was disturbed only for a moment by the sight of a large Turkish soldier looking at her with lust in his eyes. Irritated, she turned her eyes and tried to ignore him, hoping no one would notice.

But Chaya did. "Come along, children, our business is done here." Dvora heard the tension in her mother's voice. Before she knew it, Sam and Daniel grabbed her and hurried her toward the waiting wagon. The soldier disappeared into the crowd.

On their way back home, two days later, they passed through Neve Tzedek, a neighborhood north of Jaffa. It was bright and airy, very close to the city – and most importantly, it was all Jewish. Enchanted, Dvora knew that she had found the place she would return to when she grew up. Watching her daughter closely, Chaya Goldstein knew that Dvora would leave Zichron when the time came, and she sadly acknowledged that Dvora was not meant to be a *halutza* – a woman pioneer farmer. Dvora was proud of Zichron Yaacov, and of what it had become in the sixteen years it had existed, but the feeling of pride Dvora had for her birthplace did not belong to her – it was her parents' pride. Zichron Yaacov was their project, and she needed a project of her own.

The pride that Dvora felt toward her parents' project was shared by her five siblings as well. Sam, Daniel, Dvora, Ruth, Pnina and Aminadav – in that order – all blossomed under their father's wing, with the stories he ingrained into their souls, until they became part of their bones and in turn the consequences of their lives and choices. Every Shabbat morning was story time for Jacob Goldstein's children. After returning from morning services at the synagogue, the very synagogue he had helped to establish, always accompanied by some of the children, Jacob would lay his prayer-book on the table, fold his *Talith* neatly and sink into his big chair, humming. That was the sign they all waited for. Within a matter of seconds, no matter what they were doing, the Goldstein children gathered around him – the older ones sitting at his feet, the younger ones pressed against the huge arms of the chair, the youngest of all on his lap. While Chaya prepared lunch, Jacob sailed away with their imaginations, telling them tales about the old country and the new life they had created in Palestine. Dvora loved the stories of the first days of the little village, and she begged her Papa to tell them over and over again.

"More than anything, it was wet," Jacob began his story. "It was the middle of winter, a cold, rainy and windy December, and we walked a whole day from Haifa to our new home – men, women and beasts. The paths were filled with mud, the rain made large puddles, and the wind whistled straight into our freezing bones. The oxen struggled to pull the wagons, which were filled with anything imaginable: food, blankets, tools and seeds, even this chair that I'm sitting on. Everything we owned was contained in those wagons. It probably wasn't the best time to do this, but it was the second day of Hanukah and we all felt we were walking in the footsteps of the Maccabim, our ancient freedom fighters, rebuilding the new Jewish home for the ancient Jewish people. I was certain that their leader, Yehuda the Maccabi himself, was smiling down at us, approving this newly-found feeling of freedom that we had acquired."

The soaring spirits of the young settlers, barely in their twenties, who had come all the way from Romania to make their dream of Jewish freedom come true, were crushed to the ground when they arrived at the foot of the hill that was to become their new home.

"When we finally saw the hill, expecting to find the Garden of Eden itself, it seemed like a steep, barren mountain to us. We were shocked: only a narrow path led toward the top, winding amongst thorny bushes and huge rocks, and we had to make our way through them toward the summit. There was no way the oxen could drag the wagons uphill, even if the wagons had been empty – it was simply too steep and rocky. We had to leave the wagons behind and carry all the equipment on our backs. It was already getting dark, the wind and the rain had stopped, everything around us was pitch black and very, very silent. The only sound we could hear was a random cry of the jackals and the sneer of the hyenas that were having a good time laughing at our efforts. Many were afraid and a sense of hopelessness was in the air."

Although she had heard the story a hundred times, Dvora's eyes would always grow wider and wider when her father mentioned the laughing hyenas, causing her to shudder. She hated the hyena's cry. At night she could hear them, from a distance, laughing, threatening to come and take innocent children from their yards....

Her father continued: "Imagine our shock when we arrived at the top, expecting the hill we had just purchased with our life savings to be ours, only to discover a small, pathetic little Arab village whose few houses were actually shacks made of pieces of wood as black and as dirty as coal."

The settlers were speechless when they saw for themselves the reality of the land they had dreamt of making their own. Naïve and idealistic, the new immigrants had no knowledge of farming or of the social situation in Palestine. All they had was a vision. When they had arrived in Haifa, they had searched for a place to stay until they could find some land on which they could build a *moshava* – village – of their own. No hotel was big enough for all sixty families that had come, and as things were, they did not want to waste their money on hotels. They found a small inn to stay in, a place called Han Zachlan. It was an old stone house surrounded by a wall and it had an inner yard that was crowded with people and animals at all times. Goats, camels, mules and chicken screeched amongst children, women and men who were crowded in the tiny, dirty yard. Refusing to be beaten, they patiently waited for an opportunity to come their way, keeping their eyes and ears open to the musings of the wanderers and passersby who passed through Han Zachlan.

"It's a beautiful hill, a good piece of land, big enough for all of you, and it's for sale," a stranger was telling them. "If you hurry, you might be lucky."

"Is it far?"

"Oh, no, it's only a few hours south. And the price is good."

"Maybe, but it would mean giving up everything we have...."

"Well, someone else will buy the hill of Zamarin if you lot don't make up your minds...."

Fully aware that their entire hopes, dreams and chances for prosperity would be dependent upon the place they would settle in, the settlers started debating. How would they know that the land is good? How could they make sure that they were doing the right thing? They could not rid from their minds the fearful stories of others who had tried settling across the country, and in the course of their struggle, suffered from deathly diseases and perished.

"We will send scouts," they decided. "Two of us will go and inspect the hill. Let us hope that they bring back a favorable report."

The scouts came back with light in their eyes and passion in their hearts: "Zamarin, the land we have seen," said the scouts, "is better than anything we could possibly dream of. It is filled with olive trees, the fruits in the orchards are sweet – it is truly a land of milk and honey." One of the scouts even went as far as to say that he "swears on his beard and *peot* – sidelocks – that he saw a carob tree literally seeping with honey." The other scout vowed that the air is clean and healthy and there is plenty of water. The decision was made.

With spirits raised and hopes high, the settlers immediately purchased Zamarin from its Arab owner and prepared to start their new lives on the hill that was reported to be the true fulfillment of the promised land. They invested every penny they owned in the purchase of the land. "We knew we were returning to our Land by birthright," Jacob would say over and over again, "but we were determined to buy it from its owner for the full price, so no one could claim it and take it away from us. We learned that lesson from our patriarch Abraham, who did the same thing even though the Lord himself promised to give him the land!"

Although it was winter, they decided that since it had taken them almost a year to come this far they would not wait any longer. "You can imagine," Jacob said, "how surprised we were when instead of the honey and fruit that the scouts had promised, all we found were thorns and mud. Cutting the scout's beard and sidelocks was no consolation...."

The first year on the hill was almost unbearable. They lived in the small, run-down wooden shacks on the hill, working the land by day and guarding their investment by night. Some of the woman and children were sent back to Haifa "until the situation improved." Disease, hunger, hostile neighbors, bad weather and practically no success with the winter crops almost broke their hearts. Adding insult to injury, summer came as hot and burning as could be, drying and scorching their hands, feet and heads. With it came a messenger from Europe.

"I represent Baron Hirsch, who is extremely impressed by your efforts," said the messenger. "He is very concerned about his fellow Jews, and his ears are open to your cries. He recognizes that you are starving, and your families are depressed to the point where some of them refuse to join you and are waiting in Haifa. Your safety amongst the surrounding Arabs is very precarious, and the work you do every day is almost tantamount to pure slavery. Add to the fact that you must guard yourselves at night, and I am sure you will agree your situation is impossible." The messenger went on, ignoring the astonished expressions growing on the settlers' faces, some of them confused while others growing increasingly angry as he spoke.

"Baron Hirsch," the messenger continued, "wishes only luck and success for his Jewish brothers and sisters, but this land is a hard land, for it is made of iron and steel, and it is a barren land, bringing only suffering and destruction to its settlers. The generous Baron is willing to give each and every one of you the money necessary to return safely to your homes in Europe. His hopes are you will feel the same way."

The settlers were silent, most of them shocked, some of them raging. Their response came as sharp as a knife, the only knife they needed to conquer the land – the knife of their strong will.

"You wish to know how we feel?" they asked. "Tell your Baron that we have come to the land of our ancestors to fulfill a sacred cause, which is to build our future in our Holy Land, the greatest commandment of all. Tell your Baron that we are giving everything we have for this land, Zamarin is ours; there is no other home for us in this world and we have no intention of leaving it, even if we have to feed on rocks or die of disease!"

The determination and devotion in the settlers' voices flowed out from them, filling the land in the same way a gush of water fills a field, overflowing and covering the rocks and the plants around them, creeping hastily toward the messenger and his assistant, their horses, and crawling up their bodies to the roots of their hair, engulfing them with such a sense of completeness that there was room for nothing else. Filled with a new sense of mission, the messenger finally spoke as if he were speaking to the heavens.

"I will make sure that your days are made easier, and that you prosper and thrive," he started out with a timid, dreamy, stuttering voice. "I will leave you some money…and I will give an allowance to your families waiting in Haifa…." His voice was growing confident, he was becoming excited and could feel the gush of emotional waters turn into a sea of life. "You will also receive free medicine at our pharmacy in Haifa and I will arrange regular visits from the doctor to tend to your needs. May the Lord be with you!" And with that he left, galloping back to Haifa, leaving a small, angry, but determined congregation, none of them believing or understanding what had just happened.

To their surprise, the messenger kept his promises, and they were sustained for a short period of time. Eventually, after a whole year of hardship and desperation, they accepted the patronage of one of the greatest benefactors of the new Jewish settlements throughout the Land – the patronage of Baron Rothschild.

Slowly, enduring many hardships, pain, anger and with tremendous effort, Zamarin became not only an existing fact, but a flourishing one, taking the shape of a real village. Fifty wooden houses were brought from Romania, replacing the broken-down, leaking shacks that they lived in. The houses were placed in two rows along what was to become the main street of the growing village – "Founders Road." A synagogue was built just a short distance from the Goldstein's house, and Jacob Goldstein was its first *gabay* – the manager of synagogue affairs. They built a school that contained, in addition to small classrooms, a small pharmacy, and the house next door was occupied by the pharmacist and the village midwife. The village was complete with a Rabbi, a butcher and a doctor. There was even a house for the village gardener, and to complete the picture, they created a small public garden with a fishpond that had real goldfish swimming in it.

"Mama, look what I got at school today," little Sam was holding a small book, filled with French poems. "Let me read one to you, you'll see how I have improved…."

"More French?" Jacob had just walked in from the vineyards. "I would hope that they were teaching you more Hebrew."

"Come now, Jacob, you must admit that Hebrew is more fit for prayers," Dina, their neighbor, was kneading dough with Chaya. It was their Thursday evening ritual: together they would prepare enough dough to bake the next day into sweet challa bread for their families.

"All I know is that we are turning into a small, French-like colony," Jacob said, his anger rising, "a visitor would think he is in the wrong region of the world…"

"Don't get so worked up, my dear." Chaya's hands worked with confidence. "They are also learning the Bible."

"And we learn manners!" Sam jumped. "Our teacher says that if we learn enough French dialect we can really become part of the civilized world."

Chaya and Dina exchanged glances, knowing that Jacob was about to embark on one of his speeches.

"We are creating our own civilized world," he snapped. Chaya sighed. "We don't need foreign customs, we have our own! We must revive our Hebrew, and create new customs that will stem out of our old, traditional ones!"

"There is no harm in learning from other cultures. God forbid, they might have a good idea that we can learn once in a while," Chaya was the only one in the entire village who dared to be sarcastic with her husband. Dina concealed a smile, focusing on the dough.

"We are Jews," Jacob said stubbornly. "We have a glorious culture, why should we search for strange ways that are not ours?"

"Well, you can discuss it with the generous Baron himself," said Chaya, brushing the argument off. "He will be here next week. And our own little Daniel will be singing a song for him! Oh, don't look so appalled." She sighed, eyes rolling to the sky. "Yes, a French song, but Sam will recite a poem in pure Hebrew. Now go wash up for dinner. It's getting late."

Dvora was only three years old when Baron Rothschild came to visit for the first time. Five years after he had given them his patronage, the farmers of Zamarin were determined to show him he had made a wise investment. Everyone dressed up, the stables, barns and sheds were cleaned and the animals groomed. Huge bowls of sweet fruit, cheese, olives and bread, accompanied by jars of fresh lemonade tinted by sassy mint leaves, all made by the woman of Zamarin, filled the tables. The children were a colorful sight, dressed in their best Shabbat clothes and ribbons in their hair. Six-year-old Sam recited his poem for their distinguished guest, but Daniel, who was supposed to sing a song, hid under his parents' bed, refusing to come out. Dvora, feeling like a woman even at this early age, spontaneously walked up to the Baron and handed him a flower. The older girls of the settlement sang a song in French.

The Baron's heart was captured by Zamarin. The fresh air and beautiful landscape overlooking the fields and the Mediterranean sea below were an exceptional sight.

Moved and emotional, the Baron turned to the farmers and handed them the request that Jacob was praying for and that was published in all the Jewish papers from Haifa to Jerusalem. The Baron requested that the settlers and their families stand strong and stick to Hebrew, the ancient language of the Jews that was now being revived, the language that would be a pillar of this wondrous renaissance of Jewish continuity.

"Leave French to the French," he said emotionally, and Jacob beamed. "You are building the foundations of our newly-found nationality. Jews, speak Hebrew!"

The Baron had one more request. "This beautiful piece of land is a fine symbol of hard work and accomplishment," he continued. "I was hoping…that is…if you would kindly agree…to name it after my father, Jacob."

The settlers were quiet, glancing at each other.

"It will be a fulfillment of a dream for me," he added hastily, "and an honor."

"No, it is our honor," they answered. "It is the least we can do to show you our appreciation."

"And so Zamarin became Zichron Yaacov, the memory of Jacob. Some think it's named after me…." Jacob would wink, concluding this part of his story.

As the years went by, the family grew and so did the house. Little by little, routine and a calming structure became second nature. Jacob would disappear into the vineyards at dawn, leaving Chaya to run the house and its inhabitants during the day. Morning was time for school and household chores. The single bathroom suffered under the burden of rushing children, who would run in and out of the four small bedrooms and the yard, feeding the hens, fetching their eggs, washing, grabbing garments, combs, breakfast and books as they scattered to the winds, out through the kitchen door. Strict, precise order returned almost as soon as the young Goldsteins left as Chaya marched through the cheerful chaos, swiftly restoring her kingdom. Late morning and noon passed in a busy hum as Chaya washed, cleaned, cooked and tended the garden. Afternoon was her only time for relaxed enjoyment. Jacob still away, the children busy with homework, Chaya sat on the large porch, drinking her tea, sewing, and reading her "Tsena Ure'ena" – the traditional book of Judaism for women. The bells and soft bleating of the village herd returning to the stalls at dusk were the signs she waited for. Hearing the goats approaching, Chaya left her post on the porch and went into the kitchen for her favorite part of the day: preparing dinner for her family.

Small jars, filled with jams made of strawberries, peaches, apricots and plums, and large jars, bursting with pickles, peppers and carrots swimming in salt and garlic, crowded the kitchen shelves. With confident, swift movements, Chaya removed the tasty treasures from their neat rows on the brown shelves and placed them on the long, wooden table standing in the middle of the large, high-ceiling kitchen. Fragrant, delicious loaves of bread followed, emerging from the huge stove that glistened in the corner and were thrust onto large wooden trays. The children, busy in the backyard, under the strict supervision of Chaya's glance that followed them through the bright window facing the rear garden of the house, rushed in to wash for dinner. Selecting large onions and garlic garlands hanging from the walls and choosing fresh vegetables and eggs that lay in baskets on the floor, dinner was a rich celebration of the senses. Jacob managed to purchase an icebox, and every now and again, they indulged themselves with fresh meat and icy drinks.

Dvora was certain that the large dining room where the family ate their meals was able to stretch without limit whenever their family and friends came to dine. The table and chairs were simple, made of wood, with the exception of Jacob's chair. It was a large, comfortable piece of furniture with magnificent upholstery, and it was the only luxury they had brought with them from the old world.

The day ended when Chaya appeared with two buckets filled with warm water and soap flakes. The colorful tiles that paved the entire house shined happily after Chaya washed them, and everyone went to sleep with sweet jam in their dreams and fragrant soap crowning their heads. It was a simple farmer's household, filled only with the basic necessities of everyday life, which was perfectly all right since most of the time was spent outdoors anyway.

And how magnificent it was outside! Fruit trees that grew by the hour and carried the sweetest, juiciest fruit in the world; colorful wildflowers that smelled so sweet they made your eyes misty; shrubs that were as tall as a six-year-old child and that had parts that produced a sour, tasty saliva in your mouth; bugs and birds that dominated the ground and the air with sounds of music that made you restless; hidden treasures that lay between the rocks and lumps of earth, waiting to be discovered; and a looming danger that sometimes transpired in the hostile form of greedy, troublemaking Arabs that forced the men to stand guard and the women and children to wait behind doors. The threat of robbery was always great.

The days were busy and the nights were quiet, the air pungent with a mixture of calm and danger. The birds and bees that sang during the day were silent by night, gracefully submitting the kingdom of sound to the laughing hyenas and crying jackals, disturbed only by the dreams that floated from the children's heads and the soft hooves of the horses on guard.

Dvora grew up fully aware of how beautiful she was. Everyone in the village told her so, and her mother made sure that Dvora worked hard so her beauty wouldn't be the only thing in her head. Ruth, Dvora's younger sister, was her best friend and admirer, and they were inseparable. Together they would help their mother with the household chores – and those were plenty: in addition to the regular cooking and cleaning, the livestock needed tending – hens, goats, one mule and a dog. The boys were in charge of tending the crops, especially the vineyards, for the two scouts that were originally sent to evaluate the land of Zichron Yaacov turned out to be prophets: the water was sweet, the air was fresh and the vines were growing rapidly in the sun, capturing the light in the silvery veins of the leaves, expanding the body of their branches and allowing it to flow and shine in the dark glowing purple of the sweet, juicy red grapes and in the fresh, dancing colors of the sensuous green grapes.

Grapes were everywhere: they were in the glasses, sparkling deep and red, filling the air with the intoxicating sense of rich juice and delicate wine; they were on the table in large, earthy bowls, catching the eye with the promise of sweetness hidden within their ripe bodies; and they romanced the wheat, spread as tasty jams or cuddled in the crust of pies. Dvora used to watch her mother cook, fascinated by the processes that transformed basic ingredients into different forms, shapes, sizes and tastes. Soon, she started cooking herself, creating new recipes and inventing combinations of her own. As they grew older, Dvora would drag Ruth with her and both of them would venture out to the nearby woods to search for berries, mushrooms, herbs and wild spices. They were a cheerful sight for sore eyes, wearing their large straw hats, carrying a basket in one hand, and always with gloves so their hands would not be harmed by the bush. "The Belles of Zichron," people would call them as they watched the sisters walk by, and greetings would be accepted and given all round. They never went far, always keeping close eye contact with the village houses, always alert and listening out for familiar sounds versus sounds of danger.

One day, as they were chatting and laughing, they wandered a few steps beyond their regular route.

"Dvora, we've gone too far," Ruth's voice was nervous. "I can no longer see the rooftops of the houses."

"Just a few more minutes, I need to examine this bush…." Dvora answered, her eyes on a new kind of leaf she had never noticed before. It was dark, covered with small brown spots and had tiny, white hairs on the stem. Ignoring Ruth's obvious unease, Dvora carefully approached the bush, knowing how poisonous these leaves can sometimes be. As she examined the new leaves she suddenly heard Ruth gasp behind her. Puzzled, Dvora looked up and her eyes came face-to-face with a hyena.

The fear and disgust that spread throughout her body was overwhelming, paralyzing not only her physical being but her soul as well. She had never felt like this before. She was transfixed, noticing the animal's large head, its ridiculously shaped body, its strong legs. For a moment they stared at each other, both taken completely by surprise by this strange, unexpected encounter. Then, vaguely, as if from a distance, she heard Ruth screaming, she heard thunder and, before she knew what was happening, the hyena was lying dead at her feet.

Years later, she would listen to her husband Ish describe their first meeting to their children: "I saw a beautiful young lady being approached by the ugliest creature in the world. Naturally, I had to save this damsel in distress and make her my own. Only later did I discover that I got two women for the price one!" he laughed, then added with a fake sigh: "There was no way I could have handled TWO women like your mother, so I had to ask your uncle Lipeh to pitch in…."

Ish and Lipeh Broytman had been riding their horses all the way from Jaffa to Zichron Yaacov. The sons of a lumber merchant, they were determined to find brides amongst the women of the new Jewish farming settlements. The reputation of Zichron as being the village with the most beautiful women in the land was well known, so the brothers decided to take a trip up north. Their plan was to work on one of the farms while getting acquainted with the settlers. They thought it would take some time before they would meet any girls. They never expected to meet anyone on the way, and certainly not to fall in love. "That day, I discovered why a hyena laughs," Ish would whisper conspiratorially to his children. "He laughs not out of spite, but because he knows he can cast a spell on those who meet him: a spell of enchantment that can easily turn into exciting emotions that he preys on before he attacks. He tried it with your mother, but luckily I was the one she really saw and captured her soul. She had no chance to escape from me."

Dvora was indeed swept off her feet by Ish. Tall, strong and handsome, he picked her up on his horse and rode into Zichron. He came to court her that very same evening, and his brother Lipeh seemed very interested in Ruth. For the first time in her life, Dvora felt her face flush whenever this fine young man looked at her. He told her stories. He made her laugh. He took her to the fields to pick flowers, and at all times he was no less than a perfect gentleman.

But Dvora had to admit to herself that his main charm was that he was from the city. The very same city she had vowed she would return to. She gave Ish her undivided attention whenever he would talk to her about his life in the city and about the business his family had in Jaffa, selling lumber to carpenters and builders. "It's the best way to know what is really developing in the country," he would say. "We know who is building a new house and where, who is expanding the family, who entertains many people and, most importantly – where the new Jewish towns and neighborhoods are being built. They all need wood, and we sell it to them for a very good price."

Having a double wedding was a memorable event, and the people of Zichron Yaacov talked about it for years. Dvora and Ruth Goldstein, two sisters, daughters of the village founders, pillars of the farming community, married Ish and Lipeh Broytman, two brothers, two city boys, merchants who didn't know how to grow a cucumber.

"When a merger of this magnitude occurs between the people of the land and the people of the trade, it is a sign that we all are walking rapidly toward days of true redemption," Jacob Goldstein, the happy father of the brides, announced at the wedding. "They will build two new, strong Jewish families in our beloved Homeland. From now on we can say that the Jewish people are really sending deep and steadfast roots into the land – not by forming different, separate groups and settling experiments, not by being sporadic, private newcomers that have different customs, tongues and traditions, but by creating strong bonds among us all, visionaries and dreamers who make their dreams come true. May we all prosper and thrive!"

A week after the wedding, the four of them were on their way south toward Neve Shalom, one of the new Jewish neighborhoods surrounding Jaffa, to start their new lives.

"So how is married life?" Sam, their older brother, had come to pay the sisters a visit.

"Oh, it's wonderful!" Ruth exclaimed. "Don't you think this is the most beautiful neighborhood?"

"Well, I wouldn't exactly call it beautiful...," Sam laughed. He was right: Neve Shalom was simple and unattractive, especially when compared to Zichron.

"Oh, but we love life here," Dvora protested. "Whenever I walk outside, it's like a festival of the senses...come, let's go for a walk."

"But Dvora, we can't…" Ruth hesitated. "Our husbands will be back soon…."

"Oh, rubbish. Ish and Lipeh won't be home till evening, we have plenty of time."

Each time she walked down the main road, Dvora inhaled the combination of odors, the scent of roasting lamb, the colors of figs, dates, nuts and fruit. She loved the salty smell of the sea, the breeze that swished the sand around, the sweet smell of the orange groves. If Zichron Yaacov was the land of grapes, Jaffa and her surroundings was the land of oranges. Dvora learned how to make orange juice mixed with a sprig of mint, to freshen the mind and the soul, bake orange cakes and orange candy, mixed with chocolate and rum. She even tried making chicken with oranges the way she heard the French did. She learned how to use other fruit as well: yellow melons with hearts of honey, apricots that captured the sun in their skins and showed off a sassy light orange color, watermelons as red as blood and as sweet as sugarcane, with large, black seeds bursting with a white, tasty richness. She would place the black watermelon seeds in a large aluminum platter and leave them to dry in the sun, sprinkling salty water on them, until they became tanned and dry as the desert, salty and delicious as the sea.

Every morning, after their husbands left for work, Dvora and Ruth would have morning tea together, telling each other their daily news. The two new families lived close by, and the sisters were as inseparable as they had always been. After their shared morning tea, they would each go about performing their daily chores. Dvora had a strong sense of commitment, she never flinched from her responsibilities. She was the perfect wife – cleaning, cooking and tending to her husband's needs. She accomplished every goal that she set for herself, with a strong sense of duty, including the physical duties she knew a wife must fulfill for her husband. Practical and realistic, Dvora despised any demonstrative burst of emotions, but Ish loved her so much he didn't seem to care that his wife showed no interest in initiating any physical contact between them, leaving their nights completely up to him. On the contrary, he felt it made her a true lady and that the relationship between them was based on a deep understanding that exists between two people who love and respect each other. She always succumbed to him when he wanted to make love, passively accepting and waiting quietly till it was over. As far as he was concerned, their lovemaking was fulfilling enough, while she regarded it as a duty to be done without a fuss.

All in all, life in Neve Shalom was sweet and stimulating, and Dvora enthusiastically tried to transmit her excitement to Sam as they walked through the town, but as hard as she tried, Sam just wasn't convinced.

"Zichron is…Zichron. There's no place like it," was all he said. "This is just…another city."

"So much for the connection between farmers and city people," Dvora retorted in a mock-hurt voice, but inwardly she smiled: Neve Shalom was hers, and nothing could take it away from her.

There was only one blemish in her life: the presence of the Turkish soldiers. A daughter of the free-spirited settlement farmers, she never forgot the hardships that the Ottoman Empire had placed on their lives in Zichron Yaacov. In this respect, Neve Shalom was no different. Dvora could never get used to the way the soldiers strode through the streets, showing off their dark, decorated horses, as if they owned the place. They were the soldiers of Hassan Beck, the governor of Jaffa, and they would ride around as *Effendi's*-landlords, behaving as if everything belonged to them, tasting the foods from the stands, demanding lemonade or Tamarhindy, a sweet drink made of dates, grabbing a handful of sunflower or watermelon seeds, laughing aloud with each other, mocking the passersby and paying for nothing. Ish, who was already used to their arrogant demeanor, paid no attention to them, but Dvora thought it was a disgrace and would lock herself angrily inside the house every time she witnessed such behavior.

A year after the two sisters were married, two very important events took place: Theodore Herzl died, leaving behind a devastated, mourning Zionist movement, grief-stricken, but determined as ever to follow his dream of Jewish independence; and Dvora gave birth to a handsome, large baby boy. Nathan was everything she dreamed of: a happy, confident child, with the handsome, strong features of his father and the direct confident eyes of his mother. His rosy cheeks were a definite sign of health and his thick, blond hair was a challenge to a comb. When two years later she gave birth to a small baby girl with a large nose, thin hair and pale cheeks, she was afraid of her own reaction. She had been so taken by her son's finesse that her small girl looked plain and disappointing in comparison. Ish was unaware of his wife's feelings and was overjoyed upon the birth of his daughter: "Now I have two beautiful flowers in my life!" he danced around the room with the tiny baby in his arms. "Let us call her Shoshana, for she is as beautiful and fragrant as a rose!"

Dvora watched his happiness silently. She feared her feelings, for she knew that they were supposed to be different. She regretted feeling this way, but at the same time she couldn't change her reaction. She didn't know she would be spending the rest of her life trying to make amends for her disappointment. A year after Shoshana was born, Dvora gave birth to another baby boy, Avner, and she became so occupied that her daughter's insult completely slipped her mind. She would be reminded of it only years later, when her conscience would demand that she pay a heavy price to compensate for the insult she had given her daughter at birth. But this would be much later, when the darkest and most challenging of times would come.

Chapter 3

RIVKA

1902–1913

And so by birthright I was destined to roam, as my great-grandmothers Rivka and Dvora did, throughout my Homeland and beyond, always following dreams and chasing visions. This nomadic lifestyle was second nature to me, and might have been scary had I not known with complete confidence that the threads of the past would provide a safety net wherever I went.

I was born in Haifa and moved to Tel Aviv at the age of six months. When I was two years old, my father announced that we were leaving for America, where he was going to complete his Ph.D. studies in Los Angeles. It took him seven years, and two more children along the way, to achieve his aim. When we returned to Israel, we lived for a short while in the center of Tel Aviv, and then moved briefly to Ramat Aviv, and then to Herzliya. Between the ages of nine and twelve, a short period of three years, I had lived in two continents separated by an ocean, four different cities, and had attended five different schools. Yet it never seemed to bother me. Wherever I went I managed to find new friends, I was always occupied with new pur-

suits and pastimes, and I maintained a good grade average. It was as if I had no roots, I could go anywhere and float. Or maybe I had multiple roots that made me feel comfortable wherever I was, without ever really feeling completely at home anywhere. A Jewish feeling, embedded into my genes by my matriarchs, wrapped by an overflowing, excessive narrative that is enough to feed an entire nation.

It was actually very simple. Traveling through Europe on his way to America, Isaac met a Jew called Zalman-David Levontin, who was Theodore Herzl's assistant. Levontin was on his way to London, where he would work for the Anglo-Palestine Company bank that the Zionist movement had established under Herzl's leadership, but he was disadvantaged by the fact that he couldn't speak English. Highly impressed by Isaac's intelligence and knowledge of languages, English included, Levontin persuaded Isaac to accompany him to London and teach him English for a small fee. "You can always continue onto America from there," Levontin said, "and in the meantime you can save some money." It was only a matter of days and into-the-night conversations until Isaac was completely captivated by Zionism. It was as if an ancient longing that had been blossoming inside him had finally found its home. He was certain that the Zionist idea – the idea of rebuilding Jewish freedom in the Land of Israel as the only solution for the suffering, exiled Jewish People – had been dormant inside him forever and had only been waiting for the opportunity to be awakened. Isaac soon became Levontin's personal assistant and became increasingly involved in the new Zionist movement. And it was only a matter of a few months before Herzl, as part of a greater plan to establish a Jewish state in Palestine, asked both Zalman-David Levontin and Isaac Lipavsky to go to Jaffa and open a branch of the Anglo-Palestine Company bank there. They both agreed and started the arrangements immediately. Isaac turned and set back home to inform Rivka about their exciting new future.

It took another year, and a new baby daughter, Racheli, before the family finally arrived at the port of Jaffa. They were a colorful sight. Rivka's wide, blue dress scattered around her, flirting with the wind, and spread wings like a canopy that was carrying Rivka and baby Racheli, who was confidently nestled in her arms. As they approached the shore, Rivka watched the rooftops of Jaffa grow closer, and swallowed the salty sea air in deep breaths, absorbing the scents and sounds that awaited her in this strange, unknown place. The bright sun cast golden highlights in her hair that fell in ash-hued curls around her face; the dark blue waves of the deep sea were reflected in her eyes, rushing and gushing in rhythm with the waves. Rivka impatiently dismissed the heat and humidity of the thick, heavy sea air. She was totally absorbed in listening to the voices of her spirits, who were dancing around her and whispering in her ears. Despite all her pregnancies, she still had a slim, attractive figure that made the sailors bold. Some of them tried to come too close, but when she looked straight at them the spirits would surround them, filling their souls with a deep sense of awe, and the sailors would immediately retreat and rush to pray to their gods for forgiveness.

Ofsey and Olga, already twelve and eleven years old, stood very seriously on the forward deck of the boat, their heads close together, as they whispered conspiratorially to each other. Seven-year-old Aaron tried to capture their attention, but they were too busy in their own private world to take any notice of their younger brother. Isaac, a striking figure in his new dark suit, resembled a distinguished businessman, and showed no signs of being new to that world. When Rivka turned to look at her husband, her stomach filled with a warm ball of love that crept up to her throat, and she knew deep in her heart they were on their way to success. Her spirits told her so.

When the small fishing boats approached to bring them to shore, no less than ten boats were needed to carry all of the

Lipavsky's belongings. Rivka had packed everything she could think of and afford: white linen sheets embroidered with their initials; huge goose pillows, two for each one of them and an extra six for guests and her yet unborn, last son; soft cotton blankets; pots, pans, clothes; and even furniture, including a beautiful, maple cabinet, with glass windows stained with shapes of birds and flowers so you could glimpse in and see the fine cups and plates hidden within. This last object was a special farewell gift from her parents. They had bought it for Blooma the day before she died and decided Rivka should have it. It was the one object she would never part with, not under any circumstance.

Everything was packed into large boxes and brought to shore in a slow, rocking procession. To bystanders looking from the shore, the ten small fishing boats resembled a slow procession of floating clouds, disappearing and reappearing amongst the silvery-green waves, their sailors struggling to stay afloat without losing either their passengers or their possessions. As they came closer to shore, the dark clouds took shape and turned into large brown cases made of fine wood, three bright-eyed children, a tall, thin man in a fine suit and dark English hat, and a woman with a baby in her arms and eyes that matched the sea.

At first, they rented a small apartment in the Jewish neighborhood, Neve Shalom, a small, unattractive neighborhood that was appealing only because it was completely Jewish. If anything could be a complete opposite to what they had left behind, Neve Shalom and Jaffa qualified for the title. Hot, burning sand and salty, wet air swept through the doors, the windows and the wide porches, covering everything with an everlasting thin layer of golden dust that cunningly submitted to cleaning only to immediately return, mocking, refusing to be wiped or washed away. The heavy wood of the furniture was cheerfully decorated with glistening sand flakes, hiding cool, dry air only within its drawers that the children sometimes opened and thrust their sizzling hands in to cool. The sounds on the streets created a vivid circus of people and animals. Jews, Arabs, horses and camels were speaking, arguing and openly interacting in a fashion that in Europe would be considered worse than rude. The food was a combination of tastes and smells that seemed almost impossible, challenging old customs and traditional methods of cooking. To her own surprise, Rivka discovered that not only did she cope with the challenges of her new life, but she actually enjoyed every minute of it. For the first time in her life, she was completely independent, far from the protection of her father and the shrinking hearts of her brothers. The taste of her new freedom was sweet.

Isaac left the house every morning, dressed smartly, and walked to the bank on Ajamy Street, Jaffa's main road. It was a busy street lined with small businesses – merchants sold leather and copper goods; farmers offered the produce of their sweat; and craftsmen created a colorful dance of shoes, clothes and baked sweets. Newcomers, Jews and non-Jews alike, were everywhere, and Jaffa seemed like just another crowded, dirty cosmopolitan city, filled with people from all over the world, who spoke in twenty different languages. The streets were chaotic and business was booming.

"I have some good news!" Isaac declared as he waltzed through the door, one day after work.

"I know," Rivka smiled.

He was so excited, he didn't hear her. "The bank has decided to open another branch. Guess where?"

"In Jerusalem."

"In Jerusalem!" He still didn't hear her. "And I have requested to be the new assistant manager."

"I know. And you will be." The certainty in her voice finally penetrated his enthusiasm.

"Oh, I hope you are right!" he said, refusing as always to acknowledge her ability to predict the future. "You know how hard I have been trying to get a permit from the Turks to travel to

Jerusalem. It's unbelievable how they insist on monitoring one's every move. But now they will have no choice."

From the very moment his foot first touched the holy land of Palestine, Isaac's soul had been yearning to go to the Holy City, not for religious reasons but for a very personal one. He was determined to find his long-lost sister, Feiga. Rivka knew that now he would finally get his wish. A few weeks later, as her spirits had predicted, Rivka found herself, yet again, packing their belongings and moving all her children, her boxes and her Blooma cabinet, to Jerusalem.

The journey to Jerusalem was like travelling through ancient times. Observing the scenery on the way, Rivka experienced an almost biblical feeling, and she could feel the strong presence of her father and his holy songs taking the journey with her. The deep, sparkling green of orange groves gave way to the old, silvery gray of ancient olive trees. Light gold sand turned dark and heavy, fields of flowers rose to bushy hills and the air became sweeter, thinner and clearer. As the hills rose, the colors grew darker and older. Just as Rivka was starting to feel that the green darkness was about to envelope them entirely, the road took a sharp turn and the City of King David appeared before their eyes. "*Shehecheyanu Vekiyemanu VeHigi'anu Lazman Hazeh...*" Rivka and Isaac recited the blessing that is said when something that was long-awaited for materializes.

Isaac's eyes scanned the city through a veil of smiling dreams while Rivka stared blankly ahead.

Rundown, dirty and noisy, with a huge wall surrounding most of it, and a labyrinth of alleys that kept you winding within them helplessly forever, Jerusalem had a crazy, dizzy charm that captured your heart and soul, reeling you in and making you her willing slave. And there was something else in Jerusalem that Rivka had never encountered before. It was the only place in the world that she knew of where other people besides herself spoke to spirits.

Excited, Isaac was filled with a sense of energetic confidence. Not only was he establishing the new bank in Jerusalem, but he was about to see his long-lost sister! He was certain that he would find her. He told himself that whatever her situation, he would be able to ensure that she lived comfortably, for he was doing so well that for the first time in his life he was providing handsomely for his family. It was a sweet, mind-spinning feeling. So much so, that when they arrived in Jerusalem he insisted on hiring a *kavas* – a family butler. Isaac hired a tall, young Turkish man who was raised and trained in England. The *kavas* wore a white suit adorned with gold embroidery and carried a golden baton.

"Isaac, what is the meaning of this?" Rivka protested. "We don't need a servant!"

Isaac soothed her concerns. "All the Consuls and bank managers have a *kavas*, so we must have one as well. Otherwise," he argued, "how will they respect us?"

"Such vanity…" Rivka was genuinely worried. The spirits were moving, uneasy.

Eager to help him solidify his position at the bank, Rivka gave in, but when he bought her a pair of diamond earrings and seven gold, beautifully carved bracelets, she refused to enjoy them, hiding them deep inside the Blooma cabinet. The more he spent, the more concerned she became. Rivka could feel the good spirits frowning with worry, while the evil spirits snickered and started searching for other new, creative ways to punish her for her happiness. She tried to find ways to bring peace to the spirits. She fell into the habit of roaming the narrow alleys of Jerusalem, buying from small, rundown shops and giving to beggars. She constantly searched for Feiga, in the hope that finding her sister-in-law, whom she had never known, alive would somehow make up for the treasures hidden in her dead sister's cabinet. But she always came back as mystified as to Feiga's whereabouts as when she started. At first she thought that not being able to find Feiga was some sort of challenge, perhaps even a punishment. But then she became pregnant with twins again and she knew she had been wrong. This pregnancy, her last, was about to be the most difficult challenge she had yet to face.

Isaac was furious with the spirit ritual that had taken control of his family while Rivka vainly tried to save her unborn daughter, but more than that, he was terrified. In spite of the changes he had implemented in his life, he was still a man of faith. This ritual of ribbons and garlic was strange to his soul; it was almost as if idolatry had taken over his household, and that was a terrible, unspeakable sin. In an act of desperation, he tried on his own to sooth the Lord by making a substantial contribution to his favorite synagogue, "*Mevo Hama*" on Jaffa Road in Jerusalem. He debated long and hard with himself. He was set on leaving his mark on the synagogue, but he couldn't go back to what he considered to be "the trivial signs of the past" by donating a Torah book or Torah crowns. He wanted his contribution to express his own journey, a journey that combined the past with the future, connecting heritage and renewal, creating continuity between old traditions and the birth of new ones.

He racked his brain, trying to decide what would be the best way to show his respect for his narrative while acknowledging the new world that had brought him so many blessings, a symbol of the peace that he prayed would reign between his fellow Jews and the rest of the modern world. After eliminating many potential ideas, he finally found what he considered to be the perfect solution: he ordered a beautiful, huge sundial, to be made of copper and stone and to be placed above the entrance to the synagogue. He refused to have his name inscribed on it, as he wished it to be a gift "from a Jew to other Jews, expressing our place in the larger world." In his mind, the sundial was a symbol of logic, of critical thinking, of the passing of time that was the ultimate way of marking historical observations. "What better way," he explained, "to express the eternity of our beloved Torah, of our people, of the entire human race? The Lord created light and darkness, thus giving us a sense of time, order and direction, precisely the goals of the Jewish faith and law.

"The sundial," Isaac told Rivka, "will be the best expression of our own narrative, as well as of the renaissance of our people; a perfect combination of our past and our future, it will remain as a legacy forever."

Whatever her unspoken turmoil is, Isaac thought, it will undoubtedly be soothed when she sees this fine work of wisdom and art.

Forty-five days and forty-five nights the watchmaker worked, carving and transforming the copper into geometric shapes that confused the eyes, for when you started at one point, and tried to get to another, you always returned to the beginning, going on and on in endless pathways. It was as if he had captured eternal pathways into one circle of glowing matter. Then the locksmith came, and very carefully and firmly attached the sundial, an amazing work of art, above the synagogue entrance. All of Jerusalem came to marvel at the sundial, and when the rabbi said the *Shehecheyanu* blessing, Isaac's heart filled with joy, his eyes glistened with unshed tears and, for the first and only time in his life, he could hear Rivka's spirits calling his name, approving, spurring him to turn around. He was as certain of these voices as he was of his own being, and when he turned around he was surprised at how obvious it was when his eyes came face-to-face with another pair of eyes. Eyes that were so familiar, it was almost painful, and he gave out an involuntary cry of joy: in front of him stood, small and dark eyed, Feiga.

Feiga had left Russia at the age of thirteen, leaving behind fourteen-year-old Isaac to study and eventually find his fortune in Rivka. She had been taken away by their grandparents, who decided to travel to Jerusalem so they could die and be buried in the Holy City. She was a small girl, with alert, bright eyes that looked straight at you when she spoke. Her presence did not make heads turn, but she had a pleasant face and an inviting, warm smile. Like her brother, it was her smile that had changed her fate.

At the age of sixteen, Feiga's grandparents felt it was time to marry her off through a *Shidduch* – an arranged marriage. Luckily, an opportunity fell into their laps when a young man by the name of Reuven Rabinovitch appeared at their doorstep and expressed interest in marrying Feiga. When Reuven made his entry into their lives, Feiga's grandparents were thoroughly relieved. Reuven was renowned as being a rich industrialist and was considered to be a great catch. And what's more, he wanted Feiga! And all this without the help of a formal matchmaker and, most importantly, without the expense of one! It was more than they ever could have hoped for.

Reuven met Feiga while she was walking through the alleys of the city, in the direction of the market. She was on her way, large basket in hand, to buy groceries for Shabbat. Reuven was twenty-six years old, much older than she was, and when she looked up and saw him standing in front of her, she didn't lower her eyes like other girls did, but rather looked straight at him, blessed his day and smiled.

Reuven felt as if the sun had suddenly rushed up to him. His face burned with a red warning, drawing him to this small, smiling, pretty little creature and urging him all the while to run and jump into a cold bucket of water. He had never felt this way before, and he lost control of his legs that, of their own accord, carried him through the alleys, following Feiga like a blind man follows his dog, through the market and directly to her grandparents' house.

They were married in a modest ceremony. Feiga's grandparents felt they had accomplished their main task in looking out for their granddaughter's interests. They had married her off to a rich, successful man, a modern industrialist who, for the rest of her life, would take good care of her, leaving them to die in peace, which they both did less than a year after the marriage. Reuven was considered rich because he had a stocking filled with gold Napoleons and Bishliks – the coins of the Ottoman Empire. And he was considered an industrialist because he owned a sewing machine with which he sewed fine garments for Jerusalem's elite.

Shortly after their marriage, Feiga's neighbors noticed that she was getting thinner. Even when she became pregnant, she was thin. It was as if a knot had been tied in the middle of her slim body, for other than a meek belly, the rest of her body was like a string. The women of the neighborhood observed that Feiga went to the market only once a week, with an exact amount of money clenched in her fist. She always came back with an exact number of vegetables for two: four cucumbers – a half for each day and a whole one for Shabbat, one large lettuce head, fourteen potatoes – two for each day –a small chicken and some herbs for soup. Before long, it became patently clear to everyone around that as good a catch that they thought Reuven was, as great a miser he turned out to be. Reuven counted the drops of oil with which Feiga cooked, inspected the household goods every single day, made sure that nothing went to waste, and became very angry, sometimes violent, when he felt that money was spent frivolously. Feiga would lower her eyes and wait for her husband to calm down, and promise in a trembling voice to be more careful. The more she tried to please him, the crueler he became. He had managed to capture this smiling sunbeam, lure her into his house, make her his own, and he was now determined to keep her as hidden from the world as possible, far from other penetrating eyes that might enjoy her smile and steal its pleasures from him, their rightful owner. The light in Feiga's eyes and the smile on her face, the same smile that had drawn him to her when he first saw her, slowly faded, drying up like a fragile flower until its petals fell off and completely vanished. Her smile reappeared only when she was close to the one thing that filled her life with joy, a joy that was so overwhelming that it made everything else the size of an insignificant pea: her children.

Reuven and Feiga had two sons – Saul and Aharon. Feiga managed to protect them from their father while he was away at work, and when they were young she tried to make sure they were in bed by the time he returned home. The less they knew of their father's cruelty, she thought, the better off they would be.

Reuven didn't really care about his boys, regarding them mainly as two more mouths that needed to be fed and two more backs that needed to be clothed. When they started school, he demanded that the boys use the same notebook, claiming that they were learning the same lessons anyway. Feiga had to beg him for the few coins he gave her, and very carefully, behind her miserly husband's back, she began giving Hebrew lessons to toddlers, so that she could have a few extra Bishliks to get school supplies for the boys. Somehow, over the years, she managed to make ends meet. She never complained, and when Isaac and Rivka came to Jerusalem she found ways to conceal her real condition.

When he heard that Isaac was the manager of the new bank and financially independent, Reuven was delighted to meet his newly-found brother-in-law, hoping that his ideas for investments would find fertile ground. But Isaac was very careful. He did not know exactly what it was about his brother-in-law that bothered him so much, but it was enough for him to know that whenever Reuven was around, according to Rivka, her evil spirits gave her a headache. Soon, Reuven became reluctant to visit his new family, feeling Isaac and Rivka's disdain. But when Isaac couldn't help him get a loan from the bank – a loan he didn't need or deserve – Reuven's reluctance turned to a rage that Feiga and the boys felt very harshly. He bullied her into staying away from her brother's house for three weeks, claiming that she was ill. When she finally managed to sneak out for a visit while Reuven was away on business, Rivka was horrified at the sight that met her: Feiga looked like a small, sad ghost.

Ushering Feiga quickly into the secure, welcoming atmosphere of her home, Rivka didn't need any explanations. "You can't go back, at least not immediately," she tried to convince Feiga. "Stay here tonight."

"I can't," Feiga shook her head vigorously. "The children are alone."

"I will send the *kavas* to explain that you are too weak to walk back," Rivka said. "The neighbors can take them in for one night. They will be fine."

"No, they won't," Feiga's eyes were hollow. "Their father will be looking for me. If Reuven comes home and I'm not there, he'll go mad. God only help us then."

"But..."

"I can't." Her voice was low, but very determined. "He will harm them...I...I am always afraid that he will somehow make them disappear...I must protect them..."

"You yourself need protection!" Rivka cried out. "How can you possibly protect the children if you yourself are in danger?!"

"I always have," Feiga answered simply.

"I will call Isaac..."

"Please, Rivka, I only came for a short while to let you know we are fine. Really, everything will be fine. And please don't tell Isaac. He is so happy, I do not want to ruin things for him." Feiga would not budge.

Watching Feiga leave, Rivka was filled with sorrow, for she knew that the worst was yet to come and that no one could change Feiga's fate but Feiga herself. And Feiga was clearly in no condition to do anything decisive, at least not yet.

She was still reflecting on Feiga's pitiful situation when a cheerful, singing Isaac entered the house. Rivka knew it was a sign, and when he met her gaze, he started to laugh. For the first time in their marriage, he was not afraid of the fact that she could sense his news before he announced it. He was simply too happy to fear, and besides, he had also grown somewhat accustomed to his wife's gift. She smiled at his happiness, and when she greeted him with a "congratulations, mister manager," he turned into a ball of energy. He caught her by her hips, swung her in the air and declared: "Next stop – Beirut city!"

When the bank management decided to open a branch in the city of Beirut in Lebanon, their first and natural choice for manager was Isaac. He was already "in the neighborhood," he was considered an excellent employee, his son Ofsey was already climbing his way up in the bank world, and he knew six languages – Russian, English, French, Hebrew, German and most important, Arabic, which he quickly picked up in the short four years they had been in Palestine. Beirut was considered a wonderful place to be – a beautiful, modern city, where the rich and famous of the Middle East gathered for their vacations. It was called "the Switzerland of the Mediterranean," and the bank had promised it would be a very important position that would be crucial to the building of the renewed Jewish nation: it would make the transfer of monies from Europe to the Jewish settlers in the Ottoman region of Palestine much easier. Anyway, they would only be away for a short period of time, and then they would return home to Jerusalem. Isaac was ecstatic.

Rivka greeted his news with a warm smile. She was genuinely happy for him, but she kept her uneasy feelings to herself. She couldn't ignore her growing sense that this change had a seed of darkness in it. She easily detected the signs of trouble – Feiga coming into their lives only to be cut off again; little Moshe starting to crawl around the house, searching all the dark corners with his tiny hands, looking for his stillborn sister and challenging the angel of darkness to show him his face again; her other children being torn for the third time from a world they had just begun to understand; and herself, feeling the storm in her blue eyes grow darker, the waves in her soul chasing sleep from her nights and the spirits stirring restlessly in her stomach. Her life had taught her only too well that there was no way she could fight the magnitude of destiny, so this time, instead of confronting her spirits, she turned to them and vowed that she would make the family's time in Beirut as easy and as happy as she could. As she vowed, a vision flashing by and took her back to a long-forgotten, hallucinated biblical scene of seven fat cows, standing and smiling at her, and she was horrified – for next to them, instead of seven lean cows, stood six lean cows – and the seventh, a cow with horns, lay dead.

Life in Beirut was good. As always, they had brought everything with them, including Blooma's cabinet and their personal *kavas*. Beirut was a charming, modern city, a combination of European-style buildings and people and Middle Eastern Arab cities. The city projected an international flair, filled with large buildings, automobiles and horse-drawn carriages that moved hastily by charming houses, beautiful gardens and Middle Eastern alleyways, swarming with consuls, company administrators and bank managers. Isaac became part of Beirut's financial world, quickly adjusting to the diverse atmosphere of the metropolis. He felt he had found his destiny, his goal in life, and the excitement of being involved in the building of the new Jewish World filled him with passion.

"A head, as wonderful and as full of ideas as can be, will not survive a minute without fresh, flowing blood in its veins, blood that brings the oxygen and nutrients that are necessary for life," Isaac told his family. "Zionism is a wonderful, sacred task. We have been waiting for it for almost two thousand years, eagerly yearning for our beloved Homeland. But it will not happen without the blood that feeds all actions, the oxygen that turns dreams into reality, the one thing that can turn the idea into bricks and mortar. It will not happen without this man-made blood, and plenty of it – it will not happen without money! That is our task," he said proudly. "It is my mission in life to make sure that the blood of life keeps flowing into the heart of Zion," he concluded, his wife and children drinking in his words with the same unquestioning devotion with which they were spoken.

Meanwhile, the children were growing. Ofsey quickly became his father's right-hand man at the new bank and when he turned eighteen he was sent back to Palestine to work closely with Levontin, where he became his assistant manager at the bank in Jaffa. Both Isaac and Rivka were very proud of him. He had Isaac's head for figures, his loyalty and dignity, and his mother's straightforward gaze that made the beholder feel very confident. They knew he would be very successful.

Olga had inherited her father's talent for languages and love of stories. Isaac encouraged her studies, preceding his time by saying that she must have an education and that girls were at least as smart as boys, if not more. At seventeen she was accepted to the University of Luzanne in Switzerland, majoring in languages and literature. Rivka cried heartily the day Olga left, but she was also filled with a special pride, a pride she had never felt before – not only would one of her children become a scholar, but it would be her daughter, receiving the first university degree in the family, an unusual achievement for a woman, and a Jewish one, at that. She kissed Olga goodbye and watched in amazement as she left. Olga would be the only child in the family that the spirits would not accompany, fearing the intellectual pathway she had chosen. They left her alone.

Two years after Olga left, Aaron announced that it was his turn to leave: he wished to travel to America to study chemistry, his passion. No one was really surprised – Aaron always loved to mix things, watch them change, attempting to extract scents and colors from leaves and flowers, crushing stones and vegetables so he could add water, milk or vinegar to the powder, and see what would happen. He constantly tried to make perfumes for his mother and sisters, sometimes creating odors that forced the windows open, at other times creating scents that were so sweet, the house smelled like a candy factory. Once he succeeded in creating an aroma so sensuous that after his mother and sisters wore it in town some women came and begged him to prepare bottles for them, but he couldn't remember what he had used and how exactly he had used them. Rivka was always fearful of these experiments. Whenever she saw Aaron trying out one of his chemical ideas she saw Shlomo and Blooma standing in the corner, their bodies hollow and their faces worried, and she could smell smoke. Although she knew she would never see him again, she was relieved when Aaron left to make his hobby into a profession. She felt it would be safer.

Racheli and Moshe were growing and going to school. While Racheli was quiet, very responsible and completely reserved from a very early age, Moshe was filled with mischief and had a wonderful sense of humor. He loved playing with gadgets, taking them apart only to try to put them together again. He was constantly searching for new inventions and objects, filling his room with treasures he found and collected in the streets. His thirst for artifacts was never sated, and he always wanted more. An excited achiever, he always aimed to be the best: the best climber, the best ball player, the best student. The more he accomplished, the braver he became. He completely defied risk with a mockery that made Rivka lose sleep with worry. There was no doubt in her mind that his soul was secretly searching for his twin sister, playing dangerous games with death and showing off its courage. She vaguely remembered the prophetic whisper of the midwife who was present when Moshe was born, alarmingly aware that the Angel of Death was waiting patiently to strike unexpectedly. But Moshe was lively and free-spirited, and she was incapable of moderating his natural curiosity and mischief. Isaac had taught him Hebrew, Arabic and Yiddish, and when his parents bought a radio – a rare household appliance in those days – he quickly mastered English as well, all before the age of ten. Whenever his parents praised him for his achievements, he would only give them his childish smile and say: "Oh, that's nothing. Next time I'll do even better!"

Rivka watched him with a sigh, reassuring herself with the

certainty that her son was closely guarded by the good spirits, and she constantly prayed that they would be strong enough to keep death away.

Rivka became especially nervous before Hanukah, when the *Yahrzeit* memorial days came nearer. Every year, at the end of Rosh Hashana, the Jewish New Year, Rivka ended the holiday with a sigh, saying, "The *Yahtzeit* are coming," and the whole family knew what she meant. For two whole months, until the first evening of Hanukah, Rivka seemed as if a dybbuk – an obsession – had possessed her. She cleaned the house from top to bottom, scrubbing the floors until the children could see their freckles in the tiles, polishing the silver until it looked almost transparent, rearranging the family photos. During the two and a half months that fell between Rosh Hashana and Hanukah, she changed her habit of going once a week to the Beirut Jewish market and she went twice a week instead. On Mondays, just like every other Monday of the year, she bought food and supplies for the household: beautiful, tasty vegetables; succulent, juicy fruit, wheat, herbs and spices, fresh meat, different sorts of bread, and sweet candy for her husband and children. But on Wednesdays, she went for one reason alone: to buy the finest, tallest, most colorful candles in the market. She defied the custom of lighting plain white candles for Yahrzeits: she wanted bright candles, candles that would create a rainbow dance, candles that would capture everyone's complete attention and bring the spirits of her lost loved ones closer. Every Wednesday she bought an assortment of candles, checking their colors, the firmness of their wax, their weight; she would buy them and then she would go back to the market the following week to buy new ones and to replace some of the old ones with better, more beautiful candles.

This candle-buying-ceremony continued until the very first night of Hanukah. After lighting the Hanukah menorah, Rivka would light the Yahrzeit candles. Every single evening of the eight days of Hanukah, the six memorial candles would dance…each candle different, each representing a love story.

Shima'le's candle was always bright yellow, the color of the curls that crowned his head the day he died, just a sweet, innocent two-year-old baby. The twin girls had two twin candles, pink as the small baby outfits that they wore the day they died. Leah'le had a multi-colored candle that reminded Rivka of Leah'le's first laugh, the sound of bells that always made her smile. A dark, gray candle represented Blooma, and a beautiful white candle was lit for Moshe's unnamed twin sister, for Rivka was certain that the child was taken on her way from the womb so she would have an important role in heaven, amongst the angels, a role that could not wait even for her first breath.

"*Yitgadal Ve'Yitkadash Shmei Rabah…*" Rivka would light the Yahrzeit candles with great piety, her voice gently singing the mourner's prayer, her eyes watching the candlelight dancing around the room. She hoped that the light would help keep her family safe. And even as she watched them, she knew that dark days and travels still lay ahead, waiting patiently to transpire.

When Isaac heard that a new Jewish city was being built north of Jaffa he began sending money to Ofsey. The money was sent with very specific instructions: "The money will be spent to build a house for the family in the new city. Wait a year or two," he wrote Ofsey in a letter, "and see how the city develops. In the meantime – save this money in the bank."

A long time passed until a letter arrived from Ofsey. Isaac read its contents to Rivka, whose wonder and sense of destiny grew by the minute. In every sentence, within every single word, she heard the echo of her husband's fiery dream:

"One needs the blinding vision of a miracle to take a stretch of sizzling sand, that looks more like the shameless humps of a camel than a reasonable place for human beings to dwell in, and turn it into a beautiful, white city." Ofsey wrote, "And a miracle it is: the first Hebrew city of modern times."

It started for financial reasons. The Jews in Jaffa calculated that the rent they were paying their Arab landlords would be better spent if they used it to build their own homes and improved neighborhoods. Doing the math, and enchanted by the idea of creating a new, exclusively-Jewish city next to Jaffa, a city founded on the Hebrew language and Jewish culture, the Zionist councils of Jaffa started searching for land to purchase. Three years passed before a group of sixty-six families, who called themselves "The *Achuzat-Bayit* Society," managed to raise the money and find the proper land: a stretch of sand dunes north of Jaffa and the Jewish neighborhoods as well. With a very comfortable loan from the Anglo-Palestine Bank, the Society founded the first Hebrew city in the Land.

"And that is indeed what they openly declared they are founding," Rivka could see the smile shining in Ofsey's written words. "A city that is one hundred percent Jewish, its inhabitants speak Hebrew, they make aesthetics and cleanliness their first priority, and they are not submitting to the customs of gentiles. They even believe that the new city will become for the land of Israel what New York is for America, the main entrance… These founders are not like the *Halutzim* – the new farmers, dreaming crops out of rocks and water out of malaria. The new city is not dependent on the generosity of barons and patrons of any kind – this is a very practical, well-thought-out and calculated investment. The new farmers may be the heart of our new independence, but it looks like the city is its head.

"I joined the founders, many of them personal friends of mine, the day they raffled off the lots. It was a strange, surreal sight. Everyone was dressed up as if they were going to a ball, not what you would expect people to wear on a hot, sizzling day of Passover in the middle of sand dunes. The sun was burning, the sand shone so bright that it made your eyes hurt, and the air was too heavy to breathe. We resembled a strange group lost in a desert.

Yet no one complained. Every single person, be it men in heavy suits or women in gowns, felt like they were standing at a modern site of Exodus: they were to be the founders of the first Hebrew city, built out of a fine combination of dreams and practicality, not given to them by mercy or guilt but built by their own merit, expressing their own achievements, and the feeling of freedom that prevailed over all of them was overwhelming.

"We shall begin our raffle at once," said Weiss, the visionary founder of the Society, who was in charge. He woke up early in the morning and walked to the beach carrying two hats. He collected sixty-six pearl-white shells in one hat, and sixty-six dark-gray shells in the other. On the white shells, with black ink and in beautiful handwriting, he wrote the names of the sixty-six founding families. On the gray shells he wrote the numbers of the lots.

"Come close, children, and we shall begin." His voice was official and festive. Two children, a girl and a boy, drew the shells from the hats one by one, matching family to lot. The excitement was so rich that Ofsey could taste it, and he could almost hear the wings of eagles flying across the white ripples of the sandy sea. He was certain that the ancient prophets were all lined up, smiling, to bless this holy moment.

Thirteen months later, a new, white neighborhood emerged from the sizzling sands, stretching toward the bright blue skies. Spacious boulevards were set between the white, growing rows of houses, boulevards made of sand and dreams and filled with tender plants that the founders hoped would quickly grow into trees. Houses were built, white and airy, lined with balconies filled with flowers and people. Cafés and shops opened and burst with customers bringing hope and good business. There was even one *Lux* – a lamppost that shone bright on the one main street. The founders finally decided on the name of the city. Fully convinced that they were following his dream, they decided to name the city after Theodor Herzl's visionary book, *Altneuland* – Old-New Land, and in Hebrew: Tel Aviv.

"But the best of all is the building of the school," Ofsey's letter concluded. "The Gymnasia Herzliya school is by far the most magnificent building in the city, not only because it is well designed – its façade is designed as our Holy Temple was designed in ancient times – but because it is filled with young, creative minds, the minds of our ever-evolving future, minds of the people pouring into the city so that they can study in this great institution and become part of our history. Every day people are moving into this white miracle, this shining Jewish metropolis by the sea. Some of the houses are dream houses – especially the new ones being built on Nachalat Binyamin Street. Father, this is exactly what we have been working for, the best realization of our dreams. It is my honest belief that the time has come to start building a house for the family here in Tel Aviv, a place that will house us all and suit the family needs upon your return. I can get a good price – I have connections through the bank – and I have set my heart on a lot that will be big enough for two houses, for it is time for me to start a family as well."

Tel Aviv had become a reality – more and more people were building their homes there – and Rivka was anxious to help Ofsey start his own family. Isaac sent a letter to Ofsey, ordering him to "find the best place in this new city, this city which is the finest expression of Herzl's vision, this city that has been named Tel Aviv – find the finest place and build our family a home big enough for your dreams as well as ours."

Ofsey did as he was told, and a year later Isaac received a letter from his son announcing that the new house was starting to take shape. It was situated on a fine lot, on the corner of two central streets – Nachalat Binyamin Street and Gruzenberg Street. Every other month, Ofsey received money from his father that kept the building process going, and every other month, Ofsey sent his parents a photograph of the growing house. The pictures looked white and shiny, displaying the excitement of growth and the energy of building. But as time went by Rivka sensed the dark clouds that were hidden behind the rising bricks, closing in on her family both in Lebanon and in Palestine. Clouds that were growing to be so dark she could see no light through them. All she could see was that they were spreading like a disease, hovering like a terrible threat, shrouding everything, becoming so big that soon they would aim to swallow the entire world she knew, and more. They were the clouds of war.

Chapter 4

DVORA AND SHOSHANA

1908–1917

"Your life is exactly that – yours to mold – make your own choices and meanings," my mother's voice would ring loud and clear.

"Your life is a continuum of lives. Never forget where you came from. It is your responsibility to carry on the traditions and narrative of our people," my father would say in a very confident and resolute tone of voice.

My grandmother Shoshana wouldn't say anything. She just made sure to fill my being with the stories, sounds and thoughts she felt were necessary for my proper upbringing. Since the day I was born, she sang to me and told me stories. She would roam the kindergartens of Tel Aviv, asking the teachers to teach her all the new children's songs and fairytales, so she could pass them on to my infant ears. I was less than a year old when I started to sing in full sentences the exact same melodies my grandmother had planted in my soul, carefully nourishing them to create a beautiful concert of love for the land and *the culture that was my foundation. By the time I started preschool, at the tender age of one, I already knew all the songs and fairytales that were sung and related by the teachers.*

But the best stories that my grandmother Shoshana told me – the ones that fascinated me most, causing me to ask her to tell them again and again, even when I was much, much older – were the stories of her life growing up in young Tel Aviv. They were colorful stories, filled with sounds, smells and people. Stories of changing times, burning politics: a diverse mix of people that were suddenly thrust into one steaming pot and had to learn to swim in it or else they would drown. Stories of newborn cities, growing farms, roads and cultures being built, struggles, companionship, betrayals, births, deaths, war and triumphs. Her stories became so embedded in my soul that, like it or not, my own narrative became a direct continuation of them. Whenever something happened to me, I always knew where it had sprouted from, which ancient story preceded mine, which spirits accompanied my life. And to this day, I find it difficult to separate the ancient stories from my own, as if they are all one big tangle of threads growing day by day. A tangle becoming stronger and more threatening, at the same time. For awhile, they are filled with passion, commitment, and even a sense of romantic nostalgia toward those early days of renewal, but they are also filled with hostile eyes, a presence of something and someone who defied not only our own presence, but our very existence. A presence of evil looming in the shadows, an evil that at any moment can strike so hard it will break the entire web of my being.

It took almost two days to travel from Neve Shalom to Zichron Yaacov by wagon. Two days and a lot of prayers to keep you from the lurking robbers on the way, or two days and a handful of Bishliks to pay some Turkish soldiers for protection as you travel. Dvora and Ish always chose the latter: they didn't place much faith in prayers alone. Twice a year, they would all travel back to Zichron Yaacov – for Hanukah and for Pesach.

Nathan, Shoshana and Avner loved Hanukah in Zichron. The winter rain had already brought the anemones to life, the wind spread the fragrance of the daffodils and cyclamens would appear amongst the rocks, coloring them with beautiful shades of pink, greeting the children with a gentle, bashful curtsey of their heads. The entire Carmel Mountains were in full bloom, the fresh scent of wet leaves and muddy mushrooms was everywhere, and the air was crisp and cold.

Each of the eight days of Hanukah, Ish would take his children out for a hike in the nearby fields, filling their heads with funny stories and songs of the flowers and trees that surrounded them. The children learned to speak Yiddish from their Grandmother Chaya, whom they called Bobeh, since it was the only language she knew. But their Grandfather Jacob, whom they called Zeideh, would tell them his stories of the first days of Zichron in perfect, literary Hebrew.

Every Hanukah Bobeh would fry *latkes* – potato patties that became unbelievably delicious when served with applesauce, sour cream or sugar; and she would teach little Shoshana how to bake *sufganiyot* – sweet doughnuts filled with a thick, rich, homemade strawberry jam. Shoshana loved to watch the dough rise, smell the sweet scent of yeast, and lick the thick and sticky jam. During the winter, Bobeh would bring the small chicks into the kitchen so they wouldn't freeze outside, placing them in cages near the warm oven, and Shoshana would cuddle them in her small arms and fill their beaks with sweet jam and small pieces of bread.

They all slept on mattresses laid out on the kitchen floor so they could stay warm by the oven, children and chicks alike. It was a happy, light-filled holiday, and they always returned home with their wagon filled with jam, cakes, fruit, flowers, and at least one chick that Shoshana insisted on trying to raise in their backyard and that always mysteriously disappeared a few days after they returned.

If Hanukah was the holiday of the winter flowers, Pesach was the holiday of family ties. Everyone came back to Zichron for the Pesach Seder: Dvora and Ruth came back with their husbands and children, sometimes bringing their mutual in-laws with them. Pnina, who also married a city man and lived in Haifa, came back with her family, and Sam and Daniel came with their fiancés. Zeideh conducted the Seder dinner. He would sit on his magnificent, huge chair, surrounded by large, hand-embroidered white cushions, and read in a clear voice from the Haggadah. The smell of clean rooms, fresh garments, roasting chicken, sweet potatoes and spring air, filled with the scent of flowers and chilled by a refreshing breeze that climbed all the way up the mountain from the cooling Mediterranean Sea, would mingle with the sounds of prayer, songs, laughter and family gossip. Shoshana loved the festive atmosphere of the holiday that was laced with exciting news. Her mother, grandmother and aunts would buzz around like bees exchanging the details of events with each other, and the air was filled with the anticipation of summer that would soon free them from the indoor, damp, cold days of winter to the exciting days of the outdoors.

Young hens by now, Shoshana would feed the chicks of Hanukah, certain that they still recognized her. Now that the chicks were grown enough, and the air was warm enough for them to sleep in the henhouse, the children had more sleeping space in the kitchen and Shoshana found it too roomy to fall asleep immediately. Besides, there was too much information flowing around her, making its way from eager mouths to anticipating ears, filling in the gaps that were caused by distances that created family longing and loneliness. When her siblings and cousins were fast asleep, Shoshana would sneak out of her covers and hide in the corner near the dining room, from where she could clearly hear her mother and aunts speak without being seen.

"If you want to avoid having another baby," Pnina's voice was low, but it rang crisp and clear, "you should wash your privates with some iodine – you know, afterwards."

Shoshana heard choking laughter, but she had no idea who it belonged to until she heard Ruth whispering: "A better way is to let him be under you and retreat when the time comes."

"But that's totally unlady-like! I know he would be shocked if I were ever to suggest something like that!" Pnina's laughter was muffled.

Shoshana had no idea what exactly they were talking about, but she was certain it was something dark, secret and exciting – what other explanation could there be for their low, embarrassed laughter?

"I just don't understand, even after so many years of marriage, what all the fuss is about," Dvora was the only one whose voice wasn't hidden behind whispers. "I just do my duty as I must, and I know how to calculate the days to make sure that no more babies come out of it!" Shoshana was used to her mother's factual tone that was practical and virtually devoid of any emotion, but even she was taken aback by the coldness in her mother's voice. Her aunts remained silent. Oh, yes, Pesach was definitely fill-in-the-details time.

Everywhere she went, Dvora could feel the heavy presence of the Baron. When they decided to move from Neve Shalom to the new city of Tel Aviv, she refused to build their new house in the wide, spacious boulevard named Rothschild Boulevard only to find herself in a parallel street called Nachalat Binyamin – "The estate of Binyamin" – named after the very same Baron, Binyamin de Rothschild. The large, red-roofed house on Nachalat Binyamin Street was built for both Dvora and Ruth's families, ensuring that the two sisters could continue their lives together without changing their basic habits of tending to one another's business.

The building was made of two adjacent apartments, resembling two arms of the same body with a large, white porch running across the front where the families could mingle. The porch was higher than street level, and it had two large round columns supporting the roof. Each apartment had three small bedrooms, a living room, a dining room, a small kitchen and a bathroom. But the real treasure in Shoshana's young eyes was the spacious joint yard that stretched behind the house, opening up the whole world to satisfy the curiosity of the children. Playing in the yard, they could easily see the tip of the magnificent, large Gymnasia Herzliya School, and behind it, within a short distance, the blue waves of the sea.

Sometimes, when they were really lucky, they could see a ship passing, and they would make up stories about the people aboard the ship, imagining the places they were coming from and the destiny that awaited them.

Moving to Tel Aviv hadn't made Dvora change her daily habits, but she did refine them. Every morning, after the children were safely ensconced in kindergarten, Dvora and Ruth would sit on the front porch and have their morning tea together. They had many things to discuss: the new city was exciting, many new people came into their worlds, and their tongues were very busy. Their morning habit became so infamous that people would avoid walking by their house, saying that once you passed by the Broytman sisters' porch in the morning, you were destined to become the food on the tips of their tongues for the entire week.

The young city was growing rapidly and its inhabitants were determined to transform it into a modern metropolis, blessed with all the luxuries and enjoyments that a modern metropolis should have: small cafés, quaint shops and wide boulevards with gardens and benches to sit and relax on. They were also determined that Tel Aviv should boast a high standard of morality, so alcohol, gambling, and other immoral pursuits, were banned during those early, naïve days of the beginning of creation. For those, you would have to go to Jaffa.

Every Thursday afternoon Dvora would put on her best dress, white gloves would caress her hands and elegant shoes with a small heel would embrace her feet. She would dress the children in their best clothes and lead them to one of the cafés further down their street. It was always busy – men, women and children filled the white sandy streets of Tel Aviv while the blazing afternoon sun crept into every inch of space, illuminating the city with a bright gold and copper color. Sometimes they would go all the way down to the end of Rothschild Boulevard, where it met Herzl Street with a single streetlamp, and they would order a colored soda at one of Tel Aviv's two kiosks. A little bit of lemon juice, a little bit of raspberry juice, and a sparkling glass filled with bubbly soda – the GAZOZ was the best drink in town. It was sassier then the sweet Tamarhindy that the Jews who came from Jaffa brought with them, and younger than the plain soda that the older generation drank to help their indigestion. The kiosks thrived on the selling of gazoz, and a large sign announced, in beautiful letters in Hebrew calligraphy, that "We sell wonderful soda drinks for very reasonable prices. For alcohol, go somewhere else," just so no one would be confused.

Tel Aviv was a white city, filled with sand, salty air and sun. Sun and sand were everywhere. Sand filled the streets, jumped into the houses, tasted the food and slept in the beds. The white sand dunes that surrounded Tel Aviv became the color of the city, and they became the hiding place and playground of children by day and of lovers by night.

Tel Aviv was a friendly, sensuous city; it was a hyperactive city as well: houses were being built everywhere, and the sounds of hammers, levers, concrete and blocks were the music that filled your ears during the busy hours of the days. The city was rapidly growing, gay and bold in the sand. While the days were dedicated to physical growth, the evenings were a time of cultural creation, especially music. Sounds of gramophones screeching with amazement to the voices of opera and classical music – that miraculously came out of the point of a needle placed on a revolving disc – filled the hearts with astonishment and longing. Sounds of pianos, violins, lutes and singing voices would pour from the open windows, filling the streets with gaiety, engulfing the passersby with a magical harmony, making the young trees spread their growing branches in a happy dance and the flowers open their petals in thirst. If the soul of Jerusalem was its history and prayer, the spirit of Tel Aviv was renewal and music.

> "Here, in the beloved land of our forefathers
> All our hopes will come true
> Here we will live and here we shall create
> A life of freedom, a life of liberty.
> Here the Lord will dwell
> Here the language of the Torah will flourish…"

Music was everywhere. The teachers and students of the Gymnasia Herzliya School were the main source of melodies and lyrics, sending harmonies of romance, marches and longing that spread throughout the land, songs that were initiated in the sun-bleached classrooms, and were carried by the students as they marched through the hills on their endless field trips, and then sprang from their lips to the hills, from the hills to the valleys, from the valleys to the mountains, until everyone from north to south sang them with passion, knowing that they carried a profound message but not quite remembering where they had learned them.

The school quickly became one of the cornerstones of the city, its pride and joy. The first day of school was a festive occasion, and shortly after they moved to Tel Aviv, the big day arrived. Dvora proudly dressed her son and walked him to school. When they arrived, she suddenly stopped short, her eyes grew wide and she gasped: at the entrance to the school stood none other then Herzl himself.

Knowing that this was impossible – Herzl had been dead for six years – she took a deep breath, slowly regained her composure, and started walking into the school. She heard other parents greeting the man.

"Good morning, Dr. Mosinzon!"

"We should all have a great year, Dr. Mosinzon!"

And with a wink – "Dr. Mosinzon, I trust we will be spreading new songs throughout the land, maybe something about the Tel Aviv dunes…"

Dr. Mosinzon, the man who was the spitting image of the founder and great leader of the Zionist movement, was the principal of the school. Dvora wasn't the only one thrown off by his image. Many in Tel Aviv were certain that it was a heavenly sign: The first Hebrew city, that was named after Herzl's famous book, was home to the first Hebrew school, that was named after Herzl himself and lead by a principal who looked just like him. What other signs do we need, argued the passionate believers in mysticism, to convince us that these are indeed days of redemption?!

Dvora quickly adjusted herself to city manners, at least in the way she perceived them. Little Shoshana was dressed in lace and velvet, with matching gloves, shining lacquer shoes on her feet and a small hat on her head. Dvora was very strict regarding her children's manners, and they were all reared to be polite and graceful. Dvora surrounded her family with beauty: porcelain dolls and dishes, thin glass tea cups and embroidered tablecloths filled the house. When Shoshana was five years old, Dvora made Ish purchase a beautiful piano from one of the Russian Jewish families that had just arrived, and Shoshana was sent for piano lessons and to study music before she knew how to read.

But more than anything, the house was filled with books. Leather-covered books in all colors and sizes that emitted a smell of adventure and romance, filling the children's imagination with stories of faraway places and times. Bedtime was their favorite part of the day. Ish would come into their room, always with a book in hand, and he would read to them about princesses and kings and forests and duels, adding a flavor of his own and coloring them with a festive, theatrical interpretation. By the time she started school, Shoshana knew more about history, the Bible and music than all of her peers and, indeed, most of the students in the entire school.

One day, Shoshana woke up to the sound of hammers that were very close, much closer than usual. A short investigation resulted in the discovery that the empty lot behind their house, the last lot on the street – the corner of Nachalat Binyamin and Gruzenberg Streets –was empty no more: builders were there, pouring cement, stabilizing iron and hammering wood. A new house was being born.

Nathan, Shoshana and Avner were very excited – soon there would be a new family living beside them, and a new family brought the possibility of new children and new adventures. Every day, on their way home from school, Shoshana and Nathan would pass the site of the new house that was being built behind their own house. Shoshana was fascinated with the way work was progressing. Every day something new was added to the structure – another row of blocks, a rectangular frame that suddenly formed the shape of a window, a space that was being built around and miraculously developed into a door. Bright, colorful glass was put into these spaces, creating shapes that only existed in one's imagination, and when the builders started building a second floor on top of the first – she was sure she was dreaming. She would watch wide-eyed as the Arab builders would laugh, yell and cry out to each other as they created this amazing huge dollhouse right in front of her eyes.

She tried to picture the family that was building this house. She heard the adults say that they were a family of bankers with several children and even a *kavas* – a Turkish servant whose only duty in the world was to be dressed in gold and white and to open doors for people. She could imagine the toys they would probably bring with them, the beautiful garden they would have, and she secretly hoped that the mother would have lace tablecloths and porcelain dishes finer then those that her family owned. Just imagine the wonderful dinners you could have with such riches! How beautifully you could host with such accessories! Shoshana was certain that the cakes, pastries and drinks would taste differently in such a home.

Most of all, Shoshana enjoyed watching the builders who were building the porch – an enormous space in front of the building, with beautiful pillars and colorful tiles. She would stand for hours on the sidewalk, gazing at the workers' hands, watching as they built. One of them, a tall young Turk with eyes the shape and color of coffee beans and arms as long as Eucalyptus branches, would smile warmly at her. He used to hum Turkish music and work swiftly. A little uneasy, she would always smile back. The young Turk always looked around to see if Shoshana was there and he would wave his hand at her. "Ahalan, binti!" he would yell, "Hello, my daughter" – and go back to work.

Sometimes she would see a nice-looking young man come and talk to the workers. His clothes revealed that he was obviously Jewish, and it looked like he was giving them instructions, checking their progress and evaluating their job. The young Turk always accompanied the young Jew – they seemed the same age, both of them talking, smiling and shaking hands. They obviously respected each other.

When Shoshana was eight years old, well into the second decade of the twentieth century, the winds of World War I were blowing around the world and they did not overlook the young white city. Food became very scarce and the Turkish military confiscated goods from everyone: furniture, tools, horses, mules, even houses became fragile leaves that could be blown away by the fighting Ottoman Empire. Those who were Ottoman-born were spared at first: they were considered loyal citizens of the Empire, and it was the first time in her life that Dvora actually secretly blessed the fact that she, her husband and children were all native Ottoman citizens. Those who refused to become Ottoman citizens and swear their loyalty to the Empire were ordered to leave the country. Almost daily, ships took away people Shoshana had known all her life. As young as she was, Shoshana could feel the tension growing like sea weed in the air when the adults spoke. Those who were citizens strode around town with red Turkish hats – tarboosh – on their heads to show where their loyalties lay, only to become subject to swift conscription into the Turkish army and to be sent to the front, many never to return.

Worst of all, the Turkish soldiers became even meaner than before. Dvora always rushed Shoshana and the boys into the house whenever she heard the hooves of the soldiers' horses, and Ish was gone for many hours, helping those who needed food, authentic Turkish certificates or money. He himself struggled to obtain money as well. Shoshana's piano lessons were stopped. Objects from the house began to disappear, Ish taking them from the house in the morning and returning at dusk with food in a carefully-held basket instead.

Building had come to a near halt all over the city, and the house being built next to Shoshana's house was no exception. From time to time she would sneak out, looking at the abandoned, half-built porch, wishing the builders would come back and continue their magnificent work, hoping to hear the young, friendly Turk calling her again – "Ahalan, Binti!" – a call that signified a familiar, warm reassurance that everything would be all right.

At first everyone thought that the war would be short. The Ottoman Empire and the German forces would undoubtedly triumph, people said, trying to show loyalty to their government more than really believing in its strength.

During the first year of the war, the Broytman families still traveled north to Zichron when the holidays came around. But as time passed, the war became an everyday presence, crushing everything in its way. Rumors started spreading, their confidence in a swift victory vanished, and travel became very dangerous. The Turks were losing the war and, in their frustration, they harassed the Jews of Palestine more than ever, treating them like traitors and suspecting them of betrayal, even when most of them went out of their way to show their loyalty. The roads, filled with hungry Turkish soldiers searching for food, money and a scapegoat at whom they could vent their growing sense of frustration and thirst for revenge, became almost impossible to travel on. Bandits were lurking in the shadows, looking for quick and easy money, while strange, wary refugees were searching for comfort.

Dvora and Ish decided it would be too dangerous to leave Tel Aviv and travel north, so they stayed home for the holidays. News had reached Dvora of her brother Daniel: the Turks had issued a draft order for him and his three mules, an order he had no intention of fulfilling. Daniel and his mules disappeared overnight, and the family was out of its mind with worry. No one had any idea where he was – some said he was hiding in a cave, others said he was seen in another settlement further north, a place called Rosh Pina, and yet others said they had heard rumors that he had been caught by the Turks and awaited trial. Before Dvora and Ish could think of a way to get to Zichron, to find out what exactly was happening there, new rumors started spreading, rumors that left Dvora speechless with horror and made even Ish's bright and joyfully optimistic eyes grow dark: the Turks were about to evacuate Gaza, and everyone knew that Jaffa and Tel Aviv would be next.

Thread connects to thread, one path leads to another, prophecy precedes story. In a land that is dense with history, wherever you drop a pin you will hit the hearts of generations, all stacked up in a pile of endless tales.

Tarek was our gardener. He was an Arab from Taibe, a little

village about a half-hour drive to the northeast from our home in the town of Herzliya.

"Taibe was one of the few Arab villages where the people did not flee during our War of Independence in 1948," my father always used to say proudly, as if he himself had anything to do with it. "They trusted us, knowing that we can live together in harmony if we only put our mind to it. That's why I trust them right back. They are loyal to our State – Israelis just like me and you."

Tarek would come once a week, always carrying a little something for us: sweet baklava cookies, special blended coffee, a spicy rich eggplant salad. He was young, and over the years, we grew to love and respect him. His stories made us feel like we knew his entire family. He married and had children while working for my parents who, in addition to his regular salary, always gave him support that would help him raise a nice family and build a beautiful house.

One year we were all invited to his house for a meal. Having grown up listening to the stories of the legendary Arab hospitality, we were excited to be experiencing it first-hand.

Taibe was a typical mixture of old and new buildings, all of them standing on columns, some of them decorated with Jerusalem stone, some of them still standing bold in their bare cement, some with colorful, beautiful windows, and others with blue doors. The village resembled a handful of building blocks that a child had clumsily assembled, starting the process of organizing the blocks, but leaving the job undone.

Miriam, Tarek's young wife of twenty-three, already a mother of two, welcomed us at the door. It was nice and cool inside. The furniture was sparse and minimal. We noticed a large table in the dining room, all set for greeting guests. Miriam was running back and forth from the kitchen, avoiding our eyes. She made me feel uncomfortable, although I couldn't explain why – there was something very tense in the air. Tarek was giving my parents a reception fit for royalty. Trying *to be polite, my sister and I went into the kitchen and asked Miriam if we could help in any way. She turned to us sharply and, with a dark look on her face and a large, sharp kitchen knife in her hand, she waved the knife at us and said, "Go away, go on! Out!"*

I don't remember the rest of the evening. All I remember is asking my parents quietly to leave as soon as possible.

When we were in the car, safely on our way back home, we told them what had happened.

My father quickly responded: "That can't be. You must have misunderstood."

My mother was silent.

My grandmother Shoshana said: "Even if he is your best friend, you can never really trust an Arab. He will always find the first opportunity to stab you in the back. I know – I've grown up with them all my life."

And although I knew exactly why she was saying it, I still refused to believe her.

It was almost a surprise when it happened. Although the rumors had been circulating for quite sometime, no one actually took them seriously. After all, Hassan Beck himself loved to come to Tel Aviv – he personally knew many of the citizens and was always a guest of honor at the moving-pictures house. Surely he would spare them, he couldn't possibly think that the citizens of Tel Aviv posed any kind of threat to the great Ottoman Empire! As it was, they were a sad lot. Tel Aviv was almost abandoned. The long war had ravaged everything; what the war did not take, the locusts did. Coming in huge, hungry waves, the destructive locusts spread throughout the country, grabbing and munching at everything in sight, turning the poor, thin, hungry earth into a barren and devastated land, adding insult to injury, leaving nothing behind. The very notion that the poor, hungry people of Tel Aviv could be considered a threat sounded so ridiculous that most of them just nodded their heads in disbelief and let the rumors of evacuation lie quietly on the floor, swept with sand and wind until they would disappear.

But the great Empire was dangling like a dry leaf: desperate and fearful, and no mercy was shown toward the young city. Searches were conducted in the homes, people were forbidden to leave their homes after dark, and every remark or action was cause for suspicion. When the Turks caught two Arab fishermen with a handsome bribe in their pockets and their boat filled with British pamphlets, the Turks snapped with anger. The two fishermen were hung in the main square in Jaffa, and the *dalal* – the Turkish caller – called everyone to come and see what happens to those who betray the Ottoman Empire. Dvora managed to keep herself and her children hidden behind doors, in the safety of their house, sparing them from the angry crowd and the shrieks of the Turks, but Shoshana never forgot the expression in her father's eyes when he returned from the hanging: they were hollow and sad, terrified by the cruelty he had just witnessed. As the thunder of the British cannons grew closer from the south by day, the Turks became more and more desperate and vicious. The order came fierce and very clear: within a week, Jaffa and Tel Aviv were to be completely evacuated, forcing all the inhabitants into exile. Only a handful of young men were allowed to stay behind to guard the abandoned houses until their owners would be allowed to return.

They left in wagons, filled with blankets, furniture and pianos. Within a week the entire city was in motion. People were walking away desperately, looking back every few minutes, hoping for some kind of salvation that would wake them up from this unbearable nightmare. Everyone, especially those who had arrived from Europe only a few short years earlier, had an ominous feeling of déja-vu, except this time it was much worse. They were being exiled not from a place where they had always felt welcome to begin with, not from a place that refused to accept them no matter how hard they tried to belong, but from their one and only true, historic, legitimate home – a home they had been praying to return to since ancient times, a home they had built and earned with their blood, sweat and tears. They were furious.

Dvora, Ish, Ruth, Lipeh and their children were all packed into three wagons and were about to start their journey up north when Shoshana slipped away to say a last goodbye to her house and the half-built house next door. She stood there for several moments, quietly praying.

"I'll be back..." she vowed slowly and silently, and the naïve, childish determination hidden in her soul became one large ball of emotions flowing from her eyes. "I'll come back home, and I'll make sure that this unfinished house becomes a home for whoever comes to it as well! Keep our homes safe, dear Lord, they are all we have...."

She was still deep in thought and prayer when suddenly the young Turk appeared. Shoshana hadn't seen him in a while and his presence here on this particular day was a totally unexpected surprise. At once, she felt reassured; something inside her said that this was a sign that they would be fine, and things would go back to normal again – it had been nothing more than a bad dream. Instinctively, she gave him the same welcoming smile she had always given him in return for his cheerfulness.

There was no smile on his face. Shoshana couldn't read his expression – she was too young and innocent to understand what it meant. His eyes looked directly at her, cold, blazing with a freezing fire. Before she could move, he raised his hand, yelled, "*Allah Hu Akbar!*" – God is great – and with all his might, he thrust a stone at her and disappeared.

The stone hit her forehead and blood started to trickle down her face, but Shoshana didn't feel any pain. She was too numb from shock, too burning with insult, overwhelmingly disappointed by the betrayal. She returned to the wagon, silently accepting her mother's accusation, "Did you climb into the half-built house again? How many times do I have to tell you it is dangerous, that you might hurt yourself? And now you have gone and done it! Just what I needed before we leave!"

Shoshana's soul was too hurt to tell her mother what had really happened. Dvora cleaned the wound, which luckily was a shallow one, and they were on their way. The whole incident lasted no more than a few minutes. The wound left a small scar on her forehead, hardly noticeable, but the memory left a bleeding, burning mixture of feelings in her soul, and they stayed there for more than seventy years, until the day she died. These feelings seeped into her mind and watered the roots of fear, anger and resentment that she had felt by being thrown out of her own home, being forced to leave in shame, branded a traitor for reasons she could not understand, for actions she knew they were not guilty of. She would plant and nurture these feelings in the hearts of her grandchildren. She would have many friends throughout her life, some of them Arabs. She would host them, joke with them, be hosted by them and treat them with great respect. But she would never, ever trust them again.

The roads were full. They all felt like humiliated refugees. Suffering, starved, ill and dying, the refugees spread east and north. Most of the exiled families stayed in nearby Petah Tikva, but some camped in the fields on the way north. Dvora knew there was only one place they could go: she took her family home, traveling north to Zichron Yaacov. When they finally reached Zichron after two long days of travel, they discovered that the pressure of war had taken its toll on the small village on the hill: the situation at home was not much better than it was on the road. The fields were neglected, the gardens grew weeds. Hardly any livestock was left – no cows, no hens, no chicks – even the goats were gone. The Turkish army had confiscated everything in sight. Many of the refugees were forced to build huts in the yards, praying that the war would be over before the harsh winter rains would strike. Dvora's parents' house was large, and Daniel's disappearance added some more room, so Dvora and her family were spared from living in a hut. The small village seemed devastated; hunger and disease were rampant. The rough hand of the Turkish soldiers left nothing behind.

But Dvora was home, surrounded by her entire family, her children were healthy, and although it wasn't much, they still had black bread and olives on the table and a warm place to sleep. Dvora felt safe and grateful.

Some said the Turks had decided to exile all the Jews up north, far from the southern front with the British, because they were afraid that the Jews would help the British conquer Palestine. The Jews had always wanted Palestine for themselves, they argued, and now the British were promising to give it to them if only they defeated the Turks. Shortly after Dvora and her family had arrived in Zichron Yaacov, an underground group of Jewish spies was discovered by the Turks. They were a small group of men and woman whose feelings of rage toward the cruel Turkish regime, and high hopes for freedom that were fed by British promises, were translated into dangerous acts of espionage. They were young, passionate and inexperienced, and they were exposed by the Turks. Some managed to escape, others were caught. They called themselves the NILI group – an acronym for "The Eternity Of Israel Will Not Be Untrue" – and their leaders hailed from Zichron Yaacov.

Until the day she died, Shoshana never forgot the days when the Turks had caught and tortured one of the NILI leaders in Zichron Yaacov, a woman named Sara Aharonson. She was the sister of a world-famous agronomist, Aharon Aharonson, and belonged to a prominent and highly respected family. A young, passionate and wild woman, Sara decided that being part of a cause that was greater than any individual was more important than the consequences that might entail for her or her neighbors.

"How dare she!" Dina, the neighbor, exclaimed as she was standing in Bobeh's kitchen. Her angry voice made the children listen quietly, in anticipation. "Not a thought about what this would mean for the rest of us!"

"Really, Dina, don't tell me that you want the Turks to win this war."

"Of course I don't, but I am a responsible person! The armies will do their job," Dina retorted.

"NILI was trying to help the British army."

"Don't be foolish!" Dina snapped. "What can a small group of inexperienced Jewish spies achieve? All this ridiculous NILI group achieved was to bring devastation on us all!"

Dina was not the only one who was angry. Most of the people in Zichron Yaacov were furious at Sara and her friends for placing the entire village in jeopardy. Since the day the NILI group was discovered, the Turks had abused the people of Zichron, harassing them for more information, destroying the little that was left of their crops, and torturing them for being disloyal. The truth was that most of them had no idea about the small underground movement that was operating under their noses, and those who did suspect something were anxious even before the group was caught, knowing that if the Turks caught even one suspect, it would be a disaster for the entire village.

When Sara was caught, they all stood behind locked doors and closed windows, watching the Turks take her away to be questioned in one of the village's remote houses that had been turned into a prison.

"Children, come here," turning away from her mother and Dina, Dvora's voice was determined. "Come to the window and watch."

"Dvora, what are you doing?!" Bobeh was shocked. "They're too young for this."

"No, they're not," Dvora insisted. "It will be a lesson that will last them a lifetime."

Not fully understanding what Dvora was supposed to be teaching them, Nathan, Shoshana and Avner approached the window and peeked into the street through the drawn, white shutters.

Out there, they could see Sara. She was being led, humiliated, bruised, but still in high spirits, by the Turks.

"This is unspeakable!" Bobeh muttered to herself. But she knew better than to argue with her daughter. Her jaw closed tight and her head shook disapprovingly.

"Well, you and your friend can join us. Maybe you'll learn something as well."

Dvora's eyes were cold and strong as she knowingly refused to acknowledge Dina by name. She turned to her children.

"Watch closely and etch this lesson in your minds," Dvora said to them. "This is the lesson of the price of our freedom. Look at Sara and be proud. Whenever hard times come again – and they will come – always remember that it is your duty to take action to help yourselves, even when the price is high. That is what Sara is teaching us today. Her memory will be blessed." Dina and Bobeh were silent.

Shoshana remembered vividly how the young, proud Sara was dragged by the Turks, beaten and bruised, when suddenly she opened her swollen eyes and stood up. Freeing herself from the soldiers' grasp, Sara insisted on walking on her own, and started to sing in a loud and clear voice words that Shoshana, who was standing with her brothers and the rest of the village behind the half-shut shutters, couldn't hear. For a brief moment, Shoshana felt as if Sara's eyes were looking straight at her, and she was taken aback by the strong, determined look that they projected. It was the look that Shoshana had secretly wished she herself had given the young Turk who had stoned her. It was a look that would accompany Shoshana throughout her life, giving her strength and reason when the burden would become bitter, echoing in her mind with Dvora's words.

Sara was tortured in unimaginable ways. Every day the Turks would lead her from the prison through the main street to the torture house for questioning. Every day she sang the same song. And every day Dvora placed her children at the window, making them watch. After four days the Turks decided to take Sara away for further questioning, and she requested a bath. Even the Turks felt ashamed to travel with a bloodied, bruised with black and blue marks, tortured young woman, so they granted her request. Sara was tied and led through the main street all the way up to her family's house.

Shoshana watched attentively. She was only eleven years old, but the hurt and shame she felt after watching the reaction of most of the village people, and the pride she felt in her mother's reaction engulfed her, penetrating her mind and body, making her light blue eyes grow dark and painful, the pride never leaving her spirit. Slowly nurturing within her a growing sense of determination, she developed a strong will that she would nourish and pass on to future generations. It was the will of freedom fighters, and Shoshana suddenly realized that it was a will that was not brought to Palestine by the Jewish settlers from Europe. In spite of their struggle to conquer the earth, regardless of their dreams to be independent farmers in their ancient homeland, most of them were still afraid of the ruling empire, shivering in despair, as they did in the European towns from which they came. She suddenly understood that her grandparent's generation had only made half the journey and that it was her job to complete it, hers and all those who were born amidst the realization of the dream.

Some of the village people stood and stared at Sara as she was half-dragged, half-led by the Turkish soldiers. Some mumbled words of anger and shame, others showed their feelings more openly, but it seemed like no one showed any mercy toward the small young woman who had had the impertinence to defy the Ottoman Empire. Shoshana stood there with them, her feelings of anger and deliberation growing with every agonizing step Sara took. "I will always remember," she whispered to herself. "We will always remember." Transfixed, she repeated the same sentence again and again. She didn't take her eyes off Sara when the young woman turned to her and their eyes locked. For one brief moment, the determination in Sara's eyes were transferred into Shoshana's soul, and it seemed as if both were smiling knowingly at each other. It was an emotion so strong and powerful that it remained with Shoshana as a source of strength and energy until the day she died.

Several hours later, Sara managed to shoot herself, dying four days later in agony. Although Sara and her companions had been openly denounced by most, the NILI episode became a legend in the history of Zionism, and Sara Aharonson was its undeniable hero. Less than a month after the NILI organization was destroyed, the foreign minister of the British government published an official declaration stating that, after the war, Great Britain would help the Jewish people establish a national home in the Land of Israel. Among other factors, the operations of NILI became one of the catalysts that had paved the way to making such a declaration possible. For Sara and her friends, however, it was too late.

Throughout her entire life, Shoshana would always be amazed and ashamed that not one person had displayed an ounce of compassion for this brave young girl, who with a few friends, and with her own two hands, had helped bring an end to the Ottoman Empire's days in Palestine, clearing the road of one of the major obstacles that, once removed, paved the way for an independent Jewish state. She vowed to remember Sara's legacy of Jewish freedom forever.

Chapter 5

RIVKA, DVORA AND SHOSHANA

1914–1919

Zichron was the place of Sara. My grandmother saw to it that we heard her story again and again, bringing life into ghostly figures that I can always see on Founders' Road and around the Aharonson's house. I am always surprised that they are not immediately visible to others. The same can be said for Tel Aviv, Jaffa and Jerusalem. I see things that others do not notice. They have their own ghosts.

For a place has different meanings for different people, and my people have centuries of experience in imbuing deep meanings into stones, an experience that reaches the highest levels of artistic expertise where Jerusalem is concerned.

The Jaffa Gate in Jerusalem is a place of hustle and bustle. People of different religions and traditions rush in and out of the Old City, longing to inhale some of its mysteries, enchantments and charms. Thinking that they are taking with them a piece of magic, they do not realize until much later that the city is the one which has captured a piece of them. Casting her unbreakable spell upon them, sending delicate tendons that grow around their hearts and snatch their visions, the city leaves them with an unfulfilled, longing sense of love and commitment that makes the brave-hearted among them bold as knights and the weaker ones crazed with passion.

The gate opens to a colorful, busy world, filled with odors and tastes that assault the senses. Arab youngsters roll through the gate, their carts filled with large, oval-shaped and sesame-covered bagels known as "Jerusalem Bagels," baklava cakes soaking in honey and freshly-squeezed, cold lemonade that is so sweet it makes you nauseous; Jews in traditional garments walk hurriedly towards hidden entrances, their heads down, their eyes darting in different, nervous directions as they hasten their pace and disappear in the alleyways, always walking in a rigid fashion that gives them the appearance of being surrounded by a hidden wall that separates them from the rest of the world; Armenian monks walk gracefully, slowly, sometimes as if walking in a dream, filled with flowery scents and music of harps, defying the thick air and the noise of the surrounding crowd.

The gate is a place of diversity and tense pluralism, of vibrant, living, pounding hearts. But for my family, it has always been a place of tragic and painful haunting death.

The rate at which family news traveled across the world was remarkable considering that it did so without the advantages of advanced media; with roads that were difficult as well as risky to travel on at a time of a raging world war, and with moral inhibitions that demanded acquiescing silence over scandal. Rivka received the news about Feiga's family less than a week after the tragedy occurred, and would have heard it earlier had she not refused to learn Hebrew. All things considered, it was probably for the best, for had she known Hebrew she would have learned the news almost immediately and would have been subject to the humiliation of reading about it in the Jewish newspapers.

When World War I began, Feiga's firstborn son, Saul, was old enough to be drafted. He was taken to the army and Feiga was beside herself with anguish. Reuven only muttered that at least there was now one less mouth to feed during these difficult times, and that at last the Turks were taking some responsibility for the situation. Ignoring her husband, Feiga searched in vain for her son's whereabouts. Finally, after several months without a word, Saul appeared at their door one dark night. He had come for a few hours, he said, before being sent in the morning to the Antalia front.

Hearing this news, Feiga gasped. The Antalia front was a certain one-way-ticket to death. Saul looked at his mother, desperate, and for the first time in his life turned to ask his father for help: the only way to save him, he said, would be to pay off two of the Turkish officers – give them a nice *bakshish*, bribe, and he would be released.

Reuven looked at his son and yelled: "Are you out of your mind?! I would rather have you killed than give you the money! At least with the money something good can be done, what good are you?!"

Trembling, Saul said quietly: "Father, I will work hard so I can pay back every cent you give me. But if I go, I am sure to be killed."

Reuven just kept yelling: "You good-for-nothing bastard! What have you ever done to deserve my hard-earned money?! It will only go to the corrupt Turks, they will take it, laugh and mock us, so you can live at my expense and we will all end up starving! I will never give money to the Turks!"

Feiga couldn't bear it any more. For the first time since they were married, she begged her husband: "Reuven, please…I have never asked for anything, but now I am begging you…give him the money. It's not for the Turks, it's for your son. You will be saving his life."

When Reuven hurled toward her, his eyes mad and his fist in

the air, Saul finally exploded. Years of humiliation, fear, sadness and silence erupted in one great outburst. The sight of his younger brother Aaron, scurrying for a hiding place from their father's rage, and of his tiny, ghostly mother begging like a street woman, was too much for him to tolerate. Without hesitation, he lifted his gun and fired twice – one shot directly aimed at his father's heart, and then at his own head. They both died instantly.

"Sleep, my son, sleep in peace,
Mama will bring you a star
Mama will feed you with raisins and almonds,
How beautiful and loving you are…"

A peaceful, calm voice that sounded as if there were no more troubles in the world, no war, no hunger and no cruelty, was floating in the air, filling the dark alleyways of Jerusalem, soothing the babies and shining hope into the war-beaten, hunger-struck hearts of the residents. A quiet, serene feeling filled those who happened to hear the voice as it sang, a heavenly feeling that fills the believers as they listen to bells ring with the sound of a beautiful, angel-like wholeness. Morning found Feiga sitting on the floor, Saul's body in her lap, singing quietly the lullaby she used to sing to her sons when they were toddlers. Her eyes dry, her hand gently caressing Saul's blood-covered hair, Reuven dead at her feet, her whole being was as removed and detached as the heavens. It was in this state that the Turkish policemen found her. She did not hear their knocks, then banging, and finally the explusive sound of the breaking door as they burst into the house. Calling loudly, yelling at each other, and half-hysterical from the serene voice that floated from the lips of the calm woman who sat in front of them, and from the scene that surrounded her, they quickly dismissed Feiga as a complete *Majnoon* – crazy.

Immediately understanding what had happened, the Turks

removed both bodies and hung them at the entrance to the Old City at the Jaffa Gate. Feiga, who was still humming the quiet melody, cut off from reality, was forced to stand and guard the bodies while the *Dalal*, the Turkish caller, paced back and forth, announcing to the crowd what had happened, warning anybody who had thoughts of defying the Turkish army that this would be their fate, and praising Allah for punishing these traitors.

For ten days and ten nights, the bodies hung there while Feiga kept vigil, humming most of the time, stopping only for an occasional drink of water and piece of bread that merciful people managed to stealthily pass to her. After ten days, Aaron was finally allowed to bury his father and brother, taking his half-mad mother home. She never set foot outside again.

Rivka didn't tell Isaac the news when she learned what had happened to Feiga. She didn't say a word, not because she knew it would break his heart and in spite of the fact that she knew she had to tell him because she owed him the information. She knew she owed it to Feiga. Rivka didn't tell Isaac because she couldn't. Rivka couldn't tell Isaac the news because she couldn't see him: he was in a dark, deep jail cell.

The first signs were slim, hardly noticeable, and anyone without Rivka's invisible companions would not have recognized them for what they were: the expression in the eyes of the merchants at the market who suddenly looked at all strangers suspiciously; the implicit stress underlying the voices of men's discussion as they sat in the local cafés, playing backgammon, drinking strong, black coffee, the dice thrust angrily from their smoke-stained fingers; women buying rice and beans that were enough to feed their families for a long time; children being rushed off the streets and hidden behind heavy doors.

As time went by, the signs became stronger and clearer. A distinguished ambassador was hurriedly called back to his country for a consultation that did not end; invitations to dinners became rare, and when they came they were usually for a small, select group of foreigners and a handful of local leaders; the growing, endless hours that the bank required; the sudden, unexplained disappearance of their loyal *kavas*; and finally, the blunt, direct persecution that the Jews in Beirut suffered at the hands of the Turks.

When the war started ravaging around them, the Turks declared the war a religious war – a *Jihad* – and they became very suspicious of the Anglo-Palestine Bank. It was, after all, a British-based bank, and the Jewish Zionists were heretics just like the rest of the non-Muslim world. They never trusted anyone who was not Muslim, and they most certainly did not trust the bank.

It began with small harassments, then grew to bullying, culminating in an outright molestation. The Turks relentlessly searched the bank, the offices, creating chaos and disruption wherever they went, leaving behind destruction and devastation. Rivka begged Isaac to close the office before it would be too late, horrified by the memories of distant pogroms and warnings of chaotic cruelty she could see and taste all around her. But Isaac refused. He knew that closing the bank would be destructive to the Zionist movement. He wrote to Ofsey, ordering him to halt the building of their house for the moment – "until better times come." In the meantime, he could still maintain a small salary that would keep the family going, especially since food in Beirut was more abundant than in Palestine. But when the empire showed signs of losing, and the Turks started to suspect they had Jewish spies amongst them, they didn't confine their frustration to the Jews in Palestine alone: without warning they closed the bank and threw Isaac into jail, questioning and torturing him to reveal what he knew about the traitors. Rivka tried to free him, paying the few gold Napoleons and Bishliks she still had to anyone who might be helpful, knocking on the doors of consuls and army officers, contacting those who during better times took pride in calling themselves friends and now had distant, detached and fearful gazes, but it was all in vain. Like most of Europe, Beirut was in turmoil and no one really knew how to help, or who could.

The news of the chaos in Palestine did not help matters either. Rivka would overhear conversations in the market, and the rumors were terrifying: They said that the Turks were defeating the British, that the Jews were all traitors and were therefore being slaughtered, and that soon the great Ottoman Empire would rule the world and no heretic will be allowed to live without confirmation of belief in Allah and conversion to Islam.

Letters from Ofsey were few and Rivka was very worried. When finally a letter did arrive, she was confused; hardly any of it was censored, for Ofsey wrote of happy times, saying that the Turks were treating everyone in Tel Aviv well. He announced his marriage to Priscilla, describing in detail his new, American-born wife, praising her knowledge and upbringing as an aristocratic woman of the world with a higher education in zoology, writing how much he loved her and how he knew she would be an asset to him, as the job of managing the bank will definitely soon be offered to him. He went on to describe his wonderful wedding, which all the important people of Tel Aviv attended, emphasizing that food was plenty and that he was certain that the wonderful empire will soon "teach everyone a lesson and be proved to be as pure and *wholly* as this white envelope is."

Knowing that there was no way in which Ofsey could have made such a spelling mistake, it was clear to her that he was trying to convey to her something different entirely. Rivka looked carefully inside the envelope and noticed it had a slight wrinkle on the inside. Pulling at it, the envelope came apart and the real letter that Ofsey had written was revealed, hidden within. With a very light pencil and in very light handwriting, Ofsey described the real situation – the hunger, the searches, the torture, and the rumors of the upcoming exile from Tel Aviv. "When the exile will be announced, I will find refuge with friends in the hills near Petah

Tikva. We are prepared to live in tents, we know the conditions will be very difficult, but nevertheless our spirits are high for we know that soon the British will come, and with them the promises for a Jewish homeland here in Palestine will be fulfilled. Above all, I am reassured to hear that you are all safe in Beirut."

Isaac knew nothing of any spies, and after many long, painful months, the Turks were finally convinced that he would be of no use to them. They kept him in jail for a few more months and only released him when they needed the cell for some other unfortunate prisoner. He was finally free to go home. It was almost a year after he was arrested. He was released as quickly as he had been imprisoned, and he was thrown out of jail with barely a shirt on his back. Slowly, his feet sending pain up his spine with every step he took, his run-down body half the size it had been when he was arrested, and his eyes hollow, he managed to make his way through the streets of Beirut until he finally arrived home.

When Rivka saw Isaac at the door, her teeth clenched tightly, her eyes grew as dark as the night and a new, determined energy filled her arms as she went to work. She prepared for Isaac a warm bath, put soothing oils in it, and ordered him to lie still in the healing water. She prepared him a warm, healing soup, even though she knew he would hardly be able to keep it down. She then went to the Blooma cabinet, withdrew from its depth the diamond earrings that her beloved husband had bought her only several years before, and sent Racheli to trade them for a handsome price at the pawn shop. When Racheli returned with the money, Rivka finally called for the doctor. For Isaac was not only starved, but broken and battered. He was also very yellow.

From the moment the doctor set his eyes on Isaac, Rivka knew what his verdict would be. She spent the next few months nursing her husband, cleaning his wounds and his vomit, placing damp pieces of cloth on his wrists to ease the fever, and caressing the body and soul which had been so loving to her and had given her the most wonderful, pleasure-filled days and nights of her life. She told him stories and sang lullabies to him, the same lullabies she had sung to their children. She prayed to her spirits to take good care of him when he arrived in their possession. She never said a word about Feiga and her family in Jerusalem, or about Ofsey and his fate in Tel Aviv. All she wanted was to constantly make Isaac smile, the very same smile that made her fall in love with him the first time he looked at her, when she first saw him praying on the *Bima* in a time and place that seemed from another world. Three months after he was released, a short cry away from the end of the first World War that Rivka would witness, Isaac died in Rivka's arms. He was smiling.

The endless roaming, leaving the home she knew and loved, the tragedies of her sister and sister-in-law, even the deaths of her own children – none of them had prepared Rivka for the paralyzing sense of loss and emptiness she felt when Isaac was gone. It was a strange feeling, an awkward sense of hollow calm. Her blue eyes grew very dark, almost black, like a sea before a terrible storm hits. They seemed so endlessly deep and empty that Racheli became more silent and withdrawn than ever, and even Moshe stopped his endless search for his dead sister, and instead tiptoed quietly whenever he passed near his grieving mother. One day, while looking at him, Rivka said in a flat, metallic tone: "My poor little orphan…you must be strong to find your way in this world. Ofsey and Aaron are grown men. They will be your guides. As for Olga and Racheli…" she sighed, "It was not meant to be. It was just not meant to be."

Moshe had no idea what she was talking about until one day Olga suddenly appeared standing on their doorstep in Beirut. The war still gasping its last breaths, the bank still closed, Rivka struggled with the very last coins she could find. She even tried unsuccessfully to pawn the gold bracelets she still had hidden in the Blooma cabinet. She still had enough to buy food, but there was no way she could continue sending Olga money for her studies in Luzan. She wrote Olga, begging her for forgiveness and asking her to try to give lessons that would help her survive during these difficult times. She waited anxiously to hear from her daughter, and when instead of a letter Olga herself appeared at the door, they fell in each other's arms, crying, laughing and talking all at once.

"What does this mean?" Rivka examined her smart daughter's eyes carefully. "Will you be able to go back to school when times become better?"

"That won't be necessary, mother." Olga's voice revealed a hint of pride, "I have already finished school – and I have the certificate to prove it!"

Olga not only managed to obtain a double degree in languages and in literature, but she also came first in her class in spite of the hardships of the war. Rivka could clearly hear the smiles of her spirits, feeling the small light they had lit for her, and she thanked them with all her heart. When, from his exile in the sands of Petah Tikva, Ofsey managed to arrange for the whole family to return to Palestine, Rivka knew that a new beginning was awaiting her.

But not immediately. Holding the exciting letter in her hands, Olga turned to Rivka. "It's time to go back home," she said. "There is no need to stay in exile any longer."

"Not yet." Olga was surprised by the determination in her mother's voice. Misunderstanding her mother, Olga tried to convince Rivka to change her mind. "But, mother, there is nothing for us here…nothing but a meaningless stone…."

"Not yet," Rivka's voice remained adamant.

Olga was perplexed. "We must go home…we will be fine there, I know…. And, Mother, I can teach…like Father did in his early days…and earn some money to help the family."

Rivka turned to her daughter, her eyes filled with a deep sense of sorrow. "Not yet. Before we leave Beirut forever, there is one more task I must complete. Don't you understand? The Yahrzeits are coming."

Hanukah was right around the corner, and Rivka would not hear of leaving before she fulfilled her regular ritual. This year more than ever, she was determined to have the finest candles the eye had ever seen.

And so she did. When the first night of Hanukah arrived, the entire house was lit like a festival of colors dancing in a rainbow. There was a large, yellow candle for Shima'leh, twin pink candles for the twins, Leah'leh's multi-colored candle next to Blooma's dark candle, a white candle for Moshe's stillborn twin sister, and this year, less than a month after he died, a beautiful new gold candle for Isaac, gold as his heart had been – pure, loving and true. Olga dared not ask her mother how on earth she had managed to obtain such rich, obviously expensive, candles in the midst of a devastating war, telling herself that her mother is the only person who could achieve such a miracle, probably with the help she always had from her spirits. The truth was much simpler – the candle merchant, a decent man who had grown accustomed to Rivka's strange habit as the years went by, had kept the finest candles aside, waiting for Rivka, knowing she would come, and he was very happy to trade them for four of her golden bracelets.

Silently, without so much as a muscle moving in her face, Rivka lit all seven candles. She stood there, Olga, Racheli and Moshe at her side, and watched the flames. Olga patiently waited for her mother to begin reciting the mourner's *Kadish*, but Rivka was silent. Uneasy, the children looked at each other, waiting for a signal from their mother. After what seemed like a lifetime, Rivka finally opened her mouth and started to pray.

"*Yitgadal VeYitkadash, Shmei Rabbah,
Be'Almah Divrah Kir'Utei VeYamlich Malchutei...*"

Her voice was hollow, coming from a faraway hole inside her soul, drowning them all in an unbearable agony and cleansing their sorrow so it shone. When Rivka finished, no one spoke. All night they kept vigil, each one of them captured in his or her own thoughts of the different days that lay ahead. When the night was over, Rivka finally smiled, kissed the ashes that were left by Isaac's beautiful gold candle, and said to her children: "It's time. We are going home. The war is about to end."

Once again, Rivka packed all her belongings – everything that could be salvaged and taken on the long journey through a sea and a land torn and battered by a bitter war, filled with the scrapes of bodies, hunger and madness – and set out to Jaffa Port where Ofsey and all of Rivka's ghosts waited to take them to their new home and new life. The war was over.

And so stories accumulate, connect with each other in unexpected places, creating meanings, weaving a quilt of colors, sounds, scents and tastes. A quilt that has different pieces, each one with a different shape and size, each one with a mind of its own. Together they create a narrative made of flowing lives, yet greater than life itself. Hiding a greater truth, a larger picture that can only be seen when all these strange pieces are sewn together by a sewing machine, creating a bittersweet, nostalgic sense of history.

As soon as they stepped into their new house, Moshe embarked on an exploring expedition. The white house had two stories connected by a simple staircase. Each floor was a full apartment built for careful practical use. Rivka's kingdom was to be on the first floor. It had three bedrooms, a bathroom, a living room, a kitchen and a dining room. Ofsey had built the second floor to meet the needs of his newly-growing family and his position as assistant manager at the bank. The floor contained only two bedrooms but it had a large parlor for entertaining, where the third bedroom was missing. Altogether, the house was not as large as the one they had left behind in Beirut, *but it was comfortable and bright. So bright that Rivka could feel the sun following her all day, hot and humid, mixed with the salty scent of the sand and the sea and the sweet scent of oranges and crushed green leaves. It was the scent of Tel Aviv.*

After checking out the inside, Moshe ran out to the small garden to see what he could find there. Anticipating his mother's love for gardens, and his younger brother's high energy levels, Ofsey had created a small garden of fruits and vegetables planted in the yard, which also contained a swing set. The garden had a mulberry tree, an orange tree and a lemon tree, and a ficus that was sure to create some tiling problems in the coming years. It boasted a small stretch of tomato plants as well as carrots and cucumbers. All the plants were very young, thin and fragile, holding in the movement of their leaves a sweet promise of growth, flowing time and a tasty future. Ofsey had filled several of his mother's old glass jars with a variety of vegetables. Young, green cucumbers sparkling like grass in the dew, round, white cauliflower, floating like crowded clouds, fresh red peppers that stung the eyes even before you touched them. He soaked them all in salty garlic water as he had watched his mother do, hoping that it would give her a sense of home and happiness. He placed the jars outside on the windowsill to ripen in the sun, and they gave the house a colorful, gay look. The swing set was green and consisted of two simple swings hanging from a wooden structure that resembled gallows, but the best part of the yard was a small tool shack that would be a wonderful place to hide and dream in.

As he was exploring the small yard, Moshe's eye was caught by a dance of sunlight that was being performed very gaily on the other side of the garden wall. He looked at the sun dance in amazement: from the other side of the wall he could see a mop of soft, blond curls, dancing happily with the white sunrays. He was charmed by the lively duet of the curls dancing harmoniously with the hot summer sun, that ordinarily scorched everything, yet were now tenderly caressing the curls. Moshe came closer, and to his surprise, the curls turned toward him, and he found two large, light-blue eyes staring at him, smiling. They were much lighter than the blue in his mother's eyes, but they were as happy as the sun and the sky, and they gave him a comforting sense of home. For the first time since his father had died, he felt safe and confident again. He did not know it at the time, but it was very similar to the sensation that Rivka had experienced when she first met Isaac's eyes. "Shalom," said the smile of the curls. "I am Shoshana and we are neighbors."

"Shalom" he said bravely, "I'm Moshe and you will be my wife."

She didn't seem surprised. Or shy. "Ok," was all she said. They were only twelve years old, but for some reason, through some ancient bond that had connected their hearts at once, they knew that they belonged together.

The end of World War I had not sent Dvora, Ish and their children immediately back home to Tel Aviv with the other exiled families. Although she desperately wanted to return home to the city she loved, Dvora could not just up and leave when the war was over. Like the entire country, Zichron was in shambles and in desperate need of strong working hands. The British who, at the beginning of the war, had enticed the Jews with lavish promises of hopes and realizations of dreams, were now backing out of their part of the deal, surprisingly making new-found friends with the beaten, humiliated, hostile Arabs. The surprise and anger of the Jewish pioneers were growing, and the morale of the farmers was very low. Dvora and Ish decided to stay and help Bobeh and Zeideh in the fields, in the hope that life would soon return to normal.

A short while after the war had ended, as she stood by the mulberry tree in the front of the house, Dvora noticed a man coming toward her. He was walking steadily, leading three mules behind him, and a young woman was walking beside him. They were coming up the main street, and the man looked very familiar.

After a few minutes of careful attention, Dvora suddenly cried out, "Daniel!!" and ran up to her long-lost brother, who had disappeared at the beginning of the war and had been missing ever since.

Within seconds, the whole family gathered and they almost suffocated Daniel with hugs and drowned him with kisses. The questions were all asked at once, mixing exclamations with statements and wonder.

When Daniel had received the call that he was to be drafted with his three mules to the Ottoman army, he knew he had but one choice: he had to escape and hide until the war was over, his mules with him. He vanished overnight, not leaving so much as a note or any sign of his plans or whereabouts. He did not want to expose his family to any kind of danger by having them know where he was and having to hide the information from the Turks. For several months he roamed the Galilee hills, hiding out in caves, eating fruit and berries that he found on the trees, and drinking water from some of the small streams that fill the Galilee. But then it became too dangerous – too many people were roaming the same hillsides, some refugees, some hiding from the same fate he was running from, others spies seeking a few coins by giving service to the Turks. He knew he had to find a better solution.

He managed to make his way to another small village further northeast, a village called Rosh Pina. The village, one of the first Jewish settlements that was founded during the same years as Zichron Yaacov, was situated on the hills of the eastern Galilee, not far from the Kinneret – the sweet water lake of Northern Palestine and a main source of water to the entire region. Daniel was welcomed by his fellow Jews, who provided him and his mules with refuge and shelter during the years of the war. Rosh Pina also gave him a new feverish, passionate love in the shape of a young girl named Abigail. He was so absorbed in combining the art of hiding and the frenzy of love that the presence of the faraway fiancé that he had left behind in Zichron Yaacov became a vague memory that finally faded away. Drunk with love, and alert through the mastery of disguise, Daniel managed to stay very much alive and free in Rosh Pina throughout the war. When the war was over, he returned on his way to Zichron, but not before he quietly married Abigail. Daniel, his mules and his new wife returned to build their new home in Zichron next to his parents' house. It was the sign that Dvora had been waiting for. Now that Daniel had returned, and the farm was on its way to recovery, Dvora and Ish decided it was time to go back home to Tel Aviv.

Once again, they filled their wagons with their belongings and their three children, and they went on their way. It would be the one and only time that Shoshana would travel back to Tel Aviv from Zichron without a plentiful offering of fruits and vegetables or a chick by her side.

Back in Tel Aviv, life was beginning to return to normal. Shoshana's piano lessons resumed, and she was surprised to discover how much she had missed them. Ish had new, exciting stories to tell the children each night, and even Dvora seemed more relaxed. Shoshana was delighted to see that the building of the new house behind her own was renewed, and that new workers were working day and night to finish it. The small garden that was planted in the yard made her eyes smile, and the large jars that were sitting on the windowsills, creating a colorful dance of vegetables, salt, garlic and vinegar, filled her mouth with the sweet taste of anticipation. But when she noticed the swing set, her soul filled with joy – new children would be coming! She spent so many hours fantasizing about the new family that were about to become her neighbors that when they actually arrived it was as simple and as natural as if they had stepped right out of her dreamy head and materialized into flesh and blood.

One look at Moshe and she felt as if she had known him forever, and had been waiting her entire life for him to return from an errand.

They spent many hours together. Moshe would engage in long talks with Nathan, Shoshana sitting next to them, listening attentively and teasing them both. With the war over, Tel Aviv was growing again, creating new places for them to explore and discover. They walked and ran through the streets of Tel Aviv, always ending up at the sea. They spent hours gazing at the horizon, Moshe telling Shoshana stories of the faraway country that he had come from, making her eyes grow with innocent astonishment at every exaggerated detail he provided. The sand was so white it dazzled their eyes and the water was an endless changing world of colors and sounds. Early in the morning the beach was aglow with a rich, deep-blue transparent air that penetrated so deep into their skin that it felt like heaven itself was ascending downwards to greet the newborn day. In the evening, just before sunset, merchants selling corn would walk around the beach, announcing their goods and spraying the air with the sweet smell of salt mixed with sugar, so intoxicating that the taste of corn stayed in the mouth for what seemed like an eternity.

The sea was embracing. Moshe and Shoshana both loved swimming, and Moshe would always drink salty water when Shoshana would push his head in, catching him by surprise. She would cover him with sand, leaving only his head visible, and then would disappear until he yelled out loud.

Back in the house, Shoshana would play the piano while Moshe and Nathan played chess. Shoshana loved jokes, and she would make Moshe search for new jokes throughout town so he could tell them to her and she, in turn, would pass them onto her father, who in return would tell them both more stories. Moshe always asked Ish to tell them stories from the Bible, stories that made their eyes laugh and hearts yearn, stories that made them vow to someday explore the actual places where the stories had taken place. It was almost as if the war had never happened.

Tel Aviv was once again a vivid, modern city, filled with music, dancing, cinemas and schools. More restaurants and cafés opened, flourishing with new creators of literature, poetry and art.

> I haven't sung to you, my country,
> And haven't filled your name with glory
> By heroic deeds
> or endless battles
> My hands have only planted a tree....

Every week, Ish made Shoshana memorize and recite a poem in honor of Shabbat. Well-known Jewish poets and authors were a common sight in the streets of Tel Aviv, and Ish made sure that his children become well acquainted with the poetry and literature that they produced. They were the Jewish writers of the new era, of the renewing nation struggling to make a house of its own, and living the history that generations before them had dreamed of, and their words were branded in the young children's minds. Whenever they encountered any of them in the streets, Shoshana and Moshe regarded them with awe, feeling as if the new prophets of the land were walking the earth in front of their eyes.

Ish was becoming increasingly successful in his trade. The entire country was being developed: new houses and enterprises were sprouting like mushrooms after the rain, new families were arriving almost daily at Jaffa Port, newcomers from Europe were on their way to build villages, towns and cities, all of which required lumber – and plenty of it. Many of the newcomers were poor, and couldn't pay Ish for his merchandise. Again and again, Dvora would open the door to a husband who came home with fruit baskets, chickens and once even a goat that he had received in exchange for wood. Many times he would give his fellow Jews the lumber they needed, accepting a letter of purchase from them saying that they would pay him as soon as they could, giving them credit and relying on their word. They rarely disappointed him, and although Dvora scorned and warned him that the day would come when one of them would "cheat him out of his pants," his heart was large and he continued to help those who needed him, setting an example of kindness and charity that would live in his children's hearts forever. One day he came home with a huge cupboard, an incredible piece of woodwork with wide, bright drawers and beautiful stained glass doors. Seeing this magnificent creation of wood, Dvora gasped. "Where did you get this?" she exclaimed, "It is absolutely beautiful!"

"Krinitsy made it. Remember him? He used to be a local Jaffa carpenter who came in for lumber. He usually couldn't pay, but I gave him the wood anyway. He's a decent guy."

"And what have you done to deserve this?"

"Well, he's very successful now, but doesn't really have much money…and he is the head of that new city they are building east of Tel Aviv and will be leaving soon…so he paid his debt with this. What do you think?"

Dvora was silent for a minute. Then, in an uncharacteristic outburst of emotion, she asked, "When can he come for dinner?"

The new house on Nachalat Binyamin Street was starting to acquire the feeling of a home. Rivka, whose heart had never searched after material beauty, suddenly began to decorate the small apartment with accessories and Jewish emblems. It wasn't because she had suddenly developed a newfound interest in objects – she was simply obeying Isaac's wishes. Ever since Isaac had died, she had been talking to his spirit, consulting him with every decision, telling him the family news. It was he who encouraged her to fill her life with beauty. She would walk into the little shops of Jaffa, shops that were filled with confusing heaps of merchandise, piled in unorganized stacks that seemed to reach the ceiling. She would scan the piles with her eyes, carefully taking in the images, until she heard Isaac's voice saying: "Yes!" then she would detach the object from its position amongst the rest, and the expected ritual began.

"Ah, I see that Madame has exquisite taste," the merchant would coo. "Yes, indeed, this is the finest piece in my entire shop."

"And how much will be needed for you to part from this exquisite piece?"

"For you, Madame, I will make a very good price. It will practically be a gift."

"I'm sure it will be," Rivka would smile, and the negotiations began. Rivka would always offer twenty percent of the initial price, and the merchant would always act as if he was offended, saying how he needed the money for his hungry family, five children, three boys thank God. Rivka would say that it was indeed a beautiful piece, just like the one she had seen in several shops, and how she really wanted to make her purchase here because she felt he was a decent man, and how she knew he is reasonable and would be fair. The unsuspecting merchant wouldn't notice the unheard voices surrounding him until suddenly he would feel uncomfortable and, a moment before drowning in Rivka's eyes, he would settle for no more than half the original price, and both would part happy and satisfied, Rivka content that she had fulfilled Isaac's wish and the merchant relieved that she was gone.

At home, the rooms were starting to look like an elegant minuet of artifacts, each adding a graceful touch to the dance of the others. Rivka placed her Blooma cabinet in the living room, and at the Jaffa flea market she purchased a beautiful *yudenstern* – a round, metal lamp that hung from the ceiling with seven oil burners, each representing a day of the week and surrounded by a round glass bulb, all placed on the metal ring in a shape that resembled a star. The *yudenstern* was used on Shabbat: every Friday afternoon, Moshe would lower the metal ring from the ceiling. Rivka would fill the oil burners with pure olive oil, then place a cotton cord in the oil. Carefully, she lit the seven cords, and Moshe would place the lamp back in its place near the ceiling. Rivka loved watching the soft, gentle light of the *yudenstern*, caressing her cheeks and embracing her completely as her Isaac did. The oil would last all night, lighting the small apartment with a magical glow that made Racheli quieter than ever, made Moshe feel dizzy, and made Rivka's spirits feel very comfortable and at home.

They all went to one of the new schools not far from home – the Geula school, and they walked to school together, all six of them – Racheli, Moshe, Nathan, Shoshana and Avner – and Olga as well, for she had started working at the school as a French teacher. It took only a couple of weeks for the children to notice that she was avoiding coming back home with them, always saying she had to work with the literature teacher, a young man called Asher who wrote stories of his own and read them to his students during class and to Olga at night. Moshe would tease Olga, asking her what exactly does her work, teaching French, have to do with the Hebrew stories about the new pioneers that Asher told them in class. Olga always reddened, "Poof!"ed her young mischievous brother off, and went on with Asher to the nearby library or to the Rothschild Boulevard benches, under a full moon that made the young trees look silvery and shining. "He's probably reading love songs to her...." Moshe would whisper into Shoshana's ear. Rivka, who noticed the new red life in her daughter's cheeks, knew that Olga was in love and about to commit herself to a life of bitter poverty, compromising modesty and outstanding happiness. The spirits, who had always kept away from Olga knowing that they had no part in her intellectual world, had nevertheless smiled upon this young relationship, reassuring Rivka that her daughter would be happy. Poor and struggling all her days, but happy. Rivka, who had been blessed to choose whom to marry, who had known days of sorrow, hatred, riches and happiness, knew that she had survived the turmoil of her days largely because of the foundation of love that Isaac and she had shared. She watched her daughter's eyes and blessed the spirits for giving Olga the same kind of love that had brought her to life.

Olga and Asher were married in a small, modest ceremony

less than a year after Isaac had died. Few guests were invited to the ceremony, besides the family, in fact only one guest was invited. His name was Nachum, a young man who walked through the country with an easel and a pencil and sketched everything he saw. Nachum and Asher had known each other for years and they had become close friends and partners in the same passion – describing the new pioneer life that was being created, struggling, thriving and taking different turns and shapes before their very eyes, one using his pencil to create words, the other using it to create images.

It was the holiday of Shavuot, and Olga, in a plain white dress without any ornaments – they were all still in mourning – indulged herself only with a bright crown of flowers on her long, black hair. After the ceremony she carefully dried the flowers and Asher spent half a month's salary on placing the flowers in a beautiful frame. They hung the flower crown above their bed, in the small two-bedroom apartment they lived in on Sirkin Street, a short walking distance from Rivka's house. It would be their home for their entire lives, and the crown of flowers would be the only ornament hanging above their bed until the day they died.

I remember the small apartment, the crown of flowers, even the long, braided, thick gray hair that Aunt Olga had. She was a petite woman with a flair of strength and wisdom about her, and her eyes were always straightforward and bright. When she walked in her hasty, confident small steps, it was as if clarity and knowledge were walking with her.

Most of all, I remember the books. Stacks and stacks of books in every corner, on the tables, in the hallways, on shelves and on the floor. There was a familiar scent of book dust, and the sunlight that invaded the apartment from the small windows shone white and bright on the book covers, making the leather covers of even the dark brown and the black ones seem as if they were covered with silvery stardust, a stardust that would magically bring to life all the amazing characters that were hidden within the attractive pages, waiting to become alive and present in our world.

I had never met Asher – he died before I was born – but he was obviously there in the apartment with her. His desk – the same desk at which he had written all of his stories, stories that I loved reading again and again, stories that brought all the creatures that were planted in my mind to a very physical, real life, with pictures and illustrations made by Nachum – that desk was left untouched since the day he died. His pencils were still on it, some sharp and eager to write, others half-used and hiding within them endless words, sentences and characters that had flown as a young, fresh fountainhead from their tips. Pages of half-finished words and thoughts were scattered about, not daring to move, so he could continue his thread of thought from the exact place he had left it if he returned. I was never allowed to walk into his room – it was a shrine that only Aunt Olga entered – but it always gave me the exciting feeling of action, of a job that was stopped in the middle, as if the energy was still lingering in the room long after the person who had used it was gone. Only Aunt Olga entered the room, rearranging, editing, correcting and finishing, with her small handwriting, endless pages that Asher had left incomplete.

Although she was never part of the spirit dance that the rest of the women in my family enjoyed, I suspect that it was the only place where she actually tried to join it by keeping in touch with her beloved dead husband. Her own Yahrzeit creation.

The same presence came back to me the day I was married, when I received a very special gift. It was wrapped in hard, brown cardboard and had the shape of a small wall mirror. When I opened it, I discovered a signed lithography by Nachum Gutman. It depicts two men sitting at a table playing chess. One of them, the more relaxed figure, is that of a large man, his hair flipped backwards, shying away from his forehead, a pair of round spectacles on his nose. The other is obviously deep in thought, his gaze fixed on the chessboard, his thoughts flowing from the painting, deciding which move to make. My mother took one look at the strange gift and exclaimed, "What a wonderful gift! It is the sketch that Nachum did of Asher and the famous poet, Saul Tchernichovsky. They loved playing chess together." I carefully hung the lithography above my bed. It hangs there to this very day.

A few years later, I saw the same sketch in a book. Underneath, the title read, "Two soldiers playing chess between battles." It took me years to understand that both my mother's description and the title in the book meant the same thing.

Chapter 6

SHOSHANA

1919–1930

> "Here, in the beloved land of our forefathers
> all our hopes will come true...."

More than half a century after they were composed, I was still singing the songs of the pioneers with the same devotion and commitment with which they had been written. I was convinced they had written them for me, and my task was to learn more about them so I could be the next true link in their chain. They made it easy for me.

Whenever I try to map the figures in my life who have influenced me most, I am overcome by a feeling that my life is filled with distinct spaces, holes that were never empty, but always noticeable by the clamor of a strong presence of the people who used to fill them. People who had physically passed from this world long before I was even in the planning, as my mother used to say, great forefathers and unbreakable giants who walked the earth and molded the past, but whose memories had refused to depart with them to wherever it is that spirits go. They were terrified of being alone there, or worse – of *suddenly becoming insignificant among all the other spirits of the world, so they simply hung around for a few more generations, making sure that we all knew they were with us.*

It was like living surrounded by an imaginary, fine embroidery of lace, the existing threads connecting to each other via gaps that were sometimes more lively and concrete than the threads themselves. I have always loved exploring the holes, learning more about the admirable presence of my predecessors, but at the same time I knew that I must be very careful so that the delicate lace, as fragile as a spider's web, won't break.

Winds of change were blowing throughout the world, some of them bringing a sweet scent of hope, but most of them bringing the sour taste of desperation and struggle, all of them feeling like they were centralized, whether in origin or end, in one heart – the Land of Israel. While the veins of the growing Jewish community were spreading through the land, building new towns and villages in the hills and the deserts, the heart that was pumping the blood of motivation was Tel Aviv. New immigrants from faraway countries were pouring into Jaffa Port, flowing into the new Hebrew city and into the towns, bringing with them new cultures, traditions and languages. The white city was rapidly growing, both physically and emotionally. It was a common sight to see convoys of camels carrying sand, limestone and gravel, their bells sending an echo of longing into the air and their eyes soft and totally indifferent to the noise around them. The camels walked slowly through the sand on the beach, ignoring the heat and the humid, salty air, carrying their loads at a graceful, rocking pace, bringing the sources of construction to the growth-thirsty builders.

Young trees and gardens were spreading all over the city, carefully tended, and holding the promise of a green, flourishing future in their leaves. The members of the small, growing Jewish community in Palestine would assemble for endless discussions, arguments and ideological debates about the mission they all felt they were part of – renewing Jewish independence and creating a new, Hebrew culture in the land of Israel. It was a mission that was high-spirited and optimistic even during the most bitter struggles of the war and that, as the post-war years began to unravel, suddenly started to seem further than ever.

Rumors of rising anti-Semitism across Europe, especially in Russia and Poland, were swiftly followed by horrific news of persecutions, false accusations, pogroms and terrible destruction. And these, in turn, were followed by waves of Jews who came from Europe through Jaffa to Palestine, many of them settling in Tel Aviv. The more new immigrants who arrived into the country, the more hostile the Arab population was, and the more tense and uneasy were the British. Promises that were made to both Jews and Arabs by the victory-thirsty British during the war years became a dangerous three-way tango immediately after. The British Mandate, created in Palestine at the end of the war, was supposed to be a means for realizing the promise that was made during the war to create a Jewish home. The reality, however, was far different. The British were orchestrating a dangerous game of chess between the Jews and the Arabs. Restricting the number of Jews who could enter the land, the British would not allow the Jewish settlers to defend themselves, confiscating most of the already scarce weapons and ammunition they owned. "If you need help, call us. Our soldiers will defend you," they would promise, and then disappear until it was too late. The Arabs, both inside and outside of Palestine, were encouraged by British sympathy for their cause, and became even more hostile and aggressive. It was becoming increasingly obvious that the only defense the Jews in Palestine could rely on was their own.

Again and again, the small Jewish towns that decorated the land in a scattered, small exhibit of shining fireflies were attacked by ravaging Arabs, who brought aggressiveness and cruelty in their wake. Crops and household goods were stolen or ruined, water sources were blocked, and deadly attacks on innocent travelers were common events. The attacks became bolder, spreading destruction and death from north to south. The news was devastating. In the north, the small Jewish village of Tel Hai was attacked, its leaders murdered and the village abandoned. In Jerusalem, a group of Jews were brutally arrested by the British after defending themselves against their Arab attackers, who killed several of them. Widespread attacks in Jaffa resulted in the butchering of dozens, as did attacks in other areas of the land. In some cases the Jewish settlers defended themselves, successfully driving the attackers away, in other cases, where the British soldiers promised protection, that protection was given reluctantly, resulting in the loss of many lives and encouragement given to the attackers.

Whatever the scenario, the British evaluated the situation in the following way: the Arabs will never live in peace as long as they feel that the British are supporting the Jewish cause. The Jews increasingly felt that security and peace were part of a remote dream, and that their safety was dependant upon the mercy of others.

Desperate to convince the British Empire that Palestine can and should become a home for the Jewish People, the residents of the young city of Tel Aviv were excited to hear the news that Sir Winston Churchill was about to pay them a visit. Everyone wanted to be part of the welcoming committee, and everyone had their own ideas about how the distinguished guest should be greeted. Finally, after long and agonizing discussions, the decision was made. Churchill should see for himself how the Jews are truly part of the land. He should be impressed by their high level of achievements, and he should be made to feel welcome by the entire city. The head of the Tel Aviv Committee, Meir Dizengoff, thought that a ceremony facing a real forest would symbolize the growth and prosperity of the city. But Tel Aviv was still very young, its trees and greenery even younger, and a forest needs more than a couple of weeks to grow.

"It's the most ridiculous idea I have ever heard," Dvora dismissed the idea when Ish came home with the news. "I have no idea how he plans to make a forest grow overnight. That committee is made of fools who have no clue about nature. They should stick to buildings."

"Oh, but it is a remarkable idea!" exclaimed Ish. "As we speak, laborers are working in the areas surrounding Tel Aviv, where trees are plenty. They are cutting them at ground level and will bring them here. The trees will be placed between the committee building and Dizengoff's house. It will look like a real forest!"

"Even so, it will take more than a few trees to convince the British that we are rooted in this corner of the world," Dvora's voice was harsh, as it always was when she spoke of those she viewed as intruders in her life. Shoshana didn't like hearing her mother speak to her father in such a tone.

When the great day arrived, the streets were bursting with people, who had gathered to greet the honorable guest. Shoshana and Moshe were conveniently situated on the porch of one of the buildings, watching the entire scene. The forest had indeed grown overnight. Pine and cypress trees stood proudly in the sand between the buildings. An orchestra was tuning its instruments, and children waited with flowers in their hands. When the car carrying Dizengoff and Churchill came near, everyone pushed forward to capture a glimpse of their faces. The orchestra began playing cheerful marches, and chaos was about to prevail when the crowd was asked to move back by the few policemen desperately trying to keep order. The people stepped back, and Shoshana and Moshe watched with amazement as they pressed at the forest trees, leaning heavily on them, until the trees fell back, revealing trunks that were stuck into the ground with no roots. "Tel Aviv's forest is falling down, falling down, falling down…" Shoshana couldn't stop herself from singing, and Moshe was rolling on the floor with laughter.

Dizengoff, white as a sheet, leaped out of the car and started apologizing, but Churchill only laughed and said, "Mister Dizengoff, without roots it won't work.…"

"Well, in that case," Dizengoff looked directly into Churchill's eyes, "God knows we Jews have plenty of those in this Land.…"

"Here, in the beloved land of our forefathers,
all hopes will come true…"

Shoshana sang loud and clear. So clear that Churchill looked up to see where the voice was coming from. Their eyes met for less than a few seconds, and he smiled at her. Then Churchill turned, placed his arm on Dizengoff's shoulder and promised to give "a favorable report" of the small and stubborn, but highly optimistic Jewish city.

The very same year that Churchill visited Israel, in 1921, after more than a year of widespread attacks and murders, the leaders of the Yishuv – the Jewish community in Palestine – decided it was time to take additional steps to ensure their safety throughout the land. An underground organization was established, aiming to secretly equip Jewish settlements with the arms, ammunition and training necessary to defend themselves.

"We are calling the organization *Haganah*, defense, so that everyone knows what we are aiming for," said Ish to his wife. "We only want to be able to defend ourselves if necessary. We hate war, but we are not about to allow ourselves to be butchered. It's high time that those who attack us understand that we will fight back. Our fate should be in our own hands! Just wait and see. We will be supported by everyone in the Yishuv!"

But even as he pronounced those confident words, Ish was filled with mixed feelings when he read the same strength and determination in the eyes of his children. This was no game, it was a dangerous reality that everyone would have to be part of. Even the children. They would have to learn to grow up fast.

Amongst the many who joined the *Haganah* were fifteen-year-old Shoshana Broytman and Moshe Lipavsky.

School in the mornings and *Haganah* activities in the evening had become the center of their lives. Shoshana and Moshe were very young – most of the *Haganah* members were at least two years older – but were very determined to help the Zionist movement in whatever way they could. Consisting of small groups of young people, they trained in the evenings, meeting in different places each time. The meetings consisted of training sessions in a variety of defense strategies, discussions and decisions regarding local defense, and small, simple assignments, that mostly involved transferring messages to other groups.

Shoshana was sitting in class, trying to figure out what to do with the equation in front of her while desperately trying to understand why on earth she needed algebra to succeed in life, when suddenly a small, wrinkled paper ball fell on her book. She raised her eyes in time to notice Moshe, sitting only a few desks away, turn his eyes back to his book and resume the serious expression of someone whose only interest was in his studies.

She opened the crumpled piece of paper and read: "Tonight, eight, the regular place, a special surprise. M."

Moshe refused to give any further explanations on the way home, nor on their way to the house where the *Haganah* meeting was taking place.

"Are we finally going to have an assignment?" she asked, excited.

"Wait and see."

"Is one of the leaders going to be there?"

"You'll soon find out."

Impatient, she almost begged. "Come on, tell me what the surprise is!"

He only laughed, enjoying her immense curiosity, and they both kept silent the rest of the way to the meeting house. When they arrived, Shoshana was surprised to see a large group of their friends, girls and boys, standing in the yard and singing loudly. One of them was playing the accordion. Some of them formed a circle and were dancing to the music. Two British police officers who were walking down the street smiled at the celebrating youth. "Dancing and singing, eh?" they said, approvingly. "Well, carry on, carry on, as long as you don't get into trouble...."

"This is your big surprise? A sing-along?" Shoshana sounded disappointed.

"A blasting sing-along..." He smiled and, passing through the singing and dancing group, led her to the entrance to the house. He whispered a password and a minute later they were in a small room inside the house.

"This is how you take it apart...you must make sure that every part is thoroughly cleaned before you reassemble it." A young man, unknown to Shoshana, was talking to some other teenagers in the room. Shocked, she realized what he was doing: in his hands, and on the table in front of him, were the black, shining parts of a gun.

That night, for the first time in their lives, Shoshana and Moshe learned how to shoot a gun. The *Haganah* groups in Tel Aviv had managed to acquire a single gun that they transferred among them, so each group had a chance to learn how to hold it, clean it, aim – and if possible, fire. There was always loud singing and dancing in the yard, so that the sound of gunshot would not be heard on the street. Since there were several groups, and only one gun, it was a very rare event. Shoshana felt awkward holding a gun, but Moshe was titillated by the rush of the excitement and never missed a practice.

While Dvora and Ish were proud of their children's activities in the *Haganah*, Rivka was worried by Moshe's involvement in it, but nonetheless tried very hard to remain silent if not supportive, since she reluctantly realized that this was his destiny. It was another way for him to search for the angel of death, a much riskier path that involved weapons and dark, dangerous activities, as well as a halo of courage and glory, all of which were approved, to Rivka's dismay, by Isaac's voice. He supported his son's devotion to the cause, the very same cause that he himself was captivated by so many years before.

Other members of the family were either too busy to notice what Moshe and Shoshana were up to or they decided to studiously ignore it. Olga was busy teaching, supporting her tiny family with the small salary she earned, and Asher was busy writing, creating webs of reality and dreams that described the struggling life in Palestine. Both of them were occupied raising their daughter, Rivka's first granddaughter. Her name was Ayalah, Hebrew for doe, but it was a name of deception: when she was born, they decided to call her AYA – an acronym for "The Whole Land of Israel," which was considered a political statement of nationality and aspirations for freedom. Fearing that the British would harass them for such a statement – Asher was a well-known figure, therefore his daughter's name was sure to attract attention – Rivka begged them to reconsider their choice. Sensitive to her mother's stress, Olga came up with a solution: they would officially name the child Ayalah, but her nickname would be Aya.

Ofsey was always busy at the bank and his young American wife Priscilla was very busy raising cats. Her habits were very strange and misplaced, and Moshe would tease her endlessly. At four o'clock every day, she always stopped everything so she could prepare for her five o'clock tea, fully dressed in an evening gown of which the curious sand and the shameful sun of Tel Aviv made a mockery. Rivka quickly understood that whenever she wished to speak to her firstborn, she must try to make an appointment ahead of time, since Priscilla insisted on maintaining a "civilized, updated, known-in-advance" schedule. Rivka was worried by the fact that her spirits were completely silent whenever Priscilla was around, signaling neither an approval nor a dismissal of her son's match. As it was, mother-in-law and daughter-in-law hardly ever spoke, since Priscilla spoke English and some broken Hebrew, and Rivka only spoke Russian and Yiddish. In all her years in Palestine, Rivka had never learned Hebrew. The language was too strange to her ears and she was perfectly happy to communicate in her native tongues. When Priscilla gave birth to a daughter, Rivka's second grandchild, she insisted on hiring a nanny to take care of the child, to Rivka's horror. She did not want to come between her son and his wife, so she kept silent and never said a word when they decided to name the child Alona. Alona was Hebrew for an oak tree, which, in Ofsey's eyes, symbolized the strong roots that they had planted in the land; he far preferred to give his daughter a name like this than naming her after one of his female ancestors, as was the tradition in the old country. Rivka blessed the child and kept her feelings to herself.

The language spoken in Palestine was another issue to be dealt with. Many of the new influx of Jews refused to learn Hebrew, claiming it was too difficult for them to learn while defending the culture and customs they had brought with them from their old countries. Russian, German, Polish and Yiddish were heard on the streets, a mixed babble of dialects and sounds. The schoolchildren became zealous for the revival of Hebrew, becoming openly hostile toward anyone who spoke anything else. Signs of "Jews, speak Hebrew!" were posted at night so daytime revealed them decorating windows and doors. Moshe carried in his pockets eggs that were emptied and refilled with ink, Shoshana had stink bombs hidden in her purse, and they both enjoyed hurling their treasures at speakers who used any language that was not written in the Bible, casting them at surprised crowds while shouting "Speak Hebrew!!" then immediately disappearing through the streets and meeting back up again at the beach, only to stroll amongst the young couples who cuddled in the sand, making sure that the love words they whispered in each other's ears were uttered only in Hebrew.

"Follow me, Follow,
Ours is the future,
Stand for our slogan:
Jews, speak Hebrew!
Jews, speak Hebrew,
The language of our people you should nurture,
Jews, speak Hebrew,
for Hebrew is our future!"

The song came to an abrupt halt when Shoshana found herself standing face-to-face with no other than Haim Nachman Bialik, the highly-respected Jewish poet who had escaped to Palestine from Europe, where Jews faced persecution. People would come from far to hear his advice, attend to his needs and discuss his opinions as though they were written in stone. His poetry was recited at every ceremony, memorized by children and taught in the classes. This idolized giant was now right in front of her, strolling down the street with a friend, both of them deep in conversation that was conducted entirely in Russian.

Furious, Shoshana approached the poet. "How dare you speak Russian here?" she cried, "You, of all people, a symbol of our renewal, a man of distinction, who is a role model for others? You, who have so eloquently written about our suffering in exile and have joined us in our renewal in the promised land!" She became increasingly excited and her confidence grew steadily with each heated word. "All those poems you have written, those writings that give us strength and confidence in our task…I read them in Hebrew!"

Ignoring the small crowd of people that had stopped what they were doing and had begun to watch the scene, Shoshana was shaking. Surprised, Bialik didn't say a word, only touched his hat with acknowledgement, nodded toward the surrounding people and continued on his way. But the conversation switched to Hebrew. From that day on, poets, writers and teachers were encouraged by Bialik to speak only Hebrew, and the city followed his example.

Rivka loved Shoshana. All she had to do was look into Shoshana's eyes and she immediately knew that the girl had a kind heart and a giving soul; it was no wonder that her son had fallen in love at such a young age. Once again she heard the voice of the heavenly matchmakers, and she thanked the spirits for finding her little orphan such a good match. Shoshana was the only one who shared Rivka's relationship with the spirits. She could hear them, too. Rivka and Shoshana quickly became firm friends, Rivka lavishing on Shoshana the kind of motherly love that the girl craved, while Shoshana nurtured a promise within her to cherish and love Rivka's beloved Moshe for the rest of her life.

Olga became Shoshana's confidant, the two of them discussing history and literature well into the night. Asher would give them his new stories, making them his in-house editors and critics. Even remote Priscilla enjoyed spending time with Shoshana, for both of them shared a love of cats.

The only one who was very unhappy with this young love story was Racheli. Offended that her younger brother had found such a soulmate before she had, she tried to do everything she could to stop them from seeing each other or to get them into fights. Finally she tried to introduce him to one of her own friends, whispering in his ear that her friend was "experienced" and would give him a better time then Shoshana did. But Moshe was completely enraptured with Shoshana's being, rendering Racheli's efforts a waste of time.

Dvora watched her daughter with emotions that were a mixture of jealousy and amazement. She was jealous of Shoshana's relationship with Rivka, a woman who so easily connected with this daughter of hers, whom she couldn't wholeheartedly love. She was amazed that a boy – any boy – actually found her daughter attractive. Secretly, she would watch Shoshana – her small, plain figure; her dancing, ash-blond curls that surrounded her small round face, that looked like undisciplined hay scattered on a hill; and her light-blue eyes in which Moshe always drowned, but in which Dvora only saw blue milk. Nothing of what she saw could explain the deep infatuation that this young couple shared, and Dvora was suspicious and careful with her reaction.

She never gave her daughter any instructions besides telling her to be careful, saying that good girls do not let boys touch them before they are properly married. "After you are married," she would say. "you will have obligations that a wife has to her husband." Shoshana, not fully understanding what Dvora meant, was left with the feeling that any kind of touching was a dark obligation, that was absolutely forbidden before marriage but should be tolerated after. At first it did not bother her too much, but as the couple developed into young adults, and her body started to take on a womanly shape, while Moshe's voice was changing and he was turning into a young man, she started to feel uneasy. She started to hear all sorts of stories from her friends. Her best friend Tzipora, who was Nathan's sweetheart, would mock her, telling her what she had discovered from her own mother and revealing her personal passionate experiences with Nathan; Shoshana was left feeling shocked and very confused. Sensing her confusion, Moshe instinctively kept a distance from her, asking himself if she loved him at all.

Dvora, watching the two of them from a comfortable distance, decided she would put their relationship to what she considered to be the ultimate test: She invited Moshe to join them for the holiday of Pesach in Zichron. She wanted a close family opinion about the suitor of her only daughter, and she wanted to observe his conduct in her own original habitat. If the family gave him their blessing, she thought, then so would she.

Moshe came to Zichron and captivated everyone. He immediately occupied a place in Bobeh's heart when he presented her with a gift Rivka had sent – a sparkling jar filled with Rivka's homemade sweet lemon jam, accompanied by a beautiful box filled with chocolate-covered orange peels. Zeide was happy to sit and talk with Moshe for hours, enjoying the young boy's knowledge of the Bible and several languages and enchanted by Moshe's stories of the countries and cultures he had witnessed in his young life. Aminadav, Dvora's youngest brother who was only a couple of years older than Moshe himself, loved Moshe's sense of humor and, within an hour, became his best friend. Moshe was a perfect gentleman, moving the chairs for the ladies so they could sit comfortably, helping out in the kitchen. It was all so perfect that on the third day Shoshana was out of her mind with boredom and decided she had to do something to stir things up.

Conspiring with Aminadav, they invited Moshe out for a stroll in the woods. Aminadav led the way, followed by Shoshana and Moshe. Upon every turn they made, Aminadav put his hand out, stopping them, looking around very suspiciously. "What is it?" Moshe asked, alarmed. "Why are you so anxious?"

"The Debeh," Aminadav whispered, trying to sound as terrified as possible. "It's a terrible monster…it has the body and the laughter of a hyena, but it is much worse. It sneaks up on you, real quiet, so you can hardly hear it…and when you least expect it, it jumps on you and carries you away."

Moshe searched Aminadav's eyes to find even a remote flicker of sarcasm in them, but could find none. When he turned to Shoshana, she quickly added, "It's true. It has been known to take several children from their beds…. It almost took my mother once. Luckily, my father showed up and rescued her. That's how they met."

"Actually, we should feel relatively safe," Aminadav sighed. "It's good you came with us, Moshe…the Debeh has a weakness for lovers. If he feels love, he gives up. You can easily protect Shoshana that way."

Walking as they spoke, Aminadav kept up the facade of searching for danger, while Shoshana tried unsuccessfully to fall behind. But each time she tried, Moshe noticed she was slowing down and made sure he was always right behind her. In fact, from the moment she had told him of the way her parents had met, he had suddenly become very brave, searching for unexpected movement behind every bush.

He even disappeared at one point, returning after a few minutes with a faint smile dazzling in his eyes. He managed to trick them into going round one of the bushes when suddenly it moved and Aminadav cried out: "The Debeh! The Debeh! Run for your lives!" Instead of turning around and running, as they had expected him to do, and as they themselves had started, Moshe jumped up, grabbed a stick that was lying on the ground and snarled: "Where is it? Just show it to me…." and in a sudden turn and a huge thud, he hit something that was moving next to his feet.

Astonished, Aminadav and Shoshana stopped short. Moshe bent down and picked up a large, brown, ugly and completely dead, field rat. "Is this what you were looking for? I admit it looks pretty ugly, but I can't imagine it is so dangerous."

Howling with laughter, Shoshana and Aminadav had to admit that ultimately, it had been their legs that had been pulled.

Moshe's visit to Zichron was so successful that even Dvora had to reluctantly admit that his presence was as natural in their family circle as grapes are in the vineyards. But, just to be sure, she continued to carefully observe the blossoming relationship.

When they were fifteen, and Moshe finally plucked up the courage to kiss Shoshana's lips for the first time, she was horrified. She had not expected to enjoy the kiss as much as she did, especially since she had been told that they were not supposed to touch until they were married. Shoshana had presumed that since touching was an obligation to be endured, it would not be enjoyable. The fact that she had enjoyed their kiss so much could only mean one thing: she was a bad girl, with a seed of promiscuous behavior growing inside her, and she needed to be far more careful with her behavior to prevent herself from giving into temptation. The fact that she wasn't really sure what she was being careful about only added fear to her already anxious feelings. Moshe, feeling her unease, didn't attempt to kiss her again, and being young and inexperienced, accepted her explanation that they shouldn't touch each other until they were married.

"You can kiss me if you wish," she said shyly, "but nothing else. Good girls don't allow boys to…well…touch them," she said with a scarlet red face, and the hurt and puzzled look in his eyes made her add quickly, "Until we are married, that is."

Both trying very hard to put the physical contact between them on hold, they immersed themselves in other activities. Life was exciting and filled with unexpected turns. They both played endless tricks on their teachers, constantly getting into trouble, and laughing their way out of class. Moshe was constantly searching for implicit danger, mocking the British soldiers with his *Haganah* activities, dragging Shoshana through the streets of Tel Aviv to glue *Haganah* announcements on the walls by night and creeping into dark hallways for secret meetings and training during the day. He felt brave and grown up; fear was as far from him as the sun, and his unconscious hopes were that Shoshana would be impressed by his courage and fall into his arms. One day he appeared with a gun, carefully hiding it under the floor in the tool shack, making Shoshana swear she would never reveal its existence, "unless absolutely necessary." He was very excited: "It is one of a few guns that we managed to smuggle into the city," he explained. "We have been able to convince some of the orange dealers at Jaffa Port to help us smuggle more ammunition into the country. It isn't easy to find places where we can effectively hide the weapons, while giving us access to them, when we need them. As it is, we have so few options...and I have been selected to hide this baby!" he said with unhidden pride. "Now I will be the official owner of a *slick* – a hiding place for weapons! Just wait and see," he continued, "After we graduate from high school, I will join the orange export company, Pardes, and I will make sure that we get more guns and bullets to fill them with!"

"What do oranges have to do with guns?" Shoshana asked, confused.

"Nothing. But they do have something to do with crates and barrels, which are excellent hiding places," Moshe answered. He winked at her, continuing, "hiding places for anything that needs to be hidden...."

Moshe would disappear for hours on end, coming back at night dirty and hungry, saying only that he was "away on duty." Sometimes, when she knew that he was gone at night, Shoshana would sneak out of her house, climb up the wall that separated their gardens and rush to the tool shack to make sure that the gun was still there. Each time she saw the gun she felt a rush of relief, for it meant that he hadn't been arrested, or worse, that he wasn't away somewhere getting into life-threatening situations, at least not yet. When she complained that he didn't take her to any of these activities, he said only that they weren't fit for two.

Trying to fit into an adult world as quickly as possible, Moshe started asking Rivka for "wheels," only to be cut off by a wall of resistance. He used all of his persuasive power and reasoning, telling her that being mobile would mean that he could fit into his schedule many more achievements; he also tried the tactic of bribery, promising that Rivka would never have to carry heavy baskets from the market ever again; he even tried begging, saying that he would always be in debt to the family; and finally, he used his father, taking advantage of the fact that he was an orphan, saying that his father would have understood. But Rivka remained stubborn in her resistance, for she knew that this would be just one more reason for him to defy the angel of darkness.

A loud roar burst through Shoshana's window from the street. Startled, Shoshana quickly glanced outside and was surprised to see Moshe seated on a huge, dark, two-wheeled motorcycle that had the words "Harley-Davidson" written brightly on it. Knowing how reluctant Rivka had been to realize her son's dream, Shoshana learned that Moshe finally managed to come up with the ultimate threat: he had found a day job that paid handsomely. He told Rivka that he had found a job since he needed the money for a motorcycle, and that in order to keep the job, he was thinking of quitting school. Rivka finally caved in and a triumphant Moshe took a blushing and awed Shoshana for a long ride on his new prize.

Dvora was restless. She felt that her daughter was becoming too wild, too absorbed in the actions of the struggling nation, and she truly feared that Shoshana would actually forget that she was a girl. She was also haunted by her memory of Shoshana's birth, fearing that her thoughts carried such power that she was depriving her daughter the chance of becoming a beautiful young woman. As Shoshana and Moshe were approaching graduation from high school, Dvora was determined to teach her daughter the manners of a lady so she could fit into the respectable society of Tel Aviv. She managed to convince Ish that immediately after graduation, Shoshana should be sent to a girl's boarding college, a branch of the Sorbonne University located on the outskirts of Paris, for a period of two years so she could learn everything that a proper young woman should know: embroidery, table-setting, fashion and etiquette. After long inquiries, discussions and arguments with a very reluctant Shoshana, the arrangements were finalized: Shoshana was to leave Jaffa Port a month after she finished high school. Dvora knew why her daughter was so opposed to the idea. "If Moshe truly loves you," she said in her ever-practical voice, "he will wait for you."

A small party of people accompanied Shoshana as she left. Ish, his eyes showing all the longing he would feel with his daughter gone, stood tall and reassuring, handsome even with his gray hair and dressed in his best suit; Dvora's head was held high, with her fine brown hair that still showed no hint of gray, carefully piled in a bun on her head, her eyes determined and stubborn, and her hands neatly covered with white gloves; and Moshe sitting on his Harley-Davidson, his eyes troubled and his mouth twisting. "I will wait for you," he whispered into her ear, "I will work and build us the finest house in Tel Aviv…just make sure you return to me."

Shoshana stood there, dressed in a light brown dress, her golden curls swirling around her face, her blue eyes bright as the sky and crying as the clouds. She was petite, fragile-looking, and completely absorbed with Moshe. She knew that Rivka had asked some of her spirits to accompany her on her journey to ensure that she would be safe. She looked straight into Moshe's eyes and said, "There is no one else I shall ever notice. Wait and I will be back in no time. And…Moshe…since I will not be here for two years, you have my permission to…well…fulfill your physical needs with others…until I return and we're married."

And with that she was gone.

Their letters were long and full of longing. Shoshana wrote long pink words, describing her lessons, her classmates and the activities in the school. Moshe wrote poetic letters, quoting lines from books he had read, copying lines from well-known poetry and dedicating them to her, telling her how much he missed her. She wrote about the sights, sounds and smells of the faraway and very strange country she was exploring. He wrote about his first steps in the business world, excited about the new job he had secured with the orange export company in Jaffa, "Pardes Syndicate." She wrote of fancy tea parties, elegant dishes and chandeliers. He wrote about the sandy lot on Sirkin Street that her father had purchased for them and about the building plans that he had for what would be their first house. She wrote about her expanding cultural world, her ability to master five different languages and the joy she felt whenever she studied the different crafts, such as embroidery, knitting, sewing and cooking. He wrote about the satisfaction he felt as his career developed – the explicit exporting career and the implicit defense-mastery career. Neither of them wrote a word about suitors or lovers that they may have had. Those remained hidden from the eye, barely noticed by time itself.

Two years after she had left, Shoshana returned to Tel Aviv. She was greeted by a hungry Moshe, who had expressed endless yearning in his letters, and she was looking forward to a loving welcome. When he saw her at the port, he noticed how much she had matured and changed: instead of the dressed-up, but very mischievous, tomboy he had remembered, he saw a young and obviously well-behaved lady. Confused and uncertain of her feelings, he walked up to her and extended his hand for a shake. Hurt, she looked at him and cried, "What's this, Moshe? A handshake? No welcome home kiss?" Years that had felt like decades of longing and uncertainty exploded in his head. In one sweep, he grabbed her in his arms and kissed her, exploring her rosy, sweet mouth with his lips, his tongue, his breath; they stood there, wrapped in each other, not letting go, his hands running through her curls, her arms stroking his back, their faces glued by tears, anxiety and love. The sensation she felt running down her spine was overwhelming – she never knew she could feel this kind of pleasure, she had always thought it was wrong. When they finally broke away to catch their breath, Shoshana turned around and found herself standing face-to-face with the harsh, disappointed and accusing gaze of her mother.

The preparations for their wedding were one of the best and busiest times in their lives. The house on Sirkin Street was spectacular. It had two stories. The first floor was to be a kindergarten, for Moshe felt it would provide them with a nice, steady income. The second floor, separated from the first by a cement ceiling – an uncommon luxury that Moshe insisted on – was to be the apartment they would live in. It had four spacious rooms, since Moshe was determined to be able to see Shoshana's curls dance with the sun in every corner of the house. The two bedrooms were separated by a study and a large living room that opened to a large patio. The patio had a beautiful staircase that spiraled down leading to a small garden, where Moshe had plans to build a greenhouse. A large hallway separated the rooms, and a small but airy kitchen and bathroom were placed at its end. The entire apartment was bright, decorated with white wooden windows and doors. It was a place that would allow them to live, love and dream. It also allowed for several hiding places, and two different *slicks* were hidden in the house and another one in the garden.

Moshe was doing very well at Pardes. Before Shoshana had returned from Europe, he had already attained the position of manager, in charge of unloading the incoming ships, and he was earning a handsome salary. He spared no luxury from the home he was preparing for his bride, ordering merchandise out of catalogues that arrived from faraway countries such as France, Britain and America. The house was equipped with a large oven and a refrigerator, objects that were hardly seen in Tel Aviv those days. As the wedding grew close, the house started to fill up with objects of his desire. Enchanted, Shoshana watched the parade of boxes, crates, barrels, and men going in and out of the new, sparkling house, carrying deep, exciting secrets hidden within them, the products of Moshe's love for her and for beautiful treasures from faraway places. Moshe mastered the entire parade, making sure that each piece of furniture was placed in the right corner, each dish was sparkling in its design, and each ornament hanging on one of the bold white walls. A fortnight before the wedding, the wedding gifts started arriving, adding finesse and color to the already lavish house. Shoshana, Dvora and Rivka enjoyed unwrapping each box, admiring every addition that came out of it, and deciding how and where to place it. When a set of boxes arrived from Jerusalem, revealing a beautiful, full set of Armenian dishes, each painted by hand with a colorful dance of shapes, Rivka's eyes filled with tears. It was a gift from Feiga and her son Aaron. It was a sign from the past, and Rivka knew what she must do.

Carefully, she emptied the Blooma cabinet. With each grain of dust that she wiped from its drawers, and with each caress of the shelves, while cleaning them, voices and visions from the past came dancing out of its wood, enveloping her in a warm embrace. She parted from each and every one of them with compassion, knowing that they would continue to watch over her from their world, but would now escort Moshe and his bride through their life as well. The cabinet, a wedding gift from the groom's mother, was placed in the young couple's living room. While Feiga's dishes were shining on its shelves and in its drawers, the family history was the eternal food laying on them. It was the food that they would feed on every single meal. Watching the Blooma cabinet stand there, as beautiful and as grand as it had been on the day her father had given it to her, Rivka could hear Isaac's voice declaring, just as he did on the day he placed the sundial over the synagogue in Jerusalem: "…a perfect combination of our past and our future, it will remain as a legacy forever." Hearing his voice, Rivka became uneasy and disturbed. She was not sure why, but she had a dark premonition that formed itself from the depth of her childhood memories and stories: the vision of the unknown grave of a prophet placed on a hill east of the Jordan Valley. On the grave grew a beautiful bush, filled with large, red roses. They were all crying. Panicking, Rivka dismissed the vision from her eyes, refusing to explore or even acknowledge it. Years would pass before she would understand the sign that was sent to her by the spirits on her son's wedding night.

A week before the wedding came the best gift of all: a large, black Ford appeared at the doorstep of the new house. It was the wedding gift that Ish had decided to give his Shoshana and her groom. He hadn't shared this idea with anyone, not even Dvora. When Moshe saw the car, he was beside himself with excitement: it was not only a very expensive gift, but also a very rare sight in Tel Aviv those days. He immediately mastered the skill of driving, and the astonishment in Shoshana's eyes as well as the admiration of the entire neighborhood was a reward he relished.

Dvora and Rivka were both in a frenzy. The former was busy preparing her daughter for the wedding night, ensuring that every stitch in the wedding dress was properly sewn, the food was properly cooked and the tables were properly set. Dvora saw to it that every minute detail was taken care of – from the choosing of the silverware and selecting of matching tablecloths and napkins, to arranging the seating plan. The entire family was traveling across the country to attend the wedding, as were the food and drinks. Grapes, plums and peaches traveled from Zichron, accompanied by the finest wine that the little northern town had to offer, all courtesy of Zeide and Bobbeh; sweet, fragrant oranges and sour, juicy lemons arrived from the eastern orchards in Rishon LeZion, accompanied by jams, orange-flavored chocolates and freshly baked breads, all courtesy of Moshe's co-workers at "Pardes"; meat platters, decorated with vine leaves that were marinated in lemon and stuffed with rice, arrived from Jaffa, courtesy of Ish's Arab employees; fine brandy was imported all the way from England, a gift from Moshe's British friends from Jaffa Port. Dvora's spice garden was carefully combed so the best mint leaves could float in large jars of lemonade, the brightest coriander leaves could pinch the cooked dishes and the precious saffron could color the rice and raisins.

Every practical aspect was dealt with under Dvora's firm supervision, and it was with the same practical demeanor that she instructed her daughter of her wifely duties. "You must allow

Moshe to have his way with you in a dignified fashion. Remember, a lady waits for her husband to show his interest. Respect is the most important thing in a marriage – make sure you don't lose his!"

As for Rivka, she was busy talking to her spirits, enticing them with vows and gifts to forgive Moshe for his addiction to luxury and fancy gadgets and to accompany Shoshana and her son towards happiness and success through her married life.; she was filled with fear of the vengeance that awaited him by the snickering spirits. Although she wouldn't dare admit it even to herself, she was absolutely certain that this was the meaning of the sign that she had received from her spirits. Her nights would be spent listening to Isaac's comforting and approving voice, and whenever she could, she guided Shoshana through what it means to have the presence of voices in one's life, how to use them, and how to beware of them. Despite her worries and hard work, deep in her heart she knew that her kind spirits had found a soulmate in her son's bride, for Shoshana was truly a good-natured and kind-hearted girl, and Rivka knew that the kind spirits would protect her.

Everyone was in agreement that there was no bride as beautiful as Shoshana was on her wedding day, a fact that was a source of amazement for two reasons. First, Shoshana was not usually considered beautiful. Second, because everyone knew that this kind of beauty, a beauty that is born of happiness, was a sin that will bring only hardship and sorrow for the bride and groom. Each time Moshe swirled his lovely bride on the dance floor, many heads turned aside and spat against the evil eye, and they all made sure to mention that her beauty glowed from her from the minute she put on her wedding dress, and would peel off her with the dress when the evening ended, just to ensure that the evil spirits had no reason to linger.

Of all the family and guests present at the wedding, that night, Ish was the happiest. Dancing around with his daughter, then with his wife, then with every other woman in the room, his spirits were high. He offered a toast in honor of the bride and groom. "This night makes me very, very hopeful," he said, "for in front of our very eyes a true miracle is materializing. We are indeed living the times that our prophets have envisioned, that our forefathers have only been able to dream about. Moshe and Shoshana, both born here in the Land of our ancestors, both a pillar of the new creation of our modern history, are uniting tonight. Surrounding them is our entire family circle and friends who have come from near and far – Jews, Arabs and Britons. All of us are enjoying the fruit of the Land, the prosperity we have brought to this corner of the world with our own, working hands…. If this night does not show we can all live and prosper together, I don't know what will. It can only mean one thing," he continued. "They must hurry and bring the third generation of Israel-born children into this world – I want to be a young grandfather!"

When the last of the guests left, Shoshana and Moshe fell into each other's arms, exhausted, and slept through the remnants of the night. The next morning they climbed into the seats of their new Ford and drove to Jerusalem to start their honeymoon.

Chapter 7

SHOSHANA

1930-1940

I was four years old, living happily in Los Angeles, when a new addition came into my world: my baby sister who, I learned very quickly, was very beautiful. My parents, especially my father, marveled at her beauty. Inbar was indeed a very beautiful child: large green eyes, soft blond curls, a small, perfect nose, and a warm, happy smile. Everyone said she was the spitting image of my mother, while I resembled "the family features" – saying subtly that I looked more like my grandmother Shoshana. Little by little, I started to feel like the ugly duckling: not that I was ugly, but somehow in every conversation the two of us were categorized in a very definite way. My father would praise my sister's beauty, melting at every gaze she gave him, and when someone would mention something about me he would very confidently say: "Oh, yes, Liat is pretty as well, but above all, she is smart. She was born an alter-kop: a person with a wise, mature way of thinking." The result was that I always felt very dull, especially beside my ravishing sister, and she always felt stupid, especially beside her intellectual sister – me, that is. It really did us both an injustice, since I am not dull and she is not stupid. But throughout the course of my life, I longed to be, at least for a short period, a week, even a day – beautiful. And one of the greatest surprises of my life was when my great love, the man who was to become my partner for life, said to me on our second date: "How beautiful you are!" I almost stopped seeing him because of that remark, since I was so certain that he was lying to me.

Their honeymoon was a short, seven-day vacation. They spent two nights in Jerusalem and then traveled through the east side of the Jordan Valley. Only two events were worth remembering from the week-long honeymoon: the first time they had sex and a trip to the Jordan River.

On their first night in Jerusalem, Moshe was filled with anticipation while Shoshana was terrified. Remembering her mother's instructions, she quietly undressed herself and lay on the bed. Moshe felt her fear, and very slowly caressed her body, his hand barely touching her skin, as if afraid he would break her. She slowly relaxed, trying to concentrate on the sensation of his caressing hands, his warm body close to hers, his breath in her ears; but all she could think of was the dark, whispering voices of spirits that surrounded her. She tried to understand what they were telling her, not sure whether they were warning her or trying to soothe her. Kissing her gently, and running his hands through her curls, then down her spine, moving toward her shy breasts and down her small but round thighs, whispering words of love and longing into her ears, Moshe tried to recapture the moments of unleashed passion they had shared when she had returned from Europe. But Shoshana was aloof, too immersed in the voices that surrounded her, and when he penetrated her she was totally taken by surprise. Pain and insult seared through her head, and she emitted a feverish cry that swept through the walls, ran down the stairs and out to the streets, making abused wives shiver with knowledge and angry husbands crouch with shame.

Confused, Moshe quickly backed away and discovered with horror a growing pool of blood streaming slowly from between her legs. Shoshana continued to sob softly, not noticing that Moshe was starting to panic. He tried to collect the slow but firm flow of blood with a towel he had found in the room, then attempted to make her lay down with her legs high in the air, and tried to wrap a sheet around her like a diaper. The blood continued to slowly flow, and when the bed was crimson, and Shoshana's sobs wouldn't stop, he finally sent for a doctor. Embarrassed and filled with guilt, Moshe explained to the doctor what had happened. The doctor checked Shoshana's pulse, looked into her eyes, examined her tongue and fingers and said: "Bad case of anemia and anxiety. Not to worry, the flow of blood will soon stop. Feed her liver and she'll be good as new in a couple of weeks. In the meantime, young man," he turned to Moshe and winked, "you've waited this long – you can wait another fortnight!" Grateful that the fearful incident ended with a simple dose of chopped liver and fourteen days, Moshe thanked the doctor, paid him, escorted him to the door and returned to a very disappointed and guilt-stricken bride. She eagerly wanted to be able to love him, she ached with the desire to be a wonderful wife, and at the same time she was afraid she would never be able to enjoy the same kind of passion he had for her. She vowed that she would spend the rest of her days trying to make it up to him.

Two days later, they left for the Jordan Valley. They traveled the rest of the week, enjoying the scenery, bathing in the streams, Moshe bringing her fresh flowers from the fields every morning and Shoshana pampering him with fresh muffins and tea every afternoon. They were recapturing the joy of their childhood games, and time was becoming more enchanting for both of them. On the sixth day they stopped for a picnic at the Jordan River. It was afternoon, the river was overflowing with fresh, sparkling sweet water, and beautiful flowers and bushes surrounded them. Little black birds with orange wings danced in the air, chirping a gay melody, and large yellow butterflies floated about like a dreamy veil. They were completely alone, and for the first time Shoshana felt that she was indeed alone with Moshe, without any humans or spirits around. They relaxed on the green weeds, laughing, amazed by the beauty that surrounded them. Slowly, Shoshana pulled him to her, leading his lips to her breasts, caressing his hair, shyly squeezing his back. He moaned and tried to pull back – he remembered the doctor's warning from less than a week before. But she was bewitched, focusing on him alone, calming him, insisting she was all right, whispering words of passion and desire that he didn't even know she knew, and he caved in, slowly but completely. They danced in the bush, their bodies tangled and enmeshed in each other, convinced that the whole universe centered around the bank of that river. When they both lay, completely drowned and exhausted, in the weeds, he dared not look into her eyes – he was afraid he would break the magic that engulfed them. She took his silence as a sign that she had been too bold, and was now losing respect for her. She didn't know what to do or say. Finally, after a long, peaceful silence, Shoshana spoke.

"Jordan," was all she whispered. "If we ever have a son, that is what we shall call him. Jordan."

They returned to Tel Aviv the following day, and by the time they arrived, the magic had disappeared and the spirits were back, harassing Shoshana, scolding her for disappearing on them for an entire day, laughing at her for her experience, never leaving her side for even a second. Desperate, Shoshana tried to expel the evil spirits that were dancing in front of her eyes each time Moshe tried to touch her. During their first nights in the house she lay frozen, wanting desperately to respond but unable to move a limb, watching the spirits snicker and scorn whenever Moshe whispered words of love in her ears. He was baffled, hurt and surprised. She felt his frustration only too well and her female instincts told her that he would soon search for solace elsewhere. Fully aware that seeking the spirits and their advice was the real wedding gift that Rivka had given her, she tried to search for comfort and help by going to palm readers, certified witches, tarot card experts and coffee readers. But all her efforts were in vain. Not one of them managed to banish the sense of terrified nerves that she felt each night as she climbed into bed and lay stiff beside him, nor expel the sights of evil that flashed in the dark in front of her eyes, enveloping her in a pain that was so physical, she felt it crawling on her skin – a young Turk casting a stone, a beaten young woman dragged up a main street, her mother's cold, practical voice when she spoke to her father, and worse of all – her mother's cold, accusing gaze upon Shoshana's one visible moment of passion. The spirits were taking their revenge on her for allowing herself to disappear from them on the river bank, and she knew that the Jordan River was worlds away, never to return.

It seemed like everything was changing rapidly and the world they had known was far behind. The innocence of Tel Aviv's beginning was giving way to fast-paced, modern times, and the metropolis by the sea offered the energy of business and growth during the day and sensuous activities by night. Alcohol was no longer forbidden, and any kind of fun and games could be found if carefully searched for. There were still soldiers roaming the streets, but the downright rude Turks were now replaced with the politically correct rude British.

A year after Moshe and Shoshana were married, wild attacks began to spread through the country once again. In Hebron and Tzfat, full blown pogroms were inflicted on the Jews, as were attacks in many other places. In some places they defended themselves with the few weapons they had, relying mostly on sticks and stones.

Wherever the *Haganah* had power, the attackers were driven away. But wherever the settlers decided that they did not need the defense of the *Haganah*, relying solely on the protection of the British, they were literally left defenseless. Within six days, more than a hundred and thirty Jews were slaughtered by rioting Arab crowds, while thousands became homeless and destitute. There was only one conclusion that could be drawn: the defense of the Jewish villages, towns and cities should be placed in the hands of the Jews – and armed hands, for that matter. The *Haganah* should be equipped with greater reinforcements, with the ability to use weapons when necessary. Drastic action was called for, and Moshe had a brilliant plan. He was about to start a new, exciting business.

After long searches and negotiations, Moshe purchased a small shack on the Tel Aviv beach. It was a run-down, wooden structure with a large, squeaky door and small, rectangular windows that opened toward the ceiling. Every evening, after he finished his regular job at "Pardes," Moshe would go down to the shack on the beach and start working. Shoshana would join him, bringing along a cold dinner in a basket, and several friends from the *Haganah* would help out every now and again. Soon, the run-down shack took on the appearance of a combination of a sports club and pub. Bottles of beer, wine and liquor decorated the eastern wall, and a huge wooden cupboard filled with glasses of all shapes and sizes stood in the corner. The single, large room was designed as a shooting arcade: several guns stood on racks and large red targets were placed on the western wall. Moshe's connections with high-ranking British officers, as well as his financial wealth, got him the certificates necessary to open a competitive shooting club, where alcohol was served and people were allowed to come and compete for prizes. The certificates did not include permission, however, for the huge *slick* that was carefully hidden under the wooden floor.

"The British are no better than the Turks," Ish grumbled when he heard what his daughter and son-in-law were up to. "The Turks called it *bakshish*, the British call it paying for papers…basically it is the same – good old-fashioned bribery."

"Well, it's about time we had a place like this!" exclaimed a British officer, one of Moshe's friends, on the night that the club officially opened. The club was swarming with people, and from that day on, customers would come every night, enjoying the atmosphere, bragging about shooting contests, drinking, smoking and shouting into the wee hours. Overnight, the TIR club – a Hebrew acronym for "Rifle Shooting Range" – had become a great success and one of the main venues for *Haganah* practice. The setting was a perfect cover for the *Haganah* members to legitimately practice their shooting skills, but they had to be very careful not to show how good they really were when the British were around, in order not to arouse suspicion.

Every once in awhile, Moshe would go to the British police headquarters to ask for permission to purchase a new rifle. "The old one was jammed, I had to throw it away," he would explain, or he would apologize, "I'm afraid that one of your officers had a hard night with his – er – drinks, and he just walked away with it. Naturally, I couldn't insult him by accusing him of theft or of being drunk… And we wouldn't want anyone to be disappointed," he would add, winking, "when they find out we can't provide the entertainment they are used to because we don't have enough rifles, do we?" A search, if conducted, would have discovered that the so-called missing rifles lay safe and secure under the floorboards, but no one searched so no one knew. Except for the *Haganah* members, of course.

Keeping his job at "Pardes" was no longer just a matter of income. Moshe became very active in the smuggling of weapons and ammunition. His days were filled with oranges and smuggling, his nights were filled with using what he smuggled during the day.

Shoshana's days were filled with her newly acquired Parisian skills: she was the perfect lady, busy with charity, social activities, embroidery and cooking. At night she was right there with Moshe, working as the bartender at TIR. She loved the exciting, dangerous, smoke-filled and alcohol-scented atmosphere that the shooting arcade cast on its visitors. It was the only part of the day that she felt like she was an energetic, fearless and mischievous teenager again, and it was a welcome distraction from the everyday routine activities of housekeeping, cooking and embroidering tablecloths and shirts. There was only one routine that they both cherished and guarded zealously: Shabbat.

On Friday afternoon everything would stop in honor of Shabbat. Shabbat was the day that was designated for family, rest and relaxation. Shabbat dinner would be spent with Dvora and Ish, updating them with all the news of the past week.

"A new arrival came in this week," Moshe uttered softly, "and I must admit it was almost discovered. The layer of oranges was too thin. Dvora, these potatoes are absolutely delicious."

"You will end up in jail," Dvora scolded him, "have some more, there's more than enough."

"What happened?" Ish ignored his wife as he helped himself to another serving of chicken. And potatoes.

"The British soldier was sniffing around the crates like a hound dog, and was about to search them, when I noticed that he was sweating, so I offered him some orange juice and started talking to him about the damned weather. Nothing like that subject to engage them…no one bakes challah bread like yours, not even the bakery on Ajamy Street. Only the British could rant on and on about humidity and heat…. Anyway, before he noticed, the crates were gone. It was worth the risk, but we were lucky."

"You must be better prepared to deal with these kinds of situations. Luck is an elusive creature, you may not be so fortunate next time." Shoshana was genuinely concerned. She didn't eat a bite.

"Oh, we have a bunch of plans, don't worry." Moshe was confident, his mouth full. "Soon the *slick* at TIR will be completely full. I will need to create more space."

"Well, just don't let your mother in on it. She is panicking as it is." At this point, Dvora's practical voice was a soothing comfort. The potatoes were gone.

On Saturday morning they would visit Rivka, always spending Saturday afternoon with Olga and Asher. One of the creative writers of his time, Asher filled his small apartment with ideas and busy creativity: the place was always swarming with visitors, conversations, debates and political opinions. The conversations would reach their peak especially on weekends, when Shoshana and Moshe arrived, bringing whatever news they had gleaned during the week, their experiences and practical attitudes, to the doorstep of the dream-writers and storytellers.

"I am thinking of working on a new series of sketches," Nachum said, as he showed them his latest drawings. "I did these recently...." Jaffa and Tel Aviv were shining from the canvas in bright colors, naïve, almost childish, a picture of the past.

"They are wonderful!" Shoshana exclaimed. "Exactly as I remember it...." her voice trailed off.

"I want to describe life," he continued. "Our beautiful little Tel Aviv...." His voice wandered.

"Your drawings tell stories…I can literally read them...."

"Oh, no," Nachum said, smiling. "I leave the writing to Asher."

Life continued at this exhilarated pace and Shoshana enjoyed it so much that she refused to allow any other changes into her life. Whenever Dvora's eyes would search her daughter's belly for a sign of new life, Shoshana would ignore her mother's gaze and continue to chirp gaily about the fulfilling life she led. A distant conversation that she had once overheard became not only clear but very helpful, and she used it to make sure she would not become pregnant before she was absolutely ready to take on the responsibility of a child.

When Moshe tried to persuade her that maybe they should start thinking of a family, she would brush him off by asking: "What's this, Moshe? Isn't my love enough? Your love is all I need – I don't want to share you yet with anyone!" and that would be the end of the conversation. She had time.

But more than that, she was petrified. Pregnancy meant birth, which meant pain. And blood. She remembered the shame of her first night as a wife, and she was afraid.

On their fourth anniversary, Rivka approached Shoshana. In her quiet eyes lay the truth. "Don't worry, *mine kindt*," she said. "They will all guard you. It will be all right. And he will love you no less. You are his soul."

"What do you mean?" Shoshana whispered, although she already knew the answer.

"I would like to be blessed by seeing my youngest child's firstborn. It will be the last wish of my life."

Shoshana started to protest, but stopped short. Rivka's eyes were direct, honest and loving. Three weeks later Shoshana became pregnant.

It was a very easy pregnancy, hardly noticeable up until the last six weeks. For nine months, Shoshana spoke to her unborn baby, carrying on Rivka's tradition in equipping the babies of the family with tools of strength and love before birth. Certain that she was carrying a boy, she promised to shelter him from fear and pain, to always be there for him, and she told him all the family stories she had heard from her Zeide, her father and Rivka. Stories of ancient times in a newfound homeland, stories of modern struggle and of the deep roots created by that struggle. She handed her unborn baby his heritage, giving him the taste of pride that he would be a third-generation Sabra to be born in the Land of Israel – he would taste this before tasting his mother's milk. Shoshana also wanted him to know that, despite what he may feel were the undercurrents of his parents' relationship, they shared a deep, absolute love and were completely devoted to each other, a bond that was forged between them years ago, so strong that it would never break. And there was one ultimate expression of that love: she called her unborn baby Jordan.

Moshe was overflowing with emotion. He was about to become a father! All the yearning and disappointment that he had felt as a result of their clumsy physical relationship had disappeared, and he was overwhelmed by the strength of his feelings. He immediately took action. The spare bedroom started to transform itself in color and content, slowly and happily turning into a nursery. A beautiful white crib was ordered from England, accompanied by a large blue stroller, baby clothes and toys. The walls were covered with a bright flowery wallpaper, and when curtains decorated with butterflies were placed on the window the sun and wind made the room look like a bright open field with a relaxing, light blue atmosphere. When Rivka saw the nursery she turned to Moshe and asked: "Do you think the color is appropriate?"

Laughing, Moshe said: "Well, the boy will choose the color of his liking when he goes to school."

"Boy?" Rivka exclaimed blankly.

"Shoshana is certain we are having a boy."

"Nonsense. You are having a girl. But don't tell her yet. She will soon find out."

Like his father before him, Moshe knew better than to argue with his mother's premonitions.

On the wall opposite the window, Moshe hung a large, beautiful painting of teddy bears picnicking in a field. It was a beautiful picture but was more than merely a cheerful child's decoration: behind it, secure and hidden within the wall, was a *slick* with three guns and a box filled with ammunition.

At the end of spring, when the air was filled with the sweet scent of flowers and nice, salty breezes from the sea, Shoshana gave birth. It was an easy birth, as easy as was her own appearance in the world almost thirty years before. It took less than two hours, and Moshe hardly made it on time from Jaffa Port to see the birth of his first child. Rushing all the way to the Ein-Gedi Maternity Hospital, he arrived just in time to see the midwife carry a bundle out of the delivery room. "Moshe Lipavsky?" she asked with a smile," I believe this is yours."

Carefully, hesitating, he looked into the bundle. In it lay the most beautiful baby he had ever seen. It had a perfectly shaped head, laced with soft blond curls, a tiny nose and rosy lips in the middle. The baby opened its eyes for a brief moment, and Moshe noticed with astonishment that it had the same beautiful blue eyes as his mother's. Moshe was lost for words and was breathless. All he could do was stare, transfixed, at this miracle he had helped to create. "Mazal tov, it's a girl," said the midwife, and with that she and the baby disappeared into the nursery.

It's a girl, it's a girl, my beautiful baby girl – Moshe's head was still spinning when he approached Shoshana's bed. She was laying there, very pale but smiling. "Well, we did it," she said.

"Yes, we did, my little mother," he smiled. "You did most of the work."

"Are you disappointed that it isn't a boy?"

"Are you kidding?!" Moshe exclaimed, "I wouldn't trade her for a hundred boys! She is perfect. And so beautiful! She looks just like her wonderful mother."

Shoshana flinched. "Yes, she is beautiful…" Years of hidden insult, of feeling plain and insignificant, popped back into Shoshana's mind, mixed with the fear of love and intimacy that was planted in her head, with sounds of the indifferent and cold voice of her mother. Suddenly desperate, she grabbed Moshe's hand. "I want her to know how beautiful she is…." she said. "She should always know how much we love her…how much we believe she is beautiful…and smart."

Stunned by his wife's overflowing emotions, Moshe reassured her. "Of course she will…she is our princess…."

"And…Moshe…promise me that you will never stop loving me…even now, that we have our own daughter, promise me that you still love me…."

"Shoshana, my love, where is this coming from?" he cried, puzzled, "she is our princess, but you will always be my queen." He was silent for a few moments. "Well, so much for planning ahead… obviously Jordan is a name for a boy. What shall we call her?"

Shoshana looked straight into his eyes. "There is only one name we can call her. Jordana. That will be her name. Jordana."

Jordana was indeed considered a very beautiful baby, and not only Shoshana and Moshe marveled at her beauty. Whenever they strolled with her around Tel Aviv, people would stop and congratulate them for producing such a fine-looking child.

In spite of all his other activities, Moshe's whole world started to revolve around Jordana and her needs, and their carefully constructed routine of the past five years rapidly changed. He would come home from work and walk straight to her crib, picking her up, laughing, kissing and talking to her. Shoshana was almost jealous: "What's this, Moshe, you are saying hello to the baby before you greet your own wife?" But then he would turn his attention to her, and she would see the longing in his eyes and the dark shadows of their nights would make her pass a quick semi-kiss to his cheek, leaving him cold and empty hearted.

Moshe invested all his unanswered passion in Jordana. He spent days going over catalogues that displayed the best fashions of Paris and Rome, the latest activities of the royal children of London. Jordana's clothes were ordered from European catalogues, her toys from America. When she was four, a special riding suit was imported from England for her – not that there were any horses around Tel Aviv for a four year old to ride, but Moshe, who had always had a soft spot for the highlights of the English and American cultures, insisted that his daughter have at least the suit, if not the horse.

Every morning, before breakfast, Moshe would take Jordana to the beach for a swim. He taught her how to float and how to jump in the waves, catching their flow into her own movements, becoming one with the sea and rolling smoothly with them back to shore. He taught her the strong swimming strokes that made her feel like the mistress of the sea, capturing its might with her small hands and leading the way for the water itself. He taught her how to love the treasures that the sea had to offer – the colorful shells that lined the place where the water and the sand kissed each other, leaving a memory of every such kiss along the path of the waves; the smooth, warm sand that they would play in, creating endless shapes and structures, imaginary castles, fortresses, tunnels and buildings, decorated with sand drops and shell fragments; and the world that was there to discover around the rocks, where the water was trapped, creating mirrors while playing with the sun and hiding endless creatures to catch and investigate.

The people who saw them on those early morning trips always smiled, as Moshe showed off his beautiful daughter. "Her eyes are as blue as the sea!" they would exclaim, "It's almost as if she has the water of the waves trapped within them." And Moshe would think of his mother.

Jordana was as active and mischievous as the waves. Screaming with delight, she would run around the beach to catch the white foam that the sea sent with every wave, watching it disappear with astonishment saved for a small child discovering the world. She would try to grasp the wet sand only to see it slipping away between her tiny fingers, then tried to cover her Daddy with it.

One day, a red-headed woman came up to them and started chatting with Moshe. Jordana looked up from the sandcastle she was building, and felt a strange pang of jealousy – her father seemed too comfortable with this stranger, as if he knew her. On the way back home, Jordana was very quiet. When she noticed the redheaded woman walking toward them on the beach the next day, Jordana grabbed her father's hand and pulled him away. Surprised by his daughter's reaction, Moshe silently followed her lead. The red-headed woman never appeared at the beach again. Jordana never mentioned the incident to her mother. From that day on, she hated girls with red hair.

After breakfast Moshe would leave for work. Shoshana would dress Jordana up and go out to the cafés of Tel Aviv. They were both a sight to see: Shoshana in the latest Parisian fashion, her hair in beautifully combed curls, a petite hat on her forehead and her heals high; and Jordana in a miniature replica of her mother's dress, her curls running loose and her eyes wide, large and curious. Once a week they would go to have tea with Olga and Asher, always stopping at Rivka's doorstep for a blessing. Asher would sit her on his lap, telling her stories he had invented just for her, filling her head with the wonders of the pioneers and the essentials of classic childhood fairytales. Every Friday night they would go to Dvora and Ish for Shabbat dinner, and Ish would tell her the ancient stories of the Bible and history, the same stories he had told her mother years before, stories that filled her young eyes with longing and a deep sense of bonding to her home.

Jordana had inherited her father's passion for beauty, his mischievous character and his love of words. She had Shoshana's large eyes, soft blond curls and bright, free spirit. Asher's knowledge of the literary world was embedded in her soul, as was her grandfather's understanding of history and art. She could display her grandmother's aloofness when necessary, and the strong chains of steel that connected the Zichron branch to the land was wrapped around her heart. She was an amazing combination of the spirits of her family, both alive and dead.

And she had something else. Something of her own, something

that she received not from her forefathers, but from her own vivid, imaginative spirit, something that distinguished her from all the generations before her. It was hers alone, and she kept it to herself fanatically, showing it only to those she desired

Some like it mellow. A relaxed, flowing life with a well-defined structure and events that proceed in slow motion. Others like life to be hot and sizzling, changing in rapid twists and turns, so accustomed to excitement that if the waters of their lives suddenly calm down, they find new ways to generate excitement and tension, even when they are unnecessary. And sometimes, life itself presents unexpected challenges that create such an abyss you have only two choices: you can walk slowly and fall, or you can jump with all your might, breathless, to the other side.
   For years I was certain that my childhood was calm and tranquil. But as I grew up, the presence of undercurrents became clearer, casting tense excitement that was wrapped around my fists. She never made a big deal out of it, but my mother's past always felt like the present, all-encompassing, and even though she tried to ignore them, we couldn't escape the strong sounds and racing surprises that were a familiar feature in her life.

Riots were sweeping through the land once more, bringing horror and death in their wings. Ish was on his way to his lumber warehouse in Jaffa when the sound of thunder started to pound on the sidewalk. A beautiful morning in the middle of April, Ish lifted his head in astonishment, searching for the clouds in the clear blue sky, when he heard a familiar voice say in a thick, Arabic accent: "Mr. Broytman, Mr. Broytman, come quick!" and a hand grabbed at him, jerking him towards a door that slammed fast behind him.
   Moshe was at Jaffa Port when he heard the chanting. Deep, dark, hysterical voices were calling: "Allah-hu-Akbar – God is great!" and "Itbach-el-Yahud – slaughter the Jews!" Without a

second thought, he grabbed a kafiya – an Arab head wrap – threw it over his head, and a galabiya – the Arab gown – and threw it over his back and he was out and running up the street towards his father-in-law's lumber shop. He knew he must get Ish out of Jaffa and bring him safely to Tel Aviv before he came back to fight. From a distance, he saw that the lumber shop doors were smashed and a fire was blazing throughout the warehouse. Filled with horror he tried to make his way around the chanting crowd toward the shop, when the kafiya slipped from his head and his face was revealed. An angry boy pointed at him, hurled a large dark object at him that sent a shrieking pain from his arm to his eyes, cut through the crowds, and yelled: "Yahud! Yahud!" and the crowd started turning toward him. Deep in pain, Moshe stumbled forward when from the corner of his eyes he noticed a narrow alleyway opening through two shops. Mustering all the strength he had within him, he ran through it and disappeared. The alley twisted and turned until he found himself at the shore, running north on the wet sand until he saw the houses of Tel Aviv.

When he reached home and opened the door he met the grim face of his mother-in-law and a very worried wife. "Thank goodness you are alive…what's this?!" Shoshana's eyes grew dark when she saw her husband's injured arm. Quickly, she nursed his injury, cleaned the wound thoroughly, spread purple iodine on the cut and wrapped it with a clean, torn sheet she had prepared for such incidents. Luckily, the wound wasn't deep, but Moshe had lost a lot of blood and he was very weak.

"Father has disappeared," Shoshana said. "He was on his way to work this morning when the riots began. Have you seen him?"

"No." The flames of fire were dancing in front of his eyes. He decided to keep them to himself. "He must have gone into hiding. I will ask our friends to search for him."

That night, a group of four young *Haganah* members set out to Jaffa to find Ish Broytman. Armed with guns and ammunition that they had recovered from beneath the bar in a well-known, highly respected shooting arcade, kafiyas on their heads, galabiyahs on their backs, they mingled with the angry crowds that were still setting fire to shops and chanting their frenzied cries. After many long, agonizing hours, Dvora finally opened the door to greet a pale and dirty, yet very much alive, husband.

Without realizing it at first, Ish had been pushed into hiding by one of his clients – an Arab whom Ish had been working with for years, who knew that Ish would be one of the primary targets of the angry mob. Hiding in a small, inner room of his client's house throughout the day, Ish used the cloak of darkness to slip away late at night when he came across his son-in-law's messengers. He heard them ask about his shop and understood immediately why they were there. He quietly approached them, pale but smiling, "Shalom, friends. I think you are looking for me," and seeing their astonished and respectful eyes, he added: "Next time you want to look like Arabs, make sure your pants don't show under your galabiyahs…" Ish's sense of humor did not fool Dvora for one minute. She knew her husband all too well, and was fully aware of how shocked he was as a result of his ordeal. When Ish discovered that the warehouse had been burned down by a mob that only the day before he had considered as friends and clients, his heart broke into tiny pieces. A family business that was handed down to him from three generations before with instructions to work with all men as equals, regardless of their religion, nationality or skin color, a business that always held pride in its integrity and liberal thinking – that business and all it stood for went up in flames. When the port of Jaffa, the entrance to the Land he had loved and lived in during his entire life, was shut down by the Arab workers on strike, an act that drove the Jews to decide to open their own port in Tel Aviv, the tension exploded in his aching heart and he collapsed.

"A heart attack like this can only be treated with complete rest," the doctors told Dvora. "All the riots, the tension, his hard work…they all place too much stress on him. If you really love your husband, and you want him to live, you must see to it that he retires. He must stop working!"

"We have more than we need to live a happy, full life," Dvora pleaded with Ish. "You can sell the shop…it will be your grave if you don't."

Reluctant at first, Ish finally gave in to his wife's plea. His good friend, Krinitsy, persuaded him to sell his house and move to a town east of Tel Aviv, a place called Ramat Gan. "You will see," Krinitsy said, "it is by far a better place to live in than Tel Aviv. Tel Aviv has become too common, too noisy and cosmopolitan…Ramat Gan is full of fresh air and green gardens. And where else will you find a loving neighbor such as me?"

Smiling, Ish looked at Krinitsy and exclaimed: "I suppose it also won't hurt that the head of this town happens to be my best friend…all right, my friend, I will come to your turf… You can rest assured that when it becomes a fully-recognized city, and you need my vote to become mayor, you can count on me!"

Shoshana and Moshe tried to protest against Ish's decision to move to Ramat Gan. Shoshana wanted to be close to her father so that she could ensure he was obeying doctors' orders and could help take care of him and assist her mother. If her parents moved to Ramat Gan, they would have to travel out of town every time she wanted to see them, driving out every Friday night for their shared Shabbat dinners, and the roads were not safe. But their protests were in vain. Ish was not swayed by his childrens' pleas. "I will be fine," he said. "It is Jordana you should worry about." And he was right: Jordana was becoming increasingly reliant upon medical treatment.

Since she was two years old, Jordana started developing allergies. She was allergic to almost every fruit on the stands. Strawberries, tomatoes and avocado gave her a rash; cream, butter and milk were thrust from her body faster then they were let in. Shoshana would soak her in long, warm baths with strong sulphur salts that penetrated Jordana's lungs and eyes, making her sob with despair. Moshe went from one doctor to the other, trying to find a remedy for his daughter. The doctors just shook their heads, explaining again and again that time will take its course and eventually the child will outgrow her allergies. The doctor who treated Ish gave them new hope: he handed Moshe the name of an allergy specialist who practiced at the Hadassah Hospital in Jerusalem. Ramat Gan suddenly seemed very close, and the danger of the riots took on a new dimension. Traveling alone by car all the way to Jerusalem was practically a death wish: hostile Arabs were still displaying unleashed anger, Bedouins roamed the hills on the way, and the British soldiers were not to be trusted. Small cars were too vulnerable, but Ish threatened that if they didn't take Jordana to see the specialist he would go back to work. Finally, they decided to take the bus and make the trip that could help cure the child.

Unaware of the danger, Jordana was very excited – a trip on a bus, through hills and scenery she had never seen before, going to Jerusalem, a city that grandfather Ish had told her wonderful stories about – it was more than a dream come true, it was almost worth all the suffering the allergies had caused her.

Shoshana and Moshe did not share their daughter's excitement. Concealing their fear from her, they nonetheless were very alert. Shoshana held Jordana's hand tightly, while Moshe's eyes kept darting around, scanning the scenery, climbing up and down the hills, to catch any suspicious movement on the way. Every few minutes, his hand gently and secretly caressed a hidden pocket in his coat. A gun and a dozen bullets were safely hidden within.

An hour out of Tel Aviv and approaching the Kastel, a slope surrounded by high dark-green hills that were filled with strange forest scents to the eyes of a five-year-old, and looming with hidden danger to the eyes of adults, Jordana started begging them to stop – "I need to go to the bathroom," she begged, then cried, then

lain that it was impossible to stop, it was shook her head, saying that it would be ants than to run the risk of being shot at ils became so strong and fierce that the bus. "Quick," he said. "Go and return gerous to wait long. I am jeopardizing ld!"

g eyes of the bus passengers followed her one of the trees. "Hurry, child, hurry!" voices surround her. Petrified, she was and hungry, mean eyes were staring at urt her, take her away forever from her ing she loved. She returned to the bus breathless, meekly thanking the passengers who only grumbled and urged the driver to quickly continue the journey. The fear she had felt, and the shame of being accompanied by the eyes of strangers, turned into a stubborn lump of defiance in her soul. She never had allergies again.

Dark clouds were once again filling up the skies, and they were so deep that they threatened to swallow everything in sight. Rivka heard the sounds of her soulmates and knew that trouble was approaching, bigger and harder then ever before. Everyone was restless. People were appearing from the water, emerging from the sea at darkness, coming in through the mountains of the north, blending in with the native population. Refugees, making a desperate, last-minute escape from a continent that was about to burst into flames, made their way cautiously into the small, sizzling and salty land under the careful guidance of the *Haganah*. If they were lucky, the *Haganah* managed to smuggle them in and escape the British soldiers. The less lucky ones were caught and sent back to their origins, never to return.

Eager to volunteer and help ease the desperate situation in

whatever way she could, Shoshana placed Jordana in the faithful hands of a nanny so she could have a few hours to herself in the morning. The nanny – a pleasant woman named Bracha with a daughter of her own who was exactly Jordana's age – came every morning with her daughter and the three of them would enjoy the fresh morning hours.

Moshe spent hours at Pardes and TIR, carefully smuggling in whatever he could, practicing, hiding more and more ammunition that came in as a meek trickle – a few bullets here, half a rifle there; a little bit at TIR, a little bit at the house on Sirkin Street. It wasn't much, but whatever did come in was needed more than ever.

"You are risking the entire family with that ammunition you are hiding at home," Ofsey argued with Moshe. "Why don't you just keep it all at TIR? Why do you need *Slicks* in your own private house as well?"

"It is wiser to distribute our supplies," Moshe answered stubbornly. "That way, if one *slick* is discovered and lost to us, we will still have others left."

"If they find it, it's not just your head that's on the line – it's Shoshana's and the baby's as well. Aren't you thinking of them?!"

"They're exactly who I'm thinking of," Moshe said quietly.

"He's right," Asher's voice was deep and strong. "Where will we end up if we don't make sure we can defend ourselves if necessary? Look at what the British are already doing." He was becoming excited, "They are putting limits on the number of refugees that can come in legally, even though they know what fate is awaiting them in Europe with that Nazi monster in power! They are limiting the amount of land we can buy…." His voice was becoming bitter. "Even our money isn't good enough, oh, no, we are Jews, so we have to settle for less!"

"And at the same time," Moshe jumped in, "they are letting the Arabs have a free hand, promising them they will govern the land, forgetting their promises to us! Sometimes I can't help but think that the Jews who established the Irgun are right…I know you think they are extremists, but they are our Jewish brothers as well and they want Jewish freedom just like we do. They are actively resisting this situation, and what are we doing?" Moshe was becoming angrier by the minute, "We are talking, smuggling in a few people, practicing a bit with the few weapons we have, hoping to get some crumbs of recognition from the British…sometimes I feel we are still the same paupers we were in Europe."

"Don't even think about the Irgun!" Ofsey's voice thundered. The Irgun was a small group of Jews who decided to use extreme methods of fighting against the Arabs and the British, and most of the Jews in Palestine resented their violent methods. "Fine, you want to fight the British, I'll be the first to salute you when they finally leave. And our Zionist organizations are doing everything they can to make that happen." Ofsey was clear and unflinching. "Quietly, while obeying the rules and not stirring too much resistance, we have been able to organize legal defense troops, troops that can practice and make meaningful military progress with the blessing of the British commanders…and we have managed to build several new villages overnight, villages that within one day have a wall and a defense tower…I know times are hard, I know how much our people are suffering in Europe – I see evidence of it every day at the bank – but there is only so much we can do with our meager resources, and whatever we do – we must do it legally or we will be no better than common terrorists."

"We must do it however we can. And we must all be in it together, women and children as well." The calm and firm voice caught them by surprise. Shoshana was quiet, but determined. "It is our last historical chance. We must make sure we don't miss this opportunity."

The knock on the door sounded like thunder, and Jordana was awakened in a jolt. The light was harsh and bold, probing her eyes and hurting them. Three large men dressed in uniform marched boldly into her room, headed directly for her painted teddy bears, roughly moved them, to reveal a small dark door that was attached to the wall, that she never even knew was there. They opened the door and took out a package. They yelled through the window: "We found it!" "Same here!" Darkness itself was answering. Horrified, Jordana watched as one of the men put sparkling round rings round her father's wrists and with a snicker whisked Moshe out of the house.

"Mom, where is daddy?"
"He is in a faraway place called Acre. He is with friends there."
"Why is he there?"
"The British have arrested him. They discovered that we have guns, and they don't allow it. So they are punishing him."
"Like when nanny Bracha punishes me when I do something wrong?"
"Yes. Only Daddy didn't do anything wrong."
"Then why are they punishing him?"
"Daddy had guns so he could protect you if someone tries to hurt you. Does that sound wrong?"
"No."
"No, it isn't. Always remember that you have the right to protect yourself." And even when she said it, Shoshana could spot the shadow of a large Turk laughing scornfully at her in the darkness, Sara's ghost standing right behind.

Shoshana was furious. From the minute they marched through the door, confidently going directly to the *slicks* that were hidden in the house, it was obvious that someone had informed the authorities where the guns were hidden. But who? It must have been someone at Pardes, since several *Haganah* members were caught and arrested that night, all of them Pardes employees. Those who remained out of their small group gathered at the house on Sirkin Street to try to plan their next steps. They had discovered that Moshe and his friends were charged with illegal possession of weapons, a crime that incurred a penalty of at least six months in prison. Since it was their first charge, however, they received the minimal punishment with a strict warning and a handsome fine. Shoshana, Ish and the other *Haganah* members tried in vain to find ways to have Moshe released earlier. Days, weeks and months passed, and Moshe was nowhere in sight. In Jordana's young mind, he started to take the shape of a distant memory. Then one day the doorbell rang and she ran to open it. In front of her stood a thin, tall man, his face very pale and a large beard covering his chin. He was dressed in a large, brown overcoat, with big black buttons that looked like coal-covered rocks to her. She stood and stared at him, and he stared back.

"Jordana, who is it?" Shoshana was coming out from the kitchen.

"It's a peddler!" she answered, not quite understanding why this peddler's eyes were filling with tears.

"Moshe!!" Shoshana gave a cry when she saw him. Jordana, confused, looked up to this strange man. All she could say was, "You are not my father!" and with that she fled, disappearing into her room.

He slept for a week, waking only to eat hearty meals and sleep some more. Slowly, Jordana drew near, watching how the stranger gradually turned into her father again.

Time, the ultimate healer, slowly eased the pain and the anger. Once again they were at the beach, swimming and playing. Once again, Moshe became busy with work and with *Haganah* activities.

It wasn't long before Moshe started to talk about having another baby. "A boy this time," he would whisper affectionately in Shoshana's ear. "A girl for me, a boy for you," and although his chuckle sent cold shivers down her spine, she knew she must do it for him. "After Jordana starts school," she assured him. "Next year, when she's in first grade, we'll start working on having a little brother for her."

How does one make sure it's a boy? It's the least I can do to please him, she thought. She definitely couldn't ask her mother such a question. She knew what she must do: she would ask Nechama.

Dvora's youngest brother, Aminadav, married a girl from one of the villages of the north. Her name was Nechama and she quickly became the family's favorite. Sweet, smiling and hard working, Nechama's house was always open and welcoming. Being the youngest, Aminadav and his bride lived with Bobeh and Zeideh in Zichron and took charge of the farm. Technically Shoshana's uncle and aunt, they were closer in age to Shoshana and Moshe than to Aminadav's siblings. The four of them were immediate soul mates. Shoshana and Moshe would spend most of their holidays with them in Zichron. By the time Jordana was six, Nechama had already given birth to a daughter and a son, and she was very knowledgeable about earthly matters. I will ask her, Shoshana decided. Maybe she can give me some advice. During their next visit to Zichron, Shoshana took Nechama aside and discussed her dilemma with Nechama.

Nechama smiled. "There is a sure way," Nechama whispered knowingly into Shoshana's ears. "If you want a boy, you must be the first to climax."

"I guess that ends the chances of that," Shoshana thought, wryly. "I can't even climax on my own, let alone during intercourse with Moshe…we'll just have to wait and see. Next September, after Jordana goes to school."

Shoshana was certain that she was living in two worlds. The larger world, the one that touched their home through radio and large events, was turning into a fearful, unknown chaotic inferno. The closer world, the one she was born into and had known all her life, was also in chaos – but a familiar one, a world that she felt she could handle. One afternoon they were all sitting in the living room listening to the radio. Jordana was sitting on Moshe's lap when the squeaky voice that came out of the box announced that Germany had invaded Poland.

There was a moment of astonished silence. Then, slamming his fist on the table, Moshe turned to Shoshana and said, "Shoshana, prepare yourself. A world war is about to begin."

Jordana had never heard her father's voice sound like this before. It was a voice that left a scar in her head. Shoshana listened to the radio, listened to Moshe, and suddenly felt that the two worlds she was living in had merged, becoming one large universe. And that universe was very dark and threatening.

The sun was doing an unusual frenzied dance on the floors that morning, even for Tel Aviv. The dance of the sunbeams was so gay that Shoshana was forced to try and calm them in large jugs of cold lemonade, catching the beams in the ice cubes, mint leaves peacefully floating among them, jugs that she carried from the kitchen to the patio and back again to refill. Moshe, who had awakened from a ravaged sleep with a splitting headache, announced that he was ill and would not be going to work that day. Instead, he stayed home on the cool porch, going over the bills. Toward noon, his friends from the *Haganah* came by to discuss the plan of action that had been issued for the next month. Shoshana turned to the kitchen to fix some more lemonade for the guests, when she suddenly felt a rumbling and the glasses started dancing on the tray.

Jordana was in her room playing with nanny Bracha and her daughter Taly. School was out and the two girls were playing when Jordana suddenly noticed that the butterfly curtains were shaking. For a moment she watched, enchanted, as the butterflies seemed to dance around, playing hide and seek with the sunbeams that burst through them. But the curtain dance was very odd. Strange, she thought, it isn't winter yet, and there is no thunder or wind, so why is the curtain dancing? It was so bizarre that she decided to ask her mother what it meant, and she ran to the kitchen. Jordana met her mother at the kitchen door. She stopped abruptly and noticed the fear in her mother's eyes and Jordana was just about to ask her what all this means when the whole world came tumbling down.

Chapter 8

JORDANA

1940–1941

"Italian Aircrafts bombed Haifa and Tel Aviv; there were over 100 dead" (Tom Segev, *The Seventh Million*, p. 59)

Many books have been written about Tel Aviv, many more about World War II, yet in all my searches, all I could find about the bombing of Tel Aviv in September 1940 was that one sentence. In the bigger picture, it was a spec of an incident, something that came and went with the wind without really leaving an impact. Compared to the enormity of the events of the darkest days in human history, events that coincided with the outstanding struggle for renewed Jewish independence that morning in Tel Aviv just wasn't important. But for us, it was the morning that had changed the course of our lives forever.

Years later, Jordana would recall the dancing curtains, followed by long, red fingernails that raked her grave from her eyes and revealed a bright blue sky where a lifetime ago there had been a ceiling. The red fingernails removed from her face and hair pieces of dirt, white stones and sand, when she suddenly realized that they were her mother's fingers. Shoshana removed stone after stone from her daughter's face as well as from her own. The air was fiery hot, and she was amazed to hear screams and feel salty water trickling down her cheeks, stinging the path they passed, when she suddenly realized that it was she who was screaming, she was the one crying. Strangers were towering over them and removing the destruction from their torn bodies. People whom Jordana had never seen before were carrying her, holding her under her armpits, dragging her and forcing her to stand on her feet that betrayed her and completely gave in. Time was passing in slow motion and she noticed her legs – one was twisted, while the other looked like a gray piece of lumber with dark-red streaks of blood flowing down toward her ankles. She watched it with amazement, thinking how beautifully the colors red and gray contrasted with each other. She wanted to reach down and touch the life that was flowing from her leg when she suddenly began to notice the chaos around her and she was carried away by two men who were as dusty and gray as she was.

"Moshe, Moshe," Shoshana's voice was dark and broken as she cried. "Where is my Moshe?" The world started spinning, then the pain was unbearable and everything disappeared.

When Shoshana came to, she found herself in a white bed, Olga was by her side and her eyes were so filled with sorrow that Shoshana couldn't bear to look at them. "Jordana...." She whispered and Olga hushed her immediately: "Jordana is right here, beside you, in the next bed.... She's injured, but she is alive...don't speak...you both have lost a lot of blood...hush...."

"Moshe?" Shoshana managed to whisper. Olga just shook her head.

And suddenly, Shoshana knew. She knew that her Moshe was gone. She knew not because of the look in Olga's eyes, nor because she realized that they had been bombed, nor because of any other logical explanation. She knew Moshe was gone because she could suddenly hear his spirit.

The Italian aircrafts swept from the sea inland, dropping their packages from hell over the small white city that lay unsuspecting in the sand. One of the bombs fell on the house on Sirkin Street. It was a direct hit and the entire second floor was wiped out. Moshe and his friends, who were sitting on the balcony, were killed instantly. Their bodies were so badly burned and mutilated that Asher later identified his brother-in-law by the watch on his hand. Nanny Bracha and her daughter Taly were also killed on the spot. Shoshana and Jordana were the only survivors on the second floor –they were miraculously saved by the beam of the kitchen door.

Olga heard the bombs fall as if it were happening in the next room. "Stay here with grandmother," she ordered Aya in a harsh voice. "I'm going to see if Shoshana and Jordana are all right." Before Aya could protest, and before Rivka fully understood what was happening, Olga rushed through the street toward her brother's house. As she came close, the horrific scene of fire and destruction was revealed before her eyes and she started screaming: "Jordana, Jordana, where are you? What happened, my God, Jordana, where are you?" Her crying was so heartbreaking, that all the neighbors assembled around her, trying to comfort her while bringing huge buckets of water and throwing them at the fire, shouting instructions at each other, helping to remove the debris and extract her mumbling sister-in-law and niece. Rescue workers appeared, and while some of them took the injured mother and daughter to the hospital, others stopped Olga from walking over the rubble directly to where the body of her brother lay. Olga started mumbling in crazy desperation, clasping her hands to her head, shaking it from side to side. She couldn't believe the sight of horror and death that surrounded her, and her sobs became uncontrollable.

Then the terrified parents of the children in the first floor kindergarten started appearing, rushing down the street, screaming and crying the names of their children, trying to get through the rescue forces and reach their babies lying underneath the stones, the smoke and the fire. The rescue forces did their best to keep the rushing parents away when suddenly, from beneath the rubble, they heard voices crying. Quickly, with all the energy they had left, rescuers and parents worked frantically together until they revealed the first floor. They were overwhelmed with surprise when they discovered that the first floor was completely intact. The cement ceiling that Moshe had insisted on building between the two floors had stood firm and saved the lives of all 23 infants in the first floor kindergarten, including their two teachers. The sight of the live babies emerging from the fire was stunning, and in a strange way made Olga stop sobbing.

Regaining her senses, Olga left parents, babies, teachers and rescuers all crying and laughing together and went to search for Shoshana and Jordana at the Hadassah Hospital in Tel Aviv.

"The leg must go."

"Absolutely not. You must wait another day or two."

"Another day or two can cost her her life! She is suffering, if the fever doesn't drop she will develop gangrene – then it might be to late!"

From a feverish distance, through a cloud of pain and drugs, not fully understanding what she was hearing, Shoshana recognized her father's voice. She had no idea where she was or why. All she could hear was Moshe's voice in the background, soothing her, laughing with her, and then her father talking in a loud, clear and determined voice. "You will not do anything without my permission. And you will not have my permission before Professor Marcus himself sees her. I will bring him here myself."

"Mr. Broytman, please," the strange voice was pleading. "Be quick. It has been almost a week now, the fever is only rising and the leg is black with shrapnel…we must decide by morning, or the leg will finish the job that the bomb began! You don't want your granddaughter to be orphaned twice."

Ish's face grew dark and stubborn. "I will be back before you notice." He was gone, and so was Shoshana. She sank into a deep, hot world of her own.

The Jordan River was flowing beneath her and Moshe was holding her in his arms, keeping her afloat in the cool water. She felt she was slipping away from him and, frightened, clung to his neck. "Don't let go…I'm drowning!" she giggled, half-scared. "I will never let you go," he looked at her, sternly. "And I will always keep you from drowning. Don't you know that I am with you at all times?"

"Yes…you are." She closed her eyes, letting the water caress her back, slowly relaxing and spreading her arms out in the water. She felt Moshe starting to turn, both of them were turning in the water and the whole world became a funny merry-go-round until she was dizzy. Then, all at once, it stopped and she felt Moshe's warm lips on hers. The sensation of pleasure was searing within her when from a distance she heard tears, and she thought how strange it was to actually hear them. The tears were flowing, absorbing her attention, forcing her to abandon the warm pleasure of her dream. Reluctant and angry, she tried to cling on, resisting the stubborn chains that were raising her to consciousness when they suddenly became a clear, familiar voice. "Mom…Mom, wake up," and she knew that it was the one and only voice that could force her to return, the only reason that she would continue living from this point on. Jordana needed her.

She had never before seen that expression on Ish's face. In his big eyes open wide and the twist of his mouth, she read a mixture of relief, deep sadness, joy, and a harsh anger that she had never thought he was capable of. Next to him stood Professor Marcus, the best surgeon in the country. He was smiling. "Welcome back." His voice was warm. "You gave us quite a scare."

"Jordana!" She used all of her energy reserves to utter that one word.

"She's right here, in the bed beside yours. You have a very strong-willed little girl." Professor Marcus chuckled, impressed. "We wanted to move her to the children's wing of the hospital, but she raised such havoc that we had no choice but to let her stay by your side."

Shoshana gazed at the nearby bed. All she could see was a huge, white cast that covered half the bed, a large white sheet covering a tiny body, and a large bandage in the shape of half a basketball covering half of her daughter's face. One eye and half a face were visible, and it was clear that Jordana was sleeping. Her soft blond curls danced around the bandage, bringing the only sign of color and life to the little bed.

"How is she?" Shoshana turned to her father.

Ish struggled to find the right words, forcing himself to sound optimistic. "Her leg is injured and broken, and her face has been burned…but she will be fine. The doctors are taking very good care of her. The most important thing is that both of you are alive."

"Don't let them leave scars on her face…please don't let them leave scars on her face…she is so beautiful…." A pang of pain seared from her ankle through her thighs. "My leg?…" Shoshana whispered, suddenly remembering.

"You'll be dancing with me again in no time." Ish was trying to maintain his cheerful, upbeat tone.

Shoshana slept once more, an unperturbed, healing sleep.

Time is a tricky substance. It tends to have a mind of its own, sometimes creating new order, defying the fact that any well-made clock captures it in a perfect rhythm. During the months that they spent in the hospital, Jordana was certain that time had escaped from between the hands of the clock and through its glass, playing a game of hide-and-seek with her. The timetable that the outside world was living by was completely lost to her, and she calculated the days according to the new routine she lived by: a routine of doctors, nurses and drugs.

"How's our little angel today?" Nurse Tova was Jordana's favorite nurse. Always smiling herself, she knew exactly how to make Jordana happy. Every day, Nurse Tova would come to change the bandages on Jordana's face. It was a difficult procedure, and Jordana hated it. Whenever she saw Nurse Tova approaching with her large aerosol in her hand, the kind that you use to kill insects and bad bugs in the garden, Jordana felt the tears welling up in her eyes. The entire left side of her face was burned and covered with large, ugly brown wounds. The nurse had to spray the wounds every day with a stinging medicine, a remedy that was dangerous to the eyes. Every day, Nurse Tova would take off the bandages and place a round elastic cover over Jordana's eyes. Then she would spray her face thoroughly. A large quantity of the expensive, rare medicine was needed to cover the wounds, and it was sprayed on with a large aerosol container. New, fresh bandages were then placed over her wounds again and she was left alone until the next day. Grandfather Ish made sure that there was always enough medicine for her, using his considerable influence and big bank account to ensure that they kept coming from faraway America.

Shoshana's plea that Jordana's face be healed back to its original beauty was enough for Ish to scan the earth until he found the means to make sure his granddaughter received the best treatment. The fact that a raging world war was continuing, amidst all this, was not about to stop him. Three months after the bombing, Jordana's face was as beautiful and shining as before. The flesh showed no scars. Her leg was a different story. Broken as well as injured, the doctors had to combine medicine with casting. Ish used his influence to make sure that Hadassah's chief orthopedist, Professor Spiro, and his assistant, Doctor Ibner, would come personally once a week to treat Jordana's leg. Doctor Ibner always had a very large pair of scissors in his hand, and Jordana was petrified that he would accidentally cut her leg off. But he was always very careful, cutting off her cast, making her laugh by telling her jokes as he worked, watching as Professor Spiro changed the bandages that were under the cast, replacing the medicines, and then both of them wrapped her leg up again.

The days in the hospital felt interminable. Shoshana and Jordana had no idea what was going on in the world or in the rest of the country, for that matter. They were too busy focusing on healing. Treatment followed treatment, and slowly both mother and daughter started to recover. They had regular visitors. Friends came laden with gifts and chocolate in their arms. Ish would read Jordana stories from the Bible, transporting her imagination all over the land to places where her ancestors had created history. Asher also contributed to the animation of her mind by bringing her rich children's literature every day. Dvora came with pots and pans filled with food, channeling all her love, anxiety and guilt into her cooking, making sure that her daughter and granddaughter were revitalized back to health. Rivka brought the spirits, and sat next to her granddaughter, soothing her with gentle, loving songs in Yiddish that Jordana couldn't understand but knew exactly what they meant. The two of them spoke with their eyes.

A small doll, dressed as a clown, was the gift Jordana loved best. Its body was made of a matchbox covered with black and yellow velvet, from which two arms and two legs dangled out in red silk, finished by blue porcelain shoes and white porcelain fists. A tiny, porcelain head popped out of the matchbox, revealing two shiny red cheeks, big blue eyes and a large, transparent tear rolling down the clown's face. *His legs are broken like mine*, she thought. *Maybe that's why he is sad.*

Shoshana's leg had been saved, but it would take a long time before it would fully heal and she would be able to walk steadily again. The doctors managed to clean out some of the small, black shrapnel that filled her leg, but it left her in a state of considerable pain and discomfort. The fever disappeared during the day, allowing her to be lucid and coherent, but her nights were tainted with hallucinations and fiery dreams. And while the daytime visitors were cheerful and helped time pass on the way to recovery, she couldn't wait for her night-time visitor. When night fell, the hospital became quiet and Jordana was sound asleep, he would come. Every single night he was there, talking to her, laughing with her, conjuring memories of the short but wonderful marriage they had had together. Moshe would sit by her bed and show her the stars, telling her hallucinating mind stories about the world beyond. She was so deep in her conversations with him that sometimes the nurses had to come and wake her because her talking was disturbing other patients. She would wake up, smile at them and go straight back to sleep, to meet her Moshe again.

When morning came, she was exhausted but satisfied, unable to recall the contents of her dream, but she was happy in the knowledge that Moshe had been with her. As much as her mind knew Moshe was dead, in her heart and soul he was as alive as ever.

"You must tell her that her father isn't coming back," Ish's voice was soft but determined. "She needs to know."

"Not yet." Shoshana was as stubborn as her father. "When she grows stronger, I will. Now she must channel her energy into healing. Soon we will be leaving the hospital. Why rush death into her life?" And that was the end of that. Whenever Jordana asked about her father, Shoshana told her that Moshe was away because of the war, until eventually Jordana stopped asking.

One evening, three months after the bombing, Rivka appeared at the hospital carrying a large market basket. She placed it at the feet of the small table between Shoshana and Jordana's beds. Determined, with confident gestures, she started taking out its contents and putting things onto the table. First came out a snow-white tablecloth, followed by a large Hanukah Menorah with Hanukah candles. Shoshana started to protest, saying that the hospital probably doesn't allow candles to be lit on the wards. "Hush, mine kindt," Rivka said in a soothing voice. "A Jewish hospital in Eretz Yisrael, of course you can celebrate the holiday. Where else if not here?"

Shoshana dreaded what she knew was about to come. Focusing on Rivka's hands, her heart started leaping in circles within her breast as she saw the Yahrzeit candles appearing, one by one. They were all there: the large, yellow candle for Shima'le; the twin pink candles for the twins; Leah'le's multicolored candle next to Blooma's dark candle; the gold candle for Isaac; and the white candle for Moshe's still born twin sister. As the candles came dancing out of the basket, bringing joyful color into the dreary, white hospital room, Shoshana's eyes grew bigger and deeper, the blue sky in them that had captured Moshe's heart and soul so many years ago grew stormier than ever. Rivka pulled the last candle out of the basket. It was a beautiful braided Havdalah candle, that is lit to escort the Holy Shabbat to its end, just before a new week begins. The candle was blue and white. Born in Jerusalem, died in Tel Aviv, struggling for the freedom of his people throughout his entire life, Shoshana immediately realized that this was the only candle that could symbolize her beloved Moshe, and no further explanation was really necessary. The blue and white candle represented all the pressure, disappointments, agony and betrayals that had accumulated in her head throughout her entire life, crystallizing them all into one, large ball of pain that escaped her soul and turned into a heartbreaking lament.

"Recite with me," Rivka's voice was calm and clear. "*Yitgadal VeYitkadash…*"

"NO!" Shoshana cried. "He isn't dead!" her voice was filled with a stubborn agony, refusing to participate in Rivka's ceremony. "He is alive in my heart and in his daughter!"

Rivka's voice was soothing. "Hush, child, I know what you are feeling. But you must start living again. It is your duty to carry on the Yahrzeit candle lighting. You must do it for all the generations that brought him to you, and for all the generations that will come of him." And with that, she continued the prayer, "...*Bechayechon Ubeyomeichon ubechayei d'chol Beit Yisrael...*"

Shoshana just kept sobbing. Her bitter sobs crept out the hospital windows, touching the entire city: babies stopped crying, their tears drying up in fear; widows nodded in understanding, their hearts filled with a forgotten longing; husbands and wives suddenly rushed to embrace, clinging to each other's existence; and old people were filled with a sadness that comes from knowing that each day is numbered.

The only one who was left unperturbed by Shoshana's sobs was Jordana. She lay under her sheets, covering her ears and eyes, not understanding a word they said. Caught in a world of her own, she refused to read her grandmother's eyes and denied the presence of her mother's agony.

"How's our little angel today?" Nurse Tova was smiling. Jordana didn't smile back.

"My wings are broken. And look, Tolora is sick, too."

"Tolora?"

"My new doll. Mom's friends, Tola and Ora, bought her for me, so I named her after them – Tolora. Look – she is beautiful…but today she feels very bad."

"What happened to Tolora? Did she catch cold from the other dolls in the hospital?"

"No. She doesn't play with them. They make fun of her because she's an orphan."

It was to become the most important decision Dvora would ever make in her life. With no house remaining to go to, with injuries that needed to be tended and cared for over many months to come, and with a hollow, broken spirit, Shoshana didn't have the energy to think about the future. It was left to Dvora to take matters into her own hands: she announced that Shoshana and Jordana would move in with them in their apartment in Ramat Gan, at least until Shoshana could live on her own again. Since that seemed like a very distant prospect, Dvora knew that Shoshana was, in essence, coming back home. It would be the payment of the debt that she owed her daughter for the years of distance that stood between them.

Ish was delighted. His Shoshana, the apple of his eye, was about to come home again, and his beloved granddaughter with her. He immediately started making the necessary changes. A comfortable pull-out bed was placed in the living room, which was to become Shoshana's room. The extra bedroom, usually designated for guests, would become Jordana's room. It had two large doors that opened wide and would enable Jordana to enter the room with her wheelchair, which the doctors anticipated she would need to use at least until summer. The few belongings that they had managed to salvage from the bombing – as a result of the fire and the looters that swooped through the bombed street like vultures – were arranged in the apartment. Some of Jordana's toys and clothes were saved, cleaned and arranged in her new room, placed among new toys and books that Ish had bought for her. Shoshana's sewing machine, dresser and armoire, as well as the beautiful desk that Moshe used to write all his letters on, were cleaned and brought to the apartment, good as new. The Blooma cabinet was damaged beyond repair, but some of the dishes in it were saved and could be used for breakfast. One of the picture albums was only half-burned, and Ish carefully extracted the pictures that were recognizable, placing them in a new album in Shoshana's room. A small wall decoration of a young shepherd and shepherdess dancing in a field was placed in the bathroom. The shepherd had lost a leg and his face was cracked, but other than that it looked fine.

Finally, the day arrived. Shoshana, her leg still wrapped in bandages, managed to walk out of the hospital on crutches as Jordana, her leg still in a large cast, was wheeled out. Ish and Dvora took them directly to their house in Ramat Gan.

Jordana wheeled herself into her new room, placing the clown and Tolora carefully on the bed. Before she went to sleep, she asked Ish nervously, "Grandfather, where is Tel Aviv?"

"Why, it's right there, beyond the window and over the hill. Why?"

She didn't answer, but she took the pillow that was lying on her bed near the window, and moved it to the other side of the bed. She would never sleep with her head facing Tel Aviv again.

When Shoshana saw the changes her father had made to make them feel comfortable, she was very grateful. And although it was not the house she grew up in, she still felt like she had returned home. "Home is where your heart is," she said to Jordana before kissing her goodnight. "Not where your belongings are." It was a lesson that they both would carry with them for the rest of their lives.

Moshe was holding her hand and they were running on the hot sand toward the water. Splashing in the sea, the cool water eased the pain of the hot sand on her feet. They were both swimming, stroking the water in perfectly coordinated movements when suddenly a huge wave started forming in front of them, growing bigger and bigger, towering over their heads and driving them apart, when, suddenly, Shoshana felt arms pulling her back as the wave carried Moshe away. She cried out to him, warning him, watching him struggle, and she was overwhelmed with a sadness she had never known before, a sadness that was so intense it hit her in the stomach, and she woke up crying.

When she fell asleep again Moshe came back, soothing her and talking to her, and they discussed everything that had happened.

"I know you can take care of Jordana," Moshe was saying, "and I hope you will continue helping the *Haganah*. You must carry on where I left off."

"But how can I?" she begged, afraid. "If the British catch me, who will be there for Jordana?"

"If you don't, and we continue to be murdered all over the world without a proper home of our own, who will take care of Jordana then?"

"For Jordana…" she whispered. "I'll do it for Jordana."

"Yes," he said firmly, "and for all the other Jordanas of our people."

"I will if you promise to be with me."

"I am always with you." He started fading away. "It's time you told Jordana where I am."

"Don't leave," she started weeping. "I can't tell her yet…." and as he turned and smiled she opened her eyes and saw her father's sorrow gazing at her.

"It's time to go to school," Ish told Jordana less than a week after they had returned home. "You will meet new friends and learn many important things. It will be fun!"

"But how will I go? In my wheelchair?" Jordana was anxious.

"Why not? You will be the only one in your class with her own, private transportation in the room – delivering you directly to your desk!"

The next day, they all marched to school. Shoshana with her crutches, dressed in a beautiful blue dress that made her eyes look like heaven, Ish in a pressed brown suit, tall and respectful, steering an excited and scared Jordana in her wheelchair, her leg up in the cast marking the way. The first-grade teacher, a pleasant young woman named Margalit, greeted them with a smile. "Shalom, Jordana, and welcome to first grade. We were waiting for you!" Jordana smiled. Shoshana was relieved, too. She could hear Moshe approving, backed by the approving nods of other spirits, and she knew Jordana would be fine.

Margalit placed Jordana in the front row so she would be comfortable in her wheelchair. "The front row is usually for those who are shorter than others," Margalit explained. "Or for those who need to be close to the blackboard."

The desk beside her was occupied by another little girl. The girl had two very black pigtails, dark black eyes, a beautiful white dress with pink ribbons on the sleeves and a shy smile. "Shalom," she said. "I'm Rachel."

"Shalom, Rachel," Jordana answered. "I'm Jordana."

"What happened to your leg?"

"I was injured when a bomb fell on my house. That's why my mother is on crutches. She was injured, too."

Rachel was silent for a moment, allowing the information to sink in. "Does it hurt?"

"Sometimes. Especially when they change my bandages. But the doctor said that he will take the cast off in a couple of months."

"Is that why you are in a wheelchair?"

"Yes. I have to sit here so my chair won't get in the way…why are you sitting in the front row? You're tall."

"Oh, that," Rachel shrugged her shoulders. "I can't see from the other rows."

Jordana thought for a minute. "Then why don't you just get glasses? My grandfather uses them so he can see better."

"My mother says glasses are for boys. I'm a girl, and my mom says glasses make girls look ugly and I can get them only after I get married. So right now, I'm in the front row."

With Jordana at school, Dvora encouraged Shoshana to take a trip with her to Tel Aviv for the day. The sleepless, dream-shocked nights were beginning to take their toll. Dvora was desperate to bring her daughter back from night to day.

"Let's get out a bit," she said. "We can visit Olga and Asher, and maybe sit in one of the cafés on Allenby Street. It will do you good."

Shoshana was reluctant at first. Shrapnel was still coming out of her leg or flowing through her body, and when the pain seared through her, she found it difficult to walk without limping. But Dvora was determined to build a normal life for Shoshana again, and after Jordana left for school they took the bus to Tel Aviv.

The city was as alive and throbbing as Shoshana had remembered. They paid Olga and Asher a visit, and Olga was beside herself with joy to finally see her sister-in-law walking again. The small apartment was as crowded as ever with people, most of them Shoshana and Moshe's old friends. She was grateful when they treated her like a long-lost friend, without expression of pity or an elaborate mention of her ordeal.

From there they went to a small café on Allenby Street, and Dvora carefully avoided passing through Sirkin Street. The kindergarden had moved to a different location, the house had been torn down and the lot was put up for sale by Ish, with Shoshana's consent. But Shoshana wasn't yet ready to see the vacant lot with the "For Sale" sign, the only remnant from her former life.

As they walked toward the café, they passed a small shop and Shoshana stopped short. In the window sat a beautiful, porcelain doll. The doll looked painfully familiar. It was the exact same doll that Moshe had bought her as a gift for their third anniversary. It even had the same, almost invisible crack on its forehead, a crack that had upset Moshe very much when it arrived from England. One of the sleeves on the doll's dress was missing, and there were slight brown stains where it had been. The shop owner, noticing Shoshana's intense gaze, came out of his shop with a smile. "It's a remarkable piece…original British porcelain."

"What happened to its sleeve?" Shoshana's voice was strange to her own ears.

"I don't know. I bought it this way from a dealer in Jaffa. I think it is a genuine antique. But I will sell it for a good price, if you are interested."

Shoshana stood, transfixed. "It's mine," her heart was crying. "It's no antique…it was a gift from my Moshe…it's mine!" But she said nothing, only gazed at the doll. She felt helpless, tired and very much alone. Dvora, noticing her daughter's turmoil, pulled her gently away. She, too, had recognized the doll. "Let it go," she said, and Shoshana was startled. It was the first time in her life that her mother's voice was soft and gentle. "Let it go. He's in your heart, not in that doll." And with her mother's voice, Shoshana could feel Moshe's warmth in her stomach. She turned away and they left the bewildered shopkeeper on his own. The doll would become a regular visitor in Shoshana's frenzied dreams.

Jordana was enjoying her father's absence tremendously. All of her mother's friends were visiting them, each one bringing her different gifts. She had new clothes, new shoes, new school supplies and new toys. She took her new gifts to school, showing them off to her friends who stared at the new riches she kept bringing. Whenever they asked, she would say, "My father sent me these gifts from abroad. He is far away, fighting in the war and helping the British."

"See what my father sent me," Jordana was holding a beautiful leather bag, made in Egypt. "He is on the Egyptian front, that's where it came from."

"You're lying!" a freckled boy suddenly yelled at her. "Your father is dead!"

"I am not lying!" Jordana was furious. "He IS fighting in the war! And you're an ugly freckle-face!"

"Liar, liar," the boy chanted. "You're nothing but a lying orphan!"

"I'll show you who's a liar…"Jordana exploded, and with a strength that surprised even herself, she slapped the boy hard and launched her wheelchair in an attack against him.

Shoshana was called into school.

"I need to speak to you about Jordana." Margalit, the teacher, sounded very concerned.

"She is doing very well in class," she hurried to reassure Shoshana's worried eyes. "She's very bright. It is definitely helpful that she already knows how to read…and her knowledge of history and the Bible are amazing! I can see that she is very lucky to come from a family such as yours. But she is having a problem with the other children."

"What's wrong?"

Margalit pulled out a drawing. In it, a little girl was holding up a fist at a grown man. They were both surrounded with large, black teardrops. "Children can be very cruel sometimes…some of the children in class called Jordana an orphan the other day. She became so upset that she got into a fistfight with one of them, running her wheelchair at him, screaming that her father is away on an important mission for the British and that he sends her gifts all the time."

The teacher was very direct, but her voice was soft. "Have you told her that her father is dead?"

"Well, I haven't really talked to her about it yet.… I was waiting for her to grow stronger. She's been through so much."

"Indeed, she has. But keeping the truth from her is not helping her. It is making her go through even more." The teacher placed her hand softly on Shoshana's hand. "Talk to her. Tell her the truth. It's better knowing the truth from you than struggling with her friends. And I wouldn't worry too much," the teacher was smiling. "She is a strong little girl already. With your help, she will be all right."

Shoshana stood at the entrance to her parent's bedroom, enjoying the voice of her father as he told Jordana the story of David and Goliath. "You see, my child," Ish was his triumphant self, "true strength comes from within your soul. With the right cause, one can overcome anything!"

Jordana was silent for a moment. Then, Shoshana heard Jordana's voice, and it was suddenly as mature as a grown woman's voice.

"Grandfather, don't tell mom because she will be very upset, but Daddy isn't coming back."

Ish looked into his granddaughter's eyes and saw all the knowledge of the world in them. "What do you mean?" he asked carefully.

"I know he isn't fighting for the British. I know he was killed by the bomb. I know I am an orphan. But don't tell mom yet, she thinks he will be here soon. I don't want her to cry again."

There are moments in life that reveal deep understandings, moments that become the ornaments we wear proudly on our sleeves, showing them off as the pearls that define who we are, what we are made of, and what we have accomplished. These moments become detached from age, place or time. Shoshana knew that she was experiencing one of those moments. Time froze to a halt as she waltzed into the room, hugging her daughter, crying with her, both drowning in the relief of spoken knowledge and in the understanding that they will always guard each other, inseparable through whatever life will bring. From that day on, Shoshana's dreams were calmer and easier to deal with. And Jordana never lied about her father again. She knew he was an angel in heaven and that he was guarding both her and her mother forever, and in a strange way it made her feel very, very safe.

PART II

Morning

1987

The sound of the phone ringing has an extremely annoying nervousness when it blasts off in the early morning hours, especially when your nights are ravaged by uncomfortable necessities, such as rushing to the bathroom every couple of hours and finding a position in bed that is comfortable for the bulge that used to be a perfectly flat belly. This position will be comfortable for a few hours – you'll even settle for one hour– making you toss and turn quietly so that at least your loving spouse, who is of course enjoying a dreamy night right by your side, will not wake up. I finally managed to drift into a quiet slumber when the phone rang so loudly that if I could have, I would have jumped out of bed.

"Hello?" My voice was an angry muffle, so the intruder would at least feel a pang of guilt.

"I think you need to go to The Home today." It was my father.

I was surprised. "Why the sudden change of heart?"

His voice was strange. "It might be your last chance."

I woke up at once. Ben was stirring. "We'll be there." Placing the *receiver back, I leaned on the pillow for one more thought. The time had come.*

The road from Rehovot to the outskirts of Ra'anana was almost empty. It was unusually hot for December, and being nine months pregnant added an inner heat that was beginning to crawl into my head. A beautiful, sunny day, the fields were filled with white daisies and yellow chrysanthemums that were stretching their heads toward a clear, deep blue sky. A few red spots caught my eye.

"Look, anemones!" I pointed them out, excited. "I didn't think that there was enough rain this year for them to bloom."

"How appropriate," Ben answered. "Isn't that her favorite flower?"

I looked at the rainbow of cultured anemones I had bought on the way, and held onto them tightly as if they were a lifeline. They were so perfect, almost synthetic. I sighed. "I hope she likes them."

Will she like them? Will she even recognize me? It had been quite a while since I had seen her, three months to be exact, ever since she had fallen and broken her hip when trying to reach a drink near her bed. She had been at The Home ever since, it was obvious that there was no other choice. My father said she had been hallucinating most of the time, detached from her surroundings and talking to people that no one else could see. She had been talking in her sleep for years, ever since I could remember, having long and detailed conversations with the invisible creations of her dreams. So now she was conversing with them when she was awake as well. That shouldn't be too bad, should it? I hope she recognizes me. I could feel my stomach stirring, not knowing whether it was the baby or my feelings.

The white Subaru glided smoothly up the narrow dirt path leading to The Home. The sun had brought out a parade of insects and bees, humming happily in the surrounding fields. The one-story building lay calmly, stretching its wings under tall eucalyptus trees that were surrounding it like serene, dark guards, casting peaceful shadows on the roof, the garden and the cool stones that led up to a wide brown door.

The reception desk was abandoned and nurses were walking around in silent white shoes. Sounds of sobbing came from the left wing. A nurse said she would be right with us and promptly disappeared. No one else seemed to notice us or care that we were standing there. Grabbing the reception desk list of patients, Ben tried to find her name on the list. It wasn't there.

"Let's check out the right wing first," he said, and we started on our way when a voice called out, "Coming through! Move aside!" Three male nurses were carrying a huge chair that contained a small, old body, covered with a white sheet up to its shoulders. On the shoulders, a small round head, surrounded by thin white strings of hair, was placed, leaning on a pillow. Respectfully, I averted my eyes so I wouldn't invade the privacy of this tiny figure that had once been a functioning human being and was currently being treated by strange large men in white suits, when Ben put his arm around me. "Let's go," he said.

"What? Where? We have to find her first...."

He looked at me incredulously. "We just did," and all I could think was, oh, my God, I didn't recognize her.

"Oh, look, you have guests!" The nurse was talking to the small figure that had already been moved to a large bed by the time we walked in. She was trying to be cheerful in a place that had anything but joy in it. "And they brought you flowers! How lovely." I handed her the anemones, thankful for the color they would bring to this pale, death-auguring place.

"Can she hear me?" I asked the nurse, who was flitting around trying to find a vase. My eyes were stuck on the pale little head, whose eyes were now shut.

"Well, if she hasn't fallen asleep she can. Although I don't know how much she understands."

Ben's hand still on my shoulder, I slowly walked toward the bed. The figure's hand was showing through the sheet, very white, marked with blue streaks of blood vessels running up and down her arm among wrinkles, creating a strange, geographic map on her hand. I gently placed my hand on hers, softly caressing the thin, almost transparent, skin.

She opened her eyes and I was instantly struck by how blue and big they were. I wished someone had told her, when she was still fully conscious, what beautiful eyes she had.

Her eyes were staring directly at me, exploring my face, showing no sign of recognition, and completely filled with the innocence of a child that doesn't know where she is or who is with her.

"Who are you?" She whispered, astonished, and then added very simply, "You are very beautiful." And she fell asleep again. My vision became blurred.

Instinctively, I turned to Ben and stopped short. My mother was standing at the door, and her eyes, as blue as my grandmother's eyes, were filled with sorrow.

Slowly, she walked up to the bed, opened the book she had brought with her – "An Anthology of Israeli Short Stories and Poems" – and started reading out loud.

"Mom, you know she can't hear you," I said as gently as I could.

"It's morning. Morning is story time. And it is Wednesday. That's all I need to know," my mother said stubbornly, and continued reading to the breathing body beside her, refusing to be perturbed any further.

My thoughts were floating. My grandmother had always been there, tending to all our needs, filling the gaps of her life and soul with our physical expressions. I mastered the art of enjoying the engulfing protection of my mother and grandmother whenever I got into trouble, quickly learning how to dance between the two of them, instinctively understanding that whatever relationship I had with one would rapidly crawl into the threads that connected to the other. I never questioned their presence or considered what life would be like without this dynamic.

And now my grandmother was dying. I remembered the story

of my great-great-grandmother's death. Bobeh was a hundred-and-four years old when she walked out one cold December morning in Zichron to feed the hens, as was her custom every single morning since she had arrived in Zichron some eighty years earlier. The path was cold and icy. She had almost reached the henhouse when she slipped, breaking her hip and unable to rise. They found her lying there, in the cold, four hours later. Lying in her bed, Bobeh begged the doctor to save her. "Doctor, please, help me, I want to live!" she begged, but the pneumonia she had developed from lying in the cold was tricky, severe and deadly. Her daughter Dvora, my great grandmother, had peacefully died in her sleep at the ripe age of ninety-eight. My grandmother was now only eighty-two and compared to the standards that the other females of the family had set, she was too young to die.

1942–1947

Routine and structure are two different entities that can easily be confused. Routine is usually conceived as something that brings yawns to a person's life, a boring necessity that leaves the soul of the adventurous yearning for excitement and the soul of the timid afraid of change. Structure is very different. While it supplies the building blocks that may generally be considered as routine, when carefully designed, it has the reassurance of security combined with enough flexibility to be filled with an anticipation of the new and unknown. I had long learned of the routines that my grandmother Shoshana had woven into the well-defined structure that was Jordana's life in the years that followed the bombing. Not only did she put her entire soul into rebuilding their lives, but she recruited everyone around her to join in. From Rivka, Dvora and Ish, to Olga, Asher, and their friends, as well as the entire Zichron community – they all became the village that was necessary to raise

Jordana, and they did such a great job of it that Jordana never felt deprived of anything important in her life.

Morning was story time. Jordana would wake up early and scurry into her grandparents' bed.

"Grandfather, tell me a story," her voice was filled with childish cooing. Ish, already prepared, picked up his Bible. "Let's read about Noah." Ish looked through the Holy Book, and started weaving for the child a colorful, exciting story in Hebrew words that combined the ancient with the new. "Did you know that after he brought destruction on the entire world, the Lord promised that he would never do it again? That's why we have a rainbow, filled with beautiful, shining colors. The colors will bring optimism and kindness into our hearts and remind us that He is always guarding us."

Hearing this, eight-year-old Jordana looked into her grandfather's eyes, and said sorrowfully, "Well, that may be so, but I think He sometimes takes long vacations."

A hearty breakfast was Dvora's way of giving her granddaughter a good start for the day. Ever since Shoshana and Jordana had moved in, her already famous cooking had reached new peaks of richness and taste. Suddenly in charge of an entire family again, Dvora started delegating responsibilities. The household cleaning and laundry were placed in the faithful hands of Aysha, a young woman who came three times a week from one of the villages nearby. Sewing was placed in the fast fingers of Dora, a neighbor who was the same age as Shoshana. Ish dominated the market places, buying vegetables, fruit, spices and meat for the family.

But Dvora didn't trust anyone else with the role of cooking. She considered cooking an art, and art should be left to the artists, definitely not for amateurs, who would take perfectly good ingredients and reduce them into dull, unimaginative dishes. That would be a terrible waste, and Dvora could not stand things being wasted. Jordana loved watching her grandmother cook, and as she grew older, she was allowed to help. She would sit in the kitchen, watching in amazement how Dvora's confident, dexterous fingers transformed wheat, water, eggs, sugar and milk into a breathtaking dough that Jordana was allowed to cut into small ribbons. The ribbons – *farfalach* – went into a large pot of boiling water, filled with herbs, spices, a whole chicken and vegetables. The fragrance of the soup and the sweet scents of apple pie, embraced with cinnamon and vanilla, would make the stomach sing with anticipation. Dvora enjoyed watching Jordana eat, and she was certain that her healthy cooking was the reason why the child was quickly growing, strong and happy like a weed. The smells of her grandmother's dishes bid her farewell in the mornings and waited to greet her when she returned from school, filling her heart with the sense of home and security. If there was a shortage in eggs and meat throughout the land, Jordana never knew it. For her, a house full of food and warmth was natural. She didn't realize, until many years later, how much effort, time and money her grandparents and mother had invested into every single spoon and fork she put into her mouth.

School was a short, ten-minute walk away, and Jordana would go to school every day with Rachel. Although Shoshana desperately tried to remind the two energetic girls that there was a certain appropriate behavior that was expected at school, it was clear that Jordana was a natural born leader of mischief. The minute her cast came off, at the end of first grade, she discovered the joy of jumping, climbing and running wild – usually directly into trouble.

"Rachel, look," she whispered one day in class to her friend. "Niva has brought apples again and she is hiding them inside her table…she is eating them secretly…."

"I forgot my pencil sharpener at home, but she won't let me use hers," Rachel whispered back.

"She never shares anything…" Jordana sighed. "If the teacher found out, she would punish her…but Niva is always miss goody-pants for the teacher…. Why do I have to sit right behind her?"

"I know. She's really mean. I asked her what was written on the board and she refused to help me, laughing and calling me short-eyes. She really annoyed me. So I can't see well, at least I'm not as ugly as she is!"

Jordana's eyes were twinkling. "I have an idea...."

Two minutes later, Niva's carefully braided hair was unsuspectingly tied to the back of her chair.

"Children, who knows how to solve this equation?" The teacher turned to them.

Niva raised her hand in excitement and was called to the blackboard. The crash of the chair falling down with Niva on top, screaming, and all her half-eaten apples rolling out of her desk and scattering on the classroom floor to the children's delight, was definitely worth the hour of detention that Jordana and Rachel received.

Wednesdays were adventure days. After school, Shoshana and Jordana would hop on a bus to Tel Aviv. Their first stop would be Shula's Salon, on Keren Kayemet Street. Shula was a stout woman with high fluffy hair and eyes that always twinkled with laughter. Jordana would watch, wide-eyed, as her mother's hair would be thoroughly shampooed, trapped into large, colorful rolls and placed under what seemed like a hot air cooking machine. Just as Jordana was certain that one more minute would make her mother bake like a cake, Shula would take the rolls out and Shoshana would glisten like a matron.

From Shula's Salon they would go to Rivka, who was now living with Olga and Asher. The gentle old woman spoke only Yiddish, but she and Jordana communicated with some help from Shoshana and with the emotions that floated in their eyes. She always had a small gift for Jordana, and as she gave it to her she would smile and say: "*Mine Sheineh Yingaleh's Meidaleh*" – My beautiful son's daughter.

Asher carefully monitored Jordana's reading, guided by his own knowledge and the knowledge of his fellow writers. Their small apartment was always filled with the hustle and bustle of poets and writers, and Jordana loved listening to their conversations as much as they loved having her around. She nicknamed them with family titles. "Grandfather Ziskind" filled her imagination with tales of the Land, giving a clear vocal interpretation to the stories she read in his *Anthology of Hebrew Literature*. "Brother Nathan" made her laugh with amazement at his glorious, sometimes sarcastic, poems. But "Uncle Saul" was her favorite.

"So, little orphan Jordana likes to read stories?" Uncle Saul asked her.

"Yes, I do…and I like your poems, too."

"Really? Where have you read them?"

"Uncle Asher reads them to me…."

Enjoying Olga's milk and cookies, Jordana and Saul engaged in a discussion about the meaning of literature and its influence on civilization. The following week, after she had told Uncle Saul about how she was doing at school, he placed a carefully wrapped gift in her hands. "This is from me to you, little orphan Jordana," he said. "You are a very bright girl, and I want you to have this. I have inscribed it for you."

Opening the package, Jordana discovered a small, blue-leather covered book inside. *Uncle Tom's Cabin* read the title in bright, brisk Hebrew letters, and on the first page, in fine, strong handwriting, Uncle Saul had written:

"To Jordana, one of the bravest little girls I know. I am giving her this book so she can read and learn about other brave people. Sincerely, Saul Tchernikovsky." It was the first edition of the translation of *Uncle Tom's Cabin* into Hebrew.

Jordana was delighted. "Thank you, Uncle Saul! I promise to read it carefully!"

The next stop would be Axelrod's library, where Jordana would spend the favorite part of her day. She adored books. Every Wednesday, Jordana would take two books from the library, usually following Asher's recommendation, return them the next week and would take two new ones. At first, Axelrod would grumble, saying that there was no way such a young girl could devour so many words in only seven days.

The library was a small room filled with dark brown shelves that extended from the floor all the way up to the ceiling. The shelves were bursting with books and adventure, and Jordana loved watching Axelrod slide his long ladders across the floor so he could climb up and bring down the wondrous pages of stories. He would carefully question Jordana about the books she returned, making sure she had indeed read them.

"So, you managed to finish *The Three Musketeers* in one week, did you? Which one of them is your favorite?"

"Why, D'Artagnan of course." Jordana's answer was excited. "He is full of real fire! I like that."

"Is that so? Interesting...I suppose good manners doesn't count for anything these days.... And what would you like to take today?"

"Well...I was hoping to read *Jane Eyre* and *Wuthering Heights*... Asher said I would enjoy them...and...." She hesitated.

"Yes?" Axelrod's eyebrows met his thinning hairline.

She spoke quickly, before she lost her nerve. "Mr. Axelrod, I usually finish both books by Sunday, and then I have to wait until Wednesday to read again, so I was hoping you would allow me to take three books." There, she had said it. She took a deep breath and waited.

Axelrod gave her a hard look, then said in a strange voice: "Hmm. Against all library rules...and against my better judgment... books are a serious matter, young lady!" And looking straight into her eyes, he added, "I will allow it this once, and we shall see what happens.... If you don't prove you have read all three, you will be back to two in a heartbeat!"

Beaming, Jordana left the library with Jane, Cathy and Agnes held tight in her arms. And although he seemed to be bothered, she was certain she had caught Axelrod smiling secretly to himself. After she returned all three books the following week, and had answered all of Axelrod's questions about the legacy of the Bronte sisters to his satisfaction, she left with a pile of Daphne Du Maurier's writings for the following week. From that week on, she was always allowed to take three books. It was as if a rich treasure box of stories was rapidly filling and floating in her head, bringing life to the sentences that created them, invading her dreams with a mixture of adventure and romance. Whenever she awoke with the taste of book dust in her mouth, she knew she had once again dreamed a story.

Ice cream at Whitman's on Allenby Road was the last stop before they returned home to Ramat Gan. Vanilla in her mouth, her eyes fixed on the first lines of the first book, her mother securely sitting by her side on the bus, transporting them to Dvora's dinner and Ish's stories, Wednesday was definitely her favorite day of the week.

I was waiting patiently for my mother to finish reading when a doctor walked in.

"It will be soon now," he said. "A matter of hours. It would be wise to…well…make the necessary arrangements."

"I already did." My mother was struggling with her emotions, trying to sound calm and practical. "I know what she wants, it has always been her wish." Surprised, I asked her what she meant. My grandfather was buried in a grave along with another hundred people who had perished from the Tel Aviv bombing, with no place for intruders. Knowing my grandmother, she would have wanted to be right there with him, a wish that would be impossible to fulfil. Where else could she be?

"Isn't it obvious?" and as Jordana said it, I knew. Shoshana wants to be in Zichron.

The yearly cycle was also filled with traditions that were a constant in Jordana's life. Hanukah and Pesach were spent in Zichron with

Bobeh, Zeideh, Aminadav and Nechama and all the cousins. Hanukah was dedicated to the mushroom search. With long sleeves to protect her from the cold and from the scraping bush, and a large basket in her hand, Jordana would search the nearby hills for Pitariches – mushrooms that turned into hot, thick soup and fragrant, rich pies under Nechama's careful supervision. Pesach was devoted to the large family *seder* and spring. A month before Pesach, Bobeh would buy a kid that would grow into a fine young goat, that would ultimately be served at the Pessach dinner. Terrified by livestock, Jordana would go into hiding every day at five o'clock in the afternoon, when all the village goats and mules came back to the stalls. She would reappear only for dinner, when the separation between animals and humans was once more intact.

"I can't understand how the great granddaughter of our people's greatest pioneers can be afraid of some silly, harmless goats," Bobeh scolded Shoshana. "We must do something."

"Well, maybe if we let her play with the kid she will see that there is nothing to be afraid of." It was a week before Pesach, and Shoshana had arrived in Zichron early to help out with the holiday preparations. "It can't hurt to try."

The following morning the kid was left in the yard and Jordana was sent to feed it with a bottle of milk. Carefully, she approached the small animal and thrust the bottle held in her hand forward to the eager mouth. Watching the kid suck gratefully gave her a sense of curious control and security, and she dared herself into petting its head. Bleating happily, the kid licked Jordana's hand and time was lost until she heard her mother calling her for lunch. The love story between Jordana and the kid continued to develop. When Pesach evening came, and Aminadav wanted to take him to the butcher, the kid was nowhere to be found. "I won't let you take him!" Jordana was yelling in tears. "He is my friend!"

"Jordana, be reasonable...."

"No! He's mine!" The havoc she created was so intense that

Nechama finally caved in and, with a strange smile in her eyes, promised to find something else to be served at the *seder*. Saved by Jordana's howling, the growing kid sat securely in Jordana's arms during the entire *seder*. That was the last time they let her tend to the livestock.

Summers were also spent in Zichron, when Jordana was sent to help out with the harvest of the grapes. The fierce sun blazed on her head and the grape gathering sent large drops of sweat that trickled down her face, stung her eyes and dripped down her back. She would walk amidst the grape vines, her gaze caught by the summer dance of the ripe purple fruit, her hands blue from work, wishing that the interminable job would finally end so she could go home, only to discover she was longing for summer again.

The only routine Jordana refused to adhere to was her mother's regular visit to the cemetery. Once a week, Shoshana would go to visit Moshe. Talking to him at night was not enough, and the firm look in Dvora's eyes made it crystal clear that she couldn't talk to him openly when Dvora and Ish were around. So she spoke to the grave, enjoying the understanding acceptance that the few people at the cemetery always had on their faces when they saw her.

But Jordana would never join her. "It's only a stone," she would say defiantly. "There's no point in talking to it. He can't answer anyway." When Hanukah came, and Shoshana would carefully light the Yahrzeit candles, Jordana would stubbornly stay away, refusing to have any connection with the spirits that were part of their lives.

But they stayed there, secretly, quietly, patiently waiting for the day she would return to them.

Shoshana was busy with charity and *Haganah* activities. Her days were filled with embroidery, donating beautiful handmade tablecloths and shirts to charity organizations, and helping them raise funds for the needy. Carrying on from where Moshe had left off, her nights were spent transferring messages and hanging up posters for the *Haganah*. She had built around herself a wall of total devotion, based on Jordana's needs, charity and the *Haganah*, a wall so sturdy that it left no crack for suitors, and if there were any to be found in sight, it was too thick to penetrate.

But there are some events that are greater than any time or place in which they occur, bigger and stronger than the physical expression in which they transpire, affecting people in places and times far and distant from their being. Living in Palestine during those days saved Shoshana and her family from being subject to the horrors that the rest of the Jews knew. While they were relatively protected in the Land of Israel, the Holocaust and its dire consequences managed to seep through into the Land and its inhabitants even before the war was over, before all the horrific stories came out, creating a deep sense of urgency.

The Yishuv was engaged in its greatest battle of all: the intensifying battle to create an independent State for the Jews in Israel.

"We must fight with the British against the dark forces of the Nazis as if there is no struggle between them and us over Jewish independence," said David Ben-Gurion, the leader of the Zionist movement. "And we must continue struggling with the British over Jewish independence as if there is no World War. World War I gave us the Balfour Declaration. World War II will give us a Jewish State."

Answering David Ben-Gurion's motivational call, the Yishuv did everything in its power to assist the British Empire. While thousands enlisted in the British Army, participating in the defense of Palestine and the struggle against Nazi Germany, the internal debate about how the Jews of Palestine should continue their struggle for independence reached new heights.

"It is shameful, that's what it is." Dvora's voice was as harsh as usual. They were sitting one night in the living room with Ofsey, Olga and Asher. "Our best men are willing to risk their lives in fighting this war, and the British are so arrogant that they don't want our help."

"Well, we'll take whatever we can. Even the jobs they are giving us will be of use some day soon." Olga was her practical reasoning self.

"Poof! What good is building bridges and driving trucks of supplies when what we really need is to learn how to fight?"

"I'm afraid it's worse than that," Ish had a strange expression on his face. Ever since the Jaffa riots that had almost ruptured his heart, his opinions had been very definite. "The British will never keep their promises to us…they are only using us, and the minute they don't need us anymore, they will forget our help. Even now, when so many Jews are being slaughtered in Europe, they won't give our people refuge, keeping the gates of Palestine closed to those who manage to escape. The Irgun was wrong to cease its attacks against the British until the war in Europe is over."

"Well, the *Haganah* managed to convince most people," Asher reasoned. "But some think we should continue our struggle for independence with more drastic measures. I have a feeling that the Irgun won't stay quiet for long…."

"If Moshe were alive now, he would probably join the Irgun – those freedom fighters will stop at nothing until they succeed in scaring the British out of here." But even as she said it, Shoshana's voice wasn't convincing. The Irgun was an underground organization that preferred armed struggle over negotiations, and many considered them no better than mere terrorists. Ofsey jumped.

"I'm not so sure he would, and neither are you," he said. "Terrorism is not our way. Especially now, since the Jewish Brigade has finally been created. Soon we will be fighting side by side with the British, and they will realize who is loyal to them, and will swiftly change their attitude."

"We tried that one world war ago, remember?" Shoshana's voice was bitter.

"Our real battle will begin after the war is over, when we demand a state for the Jews that has, for so long, been promised to us. Mark my words," Ish concluded. "When that day comes, we will be facing Arab hostility once again. And there will be no other choice but to fight. They will never come to terms with our presence. As long as Jews and Arabs both claim this Land, there will never be peace."

The sorrowful determination in his voice penetrated the walls, crept over to the bed where Jordana was wide awake in the dark, drinking in every word. It was the only time of day when she could hear the adults around her discussing "the situation," as they referred to it, for Shoshana forbade any disturbing discussions in Jordana's presence. As far as Shoshana was concerned, Jordana's life should flow in a sequence of well-known, secure events. Even the ongoing attacks by the Arabs were part of reality, a situation that was an ongoing threat one had to learn to live with. As long as she could separate between what was going on in the world and Jordana's protected life, Shoshana felt secure. That bubble burst in her face the day Jordana announced that she was joining the Ramat Gan Scouts.

Youth movements were flourishing throughout the country, teaching the children everything from Jewish heritage and myth to the practical details of survival, such as building tents, exercising order drills and mastering Morse code signals. It was a perfect, seemingly harmless, social activity that secretly trained the youth in methods of defense, and it was spreading like mushrooms after the rain. When the scout movement decided to open a branch in Ramat Gan, Jordana was determined to be among the first to join.

"You are not going. You are too young, and besides – are you really prepared for all the field trips and the arduous activities?" Shoshana was all but saying that Jordana was too spoiled to join the demanding youth movement, but she was, in reality, masking her real concern: exposing Jordana to the scouts would mean exposing her to *Haganah* activities at a very young age.

"I will be fine! Even Rachel is going, and her parents never let her do anything!" Jordana was in tears.

"You can go, I am sure you will enjoy it," Ish's interference was very unusual.

"Mom?..."

Shoshana was silent, avoiding her father's eyes. Finally, she looked at Jordana and said "All right, all right, go. But I want to speak to your *madrich*, group counselor, tonight."

"You can't keep on wrapping her up in cotton wool," Ish's voice was very soft as he spoke to Shoshana after Jordana left. "She must be part of who we are in this land, and she must be aware of the situation and realize the consequences of being a third-generation Sabra."

Shoshana was silent.

"Would you prefer it if she went to one of the political movements? The scouts is the only movement that isn't connected to one of the extreme underground groups...."

"It's connected to the *Haganah*!" Shoshana's voice was loud. "She's too young to be involved in these activities! Hasn't she been through enough?" Shoshana's eyes were filling with tears. "What's the rush? She will learn it all soon enough...."

"You already tried to protect her from the hard truth once. It was almost a disaster. Don't make the same mistake twice." And as he spoke, Shoshana was trying very hard to deny the warm presence of Moshe in her heart, whispering gently, "For all the generations that will come of us."

"I didn't want you to come," my mother was shaking her head.

"I know. But I'm glad I did."

"Why?" her voice was filled with pain. *"Why would you want to remember her like this? So small and vulnerable.... This is not who she has been to us...I wanted to protect you from this memory."*

I looked at the figure that was lying on the bed and at my mother. They had always been like two segments of the same whole. A Yin and a Yang, complementing each other, so strongly connected that I sometimes wondered whether my mother's umbilical cord had really been cut. They were the matriarchs of my life, and they both seemed huge. In any normal country, a woman's life would be filled with personal stories, some of which might, for a brief instant or incident, touch history. Ours is not a normal corner of the world. Between the two of them, my mother and my grandmother were a walking narrative of modern Jewish history, and I could never make a distinction between their own story and the story of my People. Nor did I want to. I was fully aware that if I even tried, my very foundation would be destroyed and I would be worse off than someone who disappeared: I would become insignificant.

> "Be prepared to fulfill your duty,
> Loyal to your country and homeland,
> At all times you shall help others,
> Your duty, scout, you shall keep with devotion!
> Always be prepared…"

Singing the scout's anthem with fervor, Jordana loved the scouts' activities. It was the only place where her energy was not only approved of, but actually expected. They would invent and build strange devices made of wood, reeds and ropes; they would hike the fields surrounding the city, learning about plants, birds and earth; they would spend hours in drills, exercising marches and communicating with their peers in Morse code signals; and they would listen to the underground radio, "The voice of the *Haganah*," to find out more about what was going on in the Land.

Like her mother before her, and with the increasing commitment of mature understanding, Jordana was becoming part of something bigger, something that was precious and was hers to guard and cherish with her life, something that was a result of the lives and actions of people who surrounded her – her mother, her grandparents, her friends and her family of farmers in Zichron.

Although she didn't realize it at the time, they were the living presences in her life and the only ones she was willing to acknowledge, refusing to regard the spirits that were quietly guiding her at Moshe's prompting. But whether she admitted it or not, they all took part in tying her heart very strongly to the Land.

As Ish had predicted, the end of World War II increased the Jewish struggle for independence. The world was in transit, and Holocaust survivors from all over Europe were trying to make their way to the Land of Israel. The British were as determined as ever to undermine any Jewish aspirations of freedom, refusing to let the refugees enter the Land. Under the intense leadership of the Zionist movement, Jewish refugees continued to come, some managing to be smuggled in under the noses of the British Army, others being caught and sent back to devastating concentration camps in Cyprus. At the same time, the diplomatic effort to gain recognition of the right of the Jewish People to have a state of its own was as harsh as the physical resistance which continued to sweep the Land.

"Who is it?" Shoshana wouldn't open the door to a stranger, no matter how hard he knocked.

"An unknown soldier," came the whisper. Recognizing the name that the Irgun fighters had adopted for themselves, Shoshana quickly threw the door open. In front of her stood a small man, his clothes torn and dirty, his eyes darting around with careful suspicion.

"Quick, come in," she said, locking the door behind him. "Where...?"

"The Ramat Gan police station...they discovered us...."

"How many were hurt?"

His voice was rushing as he spoke. "Most of us got away in the truck...I must meet them at the orchard, they will be waiting for me...Dov was badly injured, I don't know if he managed to escape...the British Police are after us. But we gave them hell, and we stole their ammunition straight from the police station!" His smile was weak.

A pounding knock on the door interrupted them. "Open up! Police!"

Shoshana hid the stranger under her bed, carefully covering it with a large, hand-made quilt.

"Yes? How may I help you at this late hour?" Her voice was surprisingly calm when she opened the door to find two British police officers standing there.

"Are you alone?"

"No. My daughter is sleeping in her room and my elderly parents should be home any minute. Would you like to take a look?"

"Are you sure there is no one else here?"

"Really, I should think not!" Shoshana's voice was insulted. "It's the middle of the night, who do you think I am? Who do you think I would have here?"

They obviously felt awkward. "A group of Irgun terrorists attacked the police station tonight. We killed two of them and captured their leader, but unfortunately some of them managed to get away."

"Well!" Her voice was cold and scolding, "I certainly hope you catch those no-good terrorists! Bringing shame on us all, that's what they're doing!"

"Just the same, do you mind if we search the apartment?"

"Oh, by all means, do, I wouldn't want any of them hiding in here! Just make sure you don't wake the child."

Convinced by the firmness of her tone, the policemen rapidly looked through the rooms and left.

Closing the door behind them, Shoshana turned and found her daughter standing at the bedroom door, staring at her. She could have sworn there was a twinkle of admiration in Jordana's eyes. And behind that twinkle, for one brief moment, she saw Moshe smiling, too.

When the full extent of the Nazi horrors was discovered, and the British were fed up with the ongoing resistance in Palestine, the debate about "the Jewish Problem" finally became an international issue that would be decided upon by the very young, newly founded United Nations. The proposal presented to the UN would be known as "The Partition Plan" – a plan to divide the Land between the Arabs and the Jews. This plan was welcomed by the Zionist movement as enthusiastically as it was rejected by the Arab nations. On November 29, 1947, the UN assembly gathered to vote on the fate of the tiny Land east of the Mediterranean Sea.

It was as if an invisible glue had stuck every single person in Palestine to the radio. Ish was sitting by the table, talking to himself, as he carefully calculated the votes that were cast as the United Nations were deciding the fate of his family. "We only need two-thirds of the votes…only two-thirds." Dvora was in the kitchen, fiercely cutting farfalach as if her life depended on it, her breath held in and her forehead covered with tiny drops of sweat. Shoshana was sitting in the corner, desperately listening for a sign from Moshe and the spirits, who annoyingly decided to stay silent. Carefully watching them, Jordana knew that she was witnessing a moment that would some day coalesce with all the morning stories her grandfather had told her. The tension in the air was a thick, cutting silence. Then, after some time, Ish raised his eyes to them and for the first and only time in her life Jordana watched her grandfather sob uncontrollably.

"We've got it…." he mumbled through his tears. "We have a State…*Shehecheyanu Vekiyemanu Vehigianu Lazman Hazeh*!"

The blessing for something that was long awaited was drowned in an uproar of joyous cries making their way from the street into the little apartment, and before Shoshana could stop her, Jordana ran out to join the celebrations.

"Let her go," Ish was trying to overcome his sobs. "Let her celebrate tonight. Tomorrow will bring war. But tonight, tonight she should celebrate. And so should we." Regaining his composure, he grabbed his wife and daughter by the waists and led them to the celebrating crowds, dancing and singing until dawn.

Finally she was lying peacefully. Breathing slow, deep breaths, her face was smooth again without a wrinkle in sight, wrinkles that had appeared only a couple of years before. She was finally approaching clear waters, all the turbulence of her life smoothed away. I had never seen her so peaceful before, not even in her sleep. She was always busy, always a flow of energy, a movement, a curiosity, a need to be fulfilled.

And she had always talked in her sleep. Not just mumbling words or separate sentences, oh, no – she had full conversations, discussions, and even arguments, in her sleep. Trying to convince the imaginative creatures that filled her slumber, she would talk very clearly, presenting well-developed arguments based on figures and facts. A real debater.

None of that energy was left in her now. She was so serene, she almost seemed vulnerable. Her eyes were shut and she was completely silent, her face projecting the contentment of a very young infant who has just been fed and placed on his mother's breast for a nap. Instinctively, I reached out and caressed her thin, white hair, quietly singing the lullaby she had sung to me for so many years.

"Sleep, sleep my baby,
Sleep, sleep my child...."

For a split second, her eyes opened, she looked at me and smiled. A minute later she was gone.

Noon

1987

"There is one more thing we must do." As careful as I tried to be, my mother could see right through me.

"No." My mother's voice was stern. "I have never done it before, and there is no reason to start now."

"Tonight is the first night of Hanukah. Can you honestly tell me you think it's a coincidence? We must." I was as stubborn as she was.

"Well, I don't know how to do it and I don't want to know."

"Fine. Then I know exactly where to find what I need." And with that I kissed Shoshana's forehead, said one last good-bye and turned to leave. Dropping Ben off at work, I was headed toward the one place I knew I should go: my grandmother's house in Ramat Gan.

The house was dark and the air was thick. I had struggled with the key to the door, that seemed to have temporarily sided with my mother who had refused to come or to have anything to do with this, leaving me to deal with all the preparations on my own. Opening the windows, a breeze of fresh, orange-scented air rushed in, struggling with the stifling scent of dusty books, aging upholstery and rotting wood. The morning air in the small, hidden alleyway in Ramat Gan during December was always cool and fresh, welcoming in the green scents and chirping sounds of the surrounding gardens while shutting out the smoky, noisy rush of the main streets. It was a quiet haven of countryside in the middle of the city.

The small apartment was filled with memories that were quietly residing in the floorboards, the shelves and the walls, waiting to be revisited. Years of listening made them very familiar, but touching them now gave me an awkward, confused sense of visiting a well-known friend while invading a sacred privacy. I took a deep breath and went to work, trying very hard not to let the objects surrounding me drown me into a reminiscing gaze.

The entrance opened to a long hall that was also the library. Its length was covered with brown shelves, old and crouching under the heavy burden of literally hundreds of books that were placed on them. In the middle of the wall, a door led into the one bathroom and I could see the small window placed above the sink. Stripes of yellow, half-peeled old tape created a strange decoration on the stained glass, a hurried maze of crisscrosses that a child would scribble on paper. A small wall decoration of a young shepherd and shepherdess dancing in a field was hanging near the window. The shepherd had lost a leg and his face was cracked. Three large bags filled with sand were placed under the sink, and voices that I hadn't experienced were very vividly filling my head....

1947–1962

"You can't go out. What happens if there is an air raid?"

"Then I'll be safe and secure at Rachel's shelter. They have one at home, too."

"Why don't you invite her here? You can both finish that tablecloth you are working on and if there is an air raid you will be together in the hall."

"Mom, we have done that a million times already!" Jordana's voice was impatient. "Just this once, I want to go to her! I need to get out a bit!"

And, feeling her father's eyes on her back, Shoshana reluctantly agreed to let Jordana visit Rachel. A full-blown, bitter war for the survival of the very young independent State of Israel was going on: shootings, bombings and fierce battles were taking place throughout the country, and Jordana was on her way to Rachel's house to bake brownies.

The day following the UN decision brought two important events: the Arabs began launching attacks on the entire Jewish population in the country, and Jordana joined the *Haganah*.

She had heard so many rumors about the *Haganah* that when it actually happened she was surprised by its simplicity. Expecting a dark room with a single light bulb, a lonesome table with only a Bible and a gun on it and a very mysterious, romantic atmosphere, Jordana was taken aback when she and her peer scouts were taken to an open field nearby. There was no dark room, table or gun anywhere in sight. The group counselor, a tall, good-looking youth named Zvi, gave them a piece of paper with the *Haganah* vows written on it. They all stood in line and read out loud:

"I hereby solemnly swear that I am willingly volunteering to the Hebrew Defense Organization of Eretz Yisrael, called the *Haganah*..."

And that was all. They were told that they would be called upon when necessary, a need that transpired in a single call one evening to come to *Haganah* headquarters at the Ramat Gan fire department and fulfill the very prosaic duty of waiting for messages and preparing sandwiches for the fighting troops.

The months that followed the UN decision brought vicious

attacks on the Yishuv that was preparing to declare the establishment of a Jewish State the minute the British left. The Arabs did everything in their power to revoke the Partition Plan, declaring that they would never recognize the Jewish State that was about to be born. Snipers, car bombs and explosives were used in an attempt to create chaos and fear among the Jewish settlers, bringing destruction and devastation to the land.

"It will be the end of us." Ofsey was very worried. "We must wait and find a way to achieve an agreement."

"What? How can you say that?" Dvora was busy serving cake and tea to the family gathering one Shabbat morning. Winter was sprinkling its last refreshing drops and spring was beginning to display its colors.

"Hundreds have been killed! Endless attacks on villages, snipers on the roads, you're bombed in your home and shot at when you travel! Jerusalem has been completely cut off, people there are starving, and now even the United States has withdrawn its support for the Partition Plan! Do you really think we can survive?"

"We have our local forces, the *Haganah* is striking back…this is what we have been training for, if we give up now and let this historic chance slip by, it will never happen again!" Shoshana's voice was very passionate, speaking with pathos and desperation.

"Shoshana, be reasonable. If we declare independence, the Arab nations will join the local Arabs, and the current situation will look like a field trip! There are hardly 650,000 Jews in the country. Most of us are broken survivors of the Holocaust, with no army training whatsoever. We barely have a handful of ammunition and supplies…this is all we will have to help us survive the attacks of five Arab nations who have well equipped, trained armies and millions of people!" Ofsey was as desperate as she was.

"What are you suggesting?" Asher and Olga joined the conversation.

"We must get the United States back on our side, and I believe we can do that if we negotiate a truce with the Arabs."

"So you think we shouldn't declare a State?"

"All I'm saying is that we must wait. After a truce, and with international support, the right time will come."

"No!" They were all surprised by Ish, whose fist landed violently on the table. "We have waited enough! Do you really think that the Arabs will ever agree to our presence here? They openly declare that they want to drown us all in the sea. Well, we'll give them a fight to remember! After everything our people has been through," he looked directly into the eyes of each and every person in the room, "we have nothing more to lose."

It wasn't an easy decision. After long debates, endless discussions and tiresome arguments, the members of the Jewish People's Council agreed: The State will be declared on May 14th, 1948, at four P.M., eight hours before the British Mandate over Palestine was due to end.

"We are hereby honored to invite you to the Declaration of Independence," the invitation, secretly sent to three hundred and fifty leaders of the Zionist movement, was very simple. "That will take place on the fifth day of the Hebrew month of *Iyar*, at the Tel Aviv Museum. We ask you to please keep the contents of this invitation secret. You are requested to arrive at 3:30, wearing dark, holiday clothes. Sincerely, the People's Council."

Despite the request for secrecy, the news of the upcoming declaration spread like fire through dry weeds. For the second time in less than half a year, everyone was in the streets or glued to the radio. At the Tel Aviv Museum, the building that was built almost forty years earlier by Meir Dizengoff, the preparations were feverish. A long stage was erected in the main hall, on it a long table covered with a festive blue tablecloth. The wall was covered with two long flags, the flags that had been the symbol of the Jewish People: a white cloth with two blue stripes and a large blue Star of David in between. In the middle of the wall, sitting confidently between the flags, and directly above the Council member's heads, a large picture of Theodore Herzl was hanging, watching approvingly as Ben-Gurion declared the establishment of an independent Jewish State, to be known as the State of Israel.

As they were listening to the declaration, followed by the *Shehecheyanu* blessing, and what seemed like thousands of voices singing, Shoshana embraced Jordana, Ish and Dvora were holding each other and they all joined in singing the national anthem:

> As long as deep in the hearts
> The soul of a Jew yearns
> And towards the East,
> An eye looks to Zion,
> Our hope is not yet lost
> The hope of two thousand years,
> To be free people in our land
> The land of Zion and Jerusalem.

When they had finished singing, Ish turned to take the yellow scotch tape that was waiting on the table while Shoshana turned to a pile of bags. Handing half to Jordana and taking the other half in her arms, she said, "Come, while grandfather tapes the windows, we will fill the bags with sand. They will help save us when the bombs start to fall." The urgency in her voice proved to be accurate: Egyptian airplanes bombed Tel Aviv the following morning. The State of Israel, less then twenty-four hours old, was fighting for its life.

Everything Jordana knew about the war was derived from the radio. Shoshana refused to let her set foot outside the house, fearful that she wouldn't be close enough to a shelter if she needed one. Deprived of the outdoors, the scouts, and even school, Jordana's time was divided between embroidery, reading and friends who were always welcome as long as they came to the house and stayed there. The long hall was transformed into a shelter, packed with sand bags, water bottles and preserves. After long, agonizing months of being shut away from the world, Jordana felt she was losing her mind, and started nagging her mother to let her go out. Rachel's house was close enough, Jordana begged her mother. Ish tried to convince Shoshana that there would be no harm in letting the child leave the house for a few hours, especially since Rachel's family had an in-house shelter as well. Her heart heavy, Shoshana allowed Jordana to visit Rachel one afternoon. The girls planned to bake brownies. Glancing at the clock every few minutes, praying that time would pass and Jordana would return already, Shoshana was just about to go and drag Jordana back home when the sirens went on.

Panicking, she started toward the door when, to her surprise, Ish grabbed her arm and struggled to keep her from leaving.

"Stay put!" She had never heard his voice so dark with concern. "You can't go out now!"

"But..."

"No but! She's safe in a shelter! What good will it do if you are hurt?"

His words were cut short by the sound of an explosion that was louder than usual. Shoshana, paralyzed by the horror that was filling her soul, was silently calling to all her spirits for strength. An hour later she was still staring transfixed at the door, and did not utter a word, when suddenly the sirens announced that the danger was over and Jordana walked through the door. She was not allowed to leave the house again until the war was over.

December was coming again and Hanukah with it. Rivka, who was over ninety years old, knew that her days were numbered and she wished to visit Shoshana before she died. Rivka, Ofsey, Olga and Asher made a special trip from Tel Aviv to Ramat Gan.

"This is for Jordana. I won't be around when she marries, so please give it to her on her wedding day." Shoshana looked at the gold bracelet that Rivka had placed in her hands. It was one of the three bracelets that Rivka had left of the original seven that Isaac had given her when they first came to Jerusalem. Her eyes reflecting the deep gratitude she felt, Shoshana watched as Rivka turned to prepare the Yahrzeit candles. She was surprised when a new candle was added to the ever-growing number of candles that were blazing on the table: a tall khaki-colored candle was towering over the others, its light surrounding and protecting them. "In honor of our fighting soldiers" was the only explanation that Rivka gave.

Jordana was enclosed in her room, her nose deep in a book, her ears shut, her mind absorbing every word that was uttered in the living room despite her strong efforts to stay away.

"She refuses to take any part in the Yahrzeit ceremony. She thinks it's meaningless. She doesn't believe in spirits."

Still a dark ocean, Rivka's eyes were confident as her gaze lay upon her daughter-in-law. "Don't worry," she reassured Shoshana. "She will return to them when the time is right."

"But why doesn't she understand how much they are guarding her? Why won't she come to the cemetery with me to visit her father?"

"Why, she doesn't have to," Rivka's voice was calm. "That's what she has you for."

The hall led to the living room that was large and heavily furnished: a cabinet was graciously standing by the wall; a dining table surrounded by eight heavy chairs was placed in one corner, a desk in the other, and an old Singer sewing machine by the window. Not exactly certain what I was looking for, I turned to the desk and started my search.

The first thing I noticed was a black leather notebook that was concealed under a bunch of papers hidden in the top drawer. Its pages were lined with the yellow stains of time. Opening the notebook, I discovered it contained a treasure: in it, written carefully in beautiful, round letters that looked like curls on a baby's head, were expressions of love quoted from the Bible, Shakespeare, Bialik and Wordsworth. I recognized the fine handwriting immediately, as if it had been present in my life forever. It was the handwriting of my grandfather. The notebook had been left intact, fresh as a recently shared secret, containing quotes that Moshe had carefully copied in his fine handwriting and had hidden from the intruder's eye. My eyes fell on a poem.

> *Though nothing can bring back the hour*
> *Of splendor in the grass, of glory in the flower,*
> *We will grieve not, rather find*
> *Strength in what remains behind*
> *In the primal sympathy*
> *Which having been must ever be*
> *In the soothing thoughts that spring*
> *Out of human suffering.*
> *In the faith that looks through death,*
> *In years that bring the philosophic mind.*
> *(William Wordsworth)*

If ever one of us is left alone, my love, we will always find strength in the love we leave behind, soothing thoughts that spring from our suffering, a future based on our faith, love and understanding. It is our Jordana's heritage, and fate cannot be escaped. It is a future that she will embrace.

Moshe, Tel Aviv, 1935.

Dated long before he had died, I was completely flabbergasted by how much he had understood about my mother's life. His insight was frightening.

Or was it, as he had written, a matter of fate?

The war for Israel's independence ended in triumph after a long year of bitter battle and grave loss. The first years of the State brought challenging times of growth, everyday struggle and ongoing defense, a very rapid and energetic environment for a maturing adolescent girl. The family was changing, the old generation leaving way for the new. Rivka was gone, Ofsey had died of a heart attack, and, one evening when he was over a hundred years old, Zeideh called all his relatives to Zichron and parted from them before he sank into a sleep from which he didn't wake. Before she knew it, Jordana was graduating high school and about to join the Israel Defense Forces.

Graduation was a festive event, and Jordana prepared for it like a princess. Scanning fashion magazines, Jordana insisted on having a new dress for graduation night and a new bathing suit for the graduation beach party the following day. Watching her daughter's excitement, Shoshana reflected on Jordana's toddler years in Tel Aviv, remembering how beautiful she was even then and how proud they had felt. She had grown to be an intelligent young woman, and her beauty was breathtaking.

"Please keep her safe," Shoshana was talking to her spirits. "And happy." And as she watched Jordana leave for the big event, she could see Rivka and Moshe standing by the door, nodding their hallow heads, smiling knowingly.

The beach party was packed with people. Graduates from different schools all gathered to celebrate their last days of freedom before enlisting into the young Israeli Army. Every eighteen-year-old, man and woman alike, were to complete a couple of years of army service before getting on with their lives. It was a duty that they were committed to by the ongoing necessity of defending their State. The party was one of the last chances they would have to be together before they spread to the four corners of the Land, serving in different units on different army bases. Jordana was waiting for some friends when she heard her name being called.

"Jordana, Shalom! How are you? I haven't seen you in a long time!" A girl was walking up to her.

"Shalom, Edna, I'm fine, thanks. How were the final exams?"

"Oh, forget those. I'm getting drafted next Thursday and I couldn't care less about school right now. I want you to meet a friend, David!"

Turning to the dark figure walking toward them, Jordana was paralyzed. Dressed in uniform, he was tall, with coffee-brown eyes, black hair and a shining smile. For the first time in her life she saw her grandmother's spirit standing by, smiling, and she could hear Rivka's voice, "This is your heavenly match, my child."

It can't be, she was thinking as the family matchmaking tales of her grandparents and parents came flooding into her mind, I don't believe in these things.

"Shalom." The figure was looking at her, exploring her eyes and her soul with an intensity that made her uneasy. "My name is David and you will be my wife."

To her horror, she burst into tears and fled.

He followed her and insisted on taking her home. They talked all the way from Tel Aviv to Ramat Gan, and Jordana was growing increasingly uncomfortable by the minute when she started to realize that she liked this young man. The next day, when he came to take her to the movies, she told Ish to open the door and say she wasn't home while she hid in her room. Ish took one look into his granddaughter's eyes and smiled. Opening the door, he said very loudly, "Shalom David, I am Jordana's grandfather and she is waiting for you in her room."

They were inseparable ever since. He was already a sergeant in the army and she was just starting her service. Against all rules and regulations, he came to visit her at boot camp, bringing her chocolate, Dvora's cakes and crisp, salty watermelon seeds.

"You have to leave," she begged him when he showed up one

night. "The corporal will catch us and then we'll both be in trouble."

"Then I'll say that it's all right by a sergeant's order," and she was astonished when he actually lived up to his word and got away with it.

Against all odds, and to Shoshana's pure amazement, Jordana enjoyed her army service tremendously. The same girl who would cry during scout training, who needed special food on field trips, who always fled back home after one night in a tent, was suddenly enjoying the basic, hard life that the young army required. Stationed at Army Headquarters in Ramat Gan, the everyday operations and information were exciting and interesting. When she was summoned to the officer's course, she did not hesitate for a minute. Five months after she was drafted, Jordana was off to a base in the middle of the country for a course that would make her one of the first women officers in the Israel Defense Forces.

Training in parallel to the men's course, and on the same base, the women officers' course was strenuous and demanding. Obstacle courses, cleaning rifles, practicing at the shooting range, guard duties, navigation studies, training in a variety of defense and offense methods – for the first time in her life Jordana felt so independent, vibrant and free that even the cold water of the showers and the stale food in the kitchen could not ruin her happiness.

And she was back to her old tricks of mischief.

"Yizhar, is that you?" she whispered to the sound of chirping that floated through the window in the test room. She was in the middle of an exam in topography, and she had no idea what the correct answers were.

"Yes…."

Quietly, in barely a whisper, she read a question to the voice on the other side of the window. The correct answer floated in a moment later, and the test was on its way.

"Thanks for saving my life today," she laughed when she met the owner of the voice at the canteen.

"No problem, that's what cousins are for," his smile was broad.

"Stop! You're not supposed to admit you're my cousin – all the girls think you are the most handsome guy on the base, I want them to be jealous…."

David, who was already a seargent and a student of engineering at the Technion in Haifa, visited Jordana regularly. When she came home for weekends he would always be there. Fearing Dvora's reaction more than what might actually happen if she left them alone, Shoshana wouldn't allow them to sit in a closed room and Dvora would patrol the hall every few minutes, making sure that no misbehavior seeped into the house. When night fell, Jordana would join Shoshana in her room, while David slept in Jordana's bed, his dreams filled with the spirits of her past that were floating around like masters of the house.

For David had long become familiar with the family figures of the past and felt so comfortably at home with them that even Jordana didn't mind. Shoshana revealed them to him one cold December night. Jordana was still at her officer's course and David came to bring Shoshana a holiday gift. "I came to light the Hanukah candles with you and eat some of Dvora's delicious *sufganiyot*," he said gaily.

"The best doughnuts in the land!" Ish was beaming. Shoshana smiled, took David by the hand and led him to the living room.

"It's time you learned some of our family traditions," she said softly, and turned to light the Yahrzeit candles.

Mesmerized, David watched as the rainbow of candles came to life. Shoshana explained each candle, taking him on an unknown journey through the past. When all the candles were ablaze, and her stories were floating around them, Shoshana looked into his eyes and saw everything she had always hoped to see in her daughter's eyes.

"What are you thinking?"

David shifted his eyes from the candles and, looking at Shoshana, took her by surprise. "Can we please add one more candle?"

"Of course…what…for whom?"

"My father."

After finishing the course, Jordana was sent back to army headquarters, this time as an officer. She became the chief administrating officer for a young general named Yitzhak Rabin, who called her "Little Officer" and took her with him to inspect different army bases around the country. Time flew and David started talking about setting a wedding date. Her life would have been perfect if not for a large dark cloud that was lurking in her peaceful yet exciting skies: David's mother.

David came from a very large family that had arrived from Russia at the beginning of the century. The first child to be born in the Land of Israel, Ish would tease him and call him, "a new immigrant." His family had done very well and all his uncles and aunts, ten on his father's side and four on his mother's side, were suffocatingly close. The first time he took Jordana to meet them, a parade of uncles and aunts invaded David's little room where the two of them sat chatting. They all came with the same excuse – they were looking for something that they were sure would be in David's room. One forgot his hat, the other was looking for a book, the third misplaced her coat and the fourth needed a pen…when they all started appearing for the second time saying how enchanted they were by the fine girl. David looked at Jordana and, laughing, suggested that they go to a movie. On their way out, one of the uncles came up to Jordana.

"You are the granddaughter of Ish Broytman, correct?" he asked, a twinkle in his eye.

"Yes, I am."

"Well, give him this." He placed a piece of paper in her hand:

it was an old deed declaring that Haim Taub, David's uncle, had purchased lumber from Ish Broytman and owed him a large sum of money. "Tell your grandfather that we are even: instead of money, he is getting one of our sons!"

The only one who was immune to Jordana's charms was David's mother, Beylla. Ever since her husband had died, some three years earlier, she felt she was losing control of her firm grip on David's life. He had gone and wasted his time at the officer's course, he had decided to study engineering instead of joining the family business, and now he had found this girl, who was not only an orphan but was threateningly smart and educated. Slowly, she tried to drip poison into his mind.

"She is an orphan. Who knows how she was raised normally without a father," Beylla said one day.

"So am I," David laughed. "And her grandfather is a great father figure. I talk to him a lot."

"Well, it's a shame you won't have a family with her."

"What?!"

Beylla hesitated before talking. "I don't know how to tell you this, but I heard from a reliable source that Jordana can't have children. They had to remove her uterus because of the bomb."

"Don't be ridiculous. She was hurt in her leg. That's a pretty different body area…."

"A woman that is trying to become an officer is sure to be controlling and manipulative. Are you sure you can live with that?"

"Mom, stop." David was growing tired of his mother's endless nagging.

"Well, all I'm saying is that they have no source of income, no one has been working in that family for years, and she knows you come from a rich family. You do the math."

Storming angrily out of the house, he refused to talk to her for three weeks and returned only after Shoshana convinced him that a mother is a mother, no matter what she says.

Finally, Beylla tried the ultimate weapon. She invited Shoshana over for tea.

"Jordana is a fine, bright young woman...." She began spinning her web around Shoshana's heart. "She will be a wonderful wife."

"Thank you. I certainly hope so. We all adore your son."

"Yes...And they look so happy together!"

"Well, Jordana loves David very much."

"Such a wonderful girl.... It's really a shame...." Beylla sighed and waited, in anticipation of Shoshana's response. Shoshana innocently walked directly into the trap.

"What do you mean?"

"Well, to be honest – and believe me, this hurts me very much, after all he is my son – I just think that...well, Jordana is too good for him."

"Excuse me?"

"He's still so young and immature, he doesn't really know what he wants...and so many years of study ahead of him...it would break my heart to see Jordana working hard to earn a living for both of them...."

Shoshana was silent, not fully understanding where this conversation was going.

Beylla waited for her words to sink in.

"Do you think...perhaps...you could convince Jordana against the marriage?"

Shoshana had no idea how she managed to bring the awkward meeting to an end or how she had arrived home. All she could remember was the blurry sight of colors that shone through her tears on the way.

David was so furious, he went straight to Jordana and, falling on his knees, said: "Marry me. Set the date now."

"But...."

"No buts. I love you and want to spend the rest of my life with you."

"Your mother...."

"You're not marrying my mother. You're marrying me. That is, if you're ready...." His voice was filled with a longing that sounded familiar, the kind of love that had been embedded in a curled handwriting that she had secretly read when her mother wasn't around.

"I'm ready."

The treasures that were hidden in the desk drawers were more than I had bargained for. I placed my grandfather's notebook in my bag and continued to search. I was certain she kept a diary somewhere, maybe a book of family traditions, something I could use as a guide. The events of the day and the bag of memories that was attached to them started to creep up on me – I could feel the baby stirring and I felt heavy and drained.

Deciding to lie down for a few moments, I first glanced through the rest of the desk drawers. Documents, letters and a single picture album were scattered in them in a pile of mess. I grabbed the picture album as if I had discovered an unexpected guest.

My mother had always been careless with pictures, never bothering to document our lives in picture albums or diaries, so I was eager to see what it contained. Opening it, I was surprised. It was my parent's wedding album, which I had never seen before.

My mother was smiling at me from the photograph in a white wedding dress covered with delicate lace and decorated with a large white rose on her shoulder. The rose and a single gold bracelet were the only accessories she wore. My father, in a dark tuxedo, was embracing her. The pictures revealed a joyous wedding, and I could recognize most of my late aunts and uncles when their faces were still young and happy. Long tables adorned with braided bread, food, fruit and wine were standing proudly near the walls. A tall, white wedding cake was being cut by the bride and groom. One of the aunts and my mother were carried on shoulders, connected only by the tips of a handkerchief. Another aunt was singing to the clapping rhythm of the others. Beylla was sitting at a table, and I recognized the sour smile that had barely left her face in all the time I knew her. Even Shoshana looked beautiful, swirling with my father on the dance floor. From looking at the pictures, no one would ever have guessed the monumental effort Shoshana had put into making Jordana's wedding the happiest day of her life.

A thin, aging piece of paper was attached to one of the pages: a dowry list. It was divided into two parts: the bride's side and the groom's side. I learned that all my father's uncles had pitched in to buy a refrigerator, an oven and a full dining set for twelve. Beylla had agreed to give them a small stipend to live on until my father finished the university. Shoshana had bought all the pots, pans and linen the young couple would need. The cost of the wedding itself was divided between the two mothers. Shoshana had to sell some of her belongings in order to contribute her half.

The last picture was of my parents in a decorated car, with strings of ribbons and cans with a large "just married" sign trailing on its back. They were both smiling, and I was wondering if I was the only one to notice the strange, anxious look in their eyes.

Shoshana had never spoken to Jordana about sex. Her own experience was still a haunting memory, but she was determined not to let her anxiety transfer to her daughter. She ferociously protected Jordana from Dvora's few remarks about "how good girls should behave," fearing that the inhibitions Dvora had implanted in her soul would somehow stain Jordana's life as well. When Jordana was a child, and asked how children are born, Shoshana only said "through love," and Jordana had to be content with this unsatisfying answer.

But now that Jordana was getting married, there was no escaping such a discussion. To her surprise, Jordana only laughed.

"Don't worry, mom, I know everything I need to know," she said. "And I'll discover the rest."

"But how…?"

"What do you think Nechama and I have been discussing every time I went to Zichron? She told me all about it."

Not exactly sure what Nechama had revealed, and which family examples she had used, Shoshana kept silent. In spite of her outward confidence, Jordana was anxious on her wedding night, an anxiety that only Shoshana detected in her eyes. When they returned from their honeymoon, Shoshana asked matter-of-factly, "Well? Is everything all right?"

Relieved, Jordana laughed. "Of course it is. Don't worry, I've discovered that I'm more like Rivka than like Dvora!"

Well, as long as you're not like me, Shoshana thought wryly, and that was the end of that.

Jordana didn't really know how much of Rivka she really had in her. During those first years of marriage, all my mother was willing to admit was that she had inherited Rivka's capacity for deep love and devotion, working hard so my father could study, losing herself in passion, never questioning the path they were taking. When David told her that they had an opportunity to travel across the ocean to the United States so he could study for his PhD, she discovered that she had also inherited Rivka's implicit excitement for roaming. Without hesitation, they packed everything they had, including me, and they were gone. The only thing she was certain she had left behind was Rivka's spirits. But she was wrong.

Evening

1987

I awoke with a startle. It was growing dark, and the small apartment was filled with evening shadows that danced around the walls, joined by figures and scenes that drifted out of the pictures that were all around me. I still needed to find what I was looking for, and I slowly got up to continue my quest. My mouth was dry, and as if in protest, the baby was kicking violently. I went into the kitchen for a glass of water when, stumbling over the small kitchen table, my grandmother's recipe book fell to the floor. Fumbling through recipes that were organized in alphabetic order, among detailed recipes for chicken soup, farfalach, kugels, knishes, latkes, sufganiyot, and even salty watermelon seeds, I finally found the one I had been looking for. It was the last recipe in the book.

"Recipe: Yahrzeit."

There it was, with every single detail. The colors, the texture of the wax, the height of each candle and the people they represented. The different shades of ink revealed that several descriptions for new candles were added as the years had gone by.

I vaguely recall as a child Shoshana lighting the Yahrzeit candles, her lips whispering the mourner's Kaddish as they shone. I hadn't repeated this ceremony since I was a child, and I was determined to revive each and every detail. I knew I must hurry to the candle shop before night fell. As I turned to leave, the recipe book held firmly in my hand, a postcard fell out.

It was dated 1965, stamped in the U.S. and written in Hebrew. "Dear mom, we thought you would enjoy this picture. Liat has grown so much! Inbar is becoming more beautiful by the day and is a handful.... Love, all of us." Turning the postcard, there was a cheerful picture of three little girls. I recognized myself and my baby sister. Next to us stood another girl who seemed to be about my age and looked very familiar.

1962–1987

Agreeing that they were leaving Israel for a well-defined goal, Jordana and David were determined not to become too comfortable in their exile. They refused to buy a house, invest their time in securing good jobs, or even buy anything that would tie them to this faraway land. The only steadfast connection that they made was through family: when my father's grandfather left Russia to come to Israel, his brother decided to move to America. Life in California had been good to them: they were very well-off and were respected leaders of the local Jewish community. They were delighted to welcome my parents and their baby daughter into the American branch of the family, an embrace that soon after changed my life.

While David studied, Jordana worked at the Israeli Consulate so they could make ends meet. Both of them missed home terribly. To Jordana's great surprise, not only could she hear the family spirits very vividly, but she found herself looking for their presence behind every corner. Reluctantly, she discovered that everything reminded her of home: the Californian breeze was sea-scented, the grapes and oranges were covered with landscapes that seemed like they had come straight from Zichron, and the Shabbat candles always filled the room with a fury of light that pointed to the east.

The holidays were the worst, bringing a painful longing that was almost physical, causing my mother's eyes to fill with tears. Their first Hanukah in the U.S. was approaching when she received a devastating phone call from Shoshana, informing her that Ish and Dvora had both died within the same twenty-four hours. Still refusing to have anything to do with the Yahrzeit ceremony, Jordana caught herself by surprise when on the first night of Hanukah that she celebrated far away from Israel, she lit a separate, additional candle.

"What's that for? I thought you didn't want to have anything to do with lighting Yahrzeit candles," David asked, confused.

"I don't. And I'm not," she said fiercely. "This is…different…as long as we are in exile, I will light a candle to show us the way home."

And like Rivka before her, she caressed the light that was dancing with the unseen spirits that filled the room.

This wasn't the only time that Jordana surprised herself. She was also taken aback when one day she came to the realization that she was unable to stop herself from filling my head with stories of a faraway place that I couldn't even recall.

"Remember the roller-coaster we rode at Disneyland?" she said. "It went up and down a large, fake mountain, covered with fake white snow.… There is one mountain just like that in Israel, it's called the Hermon. Here, let me show you the map…."

"Did you enjoy the Rose Parade? Do you know that your grandmother's name is Shoshana, which means Rose in Hebrew? Let me tell you where she was born …."

"Really, that pony is more afraid of you than you are of him. You shouldn't be afraid of animals, did I ever tell you about the time I fell in love with a goat…?"

Israel was a million miles away, but in my imagination it was right there, a land filled with tastes, sounds and scenes that were so alive I never once doubted that they belonged to me, waiting patiently for me to come back.

Studying, working and raising a family all at once is no easy task – or a short one. Time was passing, and my parents were learning how to adapt to their new environment and culture. The day had arrived for me to begin kindergarten.

Daddy Frank's Kindergarten was a magical place, and I loved it. The playground was filled with toys and swings, and there were always new territories to explore and enjoy.

Kim was my best friend. Together the two us plunged into stories, creating for ourselves an entire world of dolls, trolls, paper cut-outs and costumes. Everyday at Daddy Frank's, we sat next to each other, never leaving one another's side. Although we were very young, we nonetheless possessed the wisdom of knowing each other's strengths, weaknesses, desires and dreams. We dreamed of the same little boys and, with an innocence that is reserved exclusively for four-year-olds, we decided that it didn't bother us one bit, and that we would simply share them.

But the best times we shared together were, without doubt, during the winter holidays. On Halloween, we would dress up together and go trick-or-treating, first around Kim's neighborhood and then around mine. She would sleep over in my room, beds filled with candy bags, telling each other stories and eating chocolate and marshmallows until we felt sick, our hearts were bursting with the joy of sweetness. I didn't mind that we never stayed at Kim's house – her mother, a young divorced brunette, would always have a "hot date" that required that she stay out late – but it was OK, because my father would always prepare the best, biggest pancakes you could eat the morning after.

Hanukah and Christmas were definitely the peak of our joy. We exchanged gifts – I always placed a gift for Kim underneath her gigantic tree, while Kim always gave me a gift on the first night of Hanukah. Kim loved to watch the Hanukah candles, and Jordana always let her light some of her own. I adored the red stocking that was placed on Kim's mock chimney place. Kim's mother would place another one, with an embroidered "L" on it, saying that, "Maybe Santa will have something for you, too, even though you're Jewish." And he always did. We learned each other's songs – Kim singing Hanukah songs in broken Hebrew words that made my eyes cry with laughter; then it was her turn to laugh when I mastered Christmas carols. So we enjoyed each other's holiday as well as our own, and although we were practicing each other's faith without any awareness of the fact, we both knew exactly what our own heritage was and weren't the least bit confused.

We were six years old, and about to start first grade, when one day Kim told me that she was very excited – her mom had found a new father for her. Although I congratulated her with all my heart, something dark was hovering in the air, something that I was too young and protected to understand.

I lost Kim that year. She vanished. I kept asking Mom to invite her, and each time the excuses were the same: "She's too busy to play," or "Since they moved to their new house, it's too far away." I tried to be smart, saying, "Well, then, schedule something with her for a few weekends from now!" But the answer was still no. Weeks passed without a sign from her. I couldn't understand what had happened to her, and was certain that something horrible was preventing her from calling me. Finally, I learned enough reading to find her phone number in the book. When I called, a man's voice answered. "Kim can't play with you any more," he said. "She has new friends to play with. Good, solid Christians. Don't ever call her again." And he hung up. For the first time in my young life, I knew how it felt to have a broken heart.

"I'm not going to school!" I cried, deeply hurt and not understanding why they were being so stubborn. "She hates me! She's making the other children hate me!"

"Who are you talking about?" Thinking that my refusal was a result of my painful conversation with Kim's new father, my parents were confused.

"The teacher! She hates me…."

"Come on, be reasonable. Why would she hate you?"

"I don't know! Yesterday she hung everyone's drawings on the wall, except mine!"

"Did you ask her why?" My mother was desperately trying to maintain a rational tone.

"Yes…she said there was no more room!"

And I could see my parents exchange knowing glances.

The following day, my father took me to school and disappeared along with my teacher behind the principal's door. The next thing I new he came out, pale, and took me home. Feverish discussions over the phone and into the night resulted in me being taken to a new school the following morning – the Jewish day school that was five minutes away from our house. Years later I had discovered what had happened that day: since I was the only Jewish girl in her class, it was obvious that my teacher was an anti-Semite. In the interest of avoiding a scene, the principal agreed to fire her, but he couldn't guarantee that such "unfortunate incidents" wouldn't recur. "After all, Mr. Taub, we live in the real world," the principal said. In a demonstrative act my parents removed me from the school.

But this statement came with a price tag – my previous school was a public school, and my parents didn't have the means to send me to the expensive private Jewish day school. Calling upon my father's influential family, who was genuinely appalled by the story, the Jewish community rallied and raised the funds that were necessary to give me what would become my first formal, solid, Jewish and Zionistic education. Attending the Jewish day school for three years, until we returned home, I studied Hebrew, Torah, prayer, Jewish history and holidays. Combined with the foundations of family, peoplehood and Zionism that my parents nurtured in my soul, my Jewish education became the water that nourished my roots, and gave me a flowing confidence that I belong to an incredible, supportive nation, and that as long as I was in need, I would never, ever be alone.

"She's absolutely beautiful. She looks a lot like Rivka." My grandmother Shoshana was holding my baby sister while I was dancing around them. She had come for a visit, her arms filled with gifts, and her mouth filled with songs and stories. I was so excited, I didn't let her out of my sight for one minute.

"So, Shoshana, I hope you have rested enough after your flight. Are you ready to go out for ice cream?"

"Oh, yes!" she exclaimed with childish excitement. "I love ice cream…."

"Well, this is America. They have more than thirty-four flavors here. You can eat to your heart's content." My father was smiling. We were all eating banana splits when she promised, her mouth filled with chocolate and raisins, to personally pick me up from school the next day.

When school was over, I was surprised to see her standing there with a large package in her hands.

"What's this?" I was secretly hoping she had brought me some more gifts. I glanced into the bag. It was filled with long paper wraps, each one of them hiding something within. She just smiled and refused to discuss her mystery bag until we arrived home.

"Grandma, what's in the bag?" I persisted.

"Do you know what we will be doing tonight?" she answered my question with one of her own.

"Of course. We will be lighting the Hanukah Menorah, in memory of the triumph of the Maccabim." I proudly recited what I was carefully taught at school.

"And what can you tell me about that triumph?"

"Well…" I hesitated, "the Greeks tried to force us out of Israel, and they wanted us to stop being Jews…but Jehuda the Maccabi called everyone to come and fight them, and he won!"

"That's right. And why do we light the Hanukah Menorah?"

"Because the oil that was enough for only one day miraculously lasted for eight.…"

I could see that this answer did not satisfy Shoshana, so I racked my brains, trying to think of what else the teacher had said. "And…also…to remember."

"Good girl. Now think: what are we remembering, besides the triumph?"

I thought long and hard. "The Maccabim who fought for all of us?"

"Close enough," my grandmother chuckled. Then, in a serious voice, she added, "We remember that if our hearts are strong, no one can make us leave our heritage. It is the light of our identity, so we are remembering it through light."

"But these aren't Hanukah candles!" I exclaimed when she opened one of the long paper wraps to reveal a beautiful, blue-and-white braided candle.

"No, they're not. These are Yahrzeit candles and we will light them tonight together with the Hanukah candles. Let me tell you why.…"

That evening, when the candles were blazing, I could detect the presence of all the people my grandmother had told me about. When my grandmother finished lighting the candles, my mother suddenly came out of the kitchen and added one of her own. Surprised, Shoshana looked up and was about to say something when Jordana quickly turned around and disappeared back in the kitchen. She stayed away the rest of the evening.

This was the first and only time I had witnessed the Yahrzeit ceremony. Later, back in Israel, my mother wouldn't allow it, leaving my grandmother to continue the tradition on her own, waiting for the day it would be rediscovered.

The candle shop owner looked at me strangely when I handed him my list. It was a small, crowded shop, filled with a dense aroma that was a mixture of lavender, apples, peaches and wax. Feeling the full weight of my pregnancy being engulfed by the thick scents, I started to feel dizzy. He read the impatience in my eyes.

Silently, without a word, he collected the candles I had specified and placed them carefully in a bag. He continued to watch me with a very peculiar expression as I was preparing to leave, and I felt compelled to explain. "I know these are not Hanukah candles, but, you see, may family has a special tradition…."

"I know," he said, and to my surprise, added, "You are Shoshana's granddaughter. She has always bought her candles from me. Now it's your turn."

Holding tight to the large bag of candles, I hurried back to my parents' house, where I knew Ben would already be waiting, helping my parents with the funeral arrangements and getting ready for the traditional lighting of the Hanukah Menorah. Night was falling and soon it would be completely dark. I had managed to purchase everything the recipe had called for, and the bag felt heavy in my arms, as if all of the spirits were sitting inside it with their candles: Shima'leh's yellow candle, the twin pink candles, Leah'leh's multicolored candle and Blooma's dark candle, Isaac's gold candle, the white candle of my grandfather's stillborn twin sister and his own blue-and-white braided candle. A purple candle was there for my father's family's

Yahrzeits, and a khaki candle representing all the soldiers of Israel. These had been the candles that my grandmother had lit every Hanukah, year after year, until now. Today, the day she died, there was one more candle in the bag: it was a beautiful, thick red candle, and it had the fragrance of a rose.

I tried to prepare myself for the argument I knew my mother would have waiting for me when I arrived home. I hoped she wouldn't make too much of a scene. I never really completely understood why she had refused to perform the ceremony that was clearly so important to her family. I suspected it had something to do with her need to feel independent, an aspect of her life that she could control, without being dictated to by events and people that were larger than life. Now that my grandmother was gone, I knew it was my duty to reinstate the ceremony back into our lives, despite whatever my mother might say. I could hear the spirits telling me so.

I reached the house and my mother opened the door for me when my water broke.

> "The mountain air is clear as wine,
> Filled with the scent of pine trees
> Floating in the wind of dusk
> To the sound of bells
> And sleeping rocks and trees surround her,
> The city that is captured in a dream,
> The city that sits alone
> And a Wall in its heart.
> Jerusalem of Gold...."

The song had traveled from Israel all the way to California and had become the reason for the competition among all the second-graders at school. It was a new song that had been written in Israel and was rapidly becoming more important than anything else we learned at school. Jerusalem, the city that became by force divided between Israel and Jordan during the War of Independence, was always a prime subject for discussion. The half that Israel controlled was its capital, but the most important Holy Places for the Jews were in hostile Jordanian hands, out of reach and a source of longing. Our Hebrew teacher, Mrs. Tenenbaum, was determined to teach us the words of the new song about Jerusalem in Hebrew. Spring was coming, and we all tried to master the difficult words.

"It's a song that describes our longing for our eternal capital," she declared one day in a very formal, festive voice, "and you should all memorize it."

"How come you don't remember it?" One of the girls teased me. "You're an Israeli, you should know it better than all of us."

But I kept confusing the words. Another girl who had come from Israel that year seemed to have no difficulty remembering the song, and it was driving me crazy.

"We will be singing 'Jerusalem of Gold' at the end-of-year celebration. I will choose a soloist to sing one of the verses, and the rest of you will sing the chorus," Mrs. Tenenbaum announced one morning in June. "Prepare yourselves for auditions next week."

I just had to be the soloist. Running home, I was anxious to have my mother help me memorize the words, but there was no one to help me rehearse. My parents were too busy with other worries that were hanging over their heads like huge, black rocks.

"I have to go back home," my father's voice was tense. "They will need all of us." It took me a minute to understand that when he said home, he meant Israel.

"The planes are full. Everyone wants to join the Army."

"I told the Consul that I must go back, but he seems to think we are both needed here more."

"I know. And the situation is getting worse. Today we were told to prepare homes for children that might need to be evacuated. I can't believe this is happening."

The tension in the air had been building up for quite a while, and it was so thick that my seven years of life couldn't escape it. Something terrible was happening, Israel was being threatened in a way I couldn't comprehend. The Arab nations were once again threatening the Jewish State. Busy at the Israeli Consulate, both my parents would disappear for hours, coming home only for a short rest, talking about nothing else but urgent donations of food, clothes and money that they were feverishly collecting to be sent to Israel. When the fighting began on June 6, 1967, it seemed like our entire world had turned into one, small radio. When they were home my parents clung to it, day and night. It became a lifeline, a thread of fragile connection.

"Two days have passed, and we haven't heard a thing." Jordana had just returned home from the Consulate for a short night's sleep. David was preparing to replace her on the night shift. The radio was on and the Brothers Four were singing about green fields.

"I know. They're maintaining complete communication silence." My father sighed.

"Well, one message came through today. It was the usual shopping list, but one item was crossed out. Israel said it doesn't need any more shoes." My mother sounded puzzled. The music suddenly stopped.

"What?!" my father jumped. "We don't need shoes?? That's wonderful…it's the sign we were waiting for! Don't you understand what that means?! We're winning! They're running away!"

"…Attacked by Jordan, who has joined Egypt and Syria in the war they have launched against Israel." They both fell silent, absorbing the voice that was crackling over the radio. "Israel quickly responded by sending forces to Jerusalem. After fierce battles with tremendous casualties, Israel is managing to defeat the Arab armies. It has been reported and confirmed that Israeli paratroopers have reached the Temple Mount. Following General Mota Gur's announcement *'Har Habayit Beyadeinu* – we have released the

Temple Mount' – Chief Army Rabbi General Shlomo Goren blew the Jewish horn, the Shofar, and...."

David stood, transfixed, holding onto the box and watching it with disbelief, as if any moment it would disappear if he let it out of his sight or reach for even one brief minute. He reached out and increased the volume; wrinkles formed on his forehead as he tried to listen to the pandemonium that erupted from the little box. A moment later the telephone rang and he was talking, listening, rejoicing and literally dancing with it in his hand, his voice filled with amazement and excitement. It was the one and only time I had heard him so filled with emotion – not because he wasn't emotional on other occasions, but because this kind of emotion came from a different, special place. A place where the emotions for this moment had been building up for two thousand years. A place where the threads of all our ancestors' lives were so entangled with each other that they couldn't be separated. And from that very same place came another, astonishing phenomenon, something so rare that it seemed completely unreal: Jordana was crying.

Completely amazed, I watched the tears that ran down my mother's cheeks. She was crying, with choking gasps, holding her right hand up to her mouth. I remember being bewildered: my mother is left-handed, but at that magnificent moment, that moment when all the tears of a People's longing were gathering together, she instinctively used her right hand – "If I forget thee, Jerusalem, may my right arm be forgotten." At that moment, the prayer was redeemed in the tears that were collected into her right palm. Those tears burned into my soul, leaving a mark that was deeper than the scar on my grandmother's forehead, broader than the shelves on which my mother kept her books, stronger than my father's voice. That mark has been the core of my compass ever since.

"We have returned to the water holes

To the market and the square
a Shofar is blowing on Temple Mount
In the Holy Old City
Jerusalem of Gold...."

Two weeks later, at the end-of-year celebration, I was singing loud and clear. An hour after the Temple Mount had been released I had memorized the words to perfection. Four more days of battle had brought an end to what had become one of Israel's most glorious hours: The Six Day War.

We spent the first week after the war at the Israeli Consulate. My mother claimed it was because she didn't have a babysitter, but I knew the truth. The Israeli triumph was so immense, there was fear that Israelis would be attacked by angry Muslims.

Slowly, life returned to normal. My mother gave birth to my baby brother and my father completed his PhD thesis. And we began preparing for the greatest moment of all – we were going home.

Living in Israel was nothing like what my teachers in the Jewish day school in Los Angeles had said it would be. Equipped with only stories of a glorious past and a little bit of Hebrew, I was surprised to discover a place that was vibrant, loud, impertinent and rude. I invested a lot of energy in learning how to peel the rough skin of Israel and discover her inner romantic, sensitive and passionate sides as well. Good is always combined with bad, happiness walks hand-in-hand with sorrow. It was a difficult mixture of difficult people, places and events that crept into my soul, nourished by my family's history and demanding my full commitment.

It seemed like events were gushing one after the other, and I could hardly keep up with their pace. A cousin was killed by a landmine, an uncle murdered by terrorists, my *bat mitzvah* cancelled on account of the family mourning, and another devastating war was launched against Israel on Yom Kippur, the holiest day of the year for the Jewish people. New towns were being built across the country, and industry was developing. A group of hostages was released in a faraway country by the Israeli Army. It felt as if we were still struggling for our independence and right to live a peaceful life when the first ray of hope appeared in our skies: I was seventeen, only a year off from graduating from Gymnasia Herzliya, when Anuar-el-Sa'adat, the president of Egypt, declared he was willing to come to Jerusalem to begin a peace process with Israel.

That night, I joined some friends to celebrate. I walked into the crowded room where all eyes were glued to the television set, watching the miracle transpire in front of our very eyes, when a strong hand caught mine: "Shalom. My name is Ben." And in his handshake I could feel Rivka's warm smile.

Ben was sitting by my side in the delivery room. My parents were waiting outside, exhausted from the magnitude of the day's events.

"It will be soon now," the doctor announced happily, and I tried to remember where I had already heard that today. The contraction cut my thoughts.

"I'm so glad you married me," Ben whispered into my ear. "I knew the minute I saw you that you were the only one for me." Kissing my sweating forehead and holding my hand, I could feel the one thing I refused to let the doctor take from me: Rivka's gold bracelet, the bracelet that my mother had passed on to me the day I was married. I could see Rivka standing by the door, Dvora and Shoshana beside her, and I could hear my mother's voice as I tried to collect my thoughts. They were all directed at Ben.

It runs in the family, my love. We women of the Land know love the minute we see it. We can feel it, physically, knowing immediately when we see it that this is our heavenly match, greater and stronger than us. Our spirits tell us so. My great- grandmother saw it in her husband's smile, my grandmother felt it in her beloved's voice, and my mother detected it in my father's eyes.

And I noticed it in your hands. Those strong arms that brought back faded memories of bygone generations of farmers, hands that are made to work with determination, embrace with warmth and protect with a complete devotion. The minute I felt your hand, I knew.

When the time came to decide on where we would live, I insisted we go to a new town called Maccabim. Jerusalem, Tel Aviv, Zichron Yaacov were all imbedded in my soul, but they were my family's projects. Like Dvora before me, I needed a project of my own. And like Isaac's sundial, I wanted it to combine old and new, tradition with creation. Situated on the hills where the story of Hanukah actually occurred hundreds of years before, and promising to become a beautiful, new town, it was the perfect place for our dreams to come true. You were right there beside me, willing to leap into the adventure of creating a new town in Israel. Our child will be the first baby born in Maccabim.

"Remember," my mother said on my wedding day, my grandmother's voice echoing in hers, "the important things in life are not possessions. Money will come and go, and ultimately even the rich eat one breakfast. But family and love are the real commodities of life."

Every spider web has a center, a gravity point, a place that keeps the object from falling and smashing into pieces. No matter how large the threads of the web become, no matter how far they grow or how they spread, as long as the center is intact – the entire web is safe. For my family, that center was always Israel. All the roads that were traveled on before the establishment of the State of Israel ultimately led to her, and all the roads that were taken after she was created emerged from her, only to find their way back. It was where the threads of my great-grandmothers lives met, where my grandparents discovered each other, where my parents fell in love, and where I found my heart.

And now I was having my first child, my own family, a fifth generation born – where else – in Israel.

Epilogue

January, 1987

The old cemetery in Zichron Yaacov is a beautiful corner of nature and history. Gravestones surrounded by trees and flowerbeds, narrow paths winding between them, and a sea breeze that creeps up the hill from the Mediterranean Sea, were all following me as I wandered through it. It was morning, and we had come to visit Shoshana.

A delicate rose in one hand, my baby in my arms, and Ben by my side, we approached the grave. It was still a small, narrow pile of earth, waiting patiently for the gravestone my mother had picked to be placed on it.

Ben took the baby from my arms. Gently, I kissed the rose and planted it on my grandmother's grave. It will bloom when my daughter will take her first steps.

We had named her Rotem, a beautiful desert flower that blooms throughout Israel during Hanukah. It was the perfect name.

"Here, in the land of our forefather's,
All dreams will come true...."
I sang softly. I could feel a warm smile glowing inside me, a smile

of reassurance and confident love. I looked at Ben through my tears and said, "We have one more task."

Arriving at my parent's house, my bag of candles was ready. My mother was still sitting Shiva – the Jewish seven days of mourning after the death of a close relative.

It was the fifth night of Hanukah, and it will be Rotem's first candle lighting. As long as the light is preserved, the memories will be present with us.

Ben and my father were watching me as I carefully placed the Yahrzeit candles in place. The accumulating lights were spreading in a slow, rhythmic dance and Rotem opened her eyes. I was lighting the last one, a beautiful rose-red candle, when my mother appeared out of nowhere and placed her hand on my shoulder.

"Yitgadal VeYitkadash Shmei Rabbah…."

Her voice was loud and clear.

About the Author

Liat Taiber Ben-David is a forth-generation SABRA: born in Israel. Liat holds a Ph.D. in Molecular Biology from the Weizmann Institute for Science in Rehovot, and is an accomplished educator and author. After completing her Ph.D., Liat became the head of Israel's national Science and Technology Educational Program for secondary schools at the Tel Aviv University, dealing with the connections between Israeli culture and science. She has published numerous books for students, teachers and fiction for children. During the past years, Liat has worked for the Jewish Agency for Israel as an emissary in the USA and as Director General of the Agency's Israel Department. Liat and her family – husband David and 3 children, Rotem, Roy and Bar, live in Maccabim, Israel. "Yahrzeit" is her first novel.

also influence the reaction kinetics. Allosteric activation by methylated DNA was observed with human Dnmt1 MTase (85, 93). Binding of two AdoMet molecules was reported for the EcoDam (94) and PvuII MTases (74, 95), and an effector role was suggested for the second AdoMet molecule. The precise binding stoichiometry of AdoMet, as well as its double role as methyl donor and allosteric effector, remains to be fully characterized for T4Dam (45, 63). Thus, in contrast to the apparently universal ternary structure of the catalytic domains (95–99), the existing biochemical data are complex and not clear enough for generalizations to be made concerning the kinetics of the reactions catalyzed by the different DNA MTases, and further investigation is required.

Initial velocities (V) were determined at various concentrations of substrates, [^{3}H-CH$_3$]-AdoMet and 20mer duplex DNA,

5'- CAGTTTAG<u>GATCC</u>ATTTCAC - 3'
3'- GTCAAATC<u>CTAG</u>GTAAAGTG - 5'

The substrate concentrations used in these experiments were up to 5-fold above Km^{AdoMet} (=490 nM) and 15-fold above Km^{DNA} (=6.3 nM) (64). As shown in Fig. 6, both double-reciprocal plots gave a series of straight lines that intersected to the left of the 1/V axis, which rules out a ping-pong bi–bi mechanism. An ordered rapid-equilibrium mechanism is also unlikely since the double-reciprocal plot lines should have intersected at the 1/V axis for the second substrate that binds. In addition, secondary plots of the slopes and 1/V-intercepts vs. reciprocal concentrations of substrates were approximately linear (not shown), permitting calculation of conventional kinetic parameters. In accordance with graphical predictions, the experimental data fit an equation that corresponds to either a steady state ordered bi–bi or a rapid-equilibrium random bi–bi mechanism. Since the conversion step ($k_{meth} = 0.56$ s^{-1}) in the T4Dam methylation reaction (82) was much faster than the catalytic turnover constant ($k_{cat} = 0.015$ s^{-1}), a rapid-equilibrium random mechanism appears to be ruled out.

Since product inhibition studies are commonly performed to determine whether there is a preferential order of substrate binding for a particular multiple substrate reaction (100), we used this approach to determine whether T4Dam first binds substrate DNA or AdoMet. We found that both AdoHcy (as well as sinefungin, a nonreactive AdoMet analog) were competitive inhibitors with respect to AdoMet (Fig. 7A) and a noncompetitive inhibitor with respect to 20mer DNA duplex (Fig. 7B). In contrast, the other reaction product, fully methylated 20mer DNA duplex, exhibited noncompetitive inhibition with respect to both AdoMet and unmethylated 20mer DNA duplex (Figs. 7C and 7D). Secondary plots of the slopes and 1/V-intercepts vs. concentration of inhibitor were approximately linear (not shown). These results (summarized in Table III) are consistent with a steady state ordered bi–bi mechanism

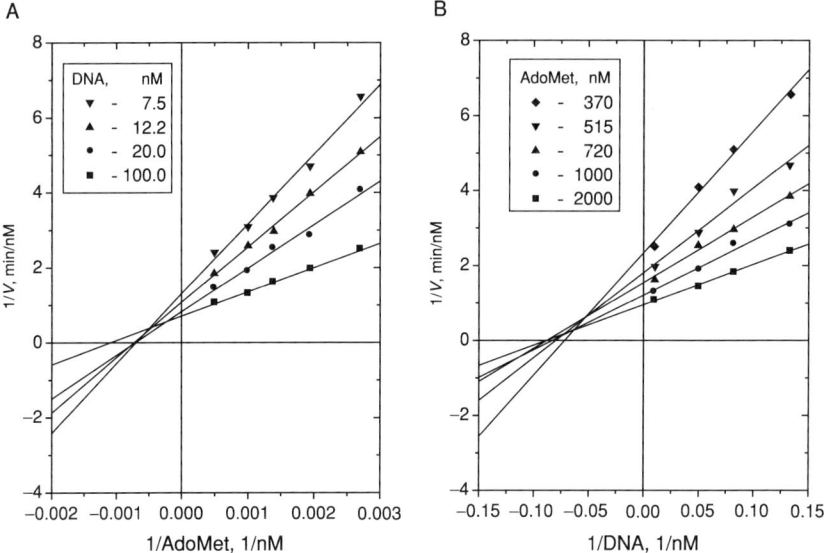

FIG. 6. Double-reciprocal plots of the initial reaction velocity vs. substrate concentration for methylation by T4Dam. (A) Varying the AdoMet concentration with the 20mer DNA duplex concentrations at the levels shown in the insert. (B) Varying the 20mer DNA duplex concentration with the AdoMet concentrations at the levels shown in the insert. The T4Dam MTase concentration was 1 nM in all cases. Least squares linear regressions for the reciprocals of the reaction velocity (1/V) vs. reciprocal substrate concentration (1/AdoMet or 1/DNA) (at fixed concentrations of the other substrate) are represented by the solid lines.

(*100*), in which the substrate binding and product release order are AdoMet ↓ DNA ↓ DNA^{Me} ↑ AdoHcy↑.

The preferential order of substrate binding proposed for T4Dam is identical to that found for several other [N6-adenine] MTases, EcoRI (*72*), EcoRV (*62*), and KpnI (*80*). The TaqI (*89*) and EcoP15I (*90*) MTases exhibit a random mechanism for substrate binding and product release. An ordered bi–bi mechanism with DNA ↓ AdoMet↓ order of substrate binding is usually assigned for the [C5-cytosine] DNA MTases; e.g., for the HhaI (*68, 76*), MspI (*69*), and murine Dnmt1 MTases (*86*). However, a random mechanism has been proposed for the human Dnmt1 MTase (*85*) and HhaI (*77*).

Generally, DNA MTases may form binary complexes with either of their reaction substrates. Binding of AdoMet in the absence of substrate DNA has been confirmed, in particular by co-crystal structures (*84, 92, 95, 98*). However, DNA MTases can also form stable, nonfunctional ("dead-end") enzyme–product–substrate ternary complexes, as has been observed for the

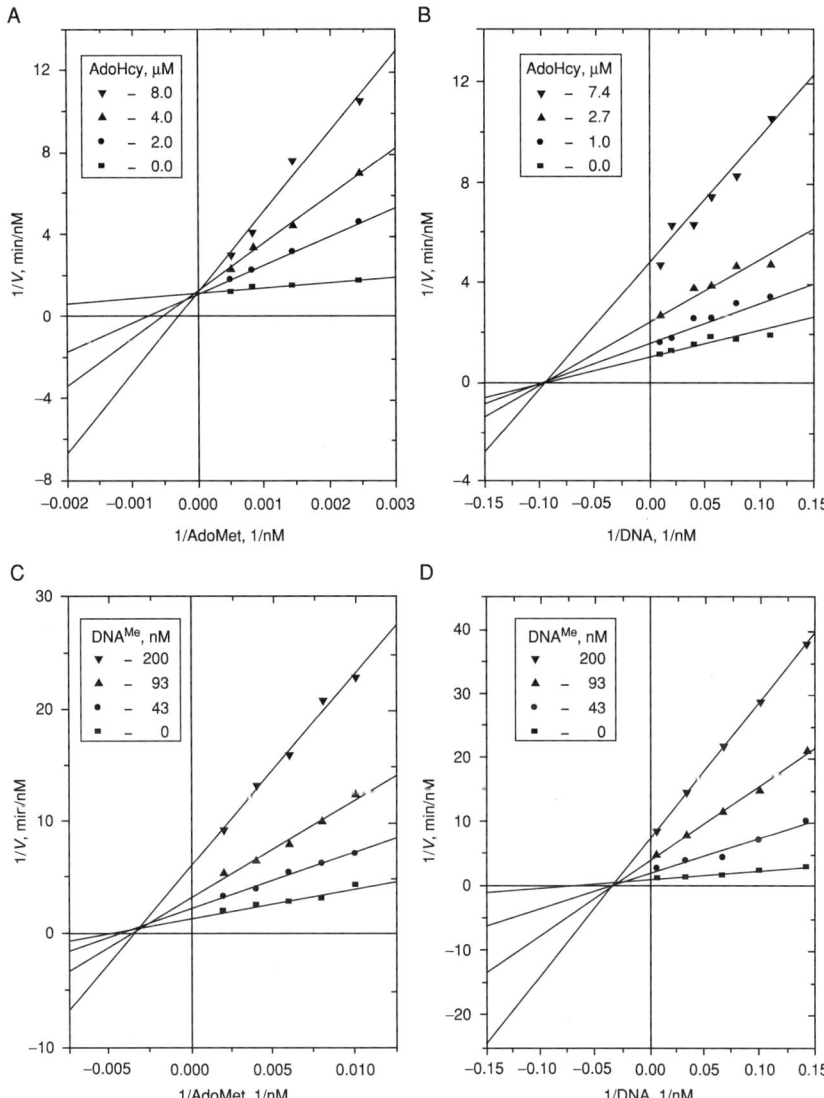

FIG. 7. Double-reciprocal plots analyzing product inhibition of the methylation reaction catalyzed by T4Dam. (A), (B) Inhibition by AdoHcy; (C), (D) Inhibition by fully methylated 20mer DNA duplex. The DNA concentration was fixed at 150 nM (A, C); the AdoMet concentration was fixed at 2 μM (B, D). The T4Dam MTase concentration was 1 nM in all cases. The concentrations of inhibitor [AdoHcy or DNA^{Me}] are given in the inserts. Least squares linear regressions for the reciprocals of the reaction velocity (1/V) vs. reciprocal substrate concentration (1/AdoMet or 1/DNA) (at fixed concentrations of AdoHcy or methylated 20mer DNA duplex) are represented by the solid lines.

TABLE III
PRODUCT INHIBITION ANALYSIS OF REACTION CATALYZED BY THE T4DAM MTASE

Inhibitor	Variable substrate	Fixed substrate	Inhibition type
AdoHcy	AdoMet	DNA	Competitive
Sinefungin	AdoMet	DNA	Competitive
AdoHcy	DNA	AdoMet	Noncompetitive
Sinefungin	DNA	AdoMet	Noncompetitive
DNA^{Me}	AdoMet	DNA	Noncompetitive
DNA^{Me}	DNA	AdoMet	Noncompetitive

MTase–AdoHcy–DNA complex of HhaI (101). Thus, if the initial concentration of the second substrate to bind were sufficiently high, a steady state ordered reaction (which has a specific order of substrate binding and product release) would show inhibition of the initial reaction velocity due to the formation of nonproductive binary and/or dead-end ternary complexes (102). In fact, at high concentrations of substrate 20-mer DNA duplex, there was a strong inhibition in T4Dam initial reaction velocity (70). This adds support to the notion of a steady state ordered bi–bi mechanism.

Increasing the concentration of substrate AdoMet did not lead to the reaction rates approaching a plateau, as would be expected for a hyperbolic dependency. Instead, the reaction rates increased almost linearly with the concentration of AdoMet (70). Catalase is another enzyme with reaction rate characteristics similar to those of T4Dam; viz., it does not exhibit any tendency to saturate at high concentrations of substrate (103). If product release is the rate-limiting step of the reaction, then this type of behavior may be explained by the binding of substrate and release of product occurring in a concerted event. Our previous results showed that product release is, in fact, the rate-limiting step in the T4Dam methylation reaction (82). We suggested that in the case of T4Dam, such a concerted event can be represented as follows:

$$EH + S \rightarrow ES + H \quad (C)$$

where AdoHcy is released last and AdoMet binding occurs first; it corresponds formally to a mechanism proposed earlier (104).

The overall kinetic scheme needed to describe all the known effects of substrates and products on the reaction rate is presented in Fig. 8. The main route in this scheme has a substrate binding and product release order of AdoMet ↓ DNA ↓ DNA^{Me} ↑ AdoHcy↑.

For example, all possible dead-end complexes are included in this scheme. It should be noted that substrate unmethylated 20-mer ODN duplex D

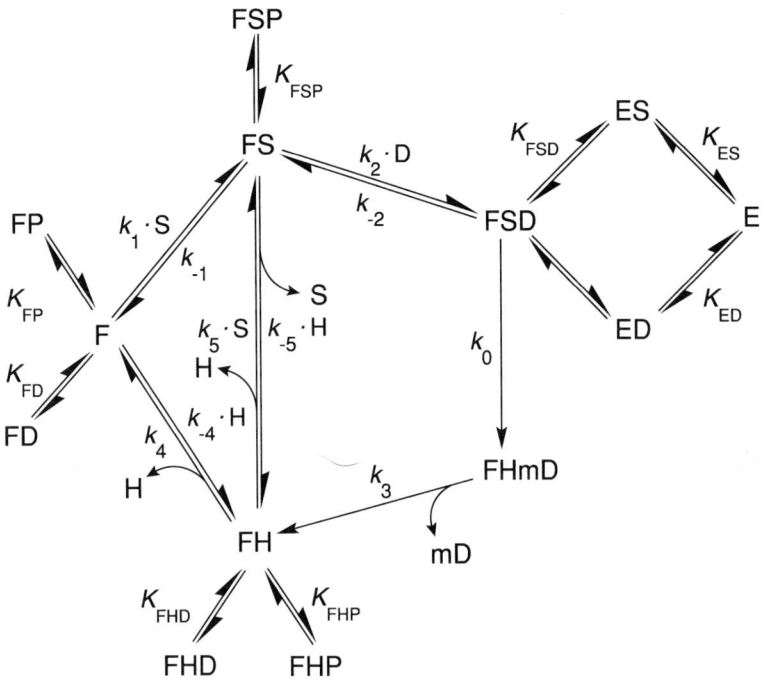

FIG. 8. Scheme for T4Dam methylation of the 20mer DNA duplex. E, T4Dam; F, an isomerized form of T4Dam; S, AdoMet; H, AdoHcy; D, (20-mer) unmethylated DNA duplex; mD, hemimethylated DNA duplex; P, fully methylated DNA duplex.

is initially converted to the hemimethylated product, mD, and not to the completely methylated duplex, P, which is an inhibitor of the reaction. Therefore, the step EHmD → EH + mD is irreversible. Furthermore, the dead-end complex EHP is introduced into the scheme, since mD and P are not identical and behave differently in the reaction. Finally, in order to account for the linear increase in the reaction rate that coincides with the increase in AdoMet concentration, we included the following reversible step, EH + S ↔ ES + H.

In addition, fluorescence studies with 2-AP substituted duplexes (Section III.B.2) indicated that after it binds AdoMet, T4Dam specificity for the DNA strand containing the adenine in GATC increased significantly (45). This suggested that after AdoMet binds, T4Dam undergoes isomerization in the ternary complex to a form (enzyme F) that has altered catalytic and binding characteristics. Therefore, we proposed that the initial enzymatic forms E, ED, and ES enter the catalytic cycle via an isomerization step, resulting in form FSD (Fig. 8).

According to the scheme, the following sequence of events occurs. Free T4Dam, initially in form E, interacts randomly with AdoMet and DNA to form binary complexes, ES and ED. These complexes interact with the second substrate to form the ternary complex, FSD, in which T4Dam has isomerized to state F. Form F is significantly different from the initial conformational state E and is specifically adapted for catalysis. After the chemical step of methyl group transfer from AdoMet to DNA, the methylated duplex dissociates relatively rapidly ($k_3 = 1.7$ s^{-1}). The dissociation of the second product, AdoHcy, appears to be the rate-limiting step of the reaction and proceeds with $k_4 = 0.018$ s^{-1}; this agrees with the value of $k_{cat} = 0.015$ s^{-1} determined previously (64). The release of AdoHcy from the FH complex can occur by two pathways. The first involves release of AdoHcy, while the enzyme remains in the isomerized F form, which preferentially binds AdoMet to form an FS complex. DNA then binds this FS complex and the catalytic cycle continues. This proposed mechanism is in contrast to the classical Iso-mechanisms, where the enzyme converts back to its initial conformational state following release of substrate, prior to the start of a new catalytic cycle.

The second pathway is one in which AdoHcy release and AdoMet binding occur as one concerted event, and the resulting enzyme–AdoMet complex remains in the F conformation ready to bind DNA and continue catalysis. Although the exact mechanism of this concerted event has not been determined, it has important biological consequences. The AdoMet concentration in *E. coli*, reported to be in the range of 30–300 μM (105) or 300–500 μM (106), is one to two orders of magnitude greater than the K_d of the T4Dam–AdoMet complex (≈ 1 μM). Therefore, the T4Dam methylation reaction *in vivo* would be predicted to be much faster than observed *in vitro* at moderate substrate concentrations.

Thus, although some details of the scheme presented in Fig. 8 may vary, it can be regarded as a good representation of the reaction mechanism of T4Dam methylation of ODN duplexes. At the present time, however, a unified picture of the reaction mechanism of DNA MTases has not emerged, despite the numerous studies done on these enzymes. However, the results of the work presented here are important not only in clarifying our understanding of the T4Dam reaction mechanism, but they also may be relevant to the mechanism of other DNA MTases. For example, conflicting data obtained with the HhaI MTase (76, 77) can be explained by assuming that this enzyme also undergoes an isomerization after formation of the ternary complex, analogous to T4Dam. Thus, it would appear that an isomerization step to make MTases catalytically active could be a common feature of these enzymes.

D. Processivity and Orientation to the Methylation Target

Since natural *in vivo* DNA substrates are much longer and contain many potential methylation sites, *in vitro* methylation of short single-site ODN duplexes is not going to take into account possible processive behavior of a DNA MTase, i.e., movement of an enzyme along polymeric DNA via one-dimensional (or linear) diffusion and carrying out multiple turnovers on the same substrate molecule (75, 79, 87). To bridge the gap between studies using short (20mer) one-site ODN substrates and natural long DNA substrates, we constructed two-site 40mer DNA duplexes to compare their substrate characteristics with those of their one-site constituents. Thus, we ligated short, defined synthetic duplexes containing complementary single-stranded overhangs (Table IV) and generated a series of 40mer duplexes with different combinations of GATC and GMTC sites (Table V).

Short component duplexes 1a/a and 2a/a

"1" "3"

5'-CAGTTTAG<u>GATC</u>CATTTCG-3'   5'-GATGCATAAG<u>GATC</u>CCTGGGT-3'
3'-GTCAAATC<u>CTAG</u>GTAAAGCCTAC-5'   3'-GTATTC<u>CTAG</u>GGACCCA-5'

"2" "4"

Ligated 40mer duplex A

"1" "3"

5'-CAGTTTAG<u>GATC</u>CATTTCGGATGCATAAG<u>GATC</u>CCTGGGT-3'
3'-GTCAAATC<u>CTAG</u>GTAAAGCCTACGTATTC<u>CTAG</u>GGACCCA-5'

"2" "4"

Consider the methylation of the 40mer duplex E (1 m/m · 2 m/a), which has only one GATC site available for methylation. At high [DNA]/[enzyme] ratios, a T4Dam monomer will bind the duplex asymmetrically at one of four possible positions (denoted "1"–"4").

```
         "1"        "3"
5' ——— GMTC ——— GMTC ——— 3'
3' ——— CTMG ——— CTAG ——— 5'
         "2"        "4"
```

If the enzyme were unable to reorient on the duplex and not act processively, then we would have expected a maximum burst value of 0.25 (number of ^{3}H-CH$_3$ groups transferred per bound T4Dam in the pre-steady state phase), because "4" is the only productive site and appropriate orientation to it is necessary for methylation. However, if the enzyme were capable of reorienting at position "3" to position "4," then the burst could be as high as 0.5. Moreover, T4Dam bound at position "1" may be capable of moving (by linear diffusion) to "3" and reorienting to "4"; perhaps it might even reorient from "2" to "1" and

TABLE IV
Synthetic Single-Site Duplexes Used to Construct 40mer
Substrates Containing Two Specific Sites

Duplex no.	Structure
1a/a	5'-CAGTTTAGGATCCATTTCG
	3'-GTCAAATCCTAGGTAAAGCCTAC
1m/a	5'-CAGTTTAGGMTCCATTTCG
	3'-GTCAAATCCTAGGTAAAGCCTAC
1a/m	5'-CAGTTTAGGATCCATTTCG
	3'-GTCAAATCCTMGGTAAAGCCTAC
1m/m	5'-CAGTTTAGGMTCCATTTCG
	3'-GTCAAATCCTMGGTAAAGCCTAC
2a/a	5'-GATGCATAAGGATCCCTGGGT
	3'-GTATTCCTAGGGACCCA
2m/a	5'-GATGCATAAGGMTCCCTGGGT
	3'-GTATTCCTAGGGACCCA

diffuse to "3," where it reorients. If some combination of these events occurs, then even higher burst values could be registered (with 1.0 as the theoretical maximum). Hence, by determining the burst value, we could ascertain whether T4Dam was able to adapt to a substrate in which a productive target site-strand represented only one-quarter of the initial binding orientations. This type of experiment was carried out with several 40mer duplexes containing differing combinations of variant sites.

The pre-steady state burst values (B) and steady state rate constants (k_{cat}) were determined for both the 40mers and stoichiometric mixtures of the unligated component duplexes used to generate each 40mer (Fig. 9 and Table V). The k_{cat} values for 40mer duplexes (with two potential sites for methylation) and the corresponding mixtures of constituents were all comparable, and they were close to the value of $k_{cat} = 0.015$ s^{-1} observed for a single-site 20mer duplex (64). Hence, it appeared that T4Dam steady state methylation of 40mer duplexes was similar to the methylation of a shorter 20mer ODN duplex, and both have the same rate-limiting step in the overall reaction. In contrast to the results for steady state methylation, the burst values differed for the 40mer duplexes vs. the stoichiometric mixtures of their component short duplexes. For example, 40mer duplex A (1a/a ∘ 2a/a) had a burst of 1.86 compared to 1.01 for the corresponding mixture of short constituents "1a/a + 2a/a." The latter burst value was also observed with a single-site 20mer duplex (82). It follows that after methylation of one A in the palindromic GATC/GATC site, T4Dam dissociates from a short

TABLE V
Kinetic Characteristics of Duplex Methylation[a]

Duplex(es)	Specific site position and methylation status	Burst values	$(k_{cat}, s^{-1}) \times 10^2$
A = 1a/a∘2a/a	- - - - A - - - - - - - - - A - - - - - - - - - A - - - - - - - - - A - - - - - -	1.86 ± 0.13	1.92 ± 0.10
1a/a + 2a/a	- - - - A - - - - - - / - - - A - - - - - - - - - A - - - - / - - - - - A - - - - - -	1.01 ± 0.09	1.57 ± 0.09
B = 1a/a∘2m/a	- - - - A - - - - - - - - - M - - - - - - - - - A - - - - - - - - - A - - - - - -	1.7 ± 0.11	1.89 ± 0.12
1a/a + 2m/a	- - - - A - - - - - - / - - - - M - - - - - - - - - A - - - - / - - - - - A - - - - - -	1.05 ± 0.12	1.93 ± 0.10
C = 1m/a∘2m/a	- - - - M - - - - - - - - - - M - - - - - - - - - A - - - - - - - - - - A - - - - - -	1.86 ± 0.09	1.45 ± 0.07
1m/a + 2m/a	- - - - M - - - - - - / - - - M - - - - - - - - - A - - - - / - - - - - A - - - - - -	1.12 ± 0.11	1.63 ± 0.16
D = 1a/m∘2m/a	- - - - A - - - - - - - - - M - - - - - - - - - M - - - - - - - - - A - - - - - -	1.74 ± 0.08	1.37 ± 0.07
1a/m + 2m/a	- - - - A - - - - - - / - - - M - - - - - - - - - M - - - - / - - - - - A - - - - - -	Not done	Not done
E = 1m/m∘2m/a	- - - - M - - - - - - - - - M- - - - - - - - - M - - - - - - - - - A - - - - - -	1.18 ± 0.09	1.33 ± 0.09
1m/m + 2m/a	- - - - M - - - - - - / - - - M - - - - - - - - - M - - - - / - - - - - A - - - - - -	0.69 ± 0.05	0.67 ± 0.04
F = 1m/m∘2a/a	- - - - M - - - - - - - - - A - - - - - - - - - M - - - - - - - - - A - - - - - -	0.97 ± 0.09	1.20 ± 0.07
1m/m + 2a/a	- - - - M - - - - - - / - - - A - - - - - - - - - M - - - - / - - - - - A - - - - - -	0.52 ± 0.05	0.73 ± 0.05

[a]The 40-mer duplexes A–F were produced by ligation of shorter duplexes (see Table IV); these are denoted with an asterisk between the two component duplexes. Pre-steady state and steady state kinetic analyses of T4Dam methylation were carried out on 40-mer duplexes and with stoichiometric amounts of their corresponding unligated component duplexes (67). Kinetic data were analyzed using the program Scientist 2.01 (MicroMath®) for regression analysis. The burst values (B, the number of [^{3}H-CH$_3$] groups incorporated per T4Dam in the pre-steady state phase) and k_{cat} values were determined using the equation [^{3}H-DNA]/[enzyme] = $B + k_{cat}t$.

duplex prior to its exchanging product AdoHcy for substrate AdoMet. In contrast, the burst value of 1.8 with 40mer duplex A suggested that after methylation of one site, T4Dam was capable of linear diffusion, release of product AdoHcy without dissociating from DNA, binding another AdoMet, and methylation of

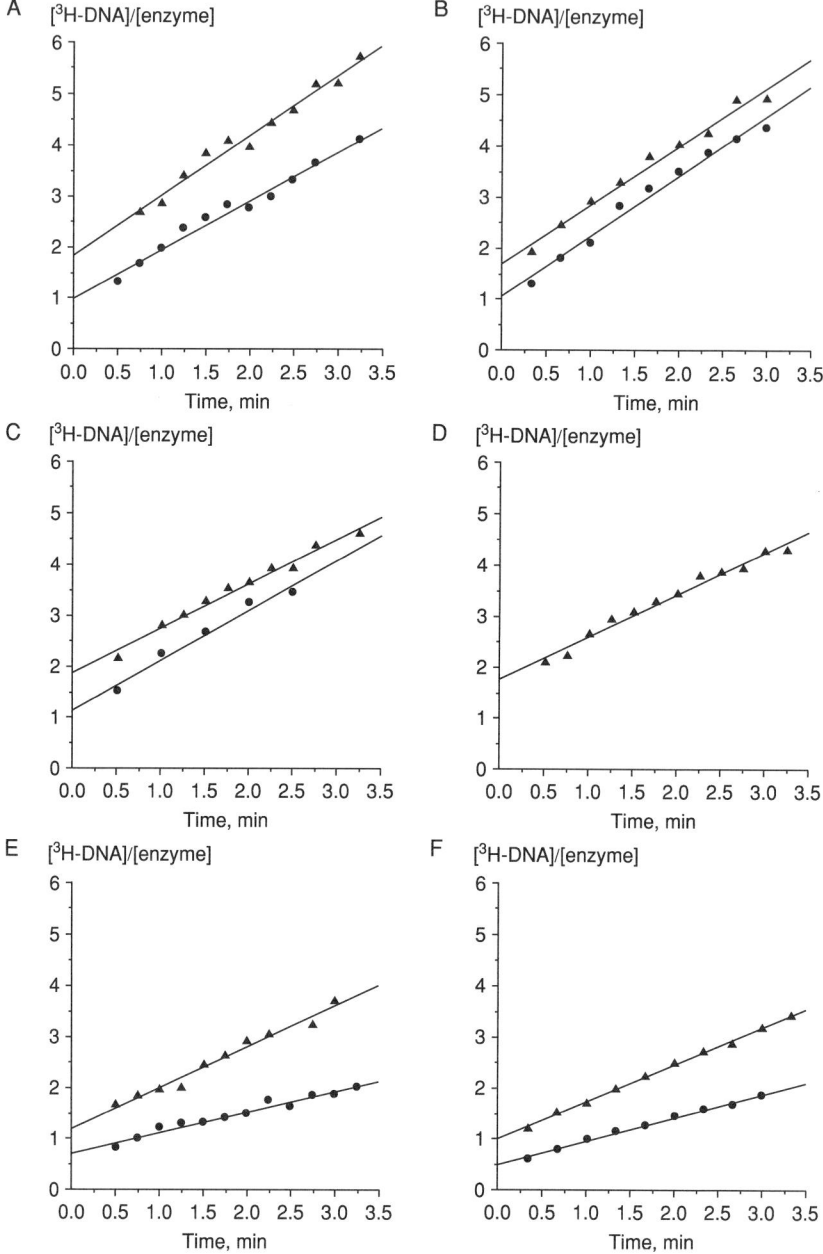

FIG. 9. Kinetics of T4Dam methylation of 40mer duplexes A–F (triangles) and corresponding stoichiometric mixtures of the unligated components (circles). The concentrations of enzyme and duplexes were 10 and 200 nM, respectively. [^{3}H-CH$_3$]AdoMet was at 5 μM. (A) duplex A; (B) duplex B; (C) duplex C; (D) duplex D; (E) duplex E; (F) duplex F.

a second site. This appeared to contradict the sequence of events observed during steady state cycles; viz., AdoMet↓ DNA↓ DNA^{Me}↑ AdoHcy↑. To reconcile this apparent discrepancy, we proposed the following series of events during the pre-steady state methylation phase of the two-site 40mer duplex A:

- T4Dam binds substrate AdoMet (AdoMet↓) and this complex binds randomly to the 40mer duplex (DNA↓) and methylation of a target GATC ensues (GATC → GMTC)
- T4Dam bound with product AdoHcy leaves the methylated site (GMTC↑); at a nonspecific DNA sequence AdoHcy rapidly dissociates from the T4Dam–DNA–AdoHcy complex (AdoHcy↑) and exchanges with AdoMet (AdoMet↓), present in excess.
- The processive steps of T4Dam action are consistent with an ordered bi–bi mechanism AdoMet↓ DNA↓ DNA^{Me}↑ AdoHcy↑. However, in contrast to the steady state, here DNA^{Me}↑ signifies departure from a methylated site, GMTC↑, without physically dissociating from the DNA molecule.
- Following methyl transfer at one site and linear diffusion to a hemimethylated site, T4Dam–AdoMet is capable of rapidly reorienting itself to the (productive) unmethylated strand. In contrast, T4Dam–AdoHcy is not capable of reorientation at an enzymatically created GMTC site.

The results with duplexes E and F were distinct from those obtained with the other 40mer duplexes. First, since they have only one methylatable site, the burst values for duplexes E and F were almost 2-fold lower. Moreover, stoichiometric mixtures of the component short duplexes (for 40mer duplexes E and F) exhibited lower k_{cat} and burst values compared to the other duplexes. This could be due to product inhibition by fully methylated short duplex "1 m/m". In contrast, judging from the increased k_{cat} values, it would appear that a fully methylated site had little inhibition potential in duplexes E and F. This suggests that T4Dam is better able to move from one site to another on the longer 40mer duplexes (via dissociation–reassociation) compared to the shorter, one-site duplexes.

The preceding results are important for refining our understanding of T4Dam methylation and its relation to the mechanisms of other processive DNA MTases. First, the ability of T4Dam to reorient to the methylation target may be a general property of processive DNA MTases. Second, in long DNA molecules the inhibition potential of fully methylated sites must be low for other DNA MTases as well. If a processive DNA MTase performs a random walk along the DNA molecule, as has been suggested (79), the enzyme passes over fully methylated sites without any kinetic delay. Finally, as with ODN

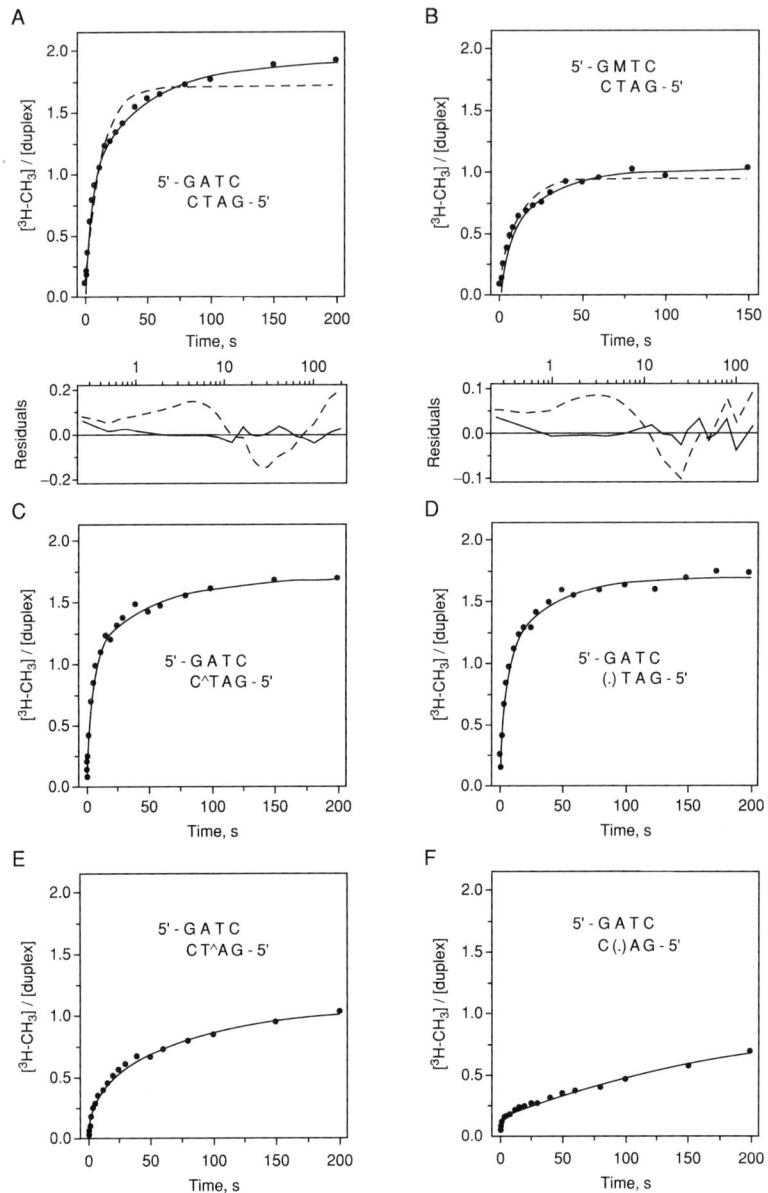

FIG. 10. Single turnover kinetics of T4Dam methylation. Shown are the recognition site structures of several representative oligonucleotide duplexes. ^ = absence of a phosphate; (.) = absence of a nucleotide. The concentrations in the resulting mixture were 2.7 µM T4Dam, 8 µM AdoMet, 0.2 µM duplex, 100 mM Tris-HCl, pH 8.0, 10 mM EDTA, 10 mM DTT, and

duplexes, the rate-limiting step with polymeric DNA substrates is dissociation of AdoHcy from T4Dam.

E. Single Turnover Analysis

Generally, DNA MTases are functional monomeric enzymes (107), although it has been reported that RsrI MTase shows partial dimerization (108), and two MTases from *Streptococcus pneumoniae* appear to exist as dimers (32). In the case of MspI MTase, the enzyme appeared to dimerize at high protein concentrations, which may reflect a tendency to aggregate rather than having functional significance (109). However, human placental DNA MTase has been shown to be dimeric in solution and active as a dimer (110). On the other hand, the DNA Ccr [N6-adenine] DNA MTase is dimeric at physiological concentrations, but it was suggested that Ccr MTase functions as a monomer (111).

T4Dam exists as a monomer in solution (40), but in the presence of substrate DNA in sub-stoichiometric concentrations, T4Dam forms dimer/oligomer structures (Section II.A). Moreover, an X-ray crystal structure of a T4Dam–DNA–AdoHcy ternary complex had an enzyme/DNA (a 12mer ODN) ratio of 2:1 (44). These results allow T4Dam to be included among a group of dissociating enzyme systems (112), in which it is supposed that dissociation/association processes play an important role in regulating cellular activity.

T4Dam methylation of various ODN duplexes was assayed under single turnover conditions; viz., AdoMet (8 μM) was saturating relative to T4Dam (2.7 μM) and both were saturating relative to the duplex (0.2 μM). Under these conditions, two T4Dam (presumably bound with AdoMet) are bound per duplex (45). In the classic case of single turnover, a substrate molecule has a single reactive group that is converted to product. The course of the methylation reaction can be described by a simple exponential function:

$$[^3\text{H-CH}_3]/[\text{duplex}] = P_{max} \cdot (1 - e^{-k_{meth} \cdot t}) \qquad (7)$$

where P_{max} is the maximum level of substrate conversion, and k_{meth} is the rate constant of the chemical stage of the reaction. However, the curves did not obey a simple exponential dependence (representative results are presented in Fig. 10 and statistical evidence is presented in (43)). All data sets were best described using Eq. 8 for two-step methylation of duplexes. Duplex 1

0.2 mg/ml BSA. Dashed curves in (A) and (B) represent fittings to the one-step reaction mechanism (Eq. 7), solid curves represent fittings to the two-step model (Eq. 8). Residual plots (data − fit) for the one step- (dashed line) and two step- (solid line) mechanisms are shown in the low panels of (A) and (B).

(Table VI) contains GATC on both strands of the target site. During a single turnover reaction, T4Dam should catalyze a methyl transfer to every duplex, and it might even methylate both Ade residues.

Since the overall DNA–MTase reaction is irreversible (68–70), it can be represented as a two-stage conversion of the initial oligonucleotide duplex containing two target Ade residues,

$$\mathrm{E \cdot D} \;\xrightarrow{k_{meth1}}\; \mathrm{E \cdot mD} \;\xrightarrow{k_{meth2}}\; \mathrm{E \cdot P} \tag{D}$$

where E is T4Dam bound with AdoMet and/or AdoHcy, D is the initial duplex, mD is the half-methylated duplex, P is the fully methylated reaction product, k_{meth1} is the rate constant of the first stage of the methylation reaction, and k_{meth2} is the rate constant of the second stage. Since the technique used only allows registration of the sum of the products of reaction [mD + P], the kinetic scheme (D) is described by Eq. 8 (113):

$$[^{3}\text{H-CH}_3]/[\text{duplex}] = P_2 - (P_1 \cdot k_{meth1} - P_2 \cdot k_{meth2}) \cdot e^{-k_{meth1} \cdot t}/(k_{meth1} - k_{meth2}) \\ - (P_2 - P_1) \cdot e^{-k_{meth2} \cdot t} \cdot k_{meth1}/(k_{meth1} - k_{meth2}) \tag{8}$$

where P_1 is the number of A residues methylated per duplex during the first stage of the reaction, and P_2 is the number of A residues methylated per duplex in the final product. For duplex 1, containing the canonical palindromic GATC/GATC site, the first stage of the single turnover reaction involves methylation of one of the two A residues (P_1 = 1.03 ^{3}H-methyl groups transferred per duplex) with rate constant k_{meth1} = 0.21 s^{-1} (43). This value is 14-fold higher than the k_{cat} under steady state conditions (64, 82). In the first stage after binding, T4Dam methylates one strand only. The second methylation stage proceeded at a rate that was an order of magnitude slower than in the first stage, and the P_2 was 1.90 methyl groups per duplex. Thus, both A residues in the canonical GATC/GATC site were methylated under single turnover conditions, where two Dam–AdoMet complexes can be bound to the duplex (43). Both curve fitting and statistical analysis showed that the two-exponential (Eq. 8) gave a better fit to the results than the single exponential (Eq. 7), although it was not ruled out that some other more complex model might better fit the data. The two-step model suggested that the two distinct k_{meth} values reflect differing methylation conditions, e.g., the second methylation is rate-limited by clearance of Dam–AdoHcy from the site on the opposite strand.

One possible explanation for the specific site of native DNA duplex 1, GATC/GATC, interacting consecutively with two T4Dam–AdoMet complexes is as follows. The binding of AdoMet induces an asymmetric state in the

TABLE VI
KINETIC PARAMETERS FOR T4DAM METHYLATION OF 20-MER DUPLEXES WITH CANONICAL GATC/GATC OR MODIFIED SITES[a]

Duplex[b] no.	Structure of recognition site	k_{cat},[c] s^{-1}	k_{meth1}, s^{-1}	k_{meth2}, s^{-1}	P_1	P_2	k_{meth}[d] s^{-1}	P[d] "burst"
1	-G-A-T-C-	0.015	0.21	0.023	1.03	1.90	0.56	0.92
[I + II]	-C-T-A-G-	(0.003)	(0.02)	(0.003)	(0.05)	(0.03)	(0.10)	(0.05)
1m	-G-M-T-C-	0.010	0.37	0.039	0.45	1.01	0.47	0.85
[Im + II]	-C-T-A-G-	(0.001)	(0.06)	(0.005)	(0.05)	(0.02)	(0.09)	(0.05)
2	-G-A-T-C-	ND	0.15	0.028	0.90	2.11		
[I + IIz]	-C-T-A-Z-		(0.05)	(0.005)	(0.24)	(0.04)		
3	-G-M-T-C-	ND	0.11	0.016	0.74	1.06		
[Im + IIz]	-C-T-A-Z-		(0.03)	(0.001)	(0.11)	(0.04)		
4	-G-A-T-C-	0.003	0.54	0.039	0.58	1.12	0.67	0.90
[I + IIn]	-C-T-N-G-	(0.001)	(0.12)	(0.008)	(0.06)	(0.03)	(0.12)	(0.03)
5	-G-A-T-C-	0.0005	0.24	0.010	0.53	1.07	0.49	0.86
[I + IX]	-C-A-T-G-	(0.0001)	(0.05)	(0.005)	(0.05)	(0.11)	(0.09)	(0.05)
6	-G-A-T-C-	0.014	0.24	0.020	1.11	1.71		
[I + IV + VII]	-C^T-A-G-	(0.001)	(0.02)	(0.004)	(0.05)	(0.03)		
7	-G-A-T-C-	0.0058	0.25	0.013	0.37	1.05		
[I + III + VIII]	-C-T^A-G-	(0.0002)	(0.04)	(0.0002)	(0.03)	(0.04)		
8	-G-A-T-C-	0.0018	0.56	0.0068	0.19	1.20		
[I + V + VI]	-C T A^G-	(0.0003)	(0.08)	(0.0007)	(0.01)	(0.06)		
9	-G-A-T-C-	0.024	0.24	0.028	1.05	1.69		
[I + VII]	(·) T-A-G-	(0.001)	(0.03)	(0.003)	(0.08)	(0.02)		
10	-G-A-T-C-	0.0029	1.17	0.0028	0.066	1.10		
[I + V]	-C-T-A (·)	(0.0002)	(0.29)	(0.0007)	(0.005)	(0.19)		
11	-G-A-T-C-	ND	0.84	0.0045	0.16	0.99		
[I + IV + VIII]	-C (·) A-G-		(0.11)	(0.0007)	(0.01)	(0.10)		

^Absence of a phosphate; (·) absence of a nucleotide; ND, not determined. Values in parentheses are the standard deviations from independent experiments.
[a]Single turnover parameters k_{meth1}, k_{meth2}, P_1, and P_2 were derived from results plotted according to Eq. (2).
[b]ODN combinations are indicated in brackets.
[c]Data from (51, 64) were for steady state conditions, where the duplex was in excess (T4Dam in monomeric form), in contrast to single turnover.
[d]Data from (43) were for pre-steady state conditions, where the duplex was in excess (T4Dam in monomeric form), in contrast to single turnover. Taken from (82) by permission of Oxford University Press.

ternary complex in which one target A residue is flipped out. The asymmetric orientation of the enzyme dimer toward one strand of the duplex may be due to steric hindrance to the simultaneous productive interaction with two target residues (71). We suggest that the presence of the second T4Dam–AdoMet in the catalytic complex may be responsible for the reduction in k_{meth1} in comparison to $k_{\text{meth}} = 0.56 \text{ s}^{-1}$, where a single T4Dam–AdoMet binds and catalyzes methylation (82).

The two-exponential equation also described the methylation of duplexes containing only one methylatable target, for example, GMTC/GATC, GMTC/ZATC, GATC/GNTC, and GATC/GTAC. For these duplexes, random T4Dam binding should result in one of two mutually exclusive orientations (productive and nonproductive) to the substrate, resulting in modification of only 50% of the duplexes. In all cases, we observed a rapid exponential phase of methyl transfer, followed by a slower increase in product accumulation. However, it must be pointed out that here k_{meth2} applies to a different process. While k_{meth1} would reflect the rate of the methylation by dimeric T4Dam–AdoMet productively oriented to the strand with the methylatable A residue, the slower k_{meth2} reflects methylation by enzyme molecules that were oriented first to the nonproductive GMTC chain and have to reorient to the opposite productive chain.

Base substitutions and deletions in the recognition site variably influenced the single turnover reaction parameters. When the GAT portion of the target sequence was interrupted, the A residue could not be methylated, although the A residue in the complementary strand GATC could be methylated. In addition, most interruptions caused a sharp decrease in the proportion of the initial, productive enzyme–substrate complexes, especially for duplexes 8, 10, and 11 (Table VI). Duplexes 8 and 11, as shown by the gel retardation method, have a greater affinity for T4Dam than the native duplex 1 (48). Therefore, the decrease in the proportion of productive complexes can not be explained by a weakened affinity for the duplex. Thus, it appears that the GAT sequences in both strands form a second order symmetrical structure that may be necessary for optimal interaction between the duplex and T4Dam–AdoMet. In contrast to interruptions in GAT, deletion of C and the adjoining 3′-sequence in the bottom strand (duplex 9) did not significantly alter the reaction parameters (Table VI).

As seen in Table VI, the k_{cat} values decreased many-fold for defective duplexes 4, 5, 7, 8, and 10, while the k_{meth1} values did not decline significantly, and some even increased (duplexes 4, 8, 10). We suggest that for the defective sites, after the rapid stage 1 methylation, release of enzyme from the site becomes the rate-limiting step. Similar defective sites in natural DNA, even if rare, might become traps for slowing down *in vivo* methylation.

F. Comparison to a DNA-[N4-cytosine]MTase

1. KINETIC MECHANISM

The amino-MTases are likely to be more closely related to one another in their mechanism of action compared to the [C5-cytosine]-MTases. Not only do they have a common modification target, an exocyclic NH_2-group, but they also possess common conserved amino acid sequences in their major structural/functional motifs (37). Moreover, with the [C5-cytosine]-MTases, the catalytic transfer of the methyl group from donor S-adenosyl-L-methionine (AdoMet) involves covalent binding of the enzyme to the target cytosine residue (68). In contrast, [adenine-N6]- and [cytosine-N4]-MTases transfer the methyl group to the exocyclic NH_2-group without formation of a transient covalent bond. On the other hand, adenine and cytosine residues are substantially different molecular targets. A number of experimental data indicate that flipping of the target nucleoside out of the DNA helix is a common property of the reactions catalyzed by all DNA–MTases (114). Since the energetic costs of flipping should differ substantially for deoxyadenosine and deoxycytidine residues, a different kinetic behavior of the [adenine-N6]- and [cytosine-N4]-MTases might be anticipated.

Earlier, it was shown that the rate of the chemical step (transfer of the methyl group to the target base) differed considerably between the EcoRI [adenine-N6] and HhaI [cytosine-C5] MTases (71, 76). The EcoRI MTase catalyzes a very rapid methyl group transfer with the k_{meth} 300-fold higher than the k_{cat}. In contrast, the HhaI MTase has a k_{meth} that is only slightly higher than k_{cat} (the rate of product release from the enzyme). It is not clear at this time what determines this difference; for example, is methyl group transfer to an exocyclic NH_2-group vs. a ring C the determining factor, or is it the nature of the target base? To approach this question, we began a study of methylation by the BamHI [cytosine-N4] MTase, which catalyzes methyl group transfer to the internal cytosine residue in the palindromic recognition site GGATCC (115). Because T4Dam modifies the adenine residue in the palindromic sequence GATC, which is contained within the BamHI target sequence GGATCC, it was possible to use the same oligonucleotide duplexes to investigate methylation by the two MTases. Such a comparison is of significant interest because the target exocyclic amino groups are on different target bases. In this regard, there appears to be a difference in the kinetic behavior of the [adenine-N6] and [cytosine-N4] MTases (64, 81, 82). For example, the rate constant of methyl group transfer from AdoMet to the [cytosine-N4] position catalyzed by BamHI MTase is one order of magnitude lower than that for T4Dam methylation of the [adenine-N6] position (81, 82). In addition, T4Dam has a higher affinity for substrate DNA duplex and AdoMet compared to BamHI MTase. However, the results of pre-steady state experiments showed that both enzymes catalyze effective transfer of the methyl group to DNA independent of which substrate was preincubated with the enzyme (*81, 82*). These results are consistent with random formation of productive ternary enzyme–substrate complexes. Thus, in spite of several important distinctions in their kinetic parameters, it was possible that BamHI and T4Dam MTases share a common kinetic mechanism.

To determine the order of BamHI MTase substrate binding and product release, we studied DNA methylation rate as a function of the substrate and product concentrations. The character of all the double-reciprocal plots were analogous to those obtained earlier with the T4Dam MTase (*70*). In summary, AdoHcy was a competitive inhibitor with regard to AdoMet, and a noncompetitive inhibitor with respect to substrate unmethylated 20-mer duplex (D). The other reaction product, fully methylated 20-mer duplex (P), was a noncompetitive inhibitor with regard to both AdoMet and unmethylated 20-mer duplex. Thus, as for the T4Dam MTase, these results are consistent with a steady state, BamHI MTase substrate binding and product release that obey the order AdoMet ↓ DNA ↓ DNA^{Me} ↑ AdoHcy↑.

Since earlier pre-steady state kinetic data (*82*) did not exclude a random route for the productive complex ESD formation, we attempted to describe the steady-state experimental data by scheme presented in Fig. 11, where BamHI MTase random binding with both substrates is permissible. This scheme, with addition of an alternative route of enzyme binding with substrate, in the order DNA↓AdoMet↓, described the experimental data (kinetic parameters and statistics of fitting are presented in (*116*)).

However, on the basis of the graphic analysis, one could suppose that there is a preferential route of central complex ESD formation, as in the case of T4Dam (Fig. 8), AdoMet ↓ DNA ↓. A fraction of this pathway in the whole reaction velocity is determined by expression (*117*):

$$f1 = \frac{k_1 \cdot S/[1 + k_{-1}/(k_3 \cdot D)]}{k_1 \cdot S/[1 + k_{-1}/(k_3 \cdot D)] + k_2 \cdot D/[1 + k_{-2}/(k_4 \cdot S)]} \quad (9)$$

We have calculated f1 values for all experimental points (not shown). With the exception of a small number of them, where the concentration of DNA was significantly higher than that of AdoMet, the f1 values were in the range 0.7–0.98. In particular, where substrate concentrations were close to their K_m values ($K_m^{DNA} = 0.2$ μM and $K_m^{AdoMet} = 1.22$ μM), the f1 values were approximately 0.95. Taken together, the results of fitting are best described by a dominant route of reaction in which the sequence of substrate binding is AdoMet ↓ DNA ↓.

In conclusion, the kinetic schemes of the reactions catalyzed by the T4Dam [adenine-N6]-MTase and the BamHI [cytosine-N4]-MTase differ significantly. A comparison of the two MTases is summarized in Table VII.

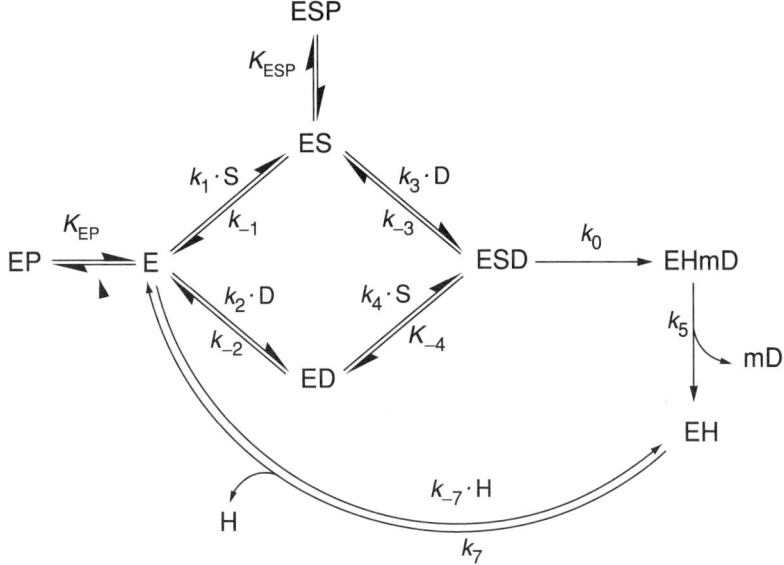

FIG. 11. Scheme for BamHI MTase methylation of the 20mer DNA duplex. E, BamHI MTase; S, AdoMet; H, AdoHcy; D, (20-mer) unmethylated DNA duplex; mD, hemimethylated DNA duplex; P, fully methylated DNA duplex.

Thus, the common chemical step of the reaction, methyl transfer from AdoMet to a free exocyclic amino group, is not sufficient to dictate a common kinetic scheme. Nonetheless, both enzymes follow the same overall reaction route, AdoMet ↓ DNA ↓ DNA^{Me} ↑ AdoHcy↑.

2. SYMMETRY ELEMENTS OF DNA STRUCTURE IMPORTANT FOR RECOGNITION

To compare the importance of specific site structural elements for recognition by BamHI and T4Dam MTases, we used the same approach of dissected DNA substrates described in Section III.A. Kinetic parameters of methyl transfer catalyzed by BamHI MTase were determined for substrate duplexes having different deletions of internucleotide phosphates or nucleotide residues, which are involved in specific site 5'-GGATCC/5'-GGATCC. In all variant duplexes, the upper chain was intact, while individual elements were deleted in the bottom strand. Figure 12 shows the influence of each deletion in the specific site on the k_{cat}/K_m value for both MTases [Zinoviev, Yakischik, Evdokimov, and Malygin, unpublished]. It is evident that a sharp decrease in activity of both MTases occurred if the structural symmetry was disrupted

TABLE VII
DIFFERENCES BETWEEN KINETIC PROPERTIES OF THE BAMHI AND T4DAM MTASES

Features	BamHI	T4Dam
General scheme of reaction	Random bi-bi	Ordered bi-bi
Inhibition of reaction by substrates	Absent	DNA at high concentration inhibits the reaction
Activation of reaction by substrates	Absent	Increasing the concentration of AdoMet leads to a progressive stimulation in the reaction rate
Limiting step of reaction	The chemical step of reaction is slowest (0.085 s^{-1}), although the effective rate of release of the products is only 2-fold higher (0.14 s^{-1})	Release of the product AdoHcy from enzyme appears to be rate-limiting in the overall reaction (at least 20-fold lower comparing with the chemical step, 0.56 s^{-1})
Enzyme isomerization	Not known	Repeating reaction cycles are catalyzed by isomerized T4Dam form, F, which is specifically adapted for catalysis

at certain sites. For the BamHI MTase, integrity of the sequence 5'-ATCC (including internucleotide phosphates) is critical, while an intact 5'-GAT sequence is necessary for activity of T4Dam. Both sequences partially overlap, have the polar relative positions, and are centered around the principal element of the recognition site–modification target (an A residue in case of T4Dam and the first C residue in the case of BamHI MTase).

IV. Structure of T4Dam

A. Alignment of Motifs and Secondary Structures

T4Dam belongs to the large family of α-group type II DNA MTases (37), in which there are at least 50 members known today and almost half of them are [N6-adenine] GATC-specific isoschizomers. This group has a characteristic motif order of motif I (Phe-x-Gly), followed by the DNA-binding target recognition domain (TRD) and motif IV (Asp-Pro-Pro-Tyr). Furthermore, the enzymes that modify the N6-amino nitrogen of adenine share not only the nine conserved motifs, but also possess striking similarity in their target recognition domains, although they have different targets; e.g., GATC, GANTC, GATATC, and nonpalindromic GGATG (98). Such homology may,

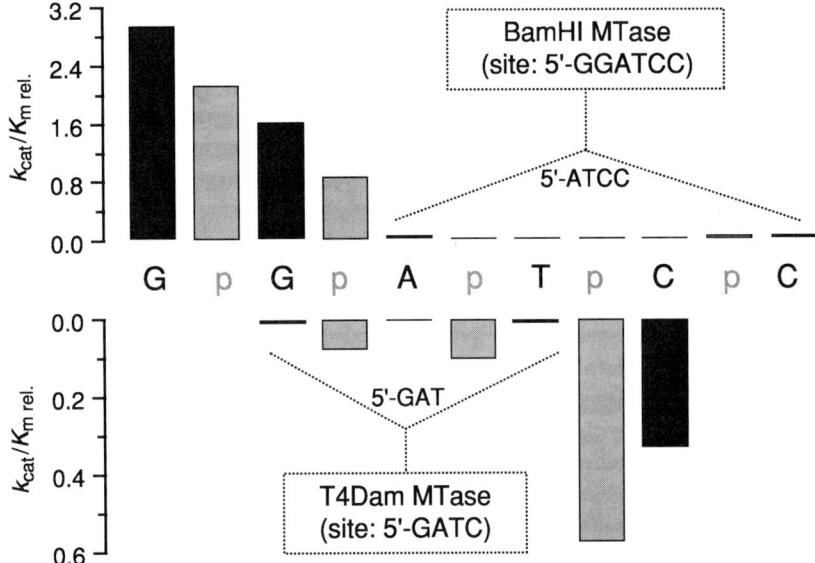

FIG. 12. Comparison of methylation capabilities of T4Dam and BamHI MTases using ODN duplexes containing defined deletions in the target site. Values k_{cat}/K_m for duplexes with deletions are normalized to k_{cat}/K_m for duplex with native site. Critical deletions are marked for both the MTases. For BamHI MTase, deletion of either G residue or the phosphate between them resulted in a marked acceleration of catalysis.

in turn, indicate that a considerable amount of similarity exists in their three-dimensional structures, as well as in their mechanism of action.

Figure 13 shows an alignment of several T4Dam orthologs. Conserved residues in the primary sequence, including sixteen invariant positions, appear scattered throughout the catalytic domain and TRD.

B. Three-Dimensional Structure from X-ray Crystallography

Recently, progress has been made in the study of DNA-[adenine] MTases. The first crystal structure for the GATC-specific DpnM MTase complexed with AdoMet was reported (98), and an extensive biochemical investigation of the GATATC-specific EcoRV MTase was performed (59, 62, 118–120). We have reported the crystal structures of T4Dam DNA MTase in a binary complex with AdoHcy and in a ternary complex with a synthetic 12 base pair DNA duplex and AdoHcy (44). T4Dam consists of two domains—the catalytic domain and the DNA binding domain. A seven-stranded catalytic domain (see legend to Fig. 13) harbors the binding site for AdoHcy, which is conserved among all the structurally characterized DNA MTases. The DNA-binding domain consists of a

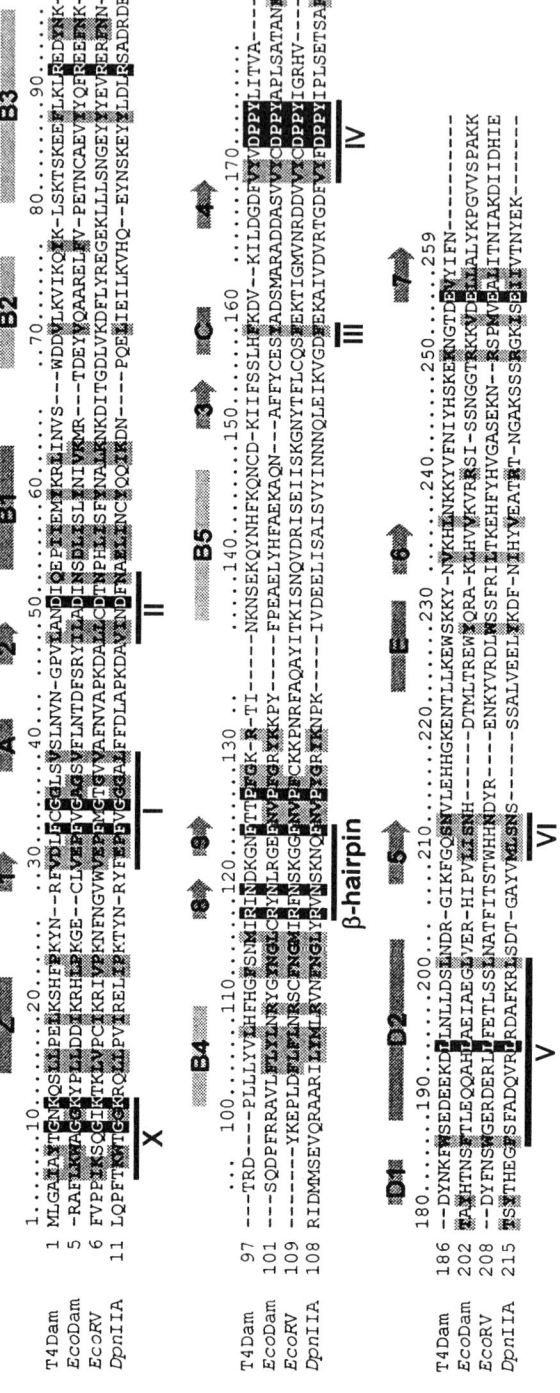

FIG. 13. Structure-based sequence alignment of the selected Dam MTase orthologs: bacteriophage T4Dam, EcoDam, restriction-modification MTases EcoRV and DpnIIA. The secondary structure of T4Dam is indicated above the sequence with rectangles and arrows for β-strands. The MTase catalytic domain is composed of the N-terminal region Z–B1, and the C-terminal region 3–7. The TRD includes α-helices B2, B3, B4, and B5. Conserved sequence motifs characteristic of the DNA–amino MTases (37) are labeled in roman numerals. Invariant amino acids are highlighted as white characters against a black background; conserved residues are highlighted in gray.

five-helix bundle and a β-hairpin that is conserved in the family of GATC-related Dam MTase orthologs. Surprisingly, the sequence-specific T4Dam bound to DNA in a nonspecific mode that contained two Dam monomers per synthetic duplex, even though the DNA contains a GATC site. The ternary structure provides a rare snapshot of an enzyme poised for linear diffusion along the DNA.

The monomeric Dam structure contains nine β-strands and 11 α-helices (Fig. 13). The N-terminal region (residues 1–52) and C-terminal region (residues 149–259) come together, forming the catalytic domain with a seven-stranded β-sheet (3 ↑ 2 ↑ 1 ↑ 4 ↑ 5 ↑ 7 ↓ 6↑)—a characteristic feature of the class-I AdoMet-dependent MTases (121). The N-terminal helices αZ and αA are located on one side of the β-sheet, and helices αC, αD1 and αD2, and αE are on the other side. Between strands β2 and β3 is the TRD, composed of a five-helix bundle (αB1–αB5) and a 25-residue segment containing a β-hairpin (β8 and β9) inserted between helices αB4 and αB5. The overall dimensions of the molecule are 55 × 34 × 28 Å, with an open cleft located between the catalytic domain and the TRD.

Conserved residues in the primary sequence, including 16 invariant positions, appear scattered throughout the catalytic domain and TRD. However, the folded structure showed that these invariant residues are clustered on two surface patches. The conserved surface patches may have functional importance, being involved in one of the three steps in the methylation reaction: AdoMet binding (Phe32 and Gly34 of motif I, Asp50 of motif II), DNA binding and sequence-specific recognition (Arg91 of αB3, Arg116 and Asn118 of the β-hairpin), and catalysis of methyl transfer (Asp-Pro-Pro-Tyr of motifIV, Lys11 of motifX, and Glu254 of β7). The N-terminal Gly9 (motifX) is involved in making a sharp turn that positions the nearby conserved residue Lys11 into the active site (see following text).

The structure of the Dam MTase offers a rationale for its conservation. For example, Pro126 (after the β-hairpin and within the TRD) is exposed on the surface together with Arg91, Arg116, and Asn118 (Fig. 2B), invariant residues that have been implicated in specific EcoRV–DNA interactions (122). It should be recalled that the Pro126Ser mutation generates the Dam^h forms of both T4Dam and T2Dam (Section I.C), which methylate noncognate sites such as the internal A in AGACC, resulting in resistance to cleavage by the EcoP1 restriction endonuclease. The altered activity of Dam^h may be due to the involvement of the surface Ser hydroxyl in extra hydrogen bonding with DNA at noncognate sites.

1. DAM–ADOHCY INTERACTIONS

In the binary Dam–AdoHcy complex, AdoHcy (added during purification) was observed at the carboxyl ends of the parallel strands β1, β2, and β4 surrounded by the conserved residues from motifs X (Tyr7), I (Phe32-Ser33-Gly34),

II (Asp50), IV (Asp171-Pro172-Pro173), and αD1 (Tyr181, Phe184, Trp185) (44). In this regard, mutation of Pro172 to Ala or Thr appeared to abolish enzyme activity *in vitro*, due to an increase in the K_m for AdoMet by 5- or 20-fold, respectively (63). Thus, when the AdoMet concentration was raised well above the K_m, the overall k_{cat} of these variants was reduced by only two-fold. Pro172 lies next to AdoHcy and the backbone carbonyl oxygen between Asp171 and Pro172 makes van der Waals contact with the homocysteine carbon $C\gamma$ (44). It is possible that the Pro172 mutations change the backbone conformation, substantially lowering the affinity for AdoMet and the rate of exchange with bound AdoHcy, thereby lowering the k_{cat}.

T4Dam–AdoHcy interactions can be grouped according to the three moieties of AdoHcy: (i) One side of the adenine ring forms edge-to-face van der Waals contacts with the phenyl ring of Phe32 after strand $\beta1$; this interaction is highly conserved among DNA MTases (97). On the other side of the adenine ring lies the side chain of Ile51 (after strand $\beta2$). The exocyclic amino group (N6) of adenine makes water-mediated hydrogen bonds to the main chain carbonyl oxygen of Phe184. The ring nitrogen N1 of Ade hydrogen bonds to the backbone amide N-H of Phe157. (ii) A strongly conserved acidic residue (Asp50) at the carboxyl-end of strand $\beta2$ forms bifurcated hydrogen bonds with the ribose hydroxyls; this is nearly universal to class-I MTases (121). In addition, Tyr7 and Gln52 each form a hydrogen bond with one of the two ribose hydroxyls. (iii) The conserved Gly34 lies underneath the homocysteine moiety, while Asp171 interacts with the amino group (NH_3^+). The AdoHcy carboxyl oxygens (COO^-) interact with the backbone amide N-H of Lys11 and the side chain hydroxyl of Ser37.

A unique interaction of T4Dam involves the short helix αD1 (after the Asp-Pro-Pro-Tyr motif), which covers the AdoHcy molecule, nearly burying it in a closed-acidic pocket. The buried AdoHcy suggests that the exchange between the methyl donor AdoMet and reaction product AdoHcy requires the movement of the 3_{10} helix and the loops flanking it, which may explain the observation that AdoMet is partially co-purified with the enzyme (44). This helix includes Trp185, which is likely to be involved in the quenching of intrinsic tryptophan fluorescence that results from T4Dam binding of either AdoMet or AdoHcy (K_d 10× higher for AdoHcy) (83). This suggests that when T4Dam binds its cofactor or methylation product, it undergoes a conformational change that alters the environment of Trp185 (the other two tryptophan residues, Trp67 and Trp226, are located more than 20 Å away from the AdoHcy). The same closed flap AdoHcy binding site is observed in the nonspecific ternary structure (see following text); in both cases, the 3_{10} helix and the flanking loops are not involved in any crystal packing contacts. An open conformation was observed in the binary M.DpnII–AdoMet structure (98), where the AdoMet is largely visible and the cover (a five-residue longer loop after strand $\beta4$) is opened up.

2. ACTIVE SITE

The active site is likely to be situated in a narrow surface pocket next to AdoHcy. The AdoHcy sulfur atom lies in the bottom of this pocket. The loop after strand β4 contributes most of the residues (Asp-Pro-Pro-Tyr of motif IV and Tyr181) in the active site pocket. In the absence of the target Ade, the active site is occupied by two ordered water molecules, one of which bridges the side chains of Asp171 and the backbone carbonyl oxygen between Pro172 and Pro173, while the other one interacts with Tyr181. Remarkably, the invariant Asp-Pro-Pro-Tyr of T4Dam is superimposable onto the corresponding motif in the ternary complex of M.TaqI (*123*), as well as the binary complex of M.DpnII (*98*) and M.RsrI (*124*) in the absence of DNA, suggesting that the conformation of Asp-Pro-Pro-Tyr is quite stable and highly conserved. In addition, an invariant Lys11 (motif X) interacts with Asp171 (via charge–charge interaction) and Tyr174 (via hydrogen bond). The Asp171–Lys11–Tyr174 interactions confer additional stability to the active site. Interestingly, the mutant of the corresponding Lys in M.EcoRV (Lys16Arg) showed an altered specificity toward the target base (*120*).

Encouraged by the similar conformations of the Asp-Pro-Pro-Tyr motif in all N6-Ade MTase structures, we superimposed the target A of the TaqI MTase onto T4Dam. This superimposition placed the flipped-out A with the target amino nitrogen atom occupying the position of a water molecule in the active site. Focusing on this amino group, it was suggested earlier (*95*) that its spinning was impeded and its pK_a altered by the formation of a pair of hydrogen bonds, one of which is to a MTase backbone carbonyl oxygen. In the case of T4Dam, this would be between Pro172 and Pro173 in the conserved Asp-Pro-Pro-Tyr of motif IV. This particular carbonyl is expected to be fairly rigid as it is between two prolines. The second proton of the target amino group makes a hydrogen bond with the side-chain of Asp171. Together, these hydrogen bonds may increase the nitrogen electron density and facilitate a nucleophilic attack on the AdoMet methylsulfonium group. In addition, the hydroxyl group of Tyr181 is between the target amino group and the AdoHcy sulfur, where the transferable methyl group will be attached in the AdoMet, potentially also facilitating the reaction.

3. DAM–DNA NONSPECIFIC INTERACTIONS

T4Dam was also crystallized in a ternary complex with AdoHcy and a GATC-containing synthetic DNA duplex (*44*). The ODN, a self-complementary 12-base pair palindrome, had the sequence 5'-ACAG<u>GATC</u>CTGT-3', where the target GATC sequence is centrally located. In the crystal, the DNA duplexes (primarily in B-form) were stacked head-to-end along the crystallographic *a* axis with an approximately 15° twist at the joint, forming a pseudo-continuous DNA duplex. Unexpectedly, a nonspecific binding mode was observed in the crystal with two Dam monomers bound to one DNA duplex. The two Dam monomer structures in the nonspecific ternary complex were quite similar to each other and to the binary structure. There were no significant conformational changes evident after nonspecific binding in the ternary complex.

Protein–phosphate interactions were primarily mediated via the TRD, i.e., a stretch of ~20 amino acids from the β-hairpin to the amino-terminal end of helix αB5. Both Dam monomers approach the DNA from the minor groove side. Although electrostatic interactions are dominant, Phe111 of the β-hairpin makes van der Waals contacts with the phosphate backbone carbons. These features—the interactions occur primarily in the minor groove side, the protein structure is maintained, virtually no sequence-specific hydrogen bonds are formed—are also shared in other examples of nonsequence specific DNA binding (125).

V. Concluding Comments

Two fundamental roles are carried out by the structural elements of a recognition site. One of them is intermolecular contact(s) with amino acid residues of the enzyme that ensure specific interactions. Another role is to support the molecular architecture necessary to ensure correct conformational movement for a catalytically productive enzyme–substrate complex. The most popular approach to investigate these functions is to change certain exterior chemical groups of nucleotides forming the recognition site and to register the effect of these changes (50). This manipulation of substrate surface permits one to calculate the thermodynamic cost of the different chemical residues that participate in the recognition process. An additional approach is eliminating various structural elements from within the recognition site (126, 127).

What are the main contacts between T4Dam and its DNA substrate? It is clear that the G residues in the top and bottom strands are critical, because their presence is essential for both binding and catalysis. Absence of the central A-T residues in the bottom strand or a double mismatch in this position did not significantly influence T4Dam binding, but strongly inhibited or completely eliminated methylation of A in the top strand. This shows that the A-T residues in the lower strand do not participate actively (or directly) in T4Dam binding with the upper strand. However, these A-T residues are strictly necessary for catalysis. Possibly, they interact directly with T4Dam residues in the complex formed or they are necessary for complementary interaction with the upper A-T during a conformational change in the complex (just before the methylated duplex is released from the enzyme).

The specific role for the C residue is unclear. Thus, the absence of C in the lower strand sharply decreased T4Dam binding, and the duplex was methylated at a 5-fold lower k_{cat}. Our general impression is that the G:C base-pairs are more important to ensure complex formation, while the central AT/TA pairing is necessary for an effective round of catalysis. In conclusion, whereas having only one-half of the recognition site element intact is sufficient for stable complex formation, the catalytic turnover process has a strict requirement for an uninterrupted GAT-sequence on both strands.

We do not understand why T4Dam failed to bind specifically with GATC sites in the ternary crystal structure (where they were separated by 12-base pairs from center to center). One explanation for the loose "nonspecific" binding between T4Dam and DNA derives from the fact that T4Dam, like *E. coli* Dam (79), methylates DNA with multiple GATC sites in a processive manner, i.e., more than one methyl group may be transferred per bound Dam monomer (67). Thus, under single-turnover conditions (Dam/DNA >1.0), a catalytically competent complex was formed that contained two Dam monomers per synthetic duplex (43). Since the rate-limiting step in the overall T4Dam methylation process is the release of product AdoHcy from the enzyme (70), it follows that after methyl transfer the Dam–AdoHcy complex must release from the target site, diffuse along the DNA, and AdoMet must exchange for AdoHcy before the next methyl transfer can occur. We suggest that in the ternary crystal structure, the T4Dam–AdoHcy complex may be positioned on the duplex in a fashion that corresponds to the stage following methyl transfer. That is, it is not in contact with the GATC target site; rather, it contacts the phosphodiester backbone and is primed for diffusion and/or exchange of AdoHcy with AdoMet. It is interesting to note that restriction-associated MTases are distributive (79), because processive methylation of DNA could interfere with the biological function of restriction-modification systems. However, the structural basis for T4Dam processivity is not obvious in comparison with M.DpnII; this pair of proteins has quite similar structures but differ substantially in their processivity. It has been suggested (128) that processive enzymes tend to more completely enclose their substrates. More structural work will be required to settle this point.

ACKNOWLEDGMENTS

This chapter is dedicated to the memory of Salvador E. Luria in whose lab it all began more than 50 years ago. This work was supported by a U.S. Public Health Service grant from the Fogarty International Center (R03 TW05755), the Russian Foundation for Basic Research (project no. 01-04-49869), and U.S. Public Health Service grant GM29227 (SH). The authors express their gratitude to the many coworkers who made important contributions to the studies described in this chapter. They include Toshio Fukasawa, Helen Revel, Joan Brooks, Samuel

Schlagman, Zoe Miner, Valeri Kossykh, Xiaodong Cheng, Victor Zinoviev, Alexey Evdokimov, Lidiya Ovechkina, Fedor Tuzikov, Norbert Reich, and William Lindstrom, Jr. Special thanks go to Alexey Evdokimov for his critical reading of the manuscript and many helpful suggestions.

References

1. Luria, S. E., and Human, M. L. (1952). A non-hereditary, host-induced variation of bacterial viruses. *J. Bacteriol.* **64,** 557–569.
2. Bertani, G., and Weigle, J. J. (1953). Host controlled variation in bacterial viruses. *J. Bacteriol.* **65,** 113–121.
3. Wyatt, G. R., and Cohen, S. S. (1952). A new pyrimidine base from bacteriophage nucleic acids. *Nature (London)* **170,** 1072–1073.
4. Lehman, I. R., and Pratt, E. A. (1960). On the structure of the glucosylated hydroxymethyl cytosine nucleotides of coliphages T2, T4, and T6. *J. Biol. Chem.* **235,** 3254–3259.
5. Greenberg, G. R., He, P., Hilfinger, J., and Tseng, M.-J. (1994). Deoxyribonucleoside triphosphate synthesis and phage T4 DNA replication. In "Molecular Biology of Bacteriophage T4" (J. D. Karam, Ed.), pp. 14–27. American Society for Microbiology Press, Washington, DC.
6. Hattman, S., and Fukasawa, T. (1963). Host-induced modification of T-even bacteriophages due to defective glucosylation of their DNA. *Proc. Natl. Acad. Sci. USA* **50,** 297–300.
7. Hattman, S. (1964). The functioning of T-even phages with unglucosylated DNA in restricting *Escherichia coli* host cells. *Virology* **24,** 333–348.
8. Arber, W. (1965). Host specificity of DNA produced by *Escherichia coli*. V. The role of methionine in the production of host specificity. *J. Mol. Biol.* **11,** 247–256.
9. Klein, A. (1965). Mechanismen der Wirtskontrollierten Modifikation des Phagen T1. *Z. Vererbungslehre* **96,** 346–363.
10. Arber, W., and Kühnlein, U. (1967). Mutationeller Verlust B-spezifischer Restriktion des Bakteriophagens fd. *Pathol. Microbiol.* **30,** 946–952.
11. Revel, H. R., and Luria, S. E. (1970). DNA-glucosylation in T-even phage: Genetic determination and role in phage-host interaction. *Annu. Rev. Genet.* **4,** 177–192.
12. Carlson, K., Raleigh, E. A., and Hattman, S. (1994). Restriction and modification. In "Molecular Biology of Bacteriophage T4" (J. D. Karam, Ed.), pp. 369–381. American Society for Microbiology Press, Washington, DC.
13. Revel, H. R., and Georgopoulos, C. P. (1969). Restriction of nonglucosylated T-even bacteriophages by prophage P1. *Virology* **39,** 1–17.
14. Dunn, D. B., and Smith, J. D. (1958). The occurrence of 6-methylaminopurine in deoxyribonucleic acids. *Nature (London)* **68,** 627–636.
15. Gefter, M., Hausmann, R., Gold, M., and Hurwitz, J. (1966). The enzymatic methylation of ribonucleic acid and deoxyribonucleic acid. X. Bacteriophage T3-induced S-adenosylmethionine cleavage. *J. Biol. Chem.* **241,** 1995–2006.
16. Fujimoto, D., Srinivasan, P. R., and Borek, E. (1965). On the nature of the deoxyribonucleic acid methylases. Biological evidence for the multiple nature of the enzymes. *Biochemistry* **4,** 2849–2855.
17. Gold, M., Hausmann, R., Maitra, U., and Hurwitz, J. (1964). The enzymatic methylation of RNA and DNA. VII. Effects of bacteriophage infection on the activity of the methylating enzymes. *Proc. Natl. Acad. Sci. USA* **52,** 292–297.
18. Hausmann, R., and Gold, M. (1966). The enzymatic methylation of ribonucleic acid and deoxyribonucleic acid. IX. Deoxyribonucleic acid methylase in bacteriophage-infected *Escherichia coli*. *J. Biol. Chem.* **241,** 1985–1994.

19. Hattman, S. (1970). DNA methylation of T-even bacteriophages and of their nonglucosylated mutants. Their role in P1-directed restriction. *Virology* **42**, 359–367.
20. Revel, H. R., and Hattman, S. M. (1971). Mutants of T2*gt* with altered DNA methylase activity: Relation to restriction by prophage P1. *Virology* **45**, 484–495.
21. Miner, Z., and Hattman, S. (1988). Molecular cloning, sequencing, and mapping of the bacteriophage T2 *dam* gene. *J. Bacteriol.* **170**, 5177–5184.
22. Hattman, S. (1981). DNA methylation. In "The Enzymes" (P. D. Boyer, Ed.), pp. 517–548. Academic Press, NY.
23. Hehlmann, R., and Hattman, S. (1972). Mutants of bacteriophage T2*gt* with altered DNA methylase activity. *J. Mol. Biol.* **67**, 351–360.
24. Hattman, S., van Ormondt, H., and de Waard, A. (1978). Sequence specificity of the wild-type (dam^+) and mutant (dam^h) forms of bacteriophage T2 DNA adenine methylase. *J. Mol. Biol.* **119**, 361–376.
25. Brooks, J. E., and Hattman, S. (1978). *In vitro* methylation of bacteriophage lambda DNA by wild type (dam^+) and mutant (dam^h) forms of the phage T2 DNA adenine methylase. *J. Mol. Biol.* **126**, 381–394.
26. Hattman, S., Brooks, J. E., and Masurekar, M. (1978). Sequence specificity of the P1 modification methylase (M. *Eco* P1) and the DNA methylase (M. *Eco dam*) controlled by the *Escherichia coli dam* gene. *J. Mol. Biol.* **126**, 367–380.
27. Schlagman, S. L., and Hattman, S. (1989). The bacteriophage T2 and T4 DNA [N6-adenine]-methyltransferase (Dam) sequence specificities are not identical. *Nucleic Acids Res.* **17**, 9101–9112.
28. Miner, Z., Schlagman, S. L., and Hattman, S. (1989). Single amino acid changes that alter the DNA sequence specificity of the DNA-[N6-adenine] methyltransferase (Dam) of bacteriophage T4. *Nucleic Acids Res.* **17**, 8149–8157.
29. Minko, I., Hattman, S., Lloyd, R. S., and Kossykh, V. (2001). Methylation by a mutant T2 DNA [N(6)-adenine] methyltransferase expands the usage of RecA-assisted endonuclease (RARE) cleavage. *Nucleic Acids Res.* **29**, 1484–1490.
30. Scherzer, E., Auer, B., and Schweiger, M. (1987). Identification, purification, and characterization of *Escherichia coli* virus T1 DNA methyltransferase. *J. Biol. Chem.* **262**, 15225–15231.
31. Brockes, J. P., Brown, P. R., and Murray, K. (1972). The deoxyribonucleic acid modification enzyme of bacteriophage P1. *Biochem. J.* **127**, 1–10.
32. de la Campa, A. G., Kale, P., Springhorn, S. S., and Lacks, S. A. (1987). Proteins encoded by the *Dpn*II restriction gene cassette. Two methylases and an endonuclease. *J. Mol. Biol.* **196**, 457–469.
33. Van Etten, J. L., Schuster, A. M., Girton, L., Burbank, D. E., Swinton, D., and Hattman, S. (1985). DNA methylation of viruses infecting a eukaryotic *Chlorella*-like green alga. *Nucleic Acids Res.* **13**, 3471–3478.
34. Schlagman, S. L., and Hattman, S. (1983). Molecular cloning of a functional dam^+ gene coding for phage T4 DNA adenine methylase. *Gene* **22**, 139–156.
35. Macdonald, P. M., and Mosig, G. (1984). Regulation of a new bacteriophage T4 gene, 69, that spans an origin of replication. *EMBO J.* **3**, 2863–2871.
36. Hattman, S., Wilkinson, J., Swinton, D., Schlagman, S. L., Macdonald, P. M., and Mosig, G. (1985). Common evolutionary origin of the phage T4 *dam* and host *Escherichia coli dam* DNA-adenine methyltransferase genes. *J. Bacteriol.* **164**, 932–937.
36a. Mannarelli, B. M., Balganesh, T. S., Greenberg, B., Springhorn, S. S., and Lacks, S. A. (1985). Nucleotide sequence of the *Dpn* II DNA methylase gene of *Streptococcus pneumoniae* and its relationship to the *dam* gene of *Escherichia coli*. *Proc. Natl. Acad. Sci. USA* **82**, 4468–4472.

37. Malone, Th., Blumenthal, R. M., and Cheng, X. (1995). Structure-guided analysis reveals nine sequence motifs conserved among DNA amino-methyltransferases, and suggests a catalytic mechanism for these enzymes. *J. Mol. Biol.* **253,** 618–632.
38. Timinskas, A., Butkus, V., and Janulaitis, A. (1995). Sequence motifs characteristic for DNA [cytosine-N4] and DNA [adenine-N6] methyltransferases. Classification of all DNA methyltransferases. *Gene* **157,** 3–11.
39. Kossykh, V. G., Schlagman, S. L., and Hattman, S. (1997). Comparative studies of the phage T2 and T4 DNA (N6-adenine)methyltransferases: Amino acid changes that affect catalytic activity. *J. Bacteriol.* **179,** 3239–3243.
40. Kossykh, V. G., Schlagman, S. L., and Hattman, S. M. (1995). Phage T4 DNA [N6-adenine]-methyltransferase. Overexpression, purification, and characterization. *J. Biol. Chem.* **270,** 14389–14393.
41. Kurganov, B. I. (1977). The theoretical analysis of kinetic behaviour of "hysteretic" allosteric enzymes. IV. Kinetics of dissociation–association processes of allosteric enzymes. *J. Theor. Biol.* **68,** 521–543.
42. Zinoviev, V. V., Ovechkina, L. G., and Malygin, E. G. (1996). Stoichiometry of phage T4 Dam–DNA-[N6-adenine]-methyltransferase binding with oligonucleotide substrates. *Mol. Biol.* **30,** 1203–1208.
43. Malygin, E. G., Lindstrom, W. M., Jr., Zinoviev, V. V., Evdokimov, A. A., Schlagman, S. L., Reich, N. O., and Hattman, S. (2003). Bacteriophage T4 Dam DNA-(Adenine-N6)-methyltransferase: Evidence for two distinct stages of methylation under single turnover conditions. *J. Biol. Chem.* **278,** 41749–41755.
44. Yang, Z., Horton, J. R., Zhou, L., Zhang, X. J., Dong, A., Zhang, X., Schlagman, S. L., Kossykh, S., Hattman, S., and Cheng, X. (2003). Structure of the bacteriophage T4 DNA adenine methyltransferase. *Nat. Struct. Biol.* **10,** 849–855.
45. Malygin, E. G., Evdokimov, A. A., Zinoviev, V. V., Ovechkina, L. G., Lindstrom, W. M., Reich, N. O., Schlagman, S. L., and Hattman, S. M. (2001). A dual role for substrate S-adenosyl-L-methionine in the methylation reaction with bacteriophage T4 Dam DNA-[N6-adenine]-methyltransferase. *Nucleic Acids Res.* **29,** 2361–2369.
46. Chen, L., MacMillan, A. M., Chang, W., Ezaz-Nikpay, K., Lane, W. S., and Verdine, G. L. (1991). Direct identification of the active-site nucleophile in a DNA (cytosine-5)-methyltransferase. *Biochemistry* **30,** 11018–11025.
47. Freese, E. (1959). The specific mutagenic effect of base analogues on phage T4. *J. Mol. Biol.* **1,** 87–105.
48. Malygin, E. G., Petrov, N. A., Gorbunov, Yu. A., Kossykh, V. G., and Hattman, S. M. (1997). Interaction of the phage T4 DNA-[N6-adenine]-(Dam)methyltransferase with oligonucleotides containing native or modified (defective) recognition sites. *Nucleic Acids Res.* **25,** 4393–4399.
49. Petrov, N. A., Gorbunov, Yu. A., Naumochkin, A. N., and Malygin, E. G. (1997). Complexes of DNA-[N6-adenine]-methyltransferases of T-even phages with their substrates which are determined by "blocking in gel" method. *Mol. Biol.* **31,** 966–972.
50. Lesser, D. R., Kurpiewski, M. R., Waters, T., Connolly, B. A., and Jen-Jacobson, L. (1993). Facilitated distortion of the DNA site enhances *Eco*RI endonuclease–DNA recognition. *Proc. Natl. Acad. Sci. USA* **90,** 7548–7552.
51. Malygin, E. G., Zinoviev, V. V., Petrov, N. A., Evdokimov, A. A., Jen-Jacobson, L., Kossykh, V. G., and Hattman, S. (1999). Effect of base analog substitutions in the specific GATC site on binding and methylation of oligonucleotide duplexes by the bacteriophage T4 Dam DNA-[N6-adenine] methyltransferase. *Nucleic Acids Res.* **27,** 1135–1144.
52. Cheng, X., Kumar, S., Posfai, J., Pflugrath, J. W., and Roberts, R. J. (1993). Crystal structure of the *Hha*I DNA methyltransferase complexed with S-adenosyl-L-methionine. *Cell* **74,** 299–307.

53. Cheng, X., Kumar, S., Klimasauskas, S., and Roberts, R. J. (1993). Crystal structure of the HhaI DNA methyltransferase. *Cold Spring Harbor Symp. Quant. Biol.* **58**, 331–338.
54. Klimasauskas, S., Kumar, S., Roberts, R. J., and Cheng, X. (1994). HhaI methyltransferase flips its target base out of the DNA helix. *Cell* **76**, 357–369.
55. Reinisch, K. M., Chen, L., Verdine, G. L., and Lipscomb, W. N. (1995). The crystal structure of HaeIII methyltransferase convalently complexed to DNA: An extrahelical cytosine and rearranged base pairing. *Cell* **82**, 143–153.
56. Allan, B. W., and Reich, N. O. (1996). Targeted base stacking disruption by the EcoRI DNA methyltransferase. *Biochemistry* **35**, 14757–14762.
57. Holz, B., Klimasauskas, S., Serva, S., and Weinhold, E. (1998). 2-Aminopurine as a fluorescent probe for DNA base flipping by methyltransferases. *Nucleic Acids Res.* **26**, 1076–1083.
58. Serva, S., Weinhold, E., Roberts, R. J., and Klimasauskas, S. (1998). Chemical display of thymine residues flipped out by DNA methyltransferases. *Nucleic Acids Res.* **26**, 3473–3479.
59. Jeltsch, A., Roth, M., and Friedrich, T. (1999). Mutational analysis of target base flipping by the EcoRV adenine-N6 DNA methyltransferase. *J. Mol. Biol.* **285**, 1121–1130.
60. Vilkaitis, G., Dong, A., Weinhold, E., Cheng, X., and Klimasauskas, S. (2000). Functional roles of the conserved threonine 250 in the target recognition domain of HhaI DNA methyltransferase. *J. Biol. Chem.* **275**, 38722–38730.
61. Szegedi, S. S., Reich, N. O., and Gumport, R. I. (2000). Substrate binding in vitro and kinetics of RsrI [N6-adenine] DNA methyltransferase. *Nucleic Acids Res.* **28**, 3962–3971.
62. Gowher, H., and Jeltsch, A. (2000). Molecular enzymology of the EcoRV DNA-(adenine-N 6)-methyltransferase: Kinetics of DNA binding and bending, kinetic mechanism and linear diffusion of the enzyme on DNA. *J. Mol. Biol.* **303**, 93–110.
63. Kossykh, V. G., Schlagman, S. L., and Hattman, S. M. (1993). Conserved sequence motif DPPY in region IV of the phage T4 Dam DNA-[N6-adenine]-methyltransferase is important for S-adenosyl-L-methionine binding. *Nucleic Acids Res.* **21**, 4659–4662.
64. Zinoviev, V. V., Evdokimov, A. A., Gorbunov, Yu. A., Malygin, E. G., Kossykh, V. G., and Hattman, S. (1998). Phage T4 DNA [N6-adenine] methyltransferase: Kinetic studies using oligonucleotides containing native or modified recognition sites. *Biol. Chem.* **379**, 481–488.
65. Lesser, D. R., Kurpiewski, M. R., and Jen-Jacobson, L. (1990). The energetic basis of specificity in the EcoRI endonuclease–DNA interaction. *Science* **250**, 776–786.
66. Szczelkun, M. D., Jones, H., and Connolly, B. A. (1995). Probing the protein–DNA interface of the EcoRV modification methyltransferase bound to its recognition sequence, GATATC. *Biochemistry* **34**, 10734–10743.
67. Zinoviev, V. V., Evdokimov, A. A., Malygin, E. G., Schlagman, S. L., and Hattman, S. (2003). Bacteriophage T4 Dam DNA-(N6-adenine)-methyltransferase. Processivity and orientation to the methylation target. *J. Biol. Chem.* **278**, 7829–7833.
68. Wu, J. C., and Santi, D. V. (1987). Kinetic and catalytic mechanism of HhaI methyltransferase. *J. Biol. Chem.* **262**, 4778–4786.
69. Bhattacharya, S. K., and Dubey, A. K. (1999). Kinetic mechanism of cytosine DNA methyltransferase MspI. *J. Biol. Chem.* **274**, 14743–14749.
70. Evdokimov, A. A., Zinoviev, V. V., Malygin, E. G., Schlagman, S. L., and Hattman, S. (2002). Bacteriophage T4 Dam DNA-[N6-adenine]methyltransferase. Kinetic evidence for a catalytically essential conformational change in the ternary complex. *J. Biol. Chem.* **277**, 279–286.
71. Reich, N. O., and Mashhoon, N. (1993). Presteady state kinetics of an S-adenosylmethionine-dependent enzyme. Evidence for a unique binding orientation requirement for EcoRI DNA methyltransferase. *J. Biol. Chem.* **268**, 9191–9193.
72. Reich, N. O., and Mashhoon, N. (1991). Kinetic mechanism of the EcoRI DNA methyltransferase. *Biochemistry* **30**, 2933–2939.

73. Gromova, E. S., Oretzkaya, T. S., Eritja, R., and Guschlbauer, W. (1994). Kinetic studies of MvaI DNA methyltransferase interaction with modified oligonucleotide duplexes. *Biochem. Mol. Biol. Intl.* **36,** 247–255.
74. Adams, G. M., and Blumenthal, R. M. (1997). The PvuII DNA (cytosine-N4)-methyltransferase comprises two trypsin-defined domains, each of which binds a molecule of S-adenosyl-L-methionine. *Biochemistry* **36,** 8284–8292.
75. Berdis, A. J., Lee, I., Coward, J. K., Stephens, C., Wright, R., Shapiro, L., and Benkovic, S. J. (1998). A cell cycle-regulated adenine DNA methyltransferase from *Caulobacter crescentus* processively methylates GANTC sites on hemimethylated DNA. *Proc. Natl. Acad. Sci. USA* **95,** 2874–2879.
76. Lindstrom, W. M., Flynn, J., and Reich, N. O. (2000). Reconciling structure and function in HhaI DNA cytosine-C-5 methyltransferase. *J. Biol. Chem.* **275,** 4912–4919.
77. Vilkaitis, G., Merkiene, E., Serva, S., Weinhold, E., and Klimasauskas, S. (2001). The mechanism of DNA cytosine-5 methylation. Kinetic and mutational dissection of HhaI methyltransferase. *J. Biol. Chem.* **276,** 20924–20934.
78. Thielking, V., Dubois, S., Eritja, R., and Guschlbauer, W. (1997). Dam methyltransferase from *Escherichia coli*: Kinetic studies using modified DNA oligomers: Nonmethylated substrates. *Biol. Chem.* **378,** 407–415.
79. Urig, S., Gowher, H., Hermann, A., Beck, C., Fatemi, M., Humeny, A., and Jeltsch, A. (2002). The *Escherichia coli* dam DNA methyltransferase modifies DNA in a highly processive reaction. *J. Mol. Biol.* **319,** 1085–1096.
80. Bheemanaik, S., Chandrashekaran, S., Nagaraja, V., and Rao, D. N. (2003). Kinetic and catalytic properties of dimeric KpnI DNA methyltransferase. *J. Biol. Chem.* **278,** 7863–7874.
81. Lindstrom, W. M., Jr., Malygin, E. G., Ovechkina, L. G., Zinoviev, V. V., and Reich, N. O. (2003). Functional analysis of BamHI DNA cytosine-N4 methyltransferase. *J. Mol. Biol.* **325,** 711–720.
82. Malygin, E. G., Lindstrom, W. M., Jr., Schlagman, S. L., Hattman, S. M., and Reich, N. O. (2000). Pre-steady state kinetics of bacteriophage T4 Dam DNA-[N6-adenine] methyltransferase: Interaction with native (GATC) or modified sites. *Nucleic Acids Res.* **28,** 4207–4211.
83. Tuzikov, F. V., Tuzikova, N. A., Naumochkin, A. N., Zinoviev, V. V., and Malygin, E. G. (1997). Fluorescence quenching study of equilibrium binding of phage T4 Dam DNA-[N6-Adenine]-methyltransferase with substrates and ligands. *Mol. Biol.* **31,** 73–76.
84. O'Gara, M., Zhang, X., Roberts, R. J., and Cheng, X. (1999). Structure of a binary complex of HhaI methyltransferase with S-adenosyl-L-methionine formed in the presence of a short nonspecific DNA oligonucleotide. *J. Mol. Biol.* **287,** 201–209.
85. Bacolla, A., Pradhan, S., Roberts, R. J., and Wells, R. D. (1999). Recombinant human DNA (cytosine-5) methyltransferase. II. Steady-state kinetics reveal allosteric activation by methylated DNA. *J. Biol. Chem.* **274,** 33011–33019.
86. Flynn, J., and Reich, N. O. (1998). Murine DNA (cytosine-C5)-methyltransferase: Steady-state and substrate trapping analyses of the kinetic mechanism. *Biochemistry* **37,** 15162–15169.
87. Allan, B. W., Reich, N. O., and Beechem, J. M. (1999). Measurement of the absolute temporal coupling between DNA binding and base flipping. *Biochemistry* **38,** 5308–5314.
88. Szilak, L., Der, A., Deak, F., and Venetianer, P. (1993). Kinetic characterization of the EcaI methyltransferase. *Eur. J. Biochem.* **218,** 727–733.
89. Wolcke, J. (1998). The kinetic mechanism of the DNA methyltransferase from *Thermus aquaticus* and selection of a DNA-binding peptide by means of phage display. Ph.D. Dissertation, University Dortmund, Germany.

90. Rao, D. N., Page, M. G., and Bickle, T. A. (1989). Cloning, overexpression, and the catalytic propeties of the *Eco*P15I modification methylase from *Escherichia coli*. *J. Mol. Biol.* **209**, 599–606.
91. Klimasauskas, S., Szyperski, T., Serva, S., and Wuthrich, K. (1998). Dynamic modes of the flipped-out cytosine during *Hha*I methyltransferase–DNA interactions in solution. *EMBO J.* **17**, 317–324.
92. Schluckebier, G., Kozak, M., Bleimling, N., Weinhold, E., and Saenger, W. (1997). Differential binding of S-adenosylmethionine, S-adenosylhomocysteine, and sinefungin to the adenine-specific DNA methyltransferase M.*Taq*I. *J. Mol. Biol.* **265**, 56–67.
93. Fatemi, M., Hermann, A., Pradhan, S., and Jeltsch, A. (2001). The activity of the murine DNA methyltransferase Dnmt1 is controlled by interaction of the catalytic domain with the N-terminal part of the enzyme leading to an allosteric activation of the enzyme after binding to methylated DNA. *J. Mol. Biol.* **309**, 1189–1199.
94. Bergerat, A., and Guschlbauer, W. (1990). The double role of methyl donor and allosteric effector of S-adenosyl-methionine for Dam methylase of *E. coli*. *Nucleic Acids Res.* **18**, 4369–4375.
95. Gong, W., O'Gara, M., Blumenthal, R. M., and Cheng, X. (1997). Structure of *Pvu*II DNA-(cytosine N4) methyltransferase, an example of domain permutation and protein fold assignment. *Nucleic Acids Res.* **25**, 2702–2715.
96. O'Gara, M., McCloy, K., Malone, Th., and Cheng, X. (1995). Structure-based sequence alignment of three AdoMet-dependent methyltransferases. *Gene* **157**, 135–138.
97. Schluckebier, G., O'Gara, M., Saenger, W., and Cheng, X. (1995). Universal catalytic domain structure of AdoMet-dependent methyltransferases. *J. Mol. Biol.* **247**, 16–20.
98. Tran, P. H., Korszun, Z. R., Cerritelli, S., Springhorn, S. S., and Lacks, S. A. (1998). Crystal structure of the *Dpn*M DNA adenine methyltransferase from the *Dpn*II restriction system of *Streptococcus pneumoniae* bound to S-adenosylmethionine. *Structure* **6**, 1563–1575.
99. Dong, A., Yoder, J. A., Zhang, X., Zhou, L., Bestor, T. H., and Cheng, X. (2001). Structure of human DNMT2, an enigmatic DNA methyltransferase homolog that displays denaturant-resistant binding to DNA. *Nucleic Acids Res.* **29**, 439–448.
100. Rudolph, F. B. (1979). Product inhibition and abortive complex formation. *Methods Enzymol.* **63**, 411–436.
101. O'Gara, M., Klimasauskas, S., Roberts, R. J., and Cheng, X. (1996). Enzymatic C5-cytosine methylation of DNA: Mechanistic implications of new crystal structures for *Hha*I methyltransferase–DNA–AdoHcy complexes. *J. Mol. Biol.* **261**, 634–645.
102. Cleland, W. W. (1979). Substrate inhibition. *Methods Enzymol.* **63**, 500–513.
103. Bonnichsen, R. K., Chance, B., and Theorell, H. (1947). Catalase activity. *Acta Chem. Scand.* **1**, 685–709.
104. Ogura, Y. (1955). Catalase activity at high concentration of hydrogen peroxide. *Arch. Biochem. Biophys.* **57**, 288–300.
105. Posnick, L. M., and Samson, L. D. (1999). Influence of S-adenosylmethionine pool size on spontaneous mutation, *dam* methylation, and cell growth of *Escherichia coli*. *J. Bacteriol.* **181**, 6756–6762.
106. Javor, G. T. (1983). Depression of adenosylmethionine content of *Escherichia coli* by thioglycerol. *Antimicrob. Agents Chemother.* **24**, 860–867.
107. Modrich, P. (1982). Studies on sequence recognition by type II restriction and modification enzymes. *CRC Crit. Rev. Biochem.* **13**, 287–323.
108. Kaszubska, W., Webb, H. K., and Gumport, R. I. (1992). Purification and characterization of the M.*Rsr*I DNA methyltransferase from *Escherichia coli*. *Gene* **118**, 5–11.

109. Dubey, A. K., Mollet, B., and Roberts, R. J. (1992). Purification and characterization of the *Msp*I DNA methyltransferase cloned and overexpressed in *E. coli*. *Nucleic Acids Res.* **20,** 1579–1585.
110. Yoo, H. Y., Noshari, J., and Lapeyre, J. N. (1987). Subunit and functional size of human placental DNA methyltransferase involved in *de novo* and maintenance methylation. *J. Biol. Chem.* **262,** 8066–8070.
111. Shier, V. K., Hancey, C. J., and Benkovic, S. J. (2001). Identification of the active oligomeric state of an essential adenine DNA methyltransferase from *Caulobacter crescentus*. *J. Biol. Chem.* **276,** 14744–14751.
112. Fersht, A. (1982). "Allosteric Enzymes. Kinetic Behaviour." John Wiley and Sons, Chichester, UK.
113. Fersht, A. (1985). "Enzyme Structure and Mechanism," pp. 133. W. H. Freeman & Co., New York, NY.
114. Cheng, X., and Roberts, R. J. (2001). AdoMet-dependent methylation, DNA methyltransferases, and base flipping. *Nucleic Acids Res.* **29,** 3784–3795.
115. Hattman, S., Keister, T., and Gottehrer, A. (1978). Sequence specificity of DNA methylases from *Bacillus amyloliquefaciens* and *Bacillus brevis*. *J. Mol. Biol.* **124,** 701–711.
116. Malygin, E. G., Zinoviev, V. V., Evodokimov, A. A., Lindstrom, W. M., Jr., Reich, N. O., and Hattman, S. (2003). DNA (cytosine-N4-)- and -(adenine-N6-)-methyltransferases have different kinetic mechanisms but the same reaction route. A comparison of M.*Bam*HI and T4 Dam. *J. Biol. Chem.* **278,** 15713–15719.
117. Malygin, E. G. (1977). Derivation of kinetic equations for steady-state enzyme reactions using multi-stage proportionate rates of enzyme form conversion. *Biofizika* **XXII,** 15–20.
118. Roth, M., Helm-Kruse, S., Friedrich, T., and Jeltsch, A. (1998). Functional roles of conserved amino acid residues in DNA methyltransferases investigated by site-directed mutagenesis of the *Eco*RV adenine-N^6-methyltransferase. *J. Biol. Chem.* **273,** 17333–17342.
119. Jeltsch, A., Friedrich, T., and Roth, M. (1998). Kinetics of methylation and binding of DNA by the *Eco*RV adenine-N^6 methyltransferase. *J. Mol. Biol.* **275,** 747–758.
120. Roth, M., and Jeltsch, A. (2001). Changing the target base specificity of the *Eco*RV DNA methyltransferase by rational *de novo* protein-design. *Nucleic Acids Res.* **29,** 3137–3144.
121. Schubert, H. L., Blumenthal, R. M., and Cheng, X. (2003). Many paths to methyltransfer: A chronicle of convergence. *Trends Biochem. Sci.* **28,** 329–335.
122. Beck, C., and Jeltsch, A. (2002). Probing the DNA interface of the *Eco*RV DNA-(adenine-N6)-methyltransferase by site-directed mutagenesis, fluorescence spectroscopy, and UV cross-linking. *Biochemistry* **41,** 14103–14110.
123. Goedecke, K., Pignot, M., Goody, R. S., Scheidig, A. J., and Weinhold, E. (2001). Structure of the N6-adenine DNA methyltransferase M*Taq*I in complex with DNA and a cofactor analog. *Nat. Struct. Biol.* **8,** 121–125.
124. Scavetta, R. D., Thomas, C. B., Walsh, M. A., Szegedi, S. S., Joachimiak, A., Gumport, R. I., and Churchill, M. E. (2000). Structure of *Rsr*I methyltransferase, a member of the N6-adenine beta class of DNA methyltransferases. *Nucleic Acids Res.* **28,** 3950–3961.
125. Murphy, F. V., and Churchill, M. E. (2000). Nonsequence-specific DNA recognition: A structural perspective. *Structure. Fold. Des.* **8,** R83–R89.
126. Zinoviev, V. V., Gorbunov, Yu. A., Baclanov, M. M., Popov, S. G., and Malygin, E. G. (1983). Structure subtraction as approach to investigation of the mechanism of restriction enzyme action. *FEBS Lett.* **154,** 282–284.
127. Buryanov, Ya. I., Zinoviev, V. V., Gorbunov, Yu. A., Tuzikov, F. V., Rechkunova, N. I., Malygin, E. G., and Bayev, A. A. (1988). Interaction of the *Eco*Dam methyltransferase with synthetic oligodeoxyribonucleotides. *Gene* **74,** 67–69.
128. Breyer, W. A., and Matthews, B. W. (2001). A structural basis for processivity. *Protein Sci.* **10,** 1699–1711.

Site-Specific Recombination and Partitioning Systems in the Stable High Copy Propagation of the 2-Micron Yeast Plasmid

MAKKUNI JAYARAM,
SHWETAL MEHTA, DINA UZRI,
YURI VOZIYANOV, AND
SOUNDARAPANDIAN
VELMURUGAN

Section of Molecular Genetics and Microbiology, University of Texas at Austin, Austin, TX 78712

I. The Flp Site-Specific Recombination System..................................	130
A. Architecture of the Flp Substrate and Organization of the Recombination Complex..	130
B. The Chemistry of the Recombination Reaction and the Flp Active Site	131
II. The Shared Active Site of Flp: DNA Cleavage in *trans*	135
A. *Trans*-Activation of a Recombinase Monomer by a Partner during Tyrosine Family Recombination..	137
B. Evolution of Site-Specific Recombination; Cryptic Ribonuclease Activities of Flp	138
C. Cryptic Ribonuclease and Topoisomerase Activities within Site-Specific Recombinases	139
III. The Geometry and Topology of Flp Recombination.........................	142
A. Deciphering DNA Architecture by the Difference Topology Assay..	146
B. The Relevance of Flp Recombination to the Biology of the 2-Micron Plasmid...	148
C. Practical Applications of Site-Specific Recombination.....................	150
IV. The 2-Micron Circle Partitioning System...	151
A. Organization and Localization of the 2-Micron Plasmid..................	152
B. Plasmid Dynamics during the Yeast Cell Cycle: Plasmid Partitioning in Mutant Yeast Strains that Show Impaired Chromosome Segregation......	152
C. Interactions among the DNA and Protein Components of the Plasmid Partitioning System	157
D. Potential Involvement of Host Factors Required in 2-Micron Circle Partitioning...	157
E. The Yeast Cohesin Complex and 2-Micron Plasmid Partitioning.........	159
F. The Specificity of 2-Micron Circle-Cohesin Association: Role of the Rep Proteins in Cohesin Recruitment	160
G. The Timing of Cohesin Recruitment to and Disassembly from the 2-Micron Plasmid as a Function of the Cell Cycle	161

128   JAYARAM ET AL.

    V. Cohesin Disassembly is a Prerequisite for Separation of
       Plasmid Clusters 161
       A. Models for Cohesin-Mediated Plasmid Segregation 164
   VI. Summary and Perspectives.. 164
       References 167

The strikingly simple genetic organization of the 2-micron plasmid of yeast belies its amazing capacity to propagate itself as a stubbornly persistent multicopy extrachromosomal element (1, 2). This remarkable feat is accomplished with a genetic endowment consisting of just four proteins (Rep1, Rep2, Flp, and Raf1) and three cis-acting loci (ORI, STB, and FRT) (Fig. 1A). The replication origin (ORI) is functionally equivalent to yeast chromosomal replication origins, and permits the replication of each plasmid molecule once per cell cycle by the host replication machine. The Rep1 and Rep2 proteins, in

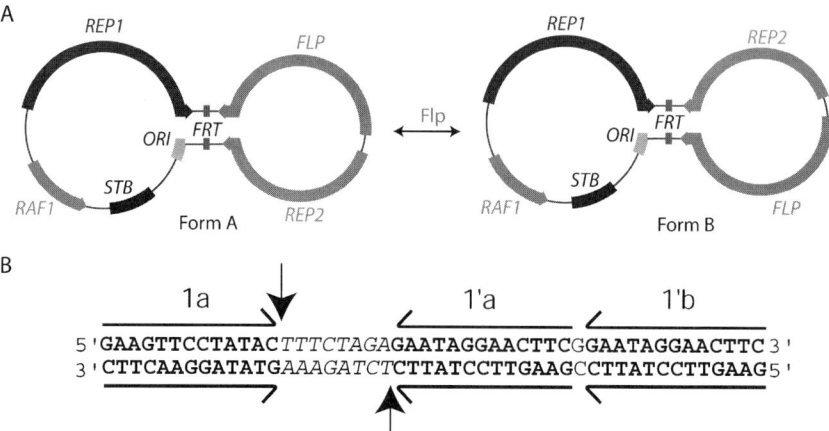

FIG. 1. The 2-micron plasmid is a double-stranded circular DNA that is often drawn as a dumbbell to highlight the 599 bp sequence that is repeated in inverted orientation (parallel lines). The open reading frames are schematically represented (FLP, REP1, REP2, and RAF1) and their transcriptional orientations are denoted by the arrowheads. The target sites for the Flp site-specific recombinase (FRT) are located within the inverted repeats. The DNA sequence and organization of the FRT site is shown below. The Flp protein binds as a monomer to each of the elements 1a, 1'a, and 1'b. Only 1a, 1'a, and the included sequence are relevant to the chemical steps of recombination. The vertical arrows denote the phosphodiester bonds that take part in the cleavage and exchange steps. The Raf1 protein appears to be a positive regulator of FLP expression. The partitioning locus, STB, acts in conjunction with the Rep1 and Rep2 proteins to mediate efficient plasmid segregation during cell division. The plasmid replication origin is marked as ORI. Flp-mediated recombination is responsible for the existence of the plasmid as an equilibrium mixture of forms A and B.

conjunction with the partitioning locus *STB*, are responsible for the even (or nearly even) distribution of the replicated molecules into the daughter cells. In case a rare missegregation event occurs, the Flp-*FRT* system amplifies the plasmid to its steady state copy number of approximately 60 per cell. Flp is a site-specific recombinase whose targets are a pair of *FRT* sites present in the plasmid genome in inverted orientation. The Raf1 protein, the least studied of all the plasmid encoded proteins, is thought to positively regulate the amplification process. The amplification step appears to be triggered by an appropriately timed recombination event during bidirectional replication of the plasmid (see following text for details).

The 2-micron circle provides a convenient model system to study mechanisms by which selfish DNA elements optimize strategies for their stable persistence in the host cell population. The plasmid does not confer any obvious advantage to its host, nor does it impose a significant disadvantage as long as the copy number does not increase well beyond the steady state value. The plasmid first came into prominence during the late 1970s and early 1980s with the advent of genetic engineering technology in yeast. Initially, it provided a convenient tool for constructing hybrid vectors for shuttling genes between yeast and *E. coli*. With a better understanding of the plasmid lifestyle came an appreciation of its utility in addressing a number of important issues in molecular and cell biology: for example, control of DNA replication and segregation, mechanisms for copy number maintenance by DNA amplification, and the potential role of cytoskeletal structures in partitioning nuclear components during cell division. A comprehensive coverage of the general physiology of the 2-micron plasmid and the early work on the mechanisms underlying its stable propagation and copy number control can be found in Broach and Volkert (2) and references therein. Later advances in our understanding of the plasmid site-specific recombination system and the partitioning system are dealt with in two reviews by Jayaram *et al.* (1, 3).

One of us (MJ) had his first encounter with the 2-micron plasmid in Dr. James Broach's laboratory, where he partook in some of the early genetic analyses of the Flp-*FRT* recombination system and the Rep-*STB* partitioning system. For a newcomer to the field of molecular genetics, this was an exciting experience that molded, in large measure, the course of his subsequent scientific career. Much of the effort of the Jayaram laboratory during past two decades has been devoted to understanding the mechanism of DNA recognition, DNA cleavage, and strand exchange mediated by the Flp recombinase. This has proven to be a rewarding exercise. In the past few years, our group has revived a longstanding, though dormant, interest in the problem of plasmid partitioning during yeast cell division. We are beginning to reveal hitherto unsuspected molecular trickeries that the plasmid resorts to in ensuring its faithful segregation into daughter cells. The years ahead promise to bring to light more such surprises. To keep roughly to the chronology of events and to maintain a historical perspective, we first describe the lessons we have learned from the Flp site-specific recombination system and then proceed to describe the progress that we have made on the partitioning front.

I. The Flp Site-Specific Recombination System

First, we describe the physicochemical attributes of the recombination reaction, as revealed by years of biochemical investigations and further refined by structural studies (3, 4). We then dwell in some detail on the active site organization of Flp and briefly speculate on its evolutionary history. Next, we allude to the topological and geometric aspects of the strand exchange reaction. They provide the basis for an analytical tool called "difference topology" that is useful in deciphering DNA paths within complex nucleic acid–protein assemblies. We discuss the relevance of the recombination system to the physiology of the 2-micron plasmid. We conclude this section by considering the practical uses of Flp in basic and applied areas of research.

A. Architecture of the Flp Substrate and Organization of the Recombination Complex

The minimal Flp substrate consists of two 13 bp Flp binding elements arranged in inverted orientation on either side of an 8 bp strand exchange region (or spacer) (Fig. 1B). The left and right binding elements have a single bp difference between them, although synthetic substrates containing identical binding elements are also active in recombination. The native *FRT* contains a third binding element, which is dispensable in recombination reactions *in vitro*. Whether this extra binding element plays any regulatory role *in vivo* in yeast is not clear. The spacer region is asymmetric in sequence, and hence confers directionality to the recombination reaction. When the DNA substrate contains a pair of *FRT* sites oriented in a head-to-head fashion, the outcome is DNA inversion between them. When the *FRT* sites are oriented in a head-to-tail fashion, the result is a deletion event. When the spacer sequence is artificially symmetrized, recombination leads to inversion or deletion with roughly equal probability. Flp is adept at carrying out intermolecular reactions as well, and utilizes supercoiled, nicked circular, and linear substrates efficiently.

The Flp protein exists as a monomer in solution and binds to DNA as a monomer, making both major and minor groove contacts. However, two monomers bound to an *FRT* site interact with each other to establish a dimer interface between them. Interactions also occur between monomers bound to partner substrates. The sum of these interactions, now revealed in atomic detail (4, 5), brings four Flp monomers and two *FRT* sites into a functional synaptic complex within which the chemistry of recombination takes place (Fig. 2A). A Flp monomer is composed of two globular domains and two protruding segments that are packed onto neighboring Flp monomers. Within the synaptic structure, each monomer forms a ring around the DNA, and the four monomers arrange themselves in a compact cyclic configuration with the two DNA partners oriented in an antiparallel configuration (more about this geometry later). The complex has a nearly square planar configuration that was already suspected from solution studies (6), and is similar to complexes formed by the Flp-related Cre recombinase with its target site *loxP* (7). The nearly perfect two-fold symmetry and only an approximate four-fold symmetry of the Flp-DNA complex are consistent with a reaction mechanism that requires two single-strand exchange steps to complete recombination (see following text). Of the four potential active sites that can be derived from the Flp tetramer, only two are in the functional state at a given time. Hence, in literature, two of the Flp monomers in the complex are designated as "active" and the other two as "inactive."

B. The Chemistry of the Recombination Reaction and the Flp Active Site

The Flp recombinase is a member of the tyrosine family of conservative site-specific recombinases (7), so named because they utilize a catalytic tyrosine to break the target phosphodiester bond during DNA exchange. The strand cleavage reaction by these proteins follows the basic type IB topoisomerase mechanism, and generates a 3' phosphotyrosyl bond and a free 5'-hydroxyl group at the break site. A recombinant strand is then formed when the 5'-hydroxyl group attacks the phosphotyrosyl bond formed on the partner substrate. Flp and related recombinases carry out a round of recombination between two DNA substrates in two temporally separate steps: first, exchanging one pair of strands to form a Holliday intermediate and then exchanging the second pair of strands to resolve this intermediate (Fig. 2B). Since the strand cleavage and joining steps are transesterification reactions, the energy of the phosphodiester bonds is conserved during recombination. Hence, the reaction proceeds without the need for an exogenous energy source such as ATP, and does not involve DNA degradation or synthesis.

The combined information from mutational analysis, solution studies, and crystal structures offers an impressively detailed picture of the active sites of Flp as well as other tyrosine recombinases (3, 4, 7). In particular, the structures of the different Cre-DNA complexes (8, 9, 10) and the Flp-DNA complex (5) provide rich insights into the possible mechanistic features of recombination. Comparison of the recombinase structures with those of vaccinia and human topoisomerases (type IB) (11, 12, 13) reveal close similarities in their active site

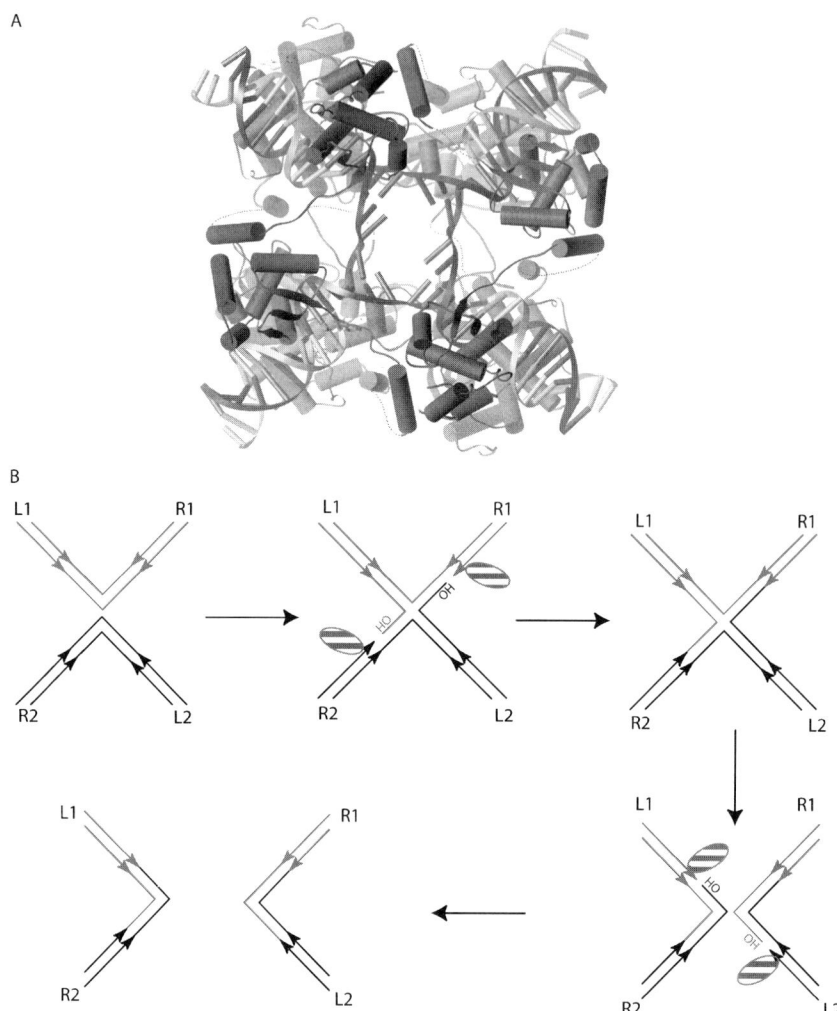

FIG. 2. (A) The structure of Flp in association with DNA shown here (5) was provided by Dr. P. A. Rice, University of Chicago. In this nearly planar complex, the four Flp monomers establish a cyclic interaction network. The green Flp monomers are adjacent to the two scissile phosphodiester bonds that are ready for cleavage, and are termed "active." The purple Flp monomers are adjacent to the phosphodiesters that are refractory to cleavage in this state, and are termed "inactive." The color scheme matches that used by Guo *et al.* (9) in their representation of the Cre-DNA structure. The Cre and Flp-DNA structures are quite similar in their overall geometry and protein–DNA interactions, consistent with a similar reaction pathway for the tyrosine recombinase family. A notable exception is that the active site tyrosines from Cre and Flp are positioned differently so that cleavage occurs in *cis* for Cre and in *trans* for Flp. In the Flp–DNA structure, it is the purple tyrosines (from the inactive monomers) that are poised to attack the target

organization, as would be expected from the common chemistry employed by these enzymes for DNA cleavage and joining.

Sequence alignments and functional characterization of Flp variants obtained by site-directed mutagenesis indicated early on that two arginines (Arg-191 and Arg-308) and a histidine (His-305) form an important catalytic triad, with Tyr-343 providing the cleavage nucleophile. In the vaccinia and human type I topoisomerases, the histidine residue is replaced by a lysine (Lys-220 and Lys-587 in the vaccinia and human enzymes, respectively). In the more generalized nomenclature proposed by Van Duyne (7), the triad residues are represented as Arg-I, His/Lys-II, and Arg-II. They are hydrogen bonded to the scissile phosphates in the Flp and Cre structures (Fig. 3). In the active conformation of an active site, the tyrosine nucleophile is well positioned for in-line attack. In the inactive conformation, though, the tyrosine is displaced from its active configuration. Recall that recombination proceeds in two steps by single strand exchanges, and only two of the active sites are functional at each step. This misorientation of tyrosine is sufficient to explain the inactive state of the active site, at least for Flp. When an exogenous small nucleophile such as hydrogen peroxide is supplied as a tyrosine mimic, strand breakage can occur at the scissile phosphate adjacent to the inactive Flp monomer (3, 14).

Two additional catalytic residues, Lysβ (Lys-223 in Flp) and His/Trp-III (Trp-330 in Flp; histidine in the topoisomerases and in the large majority of the recombinases) have been suggested by the crystal structures. Lysβ, so named because of its location between two adjacent β-strands in Cre, contacts the scissile phosphate in the active Flp monomer and forms a minor groove hydrogen bond in both Flp and Cre: with the adjacent base on the cleaved strand in Flp and on the noncleaved strand in Cre. In the inactive Flp and Cre monomers, though, the lysines are positioned quite differently. In Flp, the movement of this residue is modest, whereas in Cre it is pulled quite a distance away from the active site. Experiments with vaccinia topoisomerase using 5'-phosphorothiolate containing substrates suggest strongly that Lysβ functions as the general acid during cleavage by stabilizing the 5'-hydroxyl leaving group (15). Although there is no direct evidence, a similar function for Lysβ during Flp recombination seems quite plausible. The His/Trp-III residue (Trp-315 in Cre) forms a hydrogen bond to the scissile phosphate via the indole nitrogen in Cre and via the histidine side chain in the topoisomerases. In Flp, though, the tryptophan (Trp-330) is closer to the 5'-hydroxyl leaving group in

---

phosphates. (B) Recombination between two substrates L1-R1 and L2-R2 to yield L1-R2 and L2-R1 carried out by tyrosine recombinases in general is schematically represented. The reaction consists of two steps of cleavage and exchange between single strands. The first step produces a Holliday junction intermediate; the second step resolves it. During strand cleavage, the recombinase gets covalently attached to the 3-phosphate via the tyrosine nucleophile (shown by the DNA linked ovals). L and R refer to the left and right recombinase binding arms.

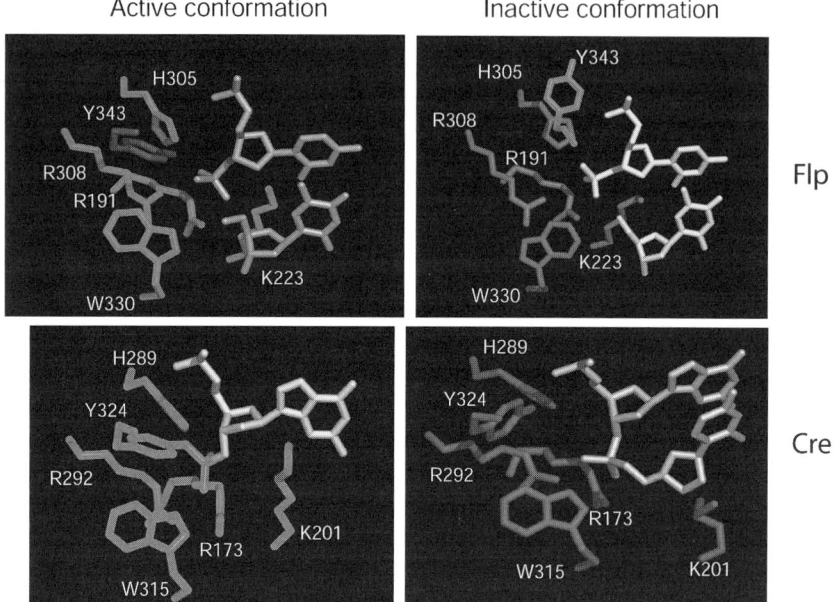

FIG. 3. Active site configurations in Flp and Cre. The active and inactive conformations of the catalytic residues for Flp (top row) and Cre (bottom row) are adapted from Chen *et al.* (2000) and Guo *et al.* (1997) (*5, 9*), respectively. The DNA and the scissile phosphate are represented in yellow. The primary distinction between the active and inactive states in both Flp and Cre is in the orientation of the tyrosine nucleophile. In Flp, the catalytic **tyrosine** is provided in *trans* by an adjacent monomer; in Cre, the tyrosine acts in *cis*. Details are given in the text. See also Fig. 4.

the active monomer, and is farther displaced from DNA in the inactive monomer.

In summary, an array of hydrogen bonds derived from a set of conserved side chains in the Flp active site can stabilize the pentacoordinate state of the scissile phosphate within the transition state. This general feature of tyrosine family recombination has prompted the suggestion that the reaction mechanism does have an electrophilic component to it (*7*). Assuming that Lysβ is the general acid during the cleavage step of tyrosine recombination, by the principle of reversibility, the same lysine may act as the general base during strand joining. What might be the general base and acid during strand cleavage and joining, respectively? The Cre structures suggest that His-II is positioned ideally to act as a proton acceptor during cleavage and a proton donor during joining. However, although mutations of His-305 in Flp show a large effect on strand joining, there is little or no effect on cleavage (*16, 17*).

II. The Shared Active Site of Flp: DNA Cleavage in *trans*

Among the well-characterized tyrosine family recombinases, Flp stands alone in the mode of assembly of its active site. As a general rule, members of this family derive all the catalytic residues for one active site from a single recombinase monomer. By contrast, an Flp active site is assembled at the interface of two monomers. In this shared active site, residues for the orientation of the scissile phosphate are provided by one monomer bound adjacent to it. In the context of the Flp structure, this is the monomer referred to as the active one. The cleavage nucleophile, Tyr-343, is supplied by a second monomer bound distal to the scissile phosphate across the spacer DNA. This monomer is referred to as inactive because the scissile phosphate next to it is not susceptible to attack by Tyr-343. The particular mode of DNA cleavage resulting from the shared configuration of the active site has been termed "*trans* cleavage" (Fig. 4A; compare to "*cis* cleavage" depicted in Fig. 4B) (3, 18). Although the idea of DNA cleavage in *trans* was greeted with a healthy dose of skepticism by the recombination community, the Flp crystal structure has fully vindicated its veracity (5). In the Flp structure (5), the helix M (that harbors Tyr-343) from a Flp monomer protrudes into the proactive site cleft formed by its partner, such that His-345 from the former is nestled between helix E and His-309 of the latter (Fig. 4B). Furthermore, His-309 stacks over Tyr-343 to orient it in its active alignment.

In the context of recombination, the shared active site provides a unifying mechanism for the strand cleavage and strand joining steps. During cleavage,

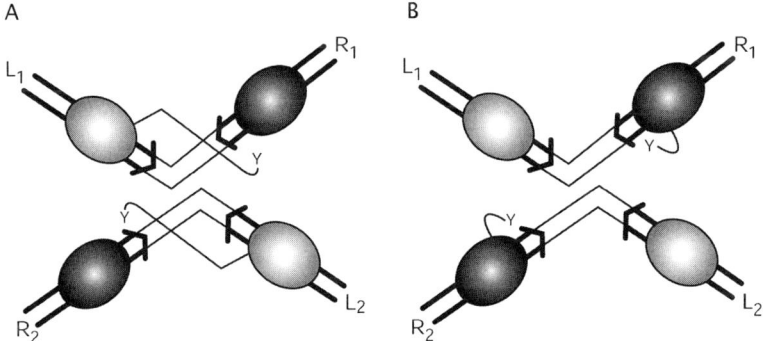

FIG. 4. DNA cleavage in *cis* or *trans* during tyrosine family site-specific recombination. Allosteric interaction between adjacent recombinase monomers is responsible for the activation of an active site for strand cleavage. A scissile phosphate is oriented by the recombinase monomer bound adjacent to it. In the case of Flp, cleavage is carried out by the tyrosine nucleophile from a monomer bound on the opposite DNA arm across the spacer (A). In the case of Cre, and other well-characterized tyrosine recombinases, the tyrosine nucleophile for cleavage is provided by the same monomer that orients the scissile phosphate (B).

an Flp monomer orients the scissile phosphodiester bond in *cis*, and a second monomer delivers Tyr-343 in *trans*. During strand union, an Flp monomer orients the 3'-O-phosphotyrosyl bond (one of the products of cleavage) in *cis*, and a 5'-hydroxyl group from the partner strand (the other cleavage product) attacks it in *trans*. Thus, strand cleavage and strand joining follow a "*cis*-orientation" and *trans*-nucleophilic attack mechanism.

Based on the active site configuration of Flp and the arrangement of the Flp tetramer within the recombination complex, the recombination reaction can be summarized as follows (Fig. 5). During the Holliday formation step, the Flp monomers bound to the left and right arms of each DNA partner (L1 and R1; L2 and R2) cooperate with each other in active site assembly. During the Holliday resolution step, the monomers switch their functional associations. Now, active site assembly is mediated by an Flp monomer bound to the left arm of one DNA partner cooperating with that bound to the right arm of the second DNA partner (R1 and L2; R2 and L1).

The swapping of functional interactions between recombinase monomers for the transition from the initiation to the termination steps of recombination is referred to as the Holliday isomerization step. For the Flp case, this involves, in addition to a scissoring of the DNA arms, rotations that force the arms into or below the plane of the junction and displace each protein monomer through $\sim\pm15°$ about the axis of the duplex to which it is bound (*4*) (Fig. 6). As a result, each monomer is translated by ~1.5 Å along the duplex axis. The direction of rotation is clockwise for the pair of diagonally related, active Flp monomers, whose catalytic centers were responsible for the first exchange step (see Fig. 6); it is counterclockwise for the second, inactive pair whose catalytic centers will be activated for the resolution step following isomerization.

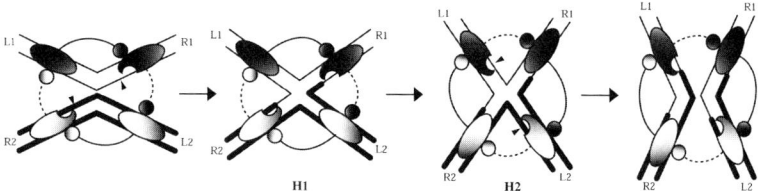

FIG. 5. Pattern of collaboration between Flp monomers during one round of recombination. Recombination is initiated by collaboration between the Flp monomers bound to the L1-R1 substrate on the one hand, and the L2-R2 substrate on the other. The resulting cleavage and exchange gives rise to the Holliday junction H1. The junction is reconfigured to H2 to accommodate collaboration between Flp monomers bound to R1 and L2 as well as R2 and L1. The resulting cleavage and exchange yields the reciprocal recombinants L1-R2 and L2-R1. The catalytically productive monomer–monomer interactions are denoted by solid curved lines with knobs at their ends. The nonproductive interactions are shown by the shorter broken curved lines ending in knobs.

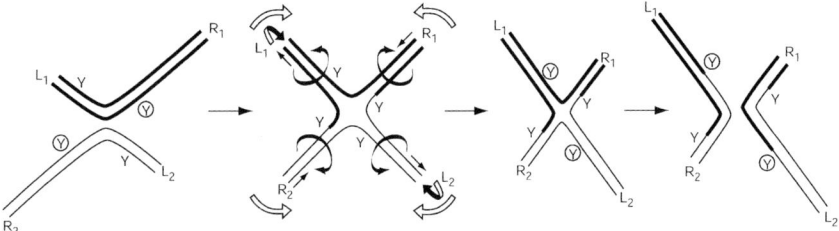

FIG. 6. Isomerization of Holliday intermediate during Flp recombination. In the reaction pathway from the parental molecules L1-R1 and L2-R2 to the recombinant products L1-R2 and L2-R1, the isomerization of the Holliday junction intermediate is highlighted. The conformational changes include the translation of each Flp monomer along the DNA axis through $\sim$1.5 Å (indicated by the thin arrows pointing toward or away from the center of the Holliday junction) and three types of rotations (shown by the distinct curved arrows) pivoting about the scissile phosphate. The scissoring of the DNA arms ($\sim$7° per arm) is coupled to their movement into or below the junction plane ($\sim$15° for each arm) and a rotation of $\sim$15° around the DNA axis. The sense of rotation for the diagonally related pair of arms that move into the junction plane is clockwise (as one looks from the end of an arm towards the junction center). For the pair of arms that move below the plane, and whose scissile phosphates then become cleavage-competent, the rotation is counterclockwise. The active tyrosine nucleophiles are circled to distinguish them from the inactive ones. A more incisive discussion of Holliday junction isomerization is given in Rice (4).

A. *Trans*-Activation of a Recombinase Monomer by a Partner during Tyrosine Family Recombination

Regardless of whether the active site is shared or not and cleavage *per se* occurs in *cis* or *trans*, the activation of a quiescent active site by interprotomer communication appears to be a general feature among the tyrosine recombinases. Structural data from Cre-DNA and Flp-DNA complexes suggest reasonable explanations for how the active or inactive state of a particular monomer is dictated by directional interactions between adjacent recombinase subunits. In particular, the turn between helices M and N and the mobility of helix M appear to be important in the regulation of catalysis. In the case of Cre, the helix M and the tyrosine nucleophile present within it function in *cis*, whereas the helix N is extended to contact the adjacent monomer in *trans* (Fig. 7A). In the case of Flp, the M helix, along with the tyrosine nucleophile, is donated in *trans* to the adjacent monomer and the N helix loops back and returns to the *cis* position (Fig. 7B). The length of the peptide linker between helices L and M appears to be important in the determination of *cis* or *trans* cleavage. A longer linker, present in Flp and related yeast site-specific recombinases, makes it possible for helix M (and the catalytic tyrosine) to reach the neighboring active site. As was proposed by Van Duyne and colleagues (*19*)

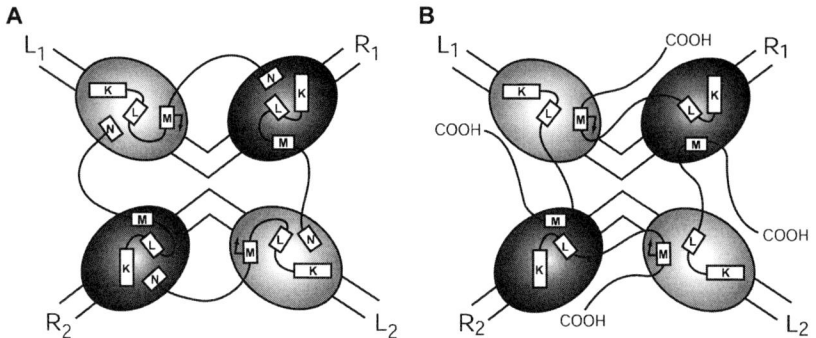

FIG. 7. Switch between *cis* and *trans* cleavages. The peptide connectivities as revealed by the crystal structures of Cre (A) and Flp (B) recombination complexes are schematically diagrammed. A switch in the peptide connectivity, between the L and M helices, can account for the transition from *cis* cleavage (A) to *trans* cleavage (B). The bent arrows extending from the M helices indicate the active tyrosines poised for cleavage. For more details, the reader is referred to Van Duyne (7) and Rice (4).

and is corroborated by the Flp crystal structure, a localized switch in the peptide connectivity can transform *cis* cleavage into *trans* with little change in the global configuration of the active site (compare Fig. 7A and B). A simple analogy can be made to a jigsaw puzzle that gives the same final solution from two different sets of pieces.

The generality of interpartner collaboration in active site assembly during tyrosine family recombination is supported by mutational studies of the *E. coli* XerC/XerD recombination system (20). Specific mutations in the presumptive donor or acceptor regions of XerC and XerD show two distinct phenotypes when assayed using synthetic Holliday junction substrates. One class of mutants activates catalysis by the partner, while impeding catalysis by self. The other class promotes catalysis by self and impairs catalysis by the partner. It is noteworthy that mutations that likely destabilize helix M packing cause activation of the mutated monomers within the tetramer; these mutations also stimulate a topoisomerase-like DNA relaxing activity of a monomer (20, 21, 22).

B. Evolution of Site-Specific Recombination; Cryptic Ribonuclease Activities of Flp

It has been suggested that the origins of homologous recombination may perhaps be traced to the need for repairing DNA damages that pose impediments to genome replication (23). Site-specific recombination, by contrast, must have emerged as a means to bringing about precise genetic rearrangements through localized action on the genome. The mechanistic differences between the two systems reflect this fundamental distinction in their physiological ends. By carrying out two steps of transesterification chemistry at specific phosphodiester bonds within well-defined short DNA sequences, a conservative site-specific recombinase performs a desired DNA rearrangement rapidly and decisively. The recombination active site must, therefore, be able to couple elementary chemical mechanisms for strand cutting and joining to the conformational transitions required for exchanging strands between two double helical partners. Given that biological catalysts have access to a fairly limited set of useful functional groups, the retention of key catalytic motifs among nucleases, topoisomerases, recombinases, and other enzymes that catalyze phosphoryl transfer reactions in nucleic acids is to be expected. The utilization by tyrosine recombinases and type IB topoisomerases of the Arg-I-His/Lys-II-Arg-II triad as an integral part of their catalytic cluster suggests mechanistic parallels to pancreatic ribonuclease and Staphylococcus nuclease reactions (24, 25).

A rather subtle structural similarity between the Integrase/Tyrosine recombinases and the AraC family of transcriptional activators has come to light (26, 27). Several of the catalytic residues of the recombinases are located within two helix–turn–helix (HTH) motifs, suggesting that an ancient DNA binding module might have duplicated and evolved to acquire enzymatic function. The tyrosine nucleophile for DNA breakage is harbored by the second helix of the carboxyl-terminal HTH in Cre. In the structures of other strand breaking and resealing enzymes (topoisomerase I, topoisomerase II, and archaeal topoisomerase VI), the catalytic tyrosine is present in an HTH region, although its position is not strictly conserved. These examples suggest parallel, independent evolution of homologous enzymatic domains with alternative placements of the catalytic residues.

The crystal structure of the NaeI restriction enzyme, an endonuclease that can be converted to a topoisomerase/recombinase by a leucine to lysine substitution, reveals a dimer with a bidomainal organization of each monomer subunit. The amino-terminal domain and the carboxyl-terminal domain contain potential DNA binding motifs corresponding to the endonuclease and topoisomerase activities, respectively (28). The NaeI structure provides support for the evolutionary divergence of DNA processing enzymes from a limited number of ancestral proteins or for the convergence of a finite set of catalytic motifs in them.

C. Cryptic Ribonuclease and Topoisomerase Activities within Site-Specific Recombinases

What simple active site might have served as the progenitor of the more complex active site that can carry out site-specific DNA recombination? Is it possible that the highly sophisticated recombinase enzymes such as Flp might have begun their existence as an elementary nuclease, for example? Could the type I topoisomerase be an intermediate in this catalytic progression? These questions have prompted us and others to examine the present-day tyrosine recombinases and topoisomerases for potential evolutionary vestiges of their presumed humble beginnings. Indeed, these efforts have unmasked rather striking RNA and DNA cleavage activities in Flp, Cre, the vaccinia topoisomerase, and the type I human topoisomerase (29, 30, 31, 32).

Two site-specific RNA cleavage activities of the Flp protein, called Flp-RNase I and Flp RNase II, have been identified by using hybrid substrates that contain specific ribonucleotide substitutions in an otherwise deoxyribooligonucleotide background (33). Flp-RNase I closely follows the normal recombination mechanism. It requires the active site tyrosine, targets the same phosphodiester bond that partakes in DNA recombination, and appears to proceed by a phosphotyrosyl intermediate (Fig. 8A and B). By contrast, Flp-RNase II mimics the pancreatic RNase mechanism Fig. 8C. It is independent of the active site tyrosine, and targets the phosphodiester immediately to the 3' side of the "recombination phosphate." The type I RNase activity (but not the type II activity) has been demonstrated in the Cre recombinase as well, and a related activity has been observed in vaccinia topoisomerase (29, 30). Furthermore, there is an intrinsic, though normally cryptic, topoisomerase activity associated with Flp. In appropriately designed DNA substrates, and under special reaction conditions, Flp can carry out relaxation of negative supercoils (32). Site-specific or even sequence-independent topoisomerase activities have also been demonstrated for Cre, XerC/XerD, and lambda Int (34, 35, 36, 37). Finally, when the catalytic tyrosine of vaccinia topoisomerase is mutated to a glutamic acid, histidine, or cysteine, the variant protein shows site-specific endonuclease activity (38).

These observations suggest that an early step in the evolution of the recombinase must have been the formation of a nuclease active site containing a group of catalytic residues, at least a subset of which has been conserved. The emergence of a precisely positioned protein nucleophile, the active site tyrosine, could then have set the stage for the maturation of this proactive site into a "topoisomerase" and further into a "recombinase" active site. A related but alternative evolutionary argument cannot be ruled out either. During the optimization of an active site intended to perform a certain chemical task, the design for a related task may be inadvertently incorporated. By this argument, the cryptic nuclease activities housed by the recombinase or topoisomerase active sites simply reflect the fact that recombination cannot proceed without the breakage of DNA strands.

The RNA cleavage reactions of recombinases and topoisomerases have also fueled speculations on the possible relevance of these activities *in vivo* (30, 39). The suggested roles include the triggering of repair pathways for the

RECOMBINATION AND PARTITIONING SYSTEMS

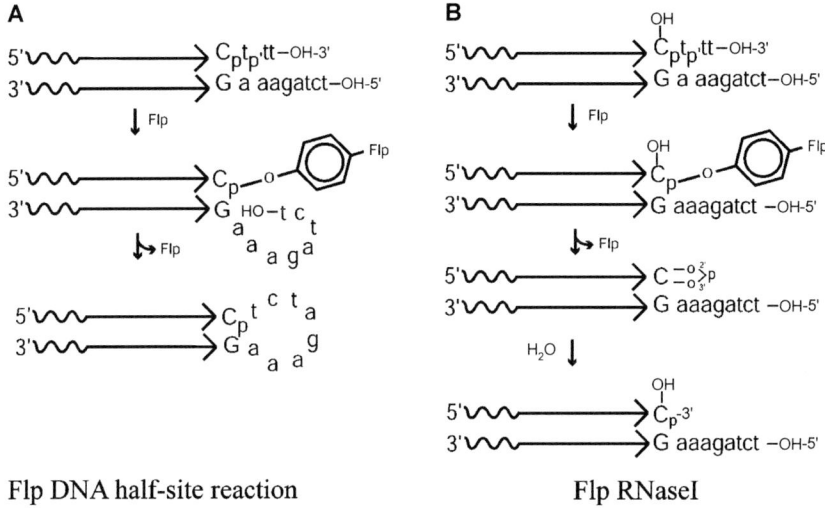

Fig. 8. The RNA cleavage activities of Flp. Recombination carried out by Flp in a half-site DNA substrate (A) is compared to its RNA cleavage activities in substrates containing ribonucleotide substitutions (B and C). In the half-site reaction (A), cleavage on the top strand followed by 5'-hydroxyl attack from the bottom strand results in a hairpin recombinant product. Since Flp cleaves DNA in *trans*, this reaction occurs in the context of two half-sites, each bound by an Flp monomer. Flp RNase I (B), like half-site recombination, is mediated by a "shared" active site, and proceeds by Tyr343-mediated cleavage at the equivalent phosphodiester position. The only difference between the two is in the nucleophile used for the subsequent step: a 5'-hydroxyl group in A and 2'-hydroxyl group in B. Flp-RNase II (C) has a different target specificity and proceeds by a distinct mechanism that bypasses the tyrosine-mediated cleavage step.

removal of ribonucleotides from DNA or involvement in RNA splicing reactions. Whether or not these enzymes once carried out reactions with which they are not presently identified, their active sites exemplify how novel and diverse activities can be derived from conserved chemical themes (40).

III. The Geometry and Topology of Flp Recombination

The crystal structures of the Cre and Flp suggest that the recombination reactions occur within an essentially planar complex, with the DNA partners organized in an antiparallel, rather than parallel, arrangement (see Fig. 9). However, this inference is not foolproof. For example, it may be argued that crystallization conditions could have, in principle, selected a nonfunctional synapse. Furthermore, in the initial Flp structure (5), because of a rather unexpected set of reactions that has occurred in the crystal, all four DNA strands are cleaved, and the spacer length has been effectively reduced from the normal 8 bp to 7 bp.

Assuming that the synapse is planar (as inferred from the crystal structure), Grainge et al. (41) have employed a topological approach to deciphering the

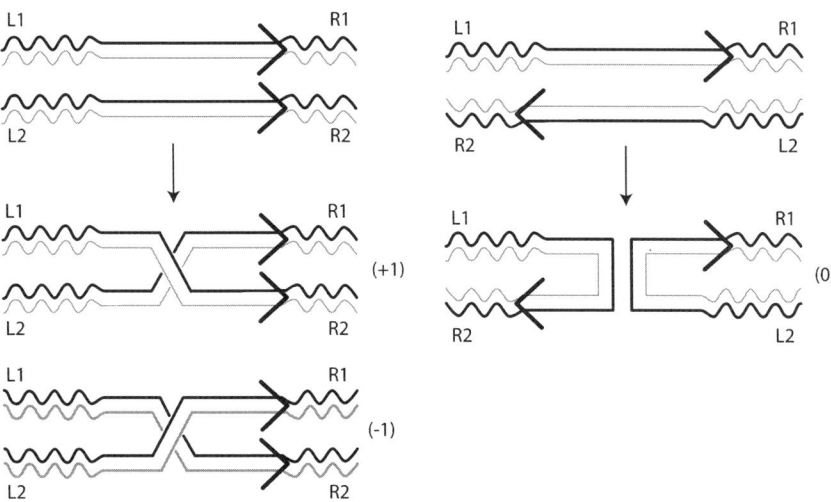

FIG. 9. Geometry of target site alignment during Flp recombination. The crystal structure of the Flp recombination complex (5) demonstrates that the two DNA partners have a virtually planar disposition. If the sites were to be arranged in parallel orientation (left), strand exchange will introduce a DNA crossing. Depending on the sense of rotation, the crossing could be +1 (right-handed) or −1 (left-handed). If the sites were to align in an antiparallel orientation (right), strand exchange will proceed without the introduction of a crossing.

arrangement of the *FRT* sites during recombination. In this analysis, the Flp reaction is carried out in circular plasmid substrates after first establishing the topologically well-characterized Tn3 resolvase synapse that entraps three negative supercoils (42). The recombination targets are hybrid *res-FRT* sites in which the accessory *res* II and *res* III sites, required for organizing the resolvase synapse, are preserved but the *res* I sites are replaced by *FRT* sites (Fig. 10, top). An inversion reaction and a deletion reaction are carried out

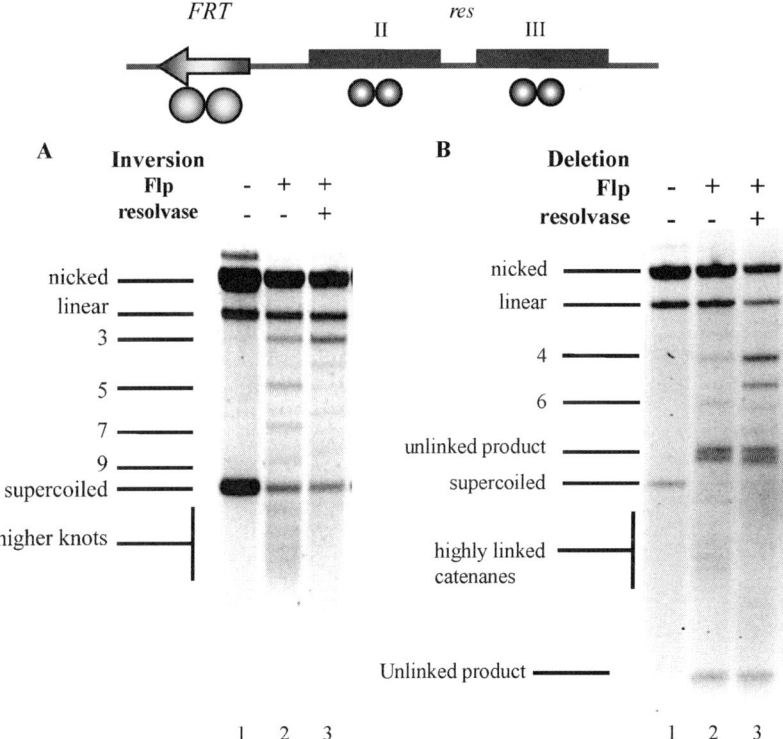

FIG. 10. Topological outcomes of recombination between two hybrid *res-FRT* sites. In the hybrid *res-FRT* site (shown schematically at the top), resolvase dimers bound to the *res* II and *res* III sites contribute to a synapse with three negative DNA crossings. The strand exchange is carried out by Flp bound to the *FRT* site. In the reactions in A, the recombination partners contain the *res* sites in direct orientation and the *FRT* sites in inverted orientation. In the reactions in B, the *res* sites and the *FRT* sites are in direct orientation. Samples are analyzed for knots or catenane products after DNase I nicking. Lanes 1: control reactions without Flp or resolvase. Lanes 2: Flp alone reactions. Lanes 3: resolvase-assisted Flp reactions. The number of knot crossings are indicated by 3, 5, 7, etc. in A, and the number of catenane crossings by 4, 6 in B. Note the specific enrichment of the 3-noded knot in lane 3 (A) and the four-noded catenane in lane 3 (B).

from a matched pair of plasmid substrates that contain the *FRT* sites in inverted and direct orientations, respectively. After removing the plasmid supercoils using human topoisomerase I, the number of knot crossings in the inversion product and the number of catenane crossings in the deletion product are determined by gel electrophoresis and comparison to marker knot and catenane ladders. In the absence of resolvase, the Flp reactions yield the unknot plus a series of knots by inversion and a pair of unlinked circles plus a series of catenanes by deletion (lanes 2, Fig. 10A and B). These product sets are expected because of the stochastic entrapment of supercoils during the synapsis of the *FRT* sites by random collision. The faint interleaved bands between the rungs of the main product ladders are due to the primary products undergoing a second round of recombination. In the resolvase-assisted Flp reactions, the three-noded knot and the four-noded catenane are enriched at the expense of the other products during inversion and deletion, respectively (lanes 3, Fig. 10A and B). As already pointed out, the slight increase in the four-noded knot and the five-noded knot in reactions with the inversion and deletion substrates, respectively, can be accounted for by a subsequent round of recombination. As will be explained, these results are most easily accommodated by an antiparallel geometry of the *FRT* sites within the Flp-mediated synapse.

For the Flp inversion substrate, the resolvase synapse with its three crossings (or any synapse with an odd number of crossings) will bring the *FRT* sites together most easily in an antiparallel orientation (Fig. 11, bottom). The recombination reaction *per se* will not add a DNA crossing, but will seal off the three crossings in the resolvase synapse and display them in the knot product. By similar arguments, the resolvase synapse will cause the direct *FRT* sites in the deletion substrate to come together in a parallel fashion. However, by introducing a fourth crossing, this will involve little energetic cost in a negatively supercoiled substrate, and the Flp protein can realign the sites to be antiparallel (Fig. 11, top). The deletion reaction will now yield a catenane with four crossings between its component circles. Similar results have been obtained for the Cre recombinase when recombination is carried out on hybrid *res-lox*P sites (*43*).

Grainge *et al.* (*44*) have further refined their analysis by carrying out the hybrid site recombinations after symmetrizing the strand exchange region of *FRT*. The reactions of the symmetrized substrate are shown in Fig. 12 along with those of the inversion and deletion substrates for comparison. As expected, the Flp alone reaction gives a ladder of bands corresponding to both knots and catenanes from the symmetrized substrate, reflecting the equal likelihood of inversion and deletion (lane 8, Fig. 12). When recombination is carried out from a pre-established resolves synapse, there is a specific enrichment of the 3-noded knot (lane 9, Fig. 12) with some increase in the band

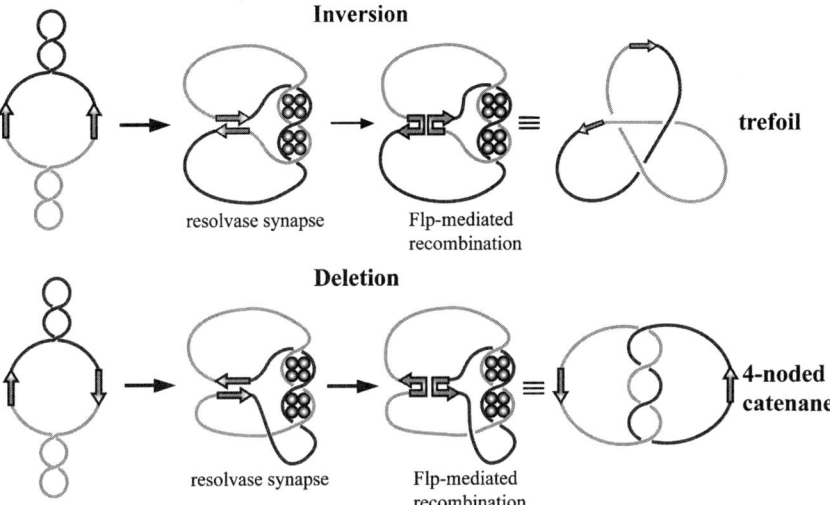

FIG. 11. Schema for the specific topology of the recombination products formed by resolvase-assisted Flp reactions. Because of the three DNA crossings introduced by the resolvase dimers bound to res II and res III, the FRT sites (indicated by the arrows) in the inversion substrate are paired in an antiparallel arrangement. Since strand exchange from this alignment does not introduce a DNA crossing, the product is a 3-noded knot (see Fig. 10). In the deletion substrate, the resolvase synapse would bring the FRT sites in parallel orientation. By trapping an additional supercoil (or a negative crossing), the FRT sites are reoriented to be antiparallel. Strand exchange then produces a 4-noded catenane (see Fig. 10). As explained in Grainge et al. (41), the observed product topologies are not consistent with parallel geometry of the FRT sites.

below it (which is likely the four-noded knot resulting from a further round of recombination). Thus, when three DNA crossings (or an odd number of crossings) are fixed in the outside synapse, the symmetrized FRT sites within the Flp synapse are treated exclusively as if they are in the inverted orientation (compare lane 9 to lanes 6 and 4 in Fig. 12). In other words, regardless of the strand exchange sequence, the functional geometry of the FRT sites is antiparallel, and the process of recombination does not introduce a DNA crossing between the product helices. Similarly, when Cre recombination is carried out on symmetrized loxP sites after organizing a different three-noded synapse (that derived from a transposition complex (45)), the enriched product again is the three-noded knot. Based on the combined topological data from the action of Flp and Cre on their native and symmetrized target sites, it is fair to generalize that antiparallel geometry of the recombination sites is a common feature of tyrosine family recombination.

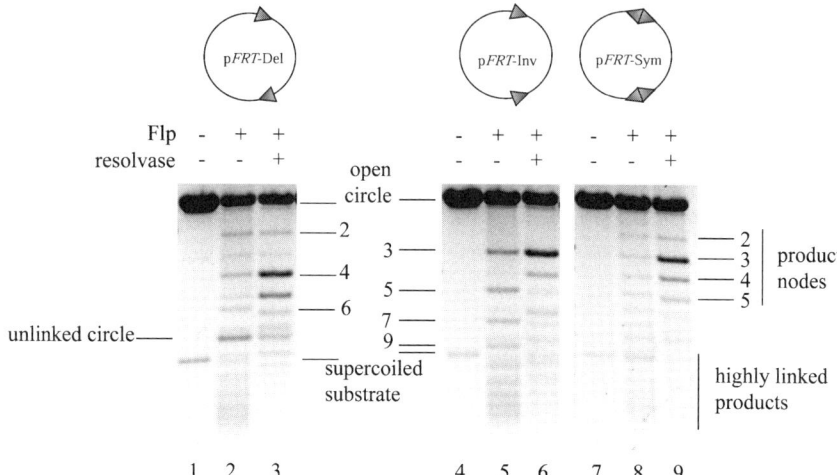

FIG. 12. Recombination between hybrid *res-FRT* sites in which the strand exchange region in *FRT* is symmetrized. The reactions with the inversion substrate (p*FRT*-Inv) and the deletion substrate (p*FRT*-Del) are similar to those shown in Fig. 10. Notice the enrichment of the 4-noded catenane from p*FRT*-Del and the 3-noded knot from p*FRT*-Inv in lanes 3 and 6, respectively. In p*FRT*-Sym, the strand exchange region in *FRT* is symmetrized. The product ladder from this substrate for the Flp alone reaction corresponds to equal probability of inversion and deletion (equal intensities of the odd and even numbered bands in lane 8). The 3-noded knot is specifically enriched when Flp recombines p*FRT*-Sym from the resolvase synapse.

A. Deciphering DNA Architecture by the Difference Topology Assay

The topology and geometry of Flp or Cre recombination derived here have formed the basis of a "difference topology" method for determining the number of crossings between two interacting DNA sites in a high order DNA–protein complex. The rationale of the analysis is as follows. Consider a case where there are n crossings between two DNA sites, n being odd. As illustrated in the resolvase case, for a circular inversion substrate, the odd number of crossings will bring two appropriately positioned *FRT* (or *lox*P) sites in the antiparallel orientation (see Fig. 11). An Flp or Cre mediated recombination will then reveal the n crossings in the "unknown synapse" as n crossings in the knot product. For the matched deletion substrate, $[|n| + 1]$ crossings are required for antiparallel geometry of the recombination sites, and these will be revealed as $[|n| + 1]$ links between the deletion circles. In other words, if the matched inversion and deletion substrates yield the $|n|$ noded inversion knot and the $[|n| + 1]$ noded deletion catenane, then n DNA crossings are trapped in the extraneous synapse, and n is odd. If the products are $|n'|$ noded catenane for deletion and $[|n'| + 1]$ noded knot for inversion, the extraneous synapse contains n' nodes, and n' is even.

Recently, the difference topology approach has been successfully applied to trace the path of DNA within the phage Mu transposition complex in which three DNA sites, attL, attR, and a transposition enhancer, must come together in a productive synapse to initiate the chemical steps of transposition (45). The inversion/deletion assays using the Cre/*loxP* recombination system reveal that the enhancer crosses the attL site once and the attR site twice. In addition, the attL and attR sites make two more crossings between them. By combining the three sets of two-site interactions, the minimal planar projection of the transposition complex can be inferred to contain five DNA crossings, as illustrated in Fig. 13.

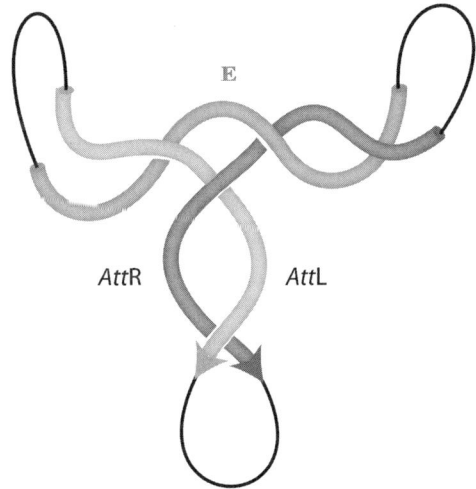

FIG. 13. The path of the DNA in the DNA transposition complex arranged by the phage Mu transposase. The Mu transposase interacts with three DNA sites to assemble the transposition synapse: the left and right ends of the phage genome (*att*L and *att*R, respectively) and a transposition enhancer, E. The five-noded synaptic architecture shown here is derived by using difference topology (45). The Cre/lox recombination system is utilized to seal off DNA crossings between a set of pairwise DNA domains separated by the crossover sites and display them in knots or catenanes (see Figs. 11–13). When the enhancer was in one domain and *att*L/*att*R in the second domain, three DNA crossings are trapped between them. When *att*L is segregated from E/*att*R, again three interdomainal crossings are trapped. When *att*R is segregated from E/*att*L, the number of crossings between the two is four. Finally, when the enhancer is topologically dissociated from the system by providing it in *trans*, *att*L and *att*R trap two crossings between them. These subtopologies are consistent with the composite topology in which E crosses *att*L once and *att*R twice, and *att*L crosses *att*R twice.

In principle, the difference topology assay is capable of revealing even a labyrinthine DNA path created by the interactions among multiple sites. First, by flanking a given site by appropriate placement of the *FRT/loxP* sites, the number of crossings it makes with the rest of the sites can be deduced by the inversion/deletion assay. The process can be iterated for each of the other sites. Superposition of these individual subtopologies should then yield an internally consistent picture of the composite topology of the whole complex. It would be interesting to apply the difference topology method to probe the DNA configurations within DNA replication, transcription, and repair complexes.

B. The Relevance of Flp Recombination to the Biology of the 2-Micron Plasmid

The types of DNA rearrangements promoted by the various tyrosine site-specific recombination systems and their physiological consequences underscore one of the fundamental attributes of life: the capacity to employ the same or similar chemical mechanisms to bring about vastly different end results. It is almost axiomatic in biology that a solution arrived at in the context of a given biochemical challenge is certain to be adopted and refined by evolution for deployment in the context of a variety of related challenges. The integration and excision reactions mediated by the lambda Int protein act as critical developmental switches in the phage's lifestyle (35). Related site-specific recombination systems are responsible for the dissemination of integrons or bacterial genes that are usually associated with antibiotic resistance or pathogenesis (46). In cyanobacterial heterocysts, tyrosine recombinases mediate site-specific deletion of intervening DNA elements to establish the functional configurations of operons involved in nitrogen fixation (47). The XerC/XerD and related recombination systems ensure the equal segregation of bacterial chromosomes and certain plasmid genomes during cell division (48). Due to homologous recombination, there is a finite probability that the duplicated circular chromosomes are present in a dimeric form or even higher oligomeric forms. The action by XerC/XerD resolves the dimer and higher oligomers into monomers that can then be partitioned into the daughter cells. The Cre recombinase is believed to play a similar partitioning role in the propagation of the unit copy bacteriophage/plasmid P1 (49).

The Flp recombinase and Flp-like recombinases encoded by the 2-micron circle and related yeast plasmids appear to be important in the copy number control of these extrachromosomal elements. In the event of a drop in plasmid copy number caused by a rare missegregation event, a replication coupled recombination reaction is thought to trigger the amplification process that restores the steady state plasmid density (50). Because the 2-micron circle replication origin is located close to one *FRT* site and away from the second, the proximal site is duplicated early during bidirectional replication. A recombination event between the unreplicated *FRT* and one of the duplicated *FRT*s inverts one fork with respect to the other. The unidirectional forks can spin out multiple copies of the plasmid by a bifurcated rolling circle mechanism. The tandem copies of the plasmid in the amplification product can be resolved into monomers by Flp recombination or by homologous recombination.

Strong experimental evidence has been provided to show that the absence of a functional Flp recombination system results in the loss of plasmid amplification (51, 52). By an elegant strategy designed to excise a wild-type copy of the 2-micron circle or a mutant version of it (containing one nonfunctional *FRT*) as a single copy from a chromosomally integrated state, Volkert and Broach (51) have demonstrated that the former plasmid is capable of elevating its copy number whereas the latter is not. Thus, there is little doubt that the act of recombination per se is central to amplification. However, there is no direct rigorous proof yet that the mechanism for amplification is as proposed by the Futcher model. For example, the replication intermediates predicted by the model have yet to be identified directly or substantiated indirectly. Electron microscopy by Petes and Williamson (53) has revealed, under elongation arrested conditions induced by the *cdc8* mutation, structures that they describe as "pince-nez" (PN). These entities are replication intermediates consisting of two circles of constant size (2 μm) linked by a growing piece of connector DNA of variable length, effectively representing an intermolecular amplifying moiety (as opposed to the intramolecular amplifying moiety in the Futcher model; see Fig. 14). The PN molecules may or may not be relevant to normal copy number control. Nevertheless, they caution against the infallibility of the Futcher model, and suggest the need for considering alternatives involving intermolecular recombination.

The 2-micron circle amplification system is normally kept repressed, and is triggered into action only when a drop in the copy number is sensed. This negative control serves as a safety mechanism to prevent uncontrolled increase in plasmid copy number. The Rep1 and Rep2 proteins appear to form a bipartite repressor whose concentration provides an indirect read out of the plasmid copy number (54). The repressor negatively regulates the expression of *FLP*, *REP1*, and *RAF1*, but apparently not *REP2*. The Raf1 protein is thought to be an antagonist of the Rep1p-Rep2p repressor, and helps to accelerate the amplification response by promoting Flp induction. The sum of these negative and positive controls helps to dampen significant deviations of plasmid copy number from the steady state value.

Circular plasmids identified in a limited set of yeast strains belonging to a common genus have structural and genetic organizations that closely resemble that of the 2-micron plasmid, even though there is a large divergence in their DNA sequences (55, 56, 57, 58, 59). All of these plasmids have apparently

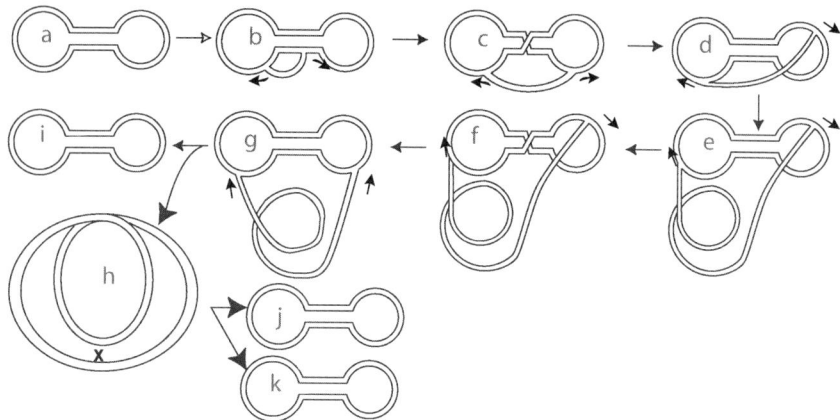

FIG. 14. The Futcher model for plasmid amplification. The schematic representation of the Futcher model (50) is adapted from Broach and Volkert (51). Bidirectional replication starting at the origin in a plasmid molecule duplicates the proximal FRT site before the distal one (a–b). An Flp-mediated inversion (c) results in two replication forks oriented in the same direction (d). Movement of the two forks around the circular template amplifies copy number (e). A second recombination event (f) restores bidirectional fork movement (g). The products of replication are a template copy (i) and an amplified moiety containing multiple tandem copies of the plasmid (h). The tandem multimer can be resolved by Flp recombination into plasmid monomers (j, k). The diagram of the Futcher model (50) shown here follows its representation by Broach and Volkert (2).

retained their own site-specific recombination and partitioning systems, suggesting that they provide a highly efficient strategy for the stable propagation of these benign parasite genomes.

C. Practical Applications of Site-Specific Recombination

Site-specific recombination provides an efficient molecular tool for engineering large genomes. The "simple" members of the tyrosine recombinases, namely, Flp and Cre, have been effectively deployed in prokaryotes and eukaryotes to mediate site-specific DNA insertions, targeted DNA deletions, and expression of proteins from selected chromosomal locales (reviewed in 3, 60). Recombination mediated activation or abolition of gene expression has proven valuable in *Drosophila*, plants, and animals for the molecular analysis of development and for the creation of transgenics. The isolation of thermostable versions of recombinases (61) and the design of ligand-dependent recombination (by using a hybrid recombinase fused to the steroid hormone ligand binding domain, for example [62]) will further enhance the utility of site-specific recombination in the genetic manipulations of higher systems.

One serious limitation in the use of site-specific recombination as a means for genome modification, though, is that the recombination target site or sites must be first inserted or must be fortuitously present (a highly unlikely situation) at the genomic locale of interest. The power of site-specific recombination in genetic engineering can be revolutionized if one is able to preselect a genomic site that resembles a native recombination target and coax the recombinase to acquire this new specificity. The feasibility of obtaining recombinase variants with "made-to-order" target specificity (*61, 63, 64, 65*) by directed evolution heralds another potentially significant advance in this direction. More recently, gene shuffling, combined with mutagenesis of Flp variants with acquired cognition for *FRT* sites harboring specific mutant positions, has yielded new variants that now functionally recognize *FRT* sites with combinatorial mutations (*66*). Based on these results, it seems likely that iterated rounds of gene shuffling and mutagenesis will lead to the evolution of recombinases for target sites that are quite diverged from native *FRT*.

IV. The 2-Micron Circle Partitioning System

The partitioning system, constituted by the Rep1 and Rep2 proteins and the cis-acting *STB* locus (see Fig. 1), is responsible for distributing replicated plasmid molecules equally or approximately equally to daughter cells. There is an apparent similarity between the general organization of the yeast plasmid partitioning system and that of bacterial plasmid partitioning systems. The latter also utilizes two partitioning proteins, one of which is an ATPase, and a centromere-like sequence with which the proteins associate to form a partitioning complex. The 2-micron circle Rep proteins also exist in tight association with the *STB* DNA, and this Rep–*STB* interaction is central to the plasmid segregation mechanism. However, the similarity ends here. All evidence points to the two systems being functionally quite disparate. For example, neither Rep1p nor Rep2p harbors standard nucleotide binding or ATPase motifs.

An immediate question is why a plasmid with as high a copy number as 60 per cell resorts to an active partitioning mechanism. At this mean copy number, random segregation should suffice, since the probability of a plasmid-free cell arising at any division event would be extremely low. Furthermore, any decrease in copy number resulting from uneven segregation can be corrected by the amplification system. Some control at the replication level will have to operate as well in order to adjust copy number in cells that receive more than their fair share of plasmids. As was suspected, and will be described, the effective copy number of the plasmid in partitioning is much lower than 60. In fact, it is close to unity. Hence, the existence of a partitioning system is eminently logical.

A. Organization and Localization of the 2-Micron Plasmid

The technique of directly visualizing reporter plasmids containing lac operator repeats in live yeast cells expressing a GFP-lac repressor fusion protein has greatly facilitated recent cell biological investigations on 2-micron circle partitioning (67, 68). The plasmid is resident in the yeast nucleus in the form of a tight knit cluster, the majority of the cells containing tetrad- or triad-shaped clusters (Fig. 15A). In some of the cells, clusters with fewer than three or more than four lobes can also be found. Although the cluster as a whole does not often change its position within the nucleus, the entities within the cluster are highly dynamic. However, despite their constant relative movement, the lobes stay together and seldom, if ever, break away from each other. When the reporter plasmid harbors the *STB* locus, the Rep1 and Rep2 proteins remain tightly associated with the plasmid cluster (Fig. 15B). In the absence of *STB*, plasmid dots that have distanced themselves from the Rep proteins can be readily seen. Plasmids without the *STB* DNA have a more spread-out organization, which is also true of *STB* containing plasmids resident in cells lacking Rep1p or Rep2p or both. When the microtubules are depolymerized using nocodazole, the Rep proteins become more widely dispersed in the nucleus; concomitantly, the plasmid cluster becomes less cohesive and more spread out. Under normal conditions, the *STB*-plasmids, but not plasmids sans *STB*, can be visualized in yeast chromosome spreads, but are not detected in spreads prepared from cells treated with nocodazole or those not expressing the Rep proteins (Fig. 15C). However, when nocodazole-treated cells are washed free of the drug and allowed to recover, plasmids are again displayed in chromosome spreads. The sum of these results suggests that the characteristic localization and organization of the 2-micron plasmid are dependent on the presence of the Rep1 and Rep2 proteins, the presence of *STB* in cis, and the integrity of the microtubules. Furthermore, the plasmid exists either in direct association with the chromosomes or is positioned at a subnuclear locale where chromosomal domains might also be anchored. We suspect that both the special organization and the nuclear location of the plasmid cluster are important for normal segregation. It is almost certain that cluster includes, in addition to Rep1p and Rep2p, chromosomally encoded proteins. It is this high-order DNA-protein complex that is the unit for partitioning.

B. Plasmid Dynamics during the Yeast Cell Cycle: Plasmid Partitioning in Mutant Yeast Strains that Show Impaired Chromosome Segregation

Time-lapse fluorescence microscopy of reporter plasmids tagged with the GFP-repressor has provided a clear picture of the dynamics of 2-micron circle segregation during the yeast cell cycle (Fig. 16). Starting with cells arrested in

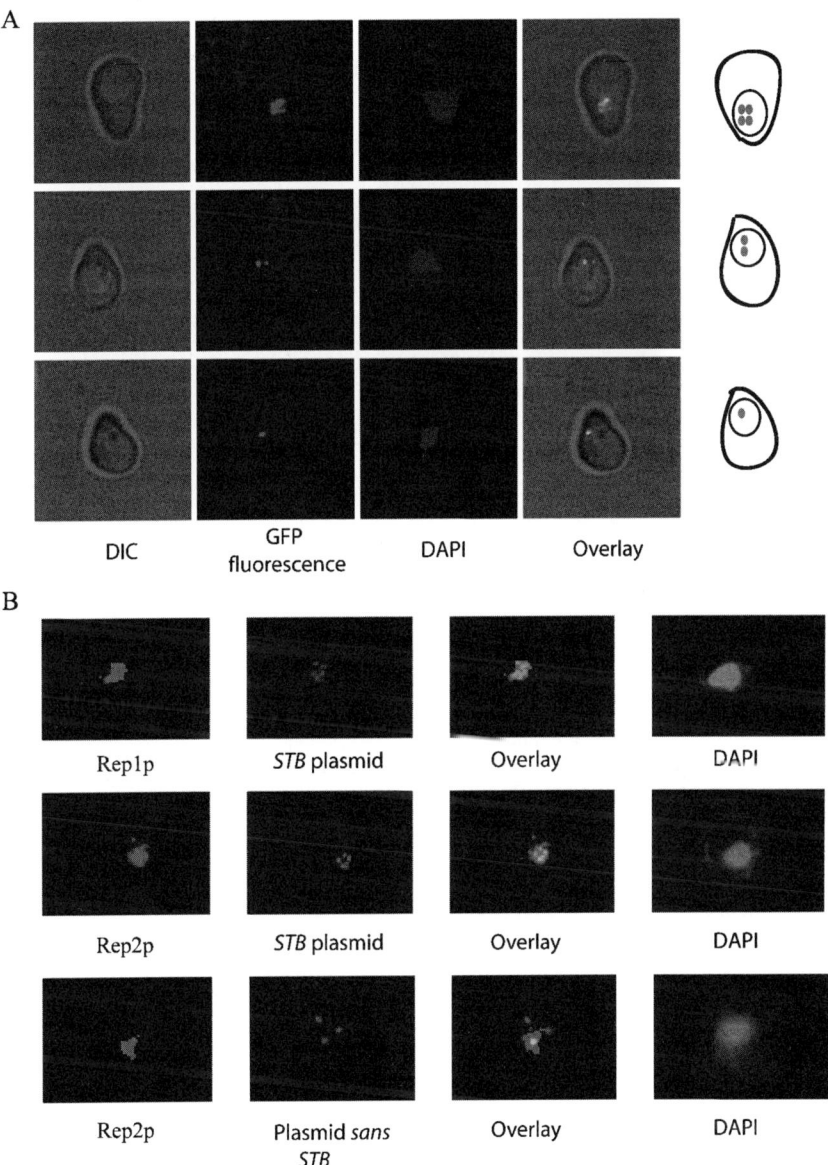

FIG. 15. (*Continued*)

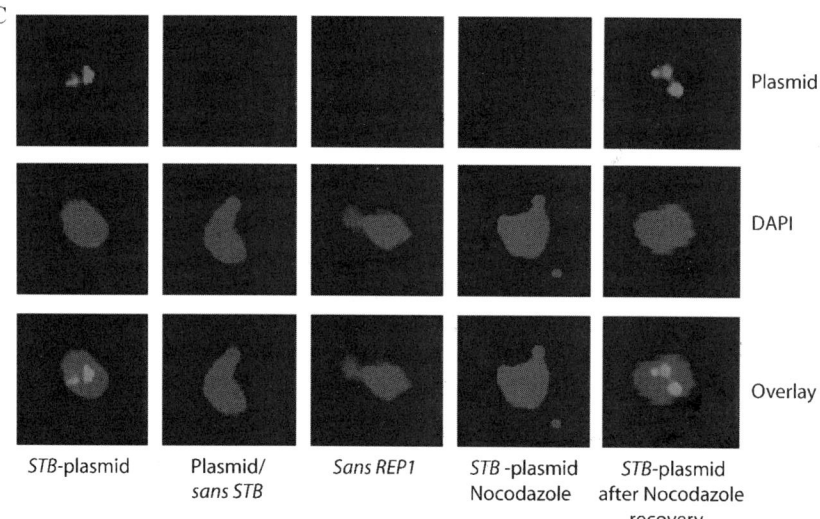

FIG. 15. Organization of the 2-micron plasmid cluster in the yeast nucleus. Reporter plasmids harboring an array of the Lac operator sequence are visualized in live cells by the fluorescence from bound GFP-Lac repressor or in fixed cells after immunostaining with antibodies against the repressor. (A) In cells arrested in G1 with alpha factor, the fluorescence-tagged plasmid is frequently seen as a tetrad shaped cluster (top row). However, clusters with two or three fluorescent dots or a single fluorescent dot are also encountered occasionally (middle and bottom rows). (B) Here the Rep1 and Rep2 proteins and the reporter plasmids are visualized by immunostaining with appropriate antibodies. The cluster of a 2-micron circle derived plasmid (containing *STB*) is tightly enveloped by the Rep1 protein (top row) and the Rep2 protein (middle row). The Rep proteins, and the associated plasmid cluster, are localized to a subzone of the DAPI staining region. A reporter plasmid lacking *STB* does not show the tight association with the Rep proteins. In the case illustrated here, a plasmid dot has broken away from the Rep2 protein zone (bottom row). (C) In chromosome spreads, an *STB* containing reporter plasmid is localized within the DAPI staining region; a plasmid lacking *STB* does not show this localization (compare columns 1 and 2). When cells lack the Rep 1 protein or when the spindle is depolymerized with nocodazole, the *STB*-plasmid is not detected in the chromosome spreads (columns 3 and 4). This is the case for the absence of the Rep2 protein as well (not shown). After nocodazole is washed off and the spindle is restored, the plasmid reappears in the spreads (column 5).

G1 with alpha factor and then released from the arrest into pheromone-free medium, one sees a rough doubling of the plasmid fluorescence during the S phase (12–18 min., Fig. 16). This is consistent with the duplication of plasmid molecules during this period. During the 42–48 min. interval, corresponding to late G2/M, the plasmid cluster separates into two, and each cluster rapidly moves away from the other to occupy the two daughter cell compartments. Comparison of the kinetics of plasmid segregation with the

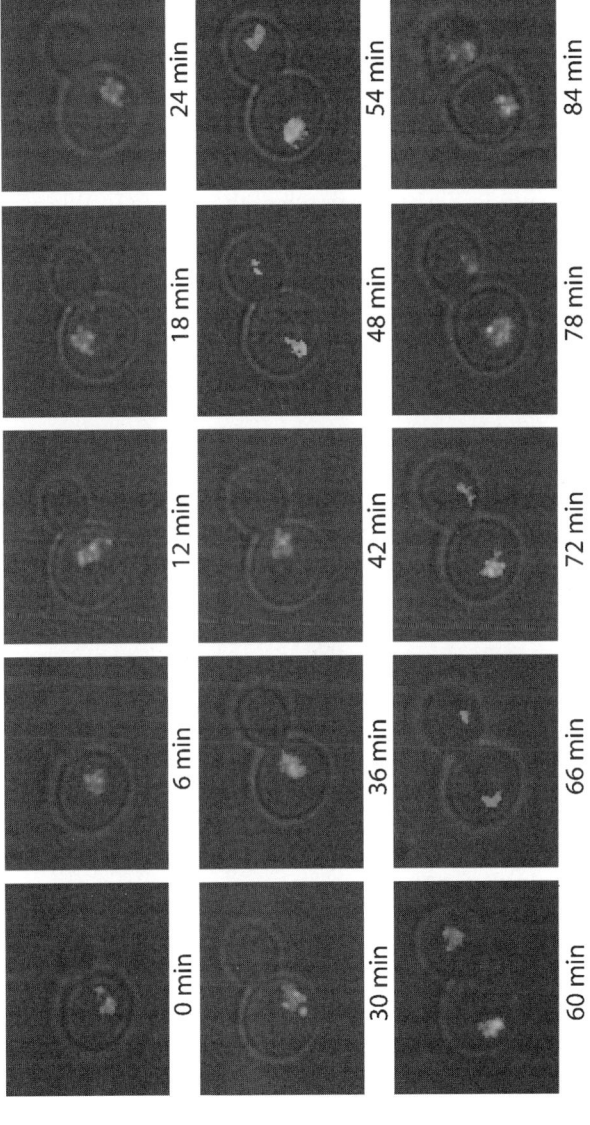

FIG. 16. Segregation of a 2-micron circle derived reporter plasmid by time-lapse fluorescence microscopy. The fluorescence-tagged plasmid is followed from the point of bud emergence (time zero) through one full division cycle. The plasmid fluorescence is doubled in the 6–18 min. period (early S phase) and plasmid partitioning occurs in the 42–48 min. interval. The observed pattern of segregation is quite similar to that of a fluorescence-tagged chromosome.

kinetics of segregation of a GFP-repressor tagged chromosome indicates that the two are nearly identical. These observations gave rise to the notion that 2-micron circle segregation and chromosome segregation may be temporally and/or spatially coupled events.

The potential connection between 2-micron circle and chromosome partitioning has been further substantiated by examining the behavior of reporter plasmids in genetic backgrounds that cause impaired chromosome segregation. In the *ipl1*–2 strain arrested at the nonpermissive temperature, the chromosomes missegregate, and so does the 2-micron plasmid (Fig. 17). Furthermore, the plasmid cluster tends to missegregate in tandem with the bulk of the chromosomes in the vast majority of the cells (67). When the *STB* locus is deleted from the reporter plasmid, the tandem missegregation of plasmid and chromosome is no longer observed. Interestingly, very similar

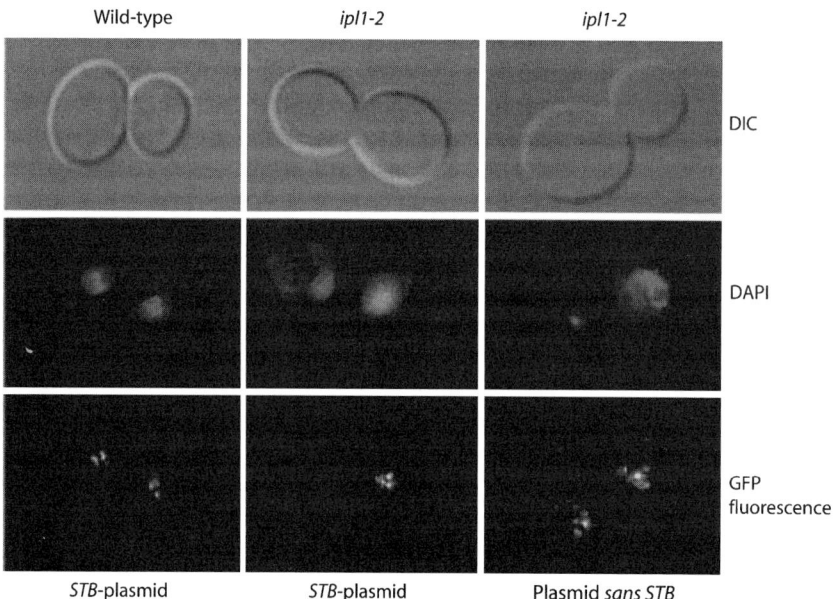

FIG. 17. Potential coupling between 2-micron plasmid and chromosome segregation. *Left*. In wild-type cells, or in *ipl1*–2 cells grown at 26°C, the 2-micron reporter plasmid and chromosome segregate normally, as indicated by the equal distribution of plasmid-associated fluorescence and the DAPI staining in the two cell compartments. *Middle*. In *ipl1*–2 cells grown at 37°C (nonpermissive for this mutant), there is gross missegregation of the chromosomes (large disparity in DAPI staining between the cell compartments). In these cells, the post-replication plasmid clusters show a strong proclivity to stay put with the bulk of the chromosomes. *Right*. Plasmids lacking *STB* are partitioned into the two cell compartments in the *ipl1-2* background at 37°C even when nearly all of the chromosomes missegregate into one compartment.

phenotypes have also been noted in other mutant strains adversely affected at distinct steps of the chromosome segregation pathway (68). Taken together, the data are consistent with the plasmid and chromosome segregation pathways being either interlinked or coordinately regulated. Perhaps the plasmid is tethered to the chromosomes, or they may exploit components of the host mitotic machinery for their own equal segregation. Or, the partitioning system may provide a checkpoint to prevent plasmid entry into a cell that lacks a full chromosome complement.

C. Interactions among the DNA and Protein Components of the Plasmid Partitioning System

Although it has been intuitively accepted that the interactions of the Rep proteins with *STB* are important for plasmid stability, there has been no direct experimental support for this notion. The colocalization of the Rep proteins in the yeast nucleus with plasmids harboring *STB*, and not those lacking *STB*, is consistent with this idea. Additional circumstantial evidence follows from the observation that the presence of Rep1p in chromosome spreads is dependent on the presence of Rep2p and vice versa (68). Using *in vivo* dihybrid assays and *in vitro* affinity trapping assays, self- and cross-interactions of the Rep proteins have now been clearly demonstrated (69, 70, 71, 72). Similarly, *in vivo* monohybrid assays have shown that Rep1p or Rep2p can associate with *STB*, and this association is not dependent on the partner Rep protein (72, 73). However, evidence for *STB* binding by the Rep proteins *in vitro* has been more difficult to establish. Partially pure Rep proteins fail to associate with *STB* when probed by standard gel mobility shift methods (74), which showed that urea-solubilized yeast cell extracts containing Rep1p or Rep2p can bind *STB*, suggesting the potential involvement of host protein(s) in this association. By using a southwestern assay, Sengupta *et al.* (70) have shown that the carboxyl-terminal portion of Rep2p has DNA binding activity. A detailed mutational analysis of the Rep1 protein (Yang and Jayaram, unpublished results) supports the functional relevance of Rep1p-Rep2p interaction and Rep1p-*STB* interaction in plasmid partitioning. Rep1p variants containing point mutations that disrupt either of the two interactions (or both) are not able to support normal plasmid maintenance.

D. Potential Involvement of Host Factors Required in 2-Micron Circle Partitioning

The loss rate of the 2-micron plasmid in a yeast population is approximately 10^{-4} to 10^{-5} per cell per generation. Or, the plasmid exhibits nearly chromosome-like stability. It has been a puzzle as to how a rudimentary partitioning system, consisting of just two proteins and a relatively short stretch of DNA, can mediate plasmid segregation with such high efficiency. Contrast this with the elaborate mitotic apparatus and multiple protein factors dedicated to ensure proper chromosome segregation. A search by yeast dihybrid and monohybrid assays for host proteins that interact with the Rep1 and/or Rep2 proteins or the *STB* locus has revealed several candidates, among which at least three are particularly interesting: the products of *BRN1*, *FUN30*, and *CST6/SHF1* (73). Whereas *BRN1* is an essential gene, both *FUN30* and *SHF1* are not. The Brn1 protein is a component of the yeast condensin complex, which plays a central role in proper chromosome segregation (75, 76). Brn1p appears to interact with Rep1p independent of Rep2p, and vice versa. Whether these interactions mirror the requirement of the condensin complex in 2-micron circle partitioning needs to be verified. Fun30p interacts with Rep1p directly but only indirectly with Rep2p, presumably through Rep1p. Both Brn1p and Fun30p can associate with *STB* in a Rep protein-dependent manner. The Shf1 protein binds to *STB* directly, as suggested by *in vivo* monohybrid results and by *in vitro* mobility retardation assays (72). In the *shf1*Δ background, there is a modest drop in the stability of a 2-micron circle-derived test plasmid. Interestingly, independent genetic assays have implicated *FUN30* as well as *SHF1* (*CST6*) to be important for chromosome partitioning (77).

The Fun30 protein contains peptide motifs characteristic of the SNF2 family of transcriptional regulators with potential chromatin remodeling activity. The Shf1 protein appears to belong to the ATF/bZIP class of transcription factors, and harbors a consensus CREB motif (72). It is likely that chromatin organization at the *STB* locus and/or its transcriptional status may affect its efficiency in plasmid partitioning. Consistent with this notion, a recent study demonstrates the requirement of the Rsc2 protein, which forms part of a chromatin remodeling complex in yeast, for the normal stability of the 2-micron circle (78). The nucleosome pattern at *STB* is altered and the association between Rep1p and *STB* is affected by the absence of Rsc2p. It is noteworthy that the region of *STB* proximal to the 2-micron circle origin, consisting of approximately six copies of a 62 bp repeat unit, is kept free of transcription by a termination signal located in the "distal" *STB* segment (79). A 24 bp silencer element, capable of suppressing the activity of a nearby promoter in an orientation-independent manner, has also been identified within the distal *STB* (80). Rather surprisingly, the 2-micron origin itself has been shown to function as a silencer, whose activity is dependent on the Sir proteins, the origin recognition complex (ORC), and the Hst3 protein, a Sir2 histone acetylase homolog (81).

It is known that transcription through eukaryotic replication origins and centromeres as well as the partitioning loci of certain bacterial plasmids can adversely affect their function (82). It is likely that the *STB* locus is also under a similar constraint, and its native location appears to have been selected to place the repeat units in a transcription-free zone. From earlier work, it is known that the stability of yeast plasmids (lacking the Rep-*STB* system) can be enhanced by the presence in *cis* of yeast telomere-associated sequences or the silencing element E associated with the unexpressed yeast mating type locus *HMRa* (83, 84, 85, 86). The partitioning activity of the subtelomeric repeats is absolutely dependent on the Rap1 protein, whereas that by the E element is mediated through the Sir1–4 proteins. The underlying common theme in both types of plasmid stabilization appears to be the organization of a silent chromatin domain. It has been suggested that the silencing complex anchors plasmids to a nuclear component that is symmetrically divided between daughter cells.

The old and new results can be accommodated by a model in which the plasmid replication is spatially restricted to a nuclear locale that facilitates the subsequent partitioning event.

E. The Yeast Cohesin Complex and 2-Micron Plasmid Partitioning

The finding that the yeast cohesin complex is recruited by the 2-micron plasmid adds an exciting new perspective to the partitioning problem. Yeast cohesin and condensin are multiprotein complexes that share homology in a subset of their subunits, and play cooperative roles in the segregation of sister chromatids during the cell cycle (87, 88, 89). As already pointed out, one of the host factors that interacts with the 2-micron circle partitioning system is the condensin subunit Brn1p. However, because of the tendency of condensin to associate nonspecifically with DNA, examining the potential role of this complex in plasmid segregation has been technically difficult to pursue. By contrast, the cohesin complex associates with the kinetochores and to consensus binding sites distributed at approximately 10 kbp intervals along the arms of chromosomes. Cohesin is loaded on to chromosomes concomitant with DNA replication, and keeps the sisters tightly paired until one of the cohesin components, Mcd1p, is cleaved by a protease during anaphase. The collapse of the cohesin bridge causes the chromosomes, attached to the spindle at their kinetochores in a bipolar manner, to be pulled apart and distributed, one each to each daughter cell. The condensin complex, on the other hand, facilitates chromosome segregation by compacting each of the sisters so as to minimize the risk of entanglement between them and the consequent self-guillotining during their separation. In a diploid eukaryotic cell, cohesin provides a mechanism for remembering a replication event as well as for accurately counting the DNA products resulting from it. Both mechanisms are important to ensure that each daughter cell arising from a given mitosis receives a full chromosome complement without accidentally acquiring two sisters instead of two homologs for any given chromosome. As described in subsequent sections, the suspicion that the 2-micron plasmid may also utilize pairing of replicated clusters via cohesin recruitment, followed later by their unpairing and segregation via cohesin disassembly, has received support from several lines of strong circumstantial evidence.

F. The Specificity of 2-Micron Circle-Cohesin Association: Role of the Rep Proteins in Cohesin Recruitment

Chromatin immunoprecipitation (ChIP) assays have demonstrated that, in exponentially growing yeast cells, the Mcd1 protein associates with the *STB* DNA of native 2-micron circles or of reporter plasmids containing *STB* (68). No association is detected with the other regions of the 2-micron circle, including *REP1*, *FLP*, or *REP2*. The plasmid origin gives a faint positive signal in the assay, presumably because of its close proximity to the STB locus. Two other cohesin components, Smc1p and Smc3p, also show a similar pattern of plasmid association. Furthermore, inactivation of Smc1p or Smc3p by T^s mutations disrupts Mcd1p-*STB* association at the nonpermissive temperature. These results are consistent with the preassembled cohesin complex being recruited by the plasmid partitioning system. Cohesin recruitment to the plasmid fails to occur when either Rep1p or Rep2p is absent. Several of the features of Mcd1p-*STB* association revealed by ChIP have been verified by probing this interaction by in vivo monohybrid assays. The combined *in vivo* and *in vitro* results satisfy two important criteria for the likely participation of the cohesin complex in plasmid segregation. First, the interaction of cohesin with the 2-micron circle is specific to the partitioning locus; plasmids lacking *STB* fail to show cohesin association. Second, cohesin recruitment by the plasmid is mediated with the combined assistance of the partitioning proteins Rep1p and Rep2p.

It should be emphasized that the mechanism of cohesin association with *STB* is clearly distinct from that of cohesin binding to chromosomal loci. There is no apparent sequence similarity between *STB* and cohesin binding sites on the chromosomes. And obviously, the Rep proteins are not required for the chromosomal recruitment of cohesin. Preliminary data also indicate that the Ctf7 protein, which is essential for cohesin assembly (but not maintenance) at chromosomal locales, is not required for cohesin assembly at *STB*. In addition, in the absence of intact nuclear microtubules, cohesin cannot be loaded on to *STB* without any deleterious effect on the acquisition of cohesin by chromosomal sites (90).

G. The Timing of Cohesin Recruitment to and Disassembly from the 2-Micron Plasmid as a Function of the Cell Cycle

As already pointed out, the chromosomes acquire cohesin as they go through DNA replication. According to available evidence, the replication machinery pauses at the cohesin binding sites and recruits a new DNA polymerase, σ, before resuming its onward movement (91, 92). The polymerase switching step is thought to be critical in mediating the association between cohesin and chromosomes (93, 94, 95). According to the latest model, an antiparallel dimer of Smc1p and Smc3p partially envelops the duplicated regions of the chromosomes, and Mcd1p closes the ring by interacting with the Smc proteins to trap the sister molecules inside (96). The cohesin chromosome association lasts until the anaphase promoting complex (APC) releases the protease that cleaves Mcd1p from its bondage by "securin" (97, 98, 99).

How does the timing of cohesin association and dissociation for the plasmid relate to the occurrence of these events on the chromosomes? Again, as determined by ChIP assays in synchronously dividing yeast cells, the periodicity of cohesin recruitment in sequential cell cycles and the lifetime of cohesin association in a given cycle are essentially identical for the plasmid and the chromosomes (Fig. 18). Thus, despite the utilization of disparate mechanisms for acquiring cohesin, the plasmid and chromosomes are well synchronized with respect to when cohesin assembles on them during the cell cycle and how long this assembly lasts. In other words, the Rep-*STB* system appears to be a clever molecular trick evolved by the plasmid to feed into the temporal program that its host has established for the cycle of cohesin association–dissociation on chromosomes. These findings provide strong grounds for seriously considering identical pathways for plasmid and chromosome segregation, or at least regulatory mechanisms that temporally coordinate the two events.

V. Cohesin Disassembly is a Prerequisite for Separation of Plasmid Clusters

The disassembly, during anaphase, of the cohesin bridge that holds sister chromatids together is mediated by specific cleavage of the Mcd1 protein. When the protease-sensitive sites within Mcd1p are mutated, cohesin fails to dissociate from the chromosomes and the cells arrest in late G2/M, with sisters remaining attached to each other (98). Although the noncleavable version of the *MCD1* gene (*MCD1*-nc) by itself would be lethal, cells harboring a copy of the wild-type *MCD1* and one of *MCD1*-nc can grow normally when the latter is kept repressed from a regulatable promoter. Is cleavage of Mcd1p important

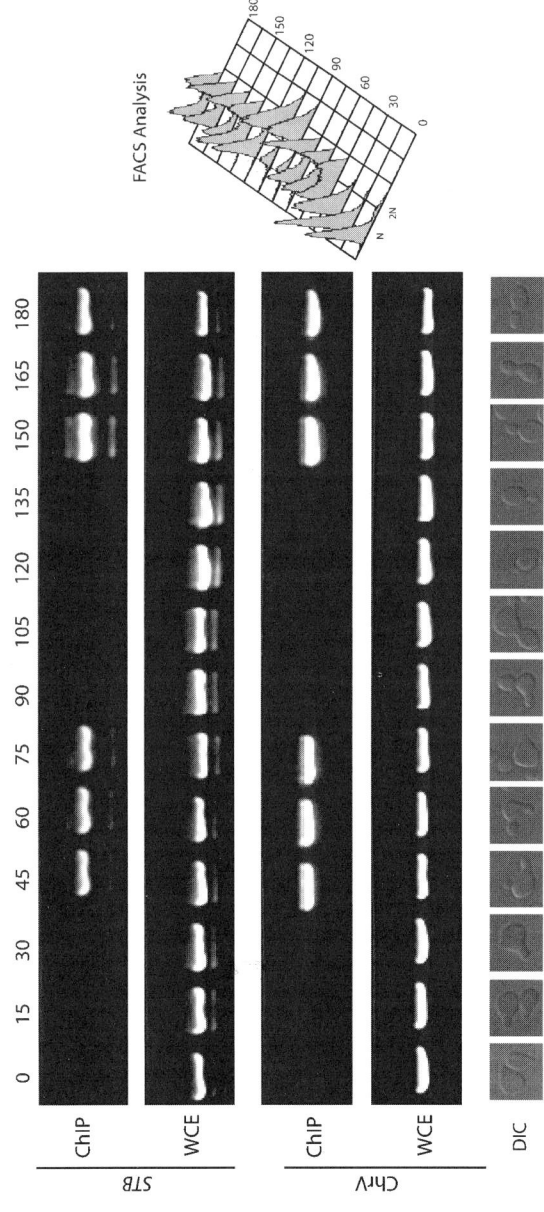

FIG. 18. Synchrony between the 2-micron plasmid and the chromosomes in cohesin recruitment during the yeast cell cycle. The presence of cohesin at *STB* or at a target site on chromosome V is followed by chromatin immunoprecipitation (ChIP) using antibodies directed to the cohesin component Mcd1p. Time zero refers to the release of cells arrested in G1 phase by α factor into pheromone-free growth medium. Cell aliquots are analyzed at the indicated time points by ChIP, light microscopy (DIC), and by FACS analysis. During each cell cycle, association of cohesin with the *STB* element occurs early in S phase and lasts until late G2/M. Note the nearly perfect synchrony between the chromosomes and the plasmid in cohesin association and dissociation. "WCE" refers to whole cell extracts used as positive controls for PCR amplification of suspected DNA targets.

for the separation of replicated 2-micron plasmid clusters, as it is for the separation of replicated chromosomes? The time-lapse assays shown in Fig. 19 are carried out with cells in which *MCD1*-nc is kept under the control of the *GAL1-10* promoter (98). In large budded cells from the dextrose

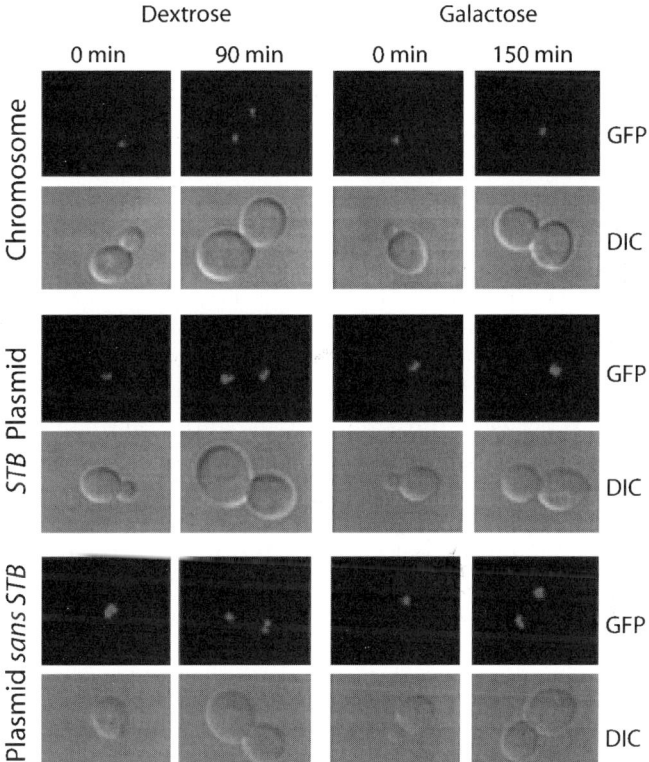

FIG. 19. Cleavage of the cohesin complex during anaphase is essential for the separation of duplicated 2-micron plasmid clusters. The fluorescence-tagged chromosome, 2-micron circle derived reporter plasmid, or plasmid lacking the *STB* sequence is resident in a host strain harboring a copy of the native *MCD1* gene and one of the non-cleavable version (*MCD1*-nc) under the *GAL10* promoter. After transferring cells from dextrose to galactose (time zero), they are followed for 150 min by time-lapse fluorescence microscopy. The control cells grown in dextrose are followed for 90 min. Representative data from 10 cells each from glucose and galactose media examined to monitor the chromosome (top two rows), the *STB*-plasmid (central two rows), or the plasmid without *STB* (bottom two rows) are shown. At 150 min., nearly 80% of the galactose grown cells show a single fluorescent dot or fluorescent cluster for the chromosome and the 2-micron reporter plasmid, respectively. By contrast, all of the galactose-grown cells containing the plasmid without *STB* show two separated plasmid clusters. Similarly, at 90 min., all the glucose-grown cells display two chromosomal dots or two plasmid clusters (for the *STB* and non-*STB* plasmids).

medium (little or no expression of *MCD1*-nc), separation of a fluorescence-tagged chromosome into two dots, and that of a similarly tagged plasmid into two clusters is readily detected. However, in the corresponding galactose-grown cells, there is neither the separation of the chromosome nor that of the plasmid in the majority of cases. These observations suggest that the cohesin recruited to the *STB* locus during the S phase is utilized to hold the replicated clusters together and that the dissociation of cohesin from *STB* is a perquisite for them to be unpaired.

A. Models for Cohesin-Mediated Plasmid Segregation

Assuming that the yeast cohesin complex plays fundamentally similar roles in the partitioning of yeast chromosomes and the 2-micron plasmid, two primary models for plasmid partitioning can be considered (Fig. 20), although several subtle variations of these themes are plausible. The first model proposes that the plasmid cluster is normally tethered to a chromosome, as is consistent with the localization of the cluster in yeast chromosome spreads. This direct physical interaction would facilitate the attachment between the new plasmid cluster and the sister chromosome formed by replication. In addition, coincident with the replication process, the sister clusters and the sister chromatids become bridged by cohesin. During anaphase, the dissolution of the cohesin bridge between the sister chromatids and the plasmid clusters would dispatch each cluster in opposite directions in association with the chromosomes. The plasmid–chromosome attachment could be mediated by cohesin itself or through other factors. If cohesin is the tethering agent, there must be some mechanism to postpone Mcd1p cleavage within this tether until after segregation has been completed. According to the second model, the two postreplication plasmid clusters are bridged by the cohesin complex but are not tethered to chromosomes. Upon disassembly of cohesin, each unpaired plasmid cluster moves to opposite cell poles without assistance from the chromosomes. This movement may be mediated by spindle attachment (a spindle associated motor protein could be involved), by an active transport system unrelated to the spindle, or by association with a subcellular entity that is evenly partitioned at cell division. Determining the precise mechanism by which the duplicated plasmid clusters are distributed to the daughter cells remains a challenge for the future.

VI. Summary and Perspectives

The 2-micron circle has provided the impetus for two important areas of research: the mechanism of site-specific DNA recombination and the mechanism of plasmid partitioning.

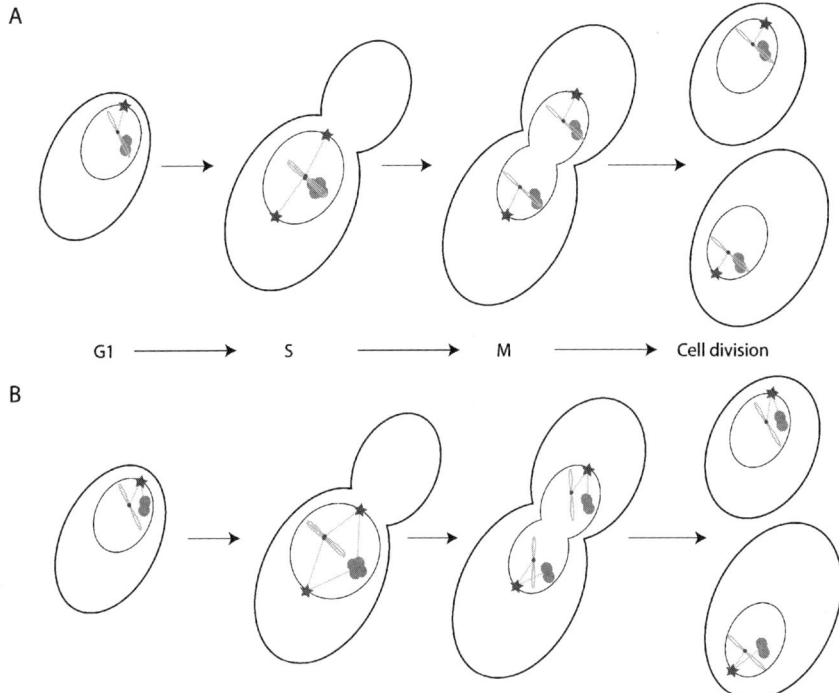

FIG. 20. Currently entertained models for 2-micron plasmid segregation. The cohesin complex appears to play analogous roles in chromosome segregation and 2-micron plasmid partitioning. (A) In one model, the plasmid cluster is tethered to a chromosome. The cohesin complex, recruited in a replication-dependent manner, bridges the duplicated plasmid clusters as it does sister chromatids. Each cluster is now attached to each of the sisters. Following cohesin disassembly in anaphase, each cluster moves toward each pole of the elongated nucleus by hitchhiking on the sister chromosomes. Nuclear division followed by karyokinesis completes the segregation pathway. (B) The basic role of cohesin in this model is the same as in A. However, there is no plasmid–chromosome tethering. Upon breakdown of the cohesin bridge, each cluster is dispatched in opposite directions independent of the chromosomes. The mechanism by which this movement is mediated (it could be by attachment to the spindle, perhaps) is not known.

The Flp recombination system has been generous in revealing the nature of DNA recognition by the recombinase, the mode of its active site assembly, and the chemical mechanisms for strand cleavage and exchange. The surprising discovery that Flp has a shared active site, causing DNA cleavage to occur in *trans*, has spurred investigation of active site organization and strand cleavage in other site-specific recombination systems and in DNA transposition systems. Among the extensively studied site-specific recombinases belonging to the tyrosine family or the serine family, Flp and Flp-like recombinases encoded by yeast plasmids are the only ones that execute *trans* DNA cleavage. Among the well-characterized transposition systems, the transposase proteins of phage Mu and Tn 5 carry out strand cutting in *trans* (*100, 101, 102, 103, 104*). The Tn10 transposase, by contrast, performs DNA cleavage in *cis* (*105*).

Since recombinases such as Flp or Cre act on sites aligned in an antiparallel fashion in a planar recombination complex, no DNA crossing is added during the strand exchange process. From this knowledge, a difference topology assay has been developed for tracing the number of crossings formed when two or more DNA sites interact within a high-order nucleoprotein complex. The mapping of DNA topology within the intermediates of the phage Mu transposition pathway illustrates the potential utility of this methodology (*45*). In principle, difference topology can be applied to follow DNA paths within replication, repair, and transcription complexes.

Flp and related site-specific recombination systems, especially Cre/lox, have been put to a number of practical applications in basic research and in biotechnology. Site-specific recombination has found seminal use in the study of development, in the construction of transgenic plants and animals, and in the insertion, deletion, or replacement of DNA at predetermined genetic loci, often in a temporally regulated manner. The construction of Flp and Cre variants with altered target site recognition promises to significantly expand the scope of site-specific recombination in directed genome manipulations.

Compared to Flp site-specific recombination, the progress on the analysis of the 2-micron circle segregation mechanism has been rather slow. The early genetic studies on plasmid partitioning were followed by a rather long lull, and interest in this area has re-emerged only recently. As outlined in this Chapter, we are beginning to unveil the mechanisms by which the rather simple Rep-*STB* system is able to raise its level of functional sophistication by taking advantage of the mitotic segregation pathway of its host.

An important question for future research is how the partitioning and amplification systems communicate with each other to sustain efficient plasmid propagation with only limited deviations from the mean plasmid copy number. Current notions on how the amplification system is kept quiescent under steady-state conditions and how it might be quickly commissioned or decommissioned depending upon the copy number status of a given cell have to be subjected to more rigorous experimental tests.

In summary, the 2-micron plasmid is a minimalist, yet carefully optimized, structural design for a selfish nucleic acid. By harboring a replication origin that is functionally equivalent to the chromosomal origins, the plasmid enjoys duplication by the host replication machinery. By pilfering host factors using components of its stability system, the plasmid apparently gains access to a highly efficient partitioning mechanism. And by preserving a recombination-mediated amplification system in readiness, the plasmid ensures that its copy number is maintained at the steady-state value. The apparent conservation of the basic 2-micron circle paradigm by the other yeast plasmids speaks to its effectiveness and evolutionary durability as a strategy for benign parasitism.

ACKNOWLEDGMENTS

The Jayaram laboratory has been sustained over the years by funds provided by the National Institutes of Health, the National Science Foundation, the Robert F. Welch foundation, the Council for Tobacco Research, the Texas Higher Education Coordinating Board, and the Human Frontiers in Science Program.

REFERENCES

1. Jayaram, M., Yang, X. M., Mehta, S., Voziyanov, Y., and Velmurugan, S. (2003). The 2 μm plasmid of *Saccharomyces cerevisiae*. In "Plasmids,"ASM Press, Washington, DC.
2. Broach, J. R., and Volkert, F. C. (1991). Circular DNA plasmids in yeasts. In "The Molecular Biology of the Yeast *Saccharomyces*; Genome Dynamics, Protein Synthesis and Energetics" (J. R. Broach, J. R. Pringle, and E. W. Jones, Eds.). Cold Spring Harbor Press, Cold Spring Harbor, NY.
3. Jayaram, M., Tribble, G., and Grainge, I. (2002). Site-specific recombination by the Flp protein of *Saccharomyces cerevisiae*. In "Mobile DNA II" (N. L. Craig, R. Craigie, M. Gellert, and A. M. Lambowitz, Eds.), pp. 192–218. ASM Press, Washington, DC.
4. Rice, P. A. (2002). Theme and variation in tyrosine recombinases: Structure of a Flp-DNA complex. In "Mobile DNA II" (N. L. Craig, R. Craigie, M. Gellert, and A. M. Lambowitz, Eds.), pp. 219–229. ASM Press, Washington, DC.
5. Chen, Y., Narendra, U., Iype, L. E., Cox, M. M., and Rice, P. A. (2000). Crystal structure of an Flp recombinase–Holliday junction complex: Assembly of an active oligomer by helix swapping. *Mol. Cell* **6**, 885–897.
6. Lee, J., Voziyanov, Y., Pathania, S., and Jayaram, M. (1998). Structural alterations and conformational dynamics in Holliday junctions induced by binding of a site-specific recombinase. *Mol. Cell* **1**, 483–493.
7. Van Duyne, G. D. (2002). A structural view of tyrosine recombinase site-specific recombination. In "Mobile DNA II" (N. L. Craig, R. Craigie, M. Gellert, and A. M. Lambowitz, Eds.), pp. 93–117. ASM Press, Washington, DC.
8. Gopaul, D. N., Guo, F., and Van Duyne, G. D. (1998). Structure of the Holliday junction intermediate in Cre-loxP site-specific recombination. *EMBO J.* **17**, 4175–4187.
9. Guo, F., Gopaul, D. N., and Van Duyne, G. D. (1997). Structure of Cre recombinase complexed with DNA in a site-specific recombination synapse. *Nature* **389**, 40–46.
10. Guo, F., Gopaul, D. N., and Van Duyne, G. D. (1999). Asymmetric DNA-bending in the Cre-loxP site-specific recombination synapse. *Proc. Natl. Acad. Sci. USA* **96**, 7143–7148.
11. Cheng, C., and Shuman, S. (1998). A catalytic domain of eukaryotic DNA topoisomerase I. *J. Biol. Chem.* **273**, 11589–11595.
12. Redinbo, M. R., Stewart, L., Kuhn, P., Champoux, J. J., and Hol, W. G. (1998). Crystal structures of human topoisomerase I in covalent and noncovalent complexes with DNA. *Science* **279**, 1504–1513.

13. Stewart, L., Redinbo, M. R., Qiu, X., Hol, W. G., and Champoux, J. J. (1998). A model for the mechanism of human topoisomerase I. *Science* **279**, 1534–1541.
14. Lee, J., Tonozuka, T., and Jayaram, M. (1997). Mechanism of active site exclusion in a site-specific recombinase: Role of the DNA substrate in conferring half-of-the-sites activity. *Genes Dev.* **11**, 3061–3071.
15. Krogh, B. O., and Shuman, S. (2000). Catalytic mechanism of DNA topoisomerase IB. *Mol. Cell* **5**, 1035–1041.
16. Pan, G., Luetke, K., and Sadowski, P. D. (1993). Mechanism of cleavage and ligation by FLP recombinase: classification of mutations in FLP protein by *in vitro* complementation analysis. *Mol. Cell. Biol.* **13**, 3167–3175.
17. Parsons, R. L., Prasad, P. V., Harshey, R. M., and Jayaram, M. (1988). Step-arrest mutants of FLP recombinase: Implications for the catalytic mechanism of DNA recombination. *Mol. Cell. Biol.* **8**, 3303–3310.
18. Lee, J., Jayaram, M., and Grainge, I. (1999). Wild-type Flp recombinase cleaves DNA in trans. *EMBO J.* **18**, 784–791.
19. Gopaul, D. N., and Van Duyne, G. D. (1999). Structure and mechanism in site-specific recombination. *Curr. Opin. Struct. Biol.* **9**, 14–20.
20. Arciszewska, L. K., Baker, R. A., Hallet, B., and Sherratt, D. J. (2000). Coordinated control of XerC and XerD catalytic activities during Holliday junction resolution. *J. Mol. Biol.* **299**, 391–403.
21. Hallet, B., Arciszewska, L. K., and Sherratt, D. J. (1999). Reciprocal control of catalysis by the tyrosine recombinases XerC and XerD: An enzymatic switch in site-specific recombination. *Mol. Cell* **4**, 949–959.
22. Spiers, A. J., and Sherratt, D. J. (1997). Relating primary structure to function in the *Escherichia coli* XerD site-specific recombinase. *Mol. Microbiol.* **24**, 1071–1082.
23. Lusetti, S. L., and Cox, M. M. (2002). The bacterial RecA protein and the recombinational DNA repair of stalled replication forks. *Ann. Rev. Biochem.* **71**, 71–100.
24. Fersht, A. (1977). "Enzyme Structure and Mechanism." W. H. Freeman, San Francisco.
25. Grainge, I., and Jayaram, M. (1999). The integrase family of recombinases: Organization and function of the active site. *Mol. Microbiol.* **33**, 449–456.
26. Gillette, W. K., Rhee, S., Rosner, J. L., and Martin, R. G. (2000). Structural homology between MarA of the AraC family of transcriptional activators and the integrase family of site-specific recombinases. *Mol. Microbiol.* **35**, 1582–1583.
27. Grishin, N. V. (2000). Two tricks in one bundle: Helix–turn–helix gains enzymatic activity. *Nucleic Acids Res.* **28**, 2229–2233.
28. Huai, Q., Colandene, J. D., Chen, Y., Luo, F., Zhao, Y., Topal, M. D., and Ke, H. (2000). Crystal structure of NaeI—An evolutionary bridge between DNA endonuclease and topoisomerase. *EMBO J.* **19**, 3110–3118.
29. Sau, A. K., Tribble, G. D., Grainge, I., Frohlich, R. F., Knudsen, B. R., and Jayaram, M. (2001). Biochemical and kinetic analysis of the RNase active sites of the Integrase/Tyrosine family site-specific DNA Recombinases. *J. Biol. Chem.* **276**, 46612–46623.
30. Sekiguchi, J., and Shuman, S. (1997). Site-specific ribonuclease activity of eukaryotic DNA topoisomerase I. *Mol. Cell* **1**, 89–97.
31. Wittschieben, J., and Shuman, S. (1997). Mechanism of DNA transesterification by vaccinia topoisomerase: Catalytic contributions of essential residues Arg-130, Gly-132, Tyr-136, and Lys-167. *Nucleic Acids Res.* **25**, 3001–3008.
32. Xu, C. J., Grainge, I., Lee, J., Harshey, R. M., and Jayaram, M. (1998). Unveiling two distinct ribonuclease activities and a topoisomerase activity in a site-specific DNA recombinase. *Mol. Cell* **1**, 729–739.

33. Xu, C. J., Ahn, Y. T., Pathania, S., and Jayaram, M. (1998). Flp ribonuclease activities. Mechanistic similarities and contrasts to site-specific DNA recombination. *J. Biol. Chem.* **273**, 30591–30598.
34. Abremsk, K. E., and Hoess, R. H. (1992). Evidence for a second conserved arginine residue in the integrase family of recombination proteins. *Protein Eng.* **5**, 87–91.
35. Azaro, M. A., and Landy, A. (2002). λ integrase and the λ int family. *In* "Mobile DNA II" (N. L. Craig, R. Craigie, M. Gellert, and A. M. Lambowitz, Eds.), pp. 118–148. ASM Press, Washington DC.
36. Cornet, F., Hallet, B., and Sherratt, D. J. (1997). Xer recombination in *Escherichia coli*. Site-specific DNA topoisomerase activity of the XerC and XerD recombinases. *J. Biol. Chem.* **272**, 21927–21931.
37. Landy, A. (1989). Dynamic, structural, and regulatory aspects of lambda site-specific recombination. *Ann. Rev. Biochem.* **58**, 913–949.
38. Wittschieben, J., Petersen, B. O., and Shuman, S. (1998). Replacement of the active site tyrosine of vaccinia DNA topoisomerase by glutamate, cysteine, or histidine converts the enzyme into a site-specific endonuclease. *Nucleic Acids Res.* **26**, 490–496.
39. Burgin, A. B., Jr. (1997). Can DNA topoisomerases be ribonucleases? *Cell* **91**, 873–874.
40. Sherratt, D. J., and Wigley, D. B. (1998). Conserved themes but novel activities in recombinases and topoisomerases. *Cell* **93**, 149–152.
41. Grainge, I., Buck, D., and Jayaram, M. (2000). Geometry of site alignment during int family recombination: Antiparallel synapsis by the Flp recombinase. *J. Mol. Biol.* **298**, 749–764.
42. Grindley, N. D. (2002). The movement of Tn3 like elements: Transposition and cointegrate resolution. *In* "Mobile DNA II" (N. L. Craig, R. Craigie, M. Gellert, and A. M. Lambowitz, Eds.), pp. 272–304. ASM Press, Washington, DC.
43. Kilbride, E., Boocock, M. R., and Stark, W. M. (1999). Topological selectivity of a hybrid site-specific recombination system with elements from Tn3 res/resolvase and bacteriophage P1 loxP/Cre. *J. Mol. Biol.* **289**, 1219–1230.
44. Grainge, I., Pathania, S., Vologodskii, A., Harshey, R. M., and Jayaram, M. (2002). Symmetric DNA sites are functionally asymmetric within Flp and Cre site-specific DNA recombination synapses. *J. Mol. Biol.* **320**, 515–527.
45. Pathania, S., Jayaram, M., and Harshey, R. M. (2002). Path of DNA within the Mu transpososome. Transposase interactions bridging two Mu ends and the enhancer trap five DNA supercoils. *Cell* **109**, 425–436.
46. Recchia, G. D., and Sherratt, D. J. (2002). Gene acquisition in bacteria by integron-mediated site-specific recombination. *In* "Mobile DNA II" (N. L. Craig, R. Craigie, M. Gellert, and A. M. Lambowitz, Eds.), pp. 162–176. ASM Press, Washington DC.
47. Carrasco, C. D., Buettner, J. A., and Golden, J. W. (1995). Programmed DNA rearrangement of a cyanobacterial hupL gene in heterocysts. *Proc. Natl. Acad. Sci. USA* **92**, 791–795.
48. Barre, F.-X., and Sherratt, D. J. (2002). Xer site-specific recombination: Promoting chromosome segregation. *In* "Mobile DNA II" (N. L. Craig, R. Craigie, M. Gellert, and A. M. Lambowitz, Eds.), pp. 149–161. ASM Press, Washington DC.
49. Austin, S., Ziese, M., and Sternberg, N. (1981). A novel role for site-specific recombination in maintenance of bacterial replicons. *Cell* **25**, 729–736.
50. Futcher, A. B. (1986). Copy number amplification of the 2-micron circle plasmid of *Saccharomyces cerevisiae*. *J. Theor. Biol.* **119**, 197–204.
51. Volkert, F. C., and Broach, J. R. (1986). Site-specific recombination promotes plasmid amplification in yeast. *Cell* **46**, 541–550.

52. Reynolds, A. E., Murray, A. W., and Szostak, J. W. (1987). Roles of the 2-micron gene products in stable maintenance of the 2-micron plasmid of *Saccharomyces cerevisiae*. *Mol. Cell. Biol.* **7**, 3566–3573.
53. Petes, T. D., and Williamson, D. H. (1994). A novel structural form of the 2-micron plasmid of the yeast *Saccharomyces cerevisiae*. *Yeast* **10**, 1341–1345.
54. Som, T., Armstrong, K. A., Volkert, F. C., and Broach, J. R. (1988). Autoregulation of 2-micron circle gene expression provides a model for maintenance of stable plasmid copy levels. *Cell* **52**, 27–37.
55. Blaisonneau, J., Sor, F., Cheret, G., Yarrow, D., and Fukuhara, H. (1997). A circular plasmid from the yeast *Torulaspora delbrueckii*. *Plasmid* **38**, 202–209.
56. Chen, X. J., Saliola, M., Falcone, C., Bianchi, M. M., and Fukuhara, H. (1986). Sequence organization of the circular plasmid pKD1 from the yeast *Kluyveromyces drosophilarum*. *Nucleic Acids Res.* **14**, 4471–4481.
57. Toh-e, A., and Utatsu, I. (1985). Physical and functional structure of a yeast plasmid, pSB3, isolated from Zygosaccharomyces bisporus. *Nucleic Acids Res.* **13**, 4267–4283.
58. Toh-e, A., Araki, H., Utatsu, I., and Oshima, Y. (1984). Plasmids resembling 2-micron DNA in the osmotolerant yeasts *Saccharomyces bailii* and *Saccharomyces bisporus*. *J. Gen. Microbiol.* **130**, 2527–2534.
59. Utatsu, I., Utsunomiya, A., and Toh-e, A. (1986). Functions encoded by the yeast plasmid pSB3 isolated from *Zygosaccharomyces rouxii* IFO 1730 (formerly *Saccharomyces bisporus var. mellis*). *J. Gen. Microbiol.* **132**, 1359–1365.
60. Sauer, B. (2002). Chromosome manipulation by Cre-lox recombination. *In* "Mobile DNA II" (N. L. Craig, R. Craigie, M. Gellert, and A. M. Lambowitz, Eds.), pp. 38–58. ASM Press, Washington DC.
61. Buchholz, F., Angrand, P. O., and Stewart, A. F. (1998). Improved properties of FLP recombinase evolved by cycling mutagenesis. *Nat. Biotechnol.* **16**, 657–662.
62. Logie, C., and Stewart, A. F. (1995). Ligand-regulated site-specific recombination. *Proc. Natl. Acad. Sci. USA* **92**, 5940–5944.
63. Rufer, A. W., and Sauer, B. (2002). Non-contact positions impose site selectivity on Cre recombinase. *Nucleic Acids Res.* **30**, 2764–2771.
64. Santoro, S. W., and Schultz, P. G. (2002). Directed evolution of the site specificity of Cre recombinase. *Proc. Natl. Acad. Sci. USA* **99**, 4185–4190.
65. Voziyanov, Y., Stewart, A. F., and Jayaram, M. (2002). A dual reporter screening system identifies the amino acid at position 82 in Flp site-specific recombinase as a determinant for target specificity. *Nucleic Acids Res.* **30**, 1656–1663.
66. Voziyanov, Y., Konieczka, H., Stewart, A. F., and Jayaram, M. (2003). Stepwise manipulation of DNA specificity in Flp recombinase: Progressively adapting Flp to individual and combinatorial mutations in its target site. *J. Mol. Biol.* **326**, 65–76.
67. Velmurugan, S., Yang, X. M., Chan, C. S., Dobson, M., and Jayaram, M. (2000). Partitioning of the 2-microm circle plasmid of *Saccharomyces cerevisiae*: Functional coordination with chromosome segregation and plasmid-encoded Rep protein distribution. *J. Cell. Biol.* **149**, 553–566.
68. Mehta, S., Yang, X. M., Chan, C. S., Dobson, M. J., Jayaram, M., and Velmurugan, S. (2002). The 2-micron plasmid purloins the yeast cohesin complex: A mechanism for coupling plasmid partitioning and chromosome segregation? *J. Cell. Biol.* **158**, 625–637.
69. Ahn, Y. T., Wu, X. L., Biswal, S., Velmurugan, S., Volkert, F. C., and Jayaram, M. (1997). The 2-micron-plasmid-encoded Rep1 and Rep2 proteins interact with each other and colocalize to the *Saccharomyces cerevisiae* nucleus. *J. Bacteriol.* **179**, 7497–7506.
70. Sengupta, A., Blomqvist, K., Pickett, A. J., Zhang, Y., Chew, J. S., and Dobson, M. J. (2001). Functional domains of yeast plasmid-encoded Rep proteins. *J. Bacteriol.* **183**, 2306–2315.

71. Scott-Drew, S., and Murray, J. A. (1998). Localization and interaction of the protein components of the yeast 2-μm circle plasmid partitioning system suggest a mechanism for plasmid inheritance. *J. Cell Sci.* **111,** 1779–1789.
72. Velmurugan, S., Ahn, Y. T., Yang, X. M., Wu, X. L., and Jayaram, M. (1998). The 2-micron plasmid stability system: Analyses of the interactions among plasmid- and host-encoded components. *Mol. Cell. Biol.* **18,** 7466–7477.
73. X. M. Yang, S. Velmurugan, and M. Jayaram, Unpublished results.
74. Hadfield, C., Mount, R. C., and Cashmore, A. M. (1995). Protein binding interactions at the *STB* locus of the yeast 2-micron plasmid. *Nucleic Acids Res.* **23,** 995–1002.
75. Lavoie, B. D., Tuffo, K. M., Oh, S., Koshland, D., and Holm, C. (2000). Mitotic chromosome condensation requires Brn1p, the yeast homologue of Barren. *Mol. Biol. Cell* **11,** 1293–1304.
76. Ouspenski, I. I., Cabello, O. A., and Brinkley, B. R. (2000). Chromosome condensation factor Brn1p is required for chromatid separation in mitosis. *Mol. Biol. Cell* **11,** 1305–1313.
77. Ouspenski, I. I., Elledge, S. J., and Brinkley, B. R. (1999). New yeast genes important for chromosome integrity and segregation identified by dosage effects on genome stability. *Nucleic Acids Res.* **27,** 3001–3008.
78. Wong, M. C., Scott-Drew, S. R., Hayes, M. J., Howard, P. J., and Murray, J. A. (2002). *RSC2*, encoding a component of the RSC nucleosome remodeling complex, is essential for 2-microcon plasmid maintenance in *Saccharomyces cerevisiae*. *Mol. Cell. Biol.* **22,** 4218–4229.
79. Sutton, A., and Broach, J. R. (1985). Signals for transcription initiation and termination in the *Saccharomyces cerevisiae* plasmid 2-micron circle. *Mol. Cell. Biol.* **5,** 2770–2780.
80. Murray, J. A., and Cesareni, G. (1986). Functional analysis of the yeast plasmid partitioning locus *STB*. *EMBO J.* **5,** 3391–3400.
81. Gunwale, A., and Ehrenhofer-Murray, A. E. (2002). A novel yeast silencer. The 2-μm origin of Saccharomyces cerevisiae has *HST3*-, *MIG1*-, and *SIR*-dependent silencing activity. *Genetics* **162,** 59–71.
82. Rodionov, O., Lobocka, M., and Yarmolinsky, M. (1999). Silencing of genes flanking the P1 plasmid centromere. *Science* **283,** 546–549.
83. Ansari, A., and Gartenberg, M. R. (1997). The yeast silent information regulator Sir4p anchors and partitions plasmids. *Mol. Cell. Biol.* **17,** 7061–7068.
84. Kimmerly, W. J., and Rine, J. (1987). Replication and segregation of plasmids containing cis-acting regulatory sites of silent mating-type genes in *Saccharomyces cerevisiae* are controlled by the *SIR* genes. *Mol. Cell. Biol.* **7,** 4225–4237.
85. Longtine, M. S., Enomoto, S., Finstad, S. L., and Berman, J. (1992). Yeast telomere repeat sequence (TRS) improves circular plasmid segregation, and TRS plasmid segregation involves the *RAP1* gene product. *Mol. Cell. Biol.* **12,** 1997–2009.
86. Longtine, M. S., Enomoto, S., Finstad, S. L., and Berman, J. (1993). Telomere-mediated plasmid segregation in *Saccharomyces cerevisiae* involves gene products required for transcriptional repression at silencers and telomeres. *Genetics* **133,** 171–182.
87. Nasmyth, K. (2001). Disseminating the genome: Joining, resolving, and separating sister chromatids during mitosis and meiosis. *Ann. Rev. Genet.* **35,** 673–745.
88. Nasmyth, K., Peters, J. M., and Uhlmann, F. (2000). Splitting the chromosome: Cutting the ties that bind sister chromatids. *Science* **288,** 1379–1385.
89. Cohen-Fix, O. (2001). The making and breaking of sister chromatid cohesion. *Cell* **106,** 137–140.
90. S. Mehta and M. Jayaram. (2003). Unpublished results.
91. Carson, D. R., and Christman, M. F. (2001). Evidence that replication fork components catalyze establishment of cohesion between sister chromatids. *Proc. Natl. Acad. Sci. USA* **98,** 8270–8275.

92. Edwards, S., Li, C. M., Levy, D. L., Brown, J., Snow, P. M., and Campbell, J. L. (2003). *Saccharomyces cerevisiae* DNA polymerase epsilon and polymerase sigma interact physically and functionally, suggesting a role for polymerase epsilon in sister chromatid cohesion. *Mol. Cell. Biol.* **23**, 2733–2748.
93. Castano, I. B., Brzoska, P. M., Sadoff, B. U., Chen, H., and Christman, M. F. (1996). Mitotic chromosome condensation in the rDNA requires *TRF4* and DNA topoisomerase I in *Saccharomyces cerevisiae*. *Genes Dev.* **10**, 2564–2576.
94. Wang, Z., and Christman, M. F. (2001). Replication-related activities establish cohesion between sister chromatids. *Cell. Biochem. Biophys.* **35**, 289–301.
95. Wang, Z., Castano, I. B., De Las Penas, A., Adams, C., and Christman, M. F. (2000). Pol kappa: A DNA polymerase required for sister chromatid cohesion. *Science* **289**, 774–779.
96. Gruber, S., Haering, C. H., and Nasmyth, K. (2003). Chromosomal cohesin forms a ring. *Cell* **112**, 765–777.
97. Rao, H., Uhlmann, F., Nasmyth, K., and Varshavsky, A. (2001). Degradation of a cohesin subunit by the N-end rule pathway is essential for chromosome stability. *Nature* **410**, 955–959.
98. Uhlmann, F., Lottspeich, F., and Nasmyth, K. (1999). Sister-chromatid separation at anaphase onset is promoted by cleavage of the cohesin subunit Scc1. *Nature* **400**, 37–42.
99. Uhlmann, F., Wernic, D., Poupart, M. A., Koonin, E. V., and Nasmyth, K. (2000). Cleavage of cohesin by the CD clan protease separin triggers anaphase in yeast. *Cell* **103**, 375–386.
100. Yang, J. Y., Jayaram, M., and Harshey, R. M. (1996). Positional information within the Mu transposase tetramer: Catalytic contributions of individual monomers. *Cell* **85**, 447–455.
101. Aldaz, H., Schuster, E., and Baker, T. A. (1996). The interwoven architecture of the Mu transposase couples DNA synapsis to catalysis. *Cell* **85**, 257–269.
102. Savilahti, H., and Mizuuchi, K. (1996). Mu transpositional recombination: Donor DNA cleavage and strand transfer in *trans* by the Mu transposase. *Cell* **85**, 271–280.
103. Naumann, T. A., and Reznikoff, W. S. (2000). Trans catalysis in Tn5 transposition. *Proc. Natl. Acad. Sci. USA* **97**, 8944–8949.
104. Namgoong, S. Y., and Harshey, R. M. (1998). The same two monomers within a MuA tetramer provide the DDE domains for the strand cleavage and strand transfer steps of transposition. *EMBO J.* **17**, 3775–3785.
105. Boland, S., and Clicker, N. (1996). The three chemical steps of Tn10/IS10 transposition involve repeated utilization of a single active site. *Cell* **84**, 223–233.

Did an Early Version of the Eukaryal Replisome Enable the Emergence of Chromatin?

GABRIEL KAUFMANN
AND TAMAR NETHANEL

Biochemistry Department, Tel Aviv University, Ramat Aviv 69978, Israel

I. Introduction	173
II. Deep-Rooted Features of Two Replisome Types	174
A. Replicative Helicases	175
B. Single-Stranded DNA Binding Proteins	179
C. Primase and the Initiating Replicase	181
D. Replicases	182
E. Replication Fork Symmetry	184
F. DNA Maturation Reactions	184
III. Coordinated Syntheses of the Opposite DNA Strands	187
A. The Bacterial Paradigm	187
B. Models of Discontinuous DNA Synthesis in Eukarya	188
C. Evidence Underlying the Nested Discontinuity Model	191
IV. Possible Implications of a Symmetrical Eukaryal Replication Fork	196
A. Could a Trombonelike Replication Loop Exist at the Eukaryal Fork?	196
B. Possible Selective Advantage of a Symmetrical Replication Fork	196
C. The Eukaryal Type Replisome and Ascent of Chromatin	196
References	199

I. Introduction[1]

The basic rules for replicating a cellular genome apply universally: parental DNA is unwound from bidirectional origins, usually defined sequences, followed by semi-discontinuous synthesis of complementary, RNA-primed DNA chains on the availed template strands (*1, 2*). Nonetheless, key replisome components, including the fork unwinding helicase, primase, and replicative

---

[1] Abbreviations used: SSB, single stranded DNA binding protein; *ori*, replication origin; Mcm, minichromosome maintenance protein; SV40, simian virus 40; LTag, large T-antigen; FRET, fluorescence resonance energy transfer; EM, electron microscopy; OBD, origin binding domain; OB-fold, oligonucleotide/oligosaccharide/oligopeptide binding fold; RPA, replication protein A; RFC, replication factor C; pol, DNA polymerase; RDP, RNA-DNA primer; OKF, Okazaki fragment; PCNA, proliferating cell nuclear antigen; FEN1, flap endonuclease/exonuclease 1; IZ, Initiation Zone (model); ND, Nested Discontinuity (model); NCP, nucleosome core particle; nt, nucleotide.

DNA polymerase (replicase) exist in two dissimilar versions. One characterizes organisms belonging to the archaeal and eukaryal domains of life, and the second prevails in bacteria. This observation underlies the notion that the two replication systems evolved independently in the progenitors of the respective cell lineages (3).

Here, we examine "deep-rooted" functional attributes that set apart the two types of replisome, focusing on components involved in parental duplex unwinding and syntheses of the new DNA strands and on the coordination of their activities. The results of this survey are integrated in a model of the eukaryal replication fork where duplex DNA is restored almost simultaneously on both of its daughter arms. Because such a property could facilitate unbiased assembly of nucleosomes on the two arms, we further suggest that the existence of a replisome endowed with this property set the stage for compacting the genome and archiving its genes in chromatin structure. Support to this notion is lent by the coincident presence of homologs of both the eukaryal core histones and the single-stranded DNA binding protein (SSB) among species of the archaeal subdivision Euryarcheota (4).

Before delving into the subject matter, we refer the reader to reviews providing broader coverage of relevant subjects, including the origin of DNA genomes and replisomes (3, 4), replication fork mechanisms in the three domains of life (5–8), structure–function relationships of specific replication proteins; those compared in this chapter, including the fork unwinding helicase (9–11), SSB (12–15), primase (16), and replicases (17, 18) as well as those mentioned in passing or left out altogether due to space considerations, such as the replicase accessory proteins (19), DNA maturation nucleases (20, 21), DNA ligases (22), and topoisomerases (23). Last but not least are suggested texts discussing the structure, replication, and possible origin of chromatin (24–29). Shared features of DNA replication likely to date back to a common ancestor of extant cell lineages are considered beyond the scope of this chapter and so are distinctive traits of eukaryal replication likely to have appeared later than chromatin. We apologize that space limits did not allow citing all relevant work.

II. Deep-Rooted Features of Two Replisome Types

The separate origins of the bacterial and eukaryal-type replisomes (3) are reflected in significant mechanistic variations, despite the common task. These variations may be better appreciated by comparing matching components of the two replisomes including the fork unwinding helicase, SSB, primase, and replicase. The selected examples represent cellular organisms from the three domains of life but also include viral paradigms providing relevant insights. Put together, these data lead us to suggest that the two replisomes coordinate the unwinding activity and syntheses of the new DNA strands in radically different ways. A section providing background information about eukaryal DNA maturation proteins concludes this part.

A. Replicative Helicases

Helicases are motor proteins known mainly for their ability to unwind nucleic acid duplexes by coupling NTP (usually ATP) hydrolysis to DNA translocation. The replicative helicases discussed here unwind the parental duplex at the replication fork. These helicases are invariably ring-shaped hexamers with an inner channel lined with positive charges suitable for binding the DNA substrate (9). Some encircle ssDNA while others accommodate dsDNA and even the two separated strands; however, only one strand is bound and translocated by the protein. Translocation occurs in a defined $3' \rightarrow '5$ or $5' \rightarrow '3$ polarity, corresponding to respective threading of the continuous or discontinuous DNA template strand. The helicase, like other components of the "replication factory," is stationary in the cell and the replicating DNA mobile (30–32). Nonetheless, for convenience, we will occasionally refer to a replication protein as if moving along the DNA template. Within the stationary replisome, the helicase interacts with SSB, primase, replicases, replicase accessory proteins, and skeletal proteins (33). In addition, a helicase ring belonging to one replication fork may interact with that assigned to the opposite fork of the same replication origin (ori) (34). Such protein–protein interactions stimulate the unwinding activity, help coordinate it with the synthesis of new DNA, and adjust the progress of the opposite replication forks.

Well-documented bacterial-type replicative helicases are E. coli DnaB (35) and homologs encoded by other bacteria, phages T7 (36) and T4 (37), or plasmid RSF1010 (38). Eukaryal-type replicative helicases include the heteromeric minichromosome maintenance proteins (Mcm2–7) conserved from yeast to humans and originally implicated only with regulation of DNA replication initiation (10, 11, 39, 40). More recently, helicase activity has been detected in a subassembly of mammalian Mcm subunits (41). Moreover, yeast Mcm subunits have been shown to move away from ori with the replication fork (42). Archaea encode homo-hexameric homologs of the eukaryal Mcm proteins with demonstrated helicase activity (43, 44). Various relevant properties of the eukaryal cell replicative helicase could be intuited by considering those of the simian virus 40 (SV40) large T antigen (LTag) helicase, which remains an important paradigm (45–47). Like Mcm, LTag figures in replication initiation and proceeds to unwind DNA at the replication forks (45). Unlike Mcm, which is attracted to ori by the origin recognition complex Orc (48, 49), LTag recognizes the SV40 ori unaided (50, 51).

The bacterial and eukaryal-type replicative helicases are not orthologs; DnaB helicases resemble in sequence and structure RecA-family recombination proteins, from which they could arise by gene duplication (52–54). Mcm and LTag helicases belong to the ubiquitous AAA+ class of ATPases that perform a variety of cellular functions (55, 56). The bacterial and eukaryal-type helicases also differ in various mechanistic attributes such as translocation polarity, nature of encircled DNA, communication between hexameric rings assigned to opposite replication forks, and, most likely, overall unwinding strategy.

DnaB family helicases translocate with a $5' \rightarrow 3'$ polarity and, thus, thread the discontinuous template strand (35, 36, 57); LTag and Mcm, which translocate with the $3' \rightarrow 5'$ polarity, pull the opposite strand (41, 43, 58–60). Since the eukaryal type helicases occlude a portion of the continuous template (30–40 nt per hexamer) (47, 61, 62), they expose the discontinuous template ahead (Fig. 1A) whereas, in bacteria, it is availed later (5). The opposite polarities likely affect the overall performance of the two replisomes. Specifically, in the eukaryal type, discontinuous DNA synthesis could precede the continuous, contrary to the situation in bacteria. In other words, the leading/lagging terminology that accurately describes the situation at the bacterial replication fork may be a misnomer when it comes to Eukarya and Archaea. Furthermore, the interactions of the eukaryal-type helicase with the SSB and initiating replicase found on the opposite template (63–65) could help couple its unwinding activity with the syntheses of the two DNA strands in a novel way.

The DNA substrates encircled by the two types of replicative helicases may also differ, judged from binding affinity, nuclease protection, chemical crosslinking, fluorescence resonance energy transfer (FRET), electron microscopy (EM), and crystallographic data (9). DnaB-family helicases bind ssDNA with far greater avidity than dsDNA. The crystal structures of the helicases encoded by phage T7 (66) and plasmid RSF 1010 (54) reveal a narrow channel fit to accommodate ssDNA. The structure of the helicase domain of bacterial DnaB has not been elucidated yet but FRET analysis indicates that it encircles in solution free ssDNA or the 5'-branch of an artificial fork structure (67). *In vitro* reconstitution studies indicate that two DnaB rings assigned to the opposite forks are loaded sequentially on *E. coli ori* (*oriC*) DNA after its partial unwinding by the replicator protein DnaA. Importantly, each DnaB ring encircles one of the two DNA strands (68, 69). On the other hand, EM visualization suggests that *E. coli* DnaB can encircle dsDNA (70). What is more, when *Thermus aquaticus* DnaB encounters a primer/template junction, it slides over and moves on the duplex portion; the movement on dsDNA displaces a bound protein and drives branch migration in an artificial Holliday structure (71). These activities may be related to a presumptive role of DnaB in homologous recombination (71, 72) but whether they are relevant to the replicative function is not known.

LTag binds both ssDNA and dsDNA and Mcm helicase could behave similarly (9, 50). EM image reconstruction and crystallography suggest a

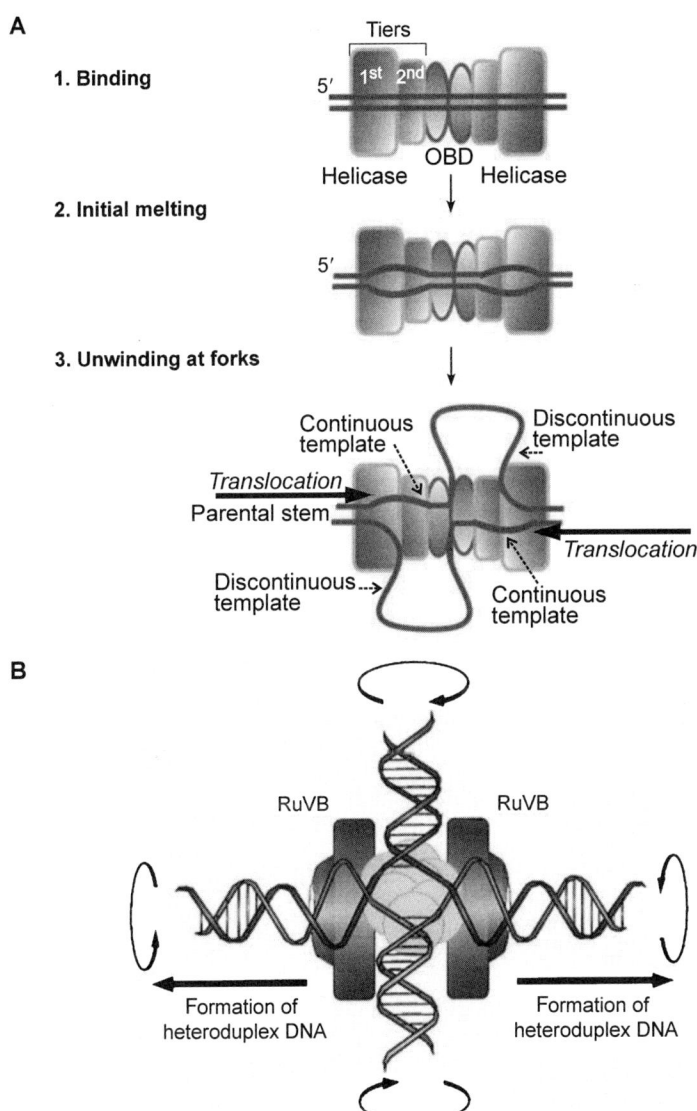

FIG. 1. (A) The LTag double-hexamer pumps in parental DNA and extrudes the ssDNA template. Due to occlusion of a portion of the continuous template, the complementary portion of the discontinuous template is exposed ahead. Adapted from Li, D., Zhao, R., Lilyestrom, W. et al. (2003) Nature **423,** 512; by permission of Dr. Chen, X. S. and Nature Publishing Group (http://www.nature.com.). (B) The RuvB DNA pump model. Adapted from West, S. C. (1996) Cell **86,** 177; by permission of Dr. West, S. C. and Elsevier Science.

complex interaction between these helicases and the encircled dsDNA substrate (47, 61, 62). LTag, which has been studied more closely, features a helicase domain divided in two sections or tiers (Fig. 1A). In the first tier, the inner channel is wide enough to encircle dsDNA; in the second, it expands into an "inner chamber" that accommodates the two separated strands. The walls of this chamber are pierced with secondary channels considered outlets for the extruded ssDNA templates. Rotation of the two tiers relative to each other could expand and constrict the inner channel, producing an "iris effect" that unwinds DNA initially at *ori* and later on at the replication forks (47).

DnaB and LTag/Mcm also differ in the interaction between single hexameric rings assigned to opposite replication forks. As mentioned, in the case of DnaB, they are loaded at *ori* separately (68, 69). Although the activities of the two rings may be coordinated, it is not known whether this communication entails direct interaction between them or is relayed by other replication proteins (17, 73, 74).

On the other hand, LTag and Mcm have been shown to exist as stable head-to-head double hexamers, both during replication initiation at *ori* and at the replication forks (34, 60, 62, 75–77). The center of the LTag double-hexamer comprises the two origin binding domains (OBD) and is flanked by the helicase domains (Fig. 1A). Bound to SV40 *ori* DNA, the LTag double-hexamer occludes over 70 bp. Its central OBD region covers the opposite pairs of recognition penta-nucleotides while the helicase domains occlude flanking sequences that unwind initially in the absence of ATP hydrolysis. EM visualization has indicated that the double hexamer sustains the DNA elongation stage, acting as a bidirectional unwinding machine (34, 75). This conclusion is reinforced by the far greater *in vitro* helicase activity of the complex compared to unassociated hexamers (78, 79). Because Mcm helicases form similar double-hexamers (60, 62, 76, 77), they could resemble LTag also in inner architecture and likewise function as bidirectional unwinding machines.

The relations between NTP hydrolysis, DNA translocation, and duplex unwinding at the replication fork are incompletely understood. However, since DnaB can assume a structure with 3-fold rotational symmetry (70), a 3-site DNA translocation model has been proposed for this helicase (9) based on the rotatory motor model of F_1, F_0-ATPase (80). In the ATPase model, 3 catalytic sites are found at any time either with bound ATP (T), bound hydrolysis products (D), or empty (E), and each site cycles between the 3 states in the T → D → E order. In the helicase model, the T- and D-states equate with respective tight and weak DNA binding and the E-state with none. Consequently, DNA is released during the ATPase cycle from one site and captured by another at a different DNA lattice; repeating the cycle causes unidirectional, processive threading of the DNA by the toroidal protein. DnaB may convert the translocation into unwinding activity by acting as a wedge, i.e., pulling the lagging template strand through, it disrupts base-pairing interactions at the parental stem and displaces the opposite strand (9).

Whether the above coupling scheme applies to DnaB-family helicases only or also to LTag and Mcm remains to be investigated. Regardless, each helicase type likely uses a different unwinding strategy; while DnaB may act as wedge, the eukaryal-type helicase may be likened to DNA pumping helicases. A relevant example seems RuvB, a bacterial DNA damage-induced $5' \rightarrow 3'$ helicase that catalyzes branch migration at DNA crossovers (81; Fig. 1B). In the DNA pump model shown, two RuvB rings oriented head-to-head encircle two diametrically opposed branches of the DNA crossover. The two rings are tethered to RuvA that binds the junction DNA and melts it into a square configuration. The two rings exert opposite rotatory forces on the DNA. Due to their immobilization by the interaction with RuvA, the encircled DNA branches are pumped outwards and free DNA branches are pulled inwards via the crossover junction, resulting in strand exchange and branch migration (81). Several features of RuvAB/DNA crossover model seem to match those expected of the LTag/replicating DNA complex (Fig. 1, compare panels A and B). Thus, the RuvB rings can be compared to the LTag helicase domains, the encircled DNA branches to the parental duplexes, and the free branches to the extruded ssDNA templates. However, the putative LTag pump acts in the reverse direction, pumping the parental duplexes in and extruding the ssDNA templates.

A different rotatory pumping model has been proposed to account for the fork unwinding activity of Mcm helicase (82). Accordingly, multiple Mcm rings align head-to-tail in two noncontiguous and oppositely oriented arrays on either side of *ori*. Their concerted movement within the arrays and their stationary state causes the parental DNA stems to rotate in opposite directions and unwind at the replication forks. This model reconciles the large molar excess of Mcm at prereplicative *ori* and absence of such concentration during S-phase at the replication forks (82, 83) by the proposed migration of Mcm to form the arrays described previously. However, whether Mcm can be loaded on DNA in this configuration instead of or in addition to the familiar head-to-head double-hexamer configuration is not known.

B. Single-Stranded DNA Binding Proteins

SSB stabilize and protect transient ssDNA stretches in DNA replication, repair, and recombination and attract during these transactions other proteins to their sites of action (12–14, 84). The SSB activity is ascribed to the OB-fold motif (oligonucleotide/oligosaccharide/oligopeptide binding) characterized by a five-stranded β-barrel abutted by an α-helix (15, 85–87). The structure of this motif diverged considerably in SSB from the three domains of life. Bacterial SSB differ from the eukaryal SSB also in subunit organization and distribution of OB-fold motifs between subunits (12, 13). The major archaeal subdivisions Crenarcheota and Euryarcheota feature bacterial-like and eukaryal-like SSB, respectively (88, 89) E. coli SSB has a single OB-fold in a 19-Kda subunit that tetramerizes only in the presence of the DNA ligand (12). The generic eukaryal SSB called replication protein A (RPA) typically contains subunits of 70, 32, and 11–14 kDa and is stable also without the DNA ligand. The large RPA subunit contains two central high affinity OB-fold domains. A third, C-proximal DNA-binding domain requires a metal for function and is important for damage recognition. The N-terminal domain of the large RPA subunit, implicated with binding other proteins, has been shown to resemble the other OB-fold domains in structure, although not in sequence, and to directly interact also with ssDNA (90). The middle subunit contains a single OB-fold domain. Yet another OB-fold motif spanning the entire small subunit is considered cryptic as it lacks detectable DNA binding activity and residues implicated with it (13, 14, 91–93). Crenarchaeal and bacterial SSB share subunit organization and presence of a single type of OB-fold domain. However, the OB-fold domain of the crenarchaeal SSB is structurally more similar to the euryarchaeal and eukaryal. Euryarchaeal SSB resemble RPA in structure and heterogeneity of the OB-fold domains; in certain species, they also resemble RPA in subunit organization (84, 88, 89). Remarkably, many of the Euryarcheota also contain homologs of the eukaryal core histones and package their DNA in a structure that corresponds to the lower level of chromatin organization (28, 94). This coincidence hints that the evolution of the eukaryal type replisome is closely related to that of chromatin.

Bacterial- and eukaryal-type SSB differ dramatically in their ssDNA binding attributes. E. coli SSB exhibits two binding modes termed $(SSB)_{65}$ and $(SSB)_{35}$ according to the number of nt occluded (12). The $(SSB)_{35}$ mode, considered relevant to DNA replication, involves two of the four subunits. The binding affinity in the $(SSB)_{35}$ mode is relatively weak (~100 nM compared to 0.1 nM with RPA and similar size target [13]). However, intertetramer cooperativity enhances the binding to longer ssDNA ligands. These properties seem tailored for rapid, processive coating of the transient, 1–3 Kb long ssDNA stretches exposed in the replicating bacterial chromosome (5), and facilitate removal of the SSB from the shrinking template. A recent kinetic study suggests that the two idle SSB subunits enable direct transfer of the tetramer from an old to a newly exposed template (95).

The four active OB-fold domains allow RPA to switch between binding modes of 8 and 30 nt (86, 91, 93, 96–100). Two OB-fold domains bind in tandem a 5'-proximal "nucleation site" of 8 nt. The remaining two likely interact with more distal portions of the 30 nt site. These modalities could allow RPA to gradually bind the ssDNA template as it becomes exposed and detach from it in the reverse order during DNA chain growth. RPA's stability as a free heterotrimer and its association with the helicase and initiating replicase (63, 101) could facilitate its direct transfer from the consumed to the newly exposed template.

RPA shows relatively high affinity to single target oligonucleotides (accommodating a single RPA molecule) but weak, if any, cooperativity in binding longer ligands (13), opposite to the bacterial SSB. These attributes, shared by the euryarchaeal homolog (84, 88), hint that RPA protects *in vivo* transient ssDNA templates corresponding to its single target site. Such a short target is availed to RPA in DNA nucleotide excision repair (102). RPA could encounter such a short target also at the replication fork, according to one view (103, 104) or a several-fold larger target in another model (7). The possible connection between the *in vitro* binding properties of a given SSB and its *in vivo* target may be further explored by determining these values for the respective bacterial-like and eukaryal-like SSB of the Crenarcheota and Euryarcheota.

C. Primase and the Initiating Replicase

Primases synthesize short RNA oligonucleotides that replicases extend with DNA. The product of a given primase is fixed in length—∼10 nt with cellular primases, as short as 4 nt with some phage primases—but of little sequence specificity, usually limited to the initial 2 residues (16, 105, 106). Bacterial DnaG-type primases are not related in sequence or protein fold to the eukaryal and archaeal Pri-primases. DnaG-type primases exist as monomers, usually associated with the fork helicase; those encoded by phages T7 and P4 even share with the helicase the same polypeptide chain (36, 107). In contrast, Pri-primases are heterodimers of catalytic and auxiliary subunits. In Eukarya, they associate with the replicative DNA polymerase (pol) α and its auxiliary subunit (108, 109). This pol α-primase complex, also referred to as initiating replicase, generates a 5'-RNA-DNA-3' product of ∼35 nt termed RNA-DNA primer (RDP, also *i*DNA, DNA primer, and primer DNA). RDP are incorporated in the continuous DNA strand as well as in intermediates of the discontinuous strand in reactions that involve an elongating replicase (110–114). As mentioned, pol-α primase associates with LTag on the opposite template strand of the SV40 replication fork (63), whereas the bacterial primase/helicase complex is confined to the lagging arm.

The dimeric Pri-primase of the archeon *Pyrococcus furiosus* is not associated with DNA polymerase. This may not surprise because the eukaryal-like replicase encoded by Archaea is more similar to the eukaryal elongating replicase pol ϵ than to pol α (115). Nonetheless, the standalone archaeal Pri-primase may be considered a functional analog of the initiating replicase since it prefers dNTP substrates and polymerizes long DNA strands *in vitro* (116, 117).

D. Replicases

Coordinated synthesis of the opposite DNA strands is accomplished in bacteria by a dimeric, asymmetrical replicase containing two catalytic pol subunits. The asymmetry is conferred by auxiliary proteins (17) or nonidentical pol subunits (118). Eukarya, in which the existence of a dimeric replicase has not been demonstrated so far, may accomplish this feat differently (119).

Bacterial replicases and the elongating eukaryal replicases consist of three distinct parts: (i) the pol core enzyme, (ii) a sliding clamp that tethers the pol to DNA and renders it more processive, and (iii) an ATPase chaperone needed to load the clamp on DNA. The bacterial clamp loader also bridges the two parts of the replicase and joins it to additional components of the replisome (17). The eukaryal clamp serves as a rather general platform for DNA elongation and maturation proteins (120, 121) and marks newly made DNA for chromatin assembly (122). The clamp and clamp loader found in the three domains of life are homologous and likely date back to a common ancestor of the extant cell lineages (3). In contrast, the bacterial and eukaryal-type replicative pols are unrelated in sequence and protein fold. The eukaryal belong to the pol family B and so does the prevalent archaeal pol. Family B also includes animal virus- and phage-encoded pols as well as the $E.$ $coli$ DNA repair protein pol II (123, 124). A crystal structure for this family, provided by a pol encoded by the T4-related phage RB69 (125), reveals an overall organization of functional units and the two-metal site to catalyze phosphoryl transfer also found in most pol families for which structures exist (124, 125). The bacterial replicative pols constitute a family of their own (family C) whose structure remains to be elucidated. Nonetheless, the canonical two-metal catalytic site has been identified in the $E.$ $coli$ protein by sequence alignment and mutational analysis (126). The common overall organization and shared catalytic site of the pols, despite their lack of sequence homology, has been attributed to independent mimicry of an ancestral ribozymic polymerase (124).

The best studied bacterial replicase is the $E.$ $coli$ pol III holoenzyme (127, 128). Its 10 different polypeptides are organized in the described 3 subassemblies. The core enzyme comprises the pol subunit DnaE or α, the editing $3' \rightarrow 5'$ exonuclease termed DnaQ or ϵ, as well as the auxiliary θ subunit that enhances editing. The ring-shaped β_2 dimer constitutes the dynamic clamp and the remaining subunits ($\chi\psi\tau_2\gamma\delta\delta'$) constitute the clamp-loader. The τ_2 component of the chaperone connects the two core enzymes to each other. τ_2 also binds the helicase, enhancing its unwinding activity (73). χ commits the clamp-loader to the lagging template by connecting it to the SSB. This asymmetrical arrangement is probably established only after the first loading event at $oriC$, where the leading pol is tethered to its template. From then on, the chaperone operates exclusively on the lagging template, loading and unloading the clamp, switching the pol repeatedly between the old and new Okazaki fragment (OKF) (17, 129). In low-GC gram-positive bacteria, the asymmetry of the replicase is conferred by the presence of two different pol subunits: a DnaE homolog implicated with lagging strand synthesis, and Pol C, another family C member assigned to the leading strand (118).

Eukaryal cell replicases include the initiating pol α-primase and elongating pol δ and pol ε (18, 130, 131). Pol α-primase seems qualified to initiate DNA chains but not complete them. It lacks an editing function and, hence, may be less faithful than the elongating replicases. However, this deficiency may be partly compensated by RPA whose interaction with pol α increases copying fidelity (132). Furthermore, pol α does not associate with the eukaryal processivity factor proliferating cell nuclear antigen (PCNA) (133). In fact, the clamp loader RFC removes pol α from the template when critical length corresponding to that of a mature RDP has been attained. PCNA is then loaded and DNA synthesis handed over to an elongating replicase (134–136).

The two elongating pols lack an associated primase but contain the editing function and both interact with PCNA, which renders them more processive (18, 137, 138). Therefore, both pol δ and pol ε seem suited for completing chains initiated by pol α-primase. Whether each acts on a different arm of the replication fork or both act on either arm is still debated (see following text). Pols δ and ε are also endowed with strand displacement activity (139, 140), which, when combined with a degradative enzyme, replaces the RNA primer moiety and, possibly, dNMP residues past the RNA–DNA junction with an all-DNA stretch (20, 21, 141, 142).

Pol δ is essential for SV40 replication whereas pol ε is not (143, 144). Due to this reason and the relative ease of studying DNA replication in the viral system, the replicative roles of pol δ are better understood. Characterization of conditional yeast mutants has suggested that both pols play important roles in cellular DNA replication (145, 146). However, more recent work suggests that in the baker and fission yeast, only pol δ is absolutely essential for replication. Namely, whereas deletion of the C-terminal checkpoint domain of pol ε (147) is lethal (148), deletion of the N-proximal DNA polymerase domain does not abolish growth, albeit severely impairs it (148, 149). Hence, the replicase function of pol ε can be substituted, possibly by pol δ. Presently, it is not known if the two elongating replicases perform different tasks at the same replication fork (e.g., continuous vs discontinuous strand synthesis) or similar tasks in different forks. Since pol δ suffices for replicating SV40 DNA as well as the DNA of yeast mutants lacking pol ε polymerase domain, pol δ seems capable of completing DNA chain synthesis on either arm of the replication fork, in both the viral and cellular systems. Accordingly, pol ε could act similarly in other cellular replicons or serve an auxiliary function in forks serviced primarily by pol δ.

A dimeric replicase complex has not been demonstrated so far in Eukarya (*119, 131*). However, the association of the helicase with the initiating replicase could provide an alternative means to coordinate the syntheses of the opposite DNA strands. For example, release of the initiating replicase from the DNA template upon completion of the RDP chain (*133*) could free the helicase to further unwind the parental duplex and allow the continuous replicase to proceed. An analogous situation exists at the replication fork of phage T7 (*150*).

All archaeal organisms whose genomes have been sequenced encode a eukaryal-like family B DNA polymerase more closely related to pol ϵ than other eukaryal replicases (*115*). Some euryarchaeal species contain a second DNA polymerase (pol D) not found among the Crenarcheota nor in the other domains of life (*8, 151*). The archaeal clamp and clamp loader interact with each other and both interact with pol B and pol D (*152*). However, pol B seems a more likely candidate for the role of the elongating replicase due to its prevalence and similarity to pol ϵ (*115*). In theory, pol D could associate with pol B to form a dimeric, asymmetric replicase, analogous to that of low-GC gram-positive bacteria (*118*). Alternatively, the idiosyncratic pol D specializes in another DNA transaction (*8*).

E. Replication Fork Symmetry

Some of the specific attributes of the replication proteins discussed in the previous sections and summarized in Table I suggest that the eukaryal-type replisome coordinates the unwinding of the parental duplex with the syntheses of the new DNA strands in ways radically different from that of the more familiar bacterial counterpart (*17*). Specifically, placement of the eukaryal-type helicase on the continuous template causes earlier exposure of the discontinuous template and, possibly, earlier DNA synthesis on it. This could yield daughter arms more similar in duplex DNA content than in bacteria, where the synthesis of the discontinuous DNA strand lags behind. The existence of a specialized eukaryal initiating replicase or functionally analogous archaeal primase could also contribute to the increased symmetry by restoring duplex structure with lesser delay than with the separately loaded bacterial primase and replicase. Furthermore, association of the initiating replicase with the helicase could postpone further unwinding until the initiating replicase completes the RDP. Unwinding of the parental duplex in RDP-size steps also agrees with the specific DNA binding properties of RPA, which seem to qualify it for binding transient ssDNA templates corresponding to the 30 nt-site occluded by this protein.

F. DNA Maturation Reactions

Reactions collectively referred to as DNA maturation are briefly discussed here to provide supplementary background information for the models to be described later. DNA maturation reactions replace with new DNA the RNA

TABLE I
IDIOSYNCRATIC FEATURES OF KEY REPLISOME COMPONENTS FROM THE THREE DOMAINS OF LIFE

Protein domain	Helicase	SSB	Primase/Init. replicase	Main replicase
Bacteria	5′ → 3′ translocation polarity	Bacterial-type OB fold	Monomeric, binds helicase	Dimeric, asymmetric holoenzyme. Contains two family C pol subunits. Binds clamp and clamp loader
	Encircles ssDNA	Homo-tetramer, stabilized by ligand	Prefers ribonucleotides, synthesizes short, 10 nt RNA primers	
	Double hexamer not detected	Low affinity to single target site		
	Unwinds as a wedge?	High cooperativity with long ligands		
Archaea	3′ → 5′ translocation polarity	In Crenarcheota, resembles the bacterial in subunit organization, the eukaryal in OB-fold structure	Heterodimer, prefers deoxyribonucleotides, able to synthesize long DNA stretches	Contains family B pol subunit, interacts with clamp and clamp loader
	Encircles dsDNA?			
	Forms double-hexamer			
	DNA pump?			Dimerization not evident
Eukarya	3′ → 5′ translocation polarity	Eukaryal-type OB-fcld	Heterodimer, binds initiating DNA polymerase	Contains family B pol subunit, interacts with clamp and clamp loader
	Encircles dsDNA	Heterotrimer, stable on its own		
	Forms double-hexamer	High affinity to single target site	Synthesizes short, 10 nt RNA primers	
	DNA pump?	Low cooperativity with long ligands		Dimerization not evident

primer moiety and, possibly, additional nucleotides past the RNA–DNA junction and join the processed DNA segments. The replacement entails degradative activities mediated by one or more 5′-end trimming nucleases that are coordinated with synthetic gap filling and/or strand displacement activities catalyzed by a pol extending a nascent chain upstream. Because the degradative and synthetic reactions translocate a nick separating the original chains, their outcome is defined as "nick-translation." Eventually, the juxtaposed DNA segments are joined by DNA ligase. Coordination of the nick translation and DNA ligase activities is necessary; otherwise, the nick would be translated indefinitely.

In *E. coli*, nick translation is catalyzed by the auxiliary replicase pol I endowed with DNA polymerase, editing 3′-exonuclease and primer trimming 5′-exonuclease activities. Other bacteria encode the pol and 5′-exonuclease as separate proteins (*1*). In Eukarya, more than one protein may be involved in either step. *In vitro* studies in the SV40 system (*143, 153*) have suggested that mammalian RNase HI removes the RNA primer moiety short of the last rNMP (*20*; see also Fig. 5). The residual rNMP or entire RNA primer plus nucleotides past the RNA–DNA junction may be removed by FEN1 (flap exo/endonuclease 1), a homolog of the 5′ exonuclease domain of *E. coli* pol I (*154*). FEN1 cleaves preferentially flapped DNA structures at or near the point of annealing but also acts as a 5′ exonuclease (*20, 141, 155, 156*). Genetic and biochemical studies in yeast have indicated that both RNase H and FEN1 partake in the degradative part of DNA maturation (*157*). However, distinct mutational spectra associated with the mutator phenotypes of FEN1 and RNase H suggest that the former plays a more critical role in replication. RNase H could have a redundant or other function (*158*). The flap utilized by FEN1 is likely generated by strand displacement by a pol since a requisite helicase has not been identified. In agreement, pol δ and FEN1 cooperate in nick-translation in an *in vitro* reconstituted system. They perform their respective functions at comparable rates, which are much slower than that of the gap-filling activity of pol δ (*141*).

A third nuclease implicated with the degradative DNA maturation step is Dna2 helicase/nuclease (*21, 159, 160–162*). Dna2 nuclease activity, which confers the essential phenotype in yeast, cleaves *in vitro* flap structures of 27 nt and above. The 5′-proximal part of this large flap may consist of RNA but the cleavage occurs only in the DNA moiety. A residual 5–7 nt flap left by Dna2 can be removed then by FEN1. Interestingly, Dna2 interacts genetically with RPA and forms, with the SSB and the long-flap containing DNA substrate, a ternary complex. The interaction with RPA stimulates Dna2 cleavage activity. On the other hand, RPA prevents FEN1 from cleaving the long flap. However, after the primary cleavage by Dna2, RPA is released and FEN1 is free to remove the residual flap. It has been inferred from such observations that pol δ strand displacement activity generates a large flap that is stabilized by RPA and then degraded by consecutive Dna2 and FEN1 reactions (*160, 162*). However, a more recent study indicates that Dna2 neither augments the nick-translation activity of a pol/δ FEN1-containing complex nor substitutes FEN1 in this reaction. Moreover, the extent of nick-translation by pol δ/FEN1 in the presence of DNA ligase I indicates that a minimal flap recognized by Dna2 is not generated by the pol (*141*). These considerations, and the fact that the elongating replicase FEN1 and the replicative DNA ligase I all interact with PCNA, strongly suggest that the latter three proteins collaborate in DNA maturation and may suffice for this function (*163*). Dna2 could become essential for DNA maturation when FEN1 is compromised and long flaps arise and/or play essential roles in other DNA transactions (*141*).

Of three cellular DNA ligases, only DNA ligase I has been implicated in DNA replication (*164*). However, DNA ligase I knockout mouse embryos develop normally to midterm before they succumb to a hematopoietic defect (*165*). Therefore, the essential functions of DNA ligase I may be substituted by another DNA ligase at the earlier stages of development or other situations where DNA ligase I is missing.

III. Coordinated Syntheses of the Opposite DNA Strands

The anti-parallel nature of DNA and uniform $5' \rightarrow 3'$ direction of its polymerization dictate assembly of one of the new DNA strands from the shorter, independently primed OKF (*166*). In replicating bacterial and phage chromosomes, OKF reach 1–3 Kb (*5*), compared to ~0.2 Kb in Eukarya and Archaea (*6, 167, 168*). Furthermore, eukaryal OKF arise from the shorter RDP (*111–114*). How RDP turn into OKF is still debated. Before addressing this problem and related aspects of eukaryal DNA elongation, we consider the more familiar bacterial paradigm.

A. The Bacterial Paradigm

The synthesis of the continuous DNA strand must be adjusted with the discontinuous, which is intrinsically slower due to the additional steps it entails: (i) protection of the transient ssDNA stretch by SSB, (ii) multiple priming events, (iii) DNA maturation reactions, and (iv) transfer of the lagging pol from a completed OKF to the new priming site. Bacteria achieve the coordination by combining a leading and a lagging pol within a dimeric, asymmetrical replicase (*17, 19*). Phage T7 couples the activities of separate leading and lagging pols by the bridging primase/helicase and SSB proteins (*150*).

The two-headed bacterial replicase is often depicted attached with other proteins to a replication fork where the lagging template strand is folded back as a loop (17, 19; Fig. 2). Growth of the current OKF inside this loop is accompanied by extrusion of new ssDNA upstream by the helicase and the loop expands. When the OKF is completed, the replicase switches to a new priming site and the loop contracts. This scheme, known as the "Trombone Model," explains how the two pols travel apart on the DNA path yet move side by side, and how the lagging pol finds its way from the completed OKF to the new priming site (169, 170). The properties of the dimeric bacterial replicase agree with this model and the predicted replication loop with an OKF growing inside has been visualized in reconstituted systems based on phage T7 (171) or phage T4 (172) replication proteins (150). The possibility that eukaryal DNA replication entails a similar loop (173, 174) will be examined next.

B. Models of Discontinuous DNA Synthesis in Eukarya

Studies on SV40 DNA replication systems provided important insights into eukaryal replication fork mechanisms at the single replicon level. Several of the proteins involved have been identified and functionally characterized using an *in vitro* reconstituted replication system. It comprised a naked DNA template,

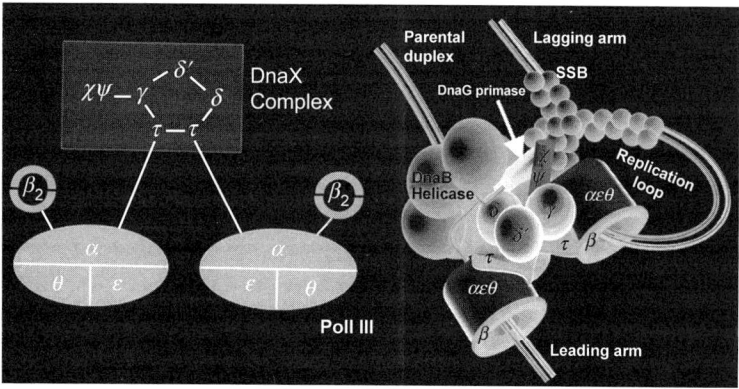

FIG. 2. Structural models of Pol III holoenzyme. *Left*. Diagram showing Pol III holoenzyme subunit stoichiometry and major protein-protein contacts. The subunits in the top left rectangle are the components of the DnaX complex, including the ATPase subunits encoded by the *dnaX* gene: τ and γ. The light gray ovals represent the two Pol III core enzymes. The ring attached to the cores represents the β_2 sliding clamp processivity factor. It is shown bound to the catalytic pol subunit α, as when assembled on DNA. β_2 is bound to δ during the 'loading' reaction prior to placement on DNA. *Right*. A model for holoenzyme subunit arrangements at the replication fork showing the τ-DnaB interaction, placement of χ-ψ on the lagging strand side of the replication fork, and the χ-SSB interaction on the lagging strand (Ref. 129). DnaB helicase approaches the parental duplex. SSB coats the exposed ssDNA template within the replication loop. Adapted from McHenry, C. S. (2003) *Mol. Microbiol.* **49**, 1157; with permission of Dr. McHencry, C. S. and Blackwell Press.

usually a plasmid with the SV40 *ori*, LTag and mammalian cell extract eventually replaced by defined proteins (6, 175–179). Closer characterization of individual replication proteins or subsets thereof entailed the use of various synthetic model DNA templates, naked or packaged into a nucleosome (21, 141, 180–183). Earlier studies using authentic replicating SV40 (or the closely related polyoma virus) chromosomes allowed visualizing nascent DNA intermediates in the natural setting (184). Such studies revealed the existence of the RDP, initially as a kinetic intermediate in OKF synthesis (110) and later as a product of pol α-primase that is further processed by an elongating replicase (112). The latter conclusions have been inferred from the selective abolition of RDP synthesis by the specific pol α inhibitor BuPdGTP (185) and pol α antibodies (186) and selective abolition of the RDP → OKF conversion by measures thought to affect the elongating replicase: addition of aphidicolin, removal of PCNA, or depletion of ATP utilized by RFC to load PCNA (103, 111, 113, 187). Pol δ is slightly more sensitive to aphidicolin than pol α when compared on a simple primed template (188). However, in hindsight it seems that the specific effect of aphidicolin on the RDP → OKF conversion resulted from selective inhibition of the strand displacement activity of pol δ, which is far more sensitive to the drug than the gap-filling activity (141, 189). Cooperation of the initiating and elongating replicases in OKF synthesis has also been deduced from results of a study that employed a synthetic primed template and proteins involved in the pol α → pol δ switch (114, 133). More recent work indicates that RFC senses that pol α polymerized 30 nt and removes it at this stage from DNA (136) prior to the loading of PCNA and recruitment of pol δ (133).

Two different models attempted to explain the RDP → OKF conversion (190). In the "Initiation Zone" (IZ) model (Fig. 3A), continuous extension of a single RDP chain by the elongating replicase yields the several-fold longer OKF. In the "Nested Discontinuity" (ND) model (Fig. 3B), RDP units are successively deposited by the initiating replicase at the fork junction. A contiguous array containing several RDP units is then converted into an OKF chain in DNA maturation reactions that entail: (i) removal of RNA primers moieties (and, possibly, additional residues past the RNA–DNA junction) between adjacent RDP units, (ii) gap-filling and/or strand displacement, and (iii) joining the juxtaposed DNA segments (164). The order and direction of these reactions across the RDP array have not been specified. It should be pointed out that the mature OKF contains the RNA primer originating from the 5′-terminal RDP unit. This moiety, which is carried onto the longer nascent chain the OKF joined to, will be removed prior to the joining of next OKF. In sum, an array containing several RDP units is assembled into OKF that, in turn, are processed and joined to form long nascent chains; hence, the term Nested Discontinuity (103, 104, 111).

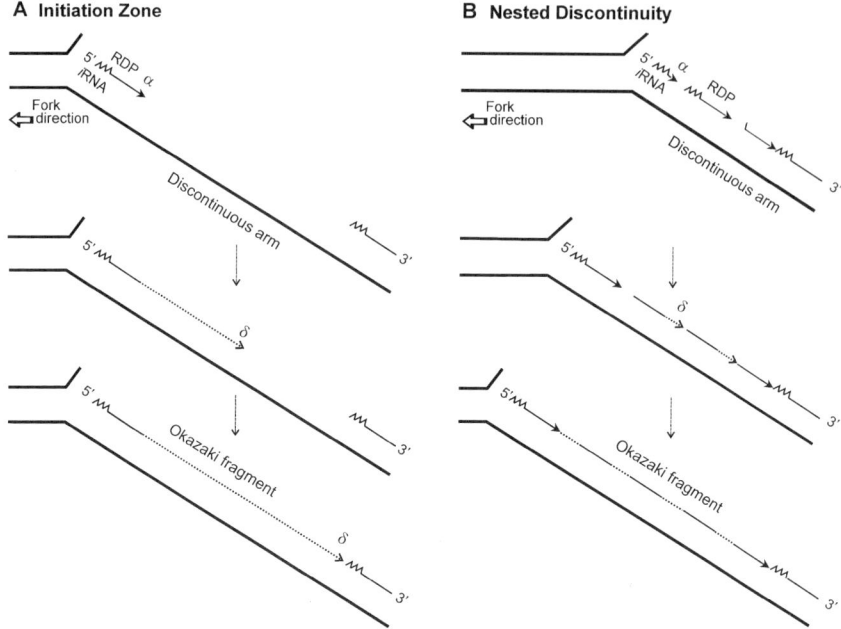

FIG. 3. Models of RDP → OKF conversion. (A). In the Initiation Zone model, the initiating replicase (α) deposits a single RDP chain at the fork junction within the OKF-sized ssDNA template. This RDP chain is continuously elongated by pol δ. (B). In the Nested Discontinuity model, RDP units are deposited successively with the unwinding of the parental duplex DNA. An array containing several RDP units is converted into an OKF by a series of DNA maturation reactions. Zigzag line represents the RNA primer moiety (iRNA), full line DNA moiety of the RDP, broken line DNA synthesized by pol δ. Arrows represent direction of chain growth.

Candidates for removing the RNA moiety between adjacent units of the RDP array are RNase HI (20), FEN1 (141, 155), and, perhaps to a lesser extent, Dna2 (21). RNase HI depends neither on PCNA nor on prior strand displacement activity. Therefore, it could act earlier than FEN1 and leave a relatively large gap. On the other hand, FEN1 interacts with PCNA, cleaves a flapped structure generated by strand displacement, and, hence, could act relatively late and leave a nick. Because Dna2 cleaves only large flaps, its nuclease activity might remove most, if not all, of the DNA stretch polymerized by pol α. However, at least in replicating SV40 and mammalian chromosomes, DNA synthesized by pol α is efficiently incorporated into more advanced intermediates (Fig. 4 and our unpublished results).

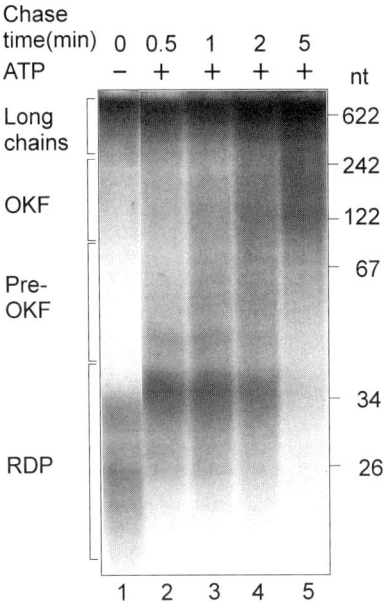

FIG. 4. Reversible arrest of RDP by depletion and restoration of ATP. Nascent SV40 DNA was pulse-labeled for 2 min from [α-^{32}P]dTTP under conditions of ATP depletion, which selectively inhibit the RDP→OKF conversion. The labeled DNA was chased with 150 molar excess of nonlabeled dTTP in the presence of 2mM ATP for the indicated time and the products separated by denaturing gel electrophoresis. Adapted from Nethanel et al. (1992). J. Virol. 66, 6634, with permission from ASM.

C. Evidence Underlying the Nested Discontinuity Model

The ND model was originally proposed to account for two observations made with replicating SV40 chromosomes. Some of its predictions could be tested experimentally or evaluated against data published by others, including attributes of the eukaryal replisome summarized in Table I.

1. Bimodal Decay of RNA Primers

A major fraction of pulse-labeled RNA primers decays during OKF growth, already at the RDP level, while a minor fraction persists in mature OKF and is carried onto the long nascent DNA chains (*111, 191, 192*; Fig. 5). The ND model accounts for this bimodal schedule by equating the short-lived fraction with internal RNA moieties of the RDP array destined to become an OKF (Fig. 3), the more persistent fraction with the 5'-terminal moiety. More difficult is to reconcile this phenomenon with the IZ model. If RNA primers were largely removed during continuous OKF growth, then only a minor

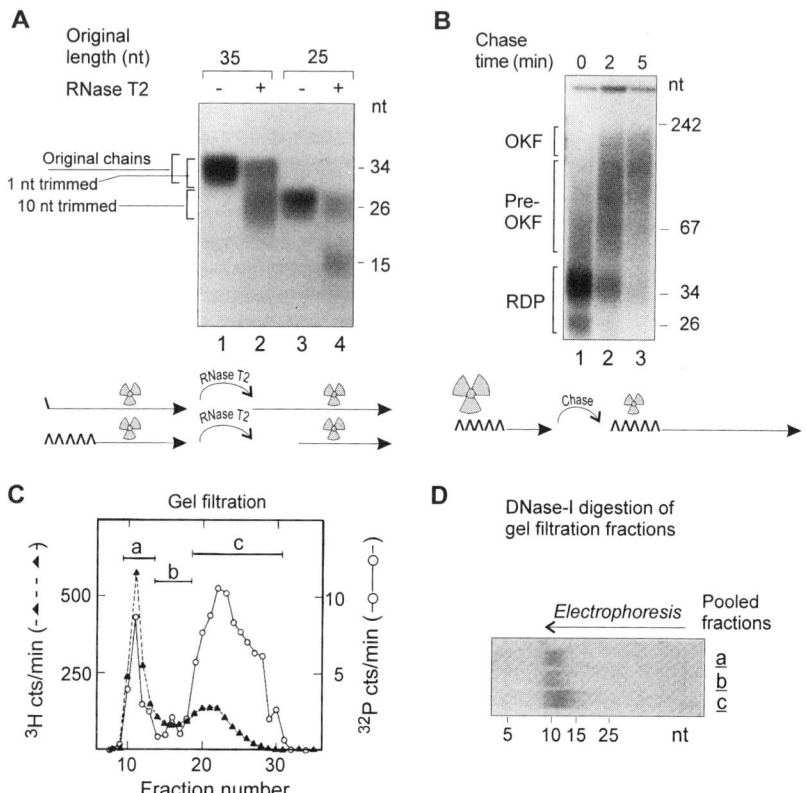

FIG. 5. Decay of RNA primers during conversion of RDP into OFK and longer nascent DNA chains. (A). Discrete fractions of RDP-sized chains pulse-labeled from [α-^{32}P] dATP in replicating chromosomes of a human fibroblast cell line were treated with RNase T2 and the products separated by denaturing gel electrophoresis. The gel mobility shift due to the RNase treatment corresponds to the loss of 1 nt or 10 nt from comparable fractions. Zigzag line represents RNA primer moiety, full line DNA moiety; ☢- indicates radioactively labeled section. (B). Partial decay of RNA primers during conversion of RDP into OFK. RDP pulse-labeled in replicating SV40 chromosomes from [α-^{32}P]rUTP were chased for the indicated time and separated as in (A). ☢, The decrease in the size of the radioactivity sign during chase signifies the partial decay of the RNA primers. (C). Nascent DNA chains obtained essentially as described in (B) but also labeled in the DNA moiety from [^{3}H]dTTP were fractionated by Sepharose 6B gel filtration. (D). The indicated pools of column fractions (panel C) were treated with DNase I and separated as in (A) to yield RNA primers carrying a few residual DNase-resistant dNMPs. Panel (B) adapted from Nethanel et al. (1992). J. Virol. 66, 6634, with permission from ASM; panels (C) and (D) were adapted from Kaufmann (1981). J. Mol. Biol. 147, 25; with permission from Elsevier Science.

fraction of the long nascent chains would contain RNA primers, contrary to the experimental evidence (103, 111, 193).

2. Arrangement of Nascent DNA Chains on the Discontinuous Template

In an attempt to measure the transient ssDNA gaps in replicating SV40 DNA (193), a heterogeneous population of short nascent DNA chains, ~135 nt in average length, was extended *in situ* by *E. coli* pol I or T4 pol lacking a 5′-exonuclease. Only products extended by pol I could be joined onto the long nascent DNA chains by T4 DNA ligase, possibly due to the need to remove the RNA primer moieties from the long chains (192). Because the short chains were extended by either pol by only a few nt, they were considered near-mature OKF (193). Surprisingly, a similar attempt to measure the gap 3′ to a newly made RDP (radio-labeled in the RNA primer moiety) yielded a value of only ~12 nt (103, 111; Fig. 6A, D). Filling this gap with pol I Klenow fragment allowed joining the newly made RDP through discrete intermediates spaced ~10 nt apart into OKF-like products but not longer chains. Hence, the newly made RDP had been separated by a gap of ~12 nt from an array of previously synthesized short chains (Fig. 6F). The long chain found downstream to this array contains an intact 5′-terminal RNA primer moiety that could prevent further ligation.

Applying the gap-filling/ligation protocol to steady-state nascent chains radiolabeled in the DNA moiety resulted in a similar extension of ~12 nt, albeit of only of a minor RDP fraction. The remaining RDP seemed to be shifted by only 1–2 nt (Fig. 4B, E). Gap filling by Klenow pol allowed joining these chains into OKF-size products (Fig. 6B), similar to the newly made RDP (Fig. 6A) or steady-state RDP that mature within authentic replicating SV40 chromosome (Fig. 6C). The different gap sizes (~12 vs 1–2 nt) could represent different stages in the maturation of the RDP array. For example, RNase H could rapidly trim the RNA primer moiety from a previous RDP upon completion of the newly synthesized RDP, creating the larger gap. Noteworthy in this regard is that about half of the steady-state RDP contain a single ribonucleotide residue, judged by the modest mobility shift after RNase treatment (Fig. 5A). The formation of the large gap could be followed by the rate-limiting steps of pol α removal by RFC (136), PCNA loading, and recruitment of pol δ, FEN1, and DNA ligase I. Rapid filling of the large gap by the elongating replicase could be followed by slow nick translation (141). However, this scenario does not explain the presence of 1–2 nt gaps rather then nicks due to the combined polδ/FEN1 activities (141). One possibility is that these small gaps arise inadvertently under the conditions employed due to an imbalance of the editing and pol activities of the replicase stalled at the nick.

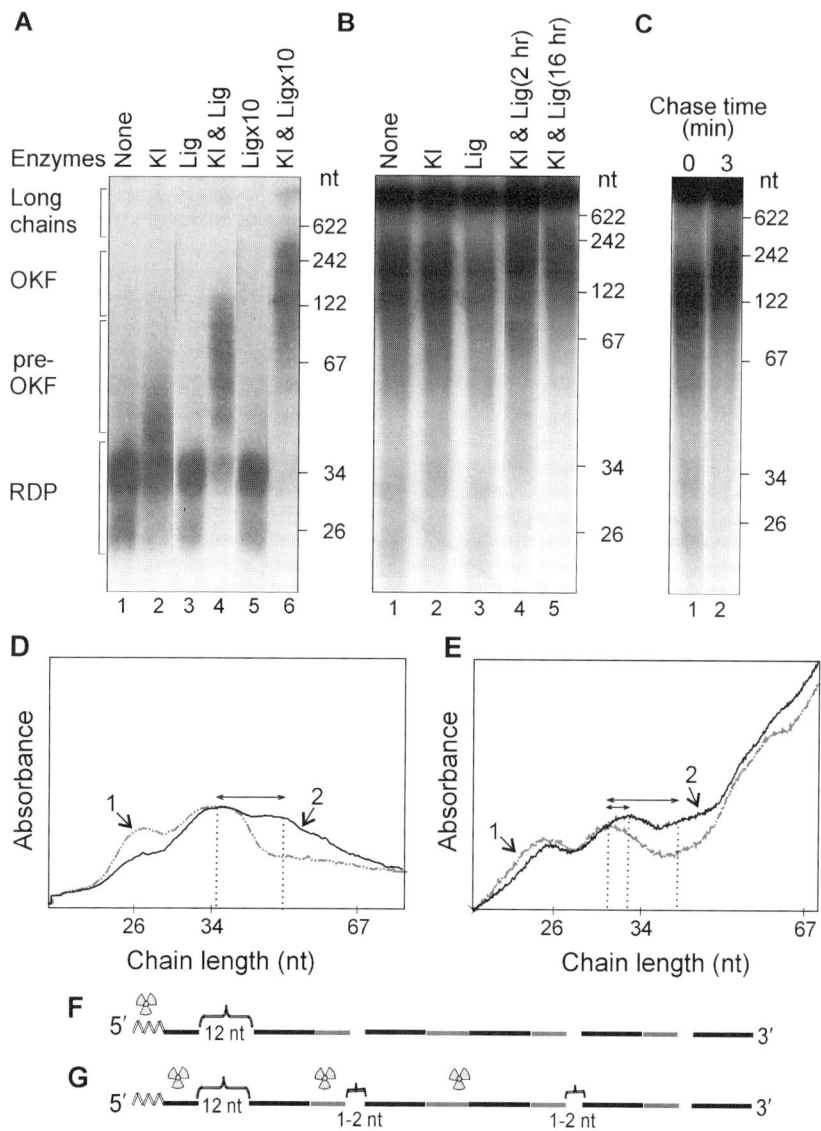

FIG. 6. Simulated RDP→OKF conversion. (A). Newly made RDP pulse-labeled form [α-^{32}P]rUTP in replicating SV40 chromosomes were incubated within the isolated replicating DNA with Klenow pol (KI) and/or indicated levels of T4 DNA ligase (Lig) and the products separated by denaturing gel electrophoresis. (B). Steady-state RDP and OKF precursors radiolabeled from [α-^{32}P]dATP were subjected to an analysis similar to that described in (A), except that a mutant Klenow fragment devoid of 3'-exonuclease activity was employed and incubation time was varied as indicated rather than DNA ligase dose. (C) Steady-state RDP and OKF described in (B) were chased within the replicating viral chromosomes. (D, E). Densitometric tracings of lanes 1 and 2 of Panels (A) and (B), respectively. Double-headed arrows represent the shift of the 34 nt

3. RPA is Poised to Interact with Growing RDP

The two models envisage different size distributions of nascent DNA populations associated with specific replication proteins. For example, RPA should face the entire spectrum of growing OKF (IZ model) or only RDP (ND model). UV-crosslinking proteins to nascent DNA within replicating SV40 chromosomes has revealed that the middle and large subunits of RPA are poised to interact with growing RDP, rather than the full spectrum of growing OKF (*104, 194*). Interestingly, the shortest RDP containing only a few dNMP residues interacted exclusively with the middle subunit, but the crosslinking preference switched with RDP growth such that the large subunit alone interacted with mature RDP. A related observation has been made in a study where purified RPA was crosslinked to the upstream primer of a synthetic gapped duplex; decreasing the gap from 19 to 9 nt switched the crosslinking preference from the middle to the large subunit (*195, 196*). Correlating the two types of crosslinking data has been taken to indicate that a mature RDP, no longer accessible to the middle subunit, faces a gap similar to that envisaged by the ND model (*103, 104, 111*). Apart from their relevance to the models examined, these data suggest that during growth of the RDP chains some of the OB-fold domains released from the template become accessible for interaction with the primer strand. How RPA competes with the initiating pol over the growing end of the RDP remains an open question.

4. Frequency of Genomic Priming Sites

Depending on the model, adjacent priming sites on the discontinuous template are separated by distances matching the size of the OKF or the RDP. The experimental evidence reveals a surprisingly high frequency of potential priming sites on the discontinuous templates in the *ori* regions of SV40, yeast, and human replicons, generally once per 10–20 nt (*197–199*). A similar frequency has been reported for an SV40 region distanced from *ori* (*200*). These patterns could be reconciled with the ND model if most of these potential priming sites were utilized in every replication cycle, and with the IZ model, if only a small subset were utilized.

5. The Initiating Replicase is Tethered to the Fork Junction

Successive deposition of RDP units envisaged by the ND model is consistent with the protein–protein interactions between the initiating replicase and its primosomal partners RPA and LTag at the SV40 replication fork (*63, 101*).

RDP peak due to the extension, by ~12 nt with newly made RDP and 1–2 nt or ~12 nt with steady-state RDP. (F, G). Presumptive RDP arrays radiolabeled, respectively, in the RNA or DNA moieties. Zigzag line represents RNA primer moieties, black line DNA segment synthesized by pol α, gray line by pol δ; ⚛, indicates radioactively labeled section. Bracket indicates gap, the number within its size in nt. Panel (A) adapted from Nethanel *et al.* (1992). *J. Virol.* **66**, 6834 with permission of ASM.

IV. Possible Implications of a Symmetrical Eukaryal Replication Fork

Distinctive properties of eukaryal-type replication proteins (Table I) and spatial/temporal attributes of nascent SV40 DNA (Section II.B,C) led us to suggest that the initiating replicase renders an RDP-sized ssDNA template double stranded before unwinding resumes. Clearly, many predictions of this model remain to be examined. Nonetheless, in what follows, we shall assume without further justification that this idea is basically correct and discuss some of its possible implications.

A. Could a Trombonelike Replication Loop Exist at the Eukaryal Fork?

According to the ND model, folding back the eukaryal discontinuous DNA template strand as a replication loop, similar to the situation at the bacterial replication fork, may be unnecessary and even impossible. Namely, the short distance traveled by the replicase on the discontinuous template does not warrant such a loop. Moreover, while it may be possible to fold a ~35 nt ssDNA segment into a loop, rendering this loop double-stranded may not be (201).

B. Possible Selective Advantage of a Symmetrical Replication Fork

A similar content of duplex DNA of progeny chromosomes at the fork junction could confer similar protection against genotoxic metabolites and ssDNA-specific nucleases. Consequently, there would be a need to allocate fewer resources for protecting the discontinuous template against deleterious damage or repair of such damage. The increased protection could, in turn, compensate for the additional investment in RNA priming and DNA maturation, compared to the thriftier bacterial replisome. The trade-off could be decided by the environmental conditions; in some cases, the advantages of greater protection could outweigh the disadvantage of slower growth due to the more cumbersome mode of replication. In other cases, the bacterial style would prevail. Once the more symmetrical mode of replication became established, its advantages could be further enhanced by consequent abilities to compact the genome and archive genes.

C. The Eukaryal Type Replisome and Ascent of Chromatin

One of the salient features of eukaryal organisms (other than dionflagellates) is the packaging of their genomes in a topologically complex superstructure known as chromatin (24). A simple form representing the most basic level of chromatin organization characterizes many of the Euryarcheota (94). As mentioned, these organisms also encode a fuller ensemble of eukaryal-like replication proteins that includes an RPA homolog absent from the Crenarcheota (94). This coincidence hints at a possible relation between the existence of a eukaryal-type replisome and the ascent of chromatin. Before examining this idea further, we briefly consider relevant properties of chromatin structure and replication, confining the discussion to the level of chromatin organization represented by the nucleosome core particle (NCP) (202).

The NCP consists of 146 bp of DNA wrapped in 1.65 superhelical turns about an octamer of the four core histones, H3, H4, H2A, and H2B. These basic proteins feature the common histone-fold motif in their C-proximal part, which plays a critical role in the organization of the particle and comprises a long α-helix separated from two shorter helices by short loops and β-strands. On the other hand, the N-proximal parts of the core histones figure in internucleosomal interactions. They are subject to various modifications that play important roles in chromatin remodeling which fates genes to be expressed or archived (203).

The histone fold is stabilized by specific dimerizations; H3 teams with H4, H2A with H2B. H3–H4 further dimerizes into a tetramer that, in turn, binds two flanking H2A–H2B heterodimers. Within the NCP, each heterodimer organizes ~30 bp of DNA but occludes a few more. The [H3–H4]$_2$ tetramer stably interacts with 73 bp DNA of the NCP DNA and loosely organizes ~120 bp. The addition of the flanking H2A–H2B heterodimer stabilizes the full-fledged NCP (202). Euryarchaeal histones are smaller, consisting solely of the 62- to 65-residue histone-fold motif. They form homo- or heterodimers and the dimers coalesce into tetramers that organize ~70 bp DNA and form with ~120 bp the loosely packed subnucleosomal particle, very much like the eukaryal [H3–H4]$_2$ tetrasome (28).

Chromatin replication entails accurate doubling not only of the parental DNA but also of its protein package. The two processes occur virtually simultaneously; meta-stable NCP are visualized on newly replicated DNA already within 1–2 nucleosomal repeats from the fork junction (204, 205). The replication of the chromatin package entails the transfer of parental histones and assembly of new nucleosomes onto the newly replicated DNA (26). The transfer of the old histones involves destabilization of one or two nucleosomes ahead of the fork junction by the advancing replication fork (205). The flanking H2A–H2B heterodimers come off and mingle with newly synthesized H2A–H2B pairs (206, 207). The [H3–H4]$_2$ tetrasome left behind may be directly transferred to the newly replicated DNA, being distributed in a random fashion between the two daughter arms. However, the transient subnucleosomal complex may be unstable since it can be partially disrupted by a vast excess of competing nonreplicating DNA (205, 208). Subsequently, the flanking H2A–H2B pairs are appended to yield a full-fledged NCP. In parallel, new nucleosomes are actively assembled from newly synthesized, acetylated histones H3–H4 followed by addition of the H2A–H2B pairs (27, 29, 209–211). Old and new H2A–H2B pairs may be randomly appended to old and new H3–H4 tetramers (206, 207). Alternatively, a more ordered distribution occurs where old H2A–H2B pairs carrying old histone modifications are added onto new tetramers devoid of such marks, and conversely. Such an ordered process could serve to evenly distribute the epigenetic information imparted by chromatin structure (212). Chromatin assembly is an active, highly regulated process involving a number of specialized chaperones, but the specific roles played by these factors in replicative nucleosome assembly and chromatin remain to be resolved (27, 29, 210, 211). Due to this uncertainty and because some of these chaperones may not be "deep-rooted," this issue is not elaborated here.

Nucleosomes are not formed on ssDNA (213). Therefore, an asymmetrical replication fork containing a long ssDNA stretch on one of its arms could impede evenhanded assembly of nucleosomes on the two arms. Conversely, a similar content of duplex DNA on the two arms would simplify the process. Furthermore, unwinding the parental duplex in steps of ~35 nt envisaged by the ND model (Section III.B) could facilitate the direct transfer of the tetrasome from old to newly replicated DNA. Accordingly, while one face of the core histone tetramer remains partially bound to the old duplex DNA, the released surface could be transferred directly or via a mediating chaperone (29) to the new duplex DNA already present on either arm of the replication fork. Although the duplex DNA of the discontinuous arm contains nicks or flapped DNA structures in the vicinity of the fork junction, these structures need not impede the assembly of the NCP and NCP package need not prevent their processing by DNA maturation enzymes (181).

As mentioned, Crenarchaea do not encode histone-fold proteins nor organize their genomes into chromatin-like structures (214). Yet, many of their replisome components are of the eukaryal type, including the helicase, primase, and the elongating replicase (8). An exception is the SSB, which resembles the bacterial in subunit organization and presence of a single type of OB-fold domain, albeit closer in structure to the euryarchaeal/eukaryal (88). Therefore, it is tempting to speculate that acquisition of an RPA-like SSB by the histone-encoding euryarchaeal species (215) was the "final touch" that rendered the replisome capable of replicating DNA organized in a primitive chromatin structure.

Acknowledgments

We thank Zvikelman Rolf Knippers, Heinz-Peter Nasheuer, and Marc Wold for useful comments and suggestions. Relevant research in the authors' laboratory was supported by grants from the Israel Cancer Research Fund and from the United States–Israel Binational Science Foundation. G.K. is an incumbent of the Louise and Nahum Barag Chain in Cancer Molecular Genetics.

References

1. Kornberg, A., and Baker, T. A. (1992). "DNA Replication." W. H. Freeman and Company, New York.
2. Baker, T. A., and Bell, S. P. (1998). Polymerases and the replisome: Machines within machines. *Cell* **92,** 295–305.
3. Leipe, D. D., Aravind, L., and Koonin, E. V. (1999). Did DNA replication evolve twice independently? *Nucleic Acids Res.* **27,** 3389–3401.
4. Forterre, P. (2002). The origin of DNA genomes and DNA replication proteins. *Curr. Opin. Microbiol.* **5,** 525–532.
5. Benkovic, S. J., Valentine, A. M., and Salinas, F. (2001). Replisome-mediated DNA replication. *Annu. Rev. Biochem.* **70,** 181–208.
6. Waga, S., and Stillman, B. (1998). The DNA replication fork in eukaryotic cells. *Annu. Rev. Biochem.* **67,** 721–751.
7. MacNeill, S. A. (2001). DNA replication: Partners in the Okazaki two-step. *Curr. Biol.* **11,** R842–R844.
8. Grabowski, B., and Kelman, Z. (2003). Archaeal DNA replication: Eukaryal proteins in a bacterial context. *Annu. Rev. Microbiol.* **57,** 487–516.
9. Patel, S. S., and Picha, K. M. (2000). Structure and function of hexameric helicases. *Annu. Rev. Biochem.* **69,** 651–697.
10. Labib, K., and Diffley, J. F. (2001). Is the MCM2-7 complex the eukaryotic DNA replication fork helicase? *Curr. Opin. Genet. Dev.* **11,** 64–70.
11. Lei, M., and Tye, B. K. (2001). Initiating DNA synthesis: From recruiting to activating the MCM complex. *J. Cell Sci.* **114,** 1447–1454.
12. Lohman, T. M., and Ferrari, M. E. (1994). *Escherichia coli* single-stranded DNA-binding protein: Multiple DNA-binding modes and cooperativities. *Annu. Rev. Biochem.* **63,** 527–570.
13. Wold, M. S. (1997). Replication protein A: A heterotrimeric, single-stranded DNA-binding protein required for eukaryotic DNA metabolism. *Annu. Rev. Biochem.* **66,** 61–92.
14. Iftode, C., Daniely, Y., and Borowiec, J. A. (1999). Replication protein A (RPA): The eukaryotic SSB. *Crit. Rev. Biochem. Mol. Biol.* **34,** 141–180.
15. Theobald, D. L., Mitton-Fry, R. M., and Wuttke, D. S. (2003). Nucleic acid recognition by OB-fold proteins. *Annu. Rev. Biophys. Biomol. Struct.* **32,** 115–133.
16. Frick, D. N., and Richardson, C. C. (2001). DNA primases. *Annu. Rev. Biochem.* **70,** 39–80.
17. McHenry, C. S. (2003). Chromosomal replicases as asymmetric dimers: Studies of subunit arrangement and functional consequences. *Mol. Microbiol.* **49,** 1157–1165.
18. Hubscher, U., Maga, G., and Spadari, S. (2002). Eukaryotic DNA polymerases. *Annu. Rev. Biochem.* **71,** 133–163.
19. O'Donnell, M., Jeruzalmi, D., and Kuriyan, J. (2001). Clamp loader structure predicts the architecture of DNA polymerase III holoenzyme and RFC. *Curr. Biol.* **11,** R935–R946.

20. Bambara, R. A., Murante, R. S., and Henricksen, L. A. (1997). Enzymes and reactions at the eukaryotic DNA replication fork. *J. Biol. Chem.* **272,** 4647–4650.
21. Hubscher, U., and Seo, Y. S. (2001). Replication of the lagging strand: A concert of at least 23 polypeptides. *Mol. Cells.* **12,** 149–157.
22. Tomkinson, A. E., and Mackey, Z. B. (1998). Structure and function of mammalian DNA ligases. *Mutat. Res.* **407,** 1–9.
23. Champoux, J. J. (2001). DNA topoisomerases: Structure, function, and mechanism. *Annu. Rev. Biochem.* **70,** 369–413.
24. Wolffe, A. P. (1998). "Chromatin Structure and Function." London, UK: Academic Press.
25. Widom, J. (1998). Structure, dynamics, and function of chromatin in vitro. *Annu. Rev. Biophys. Biomol. Struct.* **27,** 285–327.
26. Krude, T. (1999). Chromatin assembly during DNA replication in somatic cells. *Eur. J. Biochem.* **263,** 1–5.
27. Tyler, J. K. (2002). Chromatin assembly. Cooperation between histone chaperones and ATP-dependent nucleosome remodelling machines. *Eur. J. Biochem.* **269,** 2268–2274.
28. Sandman, K., Soares, D., and Reeve, J. N. (2001). Molecular components of the archaeal nucleosome. *Biochimie.* **83,** 277–281.
29. Akey, C. A., and Luger, K. (2003). Histone chaperones and nucleosome assembly. *Curr. Opin. Struct. Biol.* **13,** 6–14.
30. Jackson, D. A., and Cook, P. R. (1995). The structural basis of nuclear function. *Int. Rev. Cytol.* **162A,** 125–149.
31. Webb, D. C., Teleman, A., Gordon, S. et al. (1997). Bipolar localization of the replication origin regions of chromosomes in vegetative and sporulating cells of B. subtilis. *Cell* **88,** 667–674.
32. Lemon, K. P., and Grossman, A. D. (1998). Localization of bacterial DNA polymerase: Evidence for a factory model of replication. *Science* **282,** 1516–1519.
33. Seinsoth, S., Uhlmann-Schiffler, H., and Stahl, H. (2003). Bidirectional DNA unwinding by a ternary complex of T antigen, nucleolin, and topoisomerase I. *EMBO Rep.* **4,** 263–268.
34. Mastrangelo, I. A., Hough, P. V. C., Wall, J. S., Dodson, M., Dean, F. B., and Hurwitz, J. (1989). ATP-dependent assembly of double hexamers of SV40 T antigen at the viral origin of DNA replication. *Nature* **338,** 658–662.
35. LeBowitz, J. H., and McMacken, R. (1986). The *Escherichia coli* dnaB replication protein is a DNA helicase. *J. Biol. Chem.* **261,** 4738–4748.
36. Matson, S. W., Tabor, S., and Richardson, C. C. (1983). The gene 4 protein of bacteriophage T7. Characterization of helicase activity. *J. Biol. Chem.* **258,** 14017–14024.
37. Liu, C. C., and Alberts, B. M. (1981). Characterization of the DNA-dependent GTPase activity of T4 gene 41 protein, an essential component of the T4 bacteriophage DNA replication apparatus. *J. Biol. Chem.* **256,** 2813–2820.
38. Scherzinger, E., Ziegelin, G., Barcena, M., Carazo, J. M., Lurz, R., and Lanka, E. (1997). The RepA protein of plasmid RSF1010 is a replicative DNA helicase. *J. Biol. Chem.* **272,** 30228–30236.
39. Maine, G. T., Sinha, P., and Tye, B. K. (1984). Mutants of S. cerevisiae defective in the maintenance of minichromosomes. *Genetics* **106,** 365.
40. Romanowski, P., Madine, M. A., Rowles, A., Blow, J. J., and Laskey, R. A. (1996). The Xenopus origin recognition complex is essential for DNA replication and MCM binding to chromatin. *Curr. Biol.* **6,** 1416–1425.
41. Ishimi, Y. (1997). A DNA helicase activity is associated with an MCM4, -6, and -7 protein complex. *J. Biol. Chem.* **272,** 24508–24513.
42. Aparicio, O. M., Weinstein, D. M., and Bell, S. P. (1997). Components and dynamics of DNA replication complexes in S. cerevisiae: Redistribution of MCM proteins and Cdc45p during S phase. *Cell* **91,** 59–69.

43. Kelman, Z., Lee, J. K., and Hurwitz, J. (1999). The single minichromosome maintenance protein of Methanobacterium thermoautotrophicum Delta H contains DNA helicase activity. *Proc. Natl. Acad. Sci. USA* **96,** 14783.
44. Chong, J. P., Hayashi, M. K., Simon, M. N., Xu, R. M., and Stillman, B. A. (2000). A double-hexamer archaeal minichromosome maintenance protein is an ATP-dependent DNA helicase. *Proc. Natl. Acad. Sci. USA* **97,** 1530–1535.
45. Stahl, H., Droge, P., and Knippers, R. (1986). DNA helicase activity of SV40 large tumor antigen. *EMBO J.* **5,** 1939–1944.
46. Dean, F. B., Dodson, M., Echols, H., and Hurwitz, J. (1987). ATP-dependent formation of a specialized nucleoprotein structure by simian virus 40 (SV40) large tumor antigen at the SV40 replication origin. *Proc. Natl. Acad. Sci. USA* **84,** 8981–8985.
47. Li, D., Zhao, R., Lilyestrom, W. *et al.* (2003). Structure of the replicative helicase of the oncoprotein SV40 large tumour antigen. *Nature* **423,** 512–518.
48. Bell, S. P., and Stillman, B. (1992). ATP-dependent recognition of eukaryotic origins of DNA replication by a multiprotein complex. *Nature* **357,** 128–134.
49. Bell, S. P. (2002). The origin recognition complex: From simple origins to complex functions. *Genes Dev.* **16,** 659–672.
50. Fanning, E., and Knippers, R. (1992). Structure and function of simian virus 40 large tumor antigen. *Annu. Rev. Biochem.* **61,** 55–85.
51. Bullock, P. A. (1997). The initiation of simian virus 40 DNA replication *in vitro*. *Crit. Rev. Biochem. Mol. Biol.* **32,** 503–568.
52. Sawaya, M. R., Guo, S., Tabor, S., Richardson, C. C., and Ellenberger, T. (1999). Crystal structure of the helicase domain from the replicative helicase–primase of bacteriophage T7. *Cell* **99,** 167–177.
53. Leipe, D. D., Aravind, L., Grishin, N. V., and Koonin, E. V. (2000). The bacterial replicative helicase DnaB evolved from a RecA duplication. *Genome Res.* **10,** 5–16.
54. Niedenzu, T., Roleke, D., Bains, G., Scherzinger, E., and Saenger, W. (2001). Crystal structure of the hexameric replicative helicase RepA of plasmid RSF1010. *J. Mol. Biol.* **306,** 479–487.
55. Koonin, E. V. (1993). A common set of conserved motifs in a vast variety of putative nucleic acid-dependent ATPases including MCM proteins involved in the initiation of eukaryotic DNA replication. *Nucleic Acids Res.* **21,** 2541–2547.
56. Neuwald, A. F., Aravind, L., Spouge, J. L., and Koonin, E. V. (1999). AAA+: A class of chaperone-like ATPases associated with the assembly, operation, and disassembly of protein complexes. *Genome Res.* **9,** 27–43.
57. Venkatesan, M., Silver, L. L., and Nossal, N. G. (1982). Bacteriophage T4 gene 41 protein, required for the synthesis of RNA primers, is also a DNA helicase. *J. Biol. Chem.* **257,** 12426.
58. Goetz, G. S., Dean, F. B., Hurwitz, J., and Matson, S. W. (1988). The unwinding of duplex regions in DNA by the simian virus 40 large tumor antigen-associated DNA helicase activity. *J. Biol. Chem.* **263,** 383.
59. Wiekowski, M., Schwarz, M. W., and Stahl, H. (1988). Simian virus 40 large T antigen DNA helicase. Characterization of the ATPase-dependent DNA unwinding activity and its substrate requirements. *J. Biol. Chem.* **263,** 436.
60. Chong, J. P., Hayashi, M. K., Simon, M. N., Xu, R. M., and Stillman, B. (2000). A double-hexamer archaeal minichromosome maintenance protein is an ATP-dependent DNA helicase. *Proc. Natl. Acad. Sci. USA* **97,** 1530–1535.
61. Valle, M., Gruss, C., Halmer, L., Carazo, J. M., and Donate, L. E. (2000). Large T-antigen double hexamers imaged at the simian virus 40 origin of replication. *Mol. Cell. Biol.* **20,** 34–41.

62. Fletcher, R. J., Bishop, B. E., Leon, R. P., Sclafani, R. A., Ogata, C. M., and Chen, X. S. (2003). The structure and function of MCM from archaeal M. Thermoautotrophicum. *Nat. Struct. Biol.* **10**, 160–167.
63. Dornreiter, I., Erdile, L. F., Gilbert, I. U., Von Winkler, D., Kelly, T. J., and Fanning, E. (1992). Interaction of DNA polymerase primase with cellular replication protein A and SV40 T antigen. *EMBO J.* **11**, 769–776.
64. Carpentieri, F., De Felice, M., De Falco, M., Rossi, M., and Pisani, F. M. (2002). Physical and functional interaction between the mini-chromosome maintenance-like DNA helicase and the single-stranded DNA binding protein from the crenarchaeon sulfolobus solfataricus. *J. Biol. Chem.* **277**, 12118–12127.
65. Kneissl, M., Putter, V., Szalay, A. A., and Grummt, F. (2003). Interaction and assembly of murine pre-replicative complex proteins in yeast and mouse cells. *J. Mol. Biol.* **327**, 111–128.
66. Sawaya, M. R., Guo, S., Tabor, S., Richardson, C. C., and Ellenberger, T. (1999). Crystal structure of the helicase domain from the replicative helicase–primase of bacteriophage T7. *Cell* **99**, 167–177.
67. Jezewska, M. J., Rajendran, S., Bujalowska, D., and Bujalowski, W. (1998). Does single-stranded DNA pass through the inner channel of the protein hexamer in the complex with the *Escherichia coli* DnaB helicase? Fluorescence energy transfer studies *J. Biol. Chem.* **273**, 10515.
68. Fang, L., Davey, M. J., and O'Donnell, M. (1999). Replisome assembly at *oriC*, the replication origin of *E. coli*, reveals an explanation for initiation sites outside an origin. *Mol. Cell* **4**, 541–553.
69. Weigel, C., and Seitz, H. (2002). Strand-specific loading of DnaB helicase by DnaA to a substrate mimicking unwound *oriC*. *Mol. Microbiol.* **46**, 1149–1156.
70. Yu, X., Jezewska, M. J., Bujalowski, W., and Egelman, E. H. (1996). The hexameric *E. coli* DnaB helicase can exist in different quarternary states. *J. Mol. Biol.* **259**, 7–14.
71. Kaplan, D. R., and O'Donnell, M. (2002). DnaB drives DNA branch migration and dislodges proteins while encircling two DNA strands. *Mol. Cell* **10**, 647–657.
72. Morag, A. S., Saveson, C. J., and Lovett, S. T. (1999). Expansion of DNA repeats in *Escherichia coli*: Effects of recombination and replication functions. *J. Mol. Biol.* **289**, 21–27.
73. Kim, S., Dallmann, H. G., McHenry, C. S., and Marians, K. J. (1996). Tau couples the leading- and lagging-strand polymerases at the *Escherichia coli* DNA replication fork. *J. Biol. Chem.* **271**, 21406.
74. Gao, D., and McHenry, C. S. (2001). Tau binds and organizes *Escherichia coli* replication proteins through distinct domains. Domain IV, located within the unique C terminus of tau, binds the replication fork helicase, DnaB. *J. Biol. Chem.* **276**, 4441.
75. Wessel, R., Schweizer, J., and Stahl, H. (1992). Simian virus 40 T-antigen DNA helicase is a hexamer which forms a binary complex during bidirectional unwinding from the viral origin of DNA replication. *J. Virol.* **66**, 804–815.
76. Lee, J. K., and Hurwitz, J. (2001). Processive DNA helicase activity of the minichromosome maintenance proteins 4, 6, and 7 complex requires forked DNA structures. *Proc. Natl. Acad. Sci. USA* **98**, 54–59.
77. Schwacha, A., and Bell, S. (2001). BSP. Interactions between two catalytically distinct MCM subgroups are essential for coordinated ATP hydrolysis and DNA replication. *Mol. Cell* **8**, 1093–1104.
78. Smelkova, N. V., and Borowiec, J. A. (1997). Dimerization of simian virus 40 T-antigen hexamers activates T-antigen DNA helicase activity. *J. Virol.* **71**, 8766–8773.
79. Alexandrov, A. I., Botchan, M. R., and Cozzarelli, N. R. (2002). Characterization of simian virus 40 T-antigen double hexamers bound to a replication fork. The active form of the helicase. *J. Biol. Chem.* **277**, 44886–44897.

80. Boyer, P. D. (1997). The ATP synthase—A splendid molecular machine. *Annu. Rev. Biochem.* **66,** 717–749.
81. West, S. C. (1996). DNA helicases: New breeds of translocating motors and molecular pumps. *Cell* **86,** 177–180.
82. Laskey, R. A., and Madine, M. A. (2003). A rotary pumping model for helicase function of MCM proteins at a distance from replication forks. *EMBO Rep.* **4,** 26–30.
83. Ritzi, M., Baack, M., Musahl, C., Romanowski, P., Laskey, R. A., and Knippers, R. (1998). Human minichromosome maintenance proteins and human origin recognition complex 2 protein on chromatin. *J. Biol. Chem.* **273,** 24543–24549.
84. Chedin, F., Seitz, E. M., and Kowalczykowski, S. C. (1998). Novel homologs of replication protein A in archaea: Implications for the evolution of ssDNA-binding proteins. *Trends Biochem Sci.* **23,** 273–277.
85. Murzin, A. G. (1993). OB (oligonucleotide/oligosaccharide binding)-fold: Common structural and functional solution for non-homologous sequences. *EMBO J.* **12,** 861.
86. Bochkarev, A., Pfuetzner, R. A., Edwards, A. M., and Frappier, L. (1997). Structure of the single-stranded DNA-binding domain of replication protein A bound to DNA. *Nature* **385,** 176–181.
87. Yang, C., Curth, U., and Urbanke, C. K. C. (1997). Crystal structure of human mitochondrial single-stranded DNA binding protein at 2.4 A resolution. *Nat. Struct. Biol.* **4,** 153–157.
88. Haseltine, C. A., and Kowalczykowski, S. C. (2002). A distinctive single-stranded DNA-binding protein from the Archaeon *Sulfolobus solfataricus*. *Mol. Microbiol.* **43,** 1505–1515.
89. Kerr, I. D, Wadsworth, R. I. M., Cubeddu, L., Blankenfeldt, W., Naismith, J. H., and White, M. F. (2003). Insights into ssDNA recognition by the OB fold from a structural and thermodynamic study of Sulfolobus SSB protein. *EMBO J.* **22,** 2561.
90. Daughdrill, G. W., Ackerman, J., Isern, N. G. *et al.* (2001). The weak interdomain coupling observed in the 70 kDa subunit of human replication protein A is unaffected by ssDNA binding. *Nucl. Acids Res.* **29,** 3270–3276.
91. Philipova, D., Mullen, J. R., Maniar, H. S., Lu, J., Gu, C., and Brill, S. J. (1996). A hierarchy of SSB protomers in replication protein A. *Genes Dev.* **10,** 2222–2233.
92. Pfuetzner, R. A., Bochkarev, A., Frappier, L., and Edwards, A. M. (1997). Replication protein A. Characterization and crystallization of the DNA binding domain. *J. Biol. Chem.* **272,** 430–434.
93. Bochkarev, A., Bochkareva, E., Frappier, L., and Edwards, A. M. (1999). The crystal structure of the complex of replication protein A subunits RPA32 and RPA14 reveals a mechanism for single-stranded DNA binding. *EMBO J.* **18,** 4498–4504.
94. Pereira, S. L., Grayling, R. A., Lurz, R., and Reeve, J. N. (1997). Archaeal nucleosomes. *Proc. Natl. Acad. Sci. USA* **94,** 12633–12637.
95. Kozlov, A. G., and Lohman, T. M. (2002). Kinetic mechanism of direct transfer of *Escherichia coli* SSB tetramers between single-stranded DNA molecules. *Biochemistry* **41,** 11611–11627.
96. Kim, C., Snyder, R., and Wold, M. S. (1992). Binding properties of replication protein A from human and yeast cells. *Mol. Cell. Biol.* **12,** 3050–3059.
97. Blackwell, L. J., and Borowiec, J. A. (1994). Human replication protein A binds single-stranded DNA in two distinct complexes. *Mol. Cell. Biol.* **14,** 3993–4001.
98. Kim, C., Paulus, B. F., and Wold, M. S. (1994). Interactions of human replication protein A with oligonucleotides. *Biochemistry* **33,** 14197–14206.
99. Blackwell, L. J., Borowiec, J. A., and Masrangelo, I. A. (1996). Single-stranded DNA binding alters human replication protein A structure and facilitates interaction with DNA-dependent protein kinase. *Mol. Cell. Biol.* **16,** 4798–4807.

100. Bastin-Shanower, S. A., and Brill, S. J. (2001). Functional analysis of the four DNA binding domains of replication protein A. The role of RPA2 in ssDNA binding. *J. Biol. Chem.* **276**, 36446–36453.
101. Melendy, T., and Stillman, B. (1993). An interaction between replication protein A and SV40 T antigen appears essential for primosome assembly during SV40 DNA replication. *J. Biol. Chem.* **268**, 3389–3395.
102. Sancar, A. (1996). DNA excision repair. *Annu. Rev. Biochem.* **65**, 43–81.
103. Nethanel, T., Zlotkin, T., and Kaufmann, G. (1992). Assembly of simian virus 40 Okazaki pieces from DNA primers is reversibly arrested by ATP depletion. *J. Virol.* **66**, 6634–6640.
104. Mass, G., Nethanel, T., Lavrik, O. I., Wold, M. S., and Kaufmann, G. (2001). Replication protein A modulates its interface with the primed DNA template during RNA–DNA primer elongation in replicating SV40 chromosomes. *Nucleic Acids Res.* **29**, 3892–3899.
105. Bouche, J. P., Zechel, K., and Kornberg, A. (1975). dnaG gene product, a rifampicin-resistant RNA polymerase, initiates the conversion of a single-stranded coliphage DNA to its duplex replicative form. *J. Biol. Chem.* **250**, 5995.
106. Keck, J. L., and Berger, J. M. (2001). Primus inter pares (first among equals). *Nat. Struct. Biol.* **8**, 2–4.
107. Ziegelin, G., Scherzinger, E., Lurz, R., and Lanka, E. (1993). Phage P4 alpha protein is multifunctional with origin recognition, helicase, and primase activities. *EMBO J.* **12**, 3703–3708.
108. Conaway, R. C., and Lehman, I. R. (1982). A DNA primase activity associated with DNA polymerase alpha from *Drosophila melanogaster* embryos. *Proc. Natl. Acad. Sci. USA* **79**, 2523–2527.
109. Lehman, I. R., and Kaguni, L. S. (1989). DNA polymerase alpha. *J. Biol. Chem.* **264**, 4265–4268.
110. Eliasson, R., and Reichard, P. (1978). Replication of polyoma DNA in isolated nuclei: Synthesis and distribution of initiator RNA. *J. Biol. Chem.* **253**, 7469–7475.
111. Nethanel, T., Reisfeld, S., Dinter-Gottlieb, G., and Kaufmann, G. (1988). An Okazaki piece of simian virus 40 may be synthesized by ligation of shorter precursor chains. *J. Virol.* **62**, 2867–2873.
112. Nethanel, T., and Kaufmann, G. (1990). Two DNA polymerases may be required for synthesis of the lagging DNA strand of simian virus 40. *J. Virol.* **64**, 5912–5918.
113. Bullock, P. A., Seo, Y. S., and Hurwitz, J. (1991). Initiation of simian virus 40 DNA synthesis *in vitro*. *Mol. Cell. Biol.* **11**, 2350–2361.
114. Waga, S., and Stillman, B. (1994). Anatomy of a DNA replication fork revealed by reconstitution of SV40 DNA replication *in vitro*. *Nature* **369**, 207–212.
115. Edgell, D. R., Malik, S. B., and Doolittle, W. F. (1998). Evidence of independent gene duplications during the evolution of archaeal and eukaryotic family B DNA polymerases. *Mol. Biol. Evol.* **15**, 1207–1217.
116. Liu, L., Komori, K., Ishino, S. et al. (2001). The archaeal DNA primase: Biochemical characterization of the p41–p46 complex from Pyrococcus furiosus. *J. Biol. Chem.* **276**, 45484–45490.
117. Bocquier, A. A., Liu, L., Cann, I. K., Komori, K., Kohda, D., and Ishino, Y. (2001). Archaeal primase: Bridging the gap between RNA and DNA polymerases. *Curr. Biol.* **11**, 452–456.
118. Dervyn, E., Suski, C., Daniel, R. et al. (2001). Two essential DNA polymerases at the bacterial replication fork. *Science* **294**, 1716–1719.
119. Chilkova, O., Jonsson, B. H., and Johansson, E. (2003). The quaternary structure of DNA polymerase epsilon from *Saccharomyces cerevisiae*. *J. Biol. Chem.* **278**, 14082–14086.

120. Li, X., Li, J., Harrington, J., Lieber, M. R., and Burgers, P. M. (1995). Lagging strand DNA synthesis at the eukaryotic replication fork involves binding and stimulation of FEN-1 by proliferating cell nuclear antigen. *J. Biol. Chem.* **270,** 22109–22112.
121. Levin, D. S., Bai, W., Yao, N., O'Donnell, M., and Tomkinson, A. E. (1997). An interaction between DNA ligase I and proliferating cell nuclear antigen: Implications for Okazaki fragment synthesis and joining. *Proc. Natl. Acad. Sci. USA* **94,** 12863–12868.
122. Shibahara, K. (1999). Replication-dependent marking of DNA by PCNA facilitates CAF-1-coupled inheritance of chromatin. *Cell* **96,** 575–585.
123. Joyce, C. M., and Steitz, T. A. (1994). Function and structure relationships in DNA polymerases. *Annu. Rev. Biochem.* **63,** 777–822.
124. Steitz, T. A. (1999). DNA polymerases: Structural diversity and common mechanisms. *J. Biol. Chem.* **274,** 17395–17398.
125. Wang, J., Sattar, A. K., Wang, C. C., Karam, J. D., Konigsberg, W. H., and Steitz, T. A. (1997). Crystal structure of a pol alpha family replication DNA polymerase from bacteriophage RB69. *Cell* **89,** 1087–1099.
126. Pritchard, A. E., and McHenry, C. S. (1999). Identification of the acidic residues in the active site of DNA polymerase III. *J. Mol. Biol.* **285,** 1067–1080.
127. McHenry, C., and Kornberg, A. (1977). DNA polymerase III holoenzyme of *Escherichia coli*. Purification and resolution into subunits. *J. Biol. Chem.* **252,** 6478–6484.
128. Glover, B. P., and McHenry, C. S. (2001). The DNA polymerase III holoenzyme: An asymmetric dimeric replicative complex with leading and lagging strand polymerases. *Cell* **105,** 925–934.
129. Kelman, Z., Yuzhakov, A., Andjelkovic, J., and O'Donnell, M. (1998). Devoted to the lagging strand—The subunit of DNA polymerase III holoenzyme contacts SSB to promote processive elongation and sliding clamp assembly. *EMBO J.* **17,** 2436–2449.
130. Hubscher, U., Nasheuer, H. P., and Syvaoja, J. E. (2000). Eukaryotic DNA polymerases, a growing family. *Trends Biochem. Sci.* **25,** 143–147.
131. Pospiech, H., and Syvaoja, J. E. (2003). DNA polymerase α-More than a polymerase. *Scientific World Journal* **3,** 87–104.
132. Maga, G., Frouin, I., Spadari, S., and Hubscher, U. (2001). Replication protein A as a "fidelity clamp" for DNA polymerase alpha. *J. Biol. Chem.* **276,** 18235–18242.
133. Tsurimoto, T., Melendy, T., and Stillman, B. (1990). Sequential initiation of lagging and leading strand synthesis by two different polymerase complexes at the SV40 DNA replication origin. *Nature* **346,** 534–539.
134. Prelich, G., Tan, C. K., Kostura, M. *et al.* (1987). Functional identity of proliferating cell nuclear antigen and a DNA polymerase delta auxiliary protein. *Nature* **326,** 517–520.
135. Prelich, G., and Stillman, B. (1988). Coordinated leading and lagging DNA strand synthesis during SV40 DNA replication *in vitro* requires PCNA. *Cell* **53,** 117–126.
136. Mossi, R., Keller, R. C., Ferrari, E., and Hubscher, U. (2000). DNA polymerase switching: II. Replication factor C abrogates primer synthesis by DNA polymerase [alpha] at a critical length. *J. Mol. Biol.* **295,** 803–814.
137. Burgers, P. M. (1991). *Saccharomyces cerevisiae* replication factor C. II. Formation and activity of complexes with the proliferating cell nuclear antigen and with DNA polymerases delta and epsilon. *J. Biol. Chem.* **266,** 22698–22706.
138. Podust, V. N., Georgaki, A., Strack, B., and Hubscher, U. (1992). Calf thymus RF-C as an essential component for DNA polymerase delta and epsilon holoenzymes function. *Nucleic Acids Res.* **20,** 4159–4165.
139. Mossi, R., Ferrari, E., and Hubscher, U. (1998). DNA ligase I selectively affects DNA synthesis by DNA polymerases delta and epsilon suggesting differential functions in DNA replication and repair. *J. Biol. Chem.* **273,** 14322–14330.

140. Maga, G., Villani, G., Tillement, V. *et al.* (2001). Okazaki fragment processing: Modulation of the strand displacement activity of DNA polymerase delta by the concerted action of replication protein A, proliferating cell nuclear antigen, and flap endonuclease-1. *Proc. Natl. Acad. Sci.* **98,** 14298–14303.
141. Ayyagari, R., Gomes, X. V., Gordenin, D. A., and Burgers, P. M. J. (2003). Okazaki fragment maturation in yeast. I. Distribution of functions between FEN1 and DNA2. *J. Biol. Chem.* **278,** 1618–1625.
142. Budd, M. E., and Campbell, J. L. (1997). A yeast replicative helicase, Dna2 helicase, interacts with yeast FEN-1 nuclease in carrying out its essential function. *Mol. Cell. Biol.* **17,** 2136–2142.
143. Waga, S., Bauer, G., and Stillman, B. (1994). Reconstitution of complete SV40 DNA replication with purified replication factors. *J. Biol. Chem.* **269,** 10923–10934.
144. Zlotkin, T., Kaufmann, G., Jiang, Y. *et al.* (1996). DNA polymerase epsilon may be dispensable for SV40—but not cellular—DNA replication. *EMBO J.* **15,** 2298–2305.
145. Morrison, A., Araki, H., Clark, A. B., Hamatake, R. K., and Sugino, A. (1990). A third essential DNA polymerase in *S. cerevisiae*. *Cell* **62,** 1143–1151.
146. Budd, M. E., and Campbell, J. L. (1993). DNA polymerases delta and epsilon are required for chromosomal replication in *Saccharomyces cerevisiae*. *Mol. Cell. Biol.* **13,** 496–505.
147. Navas, T. A., Zhou, Z., and Elledge, S. J. (1995). DNA polymerase epsilon links the DNA replication machinery to the S phase checkpoint. *Cell* **80,** 29–39.
148. Kesti, T., Flick, K., Keranen, S., Syvaoja, J. E., and Wittenberg, C. (1999). DNA polymerase epsilon catalytic domains are dispensable for DNA replication, DNA repair, and cell viability. *Mol. Cell* **3,** 679–685.
149. Feng, W., and D'Urso, G. (2001). *Schizosaccharomyces pombe* cells lacking the aminoterminal catalytic domains of DNA polymerase epsilon are viable but require the DNA damage checkpoint control. *Mol. Cell. Biol.* **21,** 4495–4504.
150. Lee, J., Chastain, P. D., Kusa, T., Griffith, J. D., and Richardson, C. C. (1998). Coordinated leading and lagging strand DNA synthesis on a minicircular template. *Mol. Cell. Biol.* **1,** 1001–1010.
151. Cann, I. K., and Ishino, Y. (1999). Archaeal DNA replication. Identifying the pieces to solve a puzzle. *Genetics* **152,** 1249–1267.
152. Matsumiya, S., Ishino, S., Ishino, Y., and Morikawa, K. (2002). Physical interaction between proliferating cell nuclear antigen and replication factor C from Pyrococcus furiosus. *Genes to Cells* **7,** 911–922.
153. Turchi, J. J., Huang, L., Murante, R. S., Kim, Y., and Bambara, R. A. (1994). Enzymatic completion of mammalian lagging-strand DNA replication. *Proc. Natl. Acad. Sci.* **91,** 9803–9807.
154. Roberts, E., Nash, R. A., Robins, P., and Lindahl, T. (1994). Different active sites of mammalian DNA ligases I and II. *J. Biol. Chem.* **269,** 3789–3792.
155. Lieber, M. R. (1997). The FEN-1 family of structure-specific nucleases in eukaryotic DNA replication, recombination, and repair. *Bioessays* **19,** 233–240.
156. Rumbaugh, J. A., Henricksen, L. A., DeMott, M. S., and Bambara, R. A. (1999). Cleavage of substrates with mismatched nucleotides by Flap endonuclease-1. Implications for mammalian Okazaki fragment processing. *J. Biol. Chem.* **274,** 14602–14608.
157. Qiu, J., Qian, Y., Frank, P., Wintersberger, U., and Shen, B. (1999). *Saccharomyces cerevisiae* RNase H(35) functions in RNA primer removal during lagging-strand DNA synthesis, most efficiently in cooperation with Rad27 nuclease. *Mol. Cell. Biol.* **19,** 8361–8371.
158. Chen, J. Z., Qiu, J., Shen, B., and Holmquist, G. P. (2000). Mutational spectrum analysis of RNase H(35) deficient *Saccharomyces cerevisiae* using fluorescence-based directed termination PCR. *Nucl. Acids Res.* **28,** 3649–3656.

159. Parenteau, J., and Wellinger, R. J. (1999). Accumulation of single-stranded DNA and destabilization of telomeric repeats in yeast mutant strains carrying a deletion of RAD27. *Mol. Cell. Biol.* **19**, 4143–4152.
160. Kang, H. Y., Choi, E., Bae, S. H. *et al.* (2000). Genetic analyses of Schizosaccharomyces pombe dna2(+) reveal that dna2 plays an essential role in Okazaki fragment metabolism. *Genetics* **155**, 1055–1067.
161. Budd, M. E., Choe, W. C., and Campbell, J. L. (2000). The nuclease activity of the yeast Dna2 protein, which is related to the RecB-like nucleases, is essential *in vivo. J. Biol. Chem.* **275**, 16518–16529.
162. Bae, S. H., Bae, K. H., Kim, J. A., and Seo, Y. S. (2001). RPA governs endonuclease switching during processing of Okazaki fragments in eukaryotes. *Nature* **412**, 456–461.
163. Jonsson, Z. O., Hindges, R., and Hubscher, U. (1998). Regulation of DNA replication and repair proteins through interaction with the front side of proliferating cell nuclear antigen. *EMBO J.* **17**, 2412–2425.
164. Mackenney, V. J., Barnes, D. E., and Lindahl, T. (1997). Specific function of DNA ligase I in simian virus 40 DNA replication by human cell-free extracts is mediated by the aminoterminal non-catalytic domain. *J. Biol. Chem.* **272**, 11550–11556.
165. Bentley, D. J., Harrison, C., Ketchen, A. M. *et al.* (2002). DNA ligase I null mouse cells show normal DNA repair activity but altered DNA replication and reduced genome stability. *J. Cell Sci.* **115**, 1551–1561.
166. Okazaki, R., Okazaki, T., Sakabe, K. *et al.* (1968). *In vivo* mechanism of DNA chain growth. *Cold Spring Harbor Symp. Quant. Biol.* **33**, 129–143.
167. Fareed, G. C., and Salzman, N. P. (1972). Intermediate in SV40 DNA chain growth. *Nat. New Biol.* **238**, 274–277.
168. Matsunaga, F., Norais, C., Forterre, P., and Myllykallio, H. (2003). Identification of short "eukaryotic" Okazaki fragments synthesized from a prokaryotic replication origin. *EMBO Rep.* **4**, 154–158.
169. Alberts, B., Morris, F., Mace, D., Sinha, N., and Moran, L. (1975). Reconstruction of the T4 bacteriophage DNA replication apparatus from purified components. In "DNA Synthesis and Its Regulation" (M. Goulian and P. Hanawalt, Eds.), pp. 241–269. Benjamin, Menlo Park, CA.
170. Alberts, B. M. (1987). Prokaryotic DNA replication mechanisms. *Philos. Trans. R. Soc. Lond. B. Biol. Sci.* **317**, 395–420.
171. Park, K., Debyser, Z., Tabor, S., Richardson, C. C., and Griffith, J. D. (1998). Formation of a DNA loop at the replication fork generated by bacteriophage T7 replication proteins. *J. Biol. Chem.* **273**, 5260–5270.
172. Salinas, F., and Benkovic, S. J. (2000). Characterization of bacteriophage T4-coordinated leading- and lagging-strand synthesis on a minicircle substrate. *Proc. Natl. Acad. Sci. USA* **97**, 7196–7201.
173. Stillman, B. (1996). Comparison of DNA replication in cells from prokarya and eukarya. In "DNA Replication in Eukaryotic Cells" (M. L. DePamphilis, Ed.), pp. 435–460. Cold Spring Harbor Laboratory Press, Plainview, NY.
174. Shevelev, I. V., and Hubscher, U. (2002). The 3' 5' exonucleases. *Nat. Rev. Mol. Cell. Biol.* **3**, 364–376.
175. Li, J. J., and Kelly, T. J. (1984). Simian virus 40 DNA replication *in vitro. Proc. Natl. Acad. Sci. USA* **81**, 6973–6977.
176. Wobbe, C. R., Weissbach, L., Borowiec, J. A. *et al.* (1986). Replication of simian virus 40 origin-containing DNA with purified components. *Proc. Natl. Acad. Sci. USA* **85**, 1834–1838.
177. Stillman, B. W., and Gluzman, Y. (1985). Replication and supercoiling of simian virus 40 DNA in cell extracts from human cells. *Mol. Cell. Biol.* **5**, 2051–2060.

178. Challberg, M. D., and Kelly, T. J. (1989). Animal virus DNA replication. *Annu. Rev. Biochem.* **58,** 671–717.
179. Hurwitz, J., Dean, F. B., Kwong, A. D., and Lee, S.-H. (1990). The *in vitro* replication of DNA containing the SV40 origin. *J. Biol. Chem.* **265,** 18043–18046.
180. Chafin, D. R., Vitolo, J. M., Henricksen, L. A., Bambara, R. A., and Hayes, J. J. (2000). Human DNA ligase I efficiently seals nicks in nucleosomes. *EMBO J.* **19,** 5492–5501.
181. Huggins, C. F., Chafin, D. R., Aoyagi, S., Henricksen, L. A., Bambara, R. A., and Hayes, J. J. (2002). Flap endonuclease 1 efficiently cleaves base excision repair and DNA replication intermediates assembled into nucleosomes. *Mol. Cell* **10,** 1201–1211.
182. Kao, H. I., Henricksen, L. A., Liu, Y., and Bambara, R. A. (2002). Cleavage specificity of Saccharomyces cerevisiae flap endonuclease 1 suggests a double-flap structure as the cellular substrate. *J. Biol. Chem.* **277,** 14379–14389.
183. Jin, Y. H., Ayyagari, R., Resnick, M. A., Gordenin, D. A., and Burgers, P. M. J. (2003). Okazaki fragment maturation in yeast. II. Cooperation between the polymerase and $3'$-$5'$-exonuclease activities of pol delta in the creation of a ligatable nick. *J. Biol. Chem.* **278,** 1626–1633.
184. DePamphilis, M. L., and Bradley, M. K. (1986). Replication of SV40 and polyoma virus chromosomes. *In* "The Papovaviridae" (N. P. Salzman, Ed.), pp. 99–246. Plenum Publishing Corp.
185. Khan, N. N., Wright, G. E., Dudycz, L. W., and Brown, N. C. (1984). Butylphenyl dGTP: A selective and potent inhibitor of mammalian DNA polymerase α. *Nucleic Acids Res.* **12,** 3695–3706.
186. Tanaka, S., Hu, S.-Z., Wang, T. S. F., and Korn, D. (1982). Preparation and preliminary characterization of monoclonal antibodies against human DNA polymerase α. *J. Biol Chem.* **257,** 8386–8390.
187. Tsurimoto, T., and Stillman, B. (1991). Replication factors required for SV40 DNA replication *in vitro*. II. Switching of DNA polymerase α and δ during initiation of leading and lagging strand synthesis. *J. Biol. Chem.* **266,** 1961–1968.
188. Syvaoja, J., Suomensaari, S., Nishida, C. *et al.* (1990). DNA polymerases α, δ, and ϵ: Three distinct enzymes from HeLa cells. *Proc. Natl. Acad. Sci. USA* **87,** 6664–6668.
189. Podlutsky, A. J., Dianova, I. I., Podust, V. N., Bohr, V. A., and Dianov, G. L. (2001). Human DNA polymerase {beta} initiates DNA synthesis during long-patch repair of reduced AP sites in DNA. *EMBO J.* **20,** 1477–1482.
190. Salas, M., Miller, T. J., Leis, J., and DePamphilis, M. L. (1996). Mechanisms for priming DNA synthesis. *In* "DNA replication in eukaryotic cells" (M. L. DePamphilis, Ed.), pp. 131–176. Cold Spring Harbor Laboratory Press, Plainview, NY.
191. Kaufmann, G., Anderson, S., and DePamphilis, M. L. (1977). RNA primers in simian virus 40 DNA replication: Distribution of $5'$ terminal oligoribonucleotides in nascent DNA. *J. Mol. Biol.* **111,** 549–568.
192. Kaufmann, G. (1981). Characterization of initiator RNA from replicating simian virus 40 DNA synthesized in isolated nuclei. *J. Mol. Biol.* **147,** 25–39.
193. Anderson, S., and DePamphilis, M. L. (1979). Metabolism of Okazaki fragments during simian virus 40 DNA replication. *J. Biol. Chem.* **254,** 11495–11504.
194. Mass, G., Nethanel, T., and Kaufmann, G. (1998). The middle subunit of replication protein A contacts RNA–DNA primers within replicating SV40 chromosomes. *Mol. Cell Biol.* **18,** 6399–6410.
195. Lavrik, O. I., Nasheuer, H. P., Weisshart, K. *et al.* (1998). Subunits of human replication protein A are crosslinked by photoreactive primers synthesized by DNA polymerases. *Nucleic Acids Res.* **26,** 602–607.

196. Kolpashchikov, D. M., Khodyreva, S. N., Khlimankov, D. Y., Wold, M. S., Favre, A., and Lavrik, O. I. (2001). Polarity of human replication protein A binding to DNA. *Nucleic Acids Res.* **29,** 373–379.
197. Hay, R. T., and DePamphilis, M. L. (1982). Initiation of SV40 DNA replication *in vivo*: Location and structure of 5′ ends of DNA synthesized in the *ori* region. *Cell* **28,** 767–779.
198. Bielinsky, A. K., and Gerbi, S. A. (1998). Discrete start sites for DNA synthesis in the yeast ARS1 origin. *Science* **279,** 95–98.
199. Abdurashidova, G., Deganuto, M., Klima, R. *et al.* (2000). Start sites of bidirectional DNA synthesis at the human lamin B2 origin. *Science* **287,** 2023–2026.
200. Hay, R. T., Hendrickson, E. A., and DePamphilis, M. L. (1984). Sequence specificity for the initiation of RNA-primed SV40 DNA synthesis *in vivo*. *J. Mol. Biol.* **175,** 131–157.
201. Fire, A., and Xu, S. (1995). Rolling replication of short DNA circles. *Proc. Natl. Acad. Sci. USA* **92,** 4641–4645.
202. Luger, K., Mader, A. W., Richmond, R. K., Sargent, D. F., and Richmond, T. J. (1997). Crystal structure of the nucleosome core particle at 2.8 A resolution. *Nature* **389,** 251–260.
203. Aalfs, J. D., and Kingston, R. E. (2000). What does "chromatin remodeling" mean? *Trends Biochem. Sci.* **25,** 548–555.
204. Sogo, J. M., Stahl, H., Koller, T., and Knippers, R. (1986). Structure of replicating simian virus 40 minichromosomes. The replication fork, core histone segregation, and terminal structures. *J. Mol. Biol.* **189,** 189–204.
205. Gasser, R., Koller, T., and Sogo, J. M. (1996). The stability of nucleosomes at the replication fork. *J. Mol. Biol.* **258,** 224–239.
206. Jackson, V. (1988). Deposition of newly synthesized histones: Hybrid nucleosomes are not tandemly arranged on daughter DNA strands. *Biochemistry* **27,** 2109–2120.
207. Jackson, V. (1990). *In vivo* studies on the dynamics of histone-DNA interaction: Evidence for nucleosome dissolution during replication and transcription and a low level of dissolution independent of both. *Biochemistry* **29,** 719–731.
208. Gruss, C., Wu, J., Koller, T., and Sogo, J. M. (1993). Disruption of the nucleosomes at the replication fork. *EMBO J.* **12,** 4533–4545.
209. Smith, S., and Stillman, B. (1991). Stepwise assembly of chromatin during DNA replication *in vitro*. *EMBO J.* **10,** 971–980.
210. Kaufman, P. D. (1996). Nucleosome assembly: The CAF and the HAT. *Curr. Opin. Cell Biol.* **8,** 369–373.
211. Smith, S., and Stillman, B. (1989). Purification and characterization of CAF-I, a human cell factor required for chromatin assembly during DNA replication *in vitro*. *Cell* **58,** 15–25.
212. McNairn, A. J., and Gilbert, D. M. (2003). Epigenomic replication: Linking epigenetics to DNA replication. *Bioessays* **25,** 647–656.
213. Almouzni, G., Clark, D. J., Mechali, M., and Wolffe, A. P. (1990). Chromatin assembly on replicating DNA *in vitro*. *Nucleic Acids Res.* **18,** 5767–5774.
214. White, M. F., and Bell, S. D. (2002). Holding it together: Chromatin in the Archaea. *Trends in Genetics* **18,** 621–626.
215. Kelly, T. J., Simancek, P., and Brush, G. S. (1998). Identification and characterization of a single-stranded DNA-binding protein from the archaeon Methanococcus jannaschii. *Proc. Natl. Acad. Sci. USA* **95,** 14634–14639.

Initiation and Elongation Factors in Mammalian Mitochondrial Protein Biosynthesis

Linda L. Spremulli,
Angie Coursey, Tomas
Navratil, and Senyene
Eyo Hunter

Department of Chemistry, University of North Carolina, Chapel Hill, NC 27599-3290

I. Mammalian Mitochondrial Protein Synthesis	211
A. Roles of Mitochondria in the Cell	211
B. General Features of Mammalian Mitochondrial Protein Synthesis	212
II. Initiation of Protein Biosynthesis in Mammalian Mitochondria	214
A. Overview of the Initiation of Protein Synthesis in Prokaryotes	214
B. Mitochondrial Initiation Factor 2 (IF-2_{mt})	215
C. Mitochondrial Initiation Factor 3 (IF-3_{mt})	226
D. The Question of Initiation Factor 1 (IF-1_{mt}) in Mammalian Mitochondria	230
III. Elongation Factors in Mammalian Mitochondria	231
A. Overview of the Elongation Cycle	231
B. Mitochondrial Elongation Factor Tu (EF-Tu_{mt})	232
C. Mitochondrial Elongation Factor Ts (EF-Ts_{mt})	242
D. Mitochondrial Elongation Factor G (EF-G_{mt})	249
IV. Conclusions	252
References	253

I. Mammalian Mitochondrial Protein Synthesis

A. Roles of Mitochondria in the Cell

Mitochondria are essential subcellular compartments in eukaryotic cells which play critical roles in numerous metabolic processes. These oblong-shaped organelles are surrounded by a double membrane. The outer membrane defines the shape of the mitochondrion and is separated from the inner membrane by an intermembrane space. The inner membrane is highly invaginated, forming cristae which serve to increase the surface area of the membrane. The interior of the mitochondrion (matrix) contains many metabolic enzymes, including those required for the citric acid cycle, fatty acid degradation, the urea cycle, and heme biosynthesis. The inner membrane also plays a central role in cellular metabolism. Oxidative phosphorylation occurring in the inner membrane generates about 90% of the energy used in mammalian cells. ATP synthesis and the preceding electron transfer process are carried out through the action of five oligomeric complexes in the inner membrane and cytochrome c in the intermembrane space. In addition to these complexes, the inner membrane contains a large number of proteins, including transporters and components required for the assembly of the respiratory chain complexes. These proteins include chaperones mediating correct protein–protein interactions during the assembly of the large oligomeric complexes in the membrane and proteins required for the insertion of the cofactors involved in the electron transfer reactions used to generate energy. The inner membrane also plays an important role in the crucial process of apoptosis. A change in the permeability of the inner membrane is a key step in signaling cell death, and mitochondria are now known to coordinate many events mediating the responses of cells to viral or mutagenic damage and to developmental signals directing them to enter apoptosis (1).

The precise number of proteins in mitochondria is not known. Estimates range from about 2000 to almost 5000. In mammalian cells, all but 13 of these are the products of nuclear genes. They are synthesized in the cell cytoplasm and then imported into the organelle. The remaining 13 are encoded in the mitochondrial DNA and are synthesized within the organelle itself on a specialized translational system localized within the mitochondrion. These 13 mitochondrially encoded polypeptides are all components of the membrane-associated apparatus for electron transport and oxidative phosphorylation (2).

B. General Features of Mammalian Mitochondrial Protein Synthesis

Despite many years of research, no *in vitro* translational system has been successfully established from mammalian mitochondria. As a result, our understanding of this complex process is poorly developed. However, some of the individual reactions have been carried out *in vitro*, providing information on specific steps (3–18). The detailed sections in this chapter on the initiation and elongation factors provide a general summary of what has been learned about the auxiliary factors required for the individual steps in the translational process.

Mitochondrial ribosomes from different organisms are structurally quite diverse and range in size from 55 S to 80 S (19, 20). Mammalian mitochondrial ribosomes have low sedimentation coefficients (about 55 S) and consist of 28 S and 39 S subunits (21). They have molecular masses of about 2.6×10^6 daltons, about the size of the *E. coli* ribosome. Animal mitochondrial ribosomes have only two rRNA species, 12 S in the small subunit and 16 S in the large subunit. The bulk of the mammalian mitochondrial ribosome consists of proteins (22). Recent proteomic studies have lead to the identification of most of the proteins present in these ribosomes (23–29). The small subunit of the bovine mitochondrial ribosome has 29 proteins, while the large subunit has 48 proteins. Of these, about half are homologs of bacterial ribosomal proteins while the remainder appear to be unique to mitochondrial ribosomes.

The 13 polypeptides encoded in the mammalian mitochondrial genome are synthesized from 9 monocistronic mRNAs and 2 dicistronic mRNAs with overlapping reading frames (30, 31). The genes for these proteins are arranged in an extremely compact form generally separated by tRNA genes that serve as punctuation signals for processing of the primary transcript (32). These mRNAs are quite unusual. They have an almost complete lack of 5′ and 3′ untranslated nucleotides. The translational start codon is generally located within 3 nucleotides of the 5′ end of the mRNA (30, 33). The unusual structure of these mRNAs argues that the mechanism used by mitochondrial ribosomes to recognize the translational start site must differ significantly from the mechanisms found in bacteria and the eukaryotic cell cytoplasm. In prokaryotes, the 16 S rRNA contains a polypyrimidine tract near the 3′ end, which plays an important role in initiation complex formation by hydrogen bonding to a polypurine sequence (the Shine/Dalgarno sequence) in the mRNA (34). In contrast, eukaryotic cytoplasmic mRNAs have a 5′ cap structure. The initiation of most cytoplasmic mRNAs involves the interaction of initiation factors with the cap, which facilitates the binding of the 40 S subunit to the mRNA. The 40 S subunit then migrates in a 5′ to 3′ direction and usually initiates at the first AUG codon (35, 36). Since mitochondrial mRNAs are not capped (31) and lack a Shine/Dalgarno sequence, neither the prokaryotic nor cytoplasmic mechanism for translational initiation can be operating in this system.

One of the most interesting aspects of protein synthesis in animal mitochondria is the presence of unusual tRNAs. Animal mitochondrial tRNAs have a number of peculiar features that distinguish them from the tRNAs found in other systems. In general, mammalian mitochondrial tRNAs are shorter than their prokaryotic or eukaryotic cytoplasmic counterparts (59–75 nucleotides in length). They display numerous structural differences when compared to "normal" tRNAs. Many of these tRNAs can be folded into an L-shaped tertiary structure, but the D-loop/T-loop interactions in the elbow region do not exist or are considerably different from those of normal tRNAs (37–40). In other cases, they cannot be folded into the typical cloverleaf secondary structure and lack one or more of the invariant or semi-invariant residues found in other tRNAs (41, 42). For example, bovine tRNA$^{Ser}_{AGY}$ lacks the D-arm (40). An overall similarity in the shape of every tRNA is critical for its function on the ribosome. Information on the 3-D structures of the unusual mitochondrial tRNAs is essential for an understanding of their function in protein biosynthesis.

II. Initiation of Protein Biosynthesis in Mammalian Mitochondria

A. Overview of the Initiation of Protein Synthesis in Prokaryotes

The machinery required for the initiation of translation in mitochondria is thought to be more closely related to that of prokaryotes than to that found in the eukaryotic cell cytoplasm. Consequently, our extensive knowledge of initiation in *E. coli* can potentially serve as a model for initiation in mitochondria (43). In the current model for initiation in bacteria (Fig. 1), the 70 S ribosome is in equilibrium with its 50 S and 30 S subunits. IF-3 binds to the 30 S subunit, preventing its association with the 50 S subunit. Two routes are then proposed for the subsequent binding steps. In the first route, IF-2 binds to the 30 S:IF-3 complex with its binding enhanced by GTP (43). In the second route, IF-2 forms a complex with fMet-tRNA prior to delivering it to the P-site of the ribosome (44). IF-1 also binds to the small subunit where it is postulated to prevent premature binding of aminoacyl-tRNA to the portion of the 30 S

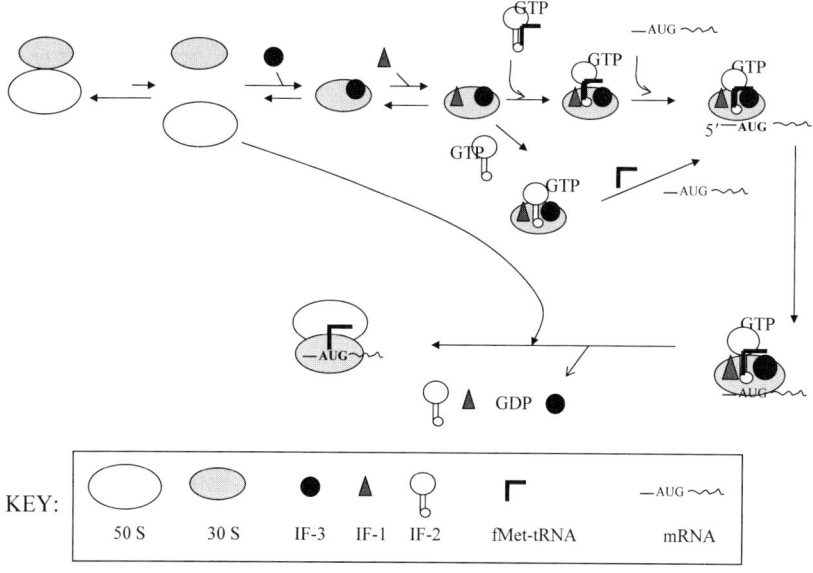

FIG. 1. Schematic diagram for the initiation of protein synthesis in bacteria. Two pathways for initiation are possible and are shown as alternative routes. In one route, IF-2 binds to the ribosome prior to fMet-tRNA binding while, in the alternative scheme, IF-2 brings fMet-tRNA to the ribosome as a binary or ternary complex.

subunit corresponding to the A-site of the 70 S ribosome (45). When both the mRNA and fMet-tRNA are present on the small subunit, an unstable pre-initiation complex forms. This complex is converted into a stable initiation complex when codon:anticodon interaction occurs. The order of binding of the mRNA and fMet-tRNA is believed to be random (43, 46). The 50 S ribosomal subunit then binds to the initiation complex, stimulating the release of IF-1 and IF-3. The release of IF-2 is accompanied by the hydrolysis of GTP. The resulting [70 S • fMet-tRNA • mRNA] complex (70 S initiation complex) is poised to enter the process of chain elongation.

B. Mitochondrial Initiation Factor 2 ($IF-2_{mt}$)

1. Purification and Characterization of Mammalian $IF-2_{mt}$

Initiation of protein synthesis in mammalian mitochondria begins with fMet-tRNA just as it does in bacteria (47). A number of years ago efforts were made to detect a factor in bovine liver mitochondria that could promote the binding of fMet-tRNA to mitochondrial ribosomes. These experiments were done with yeast cytoplasmic $fMet-tRNA_i^{Met}$ since the low abundance of mammalian mitochondrial tRNAs makes them difficult to obtain in significant amounts. $IF-2_{mt}$ was sought in the post-ribosomal supernatant of mitochondria since the ribosomes are obtained in 300 mM KCl and have a very low background of fMet-tRNA binding, suggesting that endogenous initiation factors had been removed during their preparation. Mammalian mitochondrial ribosomes have a much lower RNA content than other ribosomes, and electrostatic interactions between translational factors and ribosomes are not as strong as those observed in bacteria. Attempts to detect $IF-2_{mt}$ activity in the post-ribosomal supernatant were not successful. However, following chromatography on DEAE-cellulose, $IF-2_{mt}$ activity could be detected using an assay that measures the binding of fMet-tRNA to mitochondrial ribosomes (13). This protein was subsequently purified to homogeneity and characterized (12, 13).

Purified $IF-2_{mt}$ elutes from gel filtration columns as an 85 kDa protein. It appears to function as a monomer. In this respect, it is reminiscent of the bacterial IF-2 and distinct from the trimeric cytoplasmic factor eIF-2 that mediates $Met-tRNA_i$ binding to the 40 S subunit. Binding of fMet-tRNA to mitochondrial ribosomes requires a template such as AUG or poly(A,U,G) and is strongly stimulated by GTP (13).

2. The $IF-2_{mt}$ Gene

The human $IF-2_{mt}$ gene (MIF2) has been assigned to chromosome 2 bands p16 → p14. The gene spans just over 33,400 bp and is present as 16 exons and 15 introns (48). The transcriptional start site has been mapped to a

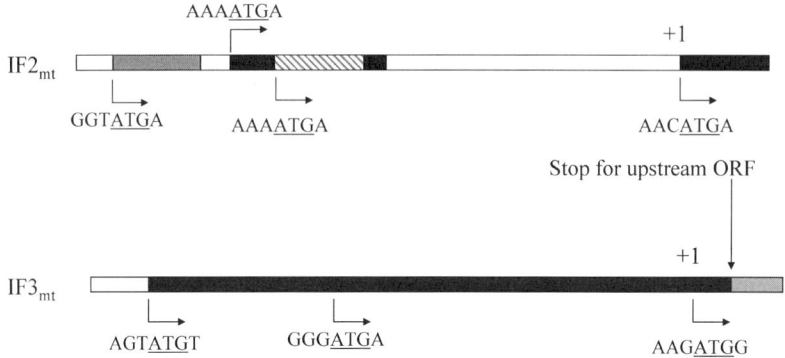

FIG. 2. 5′ untranslated regions of the IF-2_{mt} and IF-3_{mt} mRNAs. The mRNAs for both IF-2_{mt} and IF-3_{mt} have upstream AUG codons that may affect the translational efficiency of initiation at the start AUG.

cytosine residue 296 bp upstream of the AUG start codon (48). This promoter region has consensus binding sites for several transcriptional factors including Sp1, nuclear respiratory factor 1, and the estrogen receptor. Several enhancer sites have also been identified upstream of the start site.

The IF-2_{mt} transcript migrates at about 2.5 kb on Northerns (14). Analysis of the gene and cDNA sequences indicates that the 5′ untranslated region (5′ UTR) is 296 bases in length and contains 3 upstream AUG codons (Fig. 2). Two of these are in-frame with the start codon for IF-2_{mt} while the third is in an alternative reading frame. Interestingly, these upstream AUG codons are in a context rather similar to that seen with the legitimate start codon. All of them have a purine at −3 and an A at +4, positive elements in the Kozak scanning model for selection of the start codon in eukaryotic mRNAs (49). Hence, it seems likely that the upstream open reading frames (ORFs) will be expressed to some extent, leading to short polypeptide products. The presence of the upstream AUG codons may serve to reduce the amount of IF-2_{mt} synthesized. Since it is estimated that there are only 10 to 20 copies of IF-2_{mt} per mitochondrion, a low level of translational efficiency may be used to down-regulate the amount of this protein made by cells.

The abundance of the transcripts for IF-2_{mt} has been examined in various human tissues using Northern blots (14). Relatively abundant levels of the IF-2_{mt} transcript were detected in heart, skeletal muscle, and kidney. Somewhat lower levels were observed in other tissues including brain, lung, and pancreas. There appears to be a general correlation between the levels of the transcript observed and the energy demands of the tissue.

3. Sequence Analysis of IF-2_{mt}

Both human and bovine IF-2_{mt} have been cloned (14, 15), and the mature form of bovine IF-2_{mt} has been expressed in *E. coli* and purified as a C-terminally His-tagged protein. In addition, *Saccharomyces cerevisiae* IF-2_{mt} has recently been expressed in *E. coli* and purified (50). Prokaryotic IF-2 is organized into a number of discrete domains. The designations of these domains vary in different laboratories. For convenience, we will follow the domain organization and nomenclature used for *E. coli* IF-2, which is viewed as consisting of six domains (Fig. 3) (51). Domain I of *E. coli* IF-2 is present in the longest form of this factor (IF-2α). It is not present in a shorter form (IF-2β) that initiates at an in-frame GUG codon (52), nor is it present in the IF-2 from many other microorganisms. The role of Domain I is not understood. Recent structural studies (53) indicate that this domain is folded into a number of discrete subdomains. Domain II of *E. coli* IF-2 has recently been shown to be involved in the interaction of IF-2 with 30 S subunits, especially when this factor binds the ribosome in the absence of IF-1 (54, 55). This observation is surprising since Domain II is not present in the IF-2 found in a number of prokaryotes (Fig. 3). Domain III is viewed as a "linker" connecting Domains II and IV and is poorly characterized. Domain IV is the guanine nucleotide binding domain (G-domain). Domain V has been modeled as interacting with the 30 S subunit (56). Finally, the C-terminal domain (Domain VI) can be divided into two subdomains (C1 and C2). The C2 subdomain contains the fMet-tRNA recognition region (57–60).

The coding sequence of IF-2_{mt} begins with a signal peptide that specifies its import into mitochondria. The N-terminus of IF-2_{mt} is blocked but the

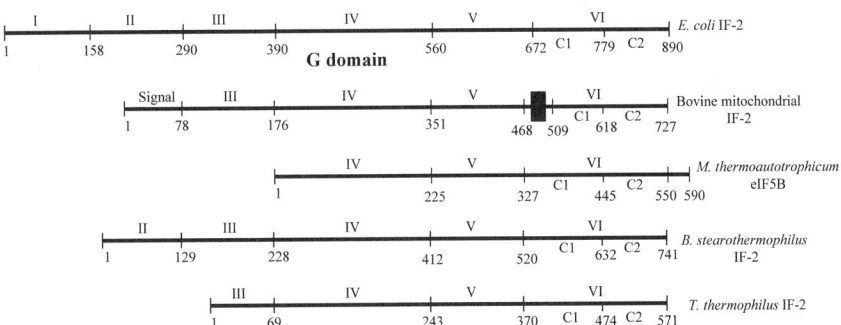

FIG. 3. Schematic organization of the domains of IF-2_{mt}. The domain organization is based on the six-domain model for *E. coli* IF-2 (151). Once the signal sequence is removed from IF-2_{mt}, the protein consists of Domains III–VI compared to *E. coli* IF-2. The numbers represent the amino acid residues at the junctions of the domains. The black box in IF-2_{mt} represents the insertion observed between Domains V and VI seen in the mitochondrial factors.

MitoProt II and PSORT programs consistently predict that the leader will be 77 residues in length. Thus, the mature form of IF-2$_{mt}$ is predicted to be 650 residues in length. Alignments of mammalian IF-2$_{mt}$ with the IF-2s from other organisms, thus, indicates that it consists essentially of Domains III–VI of *E. coli* IF-2 (Fig. 3). A similar observation has been made with the IF-2$_{mt}$ from *S. cerevisiae*, *Caenorhabditis elegans*, and *Drosophila melanogaster*. Thus, shorter forms of IF-2 may be characteristic of IF-2$_{mt}$. In contrast, alignment of IF-2 sequences from a variety of prokaryotes suggests that short forms of IF-2, beginning essentially with Domain III, are the exception rather than the rule. These shorter forms are found primarily among the extremophiles (*61*).

Since IF-2$_{mt}$ lacks Domain II, which is thought to be important for the binding of *E. coli* IF-2 to the 30 S subunit, it becomes an intriguing question of how this factor, and the shorter prokaryotic IF-2s, interact with the small subunit. Preliminary observations in our laboratory indicate that Domain III plays an important role in the interaction of IF-2$_{mt}$ with mitochondrial 28 S ribosomal subunits, particularly if fMet-tRNA is not present. In addition, GTP or a nonhydrolyzable analog of GTP which binds Domain IV is important for a stable interaction of this factor with the ribosome (Coursey and Spremulli, unpublished observations). Thus, the contacts between IF-2 and the small subunit may occur in a different manner with the mitochondrial factors than with the larger prokaryotic forms of IF-2. In this context, it should be noted that a yeast IF-2$_{mt}$ variant lacking Domain III is functional *in vivo* when overexpressed from a plasmid construct (*62*). These observations suggest that IF-2$_{mt}$ interacts with the small subunit through multiple contacts including Domain III and the initiator tRNA.

Domain III of IF-2$_{mt}$ is quite highly conserved between different species of mammals (Table I). However, a detailed analysis of the sequence of IF-2$_{mt}$ indicates that Domain III is quite poorly conserved in the mitochondrial factors found in organisms from different kingdoms in nature (Table I). Changes in the structure of the mitochondrial ribosome from different organisms, particularly in a number of the ribosomal proteins, may reflect, in part, differences in the nature of the residues of Domain III that contact the small subunit.

Domain IV, the G-domain (Fig. 3), is the most highly conserved region of IF-2 (Table I). In general, the G-domain is greater than 55% identical to the corresponding domains from the prokaryotic factors. It is over 90% identical among the known mammalian mitochondrial factors. Surprisingly, it is slightly less conserved relative to the mitochondrial factors from the lower eukaryotes than it is to the bacterial factors. A similar observation has been made with respect to the degree of conservation between the ribosomal proteins of bacteria, the mitochondria of lower eukaryotes, and mammalian mitochondrial ribosomal proteins (*27, 29*).

TABLE I
IDENTITIES OF VARIOUS DOMAINS OF IF-2 TO BOVINE IF-2$_{mt}$

Species	% Identity			
	Domain III	Domain IV	Domain V	Domain VI
Mouse mito	76	92	94	83
Homo sapiens mito	81	93	90	88
Drosophila mito	32	65	57	48
Apis mellifera mito	36	63	50	43
C. elegans mito	28	61	50	36
S. pombe mito	22	53	43	35
S. cerevisiae mito	19	53	38	33
Rickettsia	30	59	47	38
B. stearothermophilus	24	63	50	36
E. coli	22	66	51	30
T. thermophilus	26	56	35	32
B. subtilis	27	63	47	31
M. thermoautotrophicum	NA	43	19	23

All of the characteristic features found in the G-domains of other proteins are observed in bovine IF-2$_{mt}$. These include the 4 guanine nucleotide binding motifs (GXXXXGK is conserved with the prokaryotic factors as CHVDHGK, DXXGH is conserved as DTPGH, NKI/MD as NKCD, and SAL/K as SAL) and the switch 1 and switch 2 regions (Fig. 4). A model of the three-dimensional structure of the G-domain of IF-2$_{mt}$ has been created using Swiss-Model (63, 64) based on the coordinates of the G-domain of the eukaryotic cytoplasmic homolog eIF-5B (Fig. 4B). The G-domain of IF-2$_{mt}$ is 32% identical to that of eIF-5B. A large portion of the G-domain of IF-2$_{mt}$ can be fit into the coordinates of eIF-5B. The G-domain model shows significant structural similarity to eIF-5B, except for two predominantly helical regions of eIF-5B that are missing in IF-2$_{mt}$ (Fig. 4). These regions are also missing in the *E. coli* IF-2 G-domain model that closely resembles the G-domain of IF-2$_{mt}$ (65). The structural similarity of the G-domain of IF-2 to the G-domains of elongation factors EF-Tu and EF-G indicates that these translation factors share a similar interaction with the large ribosomal subunit.

Alignment of Domain V in prokaryotic and mitochondrial IF-2 indicates that it is rather highly conserved (Table I). There is generally between about 35 and 50% identity to the corresponding domains from prokaryotes. Little information is available about the biochemical function of Domain V and no

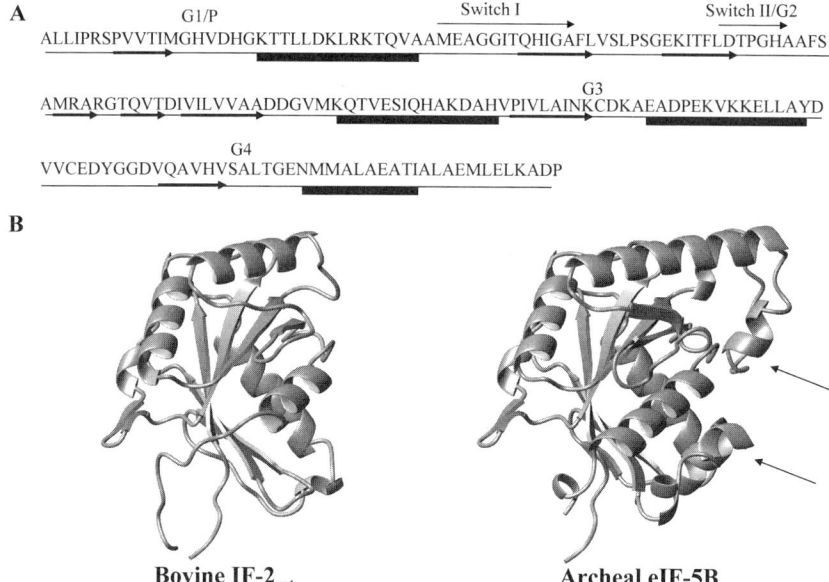

FIG. 4. Model of the G-domain of IF-2$_{mt}$ based on the crystal structure of the archeal homolog eIF-5B. (A) Primary sequence of the G-domain of bovine IF-2$_{mt}$. The four guanine nucleotide binding motifs are labeled G1 to G4. The switch 1 and switch 2 regions are indicated above the corresponding sequence. β-sheets are designated by the arrows under the sequence, while α-helices are indicated by the wide bars. (B) The coordinates of archeal eIF-5B (67) were used to construct a model of the G-domain of bovine IF-2$_{mt}$ using Swiss-Model. The PDB file used was 1G7T. Swiss-Model was used in the alignment mode and generated the G-domain model based on an alignment of the G-domain of IF-2$_{mt}$ (residues 177–350) with the sequence of M. thermoautotrophicum eIF-5B. Regions of eIF-5B that are missing in the IF-2$_{mt}$ model are indicated with an arrow.

data is available about its possible role in IF-2$_{mt}$. The structure of eIF-5B indicates that it folds into a structure similar to those observed in Domain II of EF-Tu and EF-G. It is thought to contact the small ribosomal subunit in the initiation complex (56). This domain of eIF-5B has been postulated to play an important role in mediating the ribosome-binding properties of this factor (66). It may play a similar role in IF-2$_{mt}$.

Domain V is followed by an insertion in mammalian IF-2$_{mt}$ that is at least partially present in the factors from lower eukaryotes (Figs. 3 and 5A). The precise position of this insertion depends on the number and origin of the species used in the alignment but it is clearly present in all alignments. The sequence of the insertion is quite well conserved among mammals but diverges greatly in other species both in length and in sequence (Fig. 5). This insertion is quite hydrophilic, having numerous acidic and basic residues. It is

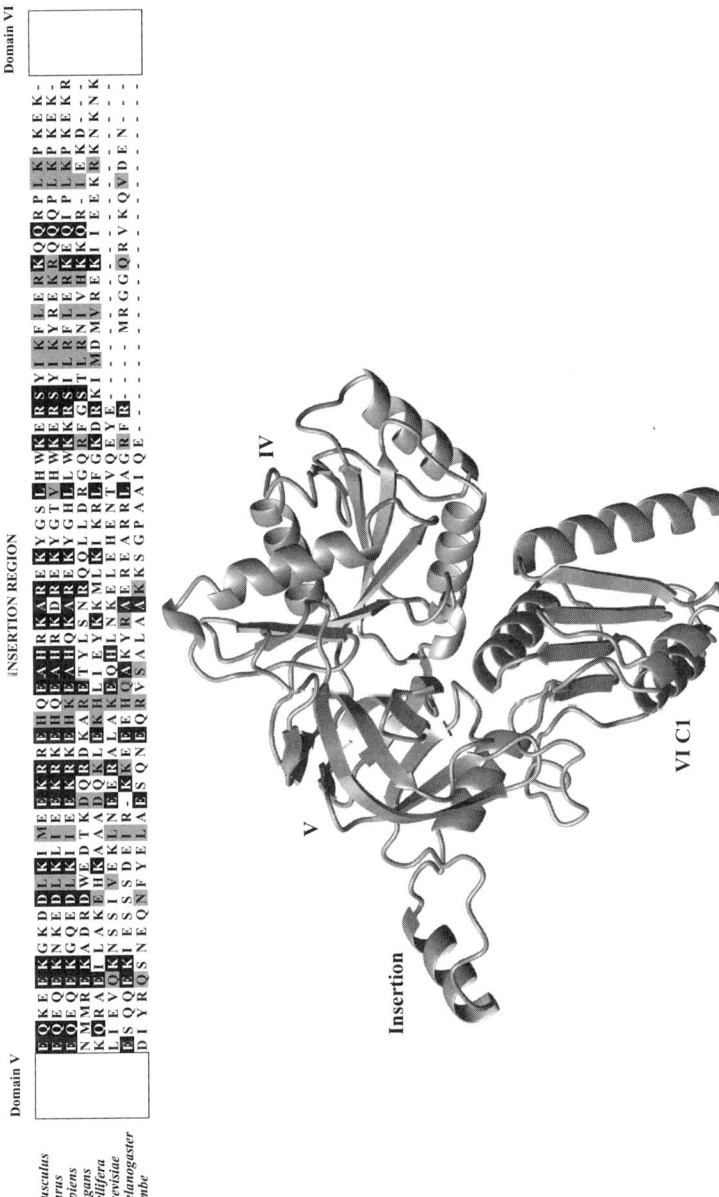

FIG. 5. Insertion region in IF-2$_{mt}$. (A) Alignment of the region between Domains V and VI of IF-2$_{mt}$ indicates that this region is longer in the mammalian mitochondrial factors than in the factors from the lower eukaryotes. (B) The insertion between Domains V and VI in bovine IF-2$_{mt}$ is modeled to project from the side of the molecule toward the small ribosomal subunit based on a recent model of IF-2 on the ribosome (56). This figure was generated using Swiss-Model in alignment mode based on an alignment of IF-2$_{mt}$, starting with the G-domain (residues 177–727) with the sequence of *M. thermoautotrophicum* eIF-5B. Domains IV–VI C1 of IF-2$_{mt}$ are modeled based on sequence similarity to Domains I–III of eIF-5B. The C2 subdomain of IF-2$_{mt}$ did not model well against Domain IV of eIF-5B due to the low sequence conservation and, therefore, was omitted in the model shown.

predicted to form a helical secondary structure. Swiss-Model suggests that this region follows helix 8 when eIF-5B is used as a possible model for the structure of IF-2_{mt} (Fig. 5B). Interestingly, this region is modeled to form a loop containing a helical stretch protruding from the surface of the protein. This view suggests that it may play an important role in the function of IF-2_{mt}. Little is known about how IF-2 binds to ribosomes. Some chemical nuclease data indicate that Domain V is in contact with the subunit interface side of the 30 S subunit (56). The insertion lying between Domains V and VI of IF-2_{mt} can actually be modeled to contact the 30 S subunit in the region close to the binding site for IF-1. Perhaps this insertion plays the role of prokaryotic IF-1 in mammalian mitochondrial translation (see following text).

Domain VI is about 30 to 40% identical between the prokaryotic and mitochondrial factors. Domain VI of IF-2 is divided into two subdomains, designated C1 and C2. These subdomains are probably separated by a long helical segment based on the crystal structure of eIF-5B (67). The C2 domain plays a critical role in the binding of fMet-tRNA (59, 60). The structure of this subdomain has been determined for *Bacillus stearothermophilus* IF-2 (68). IF-2_{mt} appears to be reasonably well aligned to the prokaryotic factors in Domain VI and presumably has a similar fold. Mutagenic studies have implicated several residues that are at or near the binding site for fMet-tRNA in the C2 subdomain of Domain VI of *B. stearothermophilus* IF-2 (57, 69). With few exceptions, these residues are conserved in IF-2_{mt}, suggesting that many of the contacts between bacterial IF-2 and fMet-tRNA have been conserved in the mammalian mitochondrial factors.

4. INTERACTION OF IF-2_{mt} WITH TRNA

The initiation of protein biosynthesis in bacteria and mitochondria generally begins with formylmethionine. Interestingly, unlike all other translational systems, animal mitochondria have a single gene for tRNA^{Met} (30). There is no evidence for the import of tRNAs in mammalian mitochondria. Hence, this gene must give rise to both the initiator tRNA (fMet-tRNA) and the elongator tRNA (Met-tRNA) in protein synthesis.

Examination of the sequence of this tRNA (Fig. 6) suggests that it has features reminiscent of a combination of features of prokaryotic and eukaryotic cytoplasmic initiator tRNAs (70, 71). However, it also has properties that allow it to interact with mitochondrial elongation factor Tu (EF-Tu$_{mt}$). Several features generally distinguish initiator tRNA species from tRNAs participating in chain elongation; (1) virtually all initiator tRNAs have three consecutive G:C base pairs at the bottom of the anticodon stem. This feature is observed in the mitochondrial tRNA^{Met}; (2) prokaryotic initiator tRNAs generally lack a Watson-Crick base pair between nucleotides 1 and 72 (numbering according to Sprinzl (72)). This feature serves as a negative determinant for interaction with EF-Tu, facilitating the exclusion of (f)Met − tRNA$_f^{Met}$ from the elongation cycle. It serves as a positive determinant for the Met-tRNA transformylase and may play a role in increasing the affinity of IF-2 for the initiator tRNA (73). In contrast, eukaryotic cytoplasmic initiator tRNAs generally have an A:U pair at this position while eukaryotic elongator tRNAs generally have a G:C pair in this position. Mammalian mitochondrial tRNA^{Met}, like cytoplasmic initiator tRNAs, has an A:U pair at the end of the acceptor stem (Fig. 6). The base pair at the end of the acceptor arm apparently allows the interaction of IF-2$_{mt}$ with fMet-tRNA while also allowing the interaction of mitochondrial Met-tRNA^{Met} with EF-Tu$_{mt}$. A large number of mammalian mitochondrial elongator tRNAs also have an A1:U72 pair at the beginning of the acceptor helix; (3) bacterial initiator tRNAs also have a purine11:pyrimidine24 base pair while other tRNAs generally have a pyrimidine11:purine24 pair. The purine11:pyrimidine24 base pair found in the prokaryotic initiator tRNA is also present in the mitochondrial initiator tRNA. This feature may be important for the recognition of this tRNA by the Met-tRNA transformylase (74); (4) eukaryotic cytoplasmic initiator tRNAs lack the TΨC sequence in loop IV and always have A54 and A60 instead of T54 and a pyrimidine at position 60. In contrast, mammalian mitochondrial tRNA^{Met} has U54 and a pyrimidine at position 60. In this respect, it resembles the prokaryotic initiator and elongator tRNAs except for the absence of the methylation of the U at position 54. The importance of these features in the mammalian mitochondrial tRNA^{Met} remains to be determined.

Most tRNAs in both prokaryotes and eukaryotes have a significant number of minor bases. In contrast, mitochondrial tRNAs have few modifications. Bovine mitochondrial tRNA^{Met} has 3 modifications, two Ψ at positions 27 and 50 and the unusual modification f^{5}C at the first position of the anticodon (71). This latter modification may be important for the ability of this tRNA to decode both AUG and AUA codons (75).

In prokaryotes and mitochondria, initiation occurs with fMet-tRNA. Early studies with yeast and E. coli (f)Met − tRNA$_i^{Met}$ indicated that bovine IF-2$_{mt}$ has a strong preference for promoting the binding of the formylated derivative to ribosomes. This preference is between 20- and 50-fold with both yeast and E. coli tRNA$_i^{Met}$ (12). No studies have yet been done with the mitochondrial Met-tRNA^{Met} directly. However, studies in yeast mitochondria have shown that initiation of protein synthesis in this organelle can occur without formylation of the initiator tRNA (76). In agreement with this observation, Garofalo et al. (50) have noted that purified yeast IF-2$_{mt}$ binds both fMet-tRNA and Met-tRNA, with the binding of the formylated derivative being only about 4-fold stronger than the binding of the unformylated Met-tRNA. The work of Tibbetts et al. (62) indicates that bovine IF-2$_{mt}$ can replace the normal yeast factor *in vivo* and that the mammalian factor can support mitochondrial

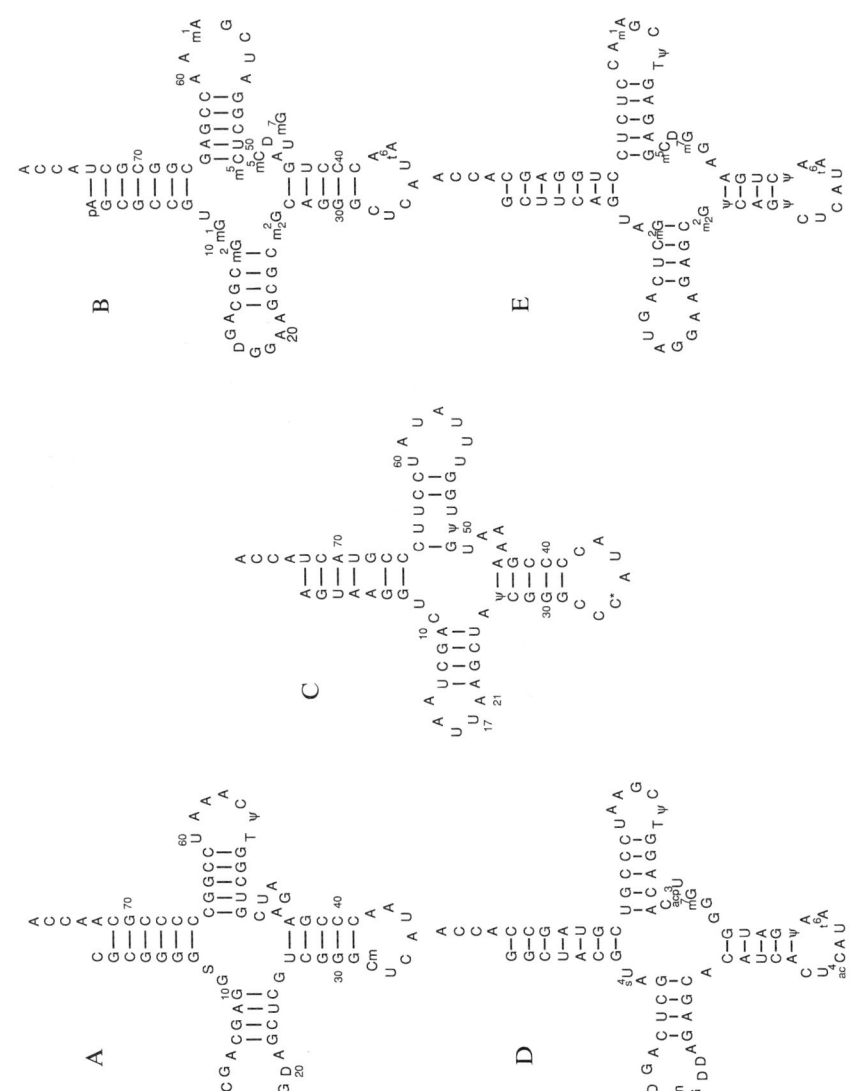

protein synthesis in the absence of formylation of the yeast mitochondrial initiator tRNA (62). These results suggest that mammalian IF-2_{mt} may also be able to initiate translation with Met-tRNA. Further studies using the homologous mammalian mitochondrial system will be required to clarify this point.

5. POSSIBLE BINDING SITE FOR IF-2_{mt} ON MITOCHONDRIAL RIBOSOMES

As has been mentioned, mammalian mitochondrial ribosomes are rich in proteins while having a lower amount of rRNA. About half of the prokaryotic small subunit ribosomal proteins have homologs in the 28 S subunit (27). IF-2 binding to ribosomes occurs first on the small subunit where it promotes the codon-dependent placement of fMet-tRNA in the P-site. It is then thought to span the region between the subunits, making contact with the 3' end of the tRNA near the peptidyl transferase center and also contacting the L7/L12 stalk, important in the activation of the GTPase activity of IF-2. Studies of *E. coli* IF-2 binding to ribosomes indicates that this factor is located on the head and platform of the small subunit (56, 61). In general, agreement with this idea is the observation that *E. coli* IF-2 can be cross-linked to ribosomal proteins S1, S2, S11, S12, S13, S14, and S19 (77, 78). Of these proteins, homologs of S2, S11, S12, and S14 are observed in mitochondrial 28 S subunits. These proteins are likely to be located near the IF-2_{mt} binding site. However, proteins S13 and S19, located in the head of the small subunit, are not present in these ribosomes and contacts between IF-2_{mt} and members of the new classes of ribosomal proteins found in mammalian mitochondria are probable.

Like IF-2 from certain prokaryotes such as *T. thermophilus*, IF-2_{mt} lacks Domain II, which is thought to be involved in binding small subunits (54). As has been mentioned, studies from our laboratory indicate that Domain III of IF-2_{mt} is critical for the binding of IF-2_{mt} to the 28 S subunit. There is no corresponding domain in eIF-5B and no information on contacts between this region of IF-2 and the small subunit are currently available. The binding of IF-2_{mt} occurs readily in the absence of fMet-tRNA. However, it appears that a nonhydrolyzable analog of GTP such as guanosine 5'-[β-γ-imido] triphosphate (GDPNP) is critical for the stable binding of IF-2_{mt} to small subunits. As indicated in Fig. 3, IF-2_{mt} contains an insertion between Domains V and VI. In current models of IF-2 or eIF-5B binding to ribosomes (56, 66), Domain V appears to be in contact with the small subunit and the insertion region may play a critical role in IF-2_{mt} binding to 28 S subunits.

FIG. 6. Structures of tRNA^{Met}. The mitochondrial tRNA^{Met} has features of both prokaryotic and eukaryotic initiator tRNAs and of tRNAs used for chain elongation. (A) *E. coli* tRNA$_f^{Met}$; (B) yeast tRNA$_i^{Met}$; (C) Bovine mitochondrial tRNA^{Met}. The ° in this sequence represents the minor base 5-formylC (71); (D) *E. coli* tRNA$_m^{Met}$; (E) yeast tRNA$_m^{Met}$.

C. Mitochondrial Initiation Factor 3 (IF-3$_{mt}$)

1. IDENTIFICATION AND EXPRESSION OF MAMMALIAN IF-3$_{mt}$

In prokaryotes, IF-3 is a small (less than 200 residue) initiation factor that has a number of roles in initiation. IF-3 binds to the 30 S subunit and inhibits its association with the 50 S subunit, thus ensuring a supply of 30 S subunits for initiation. IF-3 also promotes the conversion of the preinitiation complex to the initiation complex, at least in part, by an adjustment of the position of the mRNA on the 30 S subunit (Fig. 1) (79–82). Further, IF-3 acts to switch the decoding preference of the small ribosomal subunit from elongator tRNAs to the initiator tRNA, thus playing a proofreading role in initiation (83–85). Some studies have shown that IF-3 also plays a role in removing the deacylated tRNA from the 30 S subunit following chain termination (86).

Biochemical approaches such as those used to identify IF-2$_{mt}$ did not allow the detection of additional initiation factors. However, it seemed likely that mammalian mitochondria would contain a factor equivalent to IF-3. This idea was reinforced by the observation that, although the mammalian mitochondrial ribosome has a truncated small subunit rRNA, the portions of the rRNA where IF-3 is thought to bind are present (87). Further, the ribosomal proteins with which IF-3 interacts (S7, S11, and S18) have homologs in the 28 S subunit. Hence, it was logical to postulate that mammalian mitochondria contain a homolog of bacterial IF-3. Cyberprobing the human EST database with the amino acid sequence of IF-3 from a variety of bacterial species failed to provide any convincing evidence for mammalian IF-3$_{mt}$. However, extensive database searches with the sequences of IF-3 from the *Mycoplasma* and the IF-3 homology domain of *Euglena gracilis* chloroplast IF-3 (IF-3$_{chl}$) provided a hit in both the human and mouse EST databases.

The open reading frame encoding the region predicted to be present in the mature form of IF-3$_{mt}$ (see following text) was cloned and expressed in *E. coli* (88). The activity of the expressed protein was tested in initiation complex formation using both bacterial and mitochondrial ribosomes. IF-3$_{mt}$ stimulated fMet-tRNA binding to ribosomes in the presence of poly(A,U,G) as an mRNA and with IF-2$_{mt}$ to promote the stable binding of the initiator tRNA. In addition, it promoted the binding of fMet-tRNA to ribosomes programmed with an *in vitro* transcript of the cytochrome oxidase subunit II mRNA. The activity of IF-3$_{mt}$ in these assays appears to be largely due to its ability to promote the dissociation of the ribosome into its subunits since little stimulation was observed when isolated small subunits were used (88). Detailed studies of the properties of this factor remain to be carried out.

2. Gene Organization and Sequence Analysis of IF-3_{mt}

The gene for IF-3_{mt} is located on chromosome 13 locus q12.2. The gene spans nearly 15,800 base pairs and contains 9 exons with 8 introns (RefSeq locus 219402). The mRNA is just over 1 kb in length with a 5' UTR of 136 bases. This 5' UTR has an upstream open reading frame that terminates downstream of the AUG start codon for the IF-3_{mt} (Fig. 2). This upstream AUG has a purine at -3 but a U at $+4$, placing it in a less favorable context for initiation than the start AUG, which has the desired purine at -3 and a G at $+4$. It is possible that a certain fraction of the ribosomes loading onto the IF-3_{mt} mRNA initiate at the first AUG codon while another fraction scans past the first AUG codon and a second AUG codon in the same frame (Fig. 2) to initiate at the IF-3_{mt} start codon itself. These upstream AUG codons are likely to reduce somewhat the expression of the protein from this mRNA. This is reasonable since very low levels of IF-3_{mt} (in all likelihood, fewer than 20 copies per mitochondrion) are probably required.

The open reading frame for IF-3_{mt} encodes a 278 amino acid protein (Fig. 7). MitoProt II gives this protein a 97% probability to be localized in mitochondria and predicts that the mature protein will be 247 residues in length. Structural studies on IF-3 from *E. coli* and *Bacillus stearothermophilus* indicate that it folds into two domains (N-domain and C-domain) that are separated by a flexible linker about 45 Å in length (Fig. 7) (89–93). The C-terminal domain is capable of carrying out all of the known functions of IF-3, including binding to the 30 S subunit and promoting subunit dissociation (94). However, the N-terminal domain strongly enhances the binding of IF-3 to the small subunit (95). The mature form of IF-3_{mt} is predicted to have a 30 residue N-terminal extension (Fig. 7) when compared to *E. coli* IF-3. An N-terminal extension of about 150 residues has been noted on *E. gracilis* IF-3_{chl} (96). Heterogeneity in the length of the N-terminus is observed in the IF-3 species in various microorganisms. However, none of the prokaryotic IF-3 sequences currently available in the databases is as long as that observed with IF-3_{mt}. The longest extension observed to date is from *Wigglesworthia brevipalpis* (an obligate endocellular endosymbiont of the tsetse fly), which is 14 residues shorter than the predicted mature form of IF-3_{mt} at the N-terminus.

IF-3_{mt} also has a C-terminal extension just over 30 residues long. Overall, it is quite hydrophilic and highly charged, having 9 acidic and 5 basic residues. Most of the prokaryotic factors are 30 to 35 residues shorter than IF-3_{mt} in this region (Fig. 7). The C-terminal extension, like the N-terminal extension, is predicted to have significant helical content. A 63-residue acidic C-terminal extension on *E. gracilis* IF-3_{chl} has been shown to reduce the activity of the chloroplast factor in initiation complex formation and may serve as a potential regulatory region (97).

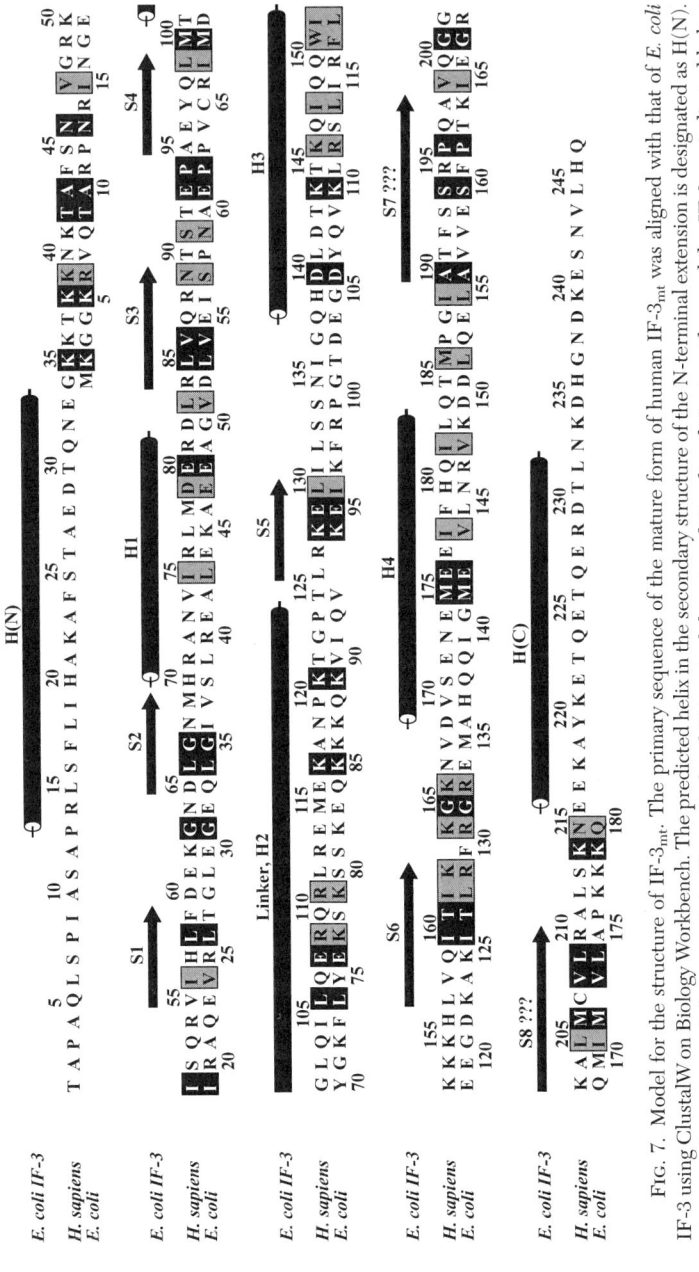

FIG. 7. Model for the structure of IF-3$_{mt}$. The primary sequence of the mature form of human IF-3$_{mt}$ was aligned with that of *E. coli* IF-3 using ClustalW on Biology Workbench. The predicted helix in the secondary structure of the N-terminal extension is designated as H(N). The secondary structural elements of the N-terminal and C-terminal domains of *E. coli* and *B. stearothermophilus* IF-3 are indicated below the amino acid sequence. The regions of this structure that can be modeled by Swiss-Model to fit the sequence of IF-3$_{mt}$ are indicated without question marks. The regions including sheets S7 and S8 that cannot be modeled in IF-3$_{mt}$ and that are not predicted to form a sheet structure using the PELE combined structure prediction program in Biology Workbench are indicated as ??. The predicted helical structure in the C-terminal extension of IF-3$_{mt}$ is indicated as H(C). The linker between the N-terminal and C-terminal domains is indicated as a helix (H2). However, NMR data obtained in solution indicates that this region is flexible *(152)*.

The region of IF-3$_{mt}$ with homology to the bacterial factors is actually not very highly conserved, showing generally less than 25% identity to its prokaryotic homologs. The most closely related prokaryotic homologs based on BLAST searches are from the *Mycoplasma*. Interestingly, somewhat greater homology is observed between human IF-3$_{mt}$ and many of the chloroplast IF-3s than between IF-3$_{mt}$ and the IF-3s from most bacterial species. No reasonable homolog of IF-3$_{mt}$ has yet been detected in *S. cerevisiae*.

The C-terminal domain of IF-3 is thought to be responsible for most of the binding interactions with the small subunit. Crystallography experiments have placed the C-terminal domain of IF-3 on the back of the platform of the small subunit (98). In contrast, cryoEM and footprinting work indicate that it is located on the side that interacts with the 50 S subunit (87, 99). Most of the residues in the C-terminal domain of IF-3 that contact the 30 S are in two helical segments, designated H3 and H4 (Fig. 7) and in several loop regions (87, 98, 100). Of these residues, those in H3 appear to be conserved or are conservative replacements in IF-3$_{mt}$. Much of the C-terminal domain of IF-3$_{mt}$ is poorly conserved with respect to its prokaryotic homologs. Swiss-Model is unable to develop a 3-D portrait of the C-terminal domain of IF-3$_{mt}$. Further, secondary structure prediction programs suggest that 2 of the 4 strands of the β-sheet (S7 and S8) in the C-terminal domain of prokaryotic IF-3 may not fold into a β-sheet conformation in IF-3$_{mt}$ (Fig. 7).

In prokaryotes, IF-3 is responsible for proofreading the selection of the initiation codon and the initiator tRNA. This property can be detected in the isolated C-terminal domain of bacterial IF-3 (94), but is strongly enhanced by conserved residues in the linker region including Tyr70, Gly71, and Tyr75 (81, 101, 102). Interestingly, these highly conserved residues in prokaryotic IF-3s are not conserved in human IF-3$_{mt}$. In mammalian mitochondria, both AUG and AUA (normally an isoleucine codon) serve as initiation codons. Furthermore, the initiator tRNA must play a role in both initiation and elongation. Consequently, the proofreading properties of human IF-3$_{mt}$ could be quite different from those of the bacterial factors.

Searches of the EST databases for homologs of human IF-3$_{mt}$ indicate the presence of a homologous protein in a variety of vertebrates including mouse, cow, and puffer fish. In general, the mammalian mitochondrial proteins are greater than 65% identical to human IF-3$_{mt}$. In contrast, puffer fish IF-3$_{mt}$ is only 31% identical to the human protein while *Drosophila* IF-3$_{mt}$ is only 23% identical. A homolog is not clearly detectable in *C. elegans*. Thus, the sequence of IF-3$_{mt}$ has not been as strongly conserved as has the sequence of IF-2$_{mt}$.

D. The Question of Initiation Factor 1 (IF-1$_{mt}$) in Mammalian Mitochondria

Both IF-2 (eIF-5B) and IF-1 (eIF-1A) are considered to be universal initiation factors, being observed in prokaryotes, archaea, and eukaryotes (*103, 104*). However, no ortholog to IF-1 has been observed in mitochondria and it is currently unclear whether mammalian mitochondria have a homolog of bacterial IF-1. IF-1 is the smallest of the three initiation factors and is essential for the viability of the cell (*105*). A number of different functions have been ascribed to IF-1 including (1) enhancement of the rate of subunit association and dissociation; (2) stimulation of the activities of IF-2 and IF-3; and (3) enhancement of the interaction of IF-2 with the ribosome. The binding of IF-1 to 30 S subunits footprints to regions of the 16 S rRNA that forms the A-site, and it has been suggested that IF-1 blocks the A-site during initiation, thereby contributing to the fidelity of selection of the start site (*45*). Furthermore, the crystal structure of IF-1 bound to the 30 S subunit indicates that it affects the conformation of functionally important residues in helix 44 near the A-site. Analysis of the regions of the small subunit rRNA present in mammalian mitochondrial ribosomes indicates that, although helix 44 is shorter in mitochondrial ribosomes, residues thought to be important for IF-1 binding have been conserved (*106*).

The eukaryotic ortholog of IF-2 (eIF-5B) is thought to play a role in the joining of the large subunit during initiation (*107, 108*). The ortholog of IF-1 (eIF-1A) has a three-dimensional fold quite similar to that observed with IF-1 and has been shown to interact with eIF-5B directly (*109–111*). Since IF-1 and IF-2 appear to be "universal" factors in translational systems, and since IF-2 is clearly present in mammalian mitochondria, we would expect to find a mitochondrial equivalent of IF-1.

Two approaches present themselves in seeking to identify a putative IF-1$_{mt}$. The first is a biochemical approach in which the ability of IF-1 to stimulate initiation complex formation is used in efforts to detect such a factor in mitochondrial extracts or in fractions derived from such extracts. To date, biochemical approaches have been unsuccessful in detecting the activity of an IF-1$_{mt}$. However, such an activity could be very difficult to detect for several reasons. First, IF-1 generally stimulates formation of initiation complexes rather than being completely required. This stimulation often affects the kinetics of complex formation rather than its extent. Thus, designing the proper assay for such a factor can be rather challenging. Second, IF-1$_{mt}$, like IF-2$_{mt}$, is probably present at extremely low levels in mitochondria. It is estimated that there are only about 10 copies of IF-2$_{mt}$ per mitochondrion in bovine liver. Thus, there may be too little of the factor present to be detected by standard filter binding assays used to measure initiation complex formation.

The second approach to the identification of IF-1_{mt} is through cyber-searching, such as was used successfully to identify IF-3_{mt}. This approach has been attempted extensively using a variety of IF-1 sequences as a cyberprobe without success. However, IF-1 is a small protein (about 70 to 80 amino acids) which is not highly conserved in primary sequence. Hence, BLAST searches are not likely to pick out correct ESTs. Further, since IF-1 is less than 100 residues, it would not generally be cataloged as a protein sequence in the databases summarizing genome sequence information. Extensive searches of the simple genomes of *S. pombe* and *S. cerevisiae* have not allowed the detection of an IF-1_{mt} in these organisms, nor is an apparent IF-1 homolog cataloged in the proteins listed for these organisms.

In an effort to determine whether mammalian mitochondria might contain an IF-1 species, initiation complex formation assays using both *E. coli* 70 S and mitochondrial 55 S ribosomes were carried out with IF-2_{mt} and IF-3_{mt} in the presence and absence of *E. coli* IF-1 (88). The presence of *E. coli* IF-1 has essentially no effect on initiation complex formation on 55 S ribosomes in the presence of IF-3_{mt} and IF-2_{mt}. This observation suggests that the mitochondrial system may not require a factor directly equivalent to IF-1. Furthermore, *E. coli* IF-1 did not stimulate the activity of IF-2_{mt} on 70 S ribosomes. IF-2_{mt} alone actually stimulates initiation complex formation on 70 S ribosomes as effectively as *E. coli* IF-2 in the presence of IF-1. The activity of *E. coli* IF-3, like that of IF-2, is stimulated by IF-1. However, in the presence of saturating levels of IF-2_{mt}, *E. coli* IF-1 fails to stimulate the activity of IF-3_{mt} on 70 S ribosomes. Taken together, these results suggest that IF-2_{mt} and IF-3_{mt} function efficiently in initiation complex formation in the absence of IF-1.

Interestingly, the insertion in mammalian IF-2_{mt} observed between domains V and VI can be modeled to interact with the 28 S subunit close to the position where IF-1 is placed in the crystal structure of the 30 S • IF-1 complex (*106*). It is possible that the insertion has assumed the role of IF-1 in mammalian mitochondria. Further investigation will be required to determine whether there is a factor equivalent to IF-1 in mitochondria or whether mitochondrial systems have bypassed the need for such a factor.

III. Elongation Factors in Mammalian Mitochondria

A. Overview of the Elongation Cycle

During polypeptide chain elongation (Fig. 8), aminoacyl-tRNAs (aa-tRNAs) are brought to the decoding site on the ribosome in the form of a ternary complex consisting of Elongation Factor Tu (EF-Tu), aminoacyl-tRNA (aa-tRNA), and GTP. Upon cognate codon:anticodon interactions, the GTP in the ternary complex is hydrolyzed and EF-Tu is released from the ribosome as

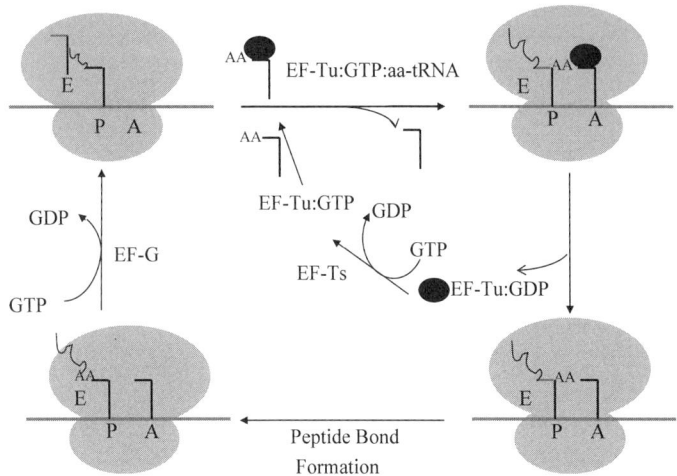

FIG. 8. Overview of the elongation cycle. The basic steps of the elongation cycle as they occur in prokaryotes and mitochondria are indicated. The large gray circles represent the large and small ribosomal subunits. The inverted "L" indicates the tRNA. The mRNA is shown as a line.

an EF-Tu • GDP complex. The exchange of GDP for GTP is catalyzed by the guanine nucleotide exchange factor, Elongation Factor Ts (EF-Ts). This exchange reaction proceeds through the formation of an intermediate EF-Tu • Ts complex. The peptide from the peptidyl-tRNA in the P-site of the ribosome is transferred to the amino acid of the aa-tRNA in the A-site through the action of the peptidyl transferase center in the 50 S subunit. Following peptide bond formation, Elongation Factor G (EF-G) catalyzes the translocation step in which the deacylated tRNA in the P-site is moved to the exit site (E-site), the peptidyl-tRNA is moved into the P-site, and the ribosome moves 3 nucleotides relative to the mRNA, exposing a new codon in the A-site. The cycle repeats with a new ternary complex entering the A-site.

Generally, the basic steps in the elongation cycle in mammalian mitochondria are the same as those observed in *E. coli*. However, several of the equilibrium dissociation constants governing the interactions of factors with their ligands are quite different from those of their *E. coli* counterparts (Table II). The properties of these factors will be discussed in more detail.

B. Mitochondrial Elongation Factor Tu (EF-Tu$_{mt}$)

1. INITIAL OBSERVATIONS

A complex of EF-Tu$_{mt}$ and EF-Ts$_{mt}$ (EF-Tu • Ts$_{mt}$) was first isolated from crude extracts of bovine liver mitochondria in the late 1980s (112). This complex was tightly associated and could not be dissociated by GDP

TABLE II
COMPARISON OF BINDING CONSTANTS OF E. COLI EF-TU AND EF-TU$_{mt}$ FOR LIGANDS

Ligand	K_d E. coli EF-Tu	K_d EF-Tu$_{mt}$	Reference
GDP	0.0077 μM	1.0 μM	(18, 154)
GTP	0.3 μM	18 μM	(18, 154)
E. coli EF-Ts	2 nM	Not detectable	(135, 154)
EF-Ts$_{mt}$	0.09 nM	5.5 nM	(17, 18)
E. coli Phe-tRNA	1.1 nM	18 nM	(17, 155)
Mitochondrial Phe-tRNA[a]	70 nM	70 nM	Unpublished

[a]From bovine liver mitochondria.

concentrations as high as 1 mM. Extensive efforts have been made to detect free EF-Tu$_{mt}$ or an EF-Tu$_{mt}$•GDP complex in extracts of mammalian mitochondria. Neither of these forms has been observed (7). Furthermore, Western blotting of mitochondrial extracts indicates that these two factors are present in a 1:1 ratio in mammalian mitochondria (7). This observation is in contrast to the 8-fold molar excess of EF-Tu over EF-Ts observed in most prokaryotic systems (113). Estimates of the amount of the EF-Tu•Ts$_{mt}$ complex present in mitochondria indicate that there are approximately 400 copies per mitochondrion. This number is in sharp contrast to the amount of EF-Tu present in E. coli (approximately 200,000 molecules/cell), which is about the same size as liver mitochondria (112). Thus, estimated intracellular concentrations of the translational factors are quite different in prokaryotes and in mammalian mitochondria.

2. SEQUENCE CONSERVATION OF EF-Tu$_{mt}$

The sequence of the cDNA for EF-Tu$_{mt}$ was determined first as a cDNA overexpressed in certain human tumors (114), and then through peptide sequencing of the purified protein from bovine liver (3). The gene for this protein is located in the nuclear genome. There are two known copies of the gene in higher mammals. The functional gene in humans is located at chromosomal position 16p11.2 while another copy, or a pseudo-gene, is located near the centromere of chromosome 17. The functional copy of the gene contains 9 introns and spans about 6000 bp. However, the mode of its transcription and potential translational regulation are unknown. EF-Tu$_{mt}$ is synthesized as a precursor with a 43-amino acid mitochondrial import sequence located at the N-terminus. The N-terminus of the mature protein has been determined directly by Edman degradation (3). The mature form of the protein is 409 amino acids in length. The major difference between the mammalian mitochondrial factor and bacterial EF-Tu is the presence of an 11-amino acid extension at the C-terminus of EF-Tu$_{mt}$.

Overall, this protein is highly conserved, being 55 to 60% identical to bacterial EF-Tu and it is divided into the same basic 3-domain structure. Domain I of EF-Tu is the guanine nucleotide binding domain (G-domain). Alignment of this region of EF-Tu with the EF-Tu from a variety of bacteria and mitochondria indicates that it contains all of the expected motifs for a guanine nucleotide binding protein (Fig. 9). The consensus amino acid sequences known to be involved in guanine nucleotide binding are GXXXXGK, DXXG, NKXD, and SALK, which interact with the phosphates, the magnesium ion coordinated to the β-phosphate group, and the guanine ring (*115, 116*). In both bovine and human EF-Tu$_{mt}$, these sequences are represented as GHVDHGK (amino acids 21 to 29 of the mature protein, Fig. 9), DCPG (amino acids 83 to 86), NKAD (amino acids 138–141), and SALC (amino acids 176–179).

The 3-D structure of the EF-Tu$_{mt}$•GDP complex has been determined at 1.94 Å resolution (Figs. 9 and 10) (*9*). As expected, the overall fold of EF-Tu$_{mt}$ is similar to that observed with the prokaryotic factors (Fig. 10A). Domain I (amino acids 1–204 of the mature form of the protein) contains the guanine nucleotide binding pocket and is formed from eight α-helices and eight β-sheets (Fig. 9). The guanine nucleotide binding pocket is structured identically to that seen in the prokaryotic factors. All of the ligands to the GDP have been conserved. A linker of 11 amino acids connects Domain I to Domain II. Domain II is composed of 11 β-sheets organized in a Greek key motif and encompasses residues 216 to 298. It is connected to Domain III by a short 6-amino acid peptide. Domain III is organized as a β-sheet formed by six β-strands folded into a jelly roll motif. Following Domain III, there is a short 11-amino acid extension which forms one helical turn. This extension seems to be specific to the mitochondrial factors and has not been observed in any of the prokaryotic factors.

When Domain I of bovine EF-Tu$_{mt}$ is overlaid on Domain I of *T. aquaticus* EF-Tu, it is clear that the structures are very similar. Domains II and III act as a rigid body and again an overlay of this region of EF-Tu$_{mt}$ with the prokaryotic factors indicates a high degree of tertiary structure conservation. However, the orientation of Domain I with respect to Domains II/III is altered in EF-Tu$_{mt}$ compared to the prokaryotic factors. This difference in orientation (19° and 12°, respectively, when comparing EF-Tu$_{mt}$•GDP to the equivalent structures from *T. aquaticus* and *E. coli*) presumably arises from slightly different surface contacts between the domains in the EF-Tu$_{mt}$ compared to bacterial EF-Tu. This slightly different orientation is accommodated by the flexible linker between the Domain I and Domain II (Fig. 10B). Since no other structures

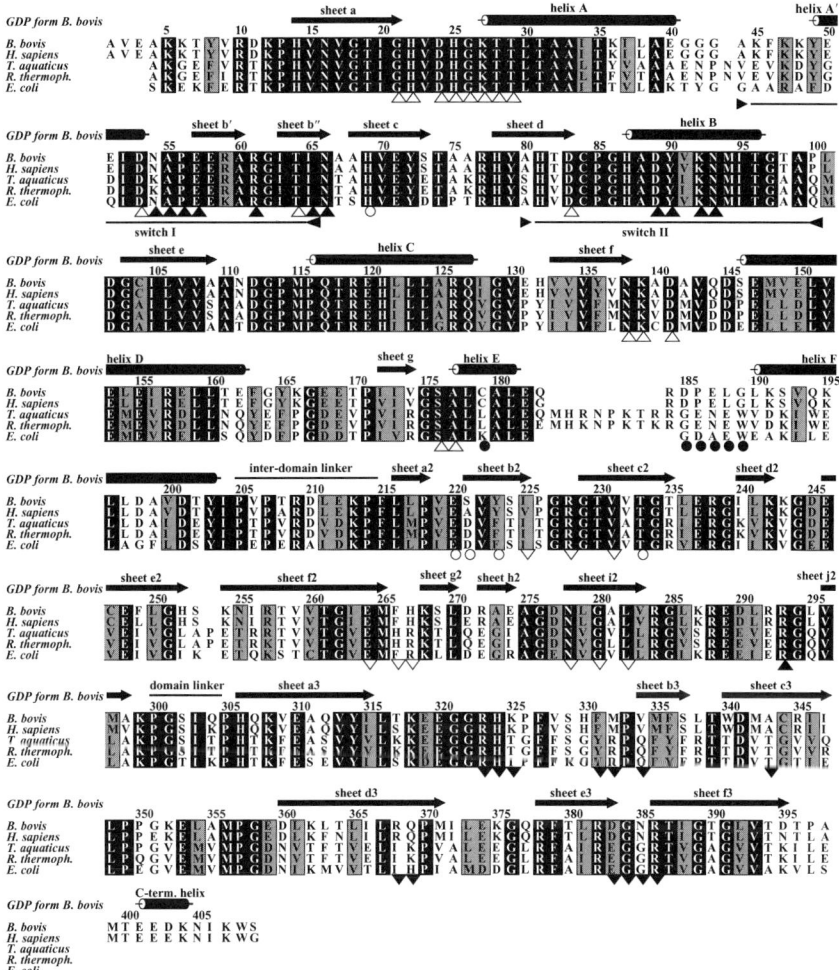

FIG. 9. The primary sequence of EF-Tu from mammalian mitochondria and prokaryotes. The sequences for the mature forms of bovine and human EF-Tu$_{mt}$ are shown aligned with those from *T. thermophilus*, *T. aquaticus*, and *E. coli*. The numbering above the figure corresponds to the residues in the mature form of bovine EF-Tu$_{mt}$. The following symbols are used: ▲, residues interacting with the acceptor stem of the aa-tRNA; ▼, residues interacting with the T-stem of the aa-tRNA; ●, residues in the mitochondrial "signature" sequence; ○ residues forming the binding pocket for the amino acid; ▽, residues interacting directly with the aminoacyl group; △, residues participating in guanine nucleotide binding. Switch 1 and switch 2 regions are underlined bounded by arrow heads.

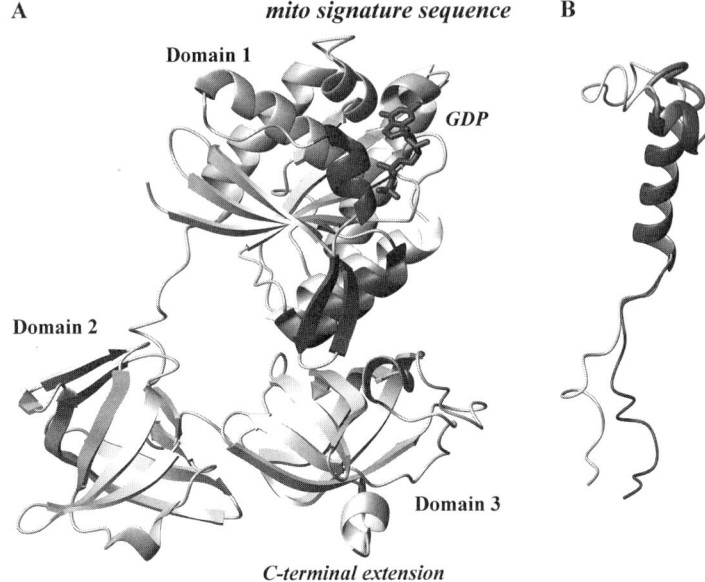

FIG. 10. Structure of EF-Tu$_{mt}$•GDP and the mitochondrial signature sequence. (A) The 3-dimensional structure of bovine EF-Tu$_{mt}$ (9) (PDB # 1D2E) is displayed using MolMol (153). Sheets are represented as flat ribbons. The GDP is shown in thick lines in Domain I. (B) The structure of the mitochondrial sequence is shown in thick dark lines with the prokaryotic sequence shown as thinner gray lines. The structure of this region of EF-Tu$_{mt}$ is superimposed on the structure of the corresponding region of *T. aquaticus* EF-Tu. The signature sequence of EF-Tu$_{mt}$ creates an alternative orientation of a surface loop.

of EF-Tu$_{mt}$ have been solved, it is unclear what implications this altered orientation of Domain I relative to Domains II/III will have on the structural transitions occurring in the formation of the EF-Tu$_{mt}$•GTP complex and the ternary complex. However, the position of Domain I in the EF-Tu$_{mt}$•GDP structure is closer to the position of Domain I in the bacterial EF-Tu complexes with GTP and aa-tRNA than to the position of Domain I in the GDP forms of the prokaryotic factors.

It is interesting to note that the region upstream of the linker connecting Domains I and II contains an entity defined by primary sequence conservation in EF-Tu$_{mt}$ and referred to as the mitochondrial signature sequence (Fig. 9, Fig. 10B) (117). This region is observed in EF-Tu$_{mt}$ from a wide variety of organisms. The residues defining the mitochondrial signature sequence are present in a loop on the surface of the protein. Overlaying the 3-D structure of bacterial EF-Tu and bovine EF-Tu$_{mt}$ in this region (Fig. 10B) illustrates that this signature sequence is present in an altered conformation in these structures. The role of the mitochondrial signature sequence has not been elucidated. However, the location of this loop on the surface of Domain I may render it accessible for possible interactions between EF-Tu$_{mt}$ and other binding partners such as components of the mitochondrial ribosome.

3. Interaction of EF-Tu$_{mt}$ with Guanine Nucleotides

Mechanistically, the mitochondrial elongation factors appear to use the same pathway for chain elongation observed with the prokaryotic and eukaryotic cytoplasmic factors (7). However, there are significant differences in the equilibrium dissociation constants that define the interaction of these factors with their ligands (Table II) (17, 18). Of particular note is the significantly weaker affinity (about 1 μM) of bovine EF-Tu$_{mt}$ for guanine nucleotides. This low affinity for GDP compared to the nM dissociation constant for the EF-Tu • Ts$_{mt}$ complex accounts for the failure of guanine nucleotides to dissociate the complex.

Although the equilibrium dissociation constant governing the interaction of EF-Tu$_{mt}$ with GDP is considerably weaker than that observed with the bacterial factors, all of the residues in EF-Tu that are directly involved in guanine nucleotide binding in the crystal structures of prokaryotic EF-Tu • GDP complexes are conserved in the sequence of EF-Tu$_{mt}$ and are placed as expected in the 3-dimensional structure of EF-Tu$_{mt}$ • GDP (9). Hence, the difference in the affinity of EF-Tu$_{mt}$ for GDP cannot arise directly from contacts between EF-Tu$_{mt}$ and GDP. One possible explanation for the weaker affinity of EF-Tu$_{mt}$ for GDP is a potential conformational flexibility of the binding pocket. For example, two Gly residues (Gly41 and Gly42 in the mature form of the factor) leading into switch 1 may make this region more flexible than the corresponding Thr38 and Tyr39 in *E. coli* EF-Tu. Another possible reason is the absence of a salt bridge (Arg171 to Glu150 in *E. coli* EF-Tu) that appears to fix part of the structure near the nucleotide binding site more firmly in place. Finally, Trp184 near the binding site for the guanine base is a glycine in EF-Tu$_{mt}$, again potentially increasing thermal motion in this region of Domain I. All of these changes could contribute to a faster k$_{off}$, leading to a weaker binding of GDP to EF-Tu$_{mt}$.

In the prokaryotic factors, EF-Tu undergoes a significant structural transition between its GDP- and GTP-bound states. This transition is characterized by secondary structure changes in Domain I and by a change in the orientation of Domain I relative to Domains II and III which act as a unit. In the GTP-form, Domain I rotates by 90° relative to Domains II and III compared to its position in the GDP-form of EF-Tu. Domains II and III retain the same orientation with respect to each other. The large opening between the domains is closed in the GTP-form and the cleft created between Domains I, II, and III forms the binding site for the aa-tRNA. The structure of EF-Tu in the

EF-Tu•GTP•Phe-tRNA^{Phe} complex is similar to its structure in the EF-Tu•GTP complex.

Two conserved switch regions, switch I (residues 40–62) and switch II (residues 80–100), are central to conformational changes that occur in the transition from the GDP to the GTP-form of EF-Tu. In the EF-Tu•GDP complex, switch I is formed by a short helix A′ (amino acids 46–50) and two short antiparallel β-strands (b′, residues 54–57, and b″, residues 60–63). In the EF-Tu•GDP form, helix B in the switch II region encompasses residues 84 to 93. Major structural rearrangements occur in the transition to the EF-Tu•GTP complex. In the switch I region β-strand, b′ is converted into a new helix A″ and β-strand b″ becomes a coiled structure. In the switch II region, helix B unwinds by one helical turn at the N-terminus and extends by 1 helical turn at the C-terminus and now comprises residues 87 to 97. This helix also tilts by 42° relative to its position in EF-Tu•GDP. The changes in the molecular switch regions in Domain I alter the surface of this domain in contact with Domain III. These switch regions are highly conserved when comparing EF-Tu$_{mt}$ with the prokaryotic factors. Hence, it is quite likely that the conformational changes observed between the GDP-bound and the GTP-bound forms of the prokaryotic factors will be present in bovine EF-Tu$_{mt}$.

4. INTERACTION OF EF-Tu$_{mt}$ WITH AA-TRNA

The crystal structures of bacterial EF-Tu in the ternary complex with GDPNP and aa-tRNA (*118, 119*) indicate that all three domains of EF-Tu are required for aa-tRNA binding. Domains I and II form the binding sites for the amino acid and the 3′ end of the aa-tRNA (Fig. 9). The extended acceptor–TΨC helix of the aa-tRNA, which is thought to contain the identity elements that distinguish initiator and elongator aa-tRNAs in prokaryotes, lies across Domain III (*120, 121*). A portion of the 3′ acceptor stem and the 5′ end of the aa-tRNA is located in a pocket formed by all three domains of EF-Tu.

Initial measurements examining the interaction of EF-Tu$_{mt}$ with aa-tRNAs were carried out using RNase protection assays and *E. coli* Phe-tRNA (*17*). As indicated in Table II, the equilibrium dissociation constant for the ternary complex of EF-Tu$_{mt}$•GTP with Phe-tRNA is about 18 nM. This value is within a factor of 2- to 3-fold of the values obtained with *E. coli* EF-Tu and several aa-tRNAs (*122*).

As indicated in Fig. 9, many of the residues in or near the aa-tRNA binding site in EF-Tu are conserved between the prokaryotic and mammalian mitochondrial factors. However, there are several interesting differences. Three of these residues are located at positions 221, 287, and 290 in *E. coli* EF-Tu. Residue 221 interacts with C75 of Cys-tRNA^{Cys} and is Ser or Thr in prokaryotic EF-Tu, but is Pro in EF-Tu$_{mt}$. Residue 287 of *E. coli* EF-Tu is adjacent to the 5′ end of the aa-tRNA and is acidic in all prokaryotic factors but is basic in

EF-Tu$_{mt}$. Residue 290 is near the conserved Arg288 that forms a salt bridge to the 5' end of aa-tRNAs. Gln290 is conserved in most prokaryotic factors while this residue is a Leu in mammalian EF-Tu$_{mt}$. Ser221, Glu287, and Gln290 were mutated in *E. coli* EF-Tu to the corresponding residues found in EF-Tu$_{mt}$, Pro, Arg, and Leu, respectively. The complementary mutations were carried out in EF-Tu$_{mt}$. The variants were expressed in *E. coli*, purified to near homogeneity and are all active in *in vitro* translation. Surprisingly, after correcting for the percentage of molecules active in ternary complex formation, each variant was able to interact with *E. coli* aa-tRNAs as well as their wild-type counterparts.

As has been discussed, one of the most interesting aspects of protein synthesis in animal mitochondria is the presence of unusual tRNAs. In general, mitochondrial tRNAs are shorter than their prokaryotic or eukaryotic cytoplasmic counterparts (59–75 nucleotides in length). They display numerous primary structural differences when compared to "normal" tRNAs. In some cases, they cannot be folded into the typical cloverleaf secondary structure and lack one or more of the invariant or semi-invariant residues found in other tRNAs (*41, 42*). Other mitochondrial tRNAs have more drastically altered shapes. For example, bovine tRNA$_{AGY}^{Ser}$ lacks the D-arm (*40*). Although many of these tRNAs can be folded into an L-shaped tertiary structure, the D-loop/T-loop interactions in the elbow region do not exist or are considerably different from those of normal tRNAs (*37–40*).

The unusual features of mammalian mitochondrial tRNAs makes it of considerable interest to examine their interactions with EF-Tu$_{mt}$. Early data using gel retardation assays (*123*) suggested that the equilibrium dissociation constants for the complex of EF-Tu$_{mt}$ • GTP with tRNA$_{AGY}^{Ser}$ is about 10 μM. However, this technique perturbs the equilibrium considerably and may overestimate the dissociation constant. Hence, we have used the RNase protection assay to obtain a better estimate of the K_d for the ternary complex between EF-Tu$_{mt}$ • GTP and bovine mitochondrial aa-tRNAs. We have selected two tRNAs for these studies (tRNA^{Phe} and tRNA$_{AGY}^{Ser}$). As indicated in Fig. 11, bovine tRNA^{Phe} can be folded into a reasonable cloverleaf, although it lacks many of the interactions that stabilize the tertiary structure of canonical tRNAs. These include conserved nucleotides in the D- and T-loops that are thought to be necessary for stable tertiary folding (*124*). In addition, mammalian mitochondrial tRNA^{Phe}, like most mitochondrial aa-tRNAs, has a higher A–U pairing and a concomitantly lower G–C pairing and has a mismatched base pair in its acceptor stem (*124, 125*). These features of animal mitochondrial tRNA^{Phe} result in the decreased stability of the tRNA compared with that of prokaryotic and cytoplasmic tRNA^{Phe} (*126*). As has been discussed, mammalian mitochondrial tRNA$_{AGY}^{Ser}$ completely lacks the D-arm, possibly creating significantly different tertiary interactions in this tRNA from those of canonical

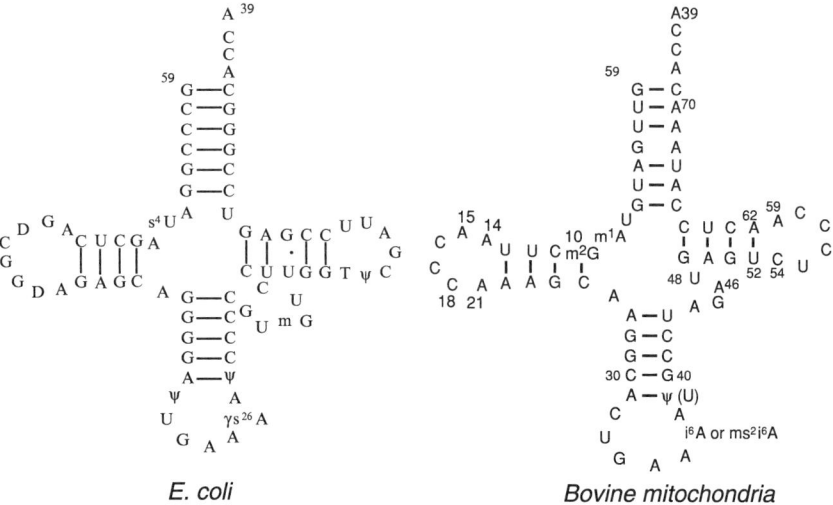

FIG. 11. Structures of bovine mitochondrial and *E. coli* tRNA[Phe]. Cloverleaf structure of *E. coli* and bovine mitochondrial tRNA[Phe].

tRNAs. This tRNA has an extra base pair in the anticodon stem and an additional nucleotide in the T-loop. In addition, the invariant nucleotides U (or Ψ) 55 and C56 that stabilize the structure of canonical tRNAs are altered in this tRNA (127). Both *E. coli* and mitochondrial EF-Tu form ternary complexes with bovine mitochondrial Phe-tRNA[Phe]. The formation of these complexes is governed by a K_d value of about 0.07 μM when the data is analyzed carefully for the percentage of EF-Tu and Phe-tRNA that is active in ternary complex formation (Table II). Somewhat weaker values were obtained for a T7 transcript of $tRNA_{AGY}^{Ser}$ ($K_d \approx 170$ μM). Preliminary observations suggest that there may be a considerable range in affinities of EF-Tu$_{mt}$ • GTP for different mitochondrial aa-tRNAs (Hunter and Spremulli, unpublished observations).

As has been described, several interesting changes in the amino acids at or near the aa-tRNA binding pocket are observed in EF-Tu$_{mt}$ (Fig. 9). The 3 mutations already described in Domain II (at positions Pro221, Glu287, and Gln290 in *E. coli* EF-Tu) were tested for their effects on the ability of EF-Tu to form ternary complexes with mitochondrial aa-tRNAs. The P269S variant of EF-Tu$_{mt}$ functions like wild-type EF-Tu$_{mt}$ in ternary complex formation with mitochondrial Phe-tRNA[Phe], while the R335E and L338Q variants show a decrease in activity in binding mitochondrial Phe-tRNA[Phe] (Hunter and Spremulli, unpublished observations). Thus, Arg335 and Leu338 must be important in the interaction between EF-Tu$_{mt}$ and mitochondrial Phe-tRNA[Phe].

Despite the similar affinity of E. coli and mitochondrial EF-Tu in binding mitochondrial aa-tRNAs, the bacterial factor is not nearly as efficient in delivering them to the A-site of the ribosome (128). Domain exchanges between E. coli EF-Tu and bovine EF-Tu$_{mt}$ indicate that the ability of the mitochondrial factor to deliver mitochondrial aa-tRNAs to the A-site of the ribosome resides primarily in Domains I and II (11). The basis for the differences observed remains to be determined. However, there are several steps in the elongation cycle that could potentially be affected. Since mitochondrial tRNAs may not form a classical L-shaped structure with the correct distance between the 3′ end and the anticodon, it is possible the E. coli EF-Tu does not position them effectively in the A-site of the ribosome. Ribosome-binding experiments in the presence of GDPNP suggest that E. coli EF-Tu is about 2-fold less active in this step of protein synthesis than is EF-Tu$_{mt}$ when provided with mitochondrial Phe-tRNA. Thus, this step may account for a portion of the reduced activity of E. coli EF-Tu with the mitochondrial aa-tRNA. However, polymerization of phenylalanine with the bacterial factor and mitochondrial Phe-tRNA is reduced about 5- to 10-fold. Thus, additional steps in the elongation cycle are likely to be affected. Once codon:anticodon interactions have taken place, the ribosome signals EF-Tu to hydrolyze GTP, allowing accommodation to occur. This communication occurs at least in part through the tRNA (129). The mitochondrial tRNAs may not trigger this communication effectively with bacterial EF-Tu, reducing the rate of GTP hydrolysis and release of the factor from the ribosome.

5. Role of the C-Terminal Extension on EF-Tu$_{mt}$

Alignments of EF-Tu from a variety of mitochondria with the corresponding prokaryotic factors indicate that the factors from animals contain extensions at the C-terminus. In bovine and human EF-Tu$_{mt}$, this extension is 11 amino acids in length and has the sequence MTEEDKNIKWS. The extreme case of a C-terminal extension on EF-Tu$_{mt}$ is represented by a variant of C. elegans EF-Tu$_{mt}$. The 57 amino acid extension (Domain III′) in C. elegans EF-Tu$_{mt}$(2) seems to represent a separate domain which confers specificity for a class of noncanonical tRNAs in nematodes which have a severely shortened T-arm and no D-arm (130). The current model suggests that the C-terminal extension of C. elegans EF-Tu$_{mt}$(2) compensates for the loss of the interaction of Domain III of EF-Tu with the T-stem of the aa-tRNA. Domain III′ may actually be located near the site where the T-arm is observed in the ternary complexes with canonical tRNAs and may provide an anchoring point for tRNAs lacking this structural feature (130).

The crystal structure of the bovine EF-Tu$_{mt}$•GDP complex indicates that the C-terminal extension has a significant α-helical content (Fig. 10) (9). This helix is connected to Domain III by a short linker of 5 amino acids. The helix is tucked under Domain III and is directed out of the plane established by Domains I, II, and III. It is possible that the orientation of this helix is different in solution than in the crystal structure. However, residues in the helix in the C-terminal extension make quite specific contacts with residues in Domain III, making it likely that the crystal structure provides a true representation of the conformation of this helix in solution.

The structure of the C-terminal helix resembles that observed in the terminal helix of the RADR zinc finger protein. This region in RADR uses a similar small surface helix to bind double-stranded DNA. The potential targets for the interaction of this helix in EF-Tu$_{mt}$ are the aa-tRNA and rRNA. Assuming the structure of the ternary complex is similar to that observed with the prokaryotic factors, the most likely target for interaction with this helix is the rRNA as the ternary complex is presented to the A-site.

Cryo-EM structures of the ternary complex in the A-site of the ribosome provide some insight into a potential role of the C-terminal helix during interaction of the EF-Tu$_{mt}$ ternary complex with the A-site (*131, 132*). Rigid body fitting of *T. aquaticus* crystal structures of the ternary complex into the cryo-EM density maps indicate that Domain III may interact with the small ribosomal subunit in the vicinity of ribosomal protein S12, while Domain I interacts with the large ribosomal subunit near the sarcin–ricin loop and ribosomal protein L11. The interaction of the ternary complex with the A-site appears to force EF-Tu into a novel conformation distinct from either its GDP or GTP form. In this conformation Domain III is rotated about 45° relative to its orientation in the ternary complex. In this orientation, the C-terminal extension on Domain III of EF-Tu$_{mt}$ would be in close contact with the 30 S subunit, suggesting that it may play a role in aa-tRNA binding to the mitochondrial ribosome.

C. Mitochondrial Elongation Factor Ts (EF-Ts$_{mt}$)

1. Sequence Analysis of EF-Ts$_{mt}$

Initial cDNA clones for bovine EF-Ts$_{mt}$ were obtained using the sequences of several peptides and an N-terminal peptide sequence. PCR was used to amplify internal portions of the coding region and the resulting PCR products were used to screen bovine cDNA libraries. The complete coding sequence was then cloned and expressed in *E. coli* with a His-tag at the C-terminus (*4*).

The EF-Ts$_{mt}$ gene maps to chromosome 12 at locus 12q13-q14. The mRNA is provisionally listed in RefSeq (entry number NM_005726) as 1253 nucleotides in length with the coding sequence covering nucleotides 31–1071. The 5′ end of the mRNA in both cows and humans is very G-rich and it is unclear at this time whether the actual 5′ end of the mRNA has been determined. AceView at NCBI suggests that there are a number of different isoforms of human EF-Ts$_{mt}$ and lists an mRNA sequence that is longer than that in RefSeq. The AceView entries generally do not result in N-terminal sequences that have a mitochondrial import signal, whereas the RefSeq entry gives a sequence with a 99% probability of being localized in mitochondria. Hence, this entry is probably more correct. The gene for EF-Ts$_{mt}$ in humans has 7 exons and 6 introns and spans 15,602 bp of DNA.

Bovine liver EF-Ts$_{mt}$ is 338 amino acids in length. The N-terminus of the mature protein has been determined using Edman degradation and indicates that removal of the 55-residue import signal leaves a mature protein of 283 amino acids (4). Primary sequence alignments with EF-Ts$_{mt}$ are somewhat of a challenge due to the limited conservation observed between the mitochondrial and prokaryotic factors. Overall, the mammalian mitochondrial factors are about 25 to 35% identical to their bacterial homologs.

2. PREDICTED STRUCTURE OF EF-Ts$_{mt}$

The crystal structure of the *E. coli* EF-Tu•Ts complex has been determined. EF-Ts interacts primarily with Domains I and III of EF-Tu, forming a broad interface between the two proteins. *E. coli* EF-Ts is organized into 4 structural modules (133): the N-terminal domain (residues 1–54), the core domain (residues 55–179 and 229–263), the dimerization domain (residues 180–228), and the C-terminal module (residues 264–282). The core domain is further divided into Subdomain N (residues 55–140) and Subdomain C (residues 141–179 and 229–263). The N-terminal domain, Subdomain N, and the C-terminal module interact with Domain 1 of EF-Tu while Subdomain C interacts with Domain III of EF-Tu (Fig. 12). Alignment of bovine EF-Ts$_{mt}$ with the *E. coli* factor indicates that the overall lengths of *E. coli* EF-Ts and the mature form of EF-Ts$_{mt}$ are the same (4).

Sequence alignments and secondary structure prediction programs suggest that EF-Ts$_{mt}$ is organized in a somewhat different way than *E. coli* EF-Ts (Fig. 12). EF-Ts$_{mt}$ aligns well with *E. coli* EF-Ts in the N-terminal domain and this region of the protein most likely folds into 3 helices, as observed for the *E. coli* factor (Fig. 12). The first 2 strands of β-sheet in Subdomain N and helices H4 and H5 are also predicted to be present in EF-Ts$_{mt}$. However, Subdomain N is interrupted by an insertion of about 20 residues. The precise position of this insertion is difficult to predict since the two proteins show very little primary sequence conservation in this region, making the alignment difficult. The remainder of Subdomain N, including helices H6 and H7 and the final strand of the β-sheet (S3), are all expected to be present. Subdomain C then begins with β-strand S4 which is followed by an insertion of about 12 residues before strands S5 and S6 and helices H8 and H12 are found. In this analysis, the dimerization domain (helices H9, H10, and H11), which is involved in contacts between two EF-Ts molecules in the crystal structure of the

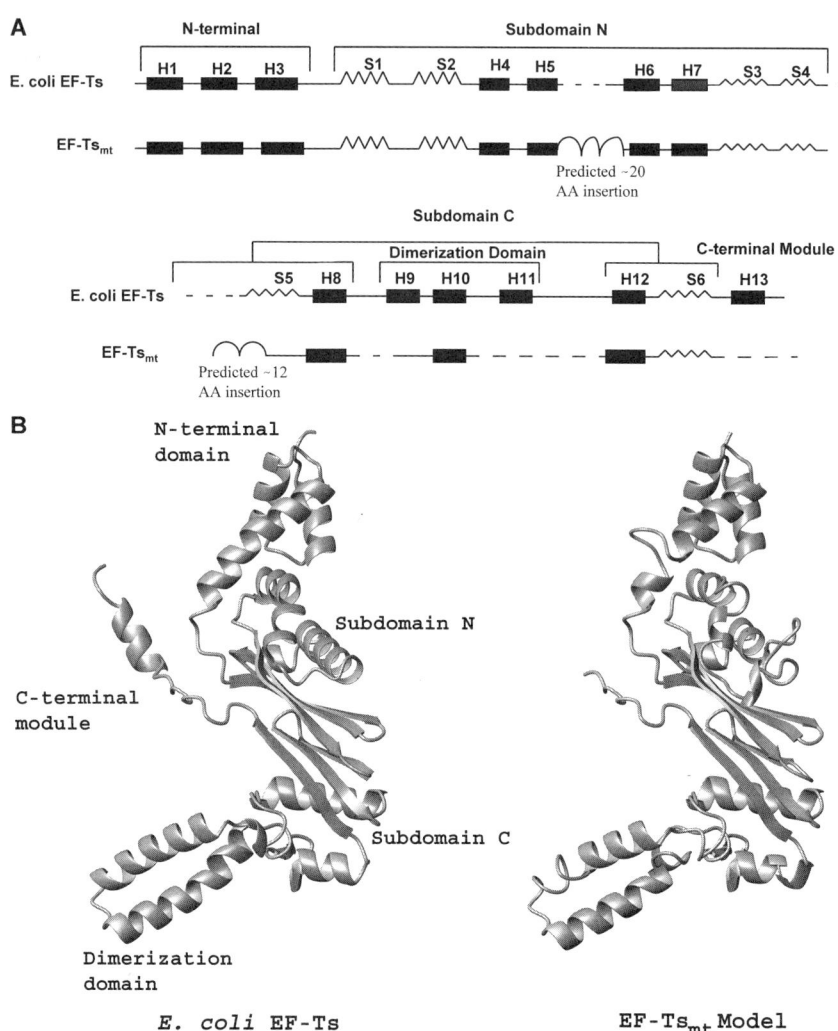

FIG. 12. Models of the possible secondary and tertiary structures of bovine EF-Ts$_{mt}$. (A) Secondary structure of *E. coli* EF-Ts determined from the crystal structure of the EF-Tu • Ts complex (133) aligned to the secondary structure predicted for EF-Ts$_{mt}$ based on multiple sequence alignments. Sequence alignments predict that there will be several insertions in the mitochondrial factor as well as a significant erosion in the "dimerization" domain. (B) Three-dimensional structure *E. coli* EF-Ts compared to a model for EF-Ts$_{mt}$ developed using the Swiss-Model software. This model predicts that a larger region of the "dimerization" domain will be present and predicts smaller insertions primarily on the side of EF-Ts that does not interact with EF-Tu.

EF-Tu•Ts complex, is largely missing from EF-Ts$_{mt}$. Only portions of what may be helix H10 appear to be present. Finally, the C-terminal module (H13) present in *E. coli* EF-Ts is missing in EF-Ts$_{mt}$.

In contrast to the predictions based on alignments and secondary structures, Swiss-Model predicts that EF-Ts$_{mt}$ will fold into a structure quite similar to that observed with *E. coli* EF-Ts (Fig. 12B). In this model, the dimerization domain is present, although smaller, in the mitochondrial factor. The C-terminal module is significantly shortened. Insertions predicted in EF-Ts$_{mt}$ are located on the back side of the molecule away from the side which forms an interface with EF-Tu. However, direct structural determinations will be required to assess more precisely the nature of the folding of this protein.

3. Expression and Characterization of EF-Ts$_{mt}$

When EF-Ts$_{mt}$ is expressed in *E. coli* as a His-tagged protein, it forms a 1:1 complex with *E. coli* EF-Tu (4). Free EF-Ts$_{mt}$ can be purified by denaturing this complex, followed by renaturation of EF-Ts$_{mt}$ (8). Free EF-Ts$_{mt}$ can also be prepared by column chromatography of the expressed protein (134). The complex formed between *E. coli* EF-Tu and EF-Ts$_{mt}$ is quite strong with an equilibrium dissociation constant of about 10^{-11} (Table II) (11). This interaction is nearly 100-fold tighter than that observed between *E. coli* EF-Tu and EF-Ts. Unlike the *E. coli* EF-Tu•Ts complex, the bovine liver EF-Tu•Ts$_{mt}$ complex cannot be dissociated in the presence of high concentrations of guanine nucleotides (112). This observation is due, at least in part, to a low affinity of EF-Tu$_{mt}$ for GDP and GTP. The equilibrium dissociation constants of the EF-Tu$_{mt}$•GDP and EF-Tu$_{mt}$•GTP complexes are about two orders of magnitude higher than those observed with *E. coli* EF-Tu (Table II) (18). Subsequent studies have shown that the equilibrium dissociation constant for the homologous EF-Tu•Ts$_{mt}$ complex is about 5.5 nM. This value is several orders of magnitude tighter than the binding of GDP to EF-Tu$_{mt}$ (Table II), accounting for failure of GDP to dissociate this complex. Interestingly, *E. coli* EF-Ts does not interact stably with EF-Tu$_{mt}$ nor does it promote polymerization with the mitochondrial factor.

The region of EF-Ts$_{mt}$ responsible for its tight binding to *E. coli* EF-Tu was evaluated using chimeric proteins prepared with different domains of the bacterial and mitochondrial factors. The results of these studies (135) indicate that Subdomain N of the core region of EF-Ts is largely responsible for this effect.

4. Residues in EF-Ts$_{mt}$ Important for Guanine Nucleotide Exchange

Examination of the structure of the *E. coli* EF-Tu•Ts complex suggests that nucleotide exchange arises, in part, because the side chains of Asp80 and Phe81 of EF-Ts intrude into the site on EF-Tu where the Mg^{2+} ion interacting with GDP is normally located (133). The resulting disruption of the Mg^{2+} ion binding site was postulated to reduce the affinity of EF-Tu for GDP (133). Mutations in these residues were prepared in both *E. coli* EF-Ts and EF-Ts$_{mt}$ (6). The D80A and F81A variants of *E. coli* EF-Ts were 2- to 3-fold less active in promoting GDP exchange with *E. coli* EF-Tu, while the D80AF81A mutant was nearly 10-fold less active. The corresponding D84A and F85A mutants of EF-Ts$_{mt}$ were also 5- to 10-fold less active in stimulating the activity of EF-Tu$_{mt}$. The double mutation completely abolished the activity of EF-Ts$_{mt}$. These data suggest that neither of these residues individually is essential for the interaction of EF-Ts with its corresponding EF-Tu or for the nucleotide exchange reaction per se. However, these residues certainly have a contributing role in the overall efficiency of EF-Ts.

The crystal structure of the *E. coli* EF-Tu•Ts complex and sequence alignments allowed a prediction of residues in EF-Ts$_{mt}$ that could be important for the interaction between these two factors and for nucleotide exchange. Site-directed mutagenesis was used to mutate these residues in an effort to examine the roles of various amino acids in the mechanism of EF-Ts$_{mt}$ (10). A number of corresponding mutations were also made in *E. coli* EF-Ts (136).

The mutated derivatives of EF-Ts$_{mt}$ have been tested in several ways with both EF-Tu$_{mt}$ and *E. coli* EF-Tu. A comparison of the effects of two of these mutants in the stimulation of poly(U)-directed polymerization is presented in Fig. 13. Interestingly, significantly different effects were observed with several mutations when tested with bacterial and mitochondrial EF-Tu. These differences appear to arise from the higher affinity of EF-Ts$_{mt}$ for *E. coli* EF-Tu ($K_d \approx 10^{-11}$) than for EF-Tu$_{mt}$ ($K_d \approx 5 \times 10^{-9}$). Mutations that weaken the interaction between EF-Ts$_{mt}$ and *E. coli* EF-Tu increased the ability of the mitochondrial factor to stimulate the activity of the bacterial EF-Tu (Fig. 13). This observation suggests that the high affinity of EF-Ts$_{mt}$ for *E. coli* EF-Tu allows it to act as a competitive inhibitor for the formation of the ternary complex following GDP release. In bacteria, the equilibrium dissociation constants for the EF-Tu•Ts complex and for the ternary complex are quite similar. The high concentration of GTP in the cell and the strong binding of the aa-tRNA then allow effective ternary complex formation in the presence of EF-Ts. However, the strong interaction between EF-Ts$_{mt}$ and *E. coli* EF-Tu inhibited formation of the ternary complex. When this interaction was weakened, but not eliminated, by mutations in EF-Ts$_{mt}$, ternary complex formation competed effectively with formation of the heterologous EF-Tu$_{Ecoli}$•Ts$_{mt}$ complex and the activity of EF-Tu in polymerization increased. Clearly, *E. coli* EF-Tu has evolved a structure that is optimally suited for a nucleotide exchange factor that has a binding constant similar to that of the ternary complex.

In contrast, most of the mutations that increase the activity of EF-Ts$_{mt}$ with *E. coli* EF-Tu actually reduce the activity of this factor with EF-Tu$_{mt}$ in

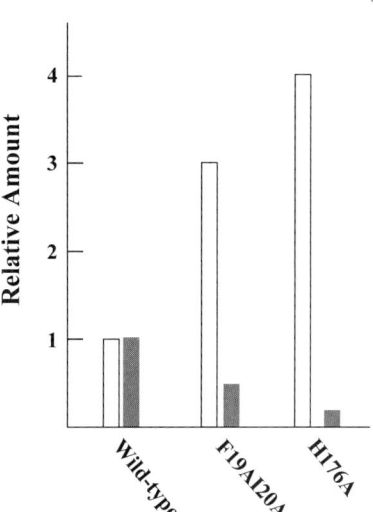

FIG. 13. Mutants of EF-Ts$_{mt}$ that have a reduced affinity for *E. coli* EF-Tu often are more active with the bacterial factor in polymerization but less active with EF-Tu$_{mt}$ in polymerization. The relative ability of wild-type EF-Ts$_{mt}$ to stimulate the activities of *E. coli* EF-Tu (open bars) and EF-Tu$_{mt}$ (gray bars) in poly(U)-dependent polymerization are set at a value of 1. The F19A120A mutant of EF-Ts$_{mt}$ has a 100-fold weaker binding to *E. coli* EF-Tu but is more active in stimulating the activity of this factor in protein synthesis. However, it is less active with EF-Tu$_{mt}$. The H176A variant of EF-Ts$_{mt}$ shows a 70-fold reduction in binding to *E. coli* EF-Tu but is more active than the wild-type factor in stimulating its activity in polymerization.

experiments using *E. coli* Phe-tRNA (Fig. 13). The K$_d$ for the homologous EF-Tu•Ts$_{mt}$ complex is about 5.5 nM while the K$_d$ for ternary complex formation with mitochondrial Phe-tRNA is comparable or somewhat weaker (about 10–70 nM, Table II). It would be of interest to examine the effects of the mutations in EF-Ts$_{mt}$ on the activity of EF-Tu$_{mt}$ with mitochondrial aa-tRNA. On the surface, it appears that both bacterial and mitochondrial EF-Tu have evolved to function with a nucleotide exchange factor that binds with an affinity comparable to that governing ternary complex formation. It should be noted that EF-Ts stabilizes the nucleotide free form of EF-Tu. This stabilization is particularly apparent with the mitochondrial factor from *C. elegans* (*137*). EF-Tu$_{mt}$ is very unstable (*112*) and a strong interaction with EF-Ts may be critical for maintaining its activity.

Many of the residues important for the activity of EF-Tu$_{mt}$ and EF-Ts$_{mt}$ are also important for the interaction of *E. coli* EF-Ts with *E. coli* EF-Tu (*136*). Thus, there appears to be conservation of important contacts when the effects of mutations in EF-Ts are examined with the EF-Tu from the corresponding system. However, EF-Ts$_{mt}$ interacts with *E. coli* EF-Tu in a significantly different manner, leading to about a 100-fold tighter interaction. As has been mentioned, EF-Tu$_{mt}$ does not bind guanine nucleotides tightly and the EF-Tu•Ts$_{mt}$ complex is not dissociated readily by either GDP or GTP (*138*). A similar situation is observed with the *T. thermophilus* (EF-Tu•Ts)$_2$ complex (*139, 140*). In contrast, the *E. coli* EF-Tu•Ts complex is easily dissociated by GDP. Subtle variations in the conformation of Domain I of EF-Tu and in the interactions among the three domains of this factor must account for these differences. Structural studies on EF-Tu$_{mt}$ and EF-Ts$_{mt}$ are underway and should help shed light on these interesting differences.

A second theme emerging from the mutagenesis of residues in EF-Ts is the importance of interactions between the N-terminal half of EF-Ts and Domain I of EF-Tu on the nucleotide exchange reaction. More essential contacts appear to occur between the N-terminal domain and Subdomain N of EF-Ts with Domain I of EF-Tu than occur between Subdomain C of EF-Ts and Domain III of EF-Tu. Of the residues examined to date, positions 19 and 20 of the mature protein have a strong preference for hydrophobic amino acids. Asp84 and Phe85 as well as His176 appear to be the most crucial for the interaction between EF-Tu$_{mt}$ and EF-Ts$_{mt}$, although they are not essential.

Analysis of the mutated derivatives prepared with both EF-Ts$_{mt}$ and *E. coli* EF-Ts indicate that mutation of these residues individually has only modest effects on the activity of EF-Ts (*6, 10, 136*). Indeed, it may be too simplistic to think that any one residue plays an essential role in the binding of EF-Ts to EF-Tu and in nucleotide exchange. Rather, the interaction of EF-Ts with EF-Tu appears to be a more global event, in which multiple small conformational changes arising from a series of side change interactions result in a significant cumulative rearrangement of the guanine nucleotide binding domain of EF-Tu, eventually promoting GDP release. Examination of the crystal structures of the EF-Tu•Ts and EF-Tu•GDP complexes indicates that EF-Ts increases the separation between Domains I and III of EF-Tu (*141*). This large-scale conformational change involves interactions of the N-terminal domain and Subdomain N of the core of EF-Ts with Domain I of EF-Tu and also the interaction of Subdomain C of EF-Ts with Domain III of EF-Tu. The structural rearrangement that arises from these interactions creates alternative conformations in a number of loops in Domain I that are involved in nucleotide binding. Thus, a widespread conformational change is propagated through Domains I and III of EF-Tu to the nucleotide binding site. Any mutation that affects the interaction of EF-Ts with EF-Tu will then be expected to have at least a small effect on nucleotide release. No mutated derivatives of EF-Ts have been observed that could bind EF-Tu but that were unable to catalyze GDP-exchange. Thus, no single residue or cluster of residues in EF-Ts is apparently responsible for the nucleotide exchange reaction. Residues in this factor important in binding EF-Tu are also important in nucleotide exchange.

A similar situation is likely to be present in the many nucleotide exchange factors found in the GTPase superfamily of proteins.

D. Mitochondrial Elongation Factor G (EF-G$_{mt}$)

1. PURIFICATION AND INITIAL CHARACTERIZATION OF EF-G$_{mt}$

The translocation step of protein biosynthesis is catalyzed by EF-G. Bovine EF-G$_{mt}$ was purified to near homogeneity from liver mitochondria over 10 years ago (142). However, the properties of this factor have never been carefully studied. Bovine EF-G$_{mt}$, like other translocases, is a single polypeptide with a molecular weight of about 80,000 on SDS-PAGE gels. It is active on E. coli ribosomes. In contrast, E. coli EF-G is not active on mitochondrial ribosomes (143).

2. SEQUENCE ANALYSIS OF EF-G$_{mt}$

Two forms of EF-G$_{mt}$ appear to be present in mammals based on examination of EST libraries (144). In humans, these genes are designated hEFG1 (AF309777) and hEFG2 (AF367997). The hEFG1 gene maps to chromosome 3q25. It consists of 18 exons and spans more than 40 kbp. The hEFG2 gene maps to chromosome 5q13 and contains 21 exons covering 45 kbp of genomic DNA. Three isoforms of EF-G2$_{mt}$ have been detected in the ESTs. One of these (Isoform 1) has a very similar length to EF-G1$_{mt}$. Isoform 2 has skipped the sequence corresponding to exon 13, while isoform 3 lacks several 3' exons and diverges considerably at the C-terminus from the other isoforms. It is unclear whether isoforms 2 and 3 actually play a physiological role. The presence of two forms of EF-G$_{mt}$ is widespread in nature and has been observed in species ranging from yeast to humans. Mutants of the yeast homolog of human EF-G1$_{mt}$ are impaired in mitochondrial protein synthesis, while mutations in the homolog of human EF-G2$_{mt}$ fail to show any clear phenotype (145).

MitoProtII predicts that EF-G1$_{mt}$ will be imported into mitochondria using a 36-residue import signal. It gives this protein a 71% probability of being localized in mitochondria. The EF-G2$_{mt}$ form is given a 68% probability of mitochondrial localization with an 81 amino acid import signal. However, cleavage at this site seems unlikely since it would create a cleavage in a region of the protein that is highly conserved with EF-G1$_{mt}$ and with the prokaryotic factors (Fig. 14). This region encompasses the first β-strand of the G-domain of EF-G (see following text) and it is unlikely that EF-G2$_{mt}$ would be missing this structural feature.

Alignment of the primary sequences of human EF-G1$_{mt}$ and human EF-G2$_{mt}$ indicates that they share considerable homology, particularly in the N-terminal halves of the proteins (Fig. 14). Overall, they are 35% identical

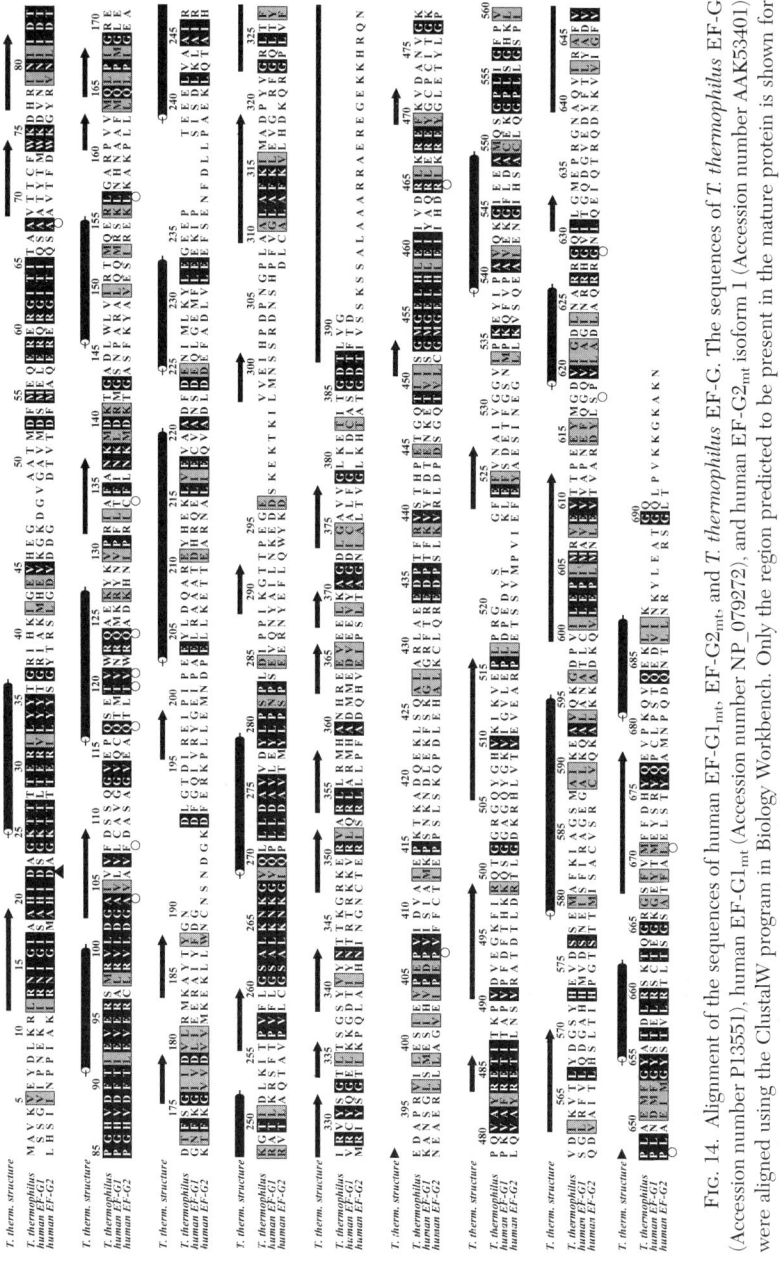

FIG. 14. Alignment of the sequences of human EF-G1mt, EF-G2mt, and T. thermophilus EF-G. The sequences of T. thermophilus EF-G (Accession number P13551), human EF-G1mt (Accession number NP_079272), and human EF-G2mt isoform 1 (Accession number AAK53401) were aligned using the ClustalW program in Biology Workbench. Only the region predicted to be present in the mature protein is shown for EF-G1mt. The corresponding region is shown for EF-G2mt. The arrow indicates the cleavage site predicted by MitoProt II for removal of the mitochondrial import signal. The secondary structural elements observed in the crystal structure of T. thermophilus EF-G are indicated above the sequence. The O indicates residues that result in fusidic acid resistance when mutated in prokaryotic EF-G (148, 150). Numbering is according to that of T. thermophilus EF-G.

TABLE III
Homology between Human EF-G1$_{mt}$, Human EF-G2$_{mt}$ and the Translocases from Other Systems

Protein	% Identity to	
	EF-G1$_{mt}$	EF-G2$_{mt}$
Human EF-G1$_{mt}$	100	35
Human EF-G2$_{mt}$	35	100
E. coli EF-G	44	37
Ricketssia EF-G	42	38
T. thermophilus EF-G	44	41
Mouse EF-G1$_{mt}$	92	35
Mouse EF-G2$_{mt}$	34	83
Yeast EF-G1$_{mt}$	53	32
Yeast EF-G2$_{mt}$	27	34
C. elegans EF-G1$_{mt}$	57	33
C. elegans EF-G2$_{mt}$	27	34
Drosophila EF-G1$_{mt}$	65	32
Drosophila EF-G2$_{mt}$	28	38

(Table III). Interestingly, these two forms of mitochondrial EF-G are actually less conserved between themselves than to the prokaryotic factors. EF-G1$_{mt}$ has been more highly conserved throughout evolution than has EF-G2$_{mt}$. For example, yeast EF-G1$_{mt}$ is 53% identical to human EF-G1$_{mt}$, while yeast EF-G2$_{mt}$ is only 34% identical to its human homolog (Table III).

EF-G is structurally divided into 5 domains (146, 147). It has a shape that is remarkably similar to that of the ternary complex of EF-Tu • GDPNP • Phe-tRNA. The first domain is analogous to Domain I of EF-Tu. It is responsible for guanine nucleotide binding. It has a fold quite similar to that of other G-domains. However, it contains an insertion termed the G'-domain. It has been speculated that this region mimics the effects of EF-Ts and serves as a built-in nucleotide exchange activity (148). This region is quite highly conserved in both EF-G1$_{mt}$ and EF-G2$_{mt}$, although EF-G2$_{mt}$ has a small insertion near the end of the G' domain.

Domain II of EF-G is quite similar to Domain II of EF-Tu, having an antiparallel β-barrel topology with 2 extra strands of β-sheet external to the barrel (146–148). This region of EF-G$_{mt}$ appears to have a similar topology. However, EF-G1$_{mt}$ appears to have a larger loop between strands 1 and 2 or an extended strand 2. In contrast, EF-G2$_{mt}$ appears to lack β-strand 2 in Domain II, but has an insertion near the end of Domain II that may compensate structurally. As has been mentioned, EF-G2$_{mt}$ appears in 3 isoforms. Isoform 2 lacks exon 13, hence, it would not contain the first 7 to 8 strands of the β-sheet in Domain II. From this perspective, it is unlikely to produce a functional product.

Domain III of EF-G is an α-β domain but is poorly resolved in the electron density map. This region appears to be present in the mitochondrial factors with a reasonable degree of conservation. Domain IV is an elongated region with an unusual fold (148) and interrupted in primary sequence by Domain V. Both of these regions are predicted to be present in EF-G1$_{mt}$ and are reasonably well conserved.

EF-G is known to be the target of the antibiotic fusidic acid. This compound acts by freezing EF-G on the ribosome. Sensitivity to fusidic acid varies over a considerable range (149). Surprisingly, EF-G$_{mt}$ is resistant to fusidic acid inhibition when assayed on bovine mitochondrial ribosomes and is only weakly inhibited by this antibiotic when tested on E. coli ribosomes (142). Several mutants of EF-G are known to be resistant to fusidic acid, allowing some idea of a possible binding site for this compound. Several of these positions are shown in Fig. 14. The residues implicated in the action of fusidic acid are distributed in three major regions in the central portion of the protein including the G-domain, Domain III, and Domain V (150). Interestingly, almost all of these residues are present in EF-G1$_{mt}$ and the apparent resistance of this factor to fusidic acid remains to be explained.

IV. Conclusions

Considerable progress has been made over the past 15 years in purifying and characterizing the initiation and elongation factors from mammalian mitochondria. Presently, two initiation factors equivalent to prokaryotic IF-2 and IF-3 have been identified. Much remains to be learned about their biochemical properties. Further, it is unclear whether additional factors are required for efficient initiation complex formation in mammalian mitochondria. Additional biochemical tests and perhaps proteomics analysis will be required to resolve this question.

Three elongation factors have been identified corresponding to EF-Tu, EF-Ts, and EF-G. The properties of both EF-Tu$_{mt}$ and EF-Ts$_{mt}$ have been studied in some detail. One of the major remaining questions about EF-Tu$_{mt}$ is the process by which it recognizes the unusual tRNAs in mammalian mitochondria. Both mutagenesis work and crystallographic studies are underway in efforts to address this question. Native EF-G$_{mt}$ has been purified and preliminary biochemical characterization has been carried out, but the protein has not been expressed in E. coli or studied in detail.

Finally, the mitochondrial ribosome has many unusual properties and the interactions of the initiation and elongation factors with mitochondrial ribosomes remains to be comprehensively analyzed.

ACKNOWLEDGMENTS

This work has been supported by funds provided by the National Institutes of Health (grant GM32734).

REFERENCES

1. Hengartner, M. O. (2000). The biochemistry of apoptosis. *Nature* **407**, 770–776.
2. Scheffler, I. (1999). "Mitochondria." Wiley-Liss, Inc., New York.
3. Woriax, V., Burkhart, W., and Spremulli, L. L. (1995). Cloning, sequence analysis, and expression of mammalian mitochondrial protein synthesis elongation factor Tu. *Biochim. Biophys. Acta* **1264**, 347–356.
4. Xin, H., Woriax, V. L., Burkhart, W., and Spremulli, L. L. (1995). Cloning and expression of mitochondrial translational elongation factor Ts from bovine and human liver. *J. Biol. Chem.* **270**, 17243–17249.
5. Woriax, V., Spremulli, G., and Spremulli, L. L. (1996). Nucleotide and aminoacyl-tRNA specificity of the mammalian mitochondrial elongation factor EF-Tu:Ts complex. *Biochim. Biophys. Acta* **1307**, 66–72.
6. Zhang, Y., Li, X., and Spremulli, L. L. (1996). Role of the conserved aspartate and phenylalanine residues in prokaryotic and mitochondrial elongation factor Ts in guanine nucleotide exchange. *FEBS Lett.* **391**, 330–332.
7. Woriax, V., Bullard, J. M., Ma, L., Yokogawa, T., and Spremulli, L. L. (1997). Mechanistic studies of the translational elongation cycle in mammalian mitochondria. *Biochim. Biophys. Acta* **1352**, 91–101.
8. Xin, H., Leanza, K., and Spremulli, L. L. (1997). Expression of bovine mitochondrial elongation factor Ts in *Escherichia coli* and characterization of the heterologous complex formed with prokaryotic elongation factor Tu. *Biochim. Biophys. Acta* **1352**, 101–112.
9. Andersen, G., Thirup, S., Spremulli, L. L., and Nyborg, J. (2000). High resolution crystal structure of bovine mitochondrial EF-Tu in complex with GDP. *J. Mol. Biol.* **297**, 421–436.
10. Zhang, Y., and Spremulli, L. L. (1998). Roles of residues in mammalian mitochondrial elongation factor Ts in the interaction with bacterial and mitochondrial elongation factor Tu. *J. Biol. Chem.* **273**, 28142–28148.
11. Bullard, J. M., Cai, Y.-C., Zhang, Y., and Spremulli, L. L. (1999). Effects of domain exchanges between *Escherichia coli* and mammalian mitochondrial EF-Tu on interactions with guanine nucleotides, aminoacyl-tRNA, and ribosomes. *Biochim. Biophys. Acta* **1446**, 102–114.
12. Liao, H.-X., and Spremulli, L. L. (1991). Initiation of protein synthesis in animal mitochondria: Purification and characterization of translational initiation factor 2. *J. Biol. Chem.* **266**, 20714–20719.
13. Liao, H.-X., and Spremulli, L. L. (1990). Identification and initial characterization of translational initiation factor 2 from bovine mitochondria. *J. Biol. Chem.* **265**, 13618–13622.
14. Ma, L., and Spremulli, L. L. (1995). Cloning and sequence analysis of the human mitochondrial translational initiation factor 2 cDNA. *J. Biol. Chem.* **270**, 1859–1865.

15. Ma, J., Farwell, M., Burkhart, W., and Spremulli, L. L. (1995). Cloning and sequence analysis of the cDNA for bovine mitochondrial translational initiation factor 2. *Biochim. Biophys. Acta* **1261,** 321–324.
16. Ma, J., and Spremulli, L. L. (1996). Expression, purification, and mechanistic studies of bovine mitochondrial translational initiation factor 2. *J. Biol. Chem.* **271,** 5805–5811.
17. Cai, Y.-C., Bullard, J. M., Thompson, N. L., and Spremulli, L. L. (2000). Interaction of mitochondrial elongation factor Tu with aminoacyl-tRNA and elongation factor Ts. *J. Biol. Chem.* **275,** 20308–20314.
18. Cai, Y.-C., Bullard, J. M., Thompson, N. L., and Spremulli, L. L. (2000). Interaction of mammalian mitochondrial elongation factor EF-Tu with guanine nucleotides. *Prot. Sci.* **9,** 1791–1800.
19. Pel, H., and Grivell, L. (1994). Protein synthesis in mitochondria. *Mol. Biol. Rep.* **19,** 183–194.
20. Kitakawa, M., and Isono, K. (1991). The mitochondrial ribosome. *Biochimie* **73,** 813–825.
21. O'Brien, T. W., Denslow, N. D., Faunce, W., Anders, J., Liu, J., and O'Brien, B. (1993). Structure and function of mammalian mitochondrial ribosomes. *In* "The Translational Apparatus: Structure, Function Regulation, and Evolution" (K. Nierhaus, F. Franceschi, A. Subramanian, V. Erdmann, and B. Wittmann-Liebold, Eds.), pp. 575–586. Plenum Press, New York.
22. Pietromonaco, S., Denslow, N., and O'Brien, T. W. (1991). Proteins of mammalian mitochondrial ribosomes. *Biochimie* **73,** 827–836.
23. Goldschmidt-Reisin, S., Kitakawa, M., Herfurth, E., Wittmann-Liebold, B., Grohmann, L., and Graack, H.-R. (1998). Mammalian mitochondrial ribosomal proteins: N-terminal amino acid sequencing, characterization, and identification of corresponding gene sequences. *J. Biol. Chem.* **273,** 34828–34836.
24. Graack, H.-R., Bryant, M., and O'Brien, T. W. (1999). Identification of mammalian mitochondrial ribosomal proteins (MRPs) by N-terminal sequencing of purified bovine MRPs and comparison to data bank sequences: The large subribosomal particle. *Biochem.* **38,** 16569–16577.
25. Koc, E. C., Blackburn, K., Burkhart, W., and Spremulli, L. L. (1999). Identification of a mammalian mitochondrial homolog of ribosomal protein S7. *Biochem. Biophys. Res. Comm.* **266,** 141–146.
26. Koc, E. C., Burkhart, W., Blackburn, K., Moseley, A., Koc, H., and Spremulli, L. L. (2000). A proteomics approach to the identification of mammalian mitochondrial small subunit ribosomal proteins. *J. Biol. Chem.* **275,** 32585–32591.
27. Koc, E. C., Burkhart, W., Blackburn, K., Moseley, A., and Spremulli, L. L. (2001). The small subunit of the mammalian mitochondrial ribosome: Identification of the full complement of ribosomal proteins present. *J. Biol. Chem.* **276,** 19363–19374.
28. Koc, E. C., Burkhart, W., Blackburn, K., Koc, H., Moseley, A., and Spremulli, L. L. (2001). Identification of four proteins from the small subunit of the mammalian mitochondrial ribosome using a proteomics approach. *Prot. Sci.* **10,** 471–481.
29. Koc, E. C., Burkhart, W., Blackburn, K., Schlatzer, D. M., Moseley, A., and Spremulli, L. L. (2001). The large subunit of the mammalian mitochondrial ribosome: Analysis of the complement of ribosomal protein present. *J. Biol. Chem.* **276,** 43958–43969.
30. Anderson, S., de Brujin, M., Coulson, A., Eperon, I., Sanger, F., and Young, I. (1982). Complete sequence of bovine mitochondrial DNA: Conserved features of the mammalian mitochondrial genome. *J. Mol. Biol.* **156,** 683–717.
31. Wolstenholme, D. (1992). Animal mitochondrial DNA. *In* "Mitochondrial Genomes" (D. Wolstenholme and K. Jeon, Eds.), pp. 173–216. Academic Press, New York.

32. Ojala, D., Montoya, J., and Attardi, G. (1981). tRNA punctuation model of RNA processing in human mitochondria. *Nature* **290**, 470–474.
33. Montoya, J., Ojala, D., and Attardi, G. (1981). Distinctive features of the 5'-terminal sequences of the human mitochondrial mRNAs. *Nature* **290**, 465–470.
34. Voorma, H. (1996). Control of translation initiation in prokaryotes. *In* "Translational Control" (J. Hershey, M. Mathews, and N. Sonenberg, Eds.), pp. 759–777. Cold Spring Harbor Laboratory Press, Cold Spring Harbor, New York.
35. Merrick, W. (1992). Mechanism and regulation of eukaryotic protein synthesis. *Micro. Rev.* **56**, 291–315.
36. Kozak, M. (1992). A consideration of alternative models for the initiation of translation in eukaryotes. *Crit. Rev. Biochem. Mol. Biol.* **27**, 385–402.
37. Steinberg, S., Gautheret, D., and Cedergren, R. (1994). Fitting the structurally diverse animal mitochondrial tRNAs^{Ser} to common three-dimensional constraints. *J. Mol. Biol.* **236**, 982–989.
38. Steinberg, S., and Cedergren, R. (1994). Structural compensation in atypical mitochondrial tRNAs. *Struct. Biol.* **1**, 507–510.
39. Yokogawa, T., Watanabe, Y.-I., Kumazawa, Y., Ueda, T., Hirao, I., Miura, K.-I., and Watanabe, K. (1991). A novel cloverleaf structure found in mammalian mitochondrial tRNA^{Ser}(UCN). *Nuc. Acids Res.* **19**, 6101–6105.
40. Watanabe, Y.-I., Kawai, G., Yokogawa, T., Hayashi, N., Kumazawa, Y., Ueda, T., Nishikawa, K., Hirao, I., Miura, K.-I., and Watanabe, K. (1994). Higher-order structure of bovine mitochondrial tRNA^{ser}UGA: Chemical modification and computer modeling. *Nuc. Acids Res.* **22**, 347–353.
41. Dirheimer, G., Keith, G., Dumas, P., and Westhof, E. (1995). Primary, secondary, and tertiary structures of tRNAs. *In* "tRNA: Structure, Biosynthesis, and Function" (U. RajBhandary and D. Soll, Eds.), pp. 93–126. ASM Press, Washington DC.
42. Martin, N. (1995). Organellar tRNAs: Biosynthesis and function. *In* "tRNA: Structure, Biosynthesis, and Function" (U. RajBhandary and D. Soll, Eds.), pp. 127–140. ASM Press, Washington DC.
43. Gualerzi, C., and Pon, C. (1990). Initiation of mRNA translation in prokaryotes. *Biochem.* **29**, 5881–5889.
44. Wu, X., and RajBhandary, U. (1997). Effect of the amino acid attached to *Escherichia coli* initiator tRNA on its affinity for the initiation factor IF2 and on the IF2 dependence of its binding to the ribosome. *J. Biol. Chem.* **272**, 1891–1895.
45. Moazed, D., Samaha, R. R., Gualerzi, C., and Noller, H. F. (1995). Specific protection of 16 S rRNA by translational initiation factors. *J. Mol. Biol.* **248**, 207–210.
46. McCarthy, J., and Brimacombe, R. (1994). Prokaryotic translation: The interactive pathway leading to initiation. *Trends Genet.* **10**, 402–407.
47. Bianchetti, R., Lucchini, G., Crosti, P., and Tortora, P. (1977). Dependence of mitochondrial protein synthesis on formylation of the initiator methionyl-tRNA$_f$. *J. Biol. Chem.* **252**, 2519–2523.
48. Overman, J., Enderle, P. J., Farrow, J. M., Wiley, J. E., and Farwell, M. A. (2003). The human mitochondrial translation initiation factor 2 gene (MTIF2): Transcriptional analysis and identification of a pseudogene. *Biochim. Biophys. Acta* **1628**, 195–205.
49. Kozak, M. (1999). Initiation of translation in prokaryotes and eukaryotes. *Gene* **234**, 187–208.
50. Garofalo, C., Trinko, R., Kramer, G., Appling, D. R., and Hardesty, B. (2003). Purification and characterization of yeast mitochondrial initiation factor 2. *Arch. Biochem. Biophys.* **413**, 243–252.

51. Laalami, S., Sacerdot, C., Vachon, G., Mortensen, K., Sperling-Petersen, H., Cenatiempo, Y., and Grunberg-Manago, M. (1991). Structural and functional domains of E. coli initiation factor IF2. *Biochimie* **73**, 1557–1566.
52. Sacerdot, C., Vachon, G., Laalami, S., Morel-Deville, F., Cenatiempo, Y., and Grunberg-Manago, M. (1992). Both forms of translational initiation factor IF-2 (α and β) are required for maximal growth of *Escherichia coli*. *J. Mol. Biol.* **225**, 67–80.
53. Laursen, B. S., Mortensen, K. K., Sperling-Petersen, H. U., and Hoffman, D. W. (2003). A conserved structural motif at the N-terminus of bacterial translation initiation factor IF2. *J. Biol. Chem.* **278**, 16320–16328.
54. Moreno, J. M. P., Dyrskjøtersen, L., Kristensen, J., Mortensen, K., and Sperling-Petersen, H. (1999). Characterization of the domains of E. coli initiation factor IF2 responsible for recognition of the ribosome. *FEBS Lett.* **455**, 130–134.
55. Moreno, J. M. P., Kildsgaard, J., Siwanowicz, I., Mortensen, K. K., and Sperling-Petersen, H. U. (1998). Binding of *E. coli* initiation factor IF2 to 30 S ribosomal subunits: A functional role for the N-terminus of the factor. *Biochem. Biophys. Res. Comm.* **252**, 465–471.
56. Marzi, S., Knight, W., Brandi, L., Caserta, E., Soboleva, N., Hill, W. E., Gualerzi, C. O., and Lodmell, J. S. (2003). Ribosomal localization of translation initiation factor IF2. *RNA* **9**, 958–969.
57. Misselwitz, R., Welfle, K., Krafft, C., Welfle, H., Brandi, L., Caserta, E., and Gualerzi, C. (1999). The fMet-tRNA binding domain of translational initiation factor IF2: Role and environment of its two cys residues. *FEBS Lett.* **459**, 332–336.
58. Szkaradkiewicz, K., Zuleeg, T., Limmer, S., and Sprinzl, M. (2000). Interaction of fMet-tRNAfMet and fMet-AMP with the C-terminal domain of *Thermus thermophilus* translation initiation factor 2. *Eur. J. Biochem.* **267**, 4290–4299.
59. Spurio, R., Brandi, L., Caserta, E., Pon, C., Gualerzi, C., Misselwitz, R., Krafft, C., Welfle, K., and Welfle, H. (2000). The C-terminal subdomain (IF2 C-2) contains the entire fMet-tRNA binding site of initiation factor IF2. *J. Biol. Chem.* **275**, 2447–2454.
60. Krafft, C., Diehl, A., Laettig, S., Behlke, J., Heinemann, U., Pon, C. L., Gualerzi, C. O., and Welfle, H. (2000). Interaction of fMet-tRNA(fMet) with the C-terminal domain of translational initiation factor IF2 from *Bacillus stearothermophilus*. *FEBS Lett.* **471**, 128–132.
61. Moreno, J. M. P., Sorensen, M., Mortensen, K. K., and Sperling-Petersen, H. U. (2000). Molecular mimicry in translation initiation: A model for the initiation factor IF2 on the ribosome. *Life* **50**, 347–354.
62. Tibbetts, A. S., Oesterlin, L., Chan, S. Y., Kramer, G., Hardesty, B., and Appling, D. R. (2003). Mammalian mitochondrial initiation factor 2 supports yeast mitochondrial translation without formylated initiator tRNA. *J. Biol. Chem.* **278**, 31774–31780.
63. Guex, N., and Peitsch, M. C. (1997). SWISS-MODEL and the Swiss-PdbViewer: An environment for comparative protein modeling. *Electrophoresis* **18**, 2714–2723.
64. Peitsch, M., Wells, T., Stampf, D., and Sussman, J. (1995). The Swiss-3D image collection and PDB-browser on the World Wide Web. *Trends Biochem. Sci.* **20**, 82–85.
65. Laursen, B. S., Siwanowicz, I., Larigauderie, G., Hedegaard, J., Ito, K., Nakamura, Y., Kenney, J. M., Mortensen, K. K., and Sperling-Petersen, H. U. (2003). Characterization of mutations in the GTP-binding domain of IF2 resulting in cold-sensitive growth of *Escherichia coli*. *J. Mol. Biol.* **326**, 543–551.
66. Shin, B. S., Maag, D., Roll-Mecak, A., Arefin, M. S., Burley, S. K., Lorsch, J. R., and Dever, T. E. (2002). Uncoupling of initiation factor eIF5B/IF2 GTPase and translational activities by mutations that lower ribosome affinity. *Cell* **111**, 1015–1025.
67. Roll-Mecak, A., Cao, C., Dever, T. E., and Burley, S. K. (2000). X-ray structures of the universal translation initiation factor IF2/eIF5B. Conformational changes on GDP and GTP binding. *Cell* **103**, 781–792.

68. Meunier, S., Spurio, R., Czisch, M., Wechselberger, R., Guenneugues, M., Gualerzi, C. O., and Boelens, R. (2000). Structure of the fMet-tRNA(fMet)-binding domain of *B. stearothermophilus* initiation factor IF2. *EMBO J.* **19,** 1918–1926.
69. Guenneugues, M., Caserta, E., Brandi, L., Spurio, R., Meunier, B., Pon, C. L., Boelens, R., and Gualerzi, C. O. (2000). Mapping the fMet-tRNA binding site of initiation factor IF2. *EMBO J.* **19,** 5233–5240.
70. RajBhandary, U., and Chow, C. (1995). Initiator tRNAs and initiation of protein synthesis. In "tRNA: Structure, Biosynthesis, and Function" (U. RajBhandary and D. Soll, Eds.), pp. 511–528. ASM Press, Washington, DC.
71. Moriya, J., Yokagawa, T., Wakita, K., Ueda, T., Nishikawa, K., Crain, P., Hashizume, T., Pomerantz, S. C., McCloskey, J. A., Kawai, G., Hayashi, N., Yokoyama, S., and Watanabe, K. (1994). A novel modified nucleoside found at the first position of the anticodon of methionine tRNA from bovine liver mitochondria. *Biochem.* **33,** 2234–2239.
72. Sprinzl, M., Horn, C., Brown, M., Ioudovitch, A., and Steinberg, S. (1998). Compilation of tRNA sequences and sequences of tRNA genes. *Nuc. Acids Res.* **26,** 148–153.
73. Mayer, C., Kohrer, C., Kenny, E., Prusko, C., and RajBhandary, U. L. (2003). Anticodon sequence mutants of *Escherichia coli* initiator tRNA: Effects of overproduction of aminoacyl-tRNA synthetases, methionyl-tRNA formyltransferase, and initiation factor 2 on activity in initiation. *Biochem.* **42,** 4787–4799.
74. Takeuchi, N., Vial, L., Panvert, M., Schmitt, E., Watanabe, K., Mechulam, Y., and Blanquet, S. (2001). Recognition of tRNAs by methionyl-tRNA transformylase from mammalian mitochondria. *J. Biol. Chem.* **276,** 20064–20068.
75. Takemoto, C., Koike, T., Yokogawa, T., Benkowski, L., Spremulli, L. L., Ueda, T., Nishikawa, K., and Watanabe, K. (1995). The ability of bovine mitochondrial transfer RNA^{met} to decode AUG and AUA codons. *Biochimie* **77,** 104–108.
76. Li, Y., Holmes, W. B., Appling, D. R., and RajBhandary, U. L. (2000). Initiation of protein synthesis in *Saccharomyces cerevisiae* mitochondria without formylation of the initiator tRNA. *J. Bact.* **182,** 2886–2892.
77. Boileau, G., Butler, P., Hershey, J. W., and Traut, R. R. (1983). Direct cross-links between initiation factors 1, 2, and 3 and ribosomal proteins promoted by 2-iminothiolane. *Biochem.* **22,** 3162–3170.
78. Bollen, A., Heimark, R. L., Cozzone, A., Traut, R. R., and Hershey, J. W. (1975). Cross-linking of initiation factor IF-2 to *Escherichia coli* 30 S ribosomal proteins with dimethylsuberimidate. *J. Biol. Chem.* **250,** 4310–4314.
79. Teana, A., Gualerzi, C., and Brimacombe, R. (1995). From stand-by to decoding site. Adjustment of the mRNA on the 30 S subunit under the influence of the initiation factors. *RNA* **1,** 772–782.
80. Hartz, D., Binkley, J., Hollingsworth, T., and Gold, L. (1990). Domains of initiator tRNA and initiation codon crucial for initiator tRNA selection by *E. coli* IF-3. *Genes Develop.* **4,** 1790–1800.
81. Sussman, J., Simons, E., and Simons, R. (1996). *Escherichia coli* translation initiation factor 3 discriminates the initiation codon *in vivo*. *Mol. Micro.* **21,** 347–360.
82. Canonaco, M., Gualerzi, C., and Pon, C. (1989). Alternative occupancy of a dual ribosomal binding site by mRNA affected by translation initiation factors. *Eur. J. Biochem.* **182,** 501–506.
83. Hartz, D., McPheeters, D., and Gold, L. (1989). Selection of the initiator tRNA by *E. coli* initiation factors. *Genes and Develop.* **3,** 1899–1912.
84. Berkhout, B., van der Laken, C. J., and van Knippenberg, P. H. (1986). Formylmethionyl-tRNA binding to 30 S ribosomes programmed with homopolynucleotides and the effect of translational initiation factor 3. *Biochim. Biophys. Acta* **866,** 144–153.

85. Shapkina, T. G., Dolan, M. A., Babin, P., and Wollenzien, P. (2000). Initiation factor 3-induced structural changes in the 30 S ribosomal subunit and in complexes containing tRNA(f)(Met) and mRNA. *J. Mol. Biol.* **299**, 615–628.
86. Karimi, R., Pavlov, M., Buckingham, R., and Ehrenberg, M. (1999). Novel roles for classical factors at the interface between translation termination and initiation. *Mol. Cell* **3**, 601–609.
87. Dallas, A., and Noller, H. F. (2001). Interaction of translation initiation factor 3 with the 30 S ribosomal subunit. *Mol. Cell* **8**, 855–864.
88. Koc, E. C., and Spremulli, L. L. (2002). Identification of mammalian mitochondrial translational initiation factor 3 and examination of its role in initiation complex formation with natural mRNAs. *J. Biol. Chem.* **277**, 35541–35549.
89. Moreau, M., de Cock, E., Fortier, P.-L., Garcia, C., Albaret, C., Blanquet, S., Lallemand, J.-Y., and Dardel, F. (1997). Heteronuclear NMR studies of *E. coli* translation initiation factor IF3. Evidence that the inter-domain region is disordered in solution. *J. Mol. Biol.* **266**, 15–22.
90. Hua, Y., and Raleigh, D. (1998). On the global architecture of initiation factor IF3: A comparative study of the linker regions from the *Escherichia coli* protein and the *Bacillus stearothermophilus* protein. *J. Mol. Biol.* **278**, 871–878.
91. Kycia, J., Biou, V., Shu, F., Gerchman, S., Graziano, V., and Ramakrishnan, V. (1995). Prokaryotic translation initiation factor IF3 is an elongated protein consisting of two crystallizable domains. *Biochem.* **34**, 6183–6187.
92. Garcia, C., Fortier, P.-L., Blanquet, S., Lallemand, J.-Y., and Dardel, F. (1995). Solution structure of the ribosome binding domain of *E. coli* translation initiation factor IF3. Homology with the UA1 protein of the eukaryotic spliceosome. *J. Mol. Biol.* **254**, 247–259.
93. Biou, V., Shu, F., and Ramakrishnan, V. (1995). X-ray crystallography shows that translational initiation factor IF3 consists of two compact α/β domains linked by an α-helix. *EMBO J.* **14**, 4056–4064.
94. Petrelli, D., LaTeana, A., Garofalo, C., Spurio, R., Pon, C. L., and Gualerzi, C. O. (2001). Translation initiation factor IF3: Two domains, five functions, one mechanism? *EMBO J.* **20**, 4560–4569.
95. Jacobs, H. (2002). From mitochondrion to nucleus and back again. *Trends Genet.* **18**, 120.
96. Lin, Q., Ma, L., Burkhart, W., and Spremulli, L. L. (1994). Isolation and characterization of cDNA clones for chloroplast translational initiation factor-3 from *Euglena gracilis*. *J. Biol. Chem.* **269**, 9436–9444.
97. Yu, N.-J., and Spremulli, L. L. (1998). Regulation of the activity of chloroplast translational initiation factor 3 by NH_2- and COOH-terminal extensions. *J. Biol. Chem.* **273**, 3871–3877.
98. Pioletti, M., Schlunzen, F., Harms, J., Zarivach, R., Gluhmann, M., Avila, H., Bashan, A., Bartels, H., Auerbach, T., Jacobi, C., Hartsch, T., Yonath, A., and Franceschi, F. (2001). Crystal structures of complexes of the small ribosomal subunit with tetracycline, edeine, and IF3. *EMBO J.* **20**, 1829–1839.
99. McCutcheon, J., Agrawal, R., Philips, S. M., Grassucci, R., Gerchman, S., Clemons, W. M., Ramakrishnan, V., and Frank, J. (1999). Location of translational initiation factor IF3 on the small ribosomal subunit. *Proc. Natl. Acad. Sci.* **96**, 4301–4306.
100. Sette, M., Spurio, R., van Tilborg, P., Gualerzi, C., and Boelens, R. (1999). Identification of the ribosome binding sites of translation initiation factor IF3 by multidimensional heteronuclear NMR spectroscopy. *RNA* **5**, 82–92.
101. de Cock, E., Springer, M., and Dardel, F. (1999). The interdomain linker of *Escherichia coli* initiation factor IF3: A possible trigger of translation initiation specificity. *Mol. Microbiol.* **32**, 193–202.

102. Sacerdot, C., de Cock, E., Engst, K., Graffe, M., Dardel, F., and Springer, M. (1999). Mutations that alter initiation codon discrimination by *Escherichia coli* initiation factor IF3. *J. Mol. Biol.* **288,** 803–810.
103. Kyrpides, N., and Woese, C. (1998). Universally conserved translation initiation factors. *Proc. Natl. Acad. Sci.* **95,** 224–228.
104. Lee, J., Choi, S.-K., Roll-Mecak, A., Burley, S., and Dever, T. (1999). Universal conservation in translation initiation revealed by human and archeal homologs of bacterial translation initiation factor IF2. *Proc. Natl. Acad. Sci.* **96,** 4342–4347.
105. Cummings, H., and Hershey, J. (1994). Translation initiation factor IF-1 is essential for cell viability in *Escherichia coli*. *J. Bact.* **176,** 198–205.
106. Carter, A. P., Clemons, J., Brodersen, D. E., Morgan-Warren, R. J., Hartsch, T., Wimberly, B. T., and Ramakrishnan, V. (2001). Crystal structure of an initiation factor bound to the 30 S ribosomal subunit. *Science* **291,** 498–501.
107. Choi, S.-K., Lee, J., Zoll, W., Merrick, W., and Dever, T. (1998). Promotion of Met-tRNA$_i^{Met}$ binding to ribosomes by yIF2, a bacterial IF2 homolog in yeast. *Science* **280,** 1757–1760.
108. Pestova, T. V., Lomakin, I. B., Lee, J. H., Choi, S. K., Dever, T. E., and Hellen, C. U. (2000). The joining of ribosomal subunits in eukaryotes requires eIF5B. *Nature* **403,** 332–335.
109. Choi, S. K., Olsen, D. S., Roll-Mecak, A., Martung, A., Remo, K. L., Burley, S. K., Hinnebusch, A. G., and Dever, T. E. (2000). Physical and functional interaction between the eukaryotic orthologs of prokaryotic translation initiation factors IF1 and IF2. *Mol. Cell Biol.* **20,** 7183–7191.
110. Sette, M., van Tilborg, P., Spurio, R., Kaptein, R., Paci, M., Gualerzi, C., and Boelens, R. (1997). The structure of the translational initiation factor IF1 from *E. coli* contains an oligomer-binding motif. *EMBO J.* **16,** 1436–1443.
111. Battiste, J. L., Pestova, T. V., Hellen, C. U., and Wagner, G. (2000). The eIF1A solution structure reveals a large RNA-binding surface important for scanning function. *Mol. Cell* **5,** 109–119.
112. Schwartzbach, C., and Spremulli, L. L. (1989). Bovine mitochondrial protein synthesis elongation factors: Identification and initial characterization of an elongation factor Tu-elongation factor Ts complex. *J. Biol. Chem.* **264,** 19125–19131.
113. Bosch, L., Kraal, B., van der Meide, P., and van Noort, J. (1983). The elongation factor Tu and its two encoding genes. *Prog. Nuc. Acid Res. Mol. Biol.* **30,** 91–126.
114. Wells, J., Henkler, F., Leversha, M., and Koshy, R. (1995). A mitochondrial elongation factor-like protein is over-expressed in tumors and differentially expressed in normal tissues. *FEBS Lett.* **358,** 119–125.
115. Wiborg, O., Andersen, C., Knudsen, C., Kristensen, T., and Clark, B. (1994). Towards an understanding of structure-function relationships of elongation factor Tu. *Biotechnol. Appl. Biochem.* **19,** 3–15.
116. Saraste, M., Sibbald, P., and Wittinghofer, A. (1990). The P-loop—A common motif in ATP and GTP binding proteins. *Trends Biochem. Sci.* **15,** 430–434.
117. Kuhlman, P., and Palmer, J. (1995). Isolation, expression, and evolution of the gene encoding mitochondrial elongation factor Tu in *Arabidopsis thaliana*. *Plant Mol. Biol.* **29,** 1057–1070.
118. Nissen, P., Kjeldgaard, M., Thirup, S., Polekhina, G., Reshetnikova, L., Clark, B., and Nyborg, J. (1995). Crystal structure of the ternary complex of Phe-tRNA^{phe}, EF-Tu and a GTP analog. *Science* **270,** 1464–1472.
119. Nissen, P., Thirup, S., Kjeldgaard, M., and Nyborg, J. (1999). The crystal structure of Cys-tRNACys-EF-Tu-GDPNP reveals general and specific features in the ternary complex and in tRNA. *Structure* **7,** 143–156.

120. Krab, I., and Parmeggiani, A. (1998). EF-Tu, a GTPase odyssey. *Biochim. Biophys. Acta* **1443**, 1–22.
121. Burkhardt, N., Junemann, R., Spahn, C. M., and Nierhaus, K. H. (1998). Ribosomal tRNA binding sites: Three-site models of translation. *Crit. Rev. Biochem. Mol. Biol.* **33**, 95–149.
122. Louie, A., Ribeiro, S., Reid, B., and Jurnak, F. (1984). Relative affinities of all *Escherichia coli* aminoacyl-tRNAs for elongation factor Tu-GTP. *J. Biol. Chem.* **259**, 5010–5016.
123. Hanada, T., Suzuki, T., Yokogawa, T., Takemoto-Hori, C., Sprinzl, M., and Watanabe, K. (2001). Translation ability of mitochondrial tRNAsSer with unusual secondary structures in an *in vitro* translation system of bovine mitochondria. *Genes Cells* **6**, 1019–1030.
124. Grosjean, H., Cedergren, R. J., and McKay, W. (1982). Structure in tRNA data. *Biochimie* **64**, 387–397.
125. Helm, M., Florentz, C., Chomyn, A., and Attardi, G. (1999). Search for differences in posttranscriptional modification patterns of mitochondrial DNA-encoded wild-type and mutant tRNA^{Lys} and tRNA$^{Leu(UUR)}$. *Nuc. Acids Res.* **27**, 756–763.
126. Hayashi, I., Kawai, G., and Watanabe, K. (1998). Higher-order structure and thermal instability of bovine mitochondrial tRNA^{Ser}UGA investigated by proton NMR spectroscopy. *J. Mol. Biol.* **284**, 57–69.
127. Helm, M., Brule, H., Friede, D., Giege, R., Putz, D., and Florentz, C. (2000). Search for characteristic structural features of mammalian mitochondrial tRNAs. *RNA* **6**, 1356–1379.
128. Kumazawa, Y., Schwartzbach, C., Liao, H.-X., Mizumoto, K., Kaziro, Y., Watanabe, K., and Spremulli, L. L. (1991). Interactions of bovine mitochondrial phenylalanyl-tRNA with ribosomes and elongation factors from mitochondria and bacteria. *Biochim. Biophys. Acta* **1090**, 167–172.
129. Piepenburg, O., Pape, T., Pleiss, J. A., Wintermeyer, W., Uhlenbeck, O. C., and Rodnina, M. V. (2000). Intact aminoacyl-tRNA is required to trigger GTP hydrolysis by elongation factor Tu on the ribosome. *Biochem.* **39**, 1734–1738.
130. Ohtsuki, T., Watanabe, Y., Takemoto, C., Kawai, G., Ueda, T., Kita, K., Kojima, S., Kaziro, Y., Nyborg, J., and Watanabe, K. (2001). An "elongated" translation elongation factor Tu for truncated tRNAs in nematode mitochondria. *J. Biol. Chem.* **276**, 21571–21577.
131. Agrawal, R. K., Spahn, C. M., Penczek, P., Grassucci, R. A., Nierhaus, K. H., and Frank, J. (2000). Visualization of tRNA movements on the *Escherichia coli* 70 S ribosome during the elongation cycle. *J. Cell Biol.* **150**, 447–460.
132. Stark, H., Rodnina, M. V., Wieden, H. J., Zemlin, F., Wintermeyer, W., and van Heel, M. (2002). Ribosome interactions of aminoacyl-tRNA and elongation factor Tu in the codon-recognition complex. *Nat. Struct. Biol.* **9**, 849–854.
133. Kawashima, T., Berthet-Colominas, C., Wulff, M., Cusack, S., and Leberman, R. (1996). The structure of the *Escherichia coli* EF-Tu:EF-Ts complex at 2.5 A resolution. *Nature* **379**, 511–518.
134. Karring, H., Andersen, G. R., Thirup, S. S., Nyborg, J., Spremulli, L. L., and Clark, B. F. C. (2002). Isolation, crystallization, and preliminary X-ray analysis of the bovine mitochondrial EF-Tu:GDP and EF-Tu:EF-Ts complexes. *Biochim. Biophys. Acta* **1601**, 172–177.
135. Zhang, Y., Sun, V., and Spremulli, L. L. (1997). Role of domains in *Escherichia coli* and mammalian mitochondrial elongation factor Ts in the interaction with elongation factor Tu. *J. Biol. Chem.* **272**, 21956–21963.
136. Zhang, Y., Yu, N.-J., and Spremulli, L. L. (1998). Mutational analysis of the roles of residues in *Escherichia coli* elongation factor Ts in the interaction with elongation factor Tu. *J. Biol. Chem.* **273**, 4556–4562.
137. Ohtsuki, T., Sakurai, M., Sato, A., and Watanabe, K. (2002). Characterization of the interaction between the nucleotide exchange factor EF-Ts from nematode mitochondria and elongation factor Tu. *Nuc. Acids Res.* **30**, 5444–5451.

138. Schwartzbach, C., and Spremulli, L. L. (1991). Interaction of animal mitochondrial EF-Tu: EF-Ts with aminoacyl-tRNA, guanine nucleotides, and ribosomes. *J. Biol. Chem.* **266**, 16324–16330.
139. Arai, K.-I., Arai, N., Nakamura, S., Oshima, T., and Kaziro, Y. (1978). Studies on polypeptide-chain-elongation factors from an extreme thermophile, *Thermus thermophilus* HB8 2. Catalytic properties. *Eur. J. Biochem.* **92**, 521–531.
140. Nakamura, S., Ohita, S., Arai, K.-I., Oshima, T., and Kaziro, Y. (1978). Studies on polypeptide chain elongation factors from an extreme thermophile, *Thermus thermophilus* HB8 3. Molecular properties. *Eur. J. Biochem.* **92**, 533–543.
141. Clark, B., and Nyborg, J. (1997). The ternary complex of EF-Tu and its role in protein synthesis. *Current Opin. Struc. Biol.* **7**, 110–116.
142. Chung, H. K., and Spremulli, L. L. (1990). Purification and characterization of elongation factor G from bovine liver mitochondria. *J. Biol. Chem.* **265**, 21000–21004.
143. Eberly, S. L., Locklear, V., and Spremulli, L. L. (1985). Bovine mitochondrial ribosomes. Elongation factor specificity. *J. Biol. Chem.* **260**, 8721–8725.
144. Hammarsund, M., Wilson, W., Corcoran, M., Merup, M., Einhorn, S., Grander, D., and Sangfelt, O. (2001). Identification and characterization of two novel human mitochondrial elongation factor genes, hEFG2 and hEFG1, phylogenetically conserved through evolution. *Hum. Genet.* **109**, 542–550.
145. Winzeler, E. A., Shoemaker, D. D., Astromoff, A., Liang, H., Anderson, K., Andre, B., Bangham, R., Benito, R., Boeke, J. D., Bussey, H., Chu, A. M., Connelly, C., Davis, K., Dietrich, F., Dow, S. W., El Bakkoury, M., Foury, F., Friend, S. H., Gentalen, E., Giaever, G., Hegemann, J. H., Jones, T., Laub, M., Liao, H., Davis, R. W. *et al.* (1999). Functional characterization of the *S. cerevisiae* genome by gene deletion and parallel analysis. *Science* **5**, 901–906.
146. Liljas, A., Ævarsson, A., Al-Karadaghi, S., Garber, M., Zheltonosova, J., and Brazhnikov, E. (1995). Crystallographic studies of elongation factor G. *Biochem. Cell Biol.* **73**, 1209–1216.
147. Al-Karadaghi, S., Ævarsson, A., Garber, M., Zheltonosova, J., and Liljas, A. (1996). The structure of elongation factor G in complex with GDP: Conformational flexibility and nucleotide exchange. *Structure* **4**, 555–565.
148. Ævarsson, A., Brazhnikov, E., Garber, M., Zheltonosova, Yu., Al-Karagaghi, A., Svensson, L., and Liljas, A. (1994). Three-dimensional structure of the ribosomal translocase: Elongation factor G from *Thermus thermophilus*. *EMBO J.* **13**, 3369–3377.
149. Breitenberger, C. A., and Spremulli, L. L. (1980). Purification of *Euglena gracilis* chloroplast elongation factor G and comparison with other prokaryotic and eukaryotic translocases. *J. Biol. Chem.* **255**, 9814–9820.
150. Johanson, U., and Hughes, D. (1994). Fusidic acid-resistant mutants define three regions in elongation factor G of *Salmonella typhimurium*. *Gene* **143**, 55–59.
151. Sperling-Petersen, H., and Mortensen, K. (1989). A structural model for initiation factor IF2. *Protein Engin.* **3**, 343–344.
152. Garcia, C., Fortier, P.-L., Blanquet, S., Lallemand, J.-Y., and Dardel, F. (1995). ^{1}H and ^{15}N resonance assignments and secondary structure of the N-terminal domain of *Escherichia coli* initiation factor 3. *Eur. J. Biochem.* **228**, 395–402.
153. Koradi, R., Billeter, M., and Wüthrich, K. (1996). MOLMOL: A program for display and analysis of macromolecular structures. *J. Mol. Graphics* **14**, 51–55.
154. Miller, D., and Weissbach, H. (1970). Studies on the purification and properties of factor Tu from *E. coli*. *Arch. Biochem. Biophys.* **141**, 26–37.
155. Louie, A., and Jurnak, F. (1985). Kinetic studies of *Escherichia coli* elongation factor Tu-guanosine 5′-triphosphate-aminoacyl-tRNA complexes. *Biochem.* **24**, 6433–6439.

Cyclin Dependent Kinase 11 in RNA Transcription and Splicing

Janeen H. Trembley,
Pascal Loyer, Dongli Hu,
Tongyuan Li, Jose Grenet,
Jill M. Lahti, and
Vincent J. Kidd

Department of Genetics and Tumor Cell Biology, St. Jude Children's Research Hospital, 332 N. Lauderdale, Memphis, TN 38105

I. Introduction 263
II. CDK11 Gene Structure and Expression 264
    A. CDK11 Gene Structure 264
    B. Alternate Promoter Usage and Alternative Splicing 267
    C. CDK11 Expression and Gene-Specific Protein Isoforms 268
    D. CDK11 is Conserved through Evolution 269
III. CDK11 Protein Isoforms and Regulation 270
    A. CDK Homology 270
    B. The CDK11 p110 Isoforms 272
    C. The p58 Isoforms 273
    D. The p46 Isoforms 274
IV. CDK Regulation of RNA Transcription 275
V. $CDK11^{p110}$ Protein Complexes and Biological Function 278
    A. $CDK11^{p110}$ Protein Complexes Contain Defined Transcriptional Elongation-Associated Factors 278
    B. $CDK11^{p110}$ Association with Transcription Complexes is Functionally Significant 278
    C. $CDK11^{p110}$ Protein Complexes Contain RNA Processing Proteins 280
    D. The $CDK11^{p110}$ Kinase Helps to Regulate Certain Pre-mRNA Splicing Events 281
VI. Alterations in $CDK11^{p110}$ Expression in Human Disease 282
References 283

I. Introduction

The explosion in signaling research data over the last two decades has helped to emphasize the fundamental importance of protein modification by phosphorylation. Changes in the phosphorylation status of numerous proteins are a central part of the cellular response to signals that mediate cell growth, differentiation, metabolism, and death. The results of the human genome sequencing project further reinforce the importance of phosphorylation in cellular function in that there are at least 518 protein kinases encoded in the human genome (1).

A key group of serine and threonine residue protein kinases is the Cyclin Dependent Kinase (CDK) family. The first CDK family members characterized were found to be catalytic subunits that formed heterodimers with regulatory partner proteins called cyclins, and binding to the cyclin protein is required for kinase activity. However, there are now members of the CDK family, defined as a CDK by amino acid sequence homology, which also interact with non-cyclin like regulatory partner proteins. For example, CDK5 is activated by interaction with two non-cyclin partners called p35 and p39 (2). Furthermore, there remain several putative CDK and cyclin family members for which no regulatory, or catalytic, partner protein has been described (see Table I). It is possible that a select few of the partnerless CDKs may function as kinases independently of regulatory partner proteins (3, 4). Finally, there are also several members of both the cyclin and CDK protein families whose cellular function is unknown (see Table I).

Although the original members of the CDK family, CDK1–4, play important roles in cell cycle control, new and diverse functions have been described for members of the CDK family. These functions include roles in RNA transcription and processing, neuronal function, cellular differentiation, protein sorting, and apoptosis (see Table I). Data published on the CDK11 protein kinases, formerly named the PITSLRE kinases, indicates that they play a role in the regulation of cell cycle, RNA transcription and processing, neuronal function, and apoptosis. The potential for CDK11 to regulate these diverse cellular activities is unique in the CDK family. The purpose of this chapter is to provide basic information regarding the CDK11 protein kinases and to describe what is currently understood about the role of CDK11 in transcription and RNA processing.

II. CDK11 Gene Structure and Expression

A. CDK11 Gene Structure

In humans, two distinct genes, *Cdc2L1* and *Cdc2L2*, encode the various isoforms of the CDK11/PITSLRE protein kinase family (*Cdc2L* is an acronym for Cell division control 2 Like). These two genes are localized in a genomic region that spans about 140 kb on human chromosome 1 band p36.3 (5). The characterization of these genes and their genomic structure was particularly difficult because of the very high level of identity between *Cdc2L1* and *Cdc2L2*. This goal was achieved by the use of several cosmid/P1/BAC clones

TABLE I
MEMBERS OF THE CDK FAMILY ARE NAMED ACCORDING TO THEIR PSTAIRE HOMOLOGY MOTIF UNTIL A CYCLIN OR REGULATORY PARTNER PROTEIN IS IDENTIFIED[a]

CDK	PSTAIRE Motif	Multiple isoforms	Cyclin class or regulatory protein	Functions defined and proposed
CDK1	PSTAIRE	No	Cyclin B	Cell cycle—G2/M, activate mitosis, repress transcription
				Apoptosis
CDK2	PSTAIRE	No	Cyclin E	Cell cycle—G1/S, DNA replication, centrosome duplication
			Cyclin A	Cell cycle—S/G2/M, DNA replication, entry into mitosis
				Apoptosis
			Cyclin J	Cell cycle—M, Drosophila entry into mitosis
CDK3	PSTAIRE	No	Cyclin E	Cell cycle—G1
CDK4	Pv/iSTVRE	No	Cyclin D	Cell cycle—G1, release cells from G1 restriction point
				Neuronal
				Apoptosis
CDK5	PSSALRE	No	p35 (p25) p39 (p29)	Neuronal development and signaling
				Differentiation
				Protein trafficking and membrane transport
				Apoptosis
CDK6	PLSTIRE	No	Cyclin D	Cell cycle—G1, release cells from G1 restriction point
				Apoptosis
CDK7	NRTALRE	No	Cyclin H	CDK activation as CAK
				RNA transcription (TFIIH)
CDK8	MSACREI	No	Cyclin C	RNA transcription
CDK9	PITALRE	Yes	Cyclins T, K	RNA transcription (P-TEFb)
				Differentiation
				Apoptosis
CDK10	PISSLRE	Yes	?	Cell cycle—G2/M
CDK11	PITSLRE	Yes	Cyclin L	Cell cycle—M
				RNA transcription and processing
				Neuronal signaling
				Apoptosis

(Continues)

TABLE I (Continued)

CDK	PSTAIRE Motif	Multiple isoforms	Cyclin class or regulatory protein	Functions defined and proposed
(CrkRS)	PITAIRE	No	?	RNA transcription and processing
	PCTAIRE-1,2,3	Yes	?	Neuronal
				Sperm development
	PFTAIRE	Yes	?	Neuronal signaling
				Testis meiosis
				Development (Drosophila)
(CHED)	PITAIRE	No	?	Hematopoiesis
	KKIALRE	Yes	?	Expressed in ovary
				Neuronal
	KKIAMRE	No	?	Expressed in testis
	NKIAMRE	No	?	(Human)
	NKIATRE	Yes	?	(Rat)

[a]Orphan cyclins include cyclins F, G, I, M, O, and P.

that were subdivided, subcloned, and then sequenced (5). The identification of a single nucleotide difference in exon 17, resulting in a Lys residue at position 625 in *Cdc2L1* and an Asn residue at the same position in *Cdc2L2*, generating an *Eco*RI site in *Cdc2L2*, provided a suitable marker to differentiate the two genes and to begin characterization. Further characterization demonstrated a total of 16 amino acid differences between *Cdc2L1* and *Cdc2L2* (5).

After extensive restriction endonuclease mapping and sequencing of the genomic fragments from these various cosmid, BAC, and P1 phage clones, it was established that this chromosomal region consists of two duplicated genomic regions, each containing a *Cdc2L* gene linked to a unique metalloprotease (MMP) gene, either *MMP21* or *MMP22*, arranged in a head-to-head configuration (Fig. 1) (6). This genomic region is also linked tightly to D1Z2, a genetic marker containing a highly polymorphic, human chromosome 1-specific VNTR (variable number tandem repeat) that consists of an unusual 40-bp repeated sequence (7, 8). This unique repetitive sequence is located at the distal end of the 140 kb region containing the human *Cdc2L* and *MMP* genes. The *Cdc2L* and *MMP* genes and the D1Z2 sequence are organized as follows: centromere-(5'-*MMP21*-3')-(3'*Cdc2L1*-5')-(5'-*Cdc2L2*-3')-(3'-*MMP22*-5')-D1Z2-telomere. This genomic configuration is consistent with the duplication of the region encompassing both the *Cdc2L* and *MMP* genes in the same p36.3 locus on chromosome 1. A series of Alu-type repeated sequences was also found near

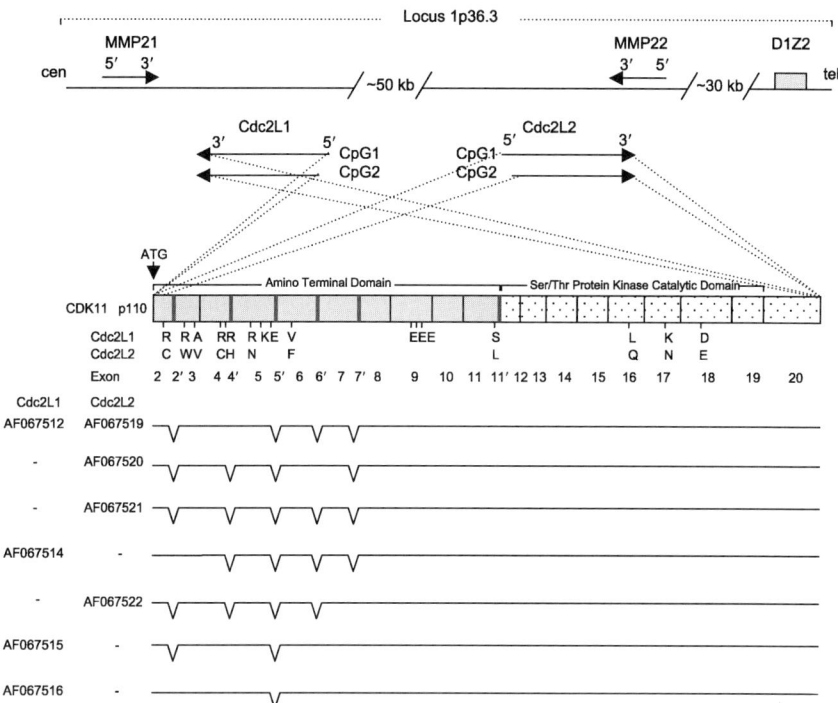

FIG. 1. At the top of the figure is a schematic representation of the human *Cdc2L1/L2* and MMP21/22 genomic structure on 1p36.3. Shown is the organization of the duplicated genomic segments, each containing a Cdc2L and MMP gene, as well as the transcriptional orientation of the genes. Just below the genomic schematic is a linear drawing of the CDK11^{p110} proteins encoded by *Cdc2L1* and *Cdc2L2*. Amino acid differences between the proteins encoded by Cdc2L1 and Cdc2L2, corresponding to nucleotide changes between the two genes, are indicated below the protein drawing. Some of the CDK11 mRNA splice variants generated by the use of alternative 3' splicing sites (depicted as bold boundaries between exons and listed as 2', 4', 5', 7', and 11') from *Cdc2L1* and/or *Cdc2L2* genes are diagramed in the lower half of the figure. Accession numbers for these splice variants are indicated on the left side of the diagrams.

the 5' end of *Cdc2L* genes as well as in several of the larger introns of these genes.

B. Alternate Promoter Usage and Alternative Splicing

The *Cdc2L1* and *Cdc2L2* genes, as well as their flanking regions, are almost identical and span approximately 40 kb per gene. Each gene consists of 20 exons and 19 introns within this 40 kb of genomic region, and they encode the sequences that comprise the most commonly expressed mRNAs of both genes. Analysis of transcripts from the human HeLa and K562 cell lines, as well as human testis, revealed that both *Cdc2L* loci are active and express nearly identical mRNAs and proteins (5). However, the identification of an alternatively spliced *Cdc2L* transcript in testis containing a unique CpG island in its 5′ UTR suggested that a distinct group of mRNAs might be expressed in specific cell types. Additional PCR analysis using primers specific for these CpG1 and CpG2 *Cdc2L* transcripts were performed and confirmed the expression of two distinct groups of transcripts which are generated from the two CpG promoter regions (5). Interestingly, the CpG1 transcripts derived from *Cdc2L1* are expressed only in testis, bone marrow, and hematopoietic cell lines.

The combination of transcription from two distinct promoters and alternative splicing generates more than 20 distinct CDK11 mRNA and protein isoforms in human cells. Six splice variants for the *Cdc2L1* gene and twelve splice variants for the *Cdc2L2* gene have been characterized to date and are partially illustrated in Fig. 1 along with their GenBank accession numbers. It is important to note that the complex alternative splicing observed for the *Cdc2L1* and *Cdc2L2* genes involves only exons encoding the amino-terminal domain, but not the protein kinase catalytic domain.

C. CDK11 Expression and Gene-Specific Protein Isoforms

It is not yet clear whether expression of certain alternatively spliced *Cdc2L* isoforms, other than those expressed from the two distinct CpG promoter regions in testis, is restricted to specific cell types, or whether these isoforms exhibit different functions during development. Moreover, we do not yet have the molecular tools to finely discriminate at the protein level between many of these isoforms. This inability to discriminate the various CDK11 isoforms generated by alternative splicing is due to the very small size of the mRNA and protein regions associated with the protein kinase isoforms. Two of the isoforms, CDK11^{p110} and CDK11^{p58}, however, have been characterized extensively. The larger CDK11^{p110} protein kinase isoform is ubiquitously expressed in all cells and cell lines examined so far, including the human cell lines Jurkat, Cem C7, HeLa, HEK 293, K562, HFF, and RNET (5, 9, 10).

Expression of the smaller, mitosis-specific CDK11^{p58} protein kinase is due to an internal ribosome entry site (IRES) sequence present in the mRNA encoding CDK11^{p110} [(11); discussed in more detail in the following text]. This IRES is similar to viral IRES sequences whose expression is limited to mitosis, and this sequence has been conserved in the CDK11^{p110} mRNAs from mouse, chicken, *Drosophila*, *Xenopus*, and *C. elegans* (GenBank accession numbers A55817; I50463; AAN12141, AAN12142, AAN12143, AAF51635; Xl.23888; NP_649521, NP_730563, NP_730564; NP_595739, respectively). The CDK11^{p58} protein is most abundant in the human cell lines K562 and HL60, but is less detectable in other cell lines, such as HepG2, HT-29, HEK293, and VA-2. CDK11^{p58} is produced during a very narrow window of mitosis and is

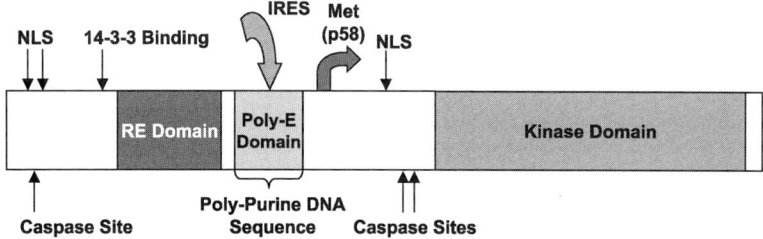

FIG. 2. Schematic diagram of the full length CDK11 protein kinase. Several of the interesting protein and nucleic acid motifs are indicated on the diagram. Only caspase cleavage sites known to be used *in vivo* are labeled. NLS, nuclear localization signal; IRES, internal ribosomal entry site; RE, arginine and glutamic acid; poly-E, poly-glutamic acid.

therefore much more difficult to detect than CDK11^{p110} (11). Although CDK11^{p58} is expressed in all cell types, its detection depends primarily on the mitotic characteristics of a particular cell type. In addition, the CDK11$^{p110/p58}$ mRNA is expressed ubiquitously in all human tissues examined, and is most abundant in human heart, brain, placenta, skeletal muscle, kidney, and pancreas (9).

Alternative splicing and transcription initiated from the two distinct promoters result in the expression of proteins with slight differences in their amino acid sequence that may affect their biological functions. Although the *Cdc2L1* and *Cdc2L2* genes encode highly similar CDK11 proteins, there are 16 amino acid residues that differ between the two longest products of 773 and 786 amino acids, respectively. Twelve of the 16 amino acid changes are located in the amino terminal domain of the CDK11^{p110} protein kinase, and the amino acid changes are listed in Fig. 1. Potentially significant differences in the amino acid sequence are found in a putative 14-3-3 consensus-binding site (12), at the caspase cleavage sites corresponding to Asp-387 and Asp-391 used to produce CDK11^{p46} during TNF- and Fas-mediated apoptosis (13, 14), and in the coiled–coiled structural motifs that are hallmarks of protein–protein interaction domains (see Fig. 2). The lack of caspase cleavage sites would render the CDK11 proteins insensitive to caspase cleavage at this site during apoptosis, while the absence of 14-3-3 binding site and coiled–coiled domains might affect protein–protein interactions and subcellular localization of the kinase. The functional relevance of these different transcripts and their corresponding proteins remains unknown at this time.

D. CDK11 is Conserved through Evolution

As mentioned briefly earlier, CDK11 is evolutionarily well conserved, as demonstrated by the fact that CDK11 genes have been found in many eukaryotic organisms with a homology >30 to 80%, compared to the human sequence (Table II). Furthermore, an antibody that was raised against the catalytic domain

TABLE II
Conservation of CDK11 During Evolution[a]

Organism	Genbank accession number cDNA	Accession number protein	% Identity to Homo sapiens protein: AAC72077
Homo sapiens	CDC2L1:AF067512	AAC72077	100
	CDCL2:AF067519	AAC72084	98.21
Mus musculus	L37092	AAA66169	95.0
Rattus norvegicus	XM235722	XP235722	89.0
Gallus gallus	AH003107	AAA67037	76.4
Xenopus laevis	BG409678 (EST)	–	–
Danio rerio	BQ074339 (EST)	–	–
Drosophila melanogaster	X99513	SP:Q9VPCD	44.0
Meloidogyne arenaria	BI747975 (EST)	–	–
Caenorhabditis elegans	NM077345	NP495617.1	39.0
Arabidopsis thaliana	NM116427	NP192105	30.0
Toxoplasma gondii	AH007454	AAD17245	38.7
Saccharomyces pombe	NC_00323	T39779	47.0°
Saccharomyces cerevisiae	SP:P00546	AAB68076	36.0°

[a] The CDK11/PITSLRE gene has been found in most organisms, including yeast. Genbank accession numbers are listed in this table for some of the organisms in which CDK11 cDNA clones exist. Among vertebrates, identity at the protein level is over 75%. The percent protein identity decreases in lower organisms, especially in the amino-terminal domain.

° Indicates organisms in which only the p58 isoform of CDK11 is found.

of the human CDK11 kinase cross-reacts with most of the CDK11 products from other species. To date, with the exception of human and chicken, only one copy of the CDK11 gene has been found in other organisms, including mouse. Multiple mRNA transcripts are detected in human and many other organisms. For example, at least 5 different CDK11 mRNAs have been detected by northern blotting at varying levels during *Drosophila melanogaster* development (15). However, not all organisms express multiple alternatively spliced mRNAs, as demonstrated by studies in mouse, which expresses very few mRNA isoforms.

III. CDK11 Protein Isoforms and Regulation

A. CDK Homology

CDK11 displays significant homology to the prototypical CDKs (CDK1 and CDK2) in the catalytic kinase domain (Figs. 2 and 3). The most important conserved amino acids include the PSTAIRE α-helix and the three

CDK11 IN RNA TRANSCRIPTION AND SPLICING

```
▼Start CDK11^P58                              ▼Start CDK11^P46
MSEDEERENENHLLVVPESRFDRDSGESEEAEEEVGEGTPQSSALTEGDYVPDSPALSPI    CDK11

ELKQELPKYLPALQGCRSVEEFQCLNRIEEGTYGVVYRAKDK..KTDEIVALKRLKMEKE    CDK11
          LGRCRSVKEFEKLNRIGEGTYGIVYRARDT..QTDEIVALKKVRMDKE    CDK10
              MEDYTKIEKIGEGTYGVVYKGRHK..TTGQVVAMKKIRLESE    CDK1
              MENFQKVEKIGEGTYGVVYKARNK..LTGEVVALKKIRLDTE    CDK2
              MQKYEKLEKIGEGTYGTVFKAKNR..ETHEIVALKRVRLDDD    CDK5
         MALDVKSRAKRYEKLDFLGEGQFATVYKARDK..NTNQIVAIKKIKLGHR    CDK7
MAKQYDSVECPFCDEVSKYEKLAKIGQGTFGEVFKARHR..KTGQKVALKKVLMENE    CDK9
MDYDFKVKLSSERERVEDLFEYEGC.KVGRGTYGHVYKAKRKDGKDDKDYALKQI.....   CDK8

KE...GFPITSLREINTILKAQHPNIVTVREIV......VGSNMDKIYIVMNYVEHDLKS   CDK11
KD...GIPISSLREITLLLRLRHPNIVELKEVV......VGNHLESIFLVMGYCEQDLAS   CDK10
EE...GVPSTAIREISLLKELRHPNIVSLQDVL........MQDSRLYLIFEFLSMDLKK   CDK1
TE...GVPSTAIREISLLKELNHPNIVKLLDVI........HTENKLYLVFEFLHQDLKK   CDK2
DE...GVPSSALREICLLKELKHKNIVRLHDVL........HSDKKLTLVFEFCDQDLKK   CDK5
SEAKDGINRTALREIKLLQELSHPNIIGLLDAF........GHKSNISLVFDFMETDLEV   CDK7
KE...GFPITALREIKILQLLKHENVVNLIEICRTKASPYNRCKGSIYLVFDFCEHDLAG   CDK9
..EGTGISMSACREIALLRELKHPNVISLQKVF......LSHADRKVWLLFDYAEHDLWH   CDK8

LM.....ETMKQP...FLPGEVKTLMIQLLRGVKHLHDNWILHRDLKTSNLLL....SHA   CDK11
LL.....ENMPTP...FSEAQVKCIVLQVLRGLQYLHRNFIIHRDLKVSNLLM....TDK   CDK10
YL.....D.SIPPGQYMDSSLVKSYLYQILQGIVFCHSRRVLHRDLKPQNLLI....DDK   CDK1
FM.....DASALTG..IPLPLIKSYLFQLLQGLAFCHSHRVLHRDLKPQNLLI....NTE   CDK2
YF.....DSC...NGDLDPEIVKSFLFQLLKGLGFCHSRNVLHRDLKPQNLLI....NRN   CDK5
II.....KDNSLV...LTPSHIKAYMLMTLQGLEYLHQHWILHRDLKPNNLLL....DEN   CDK7
LL.....SNVLV...KFTLSEIKRVMQMLLNGLYYIHRNKILHRDMKAANVLI....TRD   CDK9
IIKFHRASKANKKPVQLPRGMVKSLLYQILDGIHYLHANWVLHRDLKPANILVMGEGPER   CDK8

GILKVGDFGLAREYGS.....PLKAYTPVVVTLWYRAPELLLG...    CDK11
GCVKTADFGLARAYGV.....PVKPMTPKVVTLWYRAPELLLG...    CDK10
GTIKLADFGLARAFGI.....PIRVYTHEVVTLWYRSPEVLLG       CDK1
GAIKLADFGLARAFGV.....PVRTYTHEVVTLWYRAPEILLG...    CDK2
GELKLADFGLARAFGI.....PVRCYSAEVVTLWYRPPDVLFG...    CDK5
GVLKLADFGLAKSFGS.....PNRAYTHQVVTRWYRAPELLFG...    CDK7
GVLKLADFGLARAFSLAKNSQPNR.YTNRVVTLWYRPPELLLG...    CDK9
GRVKIADMGFARLFN..SPLKPLADLDPVVVTFWYRAPELLLG...    CDK8
```

FIG. 3. Alignment of CDK catalytic domains. The alignment begins with the first amino acid for all CDKs except CDK11. CDK11 alignment begins with the initiating methionine for the p58 isoform. The first amino acid for the CDK11 p46 isoform is indicated with an arrowhead. The conserved inhibitory threonine and tyrosine phosphorylation sites and the conserved PSTAIRE domain are boxed. Also, the activating T-loop domain is boxed and the CAK phosphorylation site is in bold type within this box.

phosphorylation sites which serve to activate or repress protein kinase activity during the cell cycle. The extensive characterization of CDK1 and CDK2 and the conservation of particular residues and domains allow us to draw a few general conclusions concerning regulation of activity in the CDK family of kinases (see Fig. 3). The structure of monomeric CDKs consists of an amino-terminal β-sheet dominated lobe and a carboxy-terminal α-helix dominated lobe. The ATP-binding pocket is located between these two lobes (16). The regulatory loop (T loop) is located in the carboxyl-terminus of CDKs, similar to other serine/threonine protein kinases, and it contains an activating phosphorylation site that is typically targeted by the CDK activating kinase (CAK) during the cell cycle (17). Structural data from several research groups on CDK2 and CDK2/cyclin A has shown how binding of a cyclin to the CDK PSTAIRE α-helix and phosphorylation of the CAK site combine to reorganize the polypeptide substrate and ATP-binding pocket, and thus regulate the corresponding protein kinase activity (16).

The two remaining conserved phosphorylation sites are located in the ATP-binding pocket, and when phosphorylated, serve to inhibit protein kinase activity. In the case of CDK1, these residues are T14 and Y15 (see Fig. 3), and the specific dephosphorylation of these sites by a CDC25 phosphatase during the G2/M cell cycle transition is necessary for maturation promoting factor (MPF) activation (17). It is of interest to note that, while phosphorylation of the activating CAK site is very important for activation of CDKs, the CAK enzyme, composed of CDK7, Cyclin H, and Mat1, is not itself cell cycle regulated. The exquisite control of cell cycle activity exhibited by several of the CDKs is actually accomplished through other mechanisms. These include cell cycle specific expression and degradation of either the cyclin or CDK proteins, regulated binding of inhibitor proteins of the Cip/Kip and INK4 families, and cell cycle controlled subcellular localization and modification of the heterodimeric proteins (16–18).

B. The CDK11 p110 Isoforms

The longest CDK11 protein isoforms are collectively referred to as "p110," due to their apparent molecular mass following protein separation by 10% SDS-PAGE (sodium dodecylsulfate-polyacrylamide gel electrophoresis) and immunoblot analysis. The $CDK11^{p110}$ protein isoforms are ubiquitously expressed in mammalian tissues and cell lines during proliferation. Moreover, $CDK11^{p110}$ continues to be detected by immunoblot in human foreskin fibroblasts (HFF) that have been serum starved into quiescence for 3 days or allowed to become quiescent following confluence and feeding for several weeks (Trembley, Loyer, and Kidd, unpublished data). Preliminary data indicates that disruption of the single murine cdc2L gene results in early embryonic lethality at the blastocyst stage of embryonic development (i.e., E3.5 post coitus) due, in part, to cellular proliferative failure (Li, Inoue, Lahti, and Kidd, in press). This portion of the embryonic lethal phenotype is consistent with $CDK11^{p110}$ function during transcription/RNA processing, which is discussed further in later sections of this chapter.

The $CDK11^{p110}$ isoforms are nuclear proteins, which localize to both splicing factor compartments (SFCs, which are also called nuclear speckles) and to the nucleoplasm (*21*). Using subcellular fractionation techniques, it has been demonstrated that there are also two distinct nuclear populations of the CDK11^{p110} protein: one population which is "soluble" (i.e., nucleoplasmic) and easily releases from the nucleus, and one population which we call "insoluble" (i.e., nuclear speckle-associated) and associates with the nuclear matrix (*21*). In addition to the nuclear localization signals, there are several well characterized protein domains in the amino terminal half of the CDK11^{p110} isoform (see Fig. 2) (*9*). These include a polyglutamic acid domain (poly-E) whose function at the amino acid level is not known. However, as mentioned earlier, the primary nucleotide sequence of this region appears to serve as the IRES sequence (See following text (*11*)). The poly-E domain encompasses a stretch of 33 amino acids, 28 of which are glutamic acids (these numbers refer to the *Cdc2L1* αSV1 isoform, GenBank accession #AF067512). Notably, the RE domain of CDK11^{p110}, which is named due to the high content of arginine (R) and aspartate (E) residues in this domain, is important both for CDK11^{p110} protein–protein interactions and nuclear localization to SFCs (*22*). For example, deletion of this domain results in the loss of interaction between CDK11^{p110} and both RNPS1 and CK2 (*21–23*). Upon induction of apoptosis in Jurkat cells, CDK11^{p110} is rapidly phosphorylated at its amino-terminal end, and is then processed by caspase 1-, 3-, and 8-like activities (*14*).

Like other CDK proteins, the activity of CDK11^{p110} appears to be regulated by a cyclin partner. Cyclin L1 has been identified as a protein partner of CDK11^{p110} by several groups. Hyman and colleagues cloned rat cyclin L1 (also called Ania 6) using a screen for genes in the rat brain responsive to cocaine stimulation (*19*). Gottesfeld and colleagues used PCR to clone human cyclin L1 from a lung cDNA library (*20*). Both groups demonstrated that cyclin L1-α associates with CDK11^{p110}. We also found cyclin L1-α associated with CDK11^{p110}; however, we found that a minor portion (less than 30%) of the CDK11^{p110} nuclear protein pool interacts with cyclin L1 in human cell lines (*66*), leaving open the possibility that CDK11^{p110} may interact with other cyclin partner proteins as well.

C. The p58 Isoforms

The first form of CDK11 identified was p58^{GTA} (i.e., galactosyltransferase-associated, although the GTA nomenclature is no longer used). This cDNA was isolated from an expression library screen using a galactosyltransferase polyclonal antiserum (*24*). Although the CDK11^{p58} protein kinase was identified via its co-purification with a mammalian glycosyltransferase, its considerable homology with CDK1 indicated a potential role in cell cycle. It is now known that CDK11^{p58} is a mitosis-specific catalytic domain isoform of CDK11, and that CDK11^{p58} is specifically translated using an IRES (see Fig. 2) during mitosis (*11*). Beyaert and colleagues mapped the IRES region to the CDK11^{p110} poly-E domain already described. CDK11^{p58} also contains a nuclear localization signal, similar to signals observed in viral and cellular oncogene sequences, in the unique amino-terminal domain that is upstream of the CDK1 kinase homology region (25). When ectopically expressed, CDK11^{p58} localizes primarily to the nucleus, but is also detected in the cytoplasm.

Mitotic abnormalities result from alterations in CDK11^{p58} expression in cultured cells. Forced expression of the CDK11^{p58} wild-type protein kinase, but not a kinase dead form of the protein, in CHO cells resulted in a longer cell-doubling time, telophase delay, and cells that were rounded-up, small, and often paired (25). Also, cells stably expressing CDK11^{p58} were found to exhibit increased micronucleation, increased aneuploidy, and a greater number of giant cells (10, 25). The decreased growth rate in CHO cells was found to be due to apoptosis, whereas the mitotic abnormalities were linked to the aberrant expression of the amino-terminal domain of CDK11^{p58} (10). As mentioned earlier in this chapter, we have observed an early embryonic lethal phenotype following disruption of both copies of the mouse *cdc2L* gene. The data indicate that this phenotype is due to cellular proliferative failure, as has been described, accompanied by mitotic arrest, and is consistent with a critical role for CDK11^{p58} during mitosis (Li, Inoue, Lahti, and Kidd, in press).

Although two cyclins are known to interact with CDK11^{p58}, only one is considered to be a potential regulator. The first cyclin identified was one of the short forms of cyclin L1, referred to as cyclin L1-β (Trembley, Loyer, and Kidd, unpublished data). These two proteins interact very strongly *in vivo*, but the *bona fide* cyclin regulator of CDK11^{p58} has not yet been identified. Cyclin D3 was cloned from a yeast two-hybrid screen as a partner protein for CDK11^{p58}, but it is viewed as an unlikely regulator of this protein kinase since the expression of cyclin D3 is restricted to mainly hematopoietic cell types and the expression of CDK11^{p58} is ubiquitous (26). It has recently been demonstrated that the interactions between CDKs and their cyclin regulatory partners are not stringently controlled (27). Thus, aberrant expression or localization of a cyclin could result in its interaction with a CDK that is not normally its partner. Therefore, the results identifying cyclin D3 as a putative regulatory partner of CDK11^{p58} are most likely an artifact of the experimental conditions used by these investigators.

D. The p46 Isoforms

During apoptosis, caspase cleavage of the CDK11^{p110} isoforms (see Fig. 2) produces the CDK11^{p46} catalytic domain isoform of CDK11, which lacks the first 52 amino acids found in the CDK11^{p58} isoform. In contrast to CDK11^{p110} and CDK11^{p58}, CDK11^{p46} localizes to the cytoplasm when ectopically expressed. However, it is important to note that when cleavage of CDK11^{p110}

occurs, the protein is in the nucleus. Induction of apoptosis in Cem-C7, Jurkat, and A375 cells by treatment with Fas monoclonal antibody induces the appearance of CDK11^{P46} (*10, 28*). Similarly, glucocorticoid- and tumor necrosis factor-induced apoptosis in T cell line cells results in appearance of the CDK11^{P46} isoform (*10, 13*). The induction of CDK11^{P46} occurs primarily due to caspase cleavage of preexisting pools of CDK11^{p110}, as opposed to translation of new CDK11 protein. CHO cells transiently expressing both wild-type and a Δ-NH2 form of p58 (that corresponds to p46 minus the first 22 amino acids) underwent apoptosis, which required a catalytically active form of the CDK11 kinase (*10*). Taken together, these results demonstrate that the CDK11^{P46} may participate in the apoptotic process, whereas CDK11^{p58} participates in mitotic processes.

While several recent publications have identified putative partner proteins for CDK11^{P46} during the cell death process, none has conclusively demonstrated definitive *in vivo* association. One publication demonstrated the association of p21-activated kinase 1 (PAK1) with CDK11^{P46} (i.e., p110C) by two-hybrid analysis (*29*). (Please note that in this publication the CDK11^{P46} isoform was not referred to appropriately, but rather as p110C, indicating the carboxy-terminal half of the CDK11^{p110} isoform.) Gu and colleagues reported that CDK11^{P46} is induced and associates with PAK1, and that PAK1 activity is inhibited by this association, during anoikis (*29*). Anoikis is a unique form of apoptosis induced by disruption of cell–matrix interactions. In addition, expression of CDK11^{P46} increased the amount of anoikis that occurred in NIH 3T3 cells. A second publication, also using two-hybrid analysis, reports a CDK11^{P46} partner protein to be the p47 subunit of Eukaryotic Initiation Factor 3 (EIF3) (*30*). Once again, the lack of convincing data demonstrating an *in vivo* interaction between these two proteins detracts from the authors' conclusions. Finally, cyclin L1-β has also been shown to interact with the CDK11^{P46} kinase isoform when expressed as a tagged-protein ectopically in cells (Trembley, Loyer, and Kidd, unpublished data). However, the significance of this observation *in vivo* is unclear; thus, to date *bona fide* CDK11^{p58} or CDK11^{P46} cyclin regulatory partners have not been identified.

IV. CDK Regulation of RNA Transcription

Participation of CDKs in the regulation of RNA production and processing is a rapidly growing area of research. RNA transcription and processing are concurrent and codependent events, during which the phosphorylation state of the carboxyl-terminal domain (CTD) of the RNA polymerase II

(RNAP II) largest subunit is actively modified. Hereafter, references to the CTD refer to the largest subunit of the RNAP II holoenzyme. The sequence of processes leading to the final mature mRNA species can be thought of as a "transcription cycle." During this transcription cycle, the RNAP II holoenzyme, in conjunction with a variable cast of associated protein factors, assembles as a preinitiation complex, binds to DNA, initiates transcription, progresses into the elongation and processing phases of RNA production, and finally terminates transcription.

Reversible phosphorylation of the RNAP II CTD plays an important role in controlling this transcription cycle. The mammalian RNAP II CTD is composed of 52 repeats of the consensus sequence YSPTSPS (*31*). In the simplest sense, the cycle begins with a preinitiation complex which contains an unphosphorylated CTD (called RNAP IIA). As the transcription cycle progresses to the elongation phase, the CTD is dynamically hyperphosphorylated (called RNAP IIO). RNAP IIO must be converted back to RNAP IIA in order for the transcription cycle to reinitiate, and at least two of the phosphatases responsible for this activity have recently been identified (*32–34*). The CTD phosphatase Fcp1 has been cloned and characterized for its ability to dephosphorylate the CTD, which has been targeted by several CDKs (*32, 33*). Protein phosphatase-1 is the second enzyme identified to co-purify with RNAP II and dephosphorylate the CTD (*34*). Thus, both kinase and phosphatase activities are required to regulate the process of mRNA production. The dynamically changing phosphorylation state of the CTD facilitates the association and disassociation of various RNA processing proteins with the RNAP II complex (*35, 36*).

CDK1, CDK7, CDK8, and CDK9 help to regulate this cycle of RNA transcription and processing events. CDK1 was the first RNAP II CTD kinase identified (*37*). CDK1/cyclin B1 is specifically activated during entry into mitosis. It is hypothesized that CDK1 phosphorylation of the RNAP II CTD may play a role in the negative regulation of RNA production during mitosis (*37, 38*). In fact, CDK1/cyclin B phosphorylates numerous transcription-related targets during mitosis, including CDK7 (TFIIH), TFIID, and the poly (A) polymerase (*39–41*). Overall, CDK1 activity has a negative effect on the transcription cycle.

CDK7, cyclin H, and Mat1 comprise the CDK-activating kinase (CAK) and are also components of Transcription Factor IIH (TFIIH) (*42, 43*). TFIIH is an essential multi-subunit general transcription factor containing ATPase, helicase, and kinase activities. TFIIH phosphorylation of the CTD via CDK7 facilitates progression of the RNAP II complex from initiation into transcriptional elongation (*44*). CDK7-mediated phosphorylation of the CTD appears to positively affect certain aspects of the transcription process.

The effect of CDK8/cyclin C phosphorylation of the RNAP II CTD is generally antagonistic for transcription. RNAP II CTD phosphorylation by CDK8 prior to the formation of the initiation complex on DNA inhibits transcription (45). Furthermore, CDK8 and cyclin C have been identified as members of purified RNAP II transcription complexes, which repress activated transcription in yeast and contain chromatin-remodeling activity in human cells (46, 47). Current models suggest that CDK8/cyclin C phosphorylates RNAP II pre-initiation complexes and thereby prevents the binding of factors required to initiate transcription. Finally, it is possible that CDK8 kinase activity may also promote the transcription of subsets of specialized genes, as has been observed in yeast (48).

CDK9 associates with four cyclin isoforms, including cyclins T1, T2a, T2b, and K (49–51). CDK9/cyclin T heterodimers phosphorylate the RNAP II CTD as part of the positive transcription elongation factor p-TEFb. As the name implies, p-TEFb phosphorylation of the CTD promotes processive transcriptional elongation (52–55). In fact, p-TEFb activity is required for transcription of most RNAP II molecules *in vivo* (56). The CDK9/cyclin T complex is unique among the CDK/cyclin complexes since the activity of this pTEFb complex is negatively regulated by its association with the small nuclear RNA 7SK (57, 58).

There is one additional CDK family member that has been shown to phosphorylate the RNAP II CTD, the CrkRS protein kinase. CrkRS is the largest CDK-related protein kinase isolated thus far (apparent molecular mass 180 kDa), and is composed of 1490 amino acids with an arginine and serine rich (RS) domain and an acidic patch in the amino terminus (3). Given that CrkRS localizes to SFCs in the nucleus and also phosphorylates the splicing factor ASF/SF2, this protein kinase may potentially play a role in pre-mRNA splicing events. Further characterization is needed to determine whether CrkRS phosphorylation of the CTD is biologically relevant.

Protein kinase modulation of mRNA production also involves phosphorylation of targets other than the CTD of the RNAP II large subunit. For example, one of the negative effects of CDK8 on RNAP II transcriptional activity is mediated through CDK8 phosphorylation of cyclin H. The ability of TFIIH to activate transcription and phosphorylate the CTD is repressed by CDK8 phosphorylation of cyclin H (59). In contrast, CK2 phosphorylation of cyclin H results in full activation of the CAK enzyme's ability to phosphorylate the CTD (60). CDK11 co-purifies with transcription protein complexes. However, unlike CDKs 1, 7, 8, and 9, CDK11 does not phosphorylate the CTD. The data published so far indicate that the CDK11^{p110} kinase functions to positively regulate the latter stages of transcription (i.e., transcriptional elongation) as well as pre-mRNA processing by regulating proteins other than the RNAP II CTD.

V. CDK11^{p110} Protein Complexes and Biological Function

A. CDK11^{p110} Protein Complexes Contain Defined Transcriptional Elongation-Associated Factors

CDK11^{p110} co-purifies and co-immunoprecipitates with transcription complexes containing the largest subunit of RNAP II and numerous transcription elongation factors. The initial indication that the CDK11^{p110} isoform might associate with transcription complexes was obtained using a yeast two-hybrid screen from which the transcription elongation factor ELL2 was cloned (23). CDK11^{p110} also associates with a Flag-tagged form of ELL2 in mammalian cells. Further co-immunoprecipitation analyses revealed that CDK11^{p110} associates with the largest subunit of RNAP II and the transcription elongation factors TFIIF and TFIIS. While the CDK11^{p110} kinase associates with both hypo-(IIA) and hyperphosphorylated (IIO) forms of the largest subunit of RNAP II, it preferentially associates with the hyperphosphorylated (IIO) form of RNAP II.

Given that CDK11^{p110} associates with and apparently regulates some aspect(s) of the function of RNAP II transcription complexes, we began to analyze and purify CDK11^{p110} complexes from the nucleoplasm. By first using fractionation of whole cell lysates over size exclusion columns, the nucleoplasmic CDK11^{p110} protein complexes were shown to elute in two major molecular mass ranges that correspond to 1 to 2 MDa and 500 to 800 KDa (23). CDK11^{p110} protein complexes were purified from the soluble HeLa nucleoplasmic fraction by using a series of cation and anion FPLC as well as affinity chromatography columns (Fig. 4). The final purified eluates were further analyzed by using two different techniques, immunoblot and electrospray LC-MS-MS, to identify any co-purifying proteins. The largest subunit of RNAP II, the SSRP1 and SPT16 subunits of the transcription elongation factor FACT, CK2, and several pre-mRNA splicing factors were identified by both techniques. We also identified the Rap30 and Rap74 subunits of TFIIF by immunoblot; however, ELL2 or TFIIS antibodies are not available, or do not react with these proteins appropriately by immunoblots, limiting this type of analysis for these proteins.

B. CDK11^{p110} Association with Transcription Complexes is Functionally Significant

The initial characterization of CDK11^{p110}-containing transcription complexes prompted us to determine whether disruption of the CDK11^{p110} protein–protein interactions would have an effect on transcriptional activity. Using a standard *in vitro* transcription assay, we found that disruption of CDK11^{p110} protein:protein interactions at the carboxyl-terminal end of the

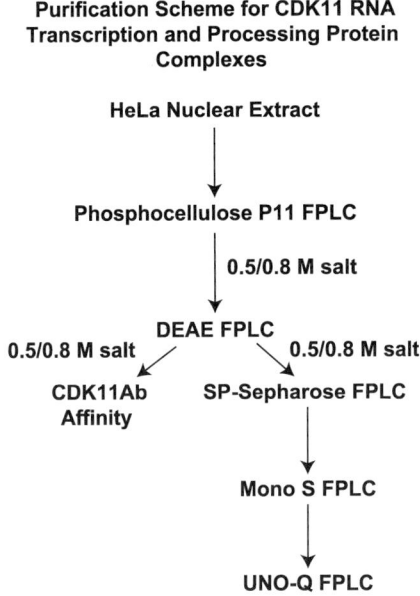

FIG. 4. Schematic for chromatographic purification of CDK11 protein complexes.

CDK11^{p110} kinase substantially reduced the amount of RNA transcript produced from both TATA-like and GC-rich promoters (23). Disruption of CDK11^{p110} protein interactions was accomplished by using both a polyclonal and a monoclonal antibody in which the targeted antigen was located within the same carboxyl-terminal segment of the CDK11^{p110} protein kinase catalytic domain. In contrast, transcriptional activity was not diminished by the addition of antibodies to the amino-terminal or the central domains of the CDK11^{p110} kinase. Addition of 6X-His epitope tagged form of CDK11^{p110} purified from insect cells to *in vitro* transcription reactions pretreated with the CDK11^{p110} carboxyl-terminal P1C antibodies resulted in the recovery of transcriptional activity. This increase in transcript production was independent of CDK11^{p110} kinase catalytic activity, suggesting that the purified protein titrated the CDK11^{p110} PIC antibodies from the transcription complexes. The *in vitro* transcription data indicate that the CDK11^{p110} protein:protein interactions and/or catalytic domain are important for transcriptional activity, and that the association of CDK11^{p110} with transcription complexes is functionally significant.

Although CDK11^{p110} does not directly phosphorylate the RNAP II CTD, CDK11^{p110} immunoprecipitates contain a CTD kinase activity that was demonstrated to be due to CK2. Protein kinase CK2 interacts either directly or indirectly with the RE domain of the CDK11^{P110} kinase. The presence of CK2 in CDK11^{P110} protein complexes was demonstrated by co-immunoprecipitation/immunoblot and by chromatographic purification and mass spectrometric identification (22). CK2 phosphorylates CDK11^{P110} as well as the RNAP II CTD; however, the functional significance of these phosphorylation events has not yet been determined. Participation of CK2 in transcriptional signaling has been reported by numerous groups and involves various signaling pathways. Many of the nuclear CK2 substrates are components of the RNAP II transcriptional machinery, and include the RNAP II CTD, cyclin H, the RAP74 subunit of TFIIF, and FCP1 (TFIIF-dependent CTD phosphatase 1) (60–64). For example, in *Xenopus laevis* cell extracts, CK2 phosphorylation enhances FCP1 CTD phosphatase activity and binding to RAP74, thereby promoting sequential transcriptional cycles (61). Finally, the mouse homologue of p110, CDK11^{P130}, was isolated as a phosphoprotein bound by a src-homology 2 (SH2) domain affinity column (65). CK2 phosphorylation of bacterially expressed GST-CDK11^{P130} *in vitro* allowed CDK11 to act as an SH2 ligand. Thus, CK2 phosphorylation of CDK11^{P110} may be relevant to its ability to function as an SH2 ligand *in vivo*.

C. CDK11^{P110} Protein Complexes Contain RNA Processing Proteins

In addition to the observation of CDK11^{P110}'s functional involvement in transcription, it has also been shown that CDK11^{P110} is coupled to the regulation of pre-mRNA splicing events, and that CDK11^{P110} protein complexes promote RNA processing (66). It has been established for some time that RNA processing events occur co-transcriptionally in cells, so it would not be surprising to have a protein kinase that couples transcriptional and pre-mRNA splicing events. The identification of splicing-associated partner proteins of the CDK11^{P110} kinase was the first indication that it was also connected to RNA processing events. Using yeast two-hybrid screening, the general splicing factors RNPS1 and 9G8 were identified as *in vivo* partners of the CDK11^{P110} kinase (21, 66). Moreover, these splicing proteins co-localize with CDK11^{P110} in the nucleus. There are numerous proteins and RNAs involved in the complex events of pre-mRNA splicing, and the SR proteins (i.e., arginine and serine-rich splicing factors) and SR-related proteins regulate both constitutive and alternative splicing events (67). RNPS1 is an SR protein-related polypeptide which functions as an activator of pre-mRNA splicing (68). RNPS1 also participates in other RNA processing events. As a component of the exon–exon junction complex (EJC), RNPS1 has a dual role in mRNA quality control and the metabolism of spliced mRNAs by mediating selective nuclear export of mature mRNA, by serving as a mark for mRNA surveillance, and by promoting mRNA translation (69–71).

9G8 is a general SR splicing factor which shuttles between the nucleus and the cytoplasm and also participates in exporting mature mRNA to the cytoplasm (72). CDK11^{p110} not only interacts with 9G8, but it also phosphorylates 9G8 *in vitro* and *in vivo* (66). Many aspects of SR protein function are controlled via reversible phosphorylation events. Two well-characterized effects of SR protein phosphorylation (e.g., by the Clk/Sty and SR protein kinases) involve a change in the nuclear localization of these SR splicing factors, as well as modification of their ability to interact with other proteins (i.e., changes in their protein:protein interactions). Furthermore, these SR protein kinases specifically phosphorylate the RS domains of SR splicing factors, and SR proteins move between SFCs and active sites of transcription and splicing in a phosphorylation-dependent manner (73). Expression of CDK11^{p110} does not result in a change in the nuclear localization of SR proteins, including 9G8, and therefore, does not regulate the nuclear localization of SR splicing factors in a manner similar to the Clk/Sty and SR protein kinases. Instead, CDK11^{p110} appears to coordinate pre-mRNA splicing events in a manner that is unique from what has been reported for these other SR protein kinases. These results indicate that CDK11^{p110} may coordinate transcriptional elongation and pre-mRNA splicing events.

D. The CDK11^{p110} Kinase Helps to Regulate Certain Pre-mRNA Splicing Events

A series of *in vitro* splicing assays were performed to determine the nature of CDK11^{p110} kinase regulation of pre-mRNA splicing events (66). A β-globin pre-mRNA substrate was used in a standard *in vitro* splicing assay to investigate whether CDK11^{p110} kinase activity influences pre-mRNA splicing activity. Immunodepletion of the CDK11^{p110} kinase from nuclear extract greatly reduced splicing activity, whereas re-addition of the CDK11^{p110} immune complexes to these CDK11^{p110} immunodepleted splicing reactions greatly enhanced splicing activity. The amino-terminal half of CDK11^{p110} is involved in protein–protein interactions (21–23, 66), while the carboxyl-terminal half is responsible for protein kinase activity. When added to *in vitro* splicing assays, a recombinant amino-terminal segment of the CDK11^{p110} kinase also substantially reduces the splicing activity in nuclear extracts (66). This result demonstrates that disruption of normal CDK11^{p110} protein:protein interactions is sufficient to disrupt and inhibit the splicing activity in this complex, and is consistent with the immunodepletion/re-addition studies. These experiments, along with the demonstration that the CDK11^{p110} kinase phosphorylates the general splicing factor 9G8 *in vivo*, indicate that CDK11^{p110} kinase activity is necessary for its effect(s) on pre-mRNA splicing events in cells. The CDK11^{p110} kinase is the first CDK to be functionally coupled to the regulation of pre-mRNA splicing.

The link between CDK11^{P110} and pre-mRNA splicing is further strengthened by data demonstrating that immunoprecipitated cyclin L1 complexes influence splicing activity. CDK11^{P110}, 9G8, and cyclin L1 are all present in the same complex within the nucleus (66). Cyclin L1 has at least three different protein isoforms that result from alternative splicing, and contains a carboxyl-terminal RS domain that is similar to those found in the SR splicing proteins (19, 20). Gottesfeld and colleagues demonstrated that recombinant GST-cyclin L1 stimulates *in vitro* splicing activity (20). Further evidence linking CDK11^{P110} kinase activity with RNA processing was obtained from research into cocaine and dopamine stimulation signaling in the rat brain striatum. In this study, Hyman and colleagues found that short and long isoforms of cyclin L1 (Ania-6a) expression are induced in specific neuronal cells by cocaine or direct dopamine agonists (19). Furthermore, the long isoform of cyclin L1 (cyclin L1-α) associates with the hyperphosphorylated form of RNAP II and CDK11^{P110} kinase, and it co-localizes with the SR splicing factor SC-35. The authors speculate that the rapid and transient induction of two alternative splice forms of cyclin L1 in the brain is a part of an acute response of neuronal cells to dopamine through regulation of pre-mRNA splicing events. The identification of cyclin L1 as an *in vivo* partner of CDK11^{P110} further strengthens the notion that the CDK11^{P110} kinase is part of a signaling pathway that coordinates the late events in transcription with pre-mRNA processing, even though the detailed mechanisms have yet to be clarified.

VI. Alterations in CDK11^{P110} Expression in Human Disease

Deletions of the short arm of chromosome 1 (i.e., 1p36.3) are among the most frequent aberrations in many human solid tumors, including neuroblastoma, colon, ovarian and breast cancer, malignant melanoma of the skin, and pheochromocytoma [(74); and references therein]. In addition, loss-of-heterozygosity (LOH) analysis revealed that the subterminal region of chromosome 1 band p36, which contains the duplicated *Cdc2L* gene locus, is frequently deleted or translocated in human tumors. A number of studies have been conducted to investigate whether the loss or rearrangement of the *Cdc2L1* and *Cdc2L2* genes occurs in various human primary tumors and their derived cell lines. Deletion of one allele of the distal region of chromosome 1 band p36.3 is consistently associated with stage IV neuroblastoma and tumor-derived cell lines with *MYCN* gene amplification, and correlates with a reduced ability of these tumors to respond to chemotherapy and a relatively poor prognosis (75, 76). In neuroblastoma cell lines, one allele of the *Cdc2L* locus is either deleted or translocated in each cell line with *MYCN* amplification analyzed in the study reported by

Lahti et al. (74). In addition, altered CDK11^{p110} protein expression was observed in many of these cell lines. In approximately 30% of primary neuroblastoma tumors from patients 1p36 LOH involves variable regions, suggesting that multiple tumor suppressors are involved (76).

Several recent reviews addressing the potential involvement of pre-mRNA splicing factors in cancer suggest that these proteins may act as mediators of tumorigenesis, since a number of published studies indicate that diminished levels of certain splicing factors have been associated with different stages of tumorigenesis (77–79). These reviews point out that changes in splicing factor abundance may not only affect the proliferative capacity of cells, but may also alter the levels of various alternatively spliced mRNAs. This subset of alternatively spliced mRNA isoforms results in the expression of variant protein isoforms, which, in turn, alter protein localization, protein:protein interactions, and/or cellular activity. It is therefore possible that by diminishing the amount of CDK11$^{p110/p58}$ kinases through deletion of one *Cdc2L* allele, the production of mRNAs, and alternatively spliced mRNAs, and as a result their corresponding proteins (e.g., what has been observed in neuroblastoma), might alter tumor cell growth (74). With regard to this point, CDK11$^{p110/p58+/-}$ heterozygote mice generated by the elimination of one *cdc2l* allele express ~20 to 30% less of the CDK11^{p110} kinase than the mouse containing both *cdc2l* alleles, suggesting that, at least in mice, a compensatory increase in the expression of the mRNA and protein from the remaining allele does not occur (Li, Inoue, Lahti, and Kidd, in press). Still, even though the human chromosome 1 band p36 LOH involving the *Cdc2L* gene loci, as well as diminished levels of the CDK11^{p110} kinase, have been observed in several different tumors (80–84), no functional relationship between these events and tumorigenesis has been demonstrated to date. However, now that the function of these protein kinases in regulating transcriptional and pre-mRNA splicing events is being revealed, this issue may be worth reexamining.

References

1. Manning, G., Whyte, D. B., Martinez, R., Hunter, T., and Sudarsanam, S. (2002). The protein kinase complement of the human genome. *Science* **298**, 1912–1934.
2. Ko, J., Humbert, S., Bronson, R. T., Takahashi, S., Kulkarni, A. B., Li, E., and Tsai, L. H. (2001). p35 and p39 are essential for cyclin-dependent kinase 5 function during neurodevelopment. *J. Neurosci.* **21**, 6758–6771.
3. Ko, T. K., Kelly, E., and Pines, J. (2001). CrkRS: A novel conserved Cdc2-related protein kinase that colocalizes with SC35 speckles. *J. Cell Sci.* **114**, 2591–2603.
4. Graeser, R., Gannon, J., Poon, R. Y. C., Dubois, T., Aitken, A., and Hunt, T. (2002). Regulation of the CDK-related protein kinase PCTAIRE-1 and its possible role in neurite outgrowth in Neuro-2A cells. *J. Cell Science* **115**, 3479–3490.

5. Gururajan, R., Lahti, J. M., Grenet, J., Easton, J., Gruber, I., Ambros, P. F., and Kidd, V. J. (1998). Duplication of a genomic region containing the Cdc2L1-2 and MMP21-22 genes on human chromosome 1p36.3 and their linkage to D1Z2. *Genome Res.* **8**, 929–939.
6. Gururajan, R., Grenet, J., Lahti, J. M., and Kidd, V. J. (1998). Isolation and characterization of two novel metalloproteinase genes linked to the *Cdc2L* locus on human chromosome 1p36.3. *Genom.* **52**, 101–106.
7. Buroker, N., Bestwick, R., Haight, G., Magenis, R. E., and Litt, M. (1987). A hypervariable repeated sequence on human chromosome 1p36. *Hum. Genet.* **77**, 175–181.
8. Nakamura, T., Julier, C., Wolff, R., Holm, T., O'Connell, P., Leppert, M., and White, R. (1987). Characterization of a human "midisatellite" sequence. *Nucleic Acids Res.* **15**, 2537–2547.
9. Xiang, J., Lahti, J. M., Grenet, J., Easton, J., and Kidd, V. J. (1994). Molecular cloning and expression of alternatively spliced PITSLRE protein kinase isoforms. *J. Biol. Chem.* **269**, 15786–15794.
10. Lahti, J. M., Xiang, J., Heath, L. S., Campana, D., and Kidd, V. J. (1995). PITSLRE protein kinase activity is associated with apoptosis. *Mol. Cell. Biol.* **15**, 1–11.
11. Cornelis, S., Bruynooghe, Y., Denecker, G., van Huffel, S., Tinton, S., and Beyaert, R. (2000). Identification and characterization of a novel cell cycle-regulated internal ribosome entry site. *Mol. Cell* **5**, 597–605.
12. Aitken, A. (1998). 14-3-3 and its possible role in coordinating multiple signaling pathways. *Trends Cell Biol.* **6**, 341–347.
13. Beyaert, R., Kidd, V. J., Cornelis, S., van de Craen, M., Denecker, G., Lahti, J. M., Gururajan, R., Vandenabeele, P., and Fiers, W. (1997). Cleavage of PITSLRE kinases by ICE/CASP-1 and CPP32/CASP-3 during apoptosis induced by tumor necrosis factor. *J. Biol. Chem.* **272**, 11694–11697.
14. Tang, D., Gururajan, R., and Kidd, V. J. (1998). Phosphorylation of PITSLRE p110 isoforms accompanies their processing by caspases during Fas-mediated cell death. *J. Biol. Chem.* **273**, 16601–16607.
15. Sauer, K., Weigmann, K., Sigrist, S., and Lehner, C. F. (1996). Novel members of the cdc2-related kinase family in *Drosophila*: cdk4/6, cdk5, PFTAIRE, and PITSLRE kinase. *Mol. Biol. Cell* **7**, 1759–1769.
16. Pavletich, N. P. (1999). Mechanisms of cyclin-dependent kinase regulation: Structures of cdks, their cyclin activators, and cip and INK4 inhibitors. *J. Mol. Biol.* **287**, 821–828.
17. Morgan, D. O. (1995). Principles of CDK regulation. *Nature* **374**, 131–134.
18. Yang, J., and Kornbluth, S. (1999). All aboard the cyclin train: Subcellular trafficking of cyclins and their CDK partners. *TICB* **9**, 207–210.
19. Berke, J. D., Sgambato, V., Zhu, P. P., Lavoie, B., Vincent, M., Krause, M., and Hyman, S. E. (2001). Dopamine and glutamate induce distinct striatal splice forms of Ania-6, an RNA polymerase II-associated cyclin. *Neuron* **32**, 277–287.
20. Dickinson, L. A., Edgar, A. J., Ehley, J., and Gottesfeld, J. M. (2002). Cyclin L is an RS domain protein involved in pre-mRNA splicing. *J. Biol. Chem.* **277**, 25465–25473.
21. Loyer, P., Trembley, J. H., Lahti, J. M., and Kidd, V. J. (1998). The RNP protein, RNPS1, associates with specific isoforms of the p34^{cdc2}-related PITSLRE protein kinase *in vivo*. *J. Cell Science* **111**, 1495–1506.
22. Trembley, J. H., Hu, D., Slaughter, C. A., Lahti, J. M., and Kidd, V. J. (2003). Casein kinase 2 interacts with cyclin-dependent kinase 11 (CDK11) *in vivo* and phosphorylates both the RNA polymerase II carboxyl-terminal domain and CDK11 *in vitro*. *J. Biol. Chem.* **278**, 2265–2270.
23. Trembley, J. H., Hu, D., Hsu, L. C., Yeung, C. Y., Slaughter, C., Lahti, J. M., and Kidd, V. J. (2002). PITSLRE p110 protein kinases associate with transcription complexes and affect their activity. *J. Biol. Chem.* **277**, 2589–2596.

24. Humphreys-Beher, M. G., Bunnell, B., van Tuinen, P., Ledbetter, D. H., and Kidd, V. J. (1986). Molecular cloning and chromosomal localization of human 4-beta-galactosyltransferase. *Proc. Natl. Acad. Sci. USA* **83,** 8918–8922.
25. Bunnell, B. A., Heath, L. S., Adams, D. E., Lahti, J. M., and Kidd, V. J. (1990). Increased expression of a 58-kDa protein kinase leads to changes in the CHO cell cycle. *Proc. Natl. Acad. Sci. USA* **87,** 7467–7471.
26. Zhang, S., Cai, M., Zhang, S., Xu, S., Chen, S., Chen, X., Chen, C., and Gu, J. (2002). Interaction of p58^{PITSLRE}, a G2/M-specific protein kinase, with cyclin D3. *J. Biol. Chem.* **277,** 35314–35322.
27. Moore, J. D., Kirk, J. A., and Hunt, T. (2003). Unmasking the S-phase-promoting potential of cyclin B1. *Science* **300,** 987–990.
28. Ariza, M. E., Broome-Powell, M., Lahti, J. M., Kidd, V. J., and Nelson, M. A. (1999). Fas-induced apoptosis in human malignant melanoma cell lines is associated with the activation of the p34(cdc2)-related PITSLRE protein kinases. *J. Biol. Chem.* **274,** 28505–28513.
29. Chen, S., Yin, X., Zhu, X., Yan, J., Ji, S., Chen, C., Cai, M., Zhang, S., Zong, H., Hu, Y. *et al.* (2003). The C-terminal kinase domain of the p34cdc2-related PITSLRE protein kinase (p110C) associates with p21-activated kinase 1 and inhibits its activity during anoikis. *J. Biol. Chem.* **278,** 20029–20036.
30. Shi, J., Feng, Y., Goulet, A. C., Vaillancourt, R. R., Sachs, N. A., Hershey, J. W., and Nelson, M. A. (2003). The p34cdc2-related cyclin-dependent kinase 11 interacts with the p47 subunit of eukaryotic initiation factor 3 during apoptosis. *J. Biol. Chem.* **278,** 5062–5071.
31. Dahmus, M. E. (1996). Reversible phosphorylation of the C-terminal domain of RNA polymerase II. *J. Biol. Chem.* **271,** 19009–19012.
32. Cho, H., Kim, T.-K., Mancebo, H. S., Lane, W. S., Flores, O., and Reinberg, D. (1999). A protein phosphatase functions to recycle RNA polymerase II. *Genes Dev.* **13,** 1540–1552.
33. Lin, P. S., Dubois, M. F., and Dahmus, M. E. (2002). TFIIF-associating carboxyl-terminal domain phosphatase dephosphorylates phosphoserines 2 and 5 of RNA polymerase II. *J. Biol. Chem.* **277,** 45949–45956.
34. Washington, K., Ammosova, T., Beullens, M., Jerebtsova, M., Kumar, A., Bollen, M., and Nekhai, S. (2002). Protein phosphatase-1 dephosphorylates the C-terminal domain of RNA polymerase-II. *J. Biol. Chem.* **277,** 40442–40448.
35. McCracken, S., Fong, N., Rosonina, E., Yankulov, K., Brothers, G., Siderovski, D., Hessel, A., Foster, S., Amgen, E. P., Shuman, S. *et al.* (1997). 5′-capping enzymes are targeted to pre-mRNA by binding to the phosphorylated carboxy-terminal domain of RNA polymerase II. *Genes Dev.* **11,** 3306–3318.
36. Ho, C. K., and Shuman, S. (1999). Distinct roles for CTD Ser-2 and Ser-5 phosphorylation in the recruitment and allosteric activation of mammalian mRNA capping enzyme. *Mol. Cell* **3,** 405–411.
37. Cisek, L. J., and Corden, J. L. (1989). Phosphorylation of RNA polymerase by the murine homologue of the cell-cycle control protein cdc2. *Nature* **339,** 679–684.
38. Zawel, L., Lu, H., Cisek, L. J., Corden, J. L., and Reinberg, D. (1993). The cycling of RNA polymerase II during transcription. *Cold Spring Harb. Symp. Quant. Biol.* **58,** 187–198.
39. Akoulitchev, S., and Reinberg, D. (98 A.D.) The molecular mechanism of mitotic inhibition of TFIIH is mediated by phosphorylation of cdk7. *Genes Dev.* **12,** 3541–3550.
40. Long, J. J., Leresche, A., Kriwacki, R. W., and Gottesfeld, J. M. (1998). Repression of TFIIH transcriptional activity and TFIIH-associated cdk7 kinase activity at mitosis. *Mol. Cell. Biol.* **18,** 1467–1476.
41. Colgan, D. F., Murthy, K. G. K., Zhao, W., Prives, C., and Manley, J. L. (1998). Inhibition of poly(A) polymerase requires p34cdc2/cyclin B phosphorylation of multiple consensus and non-consensus sites. *EMBO J.* **17,** 1053–1062.

42. Serizawa, H., Makela, T. P., Conaway, J. W., Conaway, R. C., Weinberg, R. A., and Young, R. A. (1995). Association of Cdk-activating kinase subunits with transcription factor TFIIH. *Nature* **374,** 280–282.
43. Shiekhattar, R., Mermelstein, F., Fisher, R. P., Drapkin, R., Dynlacht, B., Wessling, H. C., Morgan, D. O., and Reinberg, D. (1995). Cdk-activating kinase complex is a component of human transcription factor TFIIH. *Nature* **374,** 283–286.
44. Akoulitchev, S., Makela, T. P., Weinberg, R. A., and Reinberg, D. (1995). Requirement for TFIIH kinase activity in transcription by RNA polymerase II. *Nature* **377,** 557–560.
45. Hengartner, C. J., Myers, V. E., Liao, S. M., Wilson, C. J., Koh, S. S., and Young, R. A. (1998). Temporal regulation of RNA polymerase II by Srb10 and Kin28 cyclin-dependent kinases. *Mol. Cell* **2,** 43–53.
46. Sun, X., Zhang, Y., Cho, H., Rickert, P., Lees, E., Lane, W., and Reinberg, D. (1998). NAT, a human complex containing Srb polypeptides that functions as a negative regulator of activated transcription. *Mol. Cell* **2,** 213–222.
47. Cho, H., Orphanides, G., Sun, X., Yang, X. J., Ogryzko, V., Lees, E., Nakatani, Y., and Reinberg, D. (1998). A human RNA polymerase II complex containing factors that modify chromatin structure. *Mol. Cell. Biol.* **18,** 5355–5363.
48. Vincent, O., Kuchin, S., Hong, S. P., Townley, R., Vyas, V. K., and Carlson, M. (2001). Interaction of the Srb10 kinase with Sip4, a transcriptional activator of gluconeogenic genes in *Saccharomyces cerevisiae*. *Mol. Cell. Biol.* **21,** 5790–5796.
49. Wei, P. F., Garber ME, F. A. U., Fang SM, F. A. U., Fischer WH, F. A. U., and Jones, K. A. (1998). A novel CDK9-associated C-type cyclin interacts directly with HIV-1 Tat and mediates its high-affinity, loop-specific binding to TAR RNA. *Cell* **92,** 451–462.
50. Peng, J., Zhu, Y., Milton, J. T., and Price, D. H. (1998). Identification of multiple cyclin subunits of human P-TEFb. *Genes Dev.* **12,** 755–762.
51. Fu, T.-J., Peng, J., Lee, G., Price, D. H., and Flores, O. (1999). Cyclin K functions as a CDK9 regulatory subunit and participates in RNA polymerase II transcription. *J. Biol. Chem.* **274,** 34527–34530.
52. Marshall, N. F., Peng, J., Xie, Z., and Price, D. H. (1996). Control of RNA polymerase II elongation potential by a novel carboxyl-terminal domain kinase. *J. Biol. Chem.* **271,** 27176–27183.
53. Yang, X., Gold, M. O., Tang, D. N., Lewis, D. E., Aguilar-Cordova, E., Rice, A. P., and Herrmann, C. H. (1997). TAK, an HIV Tat-associated kinase, is a member of the cyclin-dependent family of protein kinases and is induced by activation of peripheral blood lymphocytes and differentiation of promonocytic cell lines. *Proc. Natl. Acad. Sci. USA* **94,** 12331–12336.
54. Zhou, M., Halanski, M. A., Radonovich, M. F., Kashanchi, F., Peng, J., Price, D. H., and Brady, J. N. (2000). Tat modifies the activity of CDK9 to phosphorylate serine 5 of the RNA polymerase II carboxyl-terminal domain during human immunodeficiency virus type 1 transcription. *Mol. Cell. Biol.* **20,** 5077–5086.
55. Wada, T., Takagi, T., Yamaguchi, Y., Watanabe, D., and Handa, H. (1998). Evidence that P-TEFb alleviates the negative effect of DSIF on RNA polymerase II-dependent transcription *in vitro*. *EMBO J.* **17,** 7395–7403.
56. Chao, S. H., and Price, D. H. (2001). Flavopiridol inactivates P-TEFb and blocks most RNA polymerase II transcription *in vivo*. *J. Biol. Chem.* **276,** 31793–31799.
57. Nguyen, V. T., Kiss, T., Michels, A. A., and Bensuade, O. (2003). 7SK small nuclear RNA binds to and inhibits the activity of CDK9/cyclin T complexes. *Nature* **414,** 322–325.
58. Yang, Z., Zhu, Q., Luo, K., and Zhou, Q. (2003). The 7SK small nuclear RNA inhibits the CDK9/cyclin T1 kinase to control transcription. *Nature* **414,** 317–322.
59. Akoulitchev, S., Chuikov, S., and Reinberg, D. (2000). TFIIH is negatively regulated by cdk8-containing mediator complexes. *Nature* **407,** 102–106.

60. Schneider, E., Kartarius, S., Schuster, N., and Montenarh, M. (2003). The cyclin H/cdk7/Mat1 kinase activity is regulated by CK2 phosphorylation of cyclin H. *Onc.* **21,** 5031–5037.
61. Palancade, B., Dubois, M. F., and Bensaude, O. (2002). FCP1 phosphorylation by casein kinase 2 enhances binding to TFIIF and RNA polymerase II carboxyl-terminal domain phosphatase activity. *J. Biol. Chem.* **277,** 36061–36067.
62. Rossignol, M., Keriel, A., Staub, A., and Egly, J.-M. (1999). Kinase activity and phosphorylation of the largest subunit of TFIIF transcription factor. *J. Biol. Chem.* **274,** 22387–22400.
63. Egyhazi, R., Ossoinak, A., Filhol-Cochet, O., Cochet, C., and Pigon, A. (1999). The binding of the α subunit of protein kinase CK2 and RAP74 subunit of TFIIF to protein-coding genes in living cells is DRB sensitive. *Mol. Cell. Biochem.* **191,** 149–159.
64. Payne, J. M., Laybourn, P. J., and Dahmus, M. E. (1989). The transition of RNA polymerase II from initiation to elongation is associated with phosphorylation of the carboxyl-terminal domain of subunit IIa. *J. Biol. Chem.* **264,** 19621–19629.
65. Malek, S. N., and Desiderio, S. (1994). A cyclin-dependent kinase homologue, p130^{PITSLRE}, is a phosphotyrosine-independent SH2 ligand. *J. Biol. Chem.* **269,** 33009–33020.
66. Hu, D., Mayeda, A., Trembley, J. H., Lahti, J. M., and Kidd, V. J. (2003). CDK11 complexes promote pre-mRNA splicing. *J. Biol. Chem.* **278,** 8623–8629.
67. Manley, J. L., and Tacke, R. (1996). SR proteins and splicing control. *Genes Dev.* **10,** 1569–1579.
68. Mayeda, A., Badolato, J., Kobayashi, R., Zhang, M. Q., Gardiner, E. M., and Krainer, A. R. (1999). Purification and characterization of human RNPS1: A general activator of pre-mRNA splicing. *EMBO J.* **18,** 4560–4570.
69. Le Hir, H., Izaurralde, E., Maquat, L. E., and Moore, M. J. (2000). The spliceosome deposits multiple proteins 20–24 nucleotides upstream of mRNA exon–exon junctions. *EMBO J.* **19,** 6860–6869.
70. Lykke-Andersen, J., Shu, M. D., and Steitz, J. A. (2001). Communication of the position of exon–exon junctions to the mRNA surveillance machinery by the protein RNPS1. *Science* **293,** 1836–1839.
71. Gatfield, D., and Izaurralde, E. (2002). REF1/Aly and the additional exon junction complex proteins are dispensable for nuclear mRNA export. *J. Cell Biol.* **159,** 579–588.
72. Huang, Y., and Steitz, J. A. (2001). Splicing factors SRp20 and 9G8 promote the nucleocytoplasmic export of mRNA. *Mol. Cell* **7,** 899–905.
73. Misteli, T., Caceres, J. F., and Spector, D. L. (1997). The dynamics of a pre-mRNA splicing factor in living cells. *Nature* **387,** 523–527.
74. Lahti, J. M., Valentine, M. B., Xiang, J., Joens, B., Amann, J. M., Grenet, J., Richmond, G., Look, A. T., and Kidd, V. J. (1994). Alterations in the PITSLRE protein kinase gene complex on chromosome 1p36 in childhood neuroblastoma. *Nature Gen.* **7,** 370–375.
75. Gilbert, F., Feder, M., Balaban, G., Brangman, D., Lurie, D. K., Podolsky, R., Rinaldt, V., Vinikoor, N., and Weisband, J. (1984). Human neuroblastomas and abnormalities of chromosomes 1 and 17. *Cancer Res.* **44,** 5444–5449.
76. Brodeur, G. M., Seeger, R. C., Schwab, M., Varmus, H. E., and Bishop, J. M. (1984). Amplification of N-myc in untreated human neuroblastomas correlates with advanced disease stage. *Science* **224,** 1121–1124.
77. Caceres, J. F., and Kornblihtt, A. R. (2002). Alternative splicing: Multiple control mechanisms and involvement in human disease. *Trends Genet.* **18,** 186–193.
78. Hastings, M. L., and Krainer, A. R. (2001). Pre-mRNA splicing in the new millennium. *Curr. Opin. Cell Biol.* **13,** 302–309.
79. Faustino, N. A., and Cooper, T. A. (2003). Pre-mRNA splicing and human disease. *Genes Dev.* **17,** 419–437.

80. Poetsch, M., Woenckhaus, C., Dittberner, T., Pambor, M., Lorenz, G., and Herrmann, F. H. (1998). Differences in chromosomal aberrations between nodular and superficial spreading malignant melanoma detected by interphase cytogenetics. *Lab Invest.* **78**, 883–888.
81. Poetsch, M., Woenckhaus, C., Dittberner, T., Pambor, M., Lorenz, G., and Hermann, F. H. (2003). An increased frequency of numerical chromosomal abnormalities and 1p36 deletions in isolated cells from paraffin sections of malignant melanomas by means of interphase cytogenetics. *Cancer Gen. Cytogenet.* **104**, 146–152.
82. Dave, B. J., Hess, M. M., Pickering, D. L., Zaleski, D. H., Pfeifer, A. L., Weisenburger, D. D., Armitage, J. O., and Sanger, W. G. (1999). Rearrangements of chromosome B and 1p36 in non-Hodgkin's lymphoma. *Clinical Can. Res.* **5**, 1401–1409.
83. Dave, B. J., Pickering, D. L., Hess, M. M., Weisenburger, D. D., Armitage, J. O., and Sanger, W. G. (1999). Deletion of cell division cycle 2-like 1 gene locus on 1p36 in non-Hodgkin's lymphoma. *Cancer Gen. Cytogenet.* **108**, 120–125.
84. Perlman, E. J., Valentine, M. B., Griffin, C. A., and Look, A. T. (1996). Deletion of 1p36 in childhood endodermal sinus tumors by two-color fluorescence *in situ* hybridization: A pediatric oncology group study. *Genes, Chromosomes, & Cancer* **6**, 15–20.

The Eukaryotic Ccr4-Not Complex: A Regulatory Platform Integrating mRNA Metabolism with Cellular Signaling Pathways?

MARTINE A. COLLART[*] AND
H. TH. MARC TIMMERS[§]

[*]Department of Medical Biochemistry,
CMU, 1 rue Michel Servet,
1211 Geneva 4, Switzerland

[§]Department of Physiological Chemistry,
University Medical Centre-Utrecht,
Universiteitsweg 100,
3584 CG Utrecht, The Netherlands

I. Introduction..	290
II. The Ccr4-Not Complex: Conserved in Composition and Organization..	292
A. Composition and Organization of the Core Ccr4-Not Complex	293
B. The Ccr4-Not Complex is Essential	297
III. Interaction of the Core Ccr4-Not Complex with Additional Proteins in Larger Structures...	298
A. Yeast Proteins Interacting with the Ccr4/Caf Module of the Complex	298
B. Yeast Proteins Interacting with the Not Module of the Complex.......	302
C. Genetic Links of Ccr4-Not Components in Other Eukaryotes..........	303
D. Does Human CNOT3 Link to TBP via TIP120B?........................	304
E. Relationship of Ccr4-Not Proteins with Cell Proliferation and Transcription Regulation in Higher Eukaryotes	304
IV. Role of the Yeast Ccr4-Not Complex in mRNA Metabolism................	305
A. Transcription..	306
B. mRNA Degradation	308
C. Relative Contribution of Transcription and mRNA Degradation, Coordination?..	311
V. Role of the Ccr4-Not Complex in Ubiquitylation	312
A. Not4 Proteins are Protein–Ubiquitin Ligases	312
B. Targets of Ubiquitylation Controlled by the Ccr4-Not Complex..	313
VI. Role of the Ccr4-Not Complex in Protein Modification	314
VII. The Ccr4-Not Complex as a Regulatory Platform that Senses Glucose Levels and Stress..	314
VIII. Perspectives...	316
References	317

I. Introduction

Ccr4-Not complexes are multi-subunit protein complexes, which are conserved from yeast to human. These complexes exist in several forms larger than 1 MDa and consist of at least nine core subunits (Ccr4p, Caf1p, Caf40p, Caf130p, Not1-5p in yeast, and CNOT1-10 in humans; see Table I). They play essential roles in the control of gene expression. Genes encoding the core subunits were first revealed by genetic studies of transcription in yeast. In particular, two different approaches, one that led to the identification of Ccr4p and one that led to the identification of the Not proteins, each suggested the existence of a large multisubunit complex. The specificities of the defined complexes were that the former was necessary for nonfermentative gene expression (*1–3*), while the latter repressed transcription from promoters that lacked a canonical TATA sequence preferentially (*4–6*). Purification of Ccr4p revealed a large number of associated proteins (*7*), whereas genetic interactions, phenotypic similarities, co-immunoprecipitation, and co-elution from gel filtration columns suggested that the Not proteins were in a large complex (*4–6*). It was in 1998 that the group of Clyde Denis finally demonstrated that the Ccr4 and Not complexes were one and the same (*8*).

Until 2001, namely, three years after the description of the Ccr4-Not complex and many years after the first genetic isolation of its constituents, the Ccr4-Not complex remained a molecular mystery. For a long time, it was considered to be a global transcriptional regulatory complex affecting genes both positively and negatively. Gradually, evidence linking the Not proteins to TFIID and Mediator function and, thus, to transcriptional regulation, accumulated. The link between Ccr4-Not and TFIID complexes was reinforced in 2001 by the finding that Not5p is required for the appropriate recruitment of TAF1 to promoter DNA (*9*). In the same year, Parker and colleagues discovered that the Ccr4p and Caf1p proteins are the major yeast deadenylase (*10*), thus attributing an enzymatic activity to the Ccr4-Not complex. However, this activity, surprisingly, contributes to mRNA decay rather than mRNA synthesis and takes place not in the nucleus but in specialized bodies in the cytoplasm (*11*). While this biochemical activity of Ccr4p and Caf1p has now been defined in quite some detail (*10, 12–14*), involvement of the Not proteins in the deadenylation process has not really been demonstrated. Instead, most studies have converged toward models in which Ccr4p and Caf1p, on one hand, and the Not proteins on the other, might be contributing different functions to the cell. In this model, the Ccr4-Not complex might be composed of two functional modules, which are linked to different aspects of mRNA metabolism. In 2002, this picture was modified by the finding that CNOT4, the human ortholog of Not4p, is an ubiquitin E3 ligase (*15*). This implied involvement in proteasomal protein-degradation pathways. Thus, two distinct enzymatic

TABLE I
HUMAN ORTHOLOGS OF THE CORE YEAST CCR4-NOT COMPLEX

Yeast core subunit	Aliases for yeast subunits	Human core subunit (HGNC)	Aliases for human subunits	Genbank number	Genbank/Swiss-Prot accession number
NOT1	CDC39	CNOT1	hNOT1	n.a.	n.a.
	ROS1				
	SMD6				
NOT2	CDC36	CNOT2	hNOT2	NM_014515	Q9NZN8
	DNA19				
NOT3		CNOT3S	hNOT3	AF180474	Q9NZN7
NOT5		CNOT3L		NM_014516	
NOT4	MOT2	CNOT4N	hNOT4	n.a.	O9NZN6
	SIG1	CNOT4S		n.a.	O95628
		CNOT4L		NM_013316	Q95627
CCR4	FUN27	CNOT6	hCCR4	n.a.	
	NUT21				
CAF1	POP2	CNOT7	hCAF1	NM_013354	Q9UIV1
		CNOT8	hPOP2, CALIF	NM_004779	Q9UFF9
CAF40		CNOT9	hRcd1, Rqcd1, hCAF40	NM_005444	n.a.
CAF130		CNOT10		BC002928	n.a.

activities, contributing to very distinct cellular processes, mRNA deadenylation and protein ubiquitylation, are associated within the Ccr4-Not complex. In addition, other subunits, in particular Not2p and Not5p, have very specific interactions with the general transcription factor TFIID (9, 16, 17).

As the story unfolds, the role of the Ccr4-Not complex is extending to other cellular machines. The Dhh1p RNA helicase within the decapping complex is associated with Not1p and is apparently controlled by the Ccr4-Not complex. In addition, the posttranslational modifications of the general stress transcription factor, Msn2p, and its transcriptional activation capacity, is controlled by the Ccr4-Not complex, at least in part through the interaction of the complex with a phosphatase (Collart, unpublished observations). Many other proteins (such as a subunit of the nascent-polypeptide associated complex (18)) involved in other cellular functions have been found to interact with Ccr4-Not complex subunits. However, functional control of these proteins by the Ccr4-Not complex remains to be studied. The emerging picture for the

Ccr4-Not complex is that of a regulatory platform, consisting of different functional modules controlling different cellular machines. At present, the exact role of each individual subunit, the dynamics of the interaction between the different subunits, and the reason for the association of all of these subunits in a complex, as well as the control of these dynamics by the status of the cell, remain to be characterized.

In efforts to reconcile genetic identification and interactions with the recent biochemical findings, two reviews on Ccr4-Not proteins appeared last year. These reviews emphasized the original genetic studies (*19*) or the control of mRNA metabolism by yeast Ccr4-Not subunits (*18*). In this chapter, we expand this by integrating findings in other eukaryotic systems and by extending the role of Ccr4-Not proteins to other cellular machines and pathways.

II. The Ccr4-Not Complex: Conserved in Composition and Organization

The Ccr4-Not complex was first identified in yeast cell extracts, in which it forms protein complexes of ∼1.0 MDa and ∼1.9 MDa, as assayed by gel filtration chromatography (*8*). Protein complexes of similar size have been identified in extracts of human HeLa cells (*20, 21*); Albert and Timmers, unpublished observations. Involvement of Ccr4-Not core components in the biochemical stability of the yeast complexes has been reviewed in 2003 (*18*). From these analyses, it can be concluded that the ∼1.0 MDa complex most likely represents a core consisting of 9 polypeptides, whereas the ∼1.9 MDa Ccr4-Not complexes include additional proteins. Thus far, the larger complex has been refractory to biochemical purification, which may underscore the transient nature of associations between the core complex and additional proteins.

At present, it seems that the Ccr4-Not complex, as such, does not have a single molecular function. Rather, its function in cells seems to stem from its existence as an entity, which can (transiently) associate with a number of effector molecules. Thus, the unifying theme for the different subunits of the Ccr4-Not core complex is that they are required to create the platform that mediates these diverse associations. Additionally, each subunit is required more particularly for certain interactions. Thereby, core subunits do not all perform the same or even a similar molecular function. In this section, we describe each yeast and human core subunit with regard to its known function and with regard to its importance for the integrity of the Ccr4-Not complex. In this examination, we combine findings in different eukaryotic systems, although most data come from the yeast *Saccharomyces cerevisiae*.

The nomenclature of the human Ccr4-Not proteins is rather confusing. In this chapter, we follow the nomenclature suggested by the HUGO Gene Nomenclature Committee (see http://www.gene.ucl.ac.uk/nomenclature/) and as indicated in Table I. For the human proteins, we use the HGNC name with the old name in brackets.

A. Composition and Organization of the Core Ccr4-Not Complex

In yeast extracts, the Ccr4-Not core complex consists (at least) of the five Not proteins, Ccr4p, and three Ccr4p-associated factors: Caf1p, Caf40p, and Caf130p (for reviews, see also (18, 19)). Except for Caf40p and Caf130p, identified by mass spectrometry analysis of the purified complex, all of the other core subunits were identified by genetic selections in yeast (for an extensive review on this, see (19)). Interestingly, two copies of yeast Caf1p orthologs exist in the human genome: CNOT7(hCaf1) and CNOT8(hPOP2/CALIF). And, in contrast, two CNOT3 orthologs are present in the yeast genome: Not3p and Not5p. Nevertheless, the complexes, as isolated from human cells (cervical carcinoma HeLa or diploid MRC5 cells), are quite similar in size to the yeast complex (21). Mass spectrometry of the CNOT2-tagged complex isolated from HeLa cells identified all core subunits including both CNOT7(hCaf1) and CNOT8(hPOP2/CALIF), but the CNOT4 protein was absent (20).

The largest subunit is Not1p (2108 amino acids) in yeast or CNOT1 (2376 amino acids; unpublished observations) in humans. Potential orthologs of similar size are present in all sequenced eukaryotic genomes. Inspection of the primary sequences does not reveal obvious biochemical functions. Not1p is the only protein of the core complex that is essential for yeast viability. In particular, the C-terminal end of Not1p is important for this. Removal of the last 246 amino acids is lethal (22), but deletion of the last 109 amino acids does not affect viability (Collart, unpublished observations). In contrast, removal of the first 1317 amino acids of Not1p (leaving only the C-terminal 791 amino acids) is viable, but cells expressing this truncated derivative grow extremely slowly. It has been suggested that Not1p is a scaffold for the Ccr4-Not complex. The C-terminal 791 amino acid derivative of Not1p retains this function, since it associates in protein complexes of similar apparent size as the intact Not1p (22).

All of the identified yeast core subunits can interact with Not1p by two-hybrid experiments, and the position of these other proteins relative to Not1p has been quite extensively mapped in these experiments (see Fig. 1). The nonessential Not proteins associate with the essential C-terminal region of Not1p (4–6). Not4p and Not5p can both interact with the region of Not1p comprising amino acids 1430–1862, while Not2p can associate via amino acids

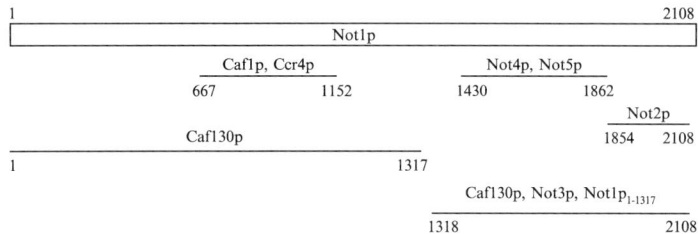

FIG. 1. Not1p is depicted at the top of the figure and, below it, the regions of Not1p that can associate with the other indicated subunits of the core complex, including the N-terminal domain of Not1p itself.

1854–2108 (9). Many experiments suggest that Not5p is particularly closely linked to Not2p (23), and thus it may associate with Not1p in between Not4p and Not2p. Not3p is more loosely associated with the complex, but also interacts with the essential region of Not1p to which the other Not proteins associate. Its association may stabilize interaction of other Not proteins, since its overexpression suppresses the *not1-1* (Trp1753Arg) assembly mutant ((24) and unpublished observations). Yeast Ccr4p, and its interacting protein Caf1p, are not essential for yeast viability (2, 3, 25) and they interact with a region of Not1p (667–1152) dispensable for yeast growth (22, 23). The association of Ccr4p with Not1p depends upon Caf1p (22, 23).

Finally, the binding of Caf40p to Not1p could not be narrowed down to any single specific region of Not1p, whereas Caf130p can independently bind both to the nonessential N-terminal region of Not1p (amino acids 1–1317) and to the essential C-terminal region of Not1p (1318–2108) (26). Whether the role of Not1p extends beyond that of a scaffold protein has not been clarified at the present time.

The current picture for the human CNOT1 is less detailed. Interactions with the C-terminal 1290 residues of CNOT1 have been reported with only a subset of human Ccr4-Not subunits (27). CNOT2, CNOT4, and CNOT8 have been found to interact in the yeast two-hybrid assay. In contrast to the situation in yeast, CNOT3S (see also following text) fails to interact directly with this part of CNOT1. CNOT3 seems to be integrated into the complex via CNOT8(hPOP2/CALIF) (27). It is not known whether the mammalian CNOT1 protein constitutes an essential protein.

After Not1p, the components of the core complex that seem most critical for yeast viability are Not2p (191 amino acids) and Not5p (560 amino acids). In human cells, a single ortholog of Not2p exists. This CNOT2 protein (540 amino acids) is substantially extended at the aminoterminal end. This extension contains short regions of homology with Not2p-orthologs of other metazoans. Yeast cells lacking Not2p or Not5p grow, but their doubling time is several-fold longer than wild-type yeast. Interestingly, cells lacking both of these two units are not less healthy compared to cells lacking one of the two subunits, which suggests that the two proteins contribute to the same function(s). Indeed, the two proteins interact tightly, and Not5p barely associates in large complexes if cells lack Not2p (22, 23). Both of these proteins contribute to support the stability of Ccr4-Not complexes, and there is less Not1p in cells lacking either Not2p or Not5p, even though the remaining Not1p can still assemble into large complexes (22, 28). Not2p and Not5p orthologs contain a unique protein motif of ~90 amino acids at their C-termini. This motif has been tentatively named the Not-box (pfam: PF04153) and the identity ranges between 20 and 40% (100) and is also present in the orthologs in higher eukaryotes. The *Ceanorhabditis elegans* (*C. elegans*) ortholog of Not2p is essential for early embryonic development (29, 30), as is the Not2p-ortholog from the fruit fly, which is essential during embryonic and early larval development (31).

Not3p (836 amino acids) is 44% identical to Not5p in its N-terminal region. This region carries a putative coiled-coiled motif (6) and both proteins have several apparent forms of about 80 kDa for Not5p and 120 kDa for Not3p. In contrast to Not5p, Not3p is not particularly important for yeast vegetative growth. Indeed, the more important function provided by Not5p lies in its C-terminal region, which harbors the Not-box. Cells expressing C-terminally truncated derivatives of Not5p grow less well at 30°C than cells lacking both Not3p and the N-terminal region of Not5p (6). Nevertheless, some cellular function is provided redundantly by the domain conserved between Not5p and Not3p. Cells become temperature sensitive for growth when they lack both Not3p and the N-terminal domain of Not5p. Even if Not5p seems more critical for yeast growth than Not3p, Not3p clearly plays a role of its own and it is associated together with Not5p in Ccr4-Not complexes. Not3p is, for instance, essential in cells lacking Not4p. This might reflect the fact that Not3p contributes to the stability of Ccr4-Not complexes (22).

Human cells and nematodes harbor only one gene orthologous to yeast Not3p and Not5p. The human CNOT3 gene expresses two isoforms: CNOT3S (609 amino acids) and CNOT3L (753 amino acids) (27, 32). The CNOT3L-specific extension carries the Not-box. Inactivation of Not3p in *C. elegans* again results in embryonic lethality (29, 30). Human CNOT3 is equally similar to yeast Not3p and Not5p (~40%) in the first 232 residues, which also harbors the coiled–coiled domain. Except for the Not-box, the rest of the Not3 proteins show a low degree homology. The CNOT3S isoform does not interact with CNOT1 in two-hybrid assays, but seems to be linked via CNOT8(hPOP2/CALIF) (27). The CNOT3L isoform has not yet been tested for interactions with Ccr4-Not core subunits.

Not4p is a protein of ~60 kDa (587 amino acids), which has a RING finger domain in its N-terminus. This domain was first recognized in its human ortholog CNOT4 (33). RING fingers have been implicated in ubiquitin modification of proteins as E3 ligases (34, 35), and this ubiquitin–protein ligase function has been demonstrated for the CNOT4 protein also (15). Yeast Not4p can probably also function as an E3 ligase. Further details and the implication of this enzymatic activity of Not4 proteins will be discussed in Section V.

The first ~240 residues of Not4 proteins have been strongly conserved throughout evolution. Surprisingly, the conserved part is not required for interaction with CNOT1, but this activity is retained in the less-conserved C-terminal half of CNOT4 (15). In yeast, the conserved first 144 amino acids of Not4p are also dispensable for interaction with Not1p (Collart, unpublished observations). Besides the RING finger, this N-terminal part also harbors an RRM (RNA-recognition motif), which is present in RNA-binding proteins like U2AF and also in DNA-binding proteins (36). Preliminary results indicate that CNOT4 is unable to bind to ds- or ss-DNA by *in vitro* experiments (de Ruwe and Timmers, unpublished observations). However, the link of the Ccr4-Not complex with mRNA deadenylation necessitates testing of RNA as a binding partner.

The human CNOT4 gene is transcribed into three alternatively spliced mRNAs, which yield three proteins: CNOT4-N (433 amino acids), CNOT4-S (575 amino acids), and CNOT4-L (642 amino acids), which have the first 418 residues in common. Interestingly, only the CNOT4-N isoform contains a bipartite nuclear localization signal at its unique C-terminal end (27). All three CNOT4 isoforms are expressed in human cells, but it is not known whether they display differential subcellular localization.

Not4p is important for appropriate yeast growth, since cells lacking Not4p grow only very slightly better than cells lacking Not2p or Not5p. Furthermore, Not4p is essential in cells lacking Not2p, Not5p, Not3p, Ccr4p, or Caf1p (22). Because Not4p seems to be located at the core of the Ccr4-Not complex (see Fig. 1), it could be that an important role of Not4p is linked to an important function in the stability of the complex, in addition to its role as an E3 ligase. Important in this respect could be the observation that CNOT4 has not been identified yet in the human Ccr4-Not complexes ((20); Albert, Winkler, and Timmers, unpublished observations).

Ccr4p and Caf1p (837 and 433 amino acids, respectively) were considered as positive transcription factors for a long time, but they were recently defined as the major yeast deadenylases (10). Both proteins contain domains of homology with known enzymatic activities, Ccr4p shares homology with a Mg^{2+}-dependent DNase/phosphatase family of proteins, and Caf1p carries a putative RNaseD domain, albeit with noncanonical residues at three of the five residues involved in formation of the catalytic site (37). Neither Ccr4p nor Caf1p appears critical for the association of Not1p in large complexes, or for the association of Not5p together with Not1p in these large complexes (22, 23). This may explain why cells lacking either or both of these proteins grow quite well. In contrast, Not5p is important for the association of Ccr4p in core Ccr4-Not complexes, probably because the N-terminal domain of Not1p interacts with the C-terminal domain of Not1p to form stable Ccr4-Not complexes (22) (see Fig. 1). Both Ccr4p and Caf1p are essential in cells lacking almost any one of the Not proteins, suggesting that Ccr4p and Caf1p nevertheless contribute to the general integrity of Ccr4-Not complexes. Alternatively, the deadenylase function might be essential in cells disrupted for the other functions mediated by the Ccr4-Not complex.

With respect to Ccr4p and Caf1p, the situation is more complicated in human cells. The CNOT6(hCcr4) protein of 558 residues is surprisingly similar to three other proteins, which all contain the signature motif of Mg^{2+}-dependent endonucleases, but in contrast to CNOT6, these paralogs do not seem to associate with the Ccr4-Not complex (38). It is likely that CNOT6 also displays mRNA deadenylase activity, but direct proof is lacking. It has been shown that, similar to yeast Ccr4p, CNOT6 requires its leucine-rich repeat to interact with the human Caf1-like proteins (38). Human cells harbor two genes encoding proteins orthologous to yeast Caf1p: CNOT7(hCAF1) and CNOT8(hPOP2/CALIF), which are 285 and 293 amino acids, respectively, and very similar (75% identity) (27). Single orthologs for Ccr4p and Caf1p seem to be present in C. elegans. Interestingly, only the Caf1p ortholog is essential for embryonic development, while inactivation of Ccr4p does not seem to have any effect (29, 30).

In contrast to the other Ccr4-Not subunits, Caf40p (373 amino acids) and Caf130p (1122 amino acids) were not isolated in any genetic selection. Also, their sequence is not associated with any defined enzymatic activity and lack of either of these subunits has no effect on yeast growth, even in the absence of other Ccr4-Not subunits (26). It would appear that these subunits are not critical elements for the stability of Ccr4-Not complexes. The human orthologous protein CNOT9(Rqcd1) and potential CNOT10 ortholog (see Table I) are 299 and 717 amino acids. Whereas these proteins are integral subunits of the human complex, interactions with other core subunits have not been mapped.

B. The Ccr4-Not Complex is Essential

There is striking evidence that the Ccr4-Not complex is essential, not so much because a single function provided by the complex is essential, but rather because the different subunits contributing to different cellular functions are assembled into a single structure. Indeed, only Not1p is essential for yeast viability, and this subunit probably acts as the scaffold of the complex.

The minimal domain that is sufficient for yeast viability provides scaffolding capacity (22). Removal of single subunits other than Not1p is not lethal, and removal of two subunits that are thought to contribute to the same cellular function (such as Ccr4p and Caf1p or Not2p and Not5p) is not lethal. In contrast, deleting two subunits that do not bind to the same portion of Not1p or that apparently contribute to different cellular functions (such as Not4p and Ccr4p) is lethal (22). As has been discussed, inactivation by RNAi of all Not-orthologs tested in the nematode C. elegans gives rise to an early embryonic lethal phenotype, and inactivation of Caf1p, but not of Ccr4p, gives this phenotype (29, 30).

Thus, the Ccr4-Not complex can be viewed as an essential platform where proteins contributing to different cellular functions are assembled. One can imagine that the purpose of such a scaffold is to perform an essential coordination function.

III. Interaction of the Core Ccr4-Not Complex with Additional Proteins in Larger Structures

While the core subunits of the 1 MDa Ccr4-Not complex have been defined as proteins that can be co-purified, many other proteins have been identified as interacting with one or the other core subunit. In some studies, it has been proposed that these interacting proteins are components of higher order Ccr4-Not complexes, which have been refractory to purification. The existing data favor a model in which the core Ccr4-Not complex may interact with many different proteins, leading to different, larger Ccr4-Notcomplexes. Nevertheless, it is also possible that individual core Ccr4-Not subunits interact with proteins outside of the complex.

Proteins interacting with Ccr4-Not complex subunits have been identified in very diverse ways. In some rare cases, interacting proteins have been isolated in genetic selections but, in general, the described interactors originate from two-hybrid experiments or large-scale proteomic approaches. In most cases, a functional connection between the endogenous proteins has not been made. Thus, we will go over the wide variety of defined interacting proteins (Table II) and discuss evidence for functional links with the Ccr4-Not proteins.

A. Yeast Proteins Interacting with the Ccr4/Caf Module of the Complex

A large-scale two-hybrid search for proteins interacting with Ccr4p (Caf for **C**cr4p **a**ssociated **f**actors) has been undertaken in the laboratory of Clyde Denis. Over time, several interacting genes have been published. After *CAF1*,

TABLE II
Proteins that Interact with Yeast Ccr4-Not Core Subunits[a]

	Genetics	Two-hybrid	Proteomics	Native co-ip
Not1p	Dhh1p[50] Spt3p[57] Spt8p[57] Srb4p[52]	Arh1p[53] TFIID[9] Srb10p[39]	Yak1p[40] Hrt1p[40] Cop1p[20] Rvb2p[20] Sec27p[20] Tfc7p[20] TAF12[41]	Dhh1p[50] TAF1[9]
Not2p	Ada2p[58]	Cap2p[51] Srb10p[39] Msb2p[53] Did4p[51] Soh1p[51] Srb9p[39]	Atp11p[20]	Ada2p[58]
Not3p	Srb4p[51]		Fas2p[20] Yra1p[20] Aha1p[20] Sam1p[20] Pdc1p[20] TFIID[41]	
Not4p	Dhh1p[50]	Met18p[51] Ubc4p[15] Ubc5p[15]		
Not5p	TFIID[9,16,17]	Nop4p[51]	TFIID[41]	TFIID[9,17]
Ccr4p	Dhh1p[46] Rad52p[47] Spt10p[25] Spt6p[25] Rpb2p[48] TFIIS[48] Spt16p[48] Spt5p[48]	Dbf2p[38] Caf4p[39] Caf16p[39] Srb9p[39] Srb10p[39]	Ubr1p[40] Cys4p[40] Sti1p[40] Tip49a[40] Rnq1p[40] YGR086C[40] Cct6p[20] Gcn1p[20] TAF4[41]	Btt1p[18] Paf1p[42] Cdc73p[42] Hpr1p[42]
Caf1p	Dhh1p[46] Srb4p[51]	Srb4p[51] Dbf2p[38]	Pol1p[20] Pol2p[20]	Dhh1p[46]

(Continues)

TABLE II (Continued)

	Genetics	Two-hybrid	Proteomics	Native co-ip
	Yak1p[56]	Yap6p[51]	Prl1p[20]	
		Reg2p[53]	Prl2p[20]	
		Std1p[51]	Kin2p[40]	
		Mob1p[54]	Tfp1p[20]	
		Csl1p[53]		
		Srb9p[39]		
Caf40p		Srb4p[51]		
		TFIIB[51]		
		Nst1p[53]		
Caf130p		Bem1p[53]		
		Btt1p[51]		

[a]The proteins designated in this table were identified in connection with the indicated core Ccr4-Not subunits. The studies in which these interactions were demonstrated are referenced for each protein in superscript, and the method by which an interaction was demonstrated defines the table columns.

the first was *DBF2*, encoding a cell cycle regulated protein kinase (*39*). Overexpressed Dbf2p was shown to co-immunoprecipitate with both Ccr4p and Caf1p and to confer kinase activity to Ccr4p immunoprecipitates, as well as to co-purify with Caf1p and Ccr4p. The functional link between Dbf2p and Ccr4p is rather weak, consisting of some similar mutant phenotypes that are rather general phenotypes, such as caffeine sensitivity or sensitivity to glycerol at 37 °C. *CAF4* and *CAF16* were the next two genes described (*40*). While they do bear motifs found in other proteins, no function has been attributed to these proteins. Like Dbf2p, Caf4p and Caf16p elute from gel filtration columns in the same fractions as the ∼1.9 MDa Ccr4-Not complex. This co-elution requires Ccr4p. Overexpressed Caf4p can co-immunoprecipitate with overexpressed Not1p, but otherwise there is no functional link between these proteins and the Ccr4-Not complex. However, a component of the RNA polymerase II holoenzyme, Srb9p, interacts with Caf16p in the two-hybrid assay, and also interacts with Not2p and Caf1p (*40*). The Srb10p kinase, associated with Srb9p in a module of the holoenzyme, also interacts by two-hybrid with Not1p and Not2p. Given components of this module and of the Ccr4-Not complex co-immunoprecipitate but only when overexpressed. Recent observations demonstrate that Srb10p is required for expression of a mutant phenotype of the Ccr4-Not complex (Collart, unpublished observations), suggesting that while interactions between the Ccr4-Not complex and the Srb10p kinase may be weak and indirect, they may nevertheless be functionally relevant.

A proteomic approach revealed several additional proteins interacting with Ccr4p: Ubr1p, a ubiquitin protein ligase; Cys4p, involved in cysteine biosynthesis; Sti1p, a chaperone; Tip49a, an ATPase within a chromatin remodeling complex; Rnq1p, a protein rich in Asn and Gln of unknown function; and YGR086C, an unknown ORF (41). A different proteomic approach using a Tap-Tagged derivative of Ccr4p identified different proteins: Cct6p, a chaperonin, and Gcn1p, important for translational activation of Gcn4p (20). Another study identified Ccr4p as a TAF4-interacting protein (42) (see Table II).

The lack of consistency between these different approaches and the fact that the interacting proteins were not identified as interacting with other Ccr4-Not core subunits might suggest that none of these proteins are true interactors of Ccr4p. Alternatively, they may not interact with Ccr4p within the Ccr4-Not complex. Ccr4p itself has been identified as a component of the Paf1p holoenzyme (43), involved in transcription elongation (44). Very recently, it was found that the Paf1p-complex participates in Set1p- and Set2p-mediated methylation of the histone H3-tail at lysines 4, 36, and 79 (45) and reviewed in (46). Yet surprisingly, none of the subunits of this Paf1p-complex were identified in any of the proteomic approaches. Finally, *ccr4* mutants display synthetic lethal interactions with several mutants of transcription elongation and other genes were identified in various genetic screens (see Table II) (25, 47–49). With the exception of Dhh1p (see following text), none of these interactions has been supported by any complementary studies.

The Dhh1p RNA helicase involved in mRNA decapping (50) holds the best cards for a functionally relevant Ccr4-Not interacting protein. Dhh1p was first isolated as a multicopy suppressor of *caf1* mutations (47). It can also suppress *ccr4* mutations and interacts with Caf1p (but not Ccr4p) in two-hybrid experiments. Dhh1p and Caf1p co-immunoprecipitate when over expressed. Dhh1p co-immunoprecipitates with Not1p, and with the nonessential N-terminal domain of Not1p, even in cells lacking Caf1p (51). Dhh1p and Not1p are associated in complexes larger than 1 MDa, and the nonessential domain of Not1p is important to maintain stable cellular levels of both Caf1p and Dhh1p. Strikingly, Dhh1p is essential in cells lacking Caf1p or Not4p, but not Ccr4p or Not5p (51).

Large scale two-hybrid experiments have defined a number of partners for Caf1p, including: Srb4p, a component of the RNA polymerase II holoenzyme, Yap6p, a bZIP transcription factor; Reg2p, a regulatory subunit of Glc7p; and Std1p, a protein that interacts with TBP and the Snf1p protein kinase (52). Based on other observations, some of these interactions deserve further study. For instance, *caf1* mutations suppress *srb4* mutations, as do mutations in *NOT1*, *NOT3*, and *NOT5* (53). In addition, mutations in *GLC7* partially suppress activation of Msn2p-dependent transcription in *ccr4-not* mutants (Collart, unpublished observations). Finally, Caf1p, Not3p, and Not5p are differentially modified under conditions where the Snf1p protein kinase becomes active (see following text). Many other proteins that might interact with Caf1p have been described (see Table II), but there is at present no data to support the relevance of all of these interactions.

Large-scale two-hybrid experiments defined Srb4p and TFIIB as interactors of Caf40p (Table II). While functional interactions between the Ccr4-Not complex and Srb4p have been described (see previous text), this is not the case for TFIIB. Nst1p, isolated in a separate selection (54), has been associated with salt tolerance, and might or might not be related to the function of the Ccr4-Not complex in the environmental stress response (see following text).

Two proteins, Bem1p and Btt1p, interact with Caf130p in the two-hybrid assay and could be relevant for Ccr4-Not function. Bem1p is an SH3 protein that binds Ste5p, a scaffold for the pheromone signaling pathway (55). Several mutants of the Ccr4-Not complex have been demonstrated to bear a constitutive pheromone response pathway (for review see (19)). Btt1p, on the other hand, is the less abundant of two homologous proteins in yeast that function as the β subunit of the nascent polypeptide-associated complex. This protein was reported to co-fractionate with Ccr4-Not complex subunits, and to co-immunoprecipitate with Ccr4p, Caf1p, and Caf40p in a Caf130p-dependent manner (18).

B. Yeast Proteins Interacting with the Not Module of the Complex

The Yak1 protein kinase, known to phosphorylate Caf1p (56), was isolated as a protein associated with Not1p, in a large-scale search for protein complexes, as was Hrt1p, a ubiquitin protein ligase (41). Purification of tagged Not1p identified other proteins implicated in diverse functions that were not isolated via other tagged core subunits (20) (see Table II). The essential Arh1 protein located on the mitochondrial inner membrane was additionally isolated by a two-hybrid screen (54). Again, the relevance of this is unknown. Clearly functionally relevant, Not1p can interact in the two-hybrid assay with all subunits of the TFIID complex, and can co-immunoprecipitate with TAF1 (9). Not1p was also identified as a TAF12-interacting protein (42). Temperature sensitivity of the *not1-2* allele can be suppressed by deleting either one of two components of the SAGA complex, namely, Spt3p or Spt8p (57), and mutations in *NOT1* can suppress a mutation in *SRB4* or *RPB2* (53).

Not2p interacts with the Ada2p subunit of the SAGA complex, as determined both by affinity chromatography and by functional assays, since Not2p can activate transcription upon promoter recruitment and this requires Ada2p (58). The functional relevance of this is supported by the observation that the *not2-4* mutant protein, which cannot interact with Ada2p, suppresses the *not1-2* allele that itself is suppressed by deletion of other SAGA subunits, as has been mentioned (57). Many other unrelated proteins were isolated in two-hybrid experiments (52, 54) or in a large-scale isolation of protein complexes (20) (see Table II).

Many potential Not3p interactors were identified in the large-scale isolation of protein complexes (20), while, in contrast, no interacting proteins have been described by the two-hybrid approaches (see Table II). Many of these proteins are involved in metabolism and Yra1p is involved in export of mRNA from nucleus to cytoplasm. The relevance of these interactions is unknown, but highly relevant is the identification of Not3p itself as a nonintegral subunit of TFIID (42).

Not4p interacts with the Ubc4p and Ubc5p E2 enzymes in the two-hybrid assays ((15); Mulder, Winkler, Timmers, and Collart, unpublished observations), as human CNOT4 can interact with the human E2 orthologs (15). These interactions with the E2s have been verified in functional assays (see Section V). Met18p involved in nucleotide excision repair and regulation of TFIIH has been identified as a Not4p-interactor in large-scale two-hybrid screen (54). This interaction has not been studied so far.

Many associations between Not5p and TAFs have been described. *not5* mutants are synthetically lethal with specific alleles of several TAF-encoding genes ((9, 17), and unpublished observations). Recombinant Not5p bound to a column can retain certain TAFs from a total cell extract (16) and can bind recombinant TAF13 *in vitro* in the absence of other TFIID or Ccr4-Not complex subunits (17). Finally, in a recent study of proteins interacting with TFIID subunits, Not5p was identified as interacting with TAF12 and TAF6 (42). Otherwise, the only other potential interacting protein for Not5p described was isolated by a two-hybrid approach and is Nop4p, a protein in the nucleolus that interestingly has an RNA recognition motif (52).

C. Genetic Links of Ccr4-Not Components in Other Eukaryotes

Additional information on Ccr4-Not components has been obtained in other eukaryotic systems. The Caf40p-ortholog in *Schizosaccharomyces pombe*, Rcd1p, was isolated in a screen for activators of *STE11* gene expression, and it was shown to be required for starvation-induced sexual development (59). In this organism, apparently Caf40p(Rcd1p) function is independent of the cAMP/protein kinase A pathway, that represses Ste11p in response to glucose or nitrogen, or the Wis1/Phh1 pathway that activates Ste11p in response to stress. The Not2p ortholog from *Drosophila melanogaster* was isolated as *Rga* (*regena*), in a screen for modifiers of position-effect variegation based on eye color (31). Many genes isolated in such screens mediate their effect via chromatin, providing a link with transcription regulation. Indeed, besides the *white*-locus, several other genes are affected by *Rga*.

Both human CNOT7(hCAF1) and CNOT8(hPOP2/CALIF) have been associated with human diseases. The CNOT8 gene maps to a region of chromosome 5q, which is deleted in a myelodysplastic syndrome (5q-syndrome) (60). The CNOT7 gene is localized on chromosome 8 at 8p21.3-p22 and this region is frequently associated with many tumor types, including colorectal cancer. However, recent analyses of 88 primary colorectal tumors detected only one heterozygous missense mutatation in the CNOT7 gene (61). Also, no aberrations in mRNA expression were observed, which indicates that CNOT7 is not the target tumor suppressor gene in this disease. In conclusion, no causal relationship of Ccr4-Not subunits with human diseases is apparent at this moment.

D. Does Human CNOT3 Link to TBP via TIP120B?

The CNOT3 gene has been isolated in a two-hybrid selection using the TBP-interaction protein 120B (TIP120B) as a bait (32). TIP120B and its paralog TIP120A can bind to TBP-affinity columns and belong to the HEAT-repeat family of proteins, which also includes the TBP-associated factors BTAF1 and Mot1p (62, 63). TIP120B is specifically expressed in muscle tissues and induced upon myoblast differentiation. TIP120B, but not TIP120A, can interact with CNOT3L. The interaction domain maps to the Not-box and, thus, CNOT3S does not interact with TIP120B (32). Thus, the TIP120B protein may link Ccr4-Not function to TBP and TFIID function in muscle tissue. The question is, what would be the outcome of this? The finding that TIP120A can stimulate transcription by the three RNA polymerases (64) but does not interact with CNOT3L could indicate that TIP120B may be inhibited by CNOT3L and/or the Ccr4-Not complex.

E. Relationship of Ccr4-Not Proteins with Cell Proliferation and Transcription Regulation in Higher Eukaryotes

Yeast two-hybrid screening provided a link of Ccr4-Not complex function with mammalian cell cycle control. CNOT7(hCAF1) was isolated with BTG1 as a bait (65, 66). BTG1 (B-cell translocation gene 1) is the founding member of the BTG/TOB family, which is characterized by two short signature motifs (for review see (67)). BTG/TOB proteins can inhibit cell proliferation (68). It was shown for the PC3 member of this family that this effect requires functional Rb-protein (69). It has been reported that mice lacking TOB have a higher incidence of chemically induced tumors of the liver and loss of TOB increases the tumor occurrence (mostly malignant lymphomas) in $p53^{-/-}$ mice (70). TOB overexpression can inhibit the cyclin D promoter and another family member, PC3, can inhibit S-phase entry, which also correlates with cyclin D inhibition (69). It was found that after overexpression, low levels of CNOT7(hCAF1) protein co-immunoprecipitate with Cdk4 and Cdc2, but not with Cdk2 (71). It was proposed that interaction of CNOT7(hCAF1) with BTG/TOB proteins could contribute to hypophosphorylation of Rb by inhibiting Cdk-activity and thereby inhibiting cell proliferation, but this hypothesis has not been tested rigorously.

BTG1 and BTG2 are closely related members of the family. Both are small (~20 kDa) and interact with CNOT7(hCAF1) as well as CNOT8(hPOP2/CALIF) in two-hybrid and GST-pull down assays (65). In addition, other members (ANA, TOB, and TOB2) can also interact with CNOT7(hCAF1) (70, 71). Interestingly, the BTG1 and BTG2 proteins contain two LXXLL-motifs, which are essential for certain coactivators to interact with nuclear hormone receptors. Indeed, BTG1 and BTG2 can regulate transcriptional stimulation by the activated estrogen receptor, ERα (72). They moderately enhance activation from a promoter containing palindromic ER-binding sites, but weakly inhibit activation from the natural ERα promoter, which contains ER half-sites. Interestingly, coexpression of both CNOT6(hCCR4) and CNOT7(hCAF1) enhance ERα activation three- to four-fold (21). Another link of BTG proteins with the Ccr4-Not complex is provided by the finding that overexpressed BTG2 co-elutes with the ~1.9 and ~1.0 MDa forms of the complex (21).

The CNOT9(hRqcd1/rcd1) protein has been shown to be involved in retinoic acid-induced differentiation of mouse F9 teratocarcinoma cells (73). Expression of this protein is induced by retinoic acid. Overexpression of CNOT9 can induce c-Jun expression, which is a marker for differentiation, and induce formation of embryoid bodies. The CNOT9 protein co-immunoprecipitates with retinoic receptors (RARs) and very strongly with the ATF-2 transcription factor. Moreover, it was shown by chromatin immunoprecipitation experiments that CNOT9 associates with the c-Jun promoter during retinoic acid-induced differentiation (73). Under these conditions, ATF-2 and RARs also bind to this promoter. Currently, it is unclear whether the other Ccr4-Not components play a role in BTG function or in the transcriptional regulation pathways mentioned.

IV. Role of the Yeast Ccr4-Not Complex in mRNA Metabolism

Strong evidence exists that the Ccr4-Not complex is essential for determining appropriate mRNA levels. Not only were most of the components isolated in yeast using selections for altered mRNA levels, but also mRNA expression profiling has been performed with strains lacking the nonessential subunits of the complex. From this, it has become clear that more than half of the genome displays altered mRNA levels when one or the other component is lacking (Collart, unpublished observations). However, while these changes would have been attributed initially to changes in transcription, either initiation or elongation, it seems likely now that at least some of the changes might be due to alterations in the rate of mRNA degradation. The question of the relative contributions of these two pathways is an important subject for future study.

A. Transcription

A role for the Ccr4-Not complex in transcription was initially attributed to the observed changes in mRNA levels in yeast *ccr4-not* mutant cells. Of the original studies, some clearly indicate that the changes in mRNA levels are due to changes in transcription. The *NOT* genes were isolated in screens for elevated *HIS3* expression (4, 5). *HIS3* is expressed from two different promoters, one containing a TATA box and one lacking a canonical TATA sequence. The resulting mRNAs are distinguished by an additional 12 nucleotides at the 5′-end of the transcript originating from the TATA-less promoter (74). The stability of these mRNAs is not known to be any different. However, their synthesis is associated with different control mechanisms (75–77). One promoter is under the control of the Gcn4p transcriptional activator, and the other (TATA-less) is particularly dependent upon certain TFIID-specific TAFs for appropriate expression (78). In *not* mutants that are recessive and loss of function mutants, transcription from the *HIS3* TATA-less promoter is specifically increased, which indicates a TATA-less-specific repressive function for the Not proteins. This has led to claims that the Ccr4-Not complex can directly control transcription, possibly by controlling TFIID function. Indeed, numerous interactions between the Ccr4-Not complex and TAFs, both physical and genetic have been reported (see previous text, and for review, see (19)). Additional support for a role in transcription is the suppression of *not1-2* by deletion of SAGA subunits (57) (see preceding text), since the SAGA complex functions as a transcriptional coregulator and can acetylate histones (for review, see (79)). Similarly, suppression of mutations in *SRB4* or *RPB2*, encoding essential components of the pol II holoenzyme (80) by mutations in several components of the Ccr4-Not complex (53), argues that the Ccr4-Not complex can control (some aspects of) transcription.

1. How is Transcription Controlled by the Ccr4-Not Complex?

While the Ccr4-Not complex has been claimed to have both a repressive and a stimulatory effect on transcription, the genetic studies mentioned here all indicate a repressive role. TAFs clearly appear as critical transcription factors that are regulated by the Ccr4-Not complex. However, it is not known in which form the TAFs might interact with the Ccr4-Not complex. All of the TAFs that have been tested can interact with Not1p in two-hybrid experiments

((9) and Collart, unpublished observations), suggesting that Not1p might interact with TFIID. However, the direct contact point could be any of the components of the Ccr4-Not complex and any component of TFIID. Not3p is the only component of the Ccr4-Not complex which has been identified as a TFIID-associated protein by multidimensional mass spectrometry (42). Nevertheless, Not5p and Not1p appeared as interacting specifically with TAF12, Not5p with TAF6, and Ccr4p with TAF4 by this same approach, as has been mentioned. *In vitro*, recombinant Not5p can retain at least TBP, TAF5, TAF6, and TAF12 from whole cell extracts, and this requires an intact TFIID complex (16). Indeed, this does not occur with extracts from the TBP(K151L, K156Y) mutant cells, in which TBP does not immunoprecipitate with all TAFs. The only known direct interaction is between Not5p and TAF13.

If the Ccr4-Not complex interacts with TFIID, or TAFs, how does this influence TAF-dependent transcription, or transcription in general? Early models for the function of the Ccr4-Not complex suggested that it might sequester TFIID to repress transcription. This model has not been extensively studied, but there has been one *in vitro* experiment that would be compatible with such a model (81). In this experiment, *in vitro* transcription from the TFIID-dependent *HIS3* TATA-less promoter could be increased by heating extracts from the *not1-1* temperature sensitive mutant. This suggests that the activity necessary for transcription from the *HIS3* TATA-less promoter is present in the extracts, but inhibited, and can be "freed" at the *not1-1* restrictive temperature.

Evidence has shown that Not5p can associate with promoter DNA, and that this association is TAF1-dependent and increases upon stress (9). Furthermore, appropriate TAF1-association with promoter DNA itself requires Not5p. Thus, it seems that the interaction of TAFs with Not5p regulates their appropriate association with promoters. A 2003 study has shown that several components of the Ccr4-Not complex (Ccr4p, Not2p, Not5p, and Caf1p, as well as Dhh1p) are recruited to the Gcn4p-dependent promoter *ARG1* by Gcn4p, consistent with the finding that Gcn4-dependent activation requires certain subunits of the Ccr4-Not complex (82). These results support the idea that the entire Ccr4-Not complex might associate with promoters. The recruitment of the Ccr4-Not complex to a core promoter by an activator, in turn, might be a means to provide a given subset of TAFs, TFIID, and/or SAGA, in appropriate levels to the core promoter for optimal activation. Interactions between the Srb4p subunit of the Mediator and certain Ccr4-Not subunits, or Not2p and the Ada2p subunit of SAGA (see Table II), could additionally all contribute to control appropriate levels of transcription initiation at core promoters. More detailed experiments will be needed to address this issue.

2. Do Ccr4p and Caf1p Contribute to Transcriptional Control?

Because Ccr4p and Caf1p are mRNA deadenylases and probably control mRNA levels by controlling mRNA decay, one can wonder whether any of the mRNA changes that have been described in *ccr4* or *caf1* mutants are due to changes in transcription. It is quite striking that Ccr4p and Caf1p bind to a nonessential central portion of Not1p, whereas the Not proteins bind to the essential C-terminal end of Not1p (Not4p and Not5p, and Not2p) (see Fig. 1). Nevertheless, the N-terminal portion of Not1p interacts with the C-terminal end (22), and thus both Caf1p and Ccr4p are likely to have every opportunity to affect interactions of Not5p with TAFs, if only by being important for the integrity of the Ccr4-Not complex. Indeed, we have evidence that Caf1p and Ccr4p are both necessary, as are the Not proteins, for the appropriate distribution TBP and TAF1 across promoters (Collart, unpublished observations). Furthermore, *caf1* is synthetically lethal with *taf1* mutants according to the same allele-specificity as *not5* ((9) and Collart, unpublished observations).

3. Transcriptional Control by Ccr4-Not Subunits in Higher Eukaryotes

The situation in higher eukaryotes is equally complicated. As has been indicated, the Caf40p ortholog CNOT9(hRqdc1/rcd1) has been proposed to act as a transcriptional coactivator for retinoic acid receptors and ATF-2 (73). Both CNOT6(hCCR4) and CNOT7(hCAF1) can potentiate ligand-dependent activation by the estrogen receptor (21). In contrast to this, promoter-targeting of CNOT6(hCCR4) does not result in activation (38). Rather, strong transcriptional repression can be observed with certain Not-subunits (100). At present, it is unclear whether the complete Ccr4-Not complex is involved in this effect. The observation that only few core components display this activity indicates that other factors outside of the complex may be involved as well. Candidates for this are the TIP120 proteins.

B. mRNA Degradation

A role for the Ccr4-Not complex in the control of mRNA degradation became evident after the discovery that Ccr4p and Caf1p act as the major yeast deadenylase. Furthermore, Dhh1p of the decapping complex interacts with, and is controlled by, the Ccr4-Not complex. In yeast, the major pathway for mRNA degradation involves shortening of the poly(A) tail, followed by decapping of the mRNA and 5′–3′ exonucleolytic activity. The importance of mRNA degradation control in the specific regulation of stable cellular mRNA levels has recently been questioned, and several revealing studies have been published (83–85). It seems that post-transcriptional processing of transcripts is an integral component of the control of the program of gene expression. Interestingly, it was shown that changes in mRNA stability can influence approximately 50% of stress-regulated genes (84). This could be quite relevant for the Ccr4-Not complex as it contributes to the control of the stress response of cells (see Section VII).

1. ENZYMATIC ACTIVITIES ASSOCIATED WITH CCR4P AND CAF1P

Mutation of the key Mg2+-binding residue in Ccr4p, which blocks endonuclease activity in other members of the family, abrogates Ccr4p function *in vivo*. It leads to many of the mutant phenotypes associated with complete removal of Ccr4p. This is also true of mutation of the residue involved in stabilizing the phosphate during catalysis or of other critically important residues (12, 13). Deletion or mutation of *CCR4* reduces approximately 1.5-fold the degradation rate of several mRNAs such as *ADH2*, *GAL1*, and *HSP12* (13), and to a greater extent of *COX17* mRNA, whose deadenylation is enhanced *in vivo* by Puf3p, a protein that binds to specific 3'-UTR sequences (12).

Epitope-tagged wild-type Ccr4p, or Ccr4p mutated at its catalytic site, were purified from yeast and tested on several DNA/RNA substrates *in vitro*. Wild-type but not mutant Ccr4p was able to function as a 3'–5' exoribonuclease, which displays a marked preference for poly(A) substrates. Its activity can be inhibited by Pab1p, a protein that binds poly(A) tails, *in vitro*. Ccr4p is most efficient with substrates that are at least 17 nucleotides long, which do not necessarily need to be adenines, and longer substrates (at least 45 nucleotides) convert Ccr4p from a distributive to a processive enzyme (86). Ccr4p is also able to function as a single-stranded DNA exonuclease but with a much slower rate of reaction, and with a preference for substrates with two A residues at its 3' end. It cannot degrade any double-stranded DNA, nor function as an endonuclease, even on an RNA molecule with 10 consecutive As within the sequence (86).

Yeast Caf1p is required for efficient *in vivo* mRNA degradation (10, 14), as defined by using a reporter plasmid encoding an *MFA2* mRNA marked with an oligo(G) tract under the control of a galactose-regulated promoter. The *MFA2* mRNA and degradation intermediates have extended poly(A) tails in the mutants. *In vitro*, a recombinant Caf1p fragment covering the RNase D motif is able to degrade a poly(A) substrate. Competition experiments clearly confirmed that the specificity of Caf1p is towards poly(A) substrates.

Even though both Caf1p and Ccr4p are important for deadenylation, Ccr4p purified from a strain lacking Caf1p is equally active *in vitro* (86). This defines Ccr4p rather than Caf1p or the Ccr4-Not complex as the major enzyme. Nevertheless, removal of both Ccr4p and Caf1p does not entirely disrupt deadenylation *in vivo*. The residual deadenylation is mostly due to the

Pan2p/Pan3p nuclease. Cells lacking both deadenylases have incredibly stable *MFA2* mRNA, confirming the importance of deadenylation for later steps in mRNA turnover. Nevertheless, because cells lacking both deadenylases are viable, mRNAs can probably be degraded by some aberrant mechanism in which decapping eventually occurs.

2. Dhh1p Involvement in mRNA Decapping and Degradation

Dhh1p was first identified as a putative RNA helicase of the DEAD box family that upon overexpression could suppress *caf1* or *ccr4* deletion strains (47). Dhh1p is not a component of the so-called core Ccr4-Not complex. Nevertheless, the evidence for association of Dhh1p with the core complex into larger complexes is compelling. Dhh1p is a cytoplasmic protein and a component of the decapping complex (50). It specifically affects mRNA turnover in the deadenylation decay pathway. Deadenylation itself is not affected by Dhh1p and cells that lack Dhh1p accumulate degradation intermediates that have lost their poly(A) tail (50, 87) but contain an intact cap structure. Dhh1p can stimulate the decapping enzyme Dcp1p in an *in vitro* decapping assay. The importance of both decapping and deadenylation in mRNA decay is evident. Indeed, inactivation of both decapping and 3′–5′ exonucleolytic degradation leads to cell death, as evidenced by inviability of *caf1 dhh1* double mutants. The initial isolation of Dhh1p as a *caf1* suppressor might be explained by an increased Dhh1p-dependent decapping that compensates for decreased deadenylation.

3. The Ccr4-Not Complex and the Control of Decapping and Deadenylation

The role of the Not proteins in decapping and deadenylation is unclear. The rate of MFA2pG degradation is only marginally reduced in cells lacking Not2p, Not3p, Not4p, and Not5p (12). It could be that the Not proteins play a regulatory role, and this role might be related to the integrity of the Ccr4-Not complexes, in which, for instance, deadenylation and decapping might be coordinately regulated. In any event, it is clear that Not1p is important to maintain stable steady-state levels of both Caf1p and Dhh1p (51). Furthermore, overexpressing Dhh1p mimics, and deletion of Dhh1p, Caf1p, or Ccr4p suppresses, a phenotype specific to only *not* mutants, namely, resistance to 3-amino triazole (AT) in cells carrying a mutant derivative of Gcn4p (51). This would suggest that the AT-resistant mutant phenotype requires decapping and deadenylation and might be mediated by deregulated decapping and/or deadenylation. Thus, the association of Dhh1p, Caf1p, and Ccr4p with the Not proteins might create a platform in which the proteins involved in mRNA decay will be timely activated or directed to their target mRNAs.

4. Where and in Which Form Does Deadenylation Occur: Localization of the Proteins

The question that remains is in which form does Ccr4p deadenylate mRNAs? Is it in the context of Ccr4-Not complexes or as a Caf1p-Ccr4p module? A major cytoplasmic localization has been described for Caf1p and Ccr4p (*12*), whereas Dhh1p, for instance, localizes to discrete cytoplasmic foci in yeast that have been called the P bodies (*11*). Originally, a nuclear localization was described for Not1p and Not2p (*5*), but recently these proteins have been shown to also localize to the cytoplasm (*10*). For some Not subunits, we have found that they can be detected in both the nuclear and cytoplasmic compartments in exponentially growing cells, but accumulate in the nucleus under stress conditions, such as glucose depletion or heat shock (Collart, unpublished observations). Localization of Caf1p or Ccr4p after stress has not been determined yet in yeast. The human homologue of Caf1p, CNOT7(hCAF1) has been found to accumulate in the nucleus under certain conditions (*66*). In another study, mouse CNOT7(hCAF1) was found to localize in both the nucleus and the cytoplasm (*65*). Cell-cycle synchronization of human cells indicated that CNOT7(hCAF1) is predominantly cytoplasmic in S-phase cells, but in G0- or G1-phase cells exclusively localizes to the nucleus and resides in the $\sim$1.9 MDa complex. In G1/S-phase cells, CNOT7(hCAF1) can also be found in the $\sim$1.0 and $\sim$0.65 MDa complexes (*21*).

It is clear that studies of Ccr4-Not complex subunit localization alone will not really address in which form Ccr4p works as a deadenylase. Even if the majority of Ccr4p is apparently cytoplasmic, Ccr4p might be delivered to the nascent mRNA in the nucleus, where other subunits of the Ccr4-Not complex might regulate transcription initiation. In such a model, Caf1p might be essential via the Ccr4-Not complex, to load Ccr4p onto the nascent mRNA. Studies determining whether Ccr4p and other subunits of the Ccr4-Not complex can be cross-linked to promoters or to coding regions with the elongating polymerase, in wild-type cells or in given *ccr4-not* mutants, will certainly be necessary to solve this issue.

C. Relative Contribution of Transcription and mRNA Degradation, Coordination?

An important question is why a single complex would control both mRNA decay and mRNA synthesis. It is very plausible that it serves to coordinate gene expression. Changing mRNA expression programs may involve degradation of preexisting mRNA pools. It seems intuitive that in exponentially growing cells in rich medium, the contribution of mRNA decay to determine the levels of specific classes of mRNAs will not be important. In contrast, under conditions of changes in environmental signals to the cell, it seems that both changes in mRNA decay and synthesis of specific mRNAs is likely to occur. To obtain a better understanding of the role of the Ccr4-Not complex in controlling total cellular mRNA levels, and furthermore the role of the individual subunits in this control, micro-array experiments will need to be performed in cells lacking each subunit of the complex. Both the stability of target transcripts and the association of the transcription machinery with target genes will need to be determined.

V. Role of the Ccr4-Not Complex in Ubiquitylation

A. Not4 Proteins are Protein–Ubiquitin Ligases

Cloning of the *NOT4* gene from yeast indicated the presence of a putative Zn-binding module at the highly conserved N-terminus of Not4p (*88*). Structural analysis of this part of human CNOT4 by NMR methods unambiguously showed the presence of two Zn-ions (*33*), which are coordinated by eight cysteine-residues organized in a cross-brace manner. This type of Zn-coordination is the hallmark for RING fingers, which most often employ a Cys_3His-Cys_4 motif for this (*89*). RING fingers have been implicated as ubiquitin–protein (E3) ligases in post-translational modification of proteins (*34, 35*). Poly-ubiquitylation via ubiquitin lysine 48-linkages destines proteins for degradation by proteasomes (for review, see (*90*)), whereas modification via other lysine residues or, alternatively, mono-ubiquitylation, has been implicated in regulatory pathways. Transfer of ubiquitin moieties involves several enzymatic steps. Activation requires ATP-hydrolysis and conjugation of ubiquitin to the E1 enzyme. Subsequently, ubiquitin is transferred to an ubiquitin-conjugating (E2) enzyme. Yeast and human cells have, respectively, 13 and more than 20 different E2 enzymes. Modification of the substrate protein involves an ubiquitin–protein (E3) ligase. These E3 ligases are critical for substrate recognition and, together with the E2 enzyme, provide the selectivity of the ubiquitin system. The many E3 ligases can be divided into monomeric E3 enzymes like c-Cbl (*91*) or multi-subunit E3 enzymes like the SCF and APC complexes (for reviews, (*92, 93*)). E3 enzymes require a RING motif or HECT domain for E2-interaction. Indeed, it was found that CNOT4 displays *in vitro* auto-ubiquitylation activity, which requires an intact RING finger (*15*).

CNOT4 interacts with a specific set of human E2 enzymes—UbcH5B, UbcH6, and UbcH9. These are closely related to the yeast Ubc4p and Ubc5p proteins, which carry redundant functions and have been involved in stress-response pathways (*94*). As expected, yUbc4p and yUbc5p proteins can interact with yeast Not4p in two-hybrid assays ((*15*) and Mulder, Winkler, Timmers, and Collart, unpublished observations). Therefore, yeast Not4p can probably also function as an E3 ligase. The human homologue CNOT4 can complement yeast cells lacking Not4p and the RING finger is essential for this (27).

B. Targets of Ubiquitylation Controlled by the Ccr4-Not Complex

The finding of an intrinsic ubiquitin–protein ligase activity associated with the Ccr4-Not complex raises several questions. What is the relevance of this enzymatic activity for Ccr4-Not function? Which are the ubiquitylation substrates for Not4p? How is the E3 activity regulated? No answers are available to date and we will speculate on these issues.

Clearly, the ubiquitin–protein ligase activity of Not4p is not essential for yeast viability. Possibly, this E3 activity is redundant with other systems. Mutants in the RING finger predicted to disrupt Ubc4p/Ubc5p-interactions *in vivo* have been created and unlike *not4* null cells these mutants grow as wild-type yeast (Mulder, Winkler, Timmers, and Collart, unpublished observations). Possibly, the activity of this E3 ligase is only required under very specific conditions.

For most of the putative E3 ligases, the *in vivo* substrates have not been identified. If Not4p-targets are within the Ccr4-Not complex, one expects that *not4* mutants might suppress other *ccr4-not* mutants. Of course, this argument is based on the assumption that Not4p-mediated ubiquitylation leads to proteosomal degradation of the substrate. This needs to be tested with mutants of Not4p that specifically affect its E3 ligase function, but not the integrity of the Ccr4-Not complex. Not3p and Not5p are candidate proteins, since the levels of these subunits have been shown to decrease after the diauxic shift in yeast (95). An alternative would be that ubiquitylation by Not4p might alter protein activity rather than abundance. In this context, it has been speculated that the TFIID and/or Mediator complexes could be targets for Not4p-mediated ubiquitylation (15). However, to our knowledge, evidence of ubiquitylation of TFIID and/or Mediator subunits is missing. As has been mentioned, many other proteins have been isolated as proteins which interact with Ccr4-Not subunits besides TFIID and Mediator subunits. This extends the possible target list and it is clear that identification of the true ubiquitylation targets will require a dedicated effort.

It is quite interesting to note that the Med8p subunit of the Mediator complex can assemble into an SCF-like ubiquitin–protein ligase complex (96). Possibly, Not4p also is integrated into a larger assembly to obtain substrate specificity. In this model, the Ccr4-Not complex would represent a similar type of assembly, which would then act as an SCF-APC-type of complex. Currently, there is little support for this model. The only backing comes from the observation that the *not4-1* allele can display a dominant-negative phenotype. This specific allele expresses a truncated version of Not4p, maintaining the conserved part including the RING and RRM domains (19). The less-conserved part of Not4p required to interact with Not1p is lacking ((15); Collart, unpublished results). However, it is unclear whether integrity of the RING is required for the dominant negative phenotype of *not4-1*. The observation that RING mutations in the context of the full-length Not4p have little effect argues against this model. In conclusion, while the ubiquitylation activity of Not4 proteins is intriguing, the functional importance of this activity should direct future research in this area.

VI. Role of the Ccr4-Not Complex in Protein Modification

The Ccr4-Not complex also seems to be involved in other post-translational modifications. Increased transcriptional activation by Msn2p was demonstrated in all *ccr4-not* mutants and this was found to correlate with altered post-translational modifications of Msn2p in *ccr4-not* mutants (95). Interestingly, this is apparently the one phenotype shared by all mutants of the core complex and also by *dhh1*, and it confers heat shock resisitance to all mutants. The observed changes in Msn2p might reflect changes in expression of protein-modifying enzymes in the mutants or they might indicate that the Ccr4-Not complex controls protein-modifying enzymes. The Glc7p phosphatase has been identified to interact with Not1p and mediate both the altered post-translational modification and increased activity of Msn2p in *ccr4-not* mutants (Collart, unpublished observations). How the Ccr4-Not complex regulates Glc7p is still unknown but, in any event, these results clearly extend the regulatory role of the Ccr4-Not complex to protein-modifying enzymes.

VII. The Ccr4-Not Complex as a Regulatory Platform that Senses Glucose Levels and Stress

As has been described, the Ccr4-Not complex can regulate transcription by interaction with TFIID and possibly SAGA, mRNA decay by interaction with Dhh1p and its mRNA deadenylases, ubiquitylation via its integral E3 ligase, and protein modification by interaction with the Glc7p phosphatase. In addition, there may be other interactions that are functionally relevant as many proteins can interact with subunits of the Ccr4-Not complex. This defines the Ccr4-Not complex as a regulatory platform for many cellular functions. As such, it may coordinate these different processes. The current evidence suggests that an important function of this complex is to contribute to the control of the cellular response to environmental stresses, such as glucose depletion and heat shock. Indeed, transcriptional activation by Msn2p, the transcription factor that mediates the environmental stress response, is increased in all mutants of the Ccr4-Not complex (95). In addition, both repression and activation of genes that occur upon glucose depletion requires different subunits of the Ccr4-Not complex. Indeed, both Caf1p and Ccr4p were identified as necessary for nonfermentative gene expression (2, 25), and mutations in NOT1 have been shown to lead to inefficient repression of genes at the diauxic shift (97). Furthermore, the Not4p E3 ligase interacts with the Ubc4p and Ubc5p E2 ligases (15), which are important for the stress response in yeast (94). Finally, the stability of heat shock mRNAs is increased in cells lacking Ccr4p.

While the role of the Ccr4-Not complex in the control of the stress response seems clearly established, the mechanism by which the response flows from the physiological stimulus to the Ccr4-Not complex, and then further to the effectors, still remains to be defined. Phosphorylation events are certainly key to some of this signal transmission. Indeed, Not1p, Not3p, Not5p, and Caf1p are phosphoproteins (56, 95, 98), and the phosphorylation status of these subunits clearly changes, for instance, as glucose is depleted from the growth medium. For Caf1p, the Yak1 protein kinase was identified as responsible for this modification that occurs on Thr97. When this amino acid is mutated, cells fail to respond by a G1 arrest in response to glucose limitation, prior to adaptation and growth under nonfermentative conditions. For Not3p and Not5p, the kinases have not been identified. However, it seems likely that both proteins are phosphorylated by PKA in exponentially growing cells. Both proteins show a two-hybrid interaction with one catalytic subunit of PKA, Tpk2p, and one form of the proteins visible on SDS PAGE requires active PKA (95). The PKA-dependent Not3p and Not5p forms disappear rapidly as PKA is inactivated upon glucose depletion. This might be a prerequisite for Caf1p phosphorylation by Yak1p, whose activity increases as PKA decreases. This possibility remains to be investigated. In any event, the stable levels of both Not3p and Not5p decrease after the diauxic shift and, in the case of Not3p, we could also show a transient decrease of the protein after heat shock (95). Thus, the change in either protein levels or phosphorylation patterns of certain subunits of the Ccr4-Not complex might alter its control of effectors.

While a lot remains to be done to understand what changes happen to the Ccr4-Not complex in response to environmental stresses, how these changes affect the different proteins that interact with the complex also needs to be addressed. Both glucose depletion and heat shock lead to nuclear accumulation of Not2p and Not5p (Collart, unpublished observations), and heat shock leads to increased association of Not5p with promoter DNA (9). Thus, one component of the response may clearly involve a change in complex localization, or a change in localization of certain subunits. At this point, we have not seen any alteration in integrity of Ccr4-Not complexes by gel filtration under stress conditions.

The role of the Ccr4-Not complex is likely to extend beyond mediating repression of the environmental stress response by PKA. Indeed, unlike the essential character of PKA that can be suppressed by deletion of Msn2p and its redundant factor Msn4p (99), growth of *not5* or *not4* null cells is by no means improved by removal of Msn2p and Msn4p (unpublished observations). A close analysis of genes deregulated in the various mutants of the Ccr4-Not complex might provide some ideas concerning which functional pathways are additionally controlled by the Ccr4-Not complex.

VIII. Perspectives

Since 1999, our knowledge about the Ccr4-Not proteins has expanded enormously. The composition of the core Ccr4-Not complex has been elucidated and many interacting proteins have been isolated. Two different enzymatic activities have been attributed to Ccr4-Not subunits. However, these findings do not provide a crystal-clear picture of the molecular and cellular functioning of the Ccr4-Not complex. It has helped, however, to direct experimental efforts. It seems most straightforward to view the Ccr4-Not complex as a protein platform, which can integrate several cellular regulatory pathways. Our current understanding of the output is in the regulation of mRNA metabolism at different levels, since even the control of Msn2p post-translational modifications by the Ccr4-Not complex ultimately controls transcription initiation. However, it is clearly important to identify the relevance of the described ubiquitylation activity of Not4p and its cognate substrates. This will require a combination of biochemical and genetic approaches. Of foremost importance will be to integrate these functions in the cell regulatory pathways, of which the environmental stress response that includes glucose depletion and heat shock may be only one of multiple signaling pathways to which the Ccr4-Not complex contributes.

Acknowledgments

We thank Bas Winkler and Cécile Deluen for critical reading of the manuscript. H. Th. M. Timmers was supported by the Netherlands Organisation for Scientific Research (NWO-MW Pionier grant 900–98–142) and the European Commission (RTN2–2001–00026) and M. A. Collart was supported by Swiss National Science Foundation grant 3100A0–100793 and OFES grant 02.0017.

References

1. Denis, C. L. (1984). Identification of new genes involved in the regulation of yeast alcohol dehydrogenase II. *Genetics* **108**, 833–834.
2. Sakai, A., Chibazakura, Y., Shimizu, Y., and Hishinuma, F. (1992). Molecular analysis of the POP2 gene, a gene required for glucose repression of *Saccharomyces cerevisiae*. *Nucleic Acids Res.* **20**, 6227–6233.
3. Draper, M. P., Salvadore, C., and Denis, C. L. (1995). Identification of a mouse protein whose homolog in *Saccharomyces cerevisiae* is a component of the CCR4 transcriptional regulatory complex. *Mol. Cell. Biol.* **15**, 3487–3495.
4. Collart, M. A., and Struhl, K. (1994). *NOT1* (*CDC39*), *NOT2* (*CDC36*), *NOT3*, and *NOT4* encode a global negative regulator of transcription that differentially affects TATA-element utilization. *Genes Dev.* **8**, 525–537.
5. Collart, M. A., and Struhl, K. (1993). CDC39, an essential nuclear protein that negatively regulates transcription and differentially affects the constitutive and inducible *HIS3* promoters. *EMBO J.* **12**, 177–186.
6. Oberholzer, U., and Collart, M. A. (1998). Characterization of *NOT5* that encodes a new component of the NOT protein complex. *Gene* **207**, 61–69.
7. Draper, M. P., Liu, H.-Y., Nelsbach, A. H., Mosley, S. P., and Denis, C. L. (1994). CCR4 is a glucose-regulated transcription factor whose leucine-rich repeat binds several proteins important for placing CCR4 in its proper promoter context. *Mol. Cell. Biol.* **14**, 4522–4531.
8. Liu, H.-Y., Badarinarayana, V., Audino, D. C., Rappsilber, J., Mann, M., and Denis, C. L. (1998). The NOT proteins are part of the CCR4 transcriptional complex and affect gene expression both positively and negatively. *EMBO J.* **17**, 1096–1106.
9. Deluen, C., James, N., Maillet, L., Molinete, M., Theiler, G., Lemaire, M., Paquet, N., and Collart, M. A. (2002). The Ccr4-Not complex and yTAF1 (yTaf(II)130p/yTaf(II)145p) present physical and functional interactions. *Mol. Cell. Biol.* **22**, 6735–6749.
10. Tucker, M., Valencia-Sanchez, M. A., Staples, R. R., Chen, J., Denis, C. L., and Parker, R. (2001). The transcription factor associated proteins, Ccr4p and Caf1p, are components of the major cytoplasmic mRNA deadenylase in *Saccharomyces cerevisiae*. *Cell* **104**, 377–386.
11. Sheth, U., and Parker, R. (2003). Decapping and decay of messenger RNA occur in cytoplasmic processing bodies. *Science* **300**, 805–808.
12. Tucker, M., Staples, R. R., Valencia-Sanchez, M. A., Muhlrad, D., and Parker, R. (2002). Ccr4p is the catalytic subunit of a Ccr4p/Pop2p/Notp mRNA deadenylase complex in *Saccharomyces cerevisiae*. *EMBO J.* **21**, 1427–1436.
13. Chen, J., Chiang, Y.-C., and Denis, C. L. (2002). CCR4, a 3′–5′ poly(A) RNA and ssDNA exonuclease, is the catalytic component of the cytoplasmic deadenylase. *EMBO J.* **21**, 1414–1426.
14. Daugeron, M.-C., Mauxion, F., and Séraphin, B. (2001). The yeast *POP2* gene encodes a nuclease involved in mRNA deadenylation. *Nucleic Acids Res.* **29**, 2448–2455.
15. Albert, T., Hanzawa, H., Legtenberg, Y. I. A., deRuwe, M. J., van der Heuvel, F. A. J., Collart, M. A., Boelens, R., and Timmers, M. H. T. (2002). Identification of a ubiquitin–protein ligase subunit within the CCR4-NOT transcription repressor complex. *EMBO J.* **21**, 355–364.
16. Badarinarayana, V., Chiang, Y.-C., and Denis, C. L. (2000). Functional interaction of CCR4-NOT proteins with TATAAA-binding protein (TBP) and its associated factors in yeast. *Genetics* **155**, 1045–1054.
17. Lemaire, M., and Collart, M. A. (2000). The TATA binding protein-associated factor yTaf$_{II}$19p functionally interacts with components of the global transcriptional regulator Ccr4-Not complex and physically interacts with the Not5 subunit. *J. Biol. Chem.* **275**, 26925–26934.

18. Denis, C. D., and Chen, J. (2003). The CCR4-NOT complex plays divers roles in mRNA metabolism. *Nucl. Acids Res. and Mol. Biol.* **73**, 221–250.
19. Collart, M. A. (2003). Global control of gene expression in yeast by the Ccr4-Not complex. *Gene* **313**, 1–16.
20. Gavin, A.-C., Bosche, M., Krause, R., Grandi, P. *et al.* (2002). Functional organization of the yeast proteome by systematic analysis of protein complexes. *Nature* **415**, 141–147.
21. Morel, A.-P., Sentis, S., Bianchin, C., Le Romancer, M., Jonard, L., Rostan, M.-C., Rimokh, R., and Corbo, L. (2003). BTG2 antiproliferative protein interacts with the human CCR4 complex existing *in vivo* in three cell cycle-regulated forms. *J. Cell Science* **116**, 2929–2936.
22. Maillet, L., Tu, C., Hong, Y. K., Shuster, E. O., and Collart, M. A. (2000). The essential function of NOT1 lies within the CCR4-NOT complex. *J. Mol. Biol.* **303**, 131–143.
23. Bai, Y., Salvadore, C., Chiang, Y.-C., Collart, M. A., Liu, H.-Y., and Denis, C. L. (1999). The CCR4 and CAF1 proteins of the CCR4-NOT complex are physically and functionally separated from NOT2, NOT4 and NOT5. *Mol. Cell. Biol.* **19**, 6642–6651.
24. Ferguson, J., Ho, T. A., Peterson, T. A., and Reed, S. I. (1986). Nucleotide sequence of the yeast cell division cycle start genes CDC28, CDC36, CDC37, and CDC39, and a structural analysis of the predicted proteins. *Nucleic Acids Res.* **14**, 6681–6697.
25. Denis, C. L., and Malvar, T. (1990). The *CCR4* gene from *Saccharomyces cerevisiae* is required for both nonfermentative and *spt*-mediated gene expression. *Genetics* **124**, 283–291.
26. Chen, J., Rappsilber, J., Chiang, Y.-C., Russell, P., Mann, M., and Denis, C. D. (2001). Purification and characterization of the 1.0 MDa Ccr4-Not complex identifies two novel components of the complex. *J. Mol. Biol.* **314**, 683–694.
27. Albert, T. K., Lemaire, M., van Berkum, N. L., Gentz, R., Collart, M. A., and Timmers, M. H. T. (2000). Isolation and characterization of human orthologs of yeast CCR4-NOT complex subunits. *Nucl. Acids Res.* **28**, 809–817.
28. Russell, P., Benson, J. D., and Denis, C. L. (2002). Characterization of mutations in NOT2 indicates that it plays an important role in maintaining the integrity of the Ccr4-Not complex. *J. Mol. Biol.* **322**, 27–39.
29. Maeda, I., Kohara, Y., Yamamoto, M., and Sugimoto, A. (2001). Large-scale analysis of gene function in Caenorhabditis elegans by high-throughput RNAi. *Current Biol.* **11**, 171–176.
30. Kamath, R. S., and Ahringer, J. (2003). Genome-wide RNAi screening in Caenorhabditis elegans. *Methods* **30**, 313–321.
31. Frolov, M. V., Benevolenskaya, E. V., and Birchler, J. A. (1998). Regena (Rga), a Drosophila homolog of the global negative transcriptional regulator CDC36 (NOT2) from yeast, modifies gene expression and suppresses position effect variegation. *Genetics* **148**, 317–329.
32. Aoki, T., Okada, N., Wakamatsu, T., and Tamura, T.-A. (2002). TBP-interaction protein 120B, which is induced in relation to myogenesis, binds to NOT3. *Biochem. Biophys. Res. Comm.* **296**, 1097–1103.
33. Hanzawa, H., de Ruwe, M. J., Albert, T. K., Van de Vliet, P. C., Timmers, M. H. T., and Boelens, R. (2001). The structure of the C4C4 ring finger of human NOT4 reveals features distinct from those of C3HC4 ring fingers. *J. Biol. Chem.* **276**, 10185–10190.
34. Freemont, P. S. (2000). RING for destruction? *Current Biol.* **10**, R84–R87.
35. Joazeiro, C. A. P., and Weissman, A. M. (2000). RING finger proteins: Mediators of ubiquitin ligase activity. *Cell* **102**, 549–552.
36. Nagai, K., Oubridge, C., Ito, N., Avis, J., and Evans, P. (1995). The RNP domain: A sequence-specific RNA-binding domain involved in processing and transport of RNA. *Trends in Biochem. Sci.* **20**, 235–240.
37. Dlakic, M. (2000). Functionally unrelated signalling proteins contain a fold similar to Mg^{2+}-dependent endonucleases. *Trends in Biochem. Sci.* **25**, 272–273.

38. Dupressoir, A., Morel, A.-P., Barbot, W., Loireau, P., Corbo, L., and Heidmann, T. (2001). Identification of four families of yCCR4- and Mg2+-dependent endonuclease-related proteins in higher eukaryotes, and characterization of orthologs of yCCR4 with a conserved leucine-rich repeat essential for hCAF1/hPOP2 binding. *BMC Genomics* **2**, 1–14.
39. Liu, H.-Y., Toyn, J. H., Chiang, Y.-C., Draper, M. P., Johnston, L. H., and Denis, C. L. (1997). DBF2, a cell cycle-regulated protein kinase, is physically and functionally associated with the CCR4 transcriptional regulatory complex. *EMBO J.* **16**, 5289–5298.
40. Liu, H.-Y., Chiang, Y.-C., Pan, J., Chen, J. *et al.* (2001). Characterization of CAF4 and CAF16 reveals a functional connection between the CCR4-NOT complex and a subset of SRB proteins of the RNA polymerase II holoenzyme. *J. Biol. Chem.* **276**, 7541–7548.
41. Ho, Y., Gruhler, A., Heibut, A., Bader, G. D. *et al.* (2002). Systematic identification of protein complexes in Saccharomyces cerevisiae by mass spectrometry. *Nature* **415**, 180–183.
42. Sanders, S. L., Jennings, J., Canutescu, A., Link, A. J., and Weil, A. P. (2002). Proteomics of the eukaryotic transcription machinery: Identification of proteins associated with components of yeast TFIID by multidimensional mass spectrometry. *Mol. Cell. Biol.* **22**, 4723–4738.
43. Chang, M., French-Cormay, D., Fan, H.-Y., Klein, H., Denis, C. L., and Jaehning, J. (1999). A complex containing RNA polymerase II, Paf1p, Cdc73p, Hpr1p, and Ccr4p plays a role in protein kinase C signaling. *Mol. Cell. Biol.* **19**, 1056–1067.
44. Squazzo, S. L., Costa, P. J., Lindstrom, D. L., Kumer, K. E., Simic, R., Jennings, J. L., Link, A. J., Arndt, K. M., and Hartzog, G. A. (2002). The Paf1 complex physically and functionally associates with transcription elongation factors *in vivo*. *EMBO J.* **21**, 1764–1774.
45. Ng, H. H., Dole, S., and Struhl, K. (2003). The Rtf1 component of the Paf1 transcriptional elongation complex is required for ubiqutination of histone H2B. *J. Biol. Chem.* **278**, 33625–33628.
46. Gerber, M., and Shilatifard, A. (2003). Transcriptional elongation by RNA polymerase II and histone methylation. *J. Biol. Chem.* **278**, 26303–26306.
47. Hata, H., Mitsui, H., Liu, H., Bai, Y., Denis, C. L., Shimizu, Y., and Sakai, A. (1998). Dhh1p, a putative RNA helicase, associates with the general transcription factors Pop2p and Ccr4p from *Saccharomyces cerevisiae*. *Genetics* **148**, 571–579.
48. Schild, D. (1995). Suppression of a new allele of the yeast *RAD52* gene by overexpression of *RAD51*, mutations in *srs2* and *ccr4*, or mating-type heterozygosity. *Genetics* **140**, 115–127.
49. Denis, C. L., Chiang, Y.-C., Cui, Y., and Chen, J. (2001). Genetic evidence supports a role for the yeast Ccr4-Not complex in transcriptional elongation. *Genetics* **158**, 627–634.
50. Fischer, N., and Weis, K. (2002). The DEAD box protein Dhh1 stimulates the decapping enzyme Dcp1. *EMBO J.* **21**, 2788–2797.
51. Maillet, L., and Collart, M. A. (2002). Interaction between Not1p, a component of the Ccr4-Not complex, a global regulator of transcription, and Dhh1p, a putative RNA helicase. *J. Biol. Chem.* **277**, 2835–2842.
52. Ito, T., Chiba, T., Ozawa, R., Yoshida, M., Hattori, M., and Sakaki, Y. (2001). A comprehensive two-hybrid analysis to explore the yeast protein interactome. *Proc. Natl. Acad. Sci. USA* **98**, 4569–4574.
53. Lee, T. I., Wyrick, J. J., Koh, S. S., Jennings, E. G., Gadbois, E. L., and Young, R. A. (1998). Interplay of positive and negative regulators in transcription initiation by RNA polymerase II holoenzyme. *Mol. Cell. Biol.* **18**, 4455–4462.
54. Uetz, P., Giot, L., Cagney, G., Mansfield, T. A. *et al.* (2001). A comprehensive analysis of protein–protein interactions in Saccharomyces cerevisiae. *Nature* **403**, 623–627.
55. Elion, E. (2001). The Ste5 scaffold. *J. Cell Science* **114**, 3967–3978.
56. Moriya, H., Shimizu-Yoshida, A., Omori, A., Iwashita, S., Katoh, M., and Sakai, A. (2001). Yak1p, a DYRK family kinase, translocates to the nucleus and phosphorylates yeast Pop2p in response to a glucose signal. *Genes Dev.* **15**, 1217–1228.

57. Collart, M. A. (1996). The NOT, SPT3, and MOT1 genes functionally interact to regulate transcription at core promoters. *Mol. Cell. Biol.* **16**, 6668–6676.
58. Benson, J. D., Benson, M., Howley, P. M., and Struhl, K. (1998). Association of distinct yeast NOT2 functional domains with components of GCN5 histone acetylase and CCR4 transcriptional regulatory complexes. *EMBO J.* **17**, 6714–6722.
59. Okazaki, N., Okazaki, K., Watanabe, Y., Kato-Hayashhi, M., Yamamoto, M., and Okayama, H. (1998). Novel factor highly conserved among eukaryotes controls sexual development in fission yeast. *Mol. Cell. Biol.* **18**, 887–895.
60. Fidler, C., Wainscoat, J. S., and Boultwood, J. (1999). The human POP2 gene: Identification, sequencing, and mapping to the critical region of the 5q-syndrome. *Genomics* **56**, 134–136.
61. Flanagan, J., Healey, S., Young, J., Whitehall, V., and Chenevix-Trench, G. (2003). Analysis of the transcriptional regulator, CNOT7, as a candidate chromosome 8 tumor suppressor gene in colorectal cancer. *Int. J. Cancer* **106**, 505–509.
62. Neuwald, A. F., and Hirano, T. (2000). HEAT repeats associated with condensins, cohesins, and other complexes involved in chromosome-related functions. *Genome Res.* **10**, 1445–1452.
63. Andrade, M. A., Perez-Iratxeta, C., and Ponting, C. P. (2001). Protein repeats: Structures, functions, and evolution. *J. Structural Biol.* **134**, 117–131.
64. Makino, Y., Yogosawa, S., Kayukawa, K., Coin, F. *et al.* (1999). TATA-binding protein-interacting protein 120, TIP120, stimulates three classes of eukaryotic transcription via a unique mechanism. *Mol. Cell. Biol.* **19**, 7951–7960.
65. Rouault, J.-P., Prévot, D., Berthet, C., Birot, A.-M., Billaud, M., Magaud, J.-P., and Corbo, L. (1998). Interaction of BTG1 and p53-regulated BTG2 gene products with mCaf1, the murine homolog of a component of the yeast CCR4 transcriptional regulatory complex. *J. Biol. Chem.* **273**, 22563–22569.
66. Bogdan, J. A., Adams-Burton, C., Pedicord, D. L., Sukovich, D. A., Benfield, P. A., Corjay, M. H., Stoltenborg, J. K., and Dicker, I. B. (1998). Human carbon catabolite repressor protein (CCR4)-associative factor 1: Cloning, expression and characterisation of its interaction with the B-cell translocation protein BTG1. *Biochem. J.* **336**, 471–481.
67. Matsuda, S., Rouault, J.-P., Magaud, J.-P., and Berthet, C. (2001). In search of a function for the TIS21/PC3/BTG1? TOB family *FEBS Letters* **497**, 67–72.
68. Suzuki, T., K-Tsuzuku, J., Ajima, R., Nakamura, T., Yoshida, Y., and Yamamoto, T. (2002). Phosphorylation of three regulatory serines of Tob by Erk1 and Erk2 is required for Ras-mediated cell proliferation and transformation. *Genes Dev.* **16**, 1356–1370.
69. Guardavaccaro, D., Corrente, G., Covone, F., Micheli, L., D'Agnano, I., Starace, G., Caruso, M., and Tirone, F. (2000). Arrest of G1-S progression by the p53 inducible gene PC3 is Rb-dependent and relies on the inhibition of cyclin D1 transcription. *Mol. Cell. Biol.* **20**, 1797–1815.
70. Yoshida, Y., Nakamura, T., Komoda, M., Satoh, H. *et al.* (2003). Mice lacking a transcriptional corepressor Tob are predisposed to cancer. *Genes Dev.* **17**, 1201–1206.
71. Ikematsu, N., Yoshida, Y., Kawamura-Tsuzuku, Y., Ohsugi, M., Onda, M., Hirai, M., Fujimoto, M., and Yamamoto, T. (1999). Tob2, a novel anti-proliferative Tob/BTG1 family member, associates with a component of the CCR4 transcriptional regulatory complex capable of binding cyclin-dependent kinases. *Oncogene* **18**, 7432–7441.
72. Prévôt, D., Morel, A.-P., Voeltzel, T., Rostan, M.-C., Rimokh, R., Magaud, J.-P., and Corbo, L. (2001). Relationships of the antiproliferative proteins Btg1 and Btg2 with CAF1, the human homolog of a component of the yeast CCR4 transcription complex. *J. Biol. Chem.* **276**, 9640–9648.

73. Hiroi, N., Ito, T., Yamamoto, H., Ochiya, T., Jinno, S., and Okayama, H. (2002). Mammalian Rcd1 is a novel transcriptional cofactor that mediates retinoic acid-induced cell differentiation. *EMBO J.* **21,** 5235–5244.
74. Struhl, K., and Hill, D. E. (1987). Two related regulatory sequences are required for maximal induction of *Saccharomyces cerevisiae HIS3* transcription. *Mol. Cell. Biol.* **7,** 104–110.
75. Mahadevan, S., and Struhl, K. (1990). T_c, an unusual promoter element required for constitutive transcription of the yeast *HIS3* gene. *Mol. Cell. Biol.* **10,** 4447–4455.
76. Harbury, P. A. B., and Struhl, K. (1989). Functional distinctions between yeast TATA elements. *Mol. Cell. Biol.* **9,** 5298–5304.
77. Ponticelli, A. S., and Struhl, K. (1990). Analysis of yeast *HIS3* transcription *in vitro*: Biochemical support for multiple mechanisms of transcription. *Mol. Cell. Biol.* **10,** 2832–2839.
78. Moqtaderi, Z., Bai, Y., Poon, D., Weil, A. P., and Struhl, K. (1996). TBP-associated factors are not generally required for transcriptional activation in yeast. *Nature* **383,** 188–191.
79. Berger, S. (2002). Histone modifications in transcriptional regulation. *Curr. Opin. Genet. Dev.* **12,** 142–148.
80. Koleske, A. J., and Young, R. A. (1994). An RNA polymerase II holoenzyme responsive to activators. *Nature* **368,** 466–469.
81. Oberholzer, U., and Collart, M. A. (1999). *In vitro* transcription of a TATA-less promoter: Negative regulation by the Not1 protein. *Biol. Chem.* **380,** 1365–1370.
82. Swanson, M. J., Hongfang, Q., Sumibcay, L., Krueger, A., Kim, S.-J., Natarjan, K., Yoon, S., and Hinnebusch, A. G. (2003). A multiplicity of coactivators is required by Gcn4p at individual promoters *in vivo*. *Mol. Cell. Biol.* **23,** 2800–2820.
83. Arava, Y., Wang, Y., Storey, J. D., Liu, C. L., Brown, P. O., and Herschlag, D. (2003). Genome-wide analysis of mRNA translation profiles in Saccharomyces cerevisiae. *Proc. Natl. Acad. Sci. USA* **100,** 3889–3894.
84. Fan, J., Yang, X., Wang, W., Wood, W. H., III, Becker, K. G., and Gorospe, M. (2002). Global analysis of stress-regulated mRNA turnover by using cDNA arrays. *Proc. Natl. Acad. Sci. USA* **99,** 10611–10616.
85. Wang, Y., Liu, C. L., Storey, J. D., Tibshirani, R. J., Herschlag, D., and Brown, P. O. (2002). Precision and functional specificity in mRNA decay. *Proc. Natl. Acad. Sci. USA* **99,** 5860–5865.
86. Viswanathan, P., Chen, J., Chiang, Y.-C., and Denis, C. D. (2003). Identification of multiple RNA features that influence CCR4 deadenylation activity. *J. Biol. Chem.* **278,** 14949–14955.
87. Coller, J. M., Tucker, M., Sheth, U., Valencia-Sanchez, M. A., and Parker, R. (2001). The DEAD box helicase, Dhh1p, functions in mRNA decapping and interacts with both the decapping and deadenylase complexes. *RNA* **12,** 1717–1727.
88. Irie, K., Yamaguchi, K., Kawase, K., and Matsumoto, K. (1994). The yeast *MOT2* gene encodes a putative zinc finger protein that serves as a global negative regulator affecting expression of several categories of genes, including mating-pheromone-responsive genes. *Mol. Cell. Biol.* **14,** 3150–3157.
89. Borden, K. L. B. (2000). RING domains: Builders of molecular scaffolds? *J. Mol. Biol.* **295,** 1103–1112.
90. Hershko, A., and Ciechanover, A. (1998). The ubiquitin system. *Ann. Rev. Biochem.* **67,** 425–479.
91. Sanjay, A., Houghton, A., Neff, L., Didomenico, E. *et al.* (2001). Cbl associates with Pyk2 and Src to regulate Src kinase activity, alpha(v)beta(3) integrin-mediated signaling, cell adhesion, and osteoclast motility. *J. Cell Biol.* **152,** 181–195.
92. Peters, J. M. (1998). SCF and APC: The yin and yang of cell cycle regulated proteolysis. *Curr. Opin. Cell Biol.* **10,** 759–768.

93. Kamura, T., Conaway, J. W., and Conaway, R. C. (2002). Roles of SCF and VHL ubiquitin ligases in regulation of cell growth. *Prog. Mol. Subcell. Biol.* **29,** 1–15.
94. Seufert, W., and Jentsch, S. (1990). Ubiquitin-conjugating enzymes UBC4 and UBC5 mediate selective degradation of short-lived and abnormal proteins. *EMBO J.* **9,** 543–550.
95. Lenssen, E., Oberholzer, U., Labarre, J., de Virgilio, C., and Collart, M. A. (2002). *Saccharomyces cerevisiae* Ccr4-Not complex contributes to the control of Msn2p-dependent transcription by the Ras/cAMP pathway. *Mol. Microbiol.* **43,** 1023–1037.
96. Sato, S., Tomomori-Sato, C., Banks, C. A., Sorokina, I. *et al.* (2003). Identification of mammalian Mediator subunits with similarities to yeast Mediator subunits Srb5, Srb6, Med11 and Rox3. *J. Biol. Chem.* **278,** 15123–15127.
97. Lemaire, M., Xie, J., Meisterernst, M., and Collart, M. A. (2000). The NC2 repressor is dispensable in yeast mutated for the Sin4p component of the holoenzyme and plays roles similar to Mot1p *in vivo*. *Mol. Microbiol.* **36,** 163–173.
98. Ficarro, S. B., McCleland, M. L., Stukenberg, P. T., Burke, D. J., Ross, M. M., Shabanowitz, J., Hunt, D. F., and White, F. M. (2002). Phosphoproteome analysis by mass spectrometry and its application to *Saccharomyces cerevisiae*. *Nature* **20,** 301–305.
99. Smith, A., Ward, M. P., and Garrett, S. (1998). Yeast PKA represses Msn2p/Msn4p-dependent gene expression to regulate growth, stress response, and glycogen accumulation. *EMBO J.* **17,** 3556–3564.
100. Zwartjes, C. G., Jayne, S., van den Berg, D. L., and Timmers, H. T. (2002). Repression of promoter activity by CNOT2, a subunit of the transcription regulatory Ccr4-Not complex. *J. Biol. Chem.* **279,** 10848–10854.

Signaling Repression of Transcription by RNA Polymerase III in Yeast

IAN M. WILLIS, NEELAM DESAI, AND RAJENDRA UPADHYA

Department of Biochemistry,
Albert Einstein College of Medicine,
1300 Morris Park Avenue,
Bronx, NY 10461

I. Introduction	323
A. Coordination of Growth and Cell Division in Yeast	323
B. Coordinate Regulation of Transcription by Pol I and Pol III	324
II. Coupling Plasma Membrane Expansion to Transcriptional Regulation of Ribosomal Components and tRNA	326
A. The Secretory Signaling Pathway	326
B. Feedback Regulation of Ribosome Biosynthesis	330
C. Relocalization of Nuclear/Nucleolar Proteins in *sec* Mutants	333
D. When Activation of Cell Integrity Signaling Does Not Repress Transcription of tRNA and rDNA	334
III. Nutrients, Starvation, and TOR Signaling	335
A. Rapamycin-Sensitive and Rapamycin-Insensitive TOR Pathways	335
B. Intersections of TOR and Cell Integrity Pathway Signaling	337
C. Examining the Role of Protein Phosphatase 2A in TOR Signaling and in the Regulation of Pol III Transcription	338
IV. Repression of Pol III Transcription in Response to DNA Damage	341
V. Maf1 and its Essential Role in Pol III Transcriptional Repression	342
A. Genetic Identification of Maf1	343
B. Genetic and Biochemical Interactions of Maf1 with Pol III	343
C. Convergence of Signaling Pathways that Repress tRNA and Ribosome Synthesis	344
D. Biochemical Effects of Maf1-Dependent Repression	345
VI. Future Studies	346
References	348

I. Introduction

A. Coordination of Growth and Cell Division in Yeast

In yeast, the production of new protein synthetic capacity determines both the growth rate and the size at which cells commit to a round of division (1–6). This coordination of growth (accumulation of cell mass) and proliferation (cell cycle progression) enables yeast to adapt within one cell cycle to changing environmental conditions (7). For a unicellular organism experiencing feast and famine, this makes good biologic sense since the synthesis of ribosomes, tRNAs, and other components of the protein synthetic machinery represents one of the major biosynthetic activities of proliferating cells and consumes a substantial amount of metabolic energy (2). The manner in which cell growth and proliferation is coordinated in yeast has provoked interest and inquiry for almost 30 years. One mechanism that has been defined involves translational control of Cln3, a G1 cyclin that functions upstream of all other cyclin-dependent kinase-regulated events involved in cell cycle entry (8). Expression of the Cln3 protein is regulated in early G1 phase by short upstream open reading frames (uORFs) in its mRNA. These uORFs reduce translational efficiency in nutritionally poor media and make the synthesis of Cln3 sensitive to both the ribosome content of the cell and the rate of translational initiation (1). Additional complexity to the coordination of growth and proliferation has been revealed from screening the viable yeast deletion strains for alterations in cell size distribution. These studies demonstrated a partial uncoupling of growth from cell cycle entry by mutations that affect ribosome biogenesis without significantly altering the growth rate (3, 4). The data indicate that the synthesis and assembly of ribosomes negatively regulates cell cycle entry and thereby enables cells to grow to a larger size before they commit to a round of cell division. Since ribosome biogenesis is intimately linked to both cell growth and division, it follows that the signaling pathways controlling transcription of the ribosome and other components of the protein synthetic machinery are critical regulators of these processes.

B. Coordinate Regulation of Transcription by Pol I and Pol III

Pols I and III are responsible for synthesizing the RNA components of the ribosome, the transfer RNA interpreters of the genetic code, and a variety of other small untranslated RNAs, some of which function in the processing of RNAs involved directly in protein synthesis (e.g., RNase P RNA and snR52) (9–11). The sole function of pol I is to synthesize a long (>5400 nucleotide) precursor molecule containing the 28S, 18S, and 5.8S RNAs from a tandem array of approximately 150 rDNA repeats. In contrast, pol III synthesizes a functionally more diverse group of transcripts, which are short (mostly <150 nucleotides), from genes that are largely dispersed throughout the genome (note that 5S rRNA genes in S. cerevisiae are found in the intergenic spacer of the rDNA repeat). In addition to the cellular complement of tRNAs, 5S rRNA, and those RNAs previously mentioned, pol III transcripts participate in processes other than protein synthesis (e.g., U6 snRNA in pre-mRNA splicing, 7SL RNA in protein secretion, 7SK RNA in transcriptional regulation, and the telomerase RNA in synthesizing telomeres (9)). However, as a group, the majority of pol III-transcribed genes function in growth-related processes. Notable exceptions include some Alu elements which are induced in response to cellular stress (12) and genes that are developmentally regulated (oocyte-specific 5S genes (13)) or cell-type specific (silk gland-specific tRNAs (14)). In proliferating cells, approximately 80% of the nucleotides consumed in nuclear gene transcription are utilized by pols I and III. The majority of this fraction (~60% of the total) is incorporated into the large ribosomal RNAs (2, 15) with another 10 to 15% consumed in tRNA synthesis (16). The high energetic cost of RNA synthesis by pols I and III and the predominant growth-related functions of their gene products likely underlies the coordinate regulation of their transcription under diverse cellular conditions (Table I). This regulation

TABLE I
CONDITIONS REPRESSING POL I AND POL III GENE TRANSCRIPTION

	References	
Cellular stress/conditions	Repression of pol I	Repression of pol III
Nutrients		
Carbon source starvation	(20)	(20)[a]
Nitrogen starvation	(20, 21)	(20)
Serum starvation	(22, 23)	(24, 25)
Growth to stationary phase	(26, 27)	(26, 28, 29)
Cell cycle regulation		
Mitotic repression	(30)	(31, 32)
Early G1 phase	(33)	(25)
Stringent response		
Amino acid starvation	(34)	(26)
Virus-mediated repression		
Poliovirus	ND	(35)
Cellular defects		
Secretory pathway defects	(36)	(16)
60S ribosomal subunit defects	(37, 38)	ND
DNA damage		
Ionizing radiation and UV	(39)	(39)
Chemical mutagenesis	(39)	(39, 40)
Chemical treatments		
Tunicamycin	(41)	(16)
Chlorpromazine	ND	(40)
Cycloheximide	(42)	(42, 43)

[a]The indicated references are representative only. Additional sources of information can be found in refs. (10) and (44). ND, not determined.

is achieved through various signaling pathways that sense and transduce changes in environment and allow a rapid adjustment of the levels of pols I and III transcription.

In yeast, two well-studied signaling pathways that regulate transcription by pols I and III (the secretory and TOR pathways) also exert a parallel response on transcription by pol II of the 137 ribosomal protein genes (2, 17, 18) and other genes involved in ribosome biogenesis (19). Thus, an understanding of these key regulatory pathways can be gained from studies on all three polymerase systems. In contrast to yeast, higher eukaryotes regulate the expression of ribosomal protein genes at the level of translation through a terminal oligopyrimidine (TOP) tract in the 5' untranslated region of their mRNAs (6). Interestingly, translational control of TOP mRNAs involves a metazoan-specific branch of the TOR signaling pathway (6).

This chapter focuses on studies in yeast dealing with the secretory and TOR signaling pathways, their regulation of transcription of the protein synthetic apparatus, and studies on pol III transcription that demonstrate the integration of these and other pathways.

II. Coupling Plasma Membrane Expansion to Transcriptional Regulation of Ribosomal Components and tRNA

A. The Secretory Signaling Pathway

In experiments reported for the first time almost 10 years ago, Mizuta and Warner (36) discovered that interruption of the secretory pathway in yeast, at various points from peptide insertion into the endoplasmic reticulum (ER) to secretory vesicle fusion with the plasma membrane, resulted in transcriptional repression of both rDNA and ribosomal protein genes. The observed transcriptional repression was not genome-wide, however, as numerous pol II genes were not affected. In addition to the many conditional *sec* mutations that were used to demonstrate the dependence on an intact secretory pathway, treatment of cells with drugs that inhibit secretion (brefeldin A and tunicamycin) produced the same result. These treatments also demonstrated that the transcriptional response was independent of the effect of a temperature shift, which was a necessary part of experiments with conditional *sec* mutants. Secretory pathway defects were subsequently shown to cause repression of tRNA and 5S rRNA genes (16). Thus, it became apparent that yeast cells contain a signaling pathway that serves to coordinately repress the transcription of all the components of the ribosome, together with its tRNA substrates, when the secretory pathway is interrupted.

The biological reason for a link between secretion and transcription of the protein synthetic machinery was not immediately obvious. However, one possibility advanced by Mizuta and Warner (36) has received growing support, namely, that a failure of the secretory pathway produces stress on the plasma membrane due to an increase in (turgor) pressure within the cell. The likely source of this increased turgor pressure, they suggested, was the continued synthesis of proteins in cells that are unable to expand their plasma membrane because of the secretory defect. The demonstration that repression of ribosomal protein gene transcription in a *sec* mutant strain could be blocked by cycloheximide treatment provided initial support for this hypothesis. Further evidence has come with identification of components of the signaling pathway that mediates the response.

Elucidation of the pathway that communicates a block in secretion to the transcription apparatus responsible for new protein synthetic capacity has involved a systematic analysis of known pathways linking transcription with secretion, ribosome synthesis, and membrane stress (45). The unfolded protein response (UPR) pathway that connects ER function to transcription was excluded since deletion of the transmembrane kinase Ire1 blocked the induction of Kar2 by tunicamycin (a hallmark of the UPR) but did not prevent repression of ribosomal protein gene transcription. The stringent response, which represses ribosome synthesis following amino acid starvation, was shown to differ from the effect of a *sec* mutation since the latter did not cause the characteristic induction of genes involved in amino acid biosynthesis. Additionally, repression due to a *sec* mutation was not prevented by constitutive activation of the protein kinase A pathway (either by overexpression of Ras2^{Val-19} or deletion of the A kinase regulatory subunit, Bcy1), which is known to increase transcription of ribosomal protein genes and rDNA (2, 46). In contrast, an examination of the pathways sensing osmotic stress led to several striking observations.

Components of the cell integrity pathway, which responds to high internal osmolarity and plasma membrane defects, but not the HOG (high-osmolarity glycerol) pathway, which responds to high external osmolarity, were needed for the repression of all ribosomal components and tRNAs when the secretory pathway was interrupted (16, 45). Specifically, deletion of protein kinase C (Pkc1), a central mediator of the cell integrity pathway, blocked repression of pol I, pol II, and pol III transcription in a *sec1-1* strain. Similarly, deletion of Wsc protein family members, (Wsc1 and Wsc2 or Wsc1 and Wsc3), considered to be the most upstream sensory components of the pathway, largely blocked repression of ribosomal protein and tRNA genes following tunicamycin treatment (residual repression was attributed to the partial functional redundancy of the remaining Wsc proteins). The link between turgor pressure, transcription, and the cell integrity pathway was also supported by experiments with the antifungal/antipsychotic compound chlorpromazine (CPZ). CPZ binds to biological membranes and causes membrane stretching (47). Thus, CPZ is thought to produce a response analogous to elevated turgor pressure (48). CPZ is a known activator of the cell integrity pathway (as determined by dual phosphorylation of the mitogen-activated protein (MAP) kinase Slt2 (48, 49) and was found to repress transcription of ribosomal protein and tRNA genes (40, 45). Consistent with these findings, Slt2 was also activated by a *sec* mutation (*sly1-1* at 33°C, a temperature below that required for a heat stress response) and by tunicamycin treatment (16). These observations, together with experiments showing that the magnitude of transcriptional repression is correlated with the severity of the *sec* defect (16, 36), have led to the view that transcription of the protein synthetic machinery is kept in balance with expansion of the plasma membrane (i.e., cell growth, as determined by the rate of secretory vesicle delivery and fusion) by a signaling pathway that includes at least some of the components of the cell integrity pathway (16, 36).

The cell integrity pathway (Fig. 1) is widely recognized for its role in sensing and responding to cell wall damage and plasma membrane stress (50, 51). The pathway is activated by a variety of extra- and intracellular inputs and conditions, which include the cell cycle regulator Cdc28, mating pheromone, heat and hypo-osmotic stress, defects in cell wall biosynthesis and, as has been noted, defects in the secretory pathway (16, 45, 50, 51). The upstream components of the cell integrity pathway (Mid2, Wsc1–4) comprise a family of putative mechano-sensors that reside in the plasma membrane and are heavily O-mannosylated on their extracellular domain (50–52). Genetic data indicate that the Wsc proteins function upstream of the redundant guanine-nucleotide exchange factors (GEFs) Rom1 and Rom2, and a two-hybrid study has demonstrated a specific interaction between Rom2 and both Mid2 and Wsc1 (52). In the case of Wsc1, this interaction is mediated through its cytoplasmic carboxy-terminus and the amino terminal domain of Rom2. Moreover, extracts of *wsc1*, *mid2*, and double mutant strains were found to be defective in catalyzing the loading of GTP in Rho1 immunoprecipitates (52). Thus, the findings support a positive role for the Wsc1/Mid2 interaction with Rom2 in stimulating nucleotide exchange on Rho1 (Fig. 1). Another GEF that contributes to cell integrity pathway signaling by activation of Rho1 is Tus1 (53). Interestingly, the function of Tus1 is not redundant with Rom1 and Rom2 since overexpressing Tus1 does not suppress the synthetic lethality of a *rom1 rom2* strain. Tus1 has been implicated in the response to heat stress (see Section III.B). However, the basis for its functional differentiation from Rom1 and Rom2 is not clear since Rom2 also participates in the heat stress response (54). Despite the limited data to distinguish the functional consequences of Tus1 and Rom1/2 action, studies in mammalian systems suggest

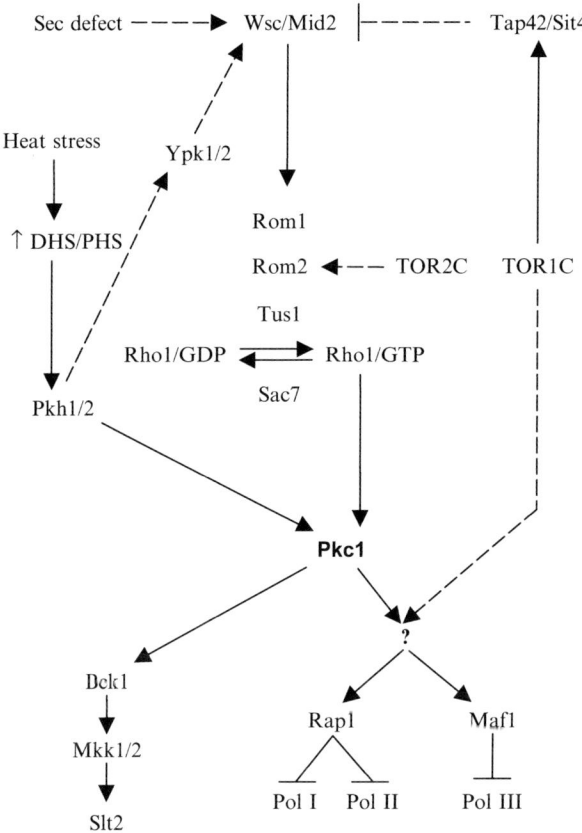

FIG. 1. Schematic representation of relationships between the cell integrity pathway, the secretory signaling pathway, and specific TOR signaling pathways. Only a small subset of cell integrity pathway inputs and outputs are shown. These include secretory defects, heat stress, and Tor kinase-mediated steps. Signaling via Pkc1 proceeds to the MAP kinase Slt2 and to a novel pathway that is responsible for repressing the transcription of all the components of the ribosome, tRNAs, and other related factors. As discussed in the text, heat stress and (presumably) signaling by TOR2C during polarized cell growth does not cause Pkc1-mediated transcriptional repression of ribosomal components. A novel TOR1C-regulated pathway that represses transcription of the protein synthetic machinery independently of Pkc1 is also shown. A solid line indicates a direct interaction/effect has been demonstrated while a dashed line represents a probable or potential interaction between proteins based on genetic and biochemical data discussed in the text and elsewhere. Arrows indicate activation; bars indicate repression.

that different GEFs may determine the downstream signaling specificity of Rho GTPases (53). In this context, it is interesting that different signaling specificities for Rho1 GTPase-activating proteins (GAPs) in yeast have been demonstrated (55).

Rho1, in addition to serving as a regulatory subunit for the integral plasma membrane enzyme β-1,3-glucan synthase, binds and activates Pkc1, which, in turn, activates a MAP kinase cascade comprising the MAP kinase kinase kinase, Bck1, a pair of redundant MAP kinase kinases, Mkk1 and Mkk2, and the MAP kinase Slt2 (50, 51). The currently known targets of Slt2 include two sequence-specific DNA binding transcription factors: Rlm1p, which is implicated in the expression of cell wall-related genes (56, 57), and SBF (Swi4/Swi6), which is required for transcriptional activation of cell cycle-regulated genes at the G1 to S transition (58). Additionally, Slt2 has been shown to phosphorylate the silent information regulator Sir3. This activity of Slt2 reduces subtelomeric silencing and shortens the replicative lifespan of yeast, surprisingly, without affecting silencing at the *HML* or rDNA loci (49, 59). While cell integrity signaling is usually depicted as a linear pathway from the Wsc proteins to the Slt2 MAP kinase, inputs can occur at different points at or above Pkc1 (Fig. 1, 50, 51). Moreover, activation of the pathway at or upstream of Pkc1 can also result in a variety of responses downstream of Pkc1. Interestingly, a growing number of these Pkc1-dependent outputs do not require the Pkc1-MAP kinase cascade (16, 54, 60–63). The data supporting this point for *sec*-mediated repression of transcription will be described.

With evidence indicating that Wsc proteins and Pkc1 are required for repression of ribosomal components and tRNAs in response to secretory defects (16, 45), experiments were conducted to examine the role of the downstream MAP kinase cascade in this regulation. Contrary to expectations at the time, deletion of *BCK1* or a catalytically inactive mutant of *SLT2*, both of which effectively abolish signaling in this pathway, failed to prevent repression of ribosomal protein and tRNA gene transcription in cells treated with tunicamycin. Since the enzymes of the Pkc1-MAP kinase cascade are not functionally redundant with other MAP kinase pathways in yeast (50) and the available genetic data (64, 65) supported the now well-established role of Pkc1 in processes other than those regulated by Bck1 and Slt2, it was concluded that the signaling pathway downstream of Pkc1 must be bifurcated (Fig. 1). Thus, interruption of the secretory pathway activates cell integrity signaling via the Wsc proteins and follows a novel Pkc1-dependent branch of the pathway to the transcription machinery regulating ribosome and tRNA synthesis (Fig. 1, 16).

B. Feedback Regulation of Ribosome Biosynthesis

In an effort to identify novel components involved in the repression of ribosome synthesis, two independent but related genetic strategies have been employed to isolate mutants that block transcriptional repression of ribosomal protein genes in response to a secretory defect. While different in detail, both screens relied on finding conditions where the expression of a reporter gene, driven by the promoter of a ribosomal protein gene, was substantially repressed in a *sec* mutant strain growing at a semipermissive temperature. This allowed the recovery of mutants that now express the reporter gene due to a failure in a component of the *sec*-mediated repression pathway. The ability to titrate expression of the reporter gene was a key feature of both strategies. In one case, the promoter of a ribosomal protein gene was fused to the bacterial gene for kanamycin resistance and cells were plated onto media containing different concentrations of G418 (37). In the other example, a promoter fusion to the *HIS3* gene was used and cells were plated onto media lacking histidine but containing 3-aminotriazole, an inhibitor of histidine biosynthesis (38). Surprisingly, these approaches yielded mutations in different ribosomal proteins, Rpl1 and Rpl11, both of which reside in the 60S subunit. Further analysis revealed that transcriptional repression induced by a *sec* defect was abolished or largely attenuated by deletion of either one of the two copies of *RPL1* or *RPL11* or of other large subunit genes (e.g., *RPL10*, *RPL20B*, and *RPL34B*). Remarkably, the ability to prevent repression by a secretory defect was specifically related to the synthesis or assembly of the 60S ribosomal subunit since deletion of several different small ribosomal subunit genes (*RPS4A*, *RPS4B*, *RPS6*, and *RPS23*) had no effect on repression. Consistent with this view, both laboratories demonstrated that defects in the assembly of 60S subunits by conditional alleles of nonribosomal proteins (*NOP4*, *TIF6*, and *RRS1*) also blocked repression of ribosomal protein gene transcription (37, 66). Interestingly, the *rrs1-1* mutation used in these experiments was isolated using the same genetic selection that yielded the mutation in *RPL11* (described previously, (66)) and was known to have a defect in the maturation of 25S rRNA similar to a loss of *TIF6* function (67). Moreover, the cold-sensitive *rrs1-1* strain accumulated 40S subunits and polyribosomes bearing an additional 43S initiation complex (halfmers) similar to the *nop4* mutant and to strains deficient in 60S ribosomal proteins (37, 66). Another important property of *rrs1-1* and deletions or mutations of large ribosomal subunit genes is that they prevent the repression of rDNA transcription that normally results from a *sec* defect or tunicamycin treatment (37, 38, 66). Whether these mutations also block *sec*-mediated repression of pol III-transcribed genes is not yet known but seems highly probable.

The mechanism by which a deficiency in 60S subunit assembly or function blocks the repression caused by a defect in secretion is still unclear. However, experimental consideration of several possible explanations has produced a well-reasoned hypothesis for the phenomenon. The data indicate that neither the reduced growth of strains with defects in 60S production nor the imbalance of 40S and 60S subunits per se contributes to the block in repression.

These differences were eliminated or substantially reduced (e.g., by growth on less favored carbon sources or by using strains deleted for both a large and a small ribosomal subunit gene, respectively) without affecting the block to transcriptional repression initiated by a secretory defect. The possibility that a shortage of ribosomes might produce feedback to prevent repression of transcription in order to restore their levels was also excluded since no general increase in ribosome synthesis was observed in a large subunit deletion strain relative to its wild-type control. The effect of *RPL* deletions or mutations could also not be attributed to lower rates of initiation of protein synthesis; conditional mutations (*prt1-1* and *tif5-1*) affecting early or late steps in initiation did not function like a deficiency in 60S subunits with respect to blocking transcriptional repression of ribosomal protein genes. However, a marked difference in the ability to attenuate repression of ribosome synthesis was seen when comparing *nmd3* and *kap120* strains. Both strains have significant defects in the synthesis of 60S subunits (68, 69) but differ in the rate at which mature 25S rRNA is degraded. The half-life of 25S rRNA in the *nmd3-4* strain (3–4 min) is greatly reduced relative to wild-type (70), whereas no difference in stability was apparent in a *kap120* strain at the end of a 10-min pulse chase (69). Nmd3 is an essential 60S subunit export factor that binds to mature, correctly folded subunits in the nucleus and escorts them into the cytoplasm (71). Surprisingly, an *nmd3-4* strain growing at a semipermissive temperature was more resistant to repression by tunicamycin than an *RPL1B* deletion strain (37). Conversely, deletion of *KAP120*, a karyopherin that is also involved in the nuclear export of 60S subunits (69), resulted in significant sensitivity to tunicamycin and repression of ribosomal protein gene transcription, although not to the same extent as in the wild-type strain (37). Given that relatively little is known so far about the function and properties of Kap120 (compared to Nmd3), these data were cautiously interpreted to suggest that some aspect of the rate, mechanism, or products of degradation of defective 60S subunits may serve to autoregulate ribosome biosynthesis.

One of the intriguing aspects of the autoregulation already described is that it appears to be specific for defects in the secretory pathway. A deficiency in 60S subunit assembly does not affect the transient repression of ribosomal protein genes by heat shock or rapamycin-mediated repression (37). The nature and selectivity of this phenomenon suggests that autoregulation of ribosome synthesis may be linked in a direct and unique way to the secretory signaling pathway (Fig. 1). However, as will be described (Sections II.D and III), heat stress and rapamycin-sensitive TOR signaling involves the most upstream components of this pathway. How then is the observed selectivity achieved? A possible explanation is that heat stress and rapamycin may activate additional pathways leading to transcriptional repression that are not subject to autoregulation of ribosome synthesis.

C. Relocalization of Nuclear/Nucleolar Proteins in *sec* Mutants

Another consequence of interfering with the secretory pathway in yeast is the inhibition of nuclear protein import and the relocalization of specific nuclear and nucleolar proteins to the cytoplasm. This response, termed the arrest of secretion response (ASR), is initiated by some of the same *sec* mutants (e.g., *sec 1*, *sec 7*, *sec 18*, and sec 63) and chemical inhibitors of secretion (brefeldin A) that have been used to study transcriptional repression of the protein synthetic machinery (*16, 36, 45, 61, 72*). Interestingly, both the repression of transcription and protein relocalization require ongoing protein synthesis and occur when secretion is interrupted between the ER and the plasma membrane but not when the block occurs between the golgi and the vacuole. ASR, like the secretory signaling pathway, also requires the Wsc proteins (primarily, Wsc2 and, to a lesser extent, Wsc1) and Pkc1 but not the downstream MAP kinase cascade (*61*) in order to respond to a secretory defect. Thus, a common set of conditions and signaling molecules appears to mediate ASR and the repression of transcription of ribosomal components and tRNA genes.

A difference between ASR and the secretory signaling pathway has been noted in cells treated with tunicamycin. ASR is reportedly not induced after 2 hours in tunicamycin (*72*), whereas transcription of the protein synthetic machinery is partially (but not maximally) repressed at this time. An important characteristic of the transcriptional response following tunicamycin treatment is the significant delay (60 min) in the onset of repression. As a result, the extent of repression after 2 hours may be as little as 50% in some strains (*16*). Given that the relocation of nuclear proteins in ASR is relatively slow in *sec* mutants (60–90 min (*61*)), it may be that a 2-hour incubation following tunicamycin addition does not reveal a conspicuous localization phenotype. An alternative possibility is that *sec* mutations and tunicamycin affect distinct but overlapping responses, both of which lead to transcriptional repression. However, this is difficult to reconcile with the observed autoregulation of rDNA and ribosomal protein gene transcription that occurs under both conditions (*37, 38*) and the fact that mutations in the most upstream components of the cell integrity pathway (the Wsc proteins) block repression by tunicamycin (*16, 45*).

While ASR was originally identified in *sec* mutants, it has since been observed in cells subject to hypertonic shock (*60*). Indeed, exposure of cells to 0.5 M salt or 1 M sorbitol produces a significantly more rapid (within 10 min) but transient relocalization of nuclear/nucleolar proteins than is seen in *sec* mutants (*60, 61*). Hypertonic shock also causes a transient decrease in the transcription of rDNA and ribosomal protein genes with similar kinetics to the ASR, suggesting that the responses are coordinate (*60, 73*). Remarkably, the signaling pathway mediating the ASR following hypertonic shock was found not to depend on components of either the HOG or cell integrity pathway MAP kinase cascades, yet required the catalytic activity and putative diacylglycerol binding site of Pkc1 (60). Thus, *sec* mutations and high osmolarity induce ASR and the repression of ribosome synthesis via a yet to be defined pathway downstream of Pkc1. Whether a common pathway mediates responses to both conditions is not yet known.

Despite the similarities noted, ASR is not seen under all conditions that repress transcription of the protein synthetic machinery (e.g., following amino acid starvation or treatment with rapamycin (60, 61)). Accordingly, it seems unlikely that ASR provides a common mechanism for the repression of pol I, pol II, or pol III transcription under diverse repressing conditions. It remains possible, however, that ASR may contribute to transcriptional repression through the nuclear export of key transcription factors under the specific conditions that induce this response.

D. When Activation of Cell Integrity Signaling Does Not Repress Transcription of tRNA and rDNA

Moderate heat stress (e.g., 25 to 37 °C) produces a rapid and precipitous, yet transient, decrease in the synthesis of ribosomal proteins that is kinetically reminiscent to, but otherwise distinct from, the effect of hypertonic stress (45, 73). Heat stress-mediated repression of ribosomal protein genes is not dependent on Pkc1 (45, 60) and there is no significant repression of rDNA or tRNA gene transcription, although the transcription of these genes has been observed to decrease slowly at elevated temperatures (37 °C) in some strain backgrounds (2, 16). The absence of a response in this case is noteworthy because transient heat stress (i) activates the cell integrity pathway and Slt2 MAP kinase activity and (ii) induces depolarization of the actin cytoskeleton through a novel Pkc1-dependent pathway that may or may not be the same as the pathway responsible for *sec*-mediated transcriptional repression (54). Thus, an explanation is needed to account for why the transcription of rDNA and tRNA genes is not repressed under these conditions. In considering this question, a more complete picture of the upstream pathway linking heat stress to cell integrity is needed.

Studies have revealed an important relationship between heat stress, sphingolipid synthesis, and the roles of two pairs of functionally redundant kinases, Pkh1/Pkh2 and Ypk1/Ypk2, in the activation of cell integrity signaling (reviewed in (74); see also Fig. 1). Heat stress in *S. cerevisiae* produces a rapid accumulation (5–10 min peak times) of molecules termed long chain bases (LCBs), which are precursors for the synthesis of ceramides and complex sphingolipids. The relevant LCB precursors for cell integrity signaling are dihydrosphingosine (DHS) and phytosphingosine (PHS). These molecules are linear alkyl chains (18 or 20 carbons in length) bearing hydroxyl groups at C-1, C-3 (DHS), and C-4 (PHS) and a C-2 amino group. Genetic and biochemical studies in yeast indicate that DHS/PHS regulation of Pkh1/Pkh2 (the homologs of mammalian 3-phosphoinositide-dependent kinase 1, PDK1) leads to activation of Pkc1 and the downstream MAP kinase cascade (74). This regulation of the Pkh kinases is further supported by the fact that sphingosine, the mammalian counterpart of PHS, is known to be a strong activator of mammalian PDK1. Pkh kinase activation of Pkc1 occurs, in part, through direct phosphorylation of T983 in the activation loop (75). Additionally, depolarization of the actin cytoskeleton following heat stress is dependent on the Ypk1/Ypk2 kinases, which are thought to function downstream of the Pkhs (75, 76). Consistent with this idea, sphingolipids have been shown to promote the phosphorylation of Ypk1 and its localization to the plasma membrane (77). The point at which the Ypk1/Ypk2 kinases activate the cell integrity pathway is not known precisely but is upstream of Rho1 since ypk lethality is suppressed by overexpression of Rom2 and Tus1. Considering the requirement for Wsc1 in signaling the effect of heat stress to the cell integrity pathway (54) and its colocalization with activated phospho-Ypk1 at the plasma membrane (77), the Wsc proteins are appealing candidates as mediators of this upstream input to the Pkc1-MAP kinase cascade (Fig. 1). Thus, it is apparent that the Pkh kinases activate Pkc1 both directly and indirectly (53). The existence of different inputs for heat stress into Pkc1-dependent signaling is potentially related to the determination of signal specificity. Selective activation of specific pathways can subsequently be achieved by several mechanisms involving scaffold proteins, signal duration and amplitude, cellular localization, or cross pathway control (78). With respect to the latter mechanism, there is now evidence for cross-talk in both directions between the cell integrity and HOG pathways. As has been noted, high osmolarity activates Pkc1-dependent relocalization of nuclear/nucleolar proteins (60). Conversely, heat stress has been found to activate the HOG pathway (79). The possible relevance of these observations for sec-mediated repression of transcription or the absence of repression (e.g., following heat stress) remains to be determined.

III. Nutrients, Starvation, and TOR Signaling

A. Rapamycin-Sensitive and Rapamycin-Insensitive TOR Pathways

One of the major signaling pathways regulating cell growth in response to nutrients in yeast, flies, and mammals employs the phosphoinositol kinase-related kinase TOR. TOR proteins are the targets of the antibiotic rapamycin, which binds to the kinase as a complex with the immunophilin FKBP12 and inhibits its activity. This ability of rapamycin is responsible for its antifungal activity, its immunosuppressive properties (which result from inhibition of T cell growth and proliferation), and its more recently discovered potential as an anticancer drug (*17, 18, 80*).

TOR signaling does not follow a single linear pathway but constitutes a group of pathways and responses to different nutritional signals and certain types of cellular stress (*17, 18, 80*). These pathways control the organization of the actin cytoskeleton, initiation of translation, amino acid permease activity, autophagy (the formation of autophagosomes for anabolic processes), and several distinct gene expression programs. The transcriptional consequences of TOR signaling or its inhibition by rapamycin affect the expression of several hundred nutrient-regulated yeast genes including those involved in glycolysis, the TCA cycle, oxidative phosphorylation, the storage of carbohydrates, the nitrogen discrimination pathway (which promotes the utilization of poor nitrogen sources), as well as genes encoding all the components of the ribosome, tRNAs, and other components related to protein synthesis (*17, 18, 21, 81, 82*). In the early 2000s, significant progress has been made in elucidating the molecules and the mechanisms responsible for TOR regulation of some of these responses (e.g., amino acid permease regulation, transcriptional control of NDP, Rtg, and Msn-regulated genes (*18, 80, 82*)). In other cases, however, the details of signaling downstream of TOR are unknown or largely incomplete.

In yeast, two partially redundant genes, *TOR1* and *TOR2*, encode the Tor kinases. Common, essential signaling functions (e.g., to translational and transcriptional targets) that are carried out by these kinases are inhibited by rapamycin. This produces a physiological response reminiscent of starvation/stationary phase. In addition, Tor2 participates in an essential rapamycin-insensitive pathway involving cell cycle-dependent polarization of the actin cytoskeleton (*18*). Organization of the actin cytoskeleton is required to direct the secretory pathway to the site of growth, namely, the bud. Studies on the protein complexes containing Tor1 and Tor2 have revealed the molecular basis for the selective inhibition of the TOR shared function by rapamycin (*83*). A complex designated TOR1C, containing either Tor1 or Tor2 together with Kog1 and Lst8, mediates the rapamycin-sensitive functions of Tor; only this complex can bind rapamycin-FKBP12. A second complex, designated TOR2C, contains Tor2, but not Tor1, together with the proteins Avo1, Avo2, Avo3, and Lst8 and mediates rapamycin-insensitive Tor2-unique signaling to the actin cytoskeleton. Given the existence of distinct TOR complexes with different sensitivities to rapamycin and different apparent functions, it was unexpected to find that a common downstream pathway, the cell integrity pathway (discussed previously) would participate in signaling events by both TOR complexes (*49, 84*).

B. Intersections of TOR and Cell Integrity Pathway Signaling

The unique function of Tor2 is exhibited in *TOR1* strains upon depletion of Tor2 or following inactivation of specific conditional *tor2* alleles (*18*). The lethal consequences of these conditions cannot be suppressed by overexpressing Tor1 and cause the cells to arrest in the G2/M phase of the cell cycle after several divisions. This is in contrast to the first cycle G1 arrest seen in *tor1 tor2* strains. Additionally, as has been noted, the polarized distribution of the actin cytoskeleton is disrupted in *TOR1 tor2* strains. Genetic and biochemical experiments indicate that this requirement for Tor2 is linked to the cell integrity pathway by Rom2 (Fig. 1). For example, overexpression of several components of the cell integrity pathway (e.g., Rom2, Rho1, Pkc1) suppresses both the growth and actin cytoskeletal defects of *tor2* strains. Moreover, the GDP/GTP exchange activity of Rom2 toward Rho1 is substantially reduced in a *tor2* mutant strain (32% of wild-type). This result, together with the fact that deletion of the Rho1 GTPase activating protein (Sac7) also suppresses a *tor2* mutation, indicates that Tor2 activates the Rho1 GTPase via Rom2 (*85*). Consistent with these findings, depletion of the Avo1 component of TOR2C inhibits growth and causes depolarization of the actin cytoskeleton as in *tor2* strains. Moreover, both of these *avo1* phenotypes can be suppressed by overexpression of Rom2, Rho1, and Pkc1 or by activating mutations in components of the MAP kinase cascade (*83*). The manner in which TOR2C function activates Rom2 to promote Rho1 GTPase has yet to be determined but it is known that both the kinase domain of Tor2 and the pleckstrin homology domain of Rom2 (which binds phosphatidylinositol derivatives) are necessary (*85*).

In addition to being activated by TOR2C, several studies have found that the cell integrity pathway is activated by rapamycin-mediated inhibition of TOR1C in a variety of yeast strain backgrounds (*49, 84*). Thus, TOR1C function is needed to suppress the activity of the Pkc1-Map kinase cascade. Unexpectedly, one of the effects of rapamycin on this pathway is depolarization of the actin cytoskeleton (*84*), a function previously thought to be unique to TOR2C (*18, 83*). While this no longer appears to be the case, it is evident that TOR1C and TOR2C function in distinctly different ways, in accordance with their different genetic and biochemical properties, to regulate the activity of the cell integrity pathway and the actin cytoskeleton. TOR2C activation of the pathway is required during polarized cell growth, whereas TOR1C inhibits the pathway under normal growth conditions and then (presumably) releases this inhibition as nutrients become limiting and the cells enter stationary phase (*18, 83, 84*). Consistent with the latter, it has been shown recently that a functional cell integrity pathway is required for cell viability following nutrient deprivation (*86*). Currently, it is not known how the two opposing functions of the TOR complexes are coordinated to provide Slt2 MAP kinase activity at the appropriate time and place. However, the differences are likely to be explained, at least in part, by the existence of distinct pathways linking TOR1C and TOR2C to cell integrity components. In this regard, the functions and interactions of the proteins that are specific to each TOR complex (Kog1, Avo1, Avo2, and Avo3), once they are known, should be informative. Other molecules that may differentiate TOR1C and TOR2C inputs into this pathway include Tap42, the type 2A-related protein phosphatase Sit4 (see Section III. C) and the Wsc/Mid2 family of plasma membrane sensors (Fig. 1). Notably, deletions of Wsc1, Mid2, and Rom2 have been shown to reduce significantly the TOR1C-mediated effect of rapamycin on the actin cytoskeleton and/or on Slt2 activation (84). Thus, through the requirement for Wsc1 and Mid2, inhibition of TOR1C is thought to induce plasma membrane stress. As has been discussed, TOR2C is known to activate Rom2 but the role, if any, of the Wsc proteins in this signaling has not been addressed.

As has been noted, deletion of *PKC1* in a *sec1-1* strain blocks or substantially attenuates repression of rDNA, tRNA, and ribosomal protein gene transcription (16, 45). Thus, the ability of rapamycin treatment to activate the cell integrity pathway and repress transcription of the protein synthetic machinery suggested that this response might also be blocked in a *pkc1Δ* strain. However, an examination of tRNA gene transcription in rapamycin-treated cells revealed no significant attenuation of repression in the absence of Pkc1 (Fig. 2). While this result does not exclude a role for Pkc1 in rapamycin-mediated transcriptional repression, it clearly indicates that an unknown Pkc1-independent pathway is responsible for the inhibition of tRNA synthesis under these conditions. Additional data supporting this view is discussed in Section III.C.

C. Examining the Role of Protein Phosphatase 2A in TOR Signaling and in the Regulation of Pol III Transcription

Tap42 is a key downstream regulator of TOR signaling that is essential for a number of TOR-mediated responses, including those affecting the stability and sorting of amino acid permeases, initiation of protein synthesis, organization of the actin cytoskeleton, and transcriptional activation of nutrient- and stress-regulated sets of genes (18, 80, 82, 84, 87). Tap42 mediates TOR signaling, in part, by its reversible association with the catalytic subunits of the type 2A and type 2A-related protein phosphatases (PP2As), Pph21/22 and Sit4, respectively, (87). The levels of these Tap42-containing complexes are regulated by nutrient availability through the activity of the Tor kinases; specifically, conditions that activate TOR promote the association of Tap42 with PP2A catalytic subunits while conditions that inhibit TOR (rapamycin or entry into stationary phase) favor complex dissociation (87). These changes in complex stability are correlated with Tor-dependent, rapamycin-sensitive

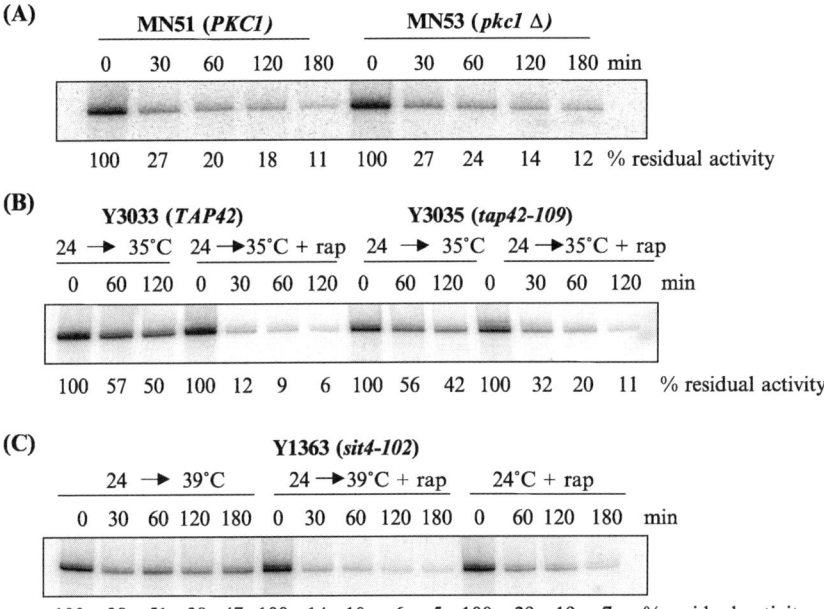

FIG. 2. Rapamycin-induced repression of pol III transcription occurs independently of PKC1, TAP42, and SIT4. (A) Strains MN51 (PKC1) and MN53 (pkc1Δ) were grown to mid-log phase (A_{600} = 0.5) in YPD medium containing 1 M sorbitol, following which rapamycin (0.2 μg/ml) was added and samples were removed for northern analysis at various times as indicated. The blot was hybridized with a pre-tRNA^{Leu} probe. Each lane contained 20 μg of total RNA. (B) Strains Y3033 (TAP42) and Y3035 (tap42-109) were transferred from 24 to 35 °C at mid-log phase, rapamycin (0.2 μg/ml) was added 20 min after the shift to the nonpermissive temperature, and samples removed at various times thereafter were subjected to northern analysis as in panel A. (C) Rapamycin (0.2 μg/ml) was added to strain Y1363 (sit4-102) (A_{600} = 0.5) either at 24 °C or 20 min after transfer to 39 °C. Samples were removed for northern analysis (as in panel A) at the indicated times, after addition of rapamycin or after the temperature shift in the experiment where no rapamycin was added.

changes in the phosphorylation state of Tap42, which is likely to be a direct substrate of TOR1C (83, 88). Thus, the phosphorylated form of Tap42 is more stably bound to the phosphatase catalytic subunits than the unphosphorylated form. Initial experiments on Tap42 suggested that it functions simply as an inhibitor of PP2As. However, several studies, including a cDNA microarray analysis of new tap42 alleles, reveal a more complex picture (82, 88, 89). The current view is that Tap42 functions as an inhibitor of phosphatase activity in some circumstances (e.g., in the regulation of Msn2/4 stress response genes) and an activator (e.g., of Gln3- and Rtg1/3-regulated genes) in others. Interestingly, the difference between these opposing functions is suggested to depend on the phosphorylation state of Tap42.

In the context of signaling to the pol III transcription machinery, the functions of Tap42 and Sit4 are of interest since both proteins have been identified as negative regulators of rapamycin-sensitive TOR signaling to the cell integrity pathway (Fig. 1) (84). This was evidenced by the fact that *tap42-11* and *sit4Δ* strains exhibit high basal levels of activated Slt2 and a disorganized actin cytoskeleton, similar to rapamycin-treated wild-type cells and *tor* mutant strains (84). Additionally, phosphatase activity is important for normal levels of pol III transcription since inactivating mutations in the regulatory A subunit of PP2A, encoded by *TPD3*, leads to a marked inhibition of tRNA synthesis *in vivo* and *in vitro* (90). Thus, repression of pol III transcription under a variety of conditions could potentially involve the inhibition of PP2A.

Conditional alleles of *TAP42* and *SIT4*, including one of the newly isolated *tap42* mutations (*tap42-109*, (82)) have been used to examine the importance of these genes for the repression of pol III transcription by rapamycin. Wild-type and *tap42-109* strains both show a modest decrease (~50%) in tRNA^{Leu} synthesis following a temperature shift, indicating that Tap42 is not required for normal levels of pol III transcription. In contrast, addition of rapamycin to wild-type and *tap42-109* cells that had previously been shifted to the nonpermissive temperature resulted in a significant reduction (~90–95%) in tRNA^{Leu} synthesis (Fig. 2, panel B). Thus, Tap42 is not required for rapamycin-induced repression of tRNA synthesis. These findings parallel those of Broach and colleagues (82), who concluded that the normal expression of ribosomal protein genes as well as the repression of these genes by rapamycin does not depend on Tap42. Analogous experiments conducted with a *sit4-102* strain produced the same results (Fig. 2, panel C). Repression of tRNA^{Leu} synthesis in the presence of rapamycin was as robust at the nonpermissive temperature as at the permissive temperature while only a modest response was observed upon temperature-shift in the absence of rapamycin. Thus, like Tap42, Sit4 is not required for tRNA gene transcription or its repression by rapamycin. The outcome of these experiments on Tap42 and Sit4 is complementary to that obtained in the *pkc1Δ* strain (Fig. 1, panel A) and these results together suggest that activation of the Slt2 MAP kinase is neither required nor sufficient for repression of pol III transcription by rapamycin. The former is consistent with the studies already discussed (Section II.A) on defects in the secretory pathway, where the repressing signal is transduced from Pkc1 to a novel downstream branch of the cell integrity pathway. As has been discussed with regard to heat stress (Section II.D), it is striking that the strong activation of Slt2 resulting from the loss of Tap42 or Sit4 is not accompanied by repression of pol III transcription, given that Slt2 activation is absolutely dependent on Pkc1. Finally, we note that experiments on rapamycin-mediated repression of both ribosomal protein and tRNA gene transcription support the concept that neither response is dependent on Tap42 or Sit4 ((82) and Fig. 2, panels B and C). The exclusion of these proteins, together with Pkc1 (Fig. 2, panel A), eliminates the well-known mediators of TOR signaling in yeast and provokes a search for the novel TOR1C-regulated pathway that signals the coordinate repression of transcription by pols I, II, and III (Fig. 1).

IV. Repression of Pol III Transcription in Response to DNA Damage

Consistent with the co-regulation of pol I and pol III under a wide range of conditions (Table I) and early reports that pol I transcription in yeast is repressed in response to DNA damage (91), later metabolic labeling studies have shown that pol I and pol III transcription in *S. cerevisiae* is repressed following UV irradiation and treatment with DNA alkylating agents (39). At the exposure levels used in this study, the resulting lesions induce a DNA damage response that includes cell cycle arrest at one of two DNA damage checkpoints. These checkpoints prevent entry into S or M phase until DNA repair is completed. Thus, the biological rationale for the repression of pol I and pol III transcription, under these conditions, may be to promote cell viability by conserving metabolic energy until the cells are able to resume cycling. The activation of DNA damage checkpoints in this response raises a question as to whether transcriptional repression occurs directly as a result of the DNA damage signal or is an indirect consequence of cell cycle arrest (32). This was resolved in favor of direct signaling to the transcription machinery by demonstrating that pol III transcription is inhibited by methylmethane sulfonate (MMS) treatment of cells previously arrested in G1 (at START) or G2/M (39).

The response to DNA damage involves a complex signal transduction network comprising sensor, transducer, and effector proteins (92, 93). Studies on the components of this network have been pursued largely from the perspective of repairing different types of DNA damage and activation of cell cycle checkpoints. Thus, it is not yet known which of the many components of the network are required for signaling to the pol III machinery. One candidate activity that is potentially important in this negative regulation is casein kinase II (CK2). In yeast and humans, CK2 functions positively to activate pol III transcription, albeit via apparently different targets (39, 94, 95). The molecular basis for CK2's stimulatory activity in yeast involves its phosphorylation of a surface exposed residue (Ser 128) on the TATA-binding protein (39, 94), one of three components of the initiation factor TFIIIB (the Brf1 subunit of this factor is a functionally important target of CK2 in humans, (95)). The exact steps in transcription that are affected by CK2-mediated TBP phosphorylation are not known, although the assembly of TFIIIB onto DNA is clearly stimulated in the presence of the enzyme and diminished in its absence (39). CK2 is well positioned to affect changes in the specific activity of pol III transcription factors since a small fraction of total cellular CK2 copurifies with TFIIIB activity, apparently in stoichiometric proportions to TBP and Brf1. Indeed, the relatively poor transcription activity of extracts derived from MMS-treated cells correlates with lower levels of TBP-associated CK2 activity and the loss of the catalytic α' subunit in TBP immunoprecipitates. A positive role for CK2 in pol III transcription is also supported by *in vivo* labeling experiments: Strains containing mutations in CK2 ($cka2^{ts}$ and $ckb1\Delta$) or the S128A mutation in TBP display lower absolute levels of pol III transcription relative to wild-type, in the absence of DNA damage. Following UV irradiation, these strains exhibit similarly repressed levels of pol III transcription as wild-type strains. The ability of mutations in CK2 or its phosphorylation site in TBP to reduce the difference in transcription between normal and DNA-damaged cells has led to the description of CK2 as a terminal effector of the signaling pathway that represses pol III transcription in response to DNA damage (39). However, it appears that this repression may, in fact, involve the reversal of CK2's effects as an activator of pol III transcription rather than a direct, positive role of CK2 in generating a transcriptional repressed state. Given this consideration, the question of whether CK2 has a positive role in signaling the DNA damage response to the pol III machinery remains open.

V. Maf1 and its Essential Role in Pol III Transcriptional Repression

As has been noted (Table I), a wide range of conditions are known to cause repression of pol III transcription. While some of these conditions may activate common signaling pathways (as demonstrated for *sec* defects and rapamycin treatment), distinct signaling pathways that impinge on the pol III transcription machinery are also likely to be involved. The novel Pkc1-independent, rapamycin-sensitive pathway already described (Sections III.B and C) and the DNA damage response pathway (92) provide two such examples. How do these pathways impact the pol III transcription machinery? Are there parallel pathways with distinct targets or do the different pathways converge? Although the existence of different pathways with distinct targets has not been excluded, several experiments demonstrate that the signaling pathways mediating repression of pol III transcription by *sec* defects, rapamycin-treatment, DNA damage, and growth to stationary phase all converge at or above a point defined by the Maf1 protein. In these situations, Maf1 is essential for signaling transcriptional repression to the pol III machinery (40).

A. Genetic Identification of Maf1

Maf1 was identified originally in a genetic screen for mutations that decreased the nonsense suppressor efficiency of *SUP11* tRNA (96). A loss of function mutation in Maf1 was found to exacerbate the anti-suppressor phenotype of a *mod5–1* strain that is specifically compromised for a tRNA base modification, namely, isopentylation of an adenosine residue (A37) immediately adjacent to the anticodon in *SUP11* and other tRNA molecules. Subsequently, the *maf1–1* mutation, as well as a *MAF1* gene deletion, was found to exhibit anti-suppressor activity independently of *mod5–1* and to confer temperature-sensitive growth on medium containing glycerol as the sole carbon source (97). Based on current knowledge, the anti-suppressor phenotype of *maf1* mutants (i.e., decreased *SUP11* function) is surprising since it is seemingly inconsistent with other properties of these strains, including their increased synthesis of tRNAs *in vivo* and *in vitro*, elevated levels of mature tRNA in total cellular RNA (98), and inability to negatively regulate pol III transcription (40). A likely explanation for the anti-suppression phenotype is that it results from reduced isopentylation of *SUP11* by Mod5, due to the excess amounts of mature tRNA, and thus less efficient decoding of nonsense mutations (98). In addition, a substrate of Mod5, dimethyallyldiphosphate (DMAPP), is also a substrate for Erg20 (farnesyl diphosphate synthase), a key enzyme in isoprenoid biosynthesis. The ability of Mod5 to compete with Erg20 for a limited pool of DMAPP may be reduced in the *maf1–1* strain since the mutation increases Erg20 mRNA and protein levels about four-fold and two-fold, respectively (99, 100)

B. Genetic and Biochemical Interactions of Maf1 with Pol III

The first indication that the function of Maf1 was related to pol III transcription came when fragments of *RPC160*, the gene encoding the largest subunit of pol III, were isolated as multicopy suppressors of the conditional growth phenotype of *maf1–1* (97). The region of *RPC160* that was critical for this effect mapped to the amino-terminal 235 amino acids. The same fragment also suppressed the anti-suppressor phenotype of *maf1–1*. Subsequently, spontaneous cold-sensitive mutations in *RPC160* were obtained as suppressors of the condition phenotype of both *maf1–1* and *maf1Δ* strains (98). Characterization of one of these mutations (*rpc160–2*) in a wild-type *MAF1* strain revealed a marked reduction in tRNA levels at the nonpermissive temperature, suggesting that the basis for its isolation in the *maf1* mutant strain was the restoration of normal cellular tRNA levels. Presumably, overexpression of the amino terminus of Rpc160 suppressed the *maf1–1* mutation in a similar manner, by limiting the concentration of pol III or its factors. In addition to these genetic interactions, reciprocal coimmunoprecipitation experiments demonstrated direct interactions between Maf1 and pol III. Approximately

15% of Maf1 in cell extracts copurified with pol III while 5 to 10% of the pol III (represented by Rpc160) was estimated to be in a complex with Maf1.

In support of the preceding genetic and biochemical interactions between Maf1 and pol III, *in vivo* pulse chase analysis revealed a three-fold increase in tRNA synthesis in the *maf1-1* strain. Smaller but reproducible effects on transcription were also seen *in vitro*, using matched extracts of wild-type and *maf1-1* strains. All together, these data supported the conclusion that Maf1 functions as a negative effector of pol III transcription (*98*).

C. Convergence of Signaling Pathways that Repress tRNA and Ribosome Synthesis

The biological context for the function of Maf1 was provided by experiments that examined its requirement for transcriptional repression following interruption of the secretory pathway. Remarkably, deletion of *MAF1* quantitatively blocked repression of pol III transcription in a *sec* mutant strain without affecting repression of rDNA and ribosomal protein genes (*40*). This result complemented earlier findings that deletion of the carboxy terminal silencing domain of Rap1 (*rap1-17*), which blocks repression of rDNA and ribosomal protein genes by a *sec* mutation (*41, 45*), does not affect repression of tRNA gene transcription under the same conditions (*16*). Thus, the secretory signaling pathway must diverge at some point downstream of Pkc1 into unique branches affecting transcription by pol III in one case and pols I and II in the other (Fig. 1).

Screening of other repressing conditions, including treatments with tunicamycin, rapamycin, MMS, and chlorpromazine, as well as growth to stationary phase, revealed that Maf1 was required in all cases for pol III transcriptional repression. Thus, at least three major signaling pathways that are independently able to regulate cell growth in response to changes in secretion, nutrient status, or DNA damage converge on Maf1, which is essential for their effects on pol III transcription (*40*). Although Maf1 is a dedicated mediator of repression in the pol III system, the signaling pathways that impinge on it are not pol III specific. Thus, it seems likely that common signaling molecules operating upstream of Maf1 may exist that are able to interface with polymerase-specific effectors to regulate all the components of the ribosome as well as the factors associated with its assembly and function (Fig. 3). Notably, while Maf1 is sufficient to mediate diverse signals to pol III, it appears that Rap1 does not perform a similarly broad role in the pol II system. In particular, the silencing domain of Rap1 that is critical for repression of rDNA and ribosomal protein genes in response to a secretory defect is not required for repression of ribosomal protein genes following nitrogen starvation (*19*). As discussed earlier, inhibition of TOR signaling represses transcription at these promoters and has been correlated kinetically with the

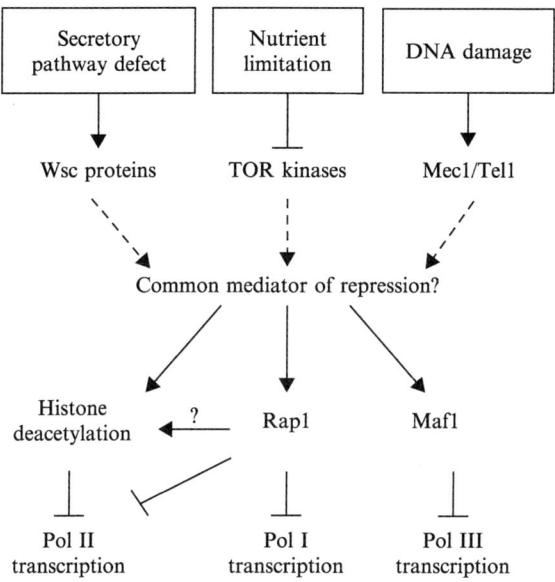

FIG. 3. Convergence of signaling pathways that repress transcription of ribosomal components and tRNAs. A minimum of three independent signaling pathways that are activated by different repressing conditions converge on a hypothetic common mediator of repression, which directs the activities of specific downstream factors in the pol I, pol II, and pol III systems. The evidence for the model is discussed in the text.

loss of Esa1 histone acetyltransferase and deacetylation of histone H4 by the Rpd3-Sin3 complex. These actions all appear to be downstream of Rap1 whose occupancy on the DNA did not change (*101*). Thus, with respect to the hypothesized common mediator of repression (Fig. 3), it seems that coordinate regulation of pols I, II, and III under different conditions may involve more than one target in the pol II machinery.

D. Biochemical Effects of Maf1-Dependent Repression

The molecular mechanism by which Maf1 brings about transcriptional repression is not yet known. However, the strict requirement for Maf1 under diverse conditions implies that a common mechanism operates to repress one or more targets in the pol III transcription machinery. Given the rapid kinetics of repression, especially with drug treatments such as chlorpromazine and rapamycin (*40*), it seems likely that the pol III machinery is regulated posttranslationally. To address these issues, *in vitro* systems that recapitulate the repression of pol III transcription seen *in vivo* have been developed using rapamycin, MMS, and chlorpromazine treatments (*39, 40, 81*). While comparable experiments in these systems are not available in all three cases, there appears to be agreement on several points: (i) mixing of control and repressed cell extracts obtained after either MMS or chlorpromazine treatment have excluded the presence of an abundant inhibitor of pol III transcription in the repressed extracts; (ii) defective transcription in treated extracts can be rescued by supplementation with a TFIIIB fraction but not with TFIIIC or pol III; and (iii) TFIIIB complex assembly is defective in repressed cell extracts (39, 40). In addition, Western blotting has established that the levels of all three subunits of TFIIIB and representative subunits of pol III and TFIIIC do not change under repressing conditions. Thus, proteolysis appears to be excluded as a mechanism of repression. It is interesting that the current data in yeast point to TFIIIB as the primary target for repression, as this factor is also targeted for repression by Rb and p53 in mammalian systems (102, 103).

Maf1 is a hydrophilic protein rich in serine and aspargine residues with a predicted molecular weight from 26 kDa (S. pombe, human) to 45 kDa (S. cerevisiae). Consistent with its interaction with pol III and its placement close to the end of the signaling pathway (Fig. 3), indirect immunofluorescence localized Maf1 to nucleus (98). Sequence comparisons of putative Maf1 orthologs in organisms from yeast to human reveal that the primary sequence of Maf1 can be subdivided into three different domains, two of which contain novel, conserved (but not invariant) signature sequences (PDYDFS and WSxxYFFYNkkxKR). This analysis suggests that the fundamental function of Maf1 in signaling pol III transcriptional repression has been conserved (98). However, at the present time, the sequence of Maf1 does not offer any clues as to its structure or mechanism of action.

VI. Future Studies

The early 2000s have witnessed important advances in our understanding about key signaling pathways that control the production of new protein synthetic capacity and thus regulate cell growth. These pathways are considered to be vitally important for the fitness and viability of cells since they enable rapid responses to nutritional and other environmental conditions and determine the biologically appropriate use of the available metabolic energy. However, compared to the considerable investment of high-energy nucleotides in ribosome and tRNA synthesis (>80% of total nuclear transcription in actively growing cells), our knowledge of the regulatory pathways and their mechanisms of action is still disproportionately small. Significant gaps exist in all of the major pathways that repress transcription of the protein synthetic machinery. Clearly, a major effort is needed to identify the missing links between the upstream components of these pathways and their ultimate downstream targets. In the case of Pkc1-independent, rapamycin-sensitive TOR1C signaling, the entire pathway has yet to be defined and there are no obvious clues as to the identity of its components (Fig. 1). With respect to the DNA damage response and its effect on pol I and pol III transcription, several candidate signal transducers are known from studies on cell cycle checkpoint control and transcriptional induction of DNA repair proteins (e.g., the ataxia telangiectasia (ATM) gene homologs Mec1 and Tel1 and downstream kinases Rad53 and Dun1). An examination of these proteins may provide a stepping-off point for further studies in this pathway. As for transcriptional repression mediated by secretory defects, it is likely that additional components remain to be identified downstream of Pkc1 and upstream of Rap1 and Maf1 (Fig. 1). In addition to these pathways, the regulation of pol I and pol III transcription by carbon source (Table I, not discussed here), presumably via protein kinase A, needs to be elaborated. It is also of great interest to know how yeast cells are able to sense changes in culture conditions during exponential growth and shut down the synthesis of ribosomes and tRNAs about three doublings before they stop dividing (2, 40). Is a specific metabolite involved and if so, what is the sensor?

Our studies on Maf1 have demonstrated the convergence of the secretory, TOR, and DNA damage response signaling pathways in the repression of tRNA synthesis and suggest that a similar convergence of these pathways occurs in the repression of rDNA and ribosomal protein gene transcription. This has led us to the hypothesis that a common mediator of repression is likely to exist upstream of Maf1, with the ability to communicate the signal to repress transcription to specific regulators in each polymerase system (Fig. 3). What might this molecule be and how might it work? Maf1 itself provides, perhaps, the best opportunity for its identification through both protein- and genetic-based approaches. This effort could also benefit from an understanding of the mechanism(s) underlying the essential role of Maf1 in pol III transcriptional repression. On this issue, there are many fundamental questions to address. For example, does Maf1 function as a stoichiometric inhibitor of pol III transcription, similar to Rb and p53 in mammalian cells, and if so, what is/are its targets? Pol III is implicated by a direct interaction with Maf1 but additional factors must be involved to account for the inhibition of TFIIIB complex assembly on tRNA genes in repressed cell extracts (40). Is the interaction of Maf1 with its transcriptional targets dependent on or enhanced under repressing conditions? The interaction of Maf1 with pol III also raises the question of its occupancy of pol III promoters, at least under repressing conditions, which needs to be examined. With the answers to these questions and a more complete description of the signaling pathways that impact ribosome and tRNA synthesis, we will be in a much better position to understand how cells achieve metabolic economy (2) and promote their viability and growth.

Acknowledgments

The authors are very grateful to Robyn Moir for numerous insightful discussions and comments on the manuscript. We also thank Jonathan Warner for his continued encouragement, support, and fruitful discussions. The research from our laboratory is supported by NIH grants GM60631 and GM42728.

References

1. Polymenis, M., and Schmidt, E. V. (1999). Coordination of cell growth with cell division. *Curr. Opin. Genet. Dev.* **9**, 76–80.
2. Warner, J. (1999). The economics of ribosome biosynthesis in yeast. *Trends Biochem. Sci.* **24**, 437–440.
3. Jorgensen, P., Nishikawa, J. L., Breitkreutz, B. J., and Tyers, M. (2002). Systematic identification of pathways that couple cell growth and division in yeast. *Science* **297**, 395–400.
4. Zhang, J., Schneider, C., Ottmers, L., Rodriguez, R., Day, A., Markwardt, J., and Schneider, B. L. (2002). Genomic scale mutant hunt identifies cell size homeostasis genes in S. cerevisiae. *Curr. Biol.* **12**, 1992–2001.
5. Grewal, S. S., and Edgar, B. A. (2003). Controlling cell division in yeast and animals: Does size matter? *J. Biol.* **2**, 5.
6. Ruggero, D., and Panadolfi, P. P. (2003). Does the ribosome translate cancer? *Nature Rev. Cancer* **3**, 179–192.
7. Fantes, P., and Nurse, P. (1977). Control of cell size at division in fission yeast by a growth-modulated size control over nuclear division. *Exp. Cell Res.* **107**, 377–386.
8. Levine, K., Tinkelenberg, A. H., and Cross, F. (1995). The CLN gene family: Central regulators of cell cycle Start in budding yeast. *Prog. Cell Cycle Res.* **1**, 101–114.
9. Willis, I. M. (1993). RNA polymerase III. Genes, factors, and transcriptional specificity. *Eur. J. Biochem.* **212**, 1–11.
10. White, R. J. (1998). RNA Polymerase III Transcription. Springer-Verlag, New York.
11. Harismendy, O., Gendrel, C. G., Soularue, P., Gidrol, X., Sentenac, A., Werner, M., and Lefebvre, O. (2003). Genome-wide location of yeast RNA polymerase III transcription machinery. *EMBO J.* **22**, 4738–4747.
12. Li, T. H., and Schmid, C. W. (2001). Differential stress induction of individual Alu loci: Implications for transcription and retrotransposition. *Gene* **276**, 135–141.
13. Wolffe, A. P. (1994). The role of transcription factors, chromatin structure, and DNA replication in 5 S RNA gene regulation. *J. Cell Sci.* **107**, 2055–2063.
14. Ouyang, C., Martinez, M. J., Young, L. S., and Sprague, K. U. (2000). TATA-binding protein–TATA interaction is a key determinant of differential transcription of silkworm constitutive and silk gland-specific tRNA(Ala) genes. *Mol. Cell. Biol.* **20**, 1329–1343.
15. Paule, M. R., and White, R. J. (2000). Survey and summary: Transcription by RNA polymerases I and III. *Nucleic Acids Res.* **28**, 1283–1298.
16. Li, Y., Moir, R. D., Sethy-Coraci, I. K., Warner, J. R., and Willis, I. M. (2000). Repression of ribosome and tRNA synthesis in secretion-defective cells is signaled by a novel branch of the cell integrity pathway. *Mol. Cell. Biol.* **20**, 3843–3851.
17. Schmelzle, T., and Hall, M. N. (2000). TOR, a central controller of cell growth. *Cell* **103**, 253–262.
18. Crespo, J. L., and Hall, M. N. (2002). Elucidating TOR signaling and rapamycin action: Lessons from Saccharomyces cerevisiae. *Microbiol. Mol. Biol. Rev.* **66**, 579–591.

19. Miyoshi, K., Shirai, C., and Mizuta, K. (2003). Transcription of genes encoding trans-acting factors required for rRNA maturation/ribosomal subunit assembly is coordinately regulated with ribosomal protein genes and involves Rap1 in Saccharomyces cerevisiae. *Nucleic Acids Res.* **31,** 1969–1973.
20. Oliver, S. G., and McLaughlin, C. S. (1977). The regulation of RNA synthesis in yeast. I: Starvation experiments. *Mol. Gen. Genet.* **154,** 145–153.
21. Powers, T., and Walter, P. (1999). Regulation of ribosome biogenesis by the rapamycin-sensitive TOR-signaling pathway in Saccharomyces cerevisiae. *Mol. Biol. Cell* **10,** 987–1000.
22. Schnapp, A., Pfleiderer, C., Rosenbauer, H., and Grummt, I. (1990). A growth-dependent transcription initiation factor (TIF-IA) interacting with RNA polymerase I regulates mouse ribosomal RNA synthesis. *EMBO J.* **9,** 2857–2863.
23. Glibetic, M., Taylor, L., Larson, D., Hannan, R., Sells, B., and Rothblum, L. (1995). The RNA polymerase I transcription factor UBF is the product of a primary response gene. *J. Biol. Chem.* **270,** 4209–4212.
24. Sinn, E., Wang, Z., Kovelman, R., and Roeder, R. G. (1995). Cloning and characterization of a TFIIIC2 subunit (TFIIIC beta) whose presence correlates with activation of RNA polymerase III-mediated transcription by adenovirus E1A expression and serum factors. *Genes Dev.* **9,** 675–685.
25. Scott, P. H., Cairns, C. A., Sutcliffe, J. E., Alzuherri, H. M., McLees, A., Winter, A. G., and White, R. J. (2001). Regulation of RNA polymerase III transcription during cell cycle entry. *J. Biol. Chem.* **276,** 1005–1014.
26. Clarke, E. M., Peterson, C. L., Brainard, A. V., and Riggs, D. L. (1996). Regulation of the RNA polymerase I and III transcription systems in response to growth conditions. *J. Biol. Chem.* **271,** 22189–22195.
27. Hannan, K. M., Kennedy, B. K., Cavanaugh, A. H., Hannan, R. D., Hirschler-Laszkiewicz, I., Jefferson, L. S., and Rothblum, L. I. (2000). RNA polymerase I transcription in confluent cells: Rb downregulates rDNA transcription during confluence-induced cell cycle arrest. *Oncogene* **19,** 3487–3497.
28. Tower, J., and Sollner-Webb, B. (1988). Polymerase III transcription factor B activity is reduced in extracts of growth-restricted cells. *Mol. Cell. Biol.* **8,** 1001–1005.
29. Sethy, I., Moir, R. D., Librizzi, M., and Willis, I. M. (1995). *In vitro* evidence for growth regulation of tRNA gene transcription in yeast. A role for transcription factor (TF)IIIB70 and TFIIIC. *J. Biol. Chem.* **270,** 28463–28470.
30. Heix, J., Vente, A., Voit, R., Budde, A., Michaelidis, T. M., and Grummt, I. (1998). Mitotic silencing of human rRNA synthesis: Inactivation of the promoter selectivity factor SL1 by cdc2/cyclin B-mediated phosphorylation. *EMBO J.* **17,** 7373–7381.
31. White, R. J., Trouche, D., Martin, K., Jackson, S. P., and Kouzarides, T. (1996). Repression of RNA polymerase III transcription by the retinoblastoma protein. *Nature* **382,** 88–90.
32. Gottesfeld, J. M., and Forbes, D. J. (1997). Mitotic repression of the transcriptional machinery. *Trends Biochem. Sci.* **22,** 197–202.
33. Klein, J., and Grummt, I. (1999). Cell cycle-dependent regulation of RNA polymerase I transcription: The nucleolar transcription factor UBF is inactive in mitosis and early G1. *Proc. Natl. Acad. Sci. USA* **96,** 6096–6101.
34. Moehle, C. M., and Hinnebusch, A. G. (1991). Association of RAP1 binding sites with stringent control of ribosomal protein gene transcription in Saccharomyces cerevisiae. *Mol. Cell. Biol.* **11,** 2723–2735.
35. Fradkin, L. G., Yoshinaga, S. K., Berk, A. J., and Dasgupta, A. (1987). Inhibition of host cell RNA polymerase III-mediated transcription by poliovirus: Inactivation of specific transcription factors. *Mol. Cell. Biol.* **7,** 3880–3887.

36. Mizuta, K., and Warner, J. R. (1994). Continued functioning of the secretory pathway is essential for ribosome synthesis. *Mol. Cell. Biol.* **14**, 2493–2502.
37. Zhao, Y., Sohn, J. H., and Warner, J. R. (2003). Autoregulation in the biosynthesis of ribosomes. *Mol. Cell. Biol.* **23**, 699–707.
38. Miyoshi, K., Tsujii, R., Yoshida, H., Maki, Y., Wada, A., Matsui, Y., Toh, E., and Mizuta, K. (2002). Normal assembly of 60 S ribosomal subunits is required for the signaling in response to a secretory defect in Saccharomyces cerevisiae. *J. Biol. Chem.* **277**, 18334–18339.
39. Ghavidel, A., and Schultz, M. C. (2001). TATA binding protein-associated CK2 transduces DNA damage signals to the RNA polymerase III transcriptional machinery. *Cell* **106**, 575–584.
40. Upadhya, R., Lee, J., and Willis, I. M. (2002). Maf1 is an essential mediator of diverse signals that repress RNA polymerase III transcription. *Mol. Cell* **10**, 1489–1494.
41. Miyoshi, K., Miyakawa, T., and Mizuta, K. (2001). Repression of rRNA synthesis due to a secretory defect requires the C-terminal silencing domain of Rap1p in Saccharomyces cerevisiae. *Nucleic Acids Res.* **29**, 3297–3303.
42. Gokal, P. K., Cavanaugh, A. H., and Thompson, E. A., Jr. (1986). The effects of cycloheximide upon transcription of rRNA, 5 S RNA, and tRNA genes. *J. Biol. Chem.* **261**, 2536–2541.
43. Dieci, G., Duimio, L., Peracchia, G., and Ottonello, S. (1995). Selective inactivation of two components of the multiprotein transcription factor TFIIIB in cycloheximide growth-arrested yeast cells. *J. Biol. Chem.* **270**, 13476–13482.
44. Paule, M. R. (1998). "Transcription of Eukaryotic Ribosomal RNA Genes by RNA Polymerase I." Springer-Verlag New York Inc., New York, NY.
45. Nierras, C. R., and Warner, J. R. (1999). Protein kinase C enables the regulatory circuit that connects membrane synthesis to ribosome synthesis in Saccharomyces cerevisiae. *J. Biol. Chem.* **274**, 13235–13241.
46. Kief, D. R., and Warner, J. R. (1981). Coordinate control of syntheses of ribosomal ribonucleic acid and ribosomal proteins during nutritional shift-up in Saccharomyces cerevisiae. *Mol. Cell. Biol.* **1**, 1007–1015.
47. Chen, J. Y., Brunauer, L. S., Chu, F. C., Helsel, C. M., Gedde, M. M., and Huestis, W. H. (2003). Selective amphipathic nature of chlorpromazine binding to plasma membrane bilayers. *Biochim. Biophys. Acta* **1616**, 95–105.
48. Kamada, Y., Jung, U. S., Piotrowski, J., and Levin, D. E. (1995). The protein kinase C-activated MAP kinase pathway of Saccharomyces cerevisiae mediates a novel aspect of the heat shock response. *Genes Dev.* **9**, 1559–1571.
49. Ai, W., Bertram, P. G., Tsang, C. K., Chan, T. F., and Zheng, X. F. (2002). Regulation of subtelomeric silencing during stress response. *Mol. Cell* **10**, 1295–1305.
50. Gustin, M. C., Albertyn, J., Alexander, M., and Davenport, K. (1998). MAP kinase pathways in the yeast Saccharomyces cerevisiae. *Microbiol. Mol. Biol. Rev.* **62**, 1264–1300.
51. Heinisch, J. J., Lorberg, A., Schmitz, H. P., and Jacoby, J. J. (1999). The protein kinase C-mediated MAP kinase pathway involved in the maintenance of cellular integrity in Saccharomyces cerevisiae. *Mol. Microbiol.* **32**, 671–680.
52. Philip, B., and Levin, D. E. (2001). Wsc1 and Mid2 are cell surface sensors for cell wall integrity signaling that act through Rom2, a guanine nucleotide exchange factor for Rho1. *Mol. Cell. Biol.* **21**, 271–280.
53. Schmelzle, T., Helliwell, S. B., and Hall, M. N. (2002). Yeast protein kinases and the RHO1 exchange factor TUS1 are novel components of the cell integrity pathway in yeast. *Mol. Cell. Biol.* **22**, 1329–1339.
54. Delley, P.-A., and Hall, M. N. (1999). Cell wall stress depolarizes cell growth via hyperactivation of RHO1. *J. Cell Biol.* **147**, 163–174.

55. Schmidt, A., Schmelzle, T., and Hall, M. N. (2002). The RHO1-GAPs SAC7, BEM2, and BAG7 control distinct RHO1 functions in Saccharomyces cerevisiae. *Mol. Microbiol.* **45**, 1433–1441.
56. Jung, U. S., and Levin, D. E. (1999). Genome-wide analysis of gene expression regulated by the yeast cell wall integrity signalling pathway. *Mol. Microbiol.* **34**, 1049–1057.
57. Jung, U. S., Sobering, A. K., Romeo, M. J., and Levin, D. E. (2002). Regulation of the yeast Rlm1 transcription factor by the Mpk1 cell wall integrity MAP kinase. *Mol. Microbiol.* **46**, 781–789.
58. Madden, K., Sheu, Y. J., Baetz, K., Andrews, B., and Snyder, M. (1997). SBF cell cycle regulator as a target of the yeast PKC-MAP kinase pathway. *Science* **275**, 1781–1784.
59. Ray, A., Hector, R. E., Roy, N., Song, J. H., Berkner, K. L., and Runge, K. W. (2003). Sir3p phosphorylation by the Slt2p pathway effects redistribution of silencing function and shortened lifespan. *Nat. Genet.* **33**, 522–526.
60. Nanduri, J., and Tartakoff, A. M. (2001). Perturbation of the nucleus: A novel Hog1p-independent, Pkc1p-dependent consequence of hypertonic shock in yeast. *Mol. Biol. Cell* **12**, 1835–1841.
61. Nanduri, J., and Tartakoff, A. M. (2001). The arrest of secretion response in yeast: Signaling from the secretory path to the nucleus via Wsc proteins and Pkc1p. *Mol. Cell* **8**, 281–289.
62. Valentini, S. R., Casolari, J. M., Oliveira, C. C., Silver, P. A., and McBride, A. E. (2002). Genetic interactions of yeast eukaryotic translation initiation factor 5A (eIF5A) reveal connections to poly(A)-binding protein and protein kinase C signaling. *Genetics* **160**, 393–405.
63. Hosotani, T., Koyama, H., Uchino, M., Miyakawa, T., and Tsuchiya, E. (2001). PKC1, a protein kinase C homologue of Saccharomyces cerevisiae, participates in microtubule function through the yeast EB1 homologue, BIM1. *Genes Cells* **6**, 775–788.
64. Errede, B., and Levin, D. E. (1993). A conserved kinase cascade for MAP kinase activation in yeast. *Curr. Opin. Cell Biol.* **5**, 254–260.
65. Helliwell, S. B., Schmidt, A., Ohya, Y., and Hall, M. N. (1998). The Rho1 effector Pkc1, but not Bni1, mediates signalling from Tor2 to the actin cytoskeleton. *Curr. Biol.* **8**, 1211–1214.
66. Tsuno, A., Miyoshi, K., Tsujii, R., Miyakawa, T., and Mizuta, K (2000). RRS1, a conserved essential gene, encodes a novel regulatory protein required for ribosome biogenesis in Saccharomyces cerevisiae. *Mol. Cell. Biol.* **20**, 2066–2074.
67. Basu, U., Si, K., Warner, J. R., and Maitra, U. (2001). The Saccharomyces cerevisiae TIF6 gene encoding translation initiation factor 6 is required for 60S ribosomal subunit biogenesis. *Mol. Cell. Biol.* **21**, 1453–1462.
68. Ho, J. H., Kallstrom, G., and Johnson, A. W. (2000). Nmd3p is a Crm1p-dependent adapter protein for nuclear export of the large ribosomal subunit. *J. Cell Biol.* **151**, 1057–1066.
69. Stage-Zimmermann, T., Schmidt, U., and Silver, P. A. (2000). Factors affecting nuclear export of the 60S ribosomal subunit *in vivo*. *Mol. Biol. Cell* **11**, 3777–3789.
70. Ho, J. H., and Johnson, A. W. (1999). NMD3 encodes an essential cytoplasmic protein required for stable 60S ribosomal subunits in Saccharomyces cerevisiae. *Mol. Cell. Biol.* **19**, 2389–2399.
71. Johnson, A. W., Lund, E., and Dahlberg, J. (2002). Nuclear export of ribosomal subunits. *Trends Biochem. Sci.* **27**, 580–585.
72. Nanduri, J., Mitra, S., Andrei, C., Liu, Y., Yu, Y., Hitomi, M., and Tartakoff, A. M. (1999). An unexpected link between the secretory path and the organization of the nucleus. *J. Biol. Chem.* **274**, 33785–33789.
73. Gasch, A. P., Spellman, P. T., Kao, C. M., Carmel-Harel, O., Eisen, M. B., Storz, G., Botstein, D., and Brown, P. O. (2000). Genomic expression programs in the response of yeast cells to environmental changes. *Mol. Biol. Cell* **11**, 4241–4257.

74. Dickson, R. C., and Lester, R. L. (2002). Sphingolipid functions in Saccharomyces cerevisiae. *Biochim. Biophys. Acta* **1583**, 13–25.
75. Inagaki, M., Schmelzle, T., Yamaguchi, K., Irie, K., Hall, M. N., and Matsumoto, K. (1999). PDK1 homologs activate the Pkc1-mitogen-activated protein kinase pathway in yeast. *Mol. Cell. Biol.* **19**, 8344–8352.
76. Casamayor, A., Torrance, P. D., Kobayashi, T., Thorner, J., and Alessi, D. R. (1999). Functional counterparts of mammalian protein kinases PDK1 and SGK in budding yeast. *Curr. Biol.* **9**, 186–197.
77. Sun, Y., Taniguchi, R., Tanoue, D., Yamaji, T., Takematsu, H., Mori, K., Fujita, T., Kawasaki, T., and Kozutsumi, Y. (2000). Sli2 (Ypk1), a homologue of mammalian protein kinase SGK, is a downstream kinase in the sphingolipid-mediated signaling pathway of yeast. *Mol. Cell. Biol.* **20**, 4411–4419.
78. Breitkreutz, A., and Tyers, M. (2002). MAPK signaling specificity: It takes two to tango. *Trends Cell Biol.* **12**, 254–257.
79. Winkler, A., Arkind, C., Mattison, C. P., Burkholder, A., Knoche, K., and Ota, I. (2002). Heat stress activates the yeast high-osmolarity glycerol mitogen-activated protein kinase pathway, and protein tyrosine phosphatases are essential under heat stress. *Eukaryot. Cell.* **1**, 163–173.
80. Rohde, J., Heitman, J., and Cardenas, M. E. (2001). The TOR kinases link nutrient sensing to cell growth. *J. Biol. Chem.* **276**, 9583–9586.
81. Zaragoza, D., Ghavidel, A., Heitman, J., and Schultz, M. C. (1998). Rapamycin induces the G0 program of transcriptional repression in yeast by interfering with the TOR signaling pathway. *Mol. Cell. Biol.* **18**, 4463–4470.
82. Duvel, K., Santhanam, A., Garrett, S., Schneper, L., and Broach, J. R. (2003). Multiple roles of Tap42 in mediating rapamycin-induced transcriptional changes in yeast. *Mol. Cell* **11**, 1467–1478.
83. Loewith, R., Jacinto, E., Wullschleger, S., Lorberg, A., Crespo, J. L., Bonenfant, D., Oppliger, W., Jenoe, P., and Hall, M. N. (2002). Two TOR complexes, only one of which is rapamycin sensitive, have distinct roles in cell growth control. *Mol. Cell* **10**, 457–468.
84. Torres, J., Di Como, C. J., Herrero, E., and De La Torre-Ruiz, M. A. (2002). Regulation of the cell integrity pathway by rapamycin-sensitive TOR function in budding yeast. *J. Biol. Chem.* **277**, 43495–43504.
85. Schmidt, A., Bickle, M., Beck, T., and Hall, M. N. (1997). The yeast phosphatidylinositol kinase homolog TOR2 activates RHO1 and RHO2 via the exchange factor ROM2. *Cell* **88**, 531–542.
86. Krause, S. A., and Gray, J. V. (2002). The protein kinase C pathway is required for viability in quiescence in Saccharomyces cerevisiae. *Curr. Biol.* **12**, 588–593.
87. Di Como, C. J., and Arndt, K. T. (1996). Nutrients, via the Tor proteins, stimulate the association of Tap42 with type 2A phosphatases. *Genes Dev.* **10**, 1904–1916.
88. Jiang, Y., and Broach, J. R. (1999). Tor proteins and protein phosphatase 2A reciprocally regulate Tap42 in controlling cell growth in yeast. *EMBO J.* **18**, 2782–2792.
89. Cutler, N. S., Pan, X., Heitman, J., and Cardenas, M. E. (2001). The TOR signal transduction cascade controls cellular differentiation in response to nutrients. *Mol. Biol. Cell* **12**, 4103–4113.
90. van Zyl, W., Huang, W., Sneddon, A. A., Stark, M., Camier, S., Werner, M., Marck, C., Sentenac, A., and Broach, J. R. (1992). Inactivation of the protein phosphatase 2A regulatory subunit A results in morphological and transcriptional defects in Saccharomyces cerevisiae. *Mol. Cell. Biol.* **12**, 4946–4959.
91. Koch, H., Waller, H., and Kiefer, J. (1976). Ultraviolet-induced inhibition of ribosomal RNA synthesis in yeast strains differing in radiation sensitivities. *Biochim. Biophys. Acta* **454**, 436–446.

92. Zhou, B. B., and Elledge, S. J. (2000). The DNA damage response: Putting checkpoints in perspective. *Nature* **408,** 433–439.
93. Rouse, J., and Jackson, S. P. (2002). Interfaces between the detection, signaling, and repair of DNA damage. *Science* **297,** 547–551.
94. Ghavidel, A., and Schultz, M. C. (1997). Casein kinase II regulation of yeast TFIIIB is mediated by the TATA-binding protein. *Genes Dev.* **11,** 2780–2789.
95. Johnston, I. M., Allison, S. J., Morton, J. P., Schramm, L., Scott, P. H., and White, R. J. (2002). CK2 forms a stable complex with TFIIIB and activates RNA polymerase III transcription in human cells. *Mol. Cell. Biol.* **22,** 3757–3768.
96. Murawski, M., Szczesniak, B., Zoladek, T., Hopper, A. K., Martin, N. C., and Boguta, M. (1994). maf1 mutation alters the subcellular localization of the Mod5 protein in yeast. *Acta Biochim. Pol.* **41,** 441–448.
97. Boguta, M., Czerska, K., and Zoladek, T. (1997). Mutation in a new gene MAF1 affects tRNA suppressor efficiency in Saccharomyces cerevisiae. *Gene* **185,** 291–296.
98. Pluta, K., Lefebvre, O., Martin, N. C., Smagowicz, W. J., Stanford, D. R., Ellis, S. R., Hopper, A. K., Sentenac, A., and Boguta, M. (2001). Maf1p, a negative effector of RNA polymerase III in Saccharomyces cerevisiae. *Mol. Cell. Biol.* **21,** 5031–5040.
99. Benko, A. L., Vaduva, G., Martin, N. C., and Hopper, A. K. (2000). Competition between a sterol biosynthetic enzyme and tRNA modification in addition to changes in the protein synthesis machinery causes altered nonsense suppression. *Proc. Natl. Acad. Sci. USA* **97,** 61–66.
100. Kaminska, J., Grabinska, K., Kwapisz, M., Sikora, J., Smagowicz, W. J., Palamarczyk, G., Zoladek, T., and Boguta, M. (2002). The isoprenoid biosynthetic pathway in Saccharomyces cerevisiae is affected in a maf1-1 mutant with altered tRNA synthesis. *FEM. Yeast Res.* **2,** 31–37.
101. Rohde, J. R., and Cardenas, M. E. (2003). The tor pathway regulates gene expression by linking nutrient sensing to histone acetylation. *Mol. Cell. Biol.* **23,** 629–635.
102. Larminie, C. G., Cairns, C. A., Mital, R., Martin, K., Kouzarides, T., Jackson, S. P., and White, R. J. (1997). Mechanistic analysis of RNA polymerase III regulation by the retinoblastoma protein. *EMBO J.* **16,** 2061–2071.
103. Crighton, D., Woiwode, A., Zhang, C., Mandavia, N., Morton, J. P., Warnock, L. J., Milner, J., White, R. J., and Johnson, D. L. (2003). p53 represses RNA polymerase III transcription by targeting TBP and inhibiting promoter occupancy by TFIIIB. *EMBO J.* **22,** 2810–2820.

Index

A

Acids, amino, 16, 73
  deletion of, 18
  groups, 335
  mitochondrial, 227, 234, 235, 240
  residues, 118
  sequence homology, 264, 269
Acids, retinoid, 21
Activator-required cofactor, human mediator complexes (hMed), 3
Activators
  co, 17, 18, 20
  transcriptional, 139, 306
  urokinase plasminogen (uPA), 21–22
AD. See Domains, activation
Adenine, 52–53
  residues, 109
AdoHcy. See S-adenosyl-L-homocysteine
AdoMet. See S-adenosyl-L-methionine
AhR. See Receptor, aryl hydrocarbon
Alanine (Asn 123), 52
Amino acids. See Acids, amino
Amplification, 149
Anaphases, 161
Androgens, 21
Angiogenesis, 19
Antibodies, 12
Antiestrogens, 16–19, 18, 19
Apoptosis, 275
AR. See Receptors
Archaea, 176, 187
Arginines, 133
Arnt. See Translocator, AhR nuclear
Arrest of secretion response (ASR), 333–334
Asn 123. See Alanine
Aspargine, 346
Ataxia telangiectasia (ATM), 347

B

Bacillus stearothermophilus, 227
Bacteria, 68, 176
Bacteriophages, 67–68
Base flipping. See Enzymes
Biosynthesis
  heme, 211
  nucleotide, 13
  ribosome, 330–332
BLAST searches, 229
Broach, James, 129
BTEB. See Proteins
BTG1. See Genes

C

CAD. See Gene promoter, carbamoylphosphate synthetase/aspartate carbamyltransferase/dihydroorotase
Carbon, ring (C5-Cyt), 68
Catalysis, 84
Ccr4-Not Complex, 289
  components, 292–298, 294, 303–304
  essential functions of, 297–298
  human, 304
  interactions of, 298–305, 299–300
  organization of, 292–298, 294
  as regulatory platform, 314–316
  relationships, 304–305
  roles of, 290–292, 291, 314
  in ubiquitylation, 312–314
  yeast, 305–312
C/D. See Domains, C-terminal
CDK. See Kinase, Cyclin Dependent
CDK11. See Kinase, Cyclin Dependent 11
CDK11^{p110}. See Kinase, Cyclin Dependent 11^{p110}

Cells, 295
  breast cancer, 5–6, 5, 14–16, 23–24
  CHO, 274
  cycle, 13, 161, 323
  division control 2 Like, 264
  division/growth of, 323–324, 326
  eukaryotic, 159, 183
  HeLa, 267–268, 292
  integrity pathways, 328, 337–338, 339
  K562, 267–268
  mass, 323
  MCF-7, 4–7, 5, 15
  mitochondria in, 211–212
  proliferation of, 4, 304–305
  prostate cancer, 16
  transactivation in, 16–17
  ZR-75, 4–6, 5, 15
Centrifugation, 73
Centromeres, 158
C5-CYT. *See* Carbon, ring
Chlorpromazine, 344, 345–346
  compound (CPZ), 328
Chromatins, 161
  replication fork symmetry and, 196–198
Chromosomes, 159–160
  centromere of, 233
  partitioning, 156–157
  phage, 187
  replicated, 163–164
  segregation, 152–157, 155
Cis-elements, 20
Citric acid cycle, 211
CK2. *See* Kinases
CKB. *See* Creatine kinase B
Coactivators, p160 steroid receptor (SRCs), 17, 18, 20
Codons
  AUA, 229
  AUG, 216, 216, 227, 229
  GUG, 217
Cofactors required for Sp1 coactivation (CRSP), 3
Cohesin, 159
  diassembly, 161–164, 163
  recruitment, 160–161, 162
Coregulators, 20
COUP-TF. *See* Transcription factors
CPZ. *See* Chlorpromazine, compound
Creatine kinase B (CKB), 1
Crenarcheota, 181, 184, 198

CRSP. *See* Cofactors required for Sp1 coactivation
Crystallography, 229
CTD. *See* Domains
Cyberprobing, 226
Cyclins, 276–277
Cytoplasms, 274
Cytosines, 69

D

Deadenylation, 310–311
Decapping, 310–311
Deoxyribonucleic acid (DNA), 166. *See also* DNA methyltransferases; Enzymes
  architecture, 49–50, 54, 146–148, 147
  bending of, 49–50, 54
  chains, 193, 191, 192, 194
  cleavage, 129, 135–142, 135, 136, 137, 138, 141
  CRE-, 131–134, 132, 134, 137, 142, 145, 150
  damage, 37–39, 38, 341–342
  deletions, 150
  destabilization, 42, 46–50, 49
  ds, 175
  elongation, 187
  genomes, 174
  glycosylases, 37–41, 38, 40, 43–44
  insertions, 150
  interactions, 7–9, 8, 157
  ligases, 174, 186–87
  maturation, 174, 184–187, 196
  methylation, *in vivo*, 70–71
  moiety, 186, 193
  nonenzymatic base pair breathing in, 41–43, 41, 42, 43
  parental, 173–174
  r, 334–335
  recognition, 111–112, 113, 129
  recombination, 139–142, 141
  RNA, 173
  ss, 175
  strands, opposite, 187–195, 188, 190, 191, 192, 194
  structure, 111–112, 113
  substrates, 71, 99, 176
  synthesis, 4
  templates, 175

INDEX

translocation, 175, 178–179
virion, 70
Dihydrosphingosine (DHS), 334–335
Dimers, 105
Diseases, human, 282–283
Dissociation
  complex, 86
  rate (k_{off}), 13, 48–49, 49
D-loops, 239
DNA methyltransferases (DNA-MTases), 67, 67. See also Enzymes; Phage, T2Dam; Phage, T4Dam
  altered, 71–72
  behavior of, 99–105, 100, 101, 102, 104, 118–119
  comparisons of, 109–112, 111, 112
  history of, 68–73
  transfer of, 76
  type II, 112–118, 114
  in vivo, 70–71
DNA polymerase (pol), 173, 174
  d, 183, 193
  T4, 193
DNA polymerase I (pol I)
  EcoDam, 193
  regulation of transcription by, 324–326, 325
DNA polymerase III (pol III)
  E.coli, 182–183
  regulation of transcription by, 324–326, 325, 338–341, 339
  repression of, 341–346, 341–347, 345
Domains
  carboxyl-terminal (CTD), 275–277
  E.coli, 27, 217–222, 219, 220, 221, 227, 231–233
  guanine nucleotide binding (G-domain), 217–219, 217, 220, 234
  inhibitory (ID), 2
  N-terminal, 227, 233–234, 243, 248
  origin binding (OBDs), 173
  Sp1, 2–3, 2
  Sp3, 2–3, 2
  target-recognition-(TRD), 67, 112, 118
Domains, activation (AD), 2
  Q-rich, 2–3, 2
  S/T rich, 2–3, 2
Domains, C-terminal (C/D), 2, 9, 183, 217, 227–229
  elongation factors and, 236, 241–242
DRE. See Response elements, dioxin

DRIPs. See Proteins
Drosophilia, 150, 229
  melanogaster, 303
Duplexes, 198
  defective, 107, 108
  40mer ODN, 99–105, 100, 101, 102, 104
  methylated, 86–92, 87, 88, 89, 91
  ODN, 73–81, 75, 78–79, 85–86, 105–108, 107
  substrate, 84–112, 87, 88, 89, 91, 94, 95, 96, 97, 100, 101, 102, 104, 107, 111, 112
  20mer ODN, 86–92, 87, 88, 89, 91
  2-AP, 97

E

E. coli DNA MTase (EcoDam), 72–73, 85–86, 114
  kinetic schemes for, 92–93
  pol I, 193
  T4 pol, 193
E. coli. See Escherichia coli
EcoDam. See E. coli DNA MTase
Edman degradation, 233
EGFR. See Receptors
EJC. See Exon-exon junction complex
Elongation Factor
  G, 232
  Ts, 232
  Tu (EF-Tu), 231–232, 232
Elongation Factor G, mitochondrial (EF-G_{mt}), 252–253
  characterization/purification of, 249
  sequence analysis of, 249–252, 250
Elongation Factor Ts, mitochondrial (EF-Ts_{mt}), 252–253
  characterization/expression of, 233, 245
  residues in, 245–249, 247
  sequence analysis of, 242–243
  structure of, 243–245, 244
Elongation Factor Tu, mitochondrial (EF-Tu_{mt}), 252–253
  aa-tRNA and, 233, 238–241, 240
  C-terminal and, 236, 241–242
  guanine nucleotides and, 233, 237–239
  observations of, 232–233, 233
  sequence conservation of, 233–237, 233, 235, 236

Elongation factors
  C/D and, 236, 241–242
  mitochondria, mammalian, 231–252, 232, 233, 235, 236, 240, 244, 247, 250, 251
  overview of, 231–232, 232
EM. *See* Microscopy
Enzymes, 39. *See also* Deoxyribonucleic acid; DNA methyltransferases
  adenine analogue, 44–46, 45, 46
  atypical base flipping of, 52–53, 53, 81–84, 82
  BamHI, 86
  BamHI Mtase, 109–112, 111, 112
  base flipping of, 37–60, 38, 43–53, 45, 46, 47, 49, 53, 54, 55, 56, 57, 59
  base pair breathing/opening of, 41–43, 41, 42, 43
  base pair stability/specific recognition of, 58–60, 59
  computational studies of, 43, 43
  EcaI, 92
  EcoP15I, 94
  EcoRI, 92, 94
  EcoRV, 92, 94
  HhaI, 86, 92, 94, 98
  human Dumt1, 92, 94
  KpnI, 86, 92, 94
  Leu 191, 51–52
  metabolic, 211
  monomeric, 105
  MspI, 86, 92
  murine Dumt1, 92
  nonpolar damaged base isosteres and, 56–58, 56, 57
  preorganized substrates in, 54–55, 54, 55
  pyrene nucleotide, 54–55, 54, 55
  pyrimidine dimer DNA (PDG), 52–53, 53
  recombinase, 139–142, 141
  resealing, 139
  RsrI, 86
  side chains, 51–52
  structural studies of, 44, 45
  TaqI, 92, 94
  Type III EcoP15I, 92
  UDG, 44–45, 45, 47, 48–53, 49, 53, 56–60, 56, 57, 59
  UDPG, 69
ER. *See* Receptor, estrogen
EREs. *See* Response elements, estrogen

Escherichia coli (*E. coli*), 68–69, 72, 214, 214
  70S, 231
  domains, 27, 217–222, 219, 220, 221, 227, 231–233
  EF-Tu/Ts, 245–249, 247
  pol III, 182–183
  XerC/XerD, 138, 148
ESD formation, 110
EST databases, 229
Estrogens, 16–19, 18, 19. *See also* receptor, estrogen
Eudonuclease mapping/sequencing, 266
Eukarya, 176, 184, 187
  DNA synthesis and, 188–190, 188, 190
Eukaryal processivity factor PCNA, 183, 187, 189–190
Eukaryotes, 68, 159, 183, 218, 223, 303–304
  higher, 304–305, 308
Euryarchaeota, 181, 197
Exon-exon junction complex (EJC), 280

F

Fatty acid degradation, 211
FEN1. *See* Flap endonuclease/exonuclease 1
5-hydroxymethylcytosine (hmC), 67
Flap endonuclease/exonuclease 1 (FEN1), 173, 186–187, 190
Fluorescence analysis, 81–84, 82
Fluorescence resonance energy transfer (FRET), 173, 176
Formylmethionine, 222
FRET. *See* Fluorescence resonance energy transfer
Futcher model, 149

G

GATC (palindromic tetranucleotide sequence), 72, 76, 117
  combinations, 99, 101
  GATC site, 106–108, 107
  mismatches, 89, 90–92, 91
  residues, 84, 119
GC sites, 4–7, 5, 6
  activation of, 12–16, 14, 17
  interactions of, 10–12, 11, 19–20, 23–24

INDEX 359

G-domain. *See* Domains
GDPNP. *See* Guanosine 5'-[b-c-imido] triphosphate
GEFs. *See* Guanine
Gel filtration analysis, 73–74
Gel shift analysis, 76–81, 78–79, 86
GenBank, 268
Gene promoter, carbamoylphosphate synthetase/aspartate carbamyltransferase/dihydroorotase (CAD), 4–5, 5
Gene promoters, 2
  E2-responsive, 10–16, 11, 14
Genes
  activation, 174
  B-cell translocation 1/2 (BTG1/2), 304–305
  Cdc2L1/Cdc2L2, 264–268, 267
  c-*fos* protooncogene, 12–13
  E2, 11, 12–13
  human (MIF2), 215–216
  IF-2$_{mt}$, 215–216, 216
  MCD1, 161–164
  metalloprotease (MMP), 266, 267
  rabbit uteroglobin, 12
  retinoid-responsive, 22
  ribosomal, 331–332
  structure/CDK11, 264–268, 267
  TOR1/TOR2, 336–341, 339
Genetics, 68, 129
Genomes
  DNA, 174
  mitochondrial, 213
  priming sites of, 195
Geometry, 146–148, 147
Glucose, 314–316
Glutaraldehyde, 74–76, 75
Glycine (His 187), 52
Glycolysis, 336
Glycosylases, 4
  DNA repair and, 37–41, 38, 40
GMTC sites, 99, 101
Growth factor
  b, transforming (TGBb), 1, 22
  vascular endothelial (VEGF), 19–20
Guanine
  domains, 217–219, 217, 220, 234
  EF-Tu$_{mt}$, 233, 237–239
  NT, 233, 237–239, 245–249, 247

  nucleotide exchange factors (GEFs), 328–329
  Rom1/Rom2, 328–329
Guanosine 5'-[b-c-imido] triphosphate (GDPNP), 225

H

Heat shock/stress, 314–316, 329, 332, 334–335
Helicases
  DnaB, 175–179, 177
  fork unwinding, 173–174
  replisomes and, 175–179, 177
Helix
  E, 135
  H6/H7, 243
  K, 138, 138
  M, 137, 138, 138
  N, 137
  PSTAIRE a-, 270
  -turn-helix (HTH), 139
Heterodimers, 197–198
Hexamers, 178
His 187. *See* Glycine
Histidines, 133
  -305, 134
  -309, 135
  345, 135
  -II, 134
Histones, 197–198
hmC. *See* 5-hydroxymethylcytosine
hMED. *See* Activator-required cofactor, human mediator complexes
Holliday formation/resolution step, 136, 176
Holliday intermediate, 131, 137
Holliday junction, 138
Homology, 175
  CDK, 270–272, 269, 271
  sequence, 264, 269
Hormones, 9, 15
HTH. *See* Helix
Hydrogen, 116
  bonding, 56–58, 56, 57
Hydrolysis
  ATP, 175, 178, 212
  GDP, 237–238
  GTP, 214–215, 225, 231, 328
  NTP, 175, 178
Hypertonic shock, 333–334

I

ID. *See* Domains
IF-2$_{mt}$. *See* Mitochondrial initiation factor 2
IGFBP-4. *See* Promoters
Inhibitors
  21, cyclin-dependent kinase, 6–7, 6
  of AdoMet, 82, 83
  product, 93–96, 95, 96
Initiation Zone model (IZ), 173, 189, 190
Initiator sites, 2
Isoforms
  p58, 269, 273–274
  p110, 269, 272–273
  protein, 268–275, 270, 269, 271
IZ. *See* Initiation Zone model

J

Jayaram laboratory, 129

K

Kinase, Cyclin Dependent (CDK), 264, 265–266
  family members, 277
  homology, 270–272, 269, 271
  regulation/RNA transcription and, 275–277
Kinase, Cyclin Dependent 11 (CDK11)
  alternate promoter usage of, 267–268, 267
  alternative splicing of, 267–268, 267
  conservation of, 269–270
  expression, 268–270, 270, 269
  gene structure, 264–268, 267
  p58 isoforms and, 269, 273–274
  p110 isoforms and, 269, 272–273
  protein isoforms and, 268–275, 270, 269, 271
Kinase, Cyclin Dependent 11^{p110} (CDK11^{p110})
  associations, 278–280
  expressions o, 282–283
  pre-mRNA splicing events and, 281–282
  protein complexes and, 278–282, 279
  RNA processing proteins and, 280–281
Kinases
  casein II (CK2), 341–342
  CDK-activating (CDK), 276–277
  functionally redundant, 334–335
  mitogen-activated protein kinase (MAPK), 15
  phosphatidylinositol-3-(P13K), 15
  Pkh1/Pkh2, 334–335
  Ypk1/Ypk2, 334–335
Kinetochores, 159
k_{off}. *See* Dissociation
Krüppel-like factors (KLFs), 3–4, 6–7

L

LCBs. *See* Long chain bases
LDLR. *See* Receptors
Loci, cis-acting
  FRT, 128, 129
  ORI, 128
  res-FRT, 143–145, 143, 145
  STB, 128, 151, 156–161
Long chain bases (LCBs), 334
Lowest energy pathway, 41
LTag. *See* T-antigen, large
Lystine b, 133

M

MAP. *See* Protein kinase
MAPK. *See* Kinases
Mcm. *See* Proteins
Metabolism, 211
  nucleotide, 4, 13, 69
Metabolism, mRNA, 213, 289
  coordination/degradation and, 308–312
  decapping/deadenylation and, 310–311
  enzymatic activities of, 309–310
  roles of, 305–312
  transcription and, 306–308, 311–312
Methylation
  DNA, 70–71
  duplex, 86–92, 87, 88, 89, 91
  T4Dam, 99–105, 100, 101, 102, 104
Methylmethane sulfonate (MMS), 341, 344, 345–346
Methyltransferases (MTases), 67–68
  amino, 109
  BamHI, 109–112, 111, 112
  C5-, 109
Michaelis constants, 84–86

INDEX

361

Microscopy
 atomic force, 45–46
 electron (EM), 149, 173, 176–177
Mitochondria, mammalian
 in cells, 211–212
 elongation factors in, 231–252, 232, 233, 235, 236, 240, 244, 247, 250, 251
 proteins in, 212, 218
 roles of, 211–212
Mitochondrial initiation factor 1 (IF-1_{mt}), 230–231
Mitochondrial initiation factor 2 (IF-2_{mt})
 AUG codons of, 216, 216, 227, 229
 binding sites of, 225
 characterization/purification of, 215
 gene, 215–216, 216
 insertion region of, 220–222, 221
 sequence analysis of, 217–222, 217, 219, 220, 221
 tRNA and, 222–225, 224
Mitochondrial initiation factor 3 (IF-3_{mt})
 expression/identification of, 226
 organization/sequence analysis of, 227–229, 228
Mitochondrial protein synthesis, mammalian, 211
 features of, 212–213
 initiation of, 214–231, 214, 216, 217, 219, 220, 221, 224, 228
MitoProt II, 218, 227, 249
MMP. *See* Genes
MMS. *See* Methylmethane sulfonate
Motifs, 112–118, 114
MTases. *See* Methyltransferases

N

NCP. *See* Nucleosome core particle
Nematodes, 295
Nested Discontinuity model (ND), 173, 189, 196, 198
 DNA chains and, 191–193, 191, 192, 194
 RDP/RPA interactions and, 195
 RNA primers and, 185, 191–193, 192
Neuroblastomas, 282
Nitrogen (N), 116, 336
NMR. *See* Spectroscopy, nuclear magnetic resonance
Northern blots, 216

NRs. *See* Receptors, nuclear
N6-methyladenine (m6A), 67, 68
NT. *See* Nucleotide
Nuclear speckles, 272–273
Nucleophiles, 135, 137, 139
Nucleoplasm, 269, 273
Nucleosome core particle (NCP), 173, 197–198
Nucleotide (NT), 107, 173
 biosynthesis, 13
 guanine, 233, 237–239, 245–249, 247
 metabolism, 4, 13, 69
 pyrene, 54–55, 54, 55

O

OB fold. *See* Oligonucleotide/oligosaccharide/oligopeptide binding fold
OBDs. *See* Domains
ODNs. *See* Oligonucleotides
Okazaki fragment (OKF), 173, 187–189, 193–195
 RDPt, 188–190, 190, 191
Oligonucleotide/oligosaccharide/oligopeptide binding fold (OB-fold), 173, 179–181
Oligonucleotides (ODNs), 12–13, 67
 combinations of, 107
 duplexes, 73–81, 75, 78–79, 85–86, 105–108, 107
 target, 181
Open reading frame (ORF), 226, 227
 upstream (uORF), 324
ORI. *See* Replication origin
Origin recognition complex (Orc), 175
Orthologs, 175

P

PBP. *See* Proteins
PC2. *See* Positive cofactor 2
PDG. *See* Enzymes
Peptides, 18, 158, 217
pERE$_3$. *See* Promoters
Phage, T2Dam
 altered, 71–72
 modification of, 68–70, 73
 in vivo, 70–71
Phage, T4Dam, 68
 AdoMet, 85–92, 87, 88, 89, 91
 analyses of, 76–84, 78–79, 82

Phage, T4Dam (*cont.*)
  binding properties of, 73–84, 75, 78–79, 82
  burst analysis of, 86–92, 87, 88, 89, 91, 100
  comparisons of, 72–73, 109–112, 111, 112
  DNA structure/recognition and, 111–112, 113
  initial binding of, 90–92
  interactions, 76–81, 78–79
  kinetic mechanism of, 109–112, 111, 112
  kinetic properties of, 84–112, 87, 88, 89, 91, 94, 95, 96, 97, 100, 101, 102, 104, 107, 111, 112
  orientation/processivity of, 99–105, 100, 101, 102, 104
  single turnover analysis of, 104, 105–108, 107
  steady state analysis of, 78–79, 84–86
  steady state mechanism of, 92–98, 94, 95, 96, 97
  structure of, 112–119, 114
  subunit structure of, 73–76, 75
Phages
  chromosome, 187
  Mu, 147, 147
  T°2, 70
  T6, 69
  T7, 176, 187
  T-even, 69
Phosphates, 107, 118
Phosphorylation, 4
  conserved, 272
  oxidative, 336
  proteins and, 263–264
  reversible, 276–277
  sites, 271–272, 271
Phytosphingosine (PHS), 334–335
Pkc1. *See* Protein kinase
Plasma membranes
  cell integrity signaling and, 334–335
  feedback regulation and, 330–332
  nuclear/nucleolar proteins and, 333–334
  secretory signaling pathway and, 326–330, 329, 333–334
Plasmids
  circular, 149–150
  partitioning, 129, 151–166, 153–154, 155, 156, 162, 163, 165
  RSF1010, 176
  segregation of, 154–156
  yeast, 148–149

Plasmids, 2-micron yeast, 127, 164–166.
  See also Proteins, Flp
  Flp recombination system and, 130–134, 132, 134, 142–151, 142, 143, 145, 146, 147, 150
  host factors and, 157–159
  interactions, 157
  localization of, 152, 153–154
  organization of, 128–130, 128, 152, 153–154
  partitioning system of, 151–166, 153–154, 155, 156, 162, 163, 165
  segregation of, 164
  yeast cohesin complex and, 159–164, 162, 163
pol. *See* DNA polymerase
Polypeptides, 213
Positive cofactor 2 (PC2), 3
PPARs. *See* Receptors
PR. *See* Receptors
Primases, 173–174, 179–181
Prokaryotes, 68, 214, 223, 226, 235
Promoters
  ERE (pERE$_3$), 17–19, 18, 19
  insulin-like growth factor binding protein 4 (IGFBP-4), 15
  p21, 6, 20–21
  thymidine kinase, 6, 7
Protein A, replication (RPA), 173, 180–181
  interactions, 195
  properties, 184
Protein kinase, 264
  C (Pkc1), 327
  Clk/Sty, 281
  CrkRS, 277
  mitogen-activated (MAP), 328–330, 335
  SR, 281
Protein-associated factors, TATA-binding (TAFs), 1, 2, 23
Proteins. *See also* Mitochondrial protein synthesis, mammalian
  basic transcription element binding (BTEB), 20–21
  complex, TFIID, 2, 291
  Ctf7, 160
  defined, 189
  Fun30, 158
  interactions, 118, 157
  isoforms and CDK11, 268–275, 270, 269, 271

KLP family of, 3–9, 5, 6, 8, 13, 23–24
minichromosome maintenance (Mcm), 173, 175–179, 177
mitochondrial, 212, 218
modification, 314
nuclear/nucleolar, 272–273, 333–334
phosphatase 2A, 338–341, 339
phosphorylation and, 263–264
proliferator-activated receptor binding (PBP), 3
Raf1, 128, 149
RecA-family recombination, 175–176
Rep1, 128, 149, 152, 157–158, 160
Rep2, 128, 149, 152, 157–158, 160
replication, 174
ribosomal, 331
RNA processing, 280–281
Rpl1/Rpl11, 331–332
synthesis, 324
TATA-binding (TBP), 1, 2, 23
TBP/TIP120B, 304
thyroid hormone receptor associated (TRAPs), 3
vitamin D interacting (DRIPs), 3
Wsc, 327–330, 335
yeast, 298–303, 299–300
zinc finger, 3–4, 10, 10
Proteins, Flp, 128, 165–166. See also Plasmids, 2-micron yeast
active site of, 131–134, 132, 134, 135, 136, 137–142, 137, 138, 141
monomers and, 136, 136
recombinase, 129–134, 132, 134, 136, 142–151, 142, 143, 145, 146, 147, 150
ribonuclease activities of, 138–139
RNA, 140–142, 141
RNase I/II, 140, 141
substrate, 129–134, 132, 134
Proteins, Maf1, 342, 347
functions of, 344–345, 345
identification of, 343
interactions of, 343–344
Proteins, single stranded DNA binding (SSBs), 173, 174
bacterial/eukaryal, 180, 187
replisomes and, 179–181
Proteins, specificity (Sp), 1, 1
ER and, 8, 9–20, 10, 11, 14, 17, 18, 19
KLF protein family and, 3–9, 5, 6, 8, 13, 23–24

Sp1 as, 2–3, 2, 4–9, 5, 6, 8
steroid hormone receptors and, 20–24
Proteins, specificity 1 (Sp1), 1
domains of, 2–3, 2
interactions of, 4–9, 5, 6, 8, 20–24
transactivation, 21
Proteins, specificity 3 (Sp3)
domains of, 2–3, 2
ER and, 19–20
interactions of, 6–7
Proton acceptor groups, 40, 40
PSORT programs, 218
Purine, 40, 40, 227
Pyrimidine, 40, 40
Pyrococcus furiosus, 181

Q

Quench instruments, 87

R

RAGE. See Receptors
Rapamycin, 340, 344, 345–346
RAR. See Receptor, retinoid acid
RDP. See RNA-DNA primer
Receptor, aryl hydrocarbon (AhR), 1, 7
Receptor, estrogen (ER), 1, 333
α, 10, 16–20, 18, 19
β, 10, 16
function of, 327
Sp proteins and, 8, 9–20, 10, 11, 14, 17, 18, 19, 23–24
Receptor, retinoid acid (RAR), 1, 9, 21–22
Receptor, retinoid X (RXR), 1, 9, 21–22
Receptors
for advanced glycation end products (RAGE), 14
androgen (AR), 21
epidermal growth factor (EGFR), 14
low density lipoprotein (LDLR), 14
orphan, 9
peroxisome proliferator-activated (PPARs), 1, 9, 21–22
progesterone (PR), 20–21
steroid hormone, 9, 20–23
thyroid hormone (TR), 21
vitamin D (VDR), 21

Receptors, nuclear (NRs), 1
  superfamily of, 9–10, 10, 18, 20–24
Recombination
  (two)2-micron yeast plasmid and, 130–134, 132, 134
  Flp protein, 129–134, 132, 134, 136, 142–151, 142, 143, 145, 146, 147, 150
  site-specific, 138–142, 141
  Tyr, 131, 137–139, 138
Regena (Rga), 303–304
Replicases, 173–174, 182–184
Replication factor C (RFC), 173
Replication fork symmetry, 184, 185, 196
  advantages of, 196
  chromatins and, 196–198
Replication origin (ORI), 128, 158–159, 173
  attraction to, 175
Replisomes
  coordinates, 184, 185
  DNA maturation and, 184–187
  features of, 174–187, 177, 185
  helicases and, 175–179, 177
  opposite DNA strands and, 187–195, 188, 190, 191, 192, 194
  primases and, 179–181
  replicases and, 182–184
  replication fork symmetry and, 196–198
  SSBs and, 179–181
  types of, 174
Repressors, 149
  GFP, 152–153, 156
Response elements, dioxin (DREs), 1, 7
Response elements, estrogen (EREs), 1, 10–12, 11
  distal, 19–20
Retinoid acids. *See* Acids, retinoid
RFC. *See* Replication factor C
Rga. *See* Regena
Ribonucleic acid (RNA). *See also* Metabolism, mRNA
  DNA, 173
  Flp proteins, 140–142, 141
  polymerase II (RNAP II), 275–277, 279–280
  pre-m, 281–282
  primers and ND, 185, 191–193, 192
  processing, 275–277
  processing proteins, 280–281

  t, 213–215, 214, 222–225, 224, 231, 238–241, 240, 326–330, 334–335
  transcription, 264, 265–266, 275–277
RING fingers, 312
RNA polymerase III (RNAP III), 323
RNA-DNA primer (RDP), 173, 181
  completion of, 184
  interactions, 195
  junction, 186
  OKF, 188–191, 190, 191
RNAP II. *See* Ribonucleic acid
RPA. *See* Protein A, replication
RXR. *See* Receptor, retinoid X

S

Saccharomyces cerevisiae, 217, 292–293
S-adenosyl-L-homocysteine (AdoHcy), 67, 68, 70, 83
  active sites of, 117–118
  binding of, 113–115, 114
  bursts of, 86, 88
  interactions, 115–116
  moieties of, 116
S-adenosyl-L-methionine (AdoMet), 67, 68, 70–71
  absence of, 80
  concentrations, 85–92, 87, 88, 89, 91
  constants for, 84
  inhibitors of, 82, 83
  reaction kinetics and, 92–98, 94, 95, 96, 97
  single turnover analysis and, 104, 105–108, 107
  values for, 73, 76
SAGA complex, 302
Salmonella typhimurium, 68
sec Mutants, 333–334
Sedimentation, 74
Serine, 264, 346
SFCs. *See* Splicing factor compartments
Shigella dysenteriae strain (Sh), 69
Shock, hypertonic, 333–334
Signaling
  cell integrity, 334–335, 337–338, 339
  cellular, 289
  pathways, 326, 346–347
  repression, 323
  research, 263

INDEX 365

secretory pathways, 326–330, 329, 333–334
TOR, 332, 335–341, 339
SMCC. See SRB/MED containing cofactor complex
SP. See Proteins, specificity
Sp1. See Proteins, specificity 1
Sp3. See Proteins, specificity 3
Spectroscopy, nuclear magnetic resonance (NMR), 41–42, 41, 42
  studies, 41–42, 41, 42, 50, 56–57, 57, 60
Sphingolipids, 334
Splicing factor compartments (SFCs), 272–273
SRB/MED containing cofactor complex (SMCC), 3
SRCs. See Coactivators, p160 steroid receptor
SSBs. See Proteins, single stranded DNA binding
Steroidgenic factor-1 (SF-1), 1, 22–23
Streptococcus pneumoniae, 72, 105
Stress, 314–316, 329, 332, 334–335
SV40. See Virus 40, simian
Swiss-Model, 222, 245

T

TAFs. See Protein-associated factors, TATA-binding
T-antigen, large (LTag), 173, 175–179, 177
TATA
TATA boxes, 2
TBP. See Proteins
TCA cycle, 336
Terminal oligoprymidine (TOP), 326, 332
TFIIH. See Transcription factors
TGBb. See Growth factor
Threonine, 264
Thymidine, 53, 58
Thyroids, 9
T-loops, 239, 271
TOP. See Terminal oligoprymidine
Topoisomerases, 174
  activities, 139–142, 141
  archaeal VI, 139
  human, 131–132, 140
  I, 139, 140
  II, 139
  type IB, 131, 139
  vaccinia, 131–132, 140
Topology, 146–148, 147, 166

TR. See Receptors
Trans-activation, 137–138, 138
Trans cleavage, 134
Transactivation, nuclear receptor-mediated, 1, 20–24. See also Proteins, specificity; Proteins, specificity 1
Transcription factors
  chicken ovalbumin upstream promoter- (COUP-TF), 22
  IIH (TFIIH), 276–277
  interactions with, 4–9, 5, 6, 8
  nuclear, 21–22
Transglutaminase, 22
Translocation rate (k_{trans}), 48–49, 49
Translocator, AhR nuclear (Arnt), 1, 7
TRAPs. See Proteins
TRD. See Domains
Trombone Model, 188
Tumors, human, 233, 282
Tunicamycin, 333, 344
Turgor pressure, 327–328
2-aminopurine (2-AP), 44–46, 45, 46, 67
  binding/substitutions of, 83–84
  duplexes, 97
Tyrosine (Tyr)
  343, 135
  recombinases, 131, 137–139, 138

U

Ubiquitylation, 312–114
Unfolded protein response (UPR), 327
Untranslated region (UTR)
  5′, 216, 326
uORF. See Open reading frame
uPA. See Activators
UPR. See Unfolded protein response
Urea cycle, 211

V

van der Waals forces, 52
VDR. See Receptors
VEGF. See Growth factor
Velocities, initial, 93, 94
Virus 40, simian (SV40), 173, 175
Vitamin D, 9, 21

W

Watson-Crick constraints, 69, 80, 222
Wigglesworthia brevipalpis, 227

X

X-ray
  crystallography, 113–118, 114

Y

Yeast, 158, 346–347. *See also* Plasma
    membranes; Plasmids, 2-micron yeast;
    RNA polymerase III
  Ccr4-Not Complex, 305–312
  cell division/growth of,
    323–324, 326
  cohesin complex, 159–160
  mutants, 183
  nutrients/starvation/Tor and,
    335–341, 339
  plasmids, 148–149
  proteins, 298–303,
    299–300
  repression, 341–346, 345
  roles of, 305–312
  secretory signaling pathways and, 326–330,
    329, 333–334
  subunits, 293–294
  transcription, 326

Z

Zinc fingers, 3–4, 10, 10
  deletions of, 16–17
  RADR, 242